Family Therapy
History, Theory, and Practice

Fourth Edition

Samuel T. Gladding

Wake Forest University

PEARSON

Merrill
Prentice Hall

Upper Saddle River, New Jersey
Columbus, Ohio

Library of Congress Cataloging in Publication Data
Gladding, Samuel T.
   Family therapy : history, theory, and practice / Samuel T. Gladding.
-- 4th ed.
      p. ; cm.
   Includes bibliographical references and index.
   ISBN 0-13-172563-7
   1. Family psychotherapy.   I. Title.
   [DNLM: 1. Family Therapy.   WM 430.5.F2 G542f 2007]
RC488.5.G535 2007
616.89'156--dc22   2006009801

Vice President and Executive Publisher: Jeffery W. Johnston
Publisher: Kevin M. Davis
Editorial Assistant: Sarah N. Kenoyer
Production Editor: Mary Harlan
Production Coordinator: Tim Flem/PublishWare
Design Coordinator: Diane C. Lorenzo
Photo Coordinator: Valerie Schultz
Cover Design: Candace Rowley
Cover Image: SuperStock
Production Manager: Laura Messerly
Director of Marketing: Ann Castel Davis
Marketing Manager: Autumn Purdy
Marketing Coordinator: Brian Mounts

This book was set in Palatino by Laserwords Private Limited, Chennai. It was printed and bound by R.R. Donnelley & Sons Company. The cover was printed by The Lehigh Press, Inc.

Chapter Opener Photo Credits: Chapter 1: © Dorling Kindersley Media Library, courtesy of Bellagio Resort Hotel, Las Vegas; Chapter 2: Rhoda Sidney/PH College; Chapter 3: Todd Yarrington/Merrill; Chapter 4: Ruth Jenkinson/© Dorling Kindersley Media Library; Chapter 5: Andy Crawford/© Dorling Kindersley Media Library; Chapter 6: David Burch/Index Stock Imagery, Inc.; Chapter 7: Patrick Watson/PH College; Chapter 8: Frank LaBua/PH College; Chapter 9: Stockbyte; Chapter 10: Scott Cunningham/Merrill; Chapter 11: Shirley Zeiberg/PH College; Chapter 12: Scott Cunningham/Merrill; Chapter 13: Todd Yarrington/Merrill; Chapter 14: Scott Cunningham/Merrill; Chapter 15: Anthony Magnacca/Merrill; Chapter 16: Bruce Forster/© Dorling Kindersley Media Library; Chapter 17: Todd Yarrington/Merrill.

Pearson Prentice Hall™ is a trademark of Pearson Education, Inc.
Pearson® is a registered trademark of Pearson plc
Prentice Hall® is a registered trademark of Pearson Education, Inc.
Merrill® is a registered trademark of Pearson Education, Inc.

Pearson Education Ltd.
Pearson Education Singapore Pte. Ltd.
Pearson Education Canada, Ltd.
Pearson Education–Japan

Pearson Education Australia Pty. Limited
Pearson Education North Asia Ltd.
Pearson Educación de Mexico, S.A. de C.V.
Pearson Education Malaysia Pte. Ltd.

PEARSON
Merrill
Prentice Hall

10 9 8 7 6 5 4 3
ISBN: 0-13-172563-7

To my family,
especially my parents,
Gertrude Barnes Templeman Gladding
and
Russell Burton Gladding,
who taught me by example
how to handle adversity,
give love,
and work for the greater good.

Preface

———————————————————— • ————————————————————

Philosophy

Therapeutic work with families is a recent scientific phenomenon but an ancient art. Throughout human history, designated persons in all cultures have helped couples and families cope, adjust, and grow. In the United States, the interest in assisting families within a healing context is both a twentieth and twenty-first century movement. Family life has always been of interest, but because of economic, social, political, and spiritual values, outsiders made little direct intervention, outside of social work, into ways of helping family functioning until the 1950s. Now, there are literally thousands of professionals who focus their attention and skills on improving family dynamics and relationships.

In examining how professionals work to assist families, the reader should keep in mind that there are as many ways of offering help as there are families. However, the most widely recognized methods are counseling, therapy, educational enrichment, and prevention. The general umbrella term for remediation work with families is *family therapy*. This concept includes the type of work done by family professionals who identify themselves by different titles, including counselors, psychologists, psychiatrists, social workers, nurses, and clergy.

Family therapy is not a perfect term; politically it gets bandied about by a number of professional associations such as the American Association for Marriage and Family Therapy (AAMFT), the American Counseling Association (ACA), the American Psychological Association (APA), and the National Association of Social Workers (NASW). Physicians who treat families also debate this term, as well as whether, as doctors, they are "family therapists" or engaged in the practice of medicine and therefore "family medical specialists." For purposes of this book, the generic term *family therapy* is used because of its wide acceptance among the public and professionals who engage in the practice of helping families. Within this term, some aspects of educational enrichment and prevention are included.

Organization

As a comprehensive text, this book focuses on multiple aspects of family therapy. Part One introduces the reader to the various ways in which families develop and the characteristics of healthy and dysfunctional families. Part Two examines the rationale and history of family therapy, its general and universal processes, plus the main theoretical approaches to working therapeutically with families: Adlerian, psychodynamic, Bowen, experiential, behavioral and cognitive-behavioral, structural, strategic, systemic (Milan), solution-focused, and narrative. Each theoretical chapter emphasizes the major theorists of the approach, premises, techniques, process/outcome, and unique aspects of the theory. A case illustration is also provided.

Part Three covers issues and dynamics in working with special family forms: single-parent families, remarried families, culturally diverse families, and addictive/abusive families and infidelity. In each of the chapters in this section, the different therapeutic approaches used in prevention and treatment are highlighted with special attention focused on the family type and background. Finally, Part Four discusses ethical, legal, and professional issues in being a family therapist. It also features a chapter on research and assessment in family therapy.

New to This Edition

The fourth edition of *Family Therapy* has been thoroughly updated with new and relevant sources—over 250 in all! A new chapter on working with couples and marriages in enriching and therapeutic ways has been added. In addition, this book has been strengthened to include a more complete discussion of issues related to diversity by highlighting Arab American and different forms of European American families, as well as expanded coverage of working with African-American, Native American Indian, Hispanic/Latino, and Asian-American families. A section has been added in the addiction/abuse chapter on dealing with infidelity. Transition issues, such as military deployment or extended work assignments, are covered in this edition as well and there is additional coverage on managed care.

A Personal Note

In undertaking the writing of this work, I have been informed not only by massive amounts of reading in the rapidly growing field of family therapy but also by my own experiences during the past 30 years of therapeutically working with families. Both my family of origin and current family of procreation have influenced me as well. In addition, because I belong to the AAMFT, the International Association for Marriage and Family Counselors (IAMFC), and Division 43 (Family Psychology) of the APA, I have tried to view families and family therapy from the broadest base possible. Readers should find information within this work that will help them gain a clear perspective on the field of family therapy and those involved with it.

Like the authors of most books, I truly hope you as a reader enjoy and benefit from the contents of this text. It is my wish that when you complete your reading, you will have gained a greater knowledge of family therapy, including aspects of prevention, enrichment, and therapy that affect you personally as well as professionally. If such is the case, then you will have benefited and possibly changed, and I, as an author, will have accomplished the task that I set out to do.

Acknowledgments

I am grateful to the reviewers who spent many hours critiquing the first edition of this book: James Bitter, California State University at Fullerton; Donald Bubenzer, Kent State University; Harper Gaushell, Northeast Louisiana University; J. Scott Hinkle, University of North Carolina at Greensboro; Gloria Lewis, Loyola University of Chicago; Donald Mattson, University of South Dakota; Eugene R. Moan, Northern Arizona University; and Tom Russo, University of Wisconsin, River Falls.

I also gratefully acknowledge the contributions of time and insightful suggestions from reviewers for the second edition: Charles P. Barnard, University of Wisconsin–Stout; Peter Emerson, Southeastern Louisiana University; and Eugene R. Moan, Northern Arizona University.

Reviewers who provided me with valuable input for the third edition of the book were Michael Carns, Southwest Texas State University; Thomas A. Cornille, Florida State University; Merith Cosden, University of California, Santa Barbara; Vonda Jump, Utah State University; and Jeffrey M. Smith, Kent State University.

Finally, I would like to express appreciation to those who critiqued the fourth edition of this text: Joseph F. Bertinetti, University of Nebraska–Omaha; Alan Demmitt, University of Dayton; Grace Mims, University of South Dakota; William H. Quinn, University of Georgia; and David A. Spruill, Louisiana State University.

I especially want to thank Trevor Buser, my current graduate assistant, who helped me locate massive amounts of information for this edition and proofread every chapter. His work ethic and efficiency are exceptional and without him I would not have been able to revise this work so thoroughly. Virginia Perry of Summit School, my former graduate assistants, Michele Kielty-Briggs, Jenny Cole, and the current program manager of the Department of Counseling, Pamela Karr, of Wake Forest University, have been constructive and positive in their input on previous editions of this text as well. I am most grateful to them. In addition, I am indebted to my editor at Merrill/Prentice Hall, Kevin Davis, for his tireless effort, support, and assistance on my behalf.

This text is dedicated to my family, especially my parents. My father died in April 1994, at the age of 84, shortly after I completed the first edition of this text. My mother died more recently in August 2000, two months short of turning 90, just as I was finishing the third edition of the book. The love and courage of both my parents along with the legacy left to me by previous generations of my family have affected me positively. I know I am most fortunate.

Finally, and as importantly, I am indebted to my wife, Claire, for her encouragement and comfort during the writing process. She has insisted throughout this effort, and our 20 years of marriage, that we talk and build our relationship as a couple. She has employed all of her communication skills, including a generous dose of humor, to help me be a better spouse. She has also been throughout this time my partner, friend, and lover in the raising of our three children: Ben, Nate, and Tim.

Samuel T. Gladding

About the Author

———————————————— • ————————————————

 Samuel T. Gladding is chair and professor of counseling at Wake Forest University in Winston-Salem, North Carolina. He has been a practicing counselor in both public and private agencies since 1971. His leadership in the field of counseling includes service as

- president of the American Counseling Association (ACA),
- president of the Association for Counselor Education and Supervision (ACES),
- president of the Association for Specialists in Group Work (ASGW),
- president of Chi Sigma Iota (international academic and professional counseling honor society),
- vice president of the Counseling Association for Humanistic Education and Development (C-AHEAD), and
- president of the Alabama Association of Marriage and Family Therapists.

Dr. Gladding is the former editor of the *Journal for Specialists in Group Work* and the ASGW newsletter. He is also the author of more than 100 professional publications. In 1999, he was cited as being in the top 1% of contributors to the *Journal of Counseling and Development* for the 15-year period from 1978 to 1993. Some of Gladding's most recent books include *The Counseling Dictionary*, Second Edition (2006); *Counseling: A Comprehensive Profession*, Fifth Edition (2004); *Group Work: A Counseling Specialty*, Fourth Edition (2003); *The Creative Arts in Counseling*, Third Edition (2005); and this fourth edition of *Family Therapy: History, Theory, and Practice* (2007).

Dr. Gladding's previous academic appointments have been at the University of Alabama at Birmingham, Fairfield University (Connecticut), and Rockingham Community College (Wentworth, North Carolina). He was also director of Children's Services at the Rockingham County (North Carolina) Mental Health Center. Gladding received his degrees from Wake Forest (B.A., M.A. Ed.), Yale (M.A.R.), and the University of North Carolina–Greensboro (Ph.D.). He is a National Certified Counselor, a Certified Clinical Mental Health Counselor, and a Licensed Professional Counselor (North Carolina). He is a former member of the Alabama Board of Examiners in Counseling and of the Research and Assessment Corporation for Counseling (RACC).

Dr. Gladding is the recipient of numerous honors, including

- the Chi Sigma Iota Thomas J. Sweeney Professional Leadership Award,
- the Counseling Association for Humanistic Education and Development Joseph W. and Lucille U. Hollis Outstanding Publication Award,

- the Association for Counselor Education and Supervision Professional Leadership Award, and
- the Association for Specialists in Group Work Eminent Career Award.

He is also a Fellow of the Association for Specialists in Group Work.

Dr. Gladding is married to the former Claire Tillson and the father of three children—Ben, Nate, and Tim. Outside of counseling, he enjoys tennis, swimming, and humor.

Discover the Companion Website
Accompanying This Book

•

The Prentice Hall Companion Website: A Virtual Learning Environment

Technology is a constantly growing and changing aspect of our field that is creating a need for content and resources. To address this emerging need, Prentice Hall has developed an online learning environment for students and professors alike—Companion Websites—to support our textbooks.

In creating a Companion Website, our goal is to build on and enhance what the textbook already offers. For this reason, the content for each user-friendly website is organized by chapter and provides the professor and student with a variety of meaningful resources.

Common Companion Website features for students include:

- **Chapter Objectives** – outline key concepts from the text.
- **Interactive Self-quizzes** – complete with hints and automatic grading that provide immediate feedback for students. After students submit their answers for the interactive self-quizzes, the Companion Website **Results Reporter** computes a percentage grade, provides a graphic representation of how many questions were answered correctly and incorrectly, and gives a question-by-question analysis of the quiz. Students are given the option to send their quiz to up to four email addresses (professor, teaching assistant, study partner, etc.).
- **Essay Questions** – allow students to respond to themes and objectives of each chapter by applying what they have learned to real classroom situations.
- **Web Destinations** – link to www sites that relate to chapter content.

To take advantage of the many available resources, please visit the *Family Therapy: History, Theory, and Practice* Companion Website at

www.prenhall.com/gladding

Brief Contents

Contents

•

Chapter 8: Behavioral and Cognitive-Behavioral Family Therapies — 179

Chapter 9: Structural Family Therapy — 201

Note: Every effort has been made to provide accurate and current Internet information in this book. However, the Internet and information posted on it are constantly changing, so it is inevitable that some of the Internet addresses listed in this textbook will change.

Understanding Families and Family Dynamics

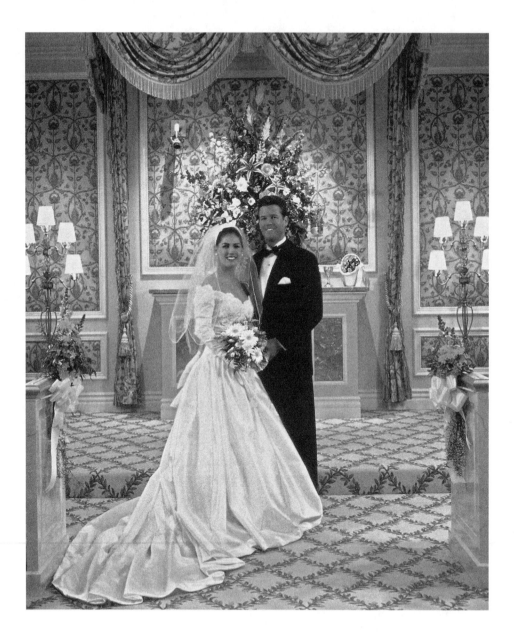

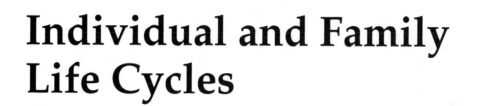

CHAPTER

1

Individual and Family Life Cycles

He was as nervous as a cat
in a room full of rockers
stiffly dressed in formal black
uptight, and afraid of moving quickly
lest he break a button
or the mood from the organ music.

She was serene
as if living a dream from childhood
dressed in layers of white with a lilac bouquet
unable to conceal her contentment
she remained poised amid the quiet
of assembled excitement.

Together they exchanged formal wedding vows,
homemade bands, and brief, expectant glances.
Then numbed, as if by Novocain,
they slowly greeted guests and themselves anew
as they whispered good-bye to innocence
and hello to the opening of a marriage.

Gladding, 1993a

F amilies have historically played an important part in the life and development of people and nations. The origin of families "dates back to prehistoric times when our hominid ancestors developed the original family unit. Although the family has evolved, it has maintained many of its original functions. It produces and socializes children, acts as a unit of economic cooperation, gives us significant roles as children, husbands, wives, and parents, and provides a source of intimacy" (Strong & DeVault, 1986, p. 4). Furthermore, a family provides some of the deepest and most satisfactory emotional experiences of life, such as love, devotion, attachment, belonging, fun, and joy (Framo, 1996). The family can also be therapeutic with members listening, sympathizing, assisting, and reassuring each other (Sayger, Homrich, & Horne, 2000).

The early Egyptians considered the royal family so important that they encouraged marriages among kin. In Chinese dynasties, family life was crucial to the accrual of power and survival of empires; consequently, marriages were arranged. In medieval Europe, powerful families intermarried in order to rule and maintain wealth. As a result, certain families, such as the Hapsburgs, enjoyed great success in accumulating wealth and power (Klein, 1992).

Throughout time, social and economic factors have forced modifications in the customs governing family life (Coontz, 2005). Rules have been established and/or abandoned as a result of societal changes resulting from such events as revolutions, economic turmoil, or natural disasters. For example, in the late 1800s the United States underwent a major transition from an agricultural society to an industrial one. This socioeconomic change altered the lives of American families:

> Industrial workers of agricultural backgrounds exchanged their rural "freedom" of flexible schedules, lack of control over environmental uncertainties on their work effort, and social isolation of rural living for regimented time schedules, lack of control over extreme and tedious work conditions, and city living.... In large measure, this shift resulted in an exchange of independence and economic self-reliance for social and economic dependence within families. (Orthner, Bowen, & Beare, 1990, p. 18)

In examining families and how to work with them, a professional must explore historical, societal, economic, and governmental factors that have had an impact on family life over time. This knowledge includes seeing the systemic interaction of personalities, communities, and events. It involves an appreciation of the tension that exists within the structure of families for dealing with outside environmental forces and internal relationship difficulties. After all, "families do not dance alone or in isolation" (Stevenson, 1994, p. 39). Take, for example, the following case.

──────────────────────── **CASE EXAMPLE** ────────────────────────

THE HARDY FAMILY

Family Background

The Hardy family requested family therapy because of a promiscuous and defiant teenage daughter, Hannah. Upon further investigation, the therapist found that the father, George, lost his job 2 years ago, and since then the family has been strapped for money. Currently, they are receiving food stamps and live in public housing. In addition, the family has moved from a small town to a large city, where they know very few people. The mother, Rachel, is in declining health and is now at the point where she is almost an invalid. In addition, the youngest child, Henry, a middle schooler, has taken on a star student role. He is the antithesis of his sister, who is being teased by her classmates in high school about her unkempt looks, poor dress, and lack of ability.

Family Dynamics: Implications for Therapy

Clearly, the Hardy family has multiple difficulties. Among its problems are those related to economic, social, and health complications as well as to those related to personal and interpersonal concerns. Hannah may be acting out most in regard to the stresses under which the family is now operating. However, as such, she is more the ticket that brings the family into therapy and should not be the main focus of treatment. If the family therapist makes the mistake of ignoring the more complex issues of the Hardy family and concentrates on working with Hannah, he or she will probably not be able to offer this family any meaningful help and will also have missed an opportunity to assist the family in making needed adjustments. Only when the therapist takes all of the family's interactive variables into account and looks at how each member influences the other and the family as a whole can a useful intervention be designed and delivered.

———————————————————— ● ————————————————————

Basically, families are systems in which the individuals within them stand in interaction with each other and the family unit as a whole. The movement of each person inside and outside the family environment has an impact on every family member and the way the family functions. The interrelatedness of the family, which is governed by rules, sequences, and feedback, is known as **cybernetics** (Bateson, 1971). It is artificial to try to isolate individual and family life cycles from one another or to separate interactions in a "freeze-frame" fashion. In essence, understanding the various developmental and systemic nuances of family life is the first step in the process of becoming a family therapist.

The second step involves becoming knowledgeable about the dynamics of individual and family life cycles. Families share universal and unique functions. Universally, they provide a structure for sexual, reproductive, economic, and educational endeavors (Cavan, 1969). Defining and appreciating the global and essential components of families in various contexts is critical. This process includes assessing the family's behavior patterns and the makeup and functioning of the family's **subsystems** (i.e., smaller units of the family system, such as parents or children, logically grouped together by age or function). Families attend to the specific needs of all or some of their members for better or worse.

This chapter tackles the task of exploring how a family's form and context plays a part in its well-being. Life cycles are examined from both a developmental and a systems perspective. An attempt is made to interconnect aspects of growth and interaction among family members.

What Is a Family?

Ideas about what a family is and how it should be structured vary across cultures and are constantly changing (Coontz, 1997, 2000). In the Americas, "families have been changing since the first settlers arrived on the shores of the new world" (Bird & Sporakowski, 1992, p. xiv) and even before with indigenous people. For some groups, such as many European Americans, the family includes only blood-related kin and is "nuclear." For other groups, such as many African Americans, the family tends to focus on a "wide informal network of kin and community" (Hines, Preto, McGoldrick, Almeida, & Weltman, 1999, p. 70). In such cases, the family includes anyone who is psychologically connected, such as close long-term friends (Hines & Boyd-Franklin, 1996). For yet others, such as some Asian Americans, the family includes ancestors and all descendants. In essence, the definition of a family is not monolithic. It varies according to cultural groups. Reaching a consensus on what constitutes a family is difficult at best.

Thus, in formulating a definition of a family, inclusive as well as exclusive elements need to be considered. The U.S. Bureau of the Census (2005) defines a **family** as "two or more people … related by birth, marriage, or adoption and residing together in the same housing unit" (http://www.census.gov/). This broad definition includes people who never marry, those who marry and never have children, those whose marriages end in divorce or death, and a variety of nontraditional family arrangements. In essence, this definition of a family is one that is geared toward one's **family-of-origin,** that is, the family in which a person grew up. The definition, however, excludes some forms of living arrangements that a number of people consider a family, too, such as gay or lesbian couples, close friends, or ancestors.

In this book, the definition of a family will be kept broad in order to promote an understanding of the different forms of family life available. A family here is considered to be those persons who are biologically and/or psychologically related whom historical, emotional, or economic bonds connect, and who perceive themselves as a part of a household. By broadly defining a family, a better appreciation of persons in family units will be gained. Better insight into the ways families govern themselves may also be obtained.

Overall, families in whatever form they come are characterized by economic, physical, social, and emotional functions. There is a dual emphasis on fostering the development of individuals within families while simultaneously offering family members stability, protection, and preservation of the family unit structure (Burr, Hill, Nye, & Reiss, 1979; Strong, DeVault, & Sayad, 2005). An example of these multiple emphases and what they foster can be seen in the Temple family.

--- **CASE EXAMPLE** ---

THE TEMPLE FAMILY

Balance Within the Family

The Temple family is composed of a stepfather, a biological mother, and two daughters, ages 11 and 9. Both the mother and stepfather work outside the home to provide economic and physical support for themselves and the children. Thus, all family members rise early in the morning, and it is often late at night before the parents get to bed.

Within this structure, the mother and father take joint responsibility for making sure the daughters behave properly by monitoring the time they spend doing homework and the children with whom they socialize. Both parents listen in the morning and at night to the children's recollections of the day. They reflect with them about what they may need for school, such as poster board, pencils, and paper, so they are not caught at the last minute going out late at night to get needed supplies. They let the children follow their interests in regard to most activities but have enrolled them in Girl Scout programs, on soccer teams, and in music classes.

The family routine at night for both the parents and children is supper, homework, and computer or television time. It is run by the clock and strictly monitored. Because of the demands of the week, the parents take a night out once a week to bowl and enjoy themselves as a couple. They also assess how their days have been and how the children are doing each night before they go to bed. Although there are disagreements and frustrations in the family due to unexpected events, there is usually balance. The children are well monitored and the couple takes time to be together to have fun as well as to vent and to plan.

Types of Families

Many alternative family lifestyles have emerged and are now competing for recognition as legitimate and healthy lifestyles (Pistole & Marson, 2005). "It no longer makes sense to refer to a typical American family life. Accuracy requires us to consider various types of families, with diverse organizational patterns, styles of living, and living arrangements" (Goldenberg & Goldenberg, 2002, p. 10). Consequently, in discussing the term *family,* an appreciation of differences works best. Among the many family forms, the following are the most prevalent:

- **Nuclear family:** A core family unit of husband, wife, and their child(ren). The nuclear family has traditionally been seen as the main provider of socialization for the young and as a preserver of cultural traditions. This family type has also been viewed as the social grouping in which society sanctions sexual relationships. The traditional nuclear family household is shrinking in both number and percentage.
- **Single-parent family:** A family that includes one parent, either biological or adoptive, who is solely responsible for care of self and child/children (see Chapter 12).
- **Remarried (i.e., blended, step) family:** A family created when two people marry and at least one of them has been married previously and has a child/children (see Chapter 13).

Other frequently mentioned family forms that are often variations on one of the three family forms just cited are as follows:

- **Dual-career family:** More than 50% of married couples with families have both husband and wife in the labor force (Saginak & Saginak, 2005). Those families, in which both marital partners are engaged in work that is developmental in sequence and to which they have a high commitment, are known as **dual-career couples.** (Gilbert, 1994). More than one million of these couples "commute" where "the spouses voluntarily maintain separate homes and live apart in order to accommodate career aspirations" (Rhodes, 2002, p. 399). A substantial number of these couples, too, are known as **DINKs (dual income, no kids).**

  Regardless of whether they commute, are child-free, or have children, balancing their careers and family life can lead to satisfaction as well as conflict. The extent to which participation in one domain (e.g., work) affects participation in another domain (e.g., the family) is known as **spillover** (Tennant & Sperry, 2003). Learning new skills, staying flexible, and continually assessing and revising work and family life are necessary if dual-career couples and families are to become balanced and thrive.

- **Child-free family:** Child-free couples are those who consciously decide not to have children or who remain child-free as a result of chance (such as marrying late) or biology (infertility). They make up a large percentage of all couples. For instance, approximately 22% of women born in the United States between 1956 and 1972 will never have children (U. S. Census Bureau, 2000). As a group, child-free couples have opportunities and advantages, such as having less stress, more discretionary income, and greater options to serve in the community; but they face pressures and may be stigmatized as well (Gold & Wilson, 2002). Child-free couples may also have difficulty in mourning the children they never had or in coming to terms with the choices they made not to have children (McGoldrick & Walsh, 1999).

- **Gay/lesbian family:** This type of family is made up of a same-sex couple without children, or with children from a previous marriage or as a result of artificial insemination. Census data suggest that partners of gays and lesbians are better educated and have higher incomes than heterosexual couples, which partially explains their varied lifestyles. Almost all gay/lesbian couples face some form of discrimination and prejudice in the communities in which they live (Johnson & Colucci, 1999). (See Chapter 14.)

- **Aging family:** An aging family is one headed by those 65 years old and above. The focus of this family type is on health, transition to retirement, widowhood, sexual dysfunction, dealing with adult children, grandparenting, imparting wisdom, and long-lived marriages (Walsh, 1999). Aging families are involved with the launching or relaunching of their young adult children and sometimes in the care of their grandchildren.

- **Multigenerational family:** This type of family is made up of households that include a child, a parent, and a grandparent (Harrigan, 1992). By the year 2020, many North American families will consist of at least four generations (Goldenberg & Goldenberg, 2002). Two factors, the economy and medical advancement, are influencing the increase in the number of these families.

- **Grandparent-headed family:** The total number of children younger than 18 living in the United States in 2000 was 72.1 million, of which approximately 6 million lived in grandparent-headed households (Lever & Wilson, 2005). Most of the grandparents taking care of their children's children were grandmothers, with 34.5% of this group being African American (Gibson, 2002). While the number of children being cared for by grandparents is only slightly more than 8% of the population of children in this age span, it represents a 65% increase in the number of such households since 1990. Furthermore, the number of grandparent-headed households is expected to continue to rise in the twenty-first century.

- **Military family:** There are over two million individuals who serve in the United States armed forces at any one time. Many of them are married and have children. Military families face special problems due to the nature of the work military personnel perform and the frequency of moves that military families have to make. Every few years military families face the challenge of finding support, making adjustments, and building or rebuilding relationships and a sense of community (Kay, 2003). Military families also live with the uncertainty of how world or national events may unfold and have a direct impact on one or more family members, for example, being deployed to dangerous oversea duty (Pavlicin, 2003). In addition, military families face issues that dual-career couples and single parents encounter but often in a more intense or crisis-oriented manner (Bowen & Orthner, 1990).

Individual and Family Development

Development (i.e., predictable physical, mental, and social changes over life that occur in relationship to the environment) is a powerful factor in individuals and in families. The process is often uneven, with alternating times of growth and regression. In examining the concept of development, the factors of time and stages must be addressed.

In the broadest sense, development is a "life course." As such, it refers to three different time dimensions in human life: individual time, social time, and historical time (Elder, 1975). **Individual time** is defined as the span of life between one's birth and death. Notable individual achievements are often highlighted in this perspective, for example, being recognized as "employee of the year." **Social time** is characterized by landmark social events such as marriage, parenthood, and retirement. Family milestones are a central focus here. **Historical time** is the era in which people live, that is, the culture. It consists of forces that affect and shape humanity at a particular point in time, such as during economic depression or war. For example, a Vietnam veteran may still be angry about government decisions involving the Vietnam War, and a survivor of an economic downturn may hoard money and be distrustful of banks. In both cases, memories of time influence present lifestyles (see Figure 1.1).

Everyone is influenced by the three dimensions of time, both concurrently and sequentially. The term **life cycle** is used in this text to describe life events. A life cycle presents an active way to conceptually picture time in human development because it denotes the continuous development of people over time in multiple contexts of their lives.

Life cycles have been formulated for both individuals and families. Neither people nor families develop or interact in isolation from each other or from the society in which they live (Schwartz, 1999). Rather, life cycles often juxtapose and intertwine within a particular

Figure 1.1
Three different time dimensions in human life.

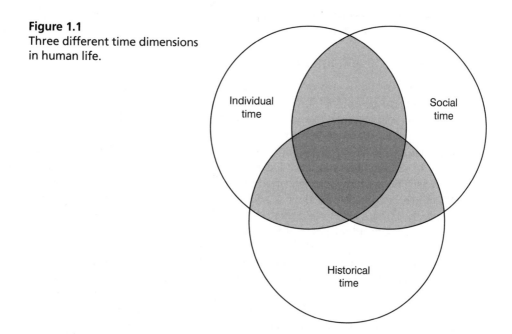

social framework. Such interactions with family members, both living and dead, influence the course of life (Bowen, 1978; Okun, 1984). For example, the choice of career and professional development is frequently connected with one's family life and history.

——————————————— CASE EXAMPLE ———————————————

LIFE DEVELOPMENT FACTORS IN PERSONAL/FAMILY HISTORY

Ida Grace Hoffman

Take the case of a 39-year-old single woman, Ida Grace Hoffman, who was named after her maiden aunt, a former schoolteacher. On multiple levels, Ida Grace has always valued education. She turned down dates in college in order to devote more time to her studies. Now her primary focus has paid off. She has been promoted to a full professor at a major public university. Her life up to this point parallels her aunt's who remained single.

In examining her life after her latest academic achievement, Ida Grace continues to take her cues from the life of her namesake. Yet, she may wonder about marriage or adopting a child. If she were to elect either of these routes, she would deviate from the life pattern she set in motion. Such a change would not be impossible but would require more effort because she has no namesake family role model to follow.

Still in her evaluation of where she is now and where she is headed, Ida Grace begins to broaden her consideration of possibilities. She thinks of her mother, a businesswoman, and of her sister, a physician. Both are married, and while her mother had two children, her sister now has one. She realizes, as she reflects, that she has most likely closed out her options prematurely up to now, but she still has possibilities, especially considering the environment in which she works and her natural gregariousness.

——————————————— ● ———————————————

Individual Life Cycle Development

Up until the 1970s, the word *development* usually referred to an individual. Part of the reason is attributable to the popularization of Erik Erikson's (1950, 1959, 1968) theory on human growth and development. Erikson was a pioneer in describing human life in terms of **stages,** sequential developmental occurrences. Following Erikson's lead, Daniel Levinson (1978), Roger Gould (1972, 1978), Gail Sheehy (1977, 1981), and Bernice Neugarten (1976) proposed adult developmental stages that focus on the individual. Indirectly reinforcing this personal emphasis has been the concentration in the helping professions on counseling individuals. With the exceptions of social work and marriage and family therapy, most helpers have traditionally worked on a one-to-one basis (Gladding, 2004).

From an individual point of view, people face predictable **developmental crises** (i.e., times of turmoil and opportunity) throughout their lives. These times involve such events as aging, retirement, birth, and marriage. The therapist should recognize how people handle and adjust to these events. The early and later phases of life and the tasks that are faced during these times result in either failure or success on many levels. Erikson's (1950, 1959, 1968) first five stages specifically focus on the formation of the person into a competent individual with adequate skills and identity. These stages are sequential, with individuals having to achieve a percentage of accomplishment in one stage before they can proceed to take on the goals of the next (Allen, 1990). The first five stages and their tasks are as follows:

Stage	Age	Task
1. Trust vs. mistrust	year 1	Emphasis on satisfying basic physical and emotional needs
2. Autonomy vs. shame/doubt	years 2–3	Emphasis on exploration and developing self-reliance
3. Initiative vs. guilt	years 4–5	Emphasis on achieving a sense of competence and initiative
4. Industry vs. inferiority	years 6–12	Emphasis on setting and attaining personal goals
5. Identity vs. role confusion	years 12–18	Emphasis on testing limits, achieving a self-identity

Gilligan (1982), McGoldrick and Carter (1999), and feminist family therapists have criticized this conceptualization of development because they believe it is centered more on men than women and that it leaves out the importance of relationships and connectedness in individuals' lives. Their points are well made and need to be considered in evaluating Erikson's model.

The last three stages of Erikson's developmental scheme are more interpersonally based and, until recently, have not been elaborated on much. The processes involved in these final stages are intimacy, generativity, and wisdom. They are tied to and dovetail with family life processes. The satisfaction people receive from intimate relationships goes a long way in influencing what they will do to help prepare the way for the next generation. Intimacy and generativity consequently relate to the total quality of life and how persons integrate overall life experiences in a healthy or unhealthy manner (Allen, 1990). Briefly, these stages can be described as follows:

Stage	Age	Task
6. Intimacy vs. isolation	years 18–35	Emphasis on achieving intimate interpersonal relationships
7. Generativity vs. stagnation	years 35–65	Emphasis on helping next generation, being productive
8. Integrity vs. despair	age 65+	Emphasis on integration of life activities, feeling worthwhile

According to Erikson (1968), other factors, in addition to the initial achievement of identity, are also important to the formation of a family. These factors, which typically increase as a person matures, are intimacy, productivity, and integration. As individuals grow into adulthood, they are challenged and tested by new conflicts that must be mastered. These conflicts come in the form of interactions with others in leisure and work settings.

Family Life Development

The **family life cycle** is the term used to describe developmental trends within the family over time (Carter & McGoldrick, 1999). This model includes all dimensions of the individual life course but emphasizes the family as a whole. Inherent in this model is tension between the person as an individual and the family as a system. Like other models, the family life cycle emphasizes some stages and aspects of life more than others. Note that what is considered an appropriate family life cycle is a social/cultural variable. Therefore, the family life cycle of many families in the United States outlined here is not universally accepted worldwide and is subject to change as society changes.

The initial version of the family life cycle was proposed by Evelyn Duvall (1977) in 1956. This model has lost some of its potency over the years as the traditional nuclear families exemplified in it have decreased in number and influence. New models have replaced Duvall's original concept and are more relevant for conceptualizing family life today. Among these are the life cycle of the intact middle-class, nuclear family; the life cycle of the single-parent family; and the life cycle of the blended family. The life cycle of the intact middle-class, nuclear family is highlighted here. (That of single-parent families and blended families are discussed in Chapters 11 and 12, respectively.)

Carter and McGoldrick (1999) outline a six-stage cycle of the intact middle-class, nuclear family that begins with the unattached adult and continues through retirement. It includes (1) single young adults, leaving home; (2) the new couple; (3) families with young children; (4) families with adolescents; (5) families launching children and moving on; and (6) families in later life. Each of the stages of this life cycle involves key adjustments, tasks, and changes that must be accomplished if the individual, family as a whole, and specific family members are going to survive and thrive. Not all intact nuclear families go through all of the stages in this model. Yet for those who do, the crucial aspects of their lives and the issues they face that might bring them into family therapy are as follows.

Single Young Adults: Leaving Home

The proportion of single young adults in the United States (those 15 years and over) is rising. According to the U.S. Census Bureau (2005), approximately 27% of the total population in the United States age 15 and over is composed of never-married adults (http://www.census.gov/; August 15, 2005). Never-married single adults, together with a large number of divorced, separated, and widowed persons (18.5% of the total United States population), make singles a significant part of the adult population in the United States (slightly less than half of all people over age 15). Singles at various stages of life have been depicted in such popular television shows as "Friends" and "Seinfeld" (for young single adults) and "Golden Girls" and "Frasier" (for older single adults).

With an increase in **singlehood** (i.e., being single), lifestyles within society are changing with a greater emphasis on individual events. Societal institutions that have been bastions for family-sponsored activities, such as churches, are being reshaped to be more accommodating to singles. The field of family therapy must change by necessity in response to the steady rise of singles. For instance, the importance of treating the individual from a family systems perspective will take on increased importance.

Being a single young adult and leaving home is one stage that individual and family life cycle theorists both emphasize. A major task of this period is to disconnect and reconnect with one's family on a different level while simultaneously establishing one's self as a person (Haley, 1980). Developing such an identity—what Murray Bowen (1978) calls "a **solid self'** (i.e., a sense of one's own beliefs and convictions that are not simply adaptive to others)"—is difficult at best and requires emotional maturity (Gerson, 1995, p. 96).

Being single requires a person to strike a balance between a career and/or marriage ambitions and a desire for personal autonomy. An increasing number of young adults in recent years have tried to achieve such a balance through **cohabitation,** living together without being married. For instance, in 2003 there were 10 million people living with an unmarried partner of the opposite sex, which translates to 8% of the couple households in the United States living in such an arrangement (http://www.census.gov/, August 15, 2005). In fact, at the beginning of the twenty-first century "more than 50% of opposite-sex couples tying the knot lived together first" (Peterson, 2000b, p. D1).

Cohabitation as an alternative to marriage and among European Americans is sometimes characterized as a "trial marriage" (Phillips & Sweeney, 2005). It has positive, neutral, and negative aspects to it.

On the positive side, it allows young adults the freedom to leave a relationship that is not working without becoming involved or embroiled in the legal system. It also allows more individual freedom for the persons involved in the relationship because there is no legal commitment to it.

On the neutral side, cohabitation does not seem to have a disruptive effect on African Americans and Mexican Americans. The majority of individuals in these groups, who cohabitate, marry (Phillips & Sweeney, 2005).

On the negative side, however, cohabitation can undermine marriage and the parenting of children (Jayson, 2005b; National Marriage Project, 2005, http://marriage.rutgers.edu/). In fact, European American couples who cohabitate and then marry are more likely to divorce than those who do not (Peterson, 2000b; Phillips & Sweeney, 2005). Research suggests that the breakup of these relationships is due to a lack of trust and commitment to marriage and a more positive perception about divorce (Larson & Lamont, 2005). Cohabitation therefore is a heterogeneous factor with the choice to cohabitate having an impact on other choices young single adults wish to make depending on their background.

Another alternative is remaining single, which is now more accepted than it was in the past. Like cohabitation, its popularity as a lifestyle appears to be growing. Indeed, "the number of never-married men and women doubled or tripled in various age groups since 1970. Among people 35 to 39 years old, the rate has more than doubled for women (from 5 percent to 13 percent) and tripled for men (from 7 percent to 19 percent)" (Carter & McGoldrick, 1999, p. 13). At the same time, only 54% of adult Americans were married compared with a record high of 74% in 1960 (U.S. Census, 2000). In 1995, more than 24 million Americans lived alone, and the number is expected to increase to 31 million by 2010 (Carey & Bryant, 1996a).

Singlehood is a viable alternative to marriage. Indeed, singles are usually the second-happiest group (married couples being the happiest), ranking above unmarried couples and others. Singlehood can be as fulfilling as marriage, depending on the needs and interests of the individual. Being single and mentally healthy requires that individuals establish social networks, find meaning in their work or avocations, and live a balanced life physically and psychologically. Singles must also develop coping strategies so as not to become distressed (Kleinke, 2002). Living a healthy single life in the United States requires making adjustments to cultural demands and realizing that culture is a phenomenon that one must accommodate.

A major challenge for singles is overcoming internal and external pressures to marry. They must also find ways to deal with loneliness. On the other hand, the personal freedom to choose one's actions is a major attraction and benefit to this style of life.

Issues that are likely to prompt singles to seek family therapy are those connected with the following:

- a weak personal sense of self
- the inability to emotionally and/or physically separate from one's family of origin
- a lack of social skills to establish significant relationships with others

The New Couple: Joining of Families Through Marriage

The new-couple relationship begins with courtship, the period when individuals test their compatibility with others through dating. This process may involve a number of partners before one commits to marriage. "During courtship, partners are encouraged to present themselves as consistently attractive and desirable—while interacting frequently with each other" (Ponzetti, 2005, p. 133). Generally, individuals tend to be most comfortable with others who are at the same or similar developmental level (Santrock, 2004). Secure men tend to become involved with secure women, and anxious women tend to become involved with less committed and more disengaged men (Lopez, 1995). That is one reason why relationships between dissimilar people are prone to frequent breakups. Environmental, psychological, and situational factors can also hinder people's adjustment to marriage (see Figure 1.2).

Regardless, "healthy couples appear to be a multidimensional, complex, nonsummative unit" (Eckstein, 2004, p. 414). They usually cope well with the transitions and challenges of everyday life.

Figure 1.2
Factors that negatively influence marriage.

From Betty Carter & Monica McGoldrick (Eds). *The Changing Family Life Cycle: A Framework for Family Therapy 2e.* Published by Allyn and Bacon, Boston, MA. Copyright © 1989 by Pearson Education. Reprinted by permission of the publisher.

1. The couple meets or marries shortly after a significant loss.
2. One or both partners wish to distance from family of origin.
3. The family backgrounds of each spouse are significantly different (religion, education, social class, ethnicity, age, etc.).
4. The couple has incompatible sibling constellations.
5. The couple resides either extremely close to or at a great distance from either family of origin.
6. The couple is dependent on either extended family financially, physically, or emotionally.
7. The couple marries before age 20 or after age 30.
8. The couple marries after an acquaintanceship of less than 6 months or after more than 3 years of engagement.
9. The wedding occurs without family or friends present.
10. The wife becomes pregnant before or within the first year of marriage.
11. Either spouse has a poor relationship with his or her siblings or parents.
12. Either spouse considers his or her childhood or adolescence as an unhappy time.
13. Marital patterns in either extended family were unstable.

The early stages of a couple relationship are characterized by idealization. Both men and women in marriage initially idealize each other and relate accordingly. This phenomenon dissipates to some degree over the course of a marriage. However, some evidence indicates that individuals who report a high level of marital satisfaction also maintain a high level of **idealistic distortion** about their marriages and spouses: They report them to be better than they actually are (Fowers, Lyons, & Montel, 1996). This quality of seeing each other positively, or through "rose-colored glasses," helps married couples endure. It is just the opposite of those most likely to divorce, who see each other through "fogged lenses" and are cynical and unable to say good things about each other (Peterson, 2000a).

Overall, the new-couple stage of the family life cycle is one of adjustment and adaptation. For example, new couples must learn how to share space and meals, as well as work, leisure, and sleep activities. They must accommodate each other's wishes, requests, and fantasies. This process takes time, energy, goodwill, and the ability to compromise. For example, Bill must understand that his new wife, Maria, takes longer to get dressed than he does. At the same time, Maria must take into consideration that Bill is more meticulous about the upkeep of the house than she is.

It is not surprising that this stage of marriage is one of the most likely times for couples to divorce due to an inability of individuals to resolve differences. It is also often seen as a time of life when couples experience the greatest amount of satisfaction, especially if they later have children (Glenn & McLanahan, 1982). The new couple is free to experiment with life and to engage freely in a wide variety of activities. Financial and time constraints are the two main limitations for couples at this time.

Issues that are likely to prompt new couples to seek family therapy are those connected with:

- the inability to adjust to living as a couple instead of as an individual
- difficulty with relatives, either family of origin or in-laws
- the inability to work through interpersonal issues, such as developing adequate or optimal communication patterns
- the question of whether or not (or of when) to have children (Peterson & Jenni, 2003)

Families with Young Children

Becoming a parent is a physical, psychological, and social event that alters a couple's lifestyle dramatically. It is a joyful but tough experience (Renshaw, 2005). The arrival of a child has an impact on a couple's lifestyle (e.g., residence), marital relationship (e.g., sexual contact), and paternal/maternal stress (e.g., new demands) (Hughes & Noppe, 1991). When a newborn enters a family, the family becomes unbalanced, at least temporarily. Couples have to adjust the time they spend working outside the house, socializing with friends, and engaging in recreational activities. They also have to arrange between themselves who will take responsibility for the child, as well as when, where, and how this responsibility will be met. A crucial task in caring for an infant is ensuring that an enduring attachment bond is created (Bowlby, 1988). In the process of caregiving, a rebalancing occurs between husbands and wives in regard to their investment of time, energy, and focus (Carter, 1999). Husbands may be especially confused as to what they should do and when because "society today has given fathers confusing expectations" (Renshaw, 2005, p. 7).

After attachment tasks are settled, families with young children must accomplish other important undertakings. Those duties connected with meeting the physical and psychological demands involved in having preschool children are among the hardest. These challenges

Figure 1.3
Stressors, strains, and well-being across the family life cycle.

From "Life Cycle and Family Development," by P. Matterssich and R. Hill, in *Handbook of Marriage and the Family* (p. 447), edited by M. Sussman and S. K. Steinmetz, 1987, New York: Plenum. Copyright Plenum Press. Reprinted by permission.

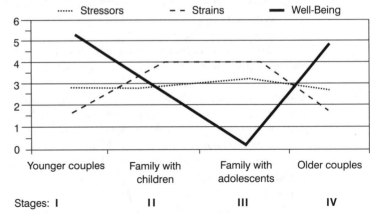

become especially great when both partners within a marriage are working outside the home. Mothers may especially feel overwhelmed because they still tend to be the primary caregiver in most families, even though 75% of them work in the labor force with approximately two-thirds of that number having preschool children (Saginak & Saginak, 2005).

Other aspects of family life where adjustments must be made include relationships with extended family, demands of work, use of leisure, and finances. Often there are strains and tension in one or more of these areas. "The strength of the marital bond (i.e., marital satisfaction) goes a long way toward mediating stress and time constraints associated with the presence of children and work" (Giblin, 1994, p. 50). Overall, as a general rule, marital satisfaction has tended to go down with each child that is added to a family (see Figure 1.3). However, it may modify as couples adjust (Mattessich & Hill, 1987).

Issues that are likely to prompt families with young children to seek family therapy are those connected with:

- "the fallout that accompanies the necessary reorganization of relationships and activities" of the married couple
- "the establishment of controls" for a young child (Minuchin, 1995, p. 115)

Families with Adolescents

Couples who have adolescents must take care of themselves, their relationship, their teenagers, and often their aging parents. Because of the squeeze they may be in psychologically and physically, they are sometimes referred to as the **sandwich generation** (Zal, 2002). According to recent statistics, there are "twenty-two million families who have at least one person who is a caregiver for an older member of the family" (Riley & Bowen, 2005, p. 52).

Regardless of whether there is an aging parent to take care of or not, this period of family life is one of the most active and exciting times in the family life cycle. It is filled with turbulence, stress, and demands that vary across families (Ellis, 1986). Some families may have trouble setting limits, defining relationships, and taking adequate care of one another. Others do just fine because they are better organized, do not have as many responsibilities, or have more congenial personalities.

The most obvious sign of stress in families with adolescents is seen in the number and kinds of disagreements between parents and teens. Increased family conflict and tension often occur during the time adolescents are in the family (Renk, Liljequist, Simpson, & Phares, 2005; Worden, 1992). The reasons for this increased conflict and tension are numerous. For one,

> [I]n families with adolescents, there seems to be a difficulty on the part of parents to make a distinction between what they want for their youngsters and what their youngsters want for themselves. This leads to parents' unwillingness to let youngsters make decisions for themselves even if they are good decisions. (Dickerson & Zimmerman, 1992, p. 341)

A second reason for the tension in these families is the process of adolescence itself. At this time of life, young adults express more of a desire and an assertiveness to be autonomous and independent (Collins, Newman, & McKenry, 1995; Fishman, 1988). Peer groups and siblings become more important for them, and parental influence decreases as conflicts with parents increase. Yet because adolescents are limited in experience, "they are restrained from seeing the multitude of possibilities available to them and are vulnerable to others' ideas ... [which they] fight against" (Dickerson & Zimmerman, 1992, p. 344). In response to this situation, families "must establish qualitatively different boundaries. ... Parents can no longer maintain complete authority" (McGoldrick & Carter, 1982, p. 183). Families with adolescents need to facilitate the recognition and acceptance of differences of family members and distinguish gender and age differences in the topics of parent-adolescent conflict. Generally, topics of parent-adolescent conflict include "everyday family matters, such as household rules and responsibilities" ... as well as "separation-individuation and autonomy issues, school-related issues, and the general values held by members of the family" (Renk et al., 2005, pp. 148–149).

If all goes well during this time in the family life cycle, adolescents develop what is known as a **planful competence,** which entails having a reasonably realistic understanding of their intellectual abilities, social skills, and personal emotional responses in interrelationships with others (Clausen, 1993). No environmental influence in the preadolescent years is as important to the development of adolescent planful competence as parenting. "Significant influences include parents paying attention to the child, providing intellectual stimulation, being supportive rather than abusive, involving the child in decision making, and conducting consistent disciplining" (Nurse, 1994, p. 36). Fathers who are as involved with their adolescents as mothers help raise psychologically healthier children who exhibit less delinquent behavior and who obtain more education (Elias, 1996).

Parenting may change during this stage as the couple relationship changes. "In the early afternoon of life—the forties, usually—many couples' relationships undergo a kind of sea change. [Either] the partners start to move closer, in ways that were not possible earlier in the marriage, or a huge amount of emotional distance begins to develop" (Scarf, 1992, p. 53). This change is related to the aging process and heightened feelings of vulnerability, "hers, about her desirability and attractiveness; his, about his virility and about physical survival itself" (Scarf, 1992, p. 53). If the couple treats each other with tenderness, empathy, and understanding, they become stronger partners and comfort each other. If, on the other hand, the couple misreads each other and does not understand the physiological changes occurring, they are likely to be rejecting and hostile toward each other.

Issues that are likely to prompt families with adolescents to seek family therapy are those connected with:

- conflict between parents and their teenage offspring, such as the setting of limits and the expression of opinions
- detachment or anger over the couple relationship as partners age developmentally and psychologically and realize dreams and opportunities are slipping away
- stress and pressure related to adequately balancing the care of aging parents with the demands of work and family life [spouse and child(ren)]

Launching Children and Moving On

As children leave home for college, careers, marriage, or other options, parents face the so-called **empty nest**—life for couples without child-rearing responsibilities. The percentage of empty nesters is increasing in the United States and will include 59% of all families by 2010, with the aging Baby Boomer generation fueling the trend (Carey & Rechin, 1996b). This time is ideal for couples to rediscover each other and have fun together. It is also a stage of vulnerability where couples may have problems over such issues as financial matters, sexual issues and ways of dealing with in-laws and grown children (Henry & Miller, 2004).

Most middle-aged women at this stage "are likely to be energetically attending to their own interests and thankful for the freedom to pursue them at last" (Scanzoni & Scanzoni, 1988, p. 535). For some women, who have mainly defined themselves as mothers and invested heavily in their children, the empty nest can be a time of sadness. In such situations, depression, despondency, and divorce may occur (Strong et al., 2005).

For men, the empty nest usually corresponds to midlife. At this time, men may focus on "their physical bodies, marriages, and occupational aspirations," as well as the new changes in the behaviors of their wives (Scanzoni & Scanzoni, 1988, p. 540). Because few studies have focused on men and the empty nest period, few data are available that report on how these men feel about the launching of their children. However, factors that correlate negatively for the happiness of men at the time of launching children are having few children, being older at the time of their children's leaving, experiencing unsatisfactory marriages, and being nurturant as fathers (Lewis, Freneau, & Roberts, 1979).

In recent years, a trend has developed where children remain with their families of origin for longer periods of time. This failure to leave or their return to the family, as **boomerang children,** is usually due to financial problems, unemployment, or an inability or reluctance to grow up (Clemens & Axelson, 1985). When children do not leave home or return home after having left, the result is often increased tension between parents and the young adult. Overall, as pointed out by Haley (1973), pathological behaviors tend to surface at points in the family life cycle when the process of disengagement of one generation from another is prevented or delayed.

Issues that are likely to prompt empty nesters to seek family therapy are those connected with:

- a sense of loss in regard to oneself, a marriage, or the moving out of a child
- a sense of conflict with a child who is not becoming independent enough
- a sense of frustration or anger in regard to one's marriage or career ambitions

Families in Later Life

The family in later life is usually composed of a couple in their final years of employment or in early retirement. The age range is from about 65 years and above. This stage of family life can cover a span of 20 or 30 years depending on the health of those involved. Within this stage are three groups: "the **young old** (65–74), the **old old** (75–84), and the **oldest old** (85 and after)" (Anderson, 1988, p. 19).

A general trend in these families is a physical decline of the individuals related to age (a gradual condition known as **senescence**) (Sharpe, 2003). Dependency may become an issue, too (Goldin & Mohr, 2000). In addition, one of the major concerns of some members of this group is finances. Older couples often worry about whether they will have enough money to take care of their needs. This concern is heightened when retirement occurs. It may be especially crucial to men who stop working or women who live long lives.

A second, equally important concern of older couples involves the loss of a spouse. Only about half the men and women over sixty-five are married; most of the others are widowed (U.S. Bureau of the Census, 2000). Recovering from the loss of a spouse is a difficult and prolonged process. It is one that women are more likely to face than men. The absence or presence of extended family at such times can make a difference in how one adjusts. The preservation of a coherent sense of self in the midst of loss is the best predictor of psychological and physiological resilience for older adults (Kaufman, 1986).

A third concern of the aging and their families is chronic illness:

> Among seniors age 65 to 84, arthritis, high blood pressure, and heart disease are most prevalent. For people over 85, the risk of cancer and the extent of disabilities increase, combined with intellectual, visual, and hearing impairment. Physical and mental deterioration may be exacerbated by depression and helplessness, reverberating with the anxiety of family members. (Walsh, 1999, p. 312)

Keeping healthy is a major task of this group.

The aging family also has advantages. One of them is being a grandparent or foster grandparent. Interacting with their children's children or other children heightens the sensitivity of many aging couples and helps them become more aware of the need for caring (Mead, 1972). The ability to do what one wants at one's pace is another advantage of this family stage. The family of later life, like the newly married couple, has the most freedom to come and go as they wish. Finally, the aging family can experience the enjoyment of having lived and participated in a number of important life cycle events. This is a time when couples can reflect on the activities they were too busy with previously.

Issues that are likely to prompt families in later life to seek family therapy are those connected with:

- a lack of meaning or enjoyment related to the loss of actively working or caring for children or the death of a spouse
- a concern over adjustments in aging, such as diminished energy or facing one's own mortality
- an inability to establish good relationships with children, in-laws, or grandchildren

A summary of family life cycle phases, stages, and crises is given in Table 1.1.

Unifying Individual and Family Life Cycles

It would seem difficult to unite individual and family life cycles in more than a superficial way. The reason is that, outwardly, stages in the individual life cycle do not always parallel and complement those within a family's development (e.g., Erikson, 1959; Gilligan, 1982; Levinson,

Table 1.1
Family Life Cycle Phases, Stages, and Crises

Phases	Family Life Cycle Stage	Practical Challenges	Emotional Challenges	Relational Challenges	Potential Crises
Coupling	Unattached young adult	Financial independence Caretaking of self	Secure sense of self Feelings of competency	Differentiation of self from family of origin	Failure to grow up
	Family formation through coupling	Finding potential mate Economic partnership Domestic cooperation Compatibility of interests	Commitment Balancing needs and expectations of self and partner	Form stable marital unit Shifting allegiances from family of origin to new family	Failure to find a mate or commit End of "honeymoon" In-law conflict
Expansion	Family with young children	Financial obligations Organizing household for raising children	Accepting new members Nurturance Parental responsibilities	Maintaining marital unit Integrating grandparents and other relatives	Marital dissatisfaction School and behavior problems
	Family with adolescents	Less predictable routines and schedules Adolescent unavailability	Flexibility with change Sense of irrelevance Loss of control	Maintaining contact between parents and adolescent Caring for elderly parents	Adolescent rebellion
Contraction	Launching children and moving on	Financial burdens (college, weddings, etc.) New financial resources Refocus on work	Loss of family life with children Aging and death of parents	Reestablishing primacy of marriage Adult relationship with children	"Empty nest" Children returning home
	Family in later life	Uncertainties of old age: economic insecurities Medical care	Coping with loss Maintaining dignity despite decline	Maintaining adequate support systems Reconciliation	Retirement Illness and death

From "The Family Life Cycle: Phases, Stages, and Crises" by R. Gerson, in *Integrating Family Therapy* (p. 96), edited by R. H. Mikesell, D.-D. Lusterman, and S. H. McDaniel, 1995, Washington, DC: American Psychological Association. Copyright © 1995 by the American Psychological Association. Reprinted with permission.

1978, 1986; Sheehy, 1977). The two life cycle concepts are unique because of the number of people involved in them, the diversity of tasks required in each, and gender distinctions. Yet, the differences in these ways of viewing life may not be as sharp or contrasting as they first appear.

One unifying emphasis of both the individual and family life cycles is the focus within each on growth and development. In most types of growth there is "change in the direction of greater awareness, competence, and authenticity" (Jourard & Landsman, 1980, p. 238). Within individuals and families, growth can be a conscious process that involves **courage,** that is, the ability to take calculated risks without knowing the exact consequences. When planned strategies and activities are outlined and accomplished as a part of growth, persons understand the past more thoroughly, live actively and fully in the present, and envision possibilities of the future more clearly.

A second unifier of individual and family life cycles is that they can both be viewed from a systemic perspective. **Systems theory** focuses on the interconnectedness of elements within all living organisms, that is, systems. It is based on the work of Ludwig von Bertalanffy (1968), a biologist, who proposed that to fully understand how a living creature operates, it is necessary to see the interfunctioning of the entire unit. A person and a family are more than the separate parts that compose them. They are a whole—a system that expresses itself through an organization, rules, and repetitive patterns.

Therefore, in working with individuals and families, therapists must emphasize **circular causality,** the idea that actions are a part of "a causal chain, each influencing and being influenced by the other" (Goldenberg & Goldenberg, 2002, p. 25). For instance, a mother overprotects her awkward and shy daughter, who stays awkward and shy due to a lack of opportunities to do otherwise, which leads to continued overprotection, which results in more awkwardness and shyness, and so forth. This idea is the opposite of **linear causality,** in which forces are seen as moving in one direction with each action causing another. In linear causality, a mother's overprotection would be targeted as the cause of her daughter's awkwardness and shyness (see Figure 1.4).

A third unifying aspect of the individual and family life cycles is that they are complementary and competitive (McGoldrick, Gerson, & Shellenberger, 1998). People within each cycle go through experiences for which they are usually developmentally ready. For example, children enter school at age 5 or 6. Most couples become parents in their late 20s or early 30s. Likewise, from interacting with their environments, the majority of individuals and families become aware of their skills and abilities. For example, from his play with peers, an adolescent may realize he is not as gifted an athlete as he previously thought. Similarly, family members may appreciate each other more from having survived a natural trauma, such as an earthquake, a flood, a hurricane, or a fire (Figley, 1989). In this sense, the challenges and associated work of one life cycle complement the challenges and work of the other.

Figure 1.4
Linear versus circular thinking.

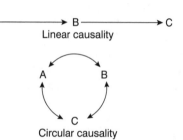

In the competitive realm, the needs and desires of individuals within the family often differ with the needs of the family to sustain itself. For example, a young couple might want to visit friends or relatives, but are distracted by the demands of their toddler who might prefer running around their host's house. A second area of conflict involves launching young people into the world. Sometimes these individuals are hesitant to go and resist leaving home (Haley, 1980). Both the family and the young adults suffer in the struggle that ensues.

Implications of Life Cycles for Family Therapy

Life cycles have a number of implications regarding family therapy. Some are more subtle than others, but all are important.

Match of Life Cycles Between Family and Therapist

The "fit" between a family's and a therapist's life cycles plays a major role in the process of helping a family change. Fit is an ever-changing variable that fluctuates according to the ages and stages of all involved in the therapeutic process. If a therapist "brings unresolved issues from a past or current life cycle stage into the clinical work with a family that is struggling to navigate the same life cycle stage, predictable problems may emerge" (Lerner, 1999, p. 512). Basically, the life cycles of a therapist and family can combine in three major ways: "(1) the therapist has not yet experienced the family's stage; (2) the therapist is currently experiencing the same stage of the life cycle as the family; and (3) the therapist has already been through that stage of the life cycle" (Simon, 1988, p. 108). While each of these global factors presents its own unique challenge, specific variables have an impact too. "The match between the therapist and the clinical family on variables such as race, ethnicity, gender, class, sibling position, and sexual orientation" must be considered for they also "influence the degree to which the life cycle issues become emotionally loaded in therapy" (Lerner, 1999, p. 513).

Particularly problematic areas include the ability to express empathy and understanding, or to establish rapport. These difficulties may be especially prevalent in cases where the therapist has not yet experienced the family's stage of development or where the therapist lacks awareness of matters related to variables such as ethnicity, class, or sexual orientation. Contempt, anxiety, or jealousy may interfere with therapists whose life cycles parallel families with whom they work or who may be of the same race or gender. On the other hand, "fit with families gets a little easier" as therapists get older and past crucial life stages (Simon, 1988, p. 110). In such circumstances, families may feel that therapists recognize and understand their problems better. However, on the downside, therapists who are beyond the life stage of their client families may have difficulties in regard to acting too knowledgeable, being out of touch with current realities, dealing with ghosts of their own pasts, and being "distant, cynical, or patronizing" (Simon, 1988, p. 111).

To compensate for a lack of fit between themselves and the families they are working with, therapists of all ages and backgrounds can do several things. First, they can work on increasing their sensitivity to particular families and issues with such families. Each family differs, and therapists, regardless of age and background, can usually be helpful if they are attuned to the specific concerns of a family. Second, therapists who do not ideally fit certain families can have their work supervised. Often, through peer consultation and clinical supervision, family therapists learn ways to overcome their deficits. Finally, a lack of fit can be addressed by continuing education programs that give therapists greater knowledge and skill in dealing with specific types of families or variables.

Ethnicity and Life Cycles

The ethnic background of families influences their concept of life cycles and their behaviors in regard to life events. It is important for clinicians to evaluate families in relation to their ethnic background and not to judge them from a limited cultural perspective (Hines et al., 1999). For example, different ethnic groups place more value on certain events and rituals such as funerals, weddings, and transitions from childhood to adulthood. Types of interaction dominant in a majority culture, such as among European Americans, may not be considered appropriate in a minority culture, such as among African Americans or Asian Americans.

In therapeutic situations, families become more attuned to their ethnic backgrounds and values. In family therapy it is important to encourage families to use their life cycle transitions to strengthen individual, family, and cultural identities (Hines et al., 1999). Through such a process, families and their members gain a greater appreciation of and sensitivity to their heritage and the role of the past in present-day life.

Family therapists, regardless of their cultural backgrounds, can work with a variety of families if they attune themselves to learning about the culture and the circumstances from whence these families came. Therapists must acquire special skills as well, through both formal training and continuing education. Finally, therapists must realize that, regardless of their best efforts, gender and ethnicity differences between themselves and their clients may enhance or detract from the therapeutic experience, at least initially (Gregory & Leslie, 1996).

Illness and Life Cycles

The onset of an illness in a family member can disrupt life cycles temporarily or permanently. The person and family may suffer only a mild setback if the illness is acute and of short duration. However, if the illness is more severe, such as AIDS, a heart condition, cancer, a chronically ill child, or a mental disorder, relationships and functioning in the family and its most directly affected members, such as the couple, will be impacted (Snyder & Whisman, 2004). In such cases, families can expect changes in the quality of the couple and family relationship, roles and responsibilities within the family, and social support. A chronic illness may wear down a family leading to a deteriorated condition and finally to separation or divorce (Cloutier, Manion, Walker, & Johnson, 2002). On the other hand, a chronic illness may, "like any other life challenge, present an opportunity for growth" and bring a couple or family closer together (Kowal, Johnson, & Lee, 2003, p. 301).

In examining illness and life cycles, therapists must examine the onset of the disorder, its course, the outcome, and its degree of incapacitation, if any (Rolland, 1999). A progressive and chronic disease, such as Alzheimer's, can put a major strain on caretakers within a family and the family as a whole. The result may be the delay of life cycle transitions, such as marriage, and the blockage of unfinished business. On the other hand, a heart condition, while putting a strain on the family, may also give family members more of a chance to communicate and bond.

Therapeutically, it is imperative that those who work with families help them assess present ways of functioning in relationships as compared with past coping strategies (Rolland,

1999). For example, a therapist may explore with family members how they previously dealt with a family illness. Thus, therapists and families may better understand present behaviors and the individuals within the family unit. Therapists may also assist families in resolving the developmental disruptions that occur in dealing with diseases. There is a growing movement in family therapy to focus on mental and physical issues in families (Cloutier et al., 2002; Wynne, Shields, & Sirkin, 1992). To work best in this domain and be effective, family therapists must prepare themselves through direct educational and supervisory experiences.

Poverty, Professionalism, and Life Cycles

As indicated throughout this chapter, individuals and families are affected by economic as well as social factors. Dual-career professional families and low-income families do not go through life cycle stages in the same way or at the same rate as other families. There is an "extreme elongation of the process of forming the family in the professional class and an extreme acceleration in the lower class" (Fulmer, 1988, p. 548).

Poverty and professionalism have several implications for family therapy. One of the most obvious is for therapists to realize that the structure of these two types of families differs. Families in poverty are generally larger, more dependent on kin, and maternal. They struggle and are stressed to obtain the necessities of life and make ends meet (Brown, 2002). Continuing poverty pushes fathers away from their children and families because these men are often working two or three jobs and are simply not available (Elias, 1996). Regardless of race or cultural background, being poor or near poor brings with it a host of factors—chronic shortage of money; accumulating debts; low levels of literacy; high rates of unemployment; incarceration; substance abuse; depression and domestic violence; poor housing and unsafe neighborhoods—that places enormous stress on relationships (Ooms & Wilson, 2004). In contrast, families of professionals are generally smaller, dependent on hired help, and often more individual or career focused. They can afford to buy services and engage in a number of enriching activities. Therefore, their levels of mental health and sense of well-being tend to be higher.

In addition to structural differences, symptom formation differs, with symptoms in poor families often connected with sudden shifts and changes in life cycle events, and symptoms in professional families often connected with delays in reaching developmental milestones. The comparison of family life stages for these two types of families from ages 12 to 35 is shown in Table 1.2, as outlined by Fulmer (1988). Therapists must acquaint themselves with the issues of both types of families. To be of assistance to each, they must cognitively and psychologically learn to address their unique problems and possibilities.

Summary and Conclusion

This chapter has examined the family from an historical and a contemporary viewpoint. Historically, families have been around since before recorded time. They have served a number of functions including social, economic, and reproductive—many of the same purposes served by contemporary families. Yet today there are more family forms (dual-career, gay/lesbian, aging, etc.) and more opinions on what constitutes a family. A family may be considered in its broadest context to include those persons who are biologically and/or psychologically related, whose historical, emotional, or economic bonds connect, and who perceive themselves as a part of a household. The three most prevalent family forms are nuclear, single parent, and remarried.

Table 1.2
Comparison of Family Life Cycle Stages

Age	Professional Families	Low-Income Families
12–17	a. Prevent pregnancy b. Graduate from high school c. Parents continue support while permitting child to achieve greater independence	a. First pregnancy b. Attempt to graduate from high school c. Parent attempts strict control before pregnancy; after pregnancy, relaxation of controls and continued support of new mother and infant
18–21	a. Prevent pregnancy b. Leave parental household for college c. Adapt to parent–child separation	a. Second pregnancy b. No further education c. Young mother acquires adult status in parental household
22–25	a. Prevent pregnancy b. Develop professional identity in graduate school c. Maintain separation from parental household; begin living in serious relationship	a. Third pregnancy b. Marriage—leave parental household to establish stepfamily c. Maintain connection with kinship network
26–30	a. Prevent pregnancy b. Marriage—develop nuclear couple as separate from parents c. Intense work involvement as career begins	a. Separate from husband b. Mother becomes head of own household within kinship network
31–35	a. First pregnancy b. Renew contact with parents as grandparents c. Differentiate career and child-rearing roles between husband and wife	a. First grandchild b. Mother becomes grandmother and cares for daughter and infant

From Betty Carter & Monica McGoldrick(Eds). *The Changing Family Life Cycle: A Framework for Family Therapy 2e.* Published by Allyn and Bacon, Boston, MA. Copyright © 1989 by Pearson Education. Reprinted by permission of the publisher.

Different models of individual and family life cycles have been constructed over the years to explain tasks and potential problems of people and family units. Erik Erikson first popularized the idea of an individual life cycle through his research and writings on the eight stages of life. His work has been praised for its innovation but criticized for its limited focus on males. The idea of a family life cycle was first proposed by Evelyn Duvall, only a few years after Erikson's model was introduced. Duvall's model was based on the nuclear family of the 1950s. In more recent years, as families in the United States have become more diverse, varied models of family life cycles have been proposed. The cycles of Carter and McGoldrick (1999), which cover many different forms of family life, are among the most useful. This chapter presented the six-stage model of the intact, middle-class nuclear family. This model is used for comparison with other life cycle models, including Erikson's individual life cycle model.

Individual and family life cycles intertwine at times. Events in one impact those in the other. Individual and family life cycles are similar in their emphases on growth, development, and systemic interaction. However, they often differ in other ways, with individual life cycles focused more narrowly and family life cycles focused more systemically. Family therapists must be aware of individual issues, as well as family issues, that are brought before them.

As a rule, family therapists should be aware of how their own individual and family life stages compare with those of their clients. They must also be sensitive to health, ethnic/cultural, and socioeconomic issues as they relate to families. A general systems perspective of individuals and families allows for such a broad-based view. It permits therapists to observe dynamics within the system of the person and family without blaming or focusing on unimportant micro-issues. Family therapists can study and receive supervision to overcome deficits they may have in regard to issues surrounding a particular type of family. Overall, the family life cycle and the variables that compose it are exciting to study and complex entities with which to work.

Summary Table

Individual and Family Life Cycles

Families date back to prehistoric times and have played an important part in the development of persons and nations.

Social and economic forces, wars, national policies, and natural disasters have modified the structure and governance of families.

Families must be worked with from a developmental, systemic, and historical perspective. The dynamics of external and internal pressures and interactions should be taken into consideration.

What Is a Family?

The definition of a family varies across cultural settings and often changes over time. However, despite various definitions, the family is a system with members impacting one another in an interactive and circular way.

The U.S. Bureau of the Census (2005) gives a broad definition of a family as "a group of two or more persons related by birth, marriage, or adoption and residing together in a household." However, this definition excludes some relationships that people consider families.

For this text, a family is defined broadly as those persons who are biologically and/or psychologically related, whom historical, emotional, or economic bonds connect, and who perceive themselves as a part of a household.

Overall, families are characterized by economic, physical, social, and emotional functions. They foster development and offer stability.

Among the different types of families are nuclear, single-parent, remarried, dual-career, child-free, gay/lesbian, aging, military, and multigenerational.

Individual and Family Development

Development is an uneven and powerful factor in families.

Three different time dimensions affect personal and family life: individual time, social time, and historical time.

The term *life cycle* is used to describe personal and family life development. These two life cycles intertwine and are interactive. Dealing with them in isolation is artificial.

Individual life cycle development has been popularized in the work of Erikson and others who describe human life in terms of stages. People face developmental crises in each of these stages.

Erikson's first five stages deal with the formation of a person as a competent individual. His final three stages are more interpersonally based.

Developmental theories have focused mainly on men but are slowly being formulated for women as well.

The family life cycle is a social/cultural phenomenon that was first proposed by Duvall in 1956. It has been modified over the years, and currently life cycles are available that describe many types of families.

A family life cycle for middle-class, nuclear families proposed by Carter and McGoldrick outlines the following six stages:

1. *Single young adults—tasks:* to develop personal autonomy, leave home, establish a career, and develop a support group
2. *The new couple—tasks:* to adjust and adapt, and learn to share with partner
3. *Families with young children—tasks:* to adjust time, energy, and personal schedules to take care of child[ren], self, and other relationships
4. *Families with adolescents—tasks:* to physically and psychologically take care of self, couple relationship, child[ren], and aging parents, and successfully handle increased family tension and conflict
5. *Families launching children and moving on—tasks:* to rediscover each other as a couple, deal with midlife events, and encourage their children to be independent
6. *Families in later life—tasks:* to adjust to aging, loss of a spouse, and decreased energy

Unifying Individual and Family Life Cycles

Individual and family life cycles are characterized by:

- growth and development
- systemic interconnectedness of people
- complementary and competitive experiences occurring within a societal context

Implications of Life Cycles for Family Therapy

Life cycles impact family therapy through:

- the matching or fitting of the therapist's life stage(s) with that of the family
- the understanding, or lack thereof, between the therapist's ethnic background and that of the family
- the influence of the unexpected, such as an illness, on the stage development of the family/individual
- the uniqueness of poverty or professionalism on the rate of recovery and the resources of the family as therapy progresses

Family therapists can overcome developmental or systemic handicaps in regard to working with families through education, supervision, consultation, and experience.

CHAPTER 2

Healthy and Dysfunctional Families

———————•———————

Amid the white sterility of intensive care
and the cries of incubated newborns
I watch your parents struggle in the quiet realization
that your life hangs by a thread too thin to sustain it.
Tenuously you fight to hold onto every breath
until peacefully, in your father's arms,
you give up in exhaustion
and with a final release, almost like a whisper,
air leaves your lungs forever.

Your mother has said her gentle good-byes
only hours after your birth
with her dreams turning into nightmares
as she contemplates her loss in the thought
of going home to silence.

Life, like faith, is sometimes fragile
best personified in newness and simple acts of courage.

———————•———————

Gladding, 1992a

amily life is constantly changing, and what is considered functional and healthy in one era is not necessarily seen the same way later. In the 1890s, widespread agreement existed among middle-class European Americans, within urban centers in the United States, that a healthy and functional family was patriarchal (Footlick, 1990). Fathers were breadwinners and rule makers; mothers were bread makers and caregivers. This type of picture is still attractive to some people and is represented in television shows from the 1950s and 1960s such as "Ozzie and Harriet," "Leave It to Beaver," and "Fathers Knows Best" (Pistole & Marson, 2005).

Realistically there are, and always have been, other kinds of functional families and family-like arrangements (Coontz, 2000). What were considered nontraditional family forms (e.g., single-parent, dual-career, egalitarian, and extended) now outnumber nuclear families and have been depicted in television shows from the 1970s to the present such as "Murphy Brown," "The Cosby Show," "7th Heaven," and "Frasier" (Pistole & Marson, 2005).

Regardless of form, the health of families varies over their life spans. The fact that a family is healthy at one stage of life of its existence is no guarantee that it will remain that way (Carlson & Fullmer, 1992; Carter & McGoldrick, 1999). Achieving and maintaining health demands constant work for members of a family unit as well as the family as a whole.

Numerous events can throw families into new or unexpected ways of functioning. When such events occur, family relationships are altered, and the family as a whole is shaken up. "Destabilizing events create stress to which family systems can react in different ways. Some systems respond by transforming the rules under which they operate, thereby allowing new, more functional behaviors. In other systems, rather than changing shape, a medical or psychological symptom emerges" (Fishman, 1988, p. 15). For example, "the onset of episodes of depression and anxiety may be precipitated by a buildup of stressful life events" (Hickey et al., 2005, p. 171). Healthy families reorganize their structure and relationships to accommodate new circumstances. For instance, they may increase their social support from their families and friends and thus facilitate their problem-solving ability and enhance their communication with one another (Hickey et al., 2005). This type of readjustment keeps these families from becoming chaotic (Cuber & Harroff, 1966).

This chapter examines qualities associated with healthy and dysfunctional families. First, the family as a living system will be explored in regard to its well-being and growth. This exploration will be followed by a discussion of the qualities of healthy families. Next, family stressors, both expected and unexpected, are looked at in regard to their impact on families, and the influence of family structure on functionality is considered. Coping strategies for dealing with family stress are highlighted, too. Finally, the implications of health (especially mental health) in working with families are featured.

The Family System and Health

As briefly examined in Chapter 1, **systems theory** is the basis on which the majority of family therapists view families and around which they organize their clinical work. The theory was refined and developed by Ludwig von Bertalanffy (1934, 1968), a biologist, in an attempt to explain how organisms thrive or die in accordance with their openness or closedness to their environments (Kaplan, 2000). Bertalanffy "saw the essential phenomena of life as individual entities called 'organisms'" (Okun & Rappaport, 1980, p. 6). He defined an **organism** as a form of life "composed of mutually dependent parts and processes standing in mutual interaction" (Bertalanffy, 1968, p. 33). As such, an organism was primarily motivated behaviorally by internal mechanisms. From Bertalanffy's work, social scientists conceptualized that all living systems, including families, operate on a similar set of principles; that is, they are internally interdependent.

Therefore, in a family, members are constantly interacting and mutually affecting one another as they are in relationship to each other. When change or movement occurs in any of the members or circumstances that make up the family system, all aspects of the family are affected for better or worse. Thus, the family's well-being and ability to function are influenced by the health of all of its members.

From a healthy systems perspective, families are continuously changing and reconstituting themselves. Those that stay healthy are open and self-regulating. They are also interactive within larger social systems. The family stabilizes and maintains homeostasis by using **negative feedback loops,** which are also called **attenuating feedback loops** (or loops that promote a return to equilibrium) as shown in Figure 2.1. These loops, like a thermostat in a home heating system, allow family expansion and contraction within the limits of a range of behaviors. If for some reason the negative feedback loops do not work, the family may increase actions in which they are engaged and be better or worse for it. A comparison analogy would be such a family using **positive feedback loops,** which are also known as **amplifying feedback loops** (or loops that promote change). Times of stability and homeostasis are temporary, and a major task for families is to maintain a balance between stability and change. If there is too much stability, the family may become stagnant; if there is too much change, the family may become chaotic.

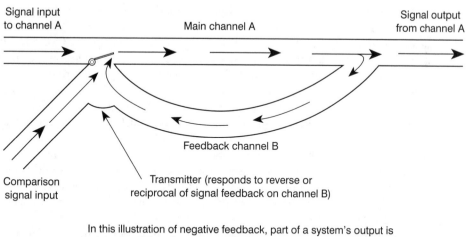

In this illustration of negative feedback, part of a system's output is reintroduced into the system as information about the output, thus governing and correcting the process. A negative signal from channel A, fed back to the sender through channel B, alters the signal in A. Feedback loops characterize all interpersonal relationships.

Figure 2.1
Negative feedback loops.
From "The Nature of Living Systems" by J. G. Miller, 1971, *Behavioral Sciences, 16,* p. 293. Reprinted by permission of the Mental Health Research Institute.

Viewing families as systems involves recognizing that the relationships formed among family members are extremely powerful and account for a considerable amount of human behavior, emotion, values, and attitudes. Moreover, like strands of a spider web, each family relationship, as well as each family member, influences all other family relationships and all other members (Figley, 1989, p. 4).

Qualities of Healthy Families

Studies reveal that functional families in virtually all cultures are able to adapt to change, set appropriate boundaries, develop relationships through open communication, promote responsibility, express confidence in themselves and their children, and are optimistic about their future (Cutler & Radford, 1999). Yet there is still disagreement as to all of the qualities of ideal healthy families. A fundamental disagreement exists over what the word *health* means. **Health** is an interactive process associated with positive relationships and outcomes (Wilcoxon, 1985). In families, health involves ethical accountability such as promoting good relationships and balancing the give-and-take among members (Boszormenyi-Nagy & Ulrich, 1981). Most families experience times of both healthy and unhealthy interactions during the family life cycle.

One cannot assume, however, that healthy individuals necessarily come from continuously healthy families (Wolin & Wolin, 1993). Highly resilient individuals who overcome adversities do well in life (Walsh, 1995). However, being in a healthy family environment is an advantage for learning productive relationships and is more helpful than not.

As a group, healthy families have a number of characteristics in common. Families that are most successful, happy, and strong are balanced in a number of ways. They seem to know what issues to address and how to address them. Furthermore, they do not operate from either an extreme cognitive or emotional framework. They exert the right amount of energy in dealing with the matters before them, and they make realistic plans. Overall, in families with a sense of well-being, multiple forces and factors interact in complex but positive ways.

One of the most vital factors underlying a healthy family is the strength and health of the marital unit (Beavers, 1985; Lavee, McCubbin, & Olson, 1987). A healthy marriage "appears to be a multidimensional, complex, nonsummative unit" (Erkstein, 2004, p. 415). It is intimate, flexible, and even synergistic (Olson & Olson, 2000). In such a relationship, partners adapt to and promote the individual growth of each other because they are healthy to begin with. Such couples get along and work at keeping the marriage exciting and open. They are able to be in touch with and express a wide array of emotions, communicate clearly, and are equalitarian and mutually supportive. "Individuals who are successful in their intimate partnerships are willing to make sacrifices and report satisfaction about sacrificing itself" (Stabb, 2005, p. 440).

Many of the characteristics that distinguish healthy couples from dysfunctional ones also separate well-functioning families from those who function less well (McCoy, 1996). According to research (Krysan, Moore, & Zill, 1990; Stinnett & DeFrain, 1985), healthy families include the following characteristics:

- commitment to the family and its individuals
- appreciation for each other (i.e., a social connection)
- willingness to spend time together
- effective communication patterns

- high degree of religious/spiritual orientation
- ability to deal with crisis in a positive manner (i.e., adaptability)
- encouragement of individuals
- clear roles

The following sections address these characteristics, along with the importance of structure and development within families.

Commitment

At the core of healthy family functioning is the idea of commitment. "In strong families, members are devoted not only to the welfare of the family but also to the growth of each of the members" (Thomas, 1992, p. 62). A commitment to the family is the basis for family members giving their time and energy to family-related activities.

Commitment involves staying loyal to the family and its members through both good and adverse life events. It is based on both emotion and intention. Couples and individuals, who have not thought through their commitment to one another or who are ambivalent about how committed they are, have difficulty staying in a marriage and working with each other. The result is often infidelity (Pittman, 1991).

Appreciation

The commitment that family members have toward one another is strengthened when they verbally or physically express their appreciation. In healthy families, "the marital partners tend to build the self-esteem of their mates by mutual love, respect, [and] compliments" (Thomas, 1992, p. 64). Other family members do likewise with each other. They avoid fights that take the form of personal attacks or violence (Wills, Weiss, & Patterson, 1974).

Willingness to Spend Time Together

Healthy families spend both quantitative and qualitative time together. "The time they spend together needs to be good time; no one enjoys hours of bickering, arguing, pouting, or bullying. Time also needs to be sufficient; quality interaction isn't likely to develop in a few minutes together" (Stinnett & DeFrain, 1985, pp. 83–84).

Events that encompass both qualitative and quantitative time abound. They range from family picnics to overnight campouts, to vacations, to special nights out that involve entertainment, such as a play, ballgame, or concert. They also encompass rituals and traditions such as celebrating birthdays and anniversaries, family interactions at mealtimes, and observing rites of passage together, such as graduations, weddings, and funerals (Giblin, 1995). The idea behind spending time together is sharing thoughts, feelings, and identities. In the process, family members come to think of themselves as a cohesive unit and not just a random group of individuals.

Effective Communication Patterns

"Communication is concerned with the delivery and reception of verbal and nonverbal information between family members. It includes skills in exchanging patterns of information within the family system" (Brock & Barnard, 1999, p. 36). When families are healthy, members attend to the messages from one another and pick up on subtle as well as obvious points.

Within these families there is support, understanding, and empathy (Giblin, 1994). There is no competition for "air time" or silence. Messages are sent and received in a sensitive or caring manner.

Brock and Barnard (1999) have delineated characteristics of optimal family communication situations. They state that in the best of circumstances, communication within families is of a high volume and includes seeking and sharing patterns. The messages between family members are clear and congruent. In addition, healthy families deal with a wide range of topics and are open to talking rather than remaining silent. When there is conflict, these families seek to work it out through discussion. Family members seek to problem-solve. They are more likely than not to communicate in a positive tone.

Religious/Spiritual Orientation

A religious/spiritual orientation to life is a characteristic of "the vast majority of the world's families" (Prest & Keller, 1993, p. 137). Involvement in the religious/spiritual dimension of life also correlates with an overall sense of marital and family health and well-being. Spiritual beliefs and practices help families cope, be resilient, as well as find meaning and moral principles by which to live (Griffith & Rotter, 1999; Walsh & Pryce, 2003). According to research, religion and spirituality have traditionally played an important part in the lives of some groups more than others. For example, collective faith has been the cornerstone by which African Americans were supported and sustained from the "oppression of slavery" to the "civil rights movement" (Hampson, Beavers, & Hulgus, 1990, p. 308).

An orientation still exists toward the religious/spiritual in regard to both organized and unorganized efforts. The elderly and adolescent, to say nothing of those in middle age, are frequently involved in life matters that can best be described as religious/spiritual (Campbell & Moyers, 1988). In addition, members of families often deal as a group with religious/spiritual questions during certain events, for example, deaths, births, and marriages. Couples, who share a common faith or orientation toward religious matters and who are intrinsically motivated in their religious/spiritual orientation, report more satisfaction in their relationships than those who are divided on these issues (Anthony, 1993).

Ability to Deal with Crisis in a Positive Manner

A number of different types of crises affect families over their life span. Usually the most common type of crisis is an expected event, which is active. An **expected event** is one that is predictable and actually occurs, for example, leaving one's family of origin to make a life for oneself, finding employment, or getting married. In these situations the general nature of the event is known but the specifics are always unique, hence the crisis. Families that function well in these times use such coping strategies as negotiating, seeking advice from those who are more experienced, rehearsing, using humor, and expressing emotions to deal with such transitions (Schlossberg, Waters, & Goodman, 1996).

There are also **nonevents,** which are passive in the sense that they are events that do not happen as envisioned or expected (Schlossberg et al., 1996). Examples of a nonevent might be the failure of a couple to have healthy children or to reach their financial goals in life. In such circumstances, families are thrown into a crisis that may or may not be recognized by others. Healthy families deal with these situations by expressing their emotions and supporting one another.

Encouragement of Individuals

Because families work as systems, they are only as strong as their weakest members. It behooves families to encourage the development of talents and abilities within their individual members. Such a process is generally done systemically and is carried out over the family life cycle (Carter & McGoldrick, 1999).

Encouragement is especially important at certain times in the life cycle. Among the most crucial times encouragement is needed are:

- with school-age children as they engage in the educational process
- with adolescents as they cope with physical changes and peer groups
- with young adults as they move from their parents' houses into their own psychological and physical spaces filled with dreams and possibilities (Lambie & Daniels-Mohring, 1993)

Clear Roles

Roles are prescribed and repetitive behaviors involving a set of reciprocal activities with other family members (Steinhauser, Santa-Barbara, & Skinner, 1984). Roles in healthy families are clear, appropriate, suitably allocated, mutually agreed on, integrated, and enacted (Minuchin, 1974). Some roles are necessary, such as the provision of material resources. Others are unique and/or unnecessary, such as the acquiring of coins for a coin collection.

The exact roles within families are determined by such factors as age, culture, and tradition. Healthy families strive to make roles as interchangeable and flexible as possible.

Growth-Producing Structure and Development Patterns

Healthy families are organized in a clear, appropriate, and growth-producing way (Lewis, Beavers, Gossett, & Phillips, 1976; McGoldrick, Gerson, & Shellenberger, 1999; Napier & Whitaker, 1978). There are no **intergenerational coalitions** (e.g., members from different generations, such as a mother and daughter, colluding as a team) or **conflictual triangles** (e.g., two individuals, such as a mother and father, arguing over and interacting in regard to a third person, such as a rebellious son, instead of attending to their relationship) as the basis for keeping the family together. Instead, parents are in charge (or, in the case of single-parent families, the single parent is in charge). **Subsystems,** such as those composed of family members logically grouped together because of age or function (e.g., parents), carry out needed tasks (e.g., parenting). Because the structure is clear, the **boundaries** (physical and psychological lines of demarcation) are and growth can take place. When a family member steps out of bounds, family pressure brings him or her back into line. This process takes place through **homeostasis**—the tendency to resist change and keep things as they are. For instance, if a teenager violates a curfew, the parents may "ground" the young person for a week or until responsibility is taken for coming home on time.

Other salient features of healthy families that center around structure are those connected with the formation and display of symptoms. Some individual dysfunctions, such as depression (Lopez, 1986), career indecisiveness (Kinnier, Brigman, & Noble, 1990), and substance abuse (West, Hosie, & Zarski, 1987), are related to family structure. In these situations, families are usually too tightly or too loosely organized, a matter that is discussed more fully later in this chapter.

Family Life Stressors

Stress is a part of every family's life. As with individuals, families attempt to keep stressful events from becoming distressful, that is, overwhelming to the point that the family cannot function (Selye, 1976). They do this through a variety of means, some of which are more healthy (such as planning ahead) than others. Sometimes families cope with stressors according to whether they are prepared to deal with the situations or not.

Carter and McGoldrick (1999) have placed family stressors into two categories: vertical and horizontal (see Figure 2.2). **Vertical stressors** are those that bring past and present issues to

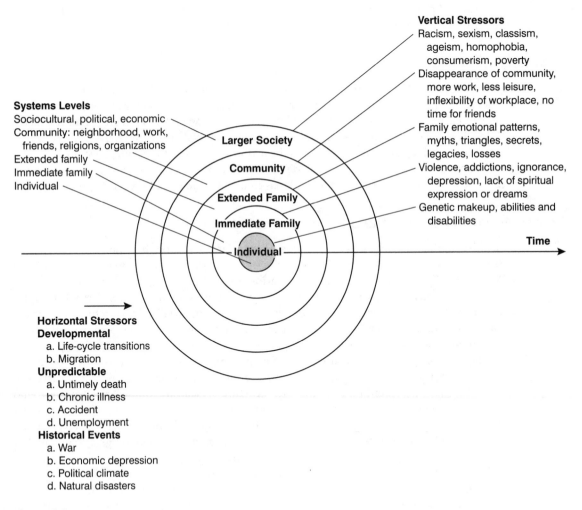

Vertical Stressors
Racism, sexism, classism, ageism, homophobia, consumerism, poverty
Disappearance of community, more work, less leisure, inflexibility of workplace, no time for friends
Family emotional patterns, myths, triangles, secrets, legacies, losses
Violence, addictions, ignorance, depression, lack of spiritual expression or dreams
Genetic makeup, abilities and disabilities

Systems Levels
Sociocultural, political, economic
Community: neighborhood, work, friends, religions, organizations
Extended family
Immediate family
Individual

Larger Society
Community
Extended Family
Immediate Family
Individual

Time

Horizontal Stressors
Developmental
  a. Life-cycle transitions
  b. Migration
Unpredictable
  a. Untimely death
  b. Chronic illness
  c. Accident
  d. Unemployment
Historical Events
  a. War
  b. Economic depression
  c. Political climate
  d. Natural disasters

Figure 2.2
Flow of stress through a family.

From Carter, B. and McGoldrick, M., in *The Expanded Family Life Cycle*, 3/e © 1999. Published by Allyn and Bacon, Boston, MA. Copyright © 1999 by Pearson Education. Reprinted by permission of the publisher.

bear reciprocally, such as family attitudes, expectations, secrets, and legacies. These stressors are historical and inherited from previous generations. They are the hand family members were dealt. **Horizontal stressors** are aspects of life that relate to the present. They are developmental and unfolding. Many are predictable and expected, including **life cycle transitions** (i.e., the transition from one stage of life to another, such as going from being a new couple to being a couple with a new child). Others are unpredictable, such as an untimely death, chronic illness, or the loss of a job.

The occurrence and impact of some developmental stressors can be predicted for the future. For example, the structure of the family and its vertical and horizontal stressors shift over time. This transition occurs in several ways, but one prevalent way is with the addition of an extra generation to the life of the family (e.g., having aging parents come and live with their grown children). Such a change tilts the family as a whole from a more horizontal to a more vertical emphasis. Likewise, if couples in the United States continue to have fewer children, "individuals in upcoming generations will have fewer siblings and cousins (horizontal dimension) and more relatives in the older generations (vertical dimension). ... Divorces and remarriages by children may multiply the vertical lines of the family" (Shields, King, & Wynne, 1995, p. 141).

Overall, the Carter and McGoldrick model of family life stressors is systemic and in line with how most family therapists view families. Families, however, are unique in their timing of transition events. Families plan for their children to grow up, leave home, and start families; but British-American families usually expect a much faster shift in these events than Italian-American families. Anticipating when events may happen helps family members prepare mentally and physically for changes. Sometimes family life stages and individual life stages complement each other (Bowen, 1978); at other times, families and individuals may become distressed and dysfunctional.

Expected Life Stressors

Families can expect a number of stressors regardless of their level of functioning. As indicated, some are **developmental stressors** (i.e., age and life-stage related), and others are **situational stressors** (i.e., interpersonal, such as dealing with feelings) (Figley, 1989). Some stressors are related to present events such as work, school, and social functions (Kaslow, 1991). Others are more historical in nature (i.e., they have family life heritage).

When surveyed, family members frequently cite prevalent stressors in their families as those associated with (1) economics and finances; (2) children's behaviors; (3) insufficient couple time; (4) communicating with children; (5) insufficient personal time; and (6) insufficient family play time (Curran, 1985). Clearly, some of these everyday stressors deal with deficiencies, such as not having enough time. In these types of stress situations, families can resolve problems through planning ahead, lowering their expectations, or both. They are then better able to cope. The flipside of this solution-based stress relief is that families and their members may experience stress from not accomplishing enough of what they planned and from overscheduling family calendars.

Unexpected Life Stressors

Some family life situations take family members by surprise or are beyond their control. If life events come too soon, are delayed, or fail to materialize, the health, happiness, and well-being of all involved may be affected (Schlossberg et al., 1996). Intensified emotionality and/or behavioral disorganization in families and their members are likely to occur as a result (Roberto, 1991).

Timing is crucial to the functioning of families and their members, especially when dealing with the unexpected. Struggle results if timing is off, or if families are "off-schedule" (Neugarten, 1979). If a first wedding is either relatively early or late in one's life (e.g., before age 20 or after age 40, respectively), the difficulty of accepting or dealing with the circumstances surrounding the event, such as interacting with the new spouse, is increased for both the persons marrying and their families (Carter & McGoldrick, 1999). If grandparents assume the task of raising their grandchildren because of unexpected circumstances, such as the incarceration of the biological parents, greater risks for all are involved (Lever & Wilson, 2005; Pinson-Milburn, Fabian, Schlossberg, & Pyle, 1996). Risks for the grandparents include increased psychological stress, financial difficulties, and health problems. Children in such circumstances are likely to suffer from a lack of consistent parenting and discipline and thus may do less well academically and socially.

Another crucial variable in dealing with the unexpected is **family development and environmental fit** (Eccles et al., 1993). Some environments are conducive to helping families develop and resolve unexpected crises. Others are not. For example, despite its best effort, a family living in an impoverished environment that experiences the loss of its major wage earner may not recover to its previous level of functioning. Such would probably not be the case with a family experiencing the same circumstance but living in a more affluent and supportive environment.

In addition to the situations just cited, families may have special difficulty in handling the following unexpected events in their life cycles (McCubbin & Figley, 1983):

1. *Happenstance:* One unpredictable aspect of the life cycle is **happenstance,** an umbrella term used to refer to all the random, chance circumstances of life, some fortunate and others not (Bandura, 1982; Gladding, 2002; Seligman, 1981). It is impossible to gauge when a person or an event may have a major impact on an individual or family that alters the style and substance of their existence. For example, members of a family on vacation may become friends with members of another family because they were housed in adjoining motel rooms. The results may be a marriage of their children, a business deal that produces wealth/frustration, or extended visits to each other's homes. Another chance event that may have a major impact on a family is the birth of a child with a disability. Such a child may strain the psychological and financial resources of a family, increase stress and, at the same time, reduce pleasant interactions and communications within the family (Seligman & Darling, 1997). It may also draw the family closer together physically and emotionally.

2. *Physical/psychological trauma:* When events of chance or happenstance take an unusually destructive and life-threatening or life-ending turn, families may find themselves suffering the effects of a physical or psychological trauma. People can be traumatized by experiencing natural events such as hurricanes, earthquakes, or fires, as well as by experiencing violent crime and physical abuse. These events may happen singularly or collectively. They share in common the fact that they are sudden, overwhelming, and often dangerous, either to one's self or significant other. These experiences are usually horrific in nature.

    Regardless of the form or circumstances, traumatic experiences have an impact on families. "Traumatized families are those who are attempting to cope with an extraordinary stressor that has disrupted their normal life routine in un-wanted ways" (Figley, 1989, p. 5). Trauma can upset the family's organizational ability and adaptability. The greater the distress of the victim(s), the greater the distress within the family as a whole. An adolescent girl may find it difficult to have a healthy relationship with her male siblings or father after suffering the trauma of a rape. Similarly, a mother and children may be unable to reorganize themselves into a functional family unit after the untimely death of the hus-band/father. Symptoms displayed by families in these circumstances include role reversals, somatization of experiences, interruption of normal developmen-tal life cycles, alienation, and inappropriate attempts at control, such as emotion-al withdrawal.

3. *Success and failure:* In his poem "If," Rudyard Kipling describes success and failure as "impostors" that should be treated just the same. Indeed, success and failure are both unsettling events for individuals and families. A family that wins a lottery or sweepstakes may find its members disagreeing over how the monies will be spent. Family members may also find themselves besieged with solicitations. In another example, a family that acquires fame and notoriety may become isolated from rou-tine interactions with friends or colleagues, thereby cutting off a social system of support and comfort.

   The experience of success or failure can leave people with mixed and volatile feelings ranging from depression to elation. The outcome may be progression or re-gression. Consequently, emotions and behaviors may be directed at increasing inti-macy, physical or psychological distancing, or the adoption of a new set of values. In any such scenarios, lifestyles and life cycle events are altered.

When anyone or anything either enters or leaves the family system, members within the family become unsettled. This point is seen graphically in the *Social Readjustment Rating Scale* (Holmes & Rahe, 1967). Of the 43 life-stress situations listed in the scale, 10 of the top 14 involve gaining or losing a family member.

In general, events such as illness, loss of a job, or inheriting a substantial amount of money are unpredictable and stressful. These occurrences add tension to the family system because of their newness, demands, and the changes they require of family members (Carter & McGoldrick, 1999). "Dysfunctional family behaviors develop when unexpected crises un-balance the system beyond its natural ability to recover" (Burgess & Hinkle, 1993, p. 134). Even in the best circumstances, certain events can cause families to behave in dysfunctional ways.

Family Structure and Functionality

In addition to stress, another factor that contributes to the health or dysfunctionality of fam-ilies is structure and organization. As seen in Chapter 1, a variety of family forms are present in society (Bubenzer, West, & Boughner, 1994). Some work better than others in handling life events. A family that is rigidly structured may respond best in a crisis situation, and one that is loosely organized may do best in recreational circumstances.

The roles family members enact are a part of a family's structure and make a difference in regard to family health. For example, in middle-class families "organized cohesiveness, sex role traditionalism, role flexibility, and shared roles" are correlated with husbands' health, and "organized cohesiveness and differentiated sharing" are correlated with wives' health

(Fisher, Ransom, Terry, & Burge, 1992, p. 399). Three common family organizational forms are (1) symmetry/complementary; (2) centripetal/centrifugal; and (3) cohesive/adaptable.

Symmetrical/Complementary Families

In Western society, families vary in the way they function. Although some are primarily symmetrical and others are mainly complementary, most successful couples show an ability to use both styles of interaction (Main & Oliver, 1988). In a **symmetrical relationship,** interaction is based on similarity of behavior. At its best, a symmetrical relationship is one where each partner is versatile and tries to become competent in doing necessary or needed tasks (Watzlawick, Beavin, & Jackson, 1967). For example, either a man or a woman can work outside the home or take care of children. This family organization is known as a **postgender relationship,** too (Knudson-Martin & Mahoney, 2005). The major time of difficulty in a symmetrical relationship is when partners do not minimize differences and instead compete with each other, or when one member of the relationship is not skilled in performing a necessary task (Sauber, L'Abate, & Weeks, 1985).

In a **complementary relationship,** family member roles are defined more rigidly, and differences are maximized. For example, one member of a couple is dominant or submissive, logical or emotional. If members fail to do their tasks, such as make decisions or nurture children, other members of the family are adversely affected. Sometimes this type of family is organized around traditional gender roles. If these roles become stereotyped, the relationship's stability and satisfaction will suffer (Knudson-Martin & Mahoney, 2005). However, as long as the prescribed roles in these relationships dovetail with each other and there is no change in the status quo, complementary families do fine.

Both symmetrical and complementary forms of family life will work as long as at least two conditions are met. First, members in the relationships must be satisfied with and competent in their roles. Second, there must be a sufficient interrelationship of roles so that necessary tasks are accomplished. In these cases, harmony results, and the family functions adequately. Meeting these two conditions, however, is not always possible, and families, and especially the couples in them, do best if they practice parallel relationships (Main & Oliver, 1988). In a **parallel relationship,** both complementary and symmetrical exchanges occur as appropriate.

Centripetal/Centrifugal Families

The term **centripetal** (directed toward a center) is used to describe a tendency to move toward family closeness. The term **centrifugal** (directed away from a center) is used to describe the tendency to move away from the family (i.e., family disengagement). In all families, periods of both closeness and distance occur during the individual and family life cycles. Some of these periods "coincide with shifts between family development tasks that require intense bonding or an inside-the-family focus," such as families with young children, and tasks that emphasize "personal identity and autonomy," such as launching children (Rolland, 1999, p. 500).

One of the strongest models that outlines the natural tendencies of three-generational families to be close to or distant from each other has been formulated by Lee Combrinck-Graham (1985) and is shown in Figure 2.3. It relates strength and health to the developmental state of the family and its individuals. It also stresses the importance of working through transitions in the family.

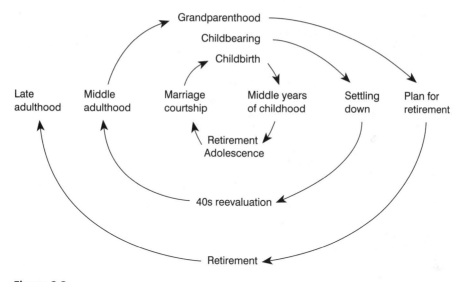

Figure 2.3
Density of the family over time.

From "A Developmental Model for Family Systems" by L. Combrinck-Graham, 1985, *Family Process, 24*, p. 142. Permission conveyed through the Copyright Clearance Center, Inc.

The work of Robert Beavers and associates at the Timberlawn Psychiatric Center in Dallas, Texas, shows that extremes in either a centripetal or centrifugal style of family interaction are likely to produce poor family functioning (Lewis et al., 1976). Figure 2.4 describes the relationship between family interaction style and family health. Families with a centripetal style have members who "view their relationship satisfactions as coming from inside the family" (Nichols & Everett, 1986, p. 77). They tend to produce children who are too tightly held by the family and who are prone to be antisocial, irresponsible, and egocentric. "Certain types of symptoms in teenagers, such as eating disorders and schizophrenia, indicate centripetal forces at work in the family" (Thomas, 1992, p. 105). Young adults who are unable or unwilling to leave home are the products of such families, too (Haley, 1980).

Families with a centrifugal style "are characterized by the tendency to expel members and view their relationship satisfactions as coming from outside the family" (Nichols & Everett, 1986, p. 77). They are likely to produce children who become socially isolated, disorganized, or withdrawn. "Adolescents who run away from home after enduring rejection or neglect and who remain on the street as casual, prematurely independent runaways would come from families in which centrifugal forces are dominant" (Thomas, 1992, p. 105).

Cohesion/Adaptability

Regardless of timing, all families have to deal with **family cohesion** (i.e., emotional bonding) and **family adaptability** (i.e., the ability to be flexible and change) (Olson, 1986; Strong, DeVault, & Sayad, 2001). In the Circumplex Model of Marital and Family Systems shown in Figure 2.5, cohesion and adaptability are highlighted. These two dimensions each have four levels (Olson, 1986). Adaptability ranges from a low to high dimension on the categories

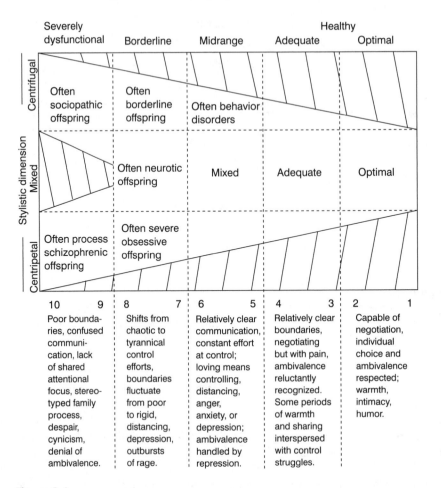

Figure 2.4
Beavers's concept of family health.

From *Successful Marriage: A Family Systems Approach to Couples Therapy* by
W. Robert Beavers, M.D., 1985 Copyright © by W. Robert Beavers. Reprinted by permission of the author.

characterized as (1) rigid, (2) structured, (3) flexible, and (4) chaotic. The structured and flexible categories are the two most moderate levels of functioning. Cohesion ranges from low
to high on these four levels: (1) disengaged, (2) separated, (3) connected, and (4) enmeshed.
Hypotheses have been advanced that high levels of enmeshment or low levels of cohesion in
the form of disengagement may be problematic for families. For example, a lack of family
cohesion, along with poor discipline, appears to raise the risk for serious delinquency in
adolescents (Gorman-Smith, Tolan, Zelli, & Huesmann, 1996). Overall, the two dimensions
of adaptability and cohesion are curvilinear. "Families that apparently are very high or very

COHESION — High
Low —

LEVELS OF FLEXIBILITY

CHAOTIC
- Lack of leadership
- Dramatic role shifts
- Erratic discipline
- Too much change

FLEXIBLE
- Shared leadership
- Democratic discipline
- Role sharing change
- Change when necessary

STRUCTURED
- Leadership sometimes shared
- Somewhat democratic discipline
- Roles stable
- Change when demanded

RIGID
- Authoritarian leadership
- Strict discipline
- Roles seldom to change
- Too little change

BALANCED
MIDRANGE
UNBALANCED

High
F L E X I B I L I T Y

CHAOTIC
- - - - - -
FLEXIBLE
- - - - - -
STRUCTURED
- - - - - -
RIGID

Low

	DISENGAGED	SEPARATED	CONNECTED	ENMESHED
CHAOTIC	CHAOTICALLY DISENGAGED	CHAOTICALLY SEPARATED	CHAOTICALLY CONNECTED	CHAOTICALLY ENMESHED
FLEXIBLE	FLEXIBLY DISENGAGED	FLEXIBLY SEPARATED	FLEXIBLY CONNECTED	FLEXIBLY ENMESHED
STRUCTURED	STRUCTURALLY DISENGAGED	STRUCTURALLY SEPARATED	STRUCTURALLY CONNECTED	STRUCTURALLY ENMESHED
RIGID	RIGIDLY DISENGAGED	RIGIDLY SEPARATED	RIGIDLY CONNECTED	RIGIDLY ENMESHED

LEVELS OF COHESION:	DISENGAGED	SEPARATED	CONNECTED	ENMESHED
I-We Balance:	I	I-we	I-We	I-WE
Closeness:	Little closeness	Low-moderate	Moderate-high	Very high closeness
Loyalty:	Little loyalty	Some loyalty	High loyalty	Very high loyalty
Independence/ Dependence:	High independence	Interdependent (More independence than dependence)	Interdependent (More dependence than independence)	High dependence

Figure 2.5
Circumplex model of family systems.

From "Circumplex Model of Family Systems: Integrating Ethnic Diversity and Other Social Systems" by Dean M. Gorall and David H. Olson, in *Integrating Family Therapy* (p. 219), edited by R. H. Mikesell, D.-D. Lusterman, and S. H. McDaniel, 1995, Washington, DC: American Psychological Association. Copyright © 1995 by the American Psychological Association. Reprinted with permission.

43

low on both dimensions seem dysfunctional, whereas families that are balanced seem to function more adequately" (Maynard & Olson, 1987, p. 502).

As previously seen (Figure 2.3) from the Combrinck-Graham diagram (1985) and as recently acknowledged by Olson, the degree of adaptability and cohesion within families is dependent on their life cycle stage and their cultural background. Therefore, caution must be exercised when stressing these two dimensions of family life in isolation from other factors.

Coping Strategies of Families

The coping strategies of healthy and dysfunctional families vary both quantitatively and qualitatively. According to Figley and McCubbin (1983), families that are generally able to cope with stress have most of the following characteristics (p. 18):

- ability to identify the stressor
- ability to view the situation as a family problem, rather than a problem of one member
- solution-oriented approach rather than blame-oriented
- tolerance for other family members
- clear expression of commitment to and affection for other family members
- open and clear communication among members
- evidence of high family cohesion
- evidence of considerable role flexibility
- appropriate utilization of resources inside and outside the family
- lack of physical violence
- lack of substance abuse

Hill's (1949) **ABCX model** illustrates whether an event is a crisis. In Hill's model, "A" represents the stressor event that happens to the family, "B" represents the resources at the family's disposal, and "C" represents the meaning or interpretation the family attaches to the experience. "X" is the combined effect of these factors (i.e., the crisis itself). This model highlights that the same type of event may be handled differently by different families. Consider two families in which a person has lost a job. In an affluent family, this event may have little impact or meaning because the family has a number of outside contacts that will readily find the unemployed person a new job. However, the same event in a poor family may provoke a considerable crisis because members do not have access to outside employment resources and the family was dependent on the income from the lost job for daily necessities.

The process that a family goes through in adjusting to a crisis is illustrated in what is sometimes referred to as the **check mark diagram** (see Figure 2.6). Families at first become disorganized and usually experience a period where they do not function well. That period stops and recovery begins once the crisis has ended. How well a family recovers depends on both the resources they have available and how well they use the resources.

Families that are unable to adjust to new circumstances try the same solutions over and over again (Watzlawick, 1978) or intensify nonproductive behaviors. In this process they fail to make needed adjustments or changes and thus become stuck or exacerbate their symptoms (Burgess & Hinkle, 1993). A family with a learning disabled child may initially talk to the child slowly and present material gradually to him or her. However, after the child has mastered some knowledge, this type of approach becomes frustrating and ineffective because the child is ready for a more challenging and mature presentation of material that he or she is supposed to master.

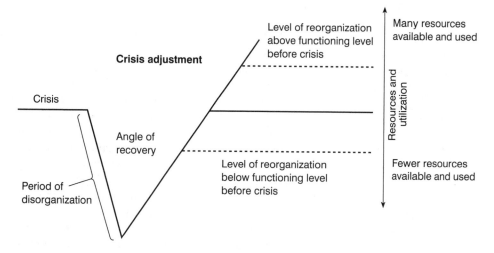

Figure 2.6
Check mark diagram: A model of a family's reaction to crisis.

From *Families Under Stress: Adjustment to the Crisis of War, Separation, and Reunion* by R. Hill, 1949, Westport, CT: Greenwood Press.

In addition to the ABCX model, the **Double ABCX model** (see Figure 2.7) provides a theoretical framework for understanding the complex interaction between situations in a family that involve more than one event. The model builds on Hill's ABCX model but focuses on family resolutions over time rather than those geared to a single happening. In essence, the

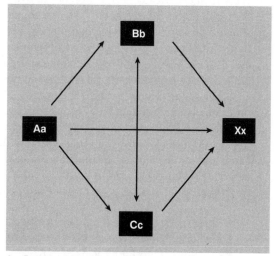

Figure 2.7
Double ABCX model.

Adapted From "The Family Stress Process: The Double ABCX Model of Adjustment and Adaptation" by H.I. McCubbin and J.M. Patterson in *Social Stress and the Family: Advances and Developments in Family Stress Theory and Research*, 1983, Binghamton, NY: Haworth Press.

Aa: Build-up of stressor events
Bb: Resources build up to deal with situation
Cc: Family perceptions of this and previous stressor events
Xx: Outcome in terms of family adaptation

Double ABCX model extends Hill's model. It addresses the issue that no event occurs in isolation and introduces the concept that stressors "pile-up" (McCubbin & Patterson, 1981). More recently, McCubbin and McCubbin (1991) proposed the **Resiliency Model of Family Stress, Adjustment, and Adaptation.** According to this model, a family's capability to meet demands is dynamic and interactional.

Ultimately, there are two levels of change that can work for families, but they need to be employed at different times for different situations. One type of change is referred to as **first-order change** (Watzlawick, Weakland, & Fisch, 1974) and is characterized by its superficial nature. For instance, dinner may be moved from being served at 6 P.M. to being served at 8 P.M., if a mother's work schedule is shifted or a father's train runs late. This type of change is appropriate in such situations. Dinner is still served. However, a first-order change that simply delays an argument from 6 P.M. to 8 P.M. is usually not going to be productive unless new ways of resolving the disagreement are found in that 2-hour span of time. Otherwise, the argument and its results still happen just like the dinner being served.

The opposite of first-order change is **second-order change.** The dynamics surrounding second-order change are those that result in a **metachange,** that is, a changing of rules sometimes referred to as a "change of change" (Watzlawick et al., 1974). In this process, a new set of rules and behaviors is introduced into the existing behavioral repertoire, often in an abrupt way (Burgess & Hinkle, 1993). The outcome is that a qualitatively new type of behavior appears.

In the previous example, a second-order change would occur if a family member engaging in a fight suggested that the family go to a therapist or a mediator to resolve their dispute, or agreed beforehand to generate possible solutions to the family's problem rather than to just voice grievances. If such changes were made, the dynamics of the situation would change. Power struggles would no longer be a part of the agenda, and divisiveness of the argument in the family would thereby be prevented.

A study of 78 French-Canadian couples who had been living together an average of 13 years further illustrates the difference between first- and second-order change. According to the result of this investigation, "when compared to nondistressed spouses, distressed spouses showed less problem solving confidence, a tendency to avoid different problem solving activities, and poor strategies to control their behavior" (Sabourin, Laporte, & Wright, 1990, p. 89). In other words, first-order change spouses were stuck in repetitive, nonproductive behaviors, but their counterparts engaged in new, productive behaviors.

Other dysfunctional patterns in families, such as sexual abuse of children, also show first-order change patterns. In families where there is **incest,** for instance, the family is "typically a closed, undifferentiated and rigid system primarily characterized by sexualized dependency" (Maddock, 1989, p. 134). In these families, the same pattern of abuse is repeated because the family unit is "insulated from critical social feedback that might influence their behavior" (Maddock, 1989, p. 134).

Other coping strategies that relieve stress in well-functioning families include:

- recognizing that stress may be positive and lead to change
- realizing that stress is usually temporary
- focusing on working together to find solutions
- realizing that stress is a normal part of life
- changing the rules to deal with stress and celebrating victories over events that led to stress (Curran, 1985)

Implications of Health in Working with Families

Studying healthy families is a complicated process (Smith & Stevens-Smith, 1992). It requires that researchers invest considerable time and effort in observing and calculating the multiple effects of numerous interactions that occur in families, such as speech and relationship patterns. In addition, to study the health of families, researchers must overcome "the individually oriented, linear causation thinking of psychopathology" as represented in the *Diagnostic and Statistical Manual of Mental Disorders* of the American Psychiatric Association (Huber, 1993, p. 70).

Both the complexity of families and the bias toward researching individuals inhibits many clinicians from carefully investigating families. Also, to the exclusion of studying healthy families, family therapists have "typically worked with clients experiencing stress and crisis in relationships, a viewpoint indicating transient dysfunctioning" (Sporakowski, 1995, p. 61). Yet, knowledge about the health of families can assist family therapists in a number of ways.

First, through studying the literature on family health, therapists can appreciate the multidimensional aspects of family life and how members influence each other systemically (Wilcoxon, 1985). This knowledge and awareness can be useful to practitioners as they interact with families experiencing difficulties. For instance, if a family member abuses alcohol, estimated by Treadway (1987) to be a factor in possibly half of the cases treated, the therapist can work to identify the problem and break the dysfunctional pattern of secrecy and silence by working in a confrontive but caring way.

A second benefit for therapists in examining healthy families is the realization that even dysfunctional families have areas of adequate or above-average performance. Because novice therapists tend to "overpathologize" client families, knowledge of healthy families is essential in gaining a balanced perspective (Barnhill, 1979). A knowledge of healthy families can be useful, for example, because it provides insight into the developmental aspects of enmeshment and disengagement that naturally occur over the family life cycle (Combrinck-Graham, 1985). This type of information can help therapists become aware of what is normal and healthy behavior and thereby focus on situations that are not normal and healthy.

A third advantage of exploring characteristics of healthy families is the realization that health and pathology are developmental (Wilcoxon, 1985). For example, in midlife, couples grow together and function with less conflict and stress as they launch their children (Blacker, 1999; McCullough & Rutenberg, 1988). Similarly, couples who maintain positive interactions during this time may be less susceptible to premature death from such disorders as hypertension, stroke, and coronary heart disease (Lynch, 1977). This type of knowledge helps clinicians realize more fully that change is possible and probable if proper therapeutic interventions are made.

A fourth implication of studying healthy families is that therapists can delineate areas of deficiency and strength (Huber, 1993). Healthy families have weaknesses and dysfunctional families have strengths. Secrets, conflict, jealousy, guilt, and scapegoating, as well as openness, cooperation, admiration, understanding, and accepting of responsibility, may occur on occasions in almost any family (Framo, 1996). Realizing the range and extent of behaviors in families gives therapists an awareness of how to potentially deal in an effective way with severely stressed families, as well as an understanding of how healthy families develop.

A final implication for studying healthy families is educational. An awareness of potential stressors in life can help therapists prepare a family and its members to deal with situations in advance. For instance, those struggling to recover from traumatic events appear to need to resolve five fundamental questions (Figley, 1989, p. 14): (1) What happened? (2) Why did it happen? (3) Why did I and others act as we did then? (4) Why did I and others act as we did since then? (5) If something like this happened again, would I be able to cope more effectively? Only by directly addressing these questions can a person or family realize to the greatest extent possible the effect of a trauma on them and their life cycle development.

Education concerning healthy families also emphasizes the values of previously tried solutions (O'Hanlon & Weiner-Davis, 1989). Families and their members sometimes do not deal appropriately with events because they fail to examine strategies they could employ or perhaps overlook strategies they have utilized at exceptional times in the past for reaching successful resolutions. By focusing on universal or unique strategies that enable them to deal with stress, families may become healthier and more satisfied with themselves and their environments.

Knowledge is not a guarantee that families will handle changes in their life cycles without turmoil and crisis. However, through educating themselves and the families they work with about potential difficulties, family therapists give families a choice as to what they do and when.

Summary and Conclusion

Exploring aspects of healthy families is important from a conceptual, ethical, and treatment basis. Clinicians can become more competent and also preempt personal and legal criticism by describing their model of healthy family functioning (Brendel & Nelson, 1999). One aspect of family life that stands out is that families go through periods of transition and develop according to general and specific milestones. Families that work best are those that plan and use their time wisely in setting up and implementing positive activities around expected and unexpected events in their lives.

This chapter examined multiple aspects of family health. First, the nature of the family as an interactive relationship system was discussed in regard to family health. Next the nature of healthy families was explored in regard to characteristics and behaviors. Healthy families are in a cycle that, when unbalanced, eventually changes in order to accommodate new situations. Family stressors were also examined. Stressors come in many forms, such as vertical and horizontal, present and past. Handling expected stressful situations, through such techniques as time management, is difficult for many families. More troublesome is the management and recovery from unexpected life stressors, such as traumas from natural disasters like a hurricane or unexpected death.

Another area explored was family structure. Families organize themselves in many different ways. However, families that are primarily symmetrical, versus those that are predominantly complementary, will vary in their ability to achieve tasks. A parallel family structure, which depends on flexibility and appropriateness of couples, seems to be most successful. Centripetal and centrifugal families differ in the ways in which they address family matters. Centripetal families depend more on family members for help, and centrifugal families focus outwardly. Both are appropriate ways for families to be structured at different times in the life cycle. A final characteristic of structure is cohesion and adaptability. Again, both of these qualities differ in families depending on their cultural background and stage of life. The point is that family therapists need to realize that there are preferred family structures at various times in the family life cycle. Therapists also need to know how family structure influences family system dynamics.

The final sections of this chapter dealt with coping strategies of families and the implication of understanding health as it pertains to family therapy. Generally, families cope the best they can. The ABCX and Double ABCX models explain how families perceive and deal with crises at a point in time and over time. Families that are able to make second-order changes, that is, try totally new responses, do a better job of marshaling their resources than those who repeat old patterns or make incremental changes regardless of the situation (first-order changes).

By studying healthy families, family therapists educate themselves to the complexity of family life and change. They also become sophisticated in realizing the developmental aspects of health. Therefore, they tend to be appropriately cautious in their assessment and treatment procedures. This type of knowledge gives therapists and the families they work with more choice in regard to what they do and how, thereby empowering all concerned in the process of change. With such information, family therapists "can take a leadership role in helping society come to terms with what is needed to create strong [and healthy] families" (Arnold & Allen, 1996, p. 84) and promote enrichment activities as well.

Summary Table

Healthy and Dysfunctional Characteristics of Families

The Family System and Health

Families are systemic in nature. Their health varies over their life span.
Healthy families readjust their rules and structure in dealing with crises and change.

Qualities of Healthy Families

Healthy families interact in a productive manner. They are characterized by:
- commitment of family members
- spending of qualitative and quantitative time together
- effective communication patterns
- a religious/spiritual orientation to life
- dealing with crises in a positive and effective manner
- clear roles and encouragement of members
- an appropriate structure and organization

Family Life Stressors

Stress is a part of family life. It may be vertical (i.e., historical) or horizontal (i.e., current), predictable (e.g., aging) or unexpected (e.g., death).
Expected life stressors are developmental and situational. They revolve around issues associated with economics, children, time, and behavior.
Unexpected life stressors are beyond a family's control and include happenstance, physical/psychological trauma, and success/failure. Timing and environmental fit are crucial factors in dealing with unexpected stress.
Stress events initially unbalance the family.

Family Structure and Functionality

The way in which a family is structured affects its ability to respond.
Three common ways families organize are:
- symmetry/complementary
- centripetal/centrifugal
- cohesive/adaptable

Coping Strategies of Families

The ability of families to cope is both a qualitative and quantitative process. Coping is characterized by:
- an ability to identify a stressor
- viewing a problem from a family perspective
- adopting a solution-oriented approach
- showing tolerance for other family members
- establishing clear communication patterns
- high family cohesion and role flexibility
- appropriate utilization of resources
- lack of physical violence and substance abuse
- use of second-order change strategies
- recognizing that stress is normal and may lead to change
- celebrating victories over events that led to stress

The ABCX model and Double ABCX model of handling a crisis help explain how families perceive and deal with events at a point in time and over time.

Implications of Health in Working with Families

Studying family health helps family therapists:
- appreciate the complexity of families
- realize that health is developmental and situational
- be less prone to pathologizing families
- be aware of families' strengths and deficits
- be more educational in assisting families with problems

PART 2

Therapeutic Approaches to Working with Families

Rationale and History of Family Therapy

In the lighting of candles and exchanging of vows
we are united as husband and wife.
In the holiday periods of nonstop visits
we are linked again briefly to our roots.
Out of crises and the mundane
we celebrate life
appreciating the novel
and accepting the routine
as we meet each other anew
amid ancestral histories and current reflections.
Families are a weaver's dream
with unique threads from the past
that are intertwined with the present
to form a colorful tapestry
of relationships in time.

Gladding, 1991a

"In 2004, 56.9 million people were seen by marriage and family therapists. This represents 19% of the entire U.S. population. Additionally, 9.4 million couples and 6.6 million families were seen by MFTs, which represents 16% of U.S. couples and 9% of families. Finally, it is estimated $338 million was spent on MFT services in that year" (Northey, 2004, p. 14). Despite the surprising trends in these statistics and sums, the practice of family therapy is relatively new, "dating back only a few decades" (Sayger, Homrich, & Horne, 2000, p. 12). Its theoretical and clinical beginnings were hammered out from the 1940s through the 1960s, while its real growth as a legitimate form of therapy occurred from the 1970s through the early part of the twenty-first century (Doherty & Simmons, 1996; Kaslow, 1991; Northey, 2002).

Family therapy differs from individual and group counseling both in its emphasis and in its clientele (Hines, 1988; Trotzer, 1988). For example, individual counseling generally focuses on a person as if the problems and resolutions for those difficulties lie within him or her. It is **intrapersonal**. Group counseling is more **interpersonal** and includes a number of individuals. However, it usually concentrates on helping people resolve select issues in life through multiple inputs and examples that group members and the group therapist offer. On the other hand, family therapy concentrates on making changes in total life **systems**. It is simultaneously intrapersonal, interpersonal, and systems focused.

The rise of family therapy as a practice and, subsequently, as a profession closely followed dramatic changes in the form, composition, and structure of the American family. These variations were a result of the family's shift from a primarily nuclear unit to a complex and varied institution, involving single parents, remarried families, and dual-career families (Pickens, 1997). Family therapy has also been connected to the influence of creative, innovative, and assertive mental health practitioners who devised and advocated new ways of providing services to their clients (Nichols, 1993).

Although some of the theories and methods employed in family therapy are similar to those used in other settings, many are different. This chapter examines the genesis and development of family therapy. The emphasis is on the people, events, and interaction processes that most contributed to the formation of the field. Before examining these historical events, the rationale for working with families and reasons for working with families, instead of individuals, is highlighted.

The Rationale for Family Therapy

One reason for conducting family therapy is the belief that most life difficulties arise and can best be addressed within families. Families are seen as powerful forces that work for either the good or the detriment of their members. Because an interconnectedness exists among family members, the actions of the members affect the health or dysfunctionality of each individual and the family as a whole.

Another reason for working therapeutically with families is the proven effectiveness of such treatment. In a landmark issue of the *Journal of Marital and Family Therapy*, edited by William Pinsof and Lyman Wynne (1995), a meta-analysis was conducted on more than 250 studies. The results showed that various forms of family therapy worked better than no treatment at all, and no study showed negative or destructive effects. In addition, family and couple therapy had a positive effect in treating such disorders as adult schizophrenia, adult alcoholism and drug abuse, depression in women who were in distressed marriages, adult hypertension, dementia, adult obesity, adolescent drug abuse, anorexia in young adolescent females, childhood conduct disorders, aggression and noncompliance in children with attention deficit disorders, childhood autism, chronic physical illnesses in adults and children, and couple distress and conflict. While couple and family therapy was not in itself sufficient to treat a number of severe and chronic mental disorders, for example, unipolar and bipolar affective disorders, it "significantly enhances the treatment packages for these disorders" (Pinsof & Wynne, 2000, p. 2).

A final rationale for family therapy concerns client satisfaction. In a national survey of family therapists and their clients, Doherty and Simmons (1996) found that over 97% of clients were satisfied with the services they received from marriage and family therapists and rated these services good to excellent. An equally large percentage of clients reported that the services they received from marriage and family therapists helped them deal more effectively with their problems; that is, they got the help they wanted.

Given the nature and origin of family troubles, as well as the effectiveness of and satisfaction with forms of family therapy, it is little wonder that this form of treatment has gained and is continuing to achieve recognition and status in the mental health field.

Reasons for Working with Families as Opposed to Working with Individuals

Besides the rationale for family therapy, there are advantages to working with entire families as a unit, rather than just the individuals within them. First, family therapy allows practitioners to "see causation as circular as well as, at times, linear" (Fishman, 1988, p. 5). This view enables clinicians to examine events broadly and in light of their complexity. It keeps therapists from being overly simplistic when offering help to those with whom they work. For example, a circular view of the problem of anorexia nervosa considers the friction within the whole family, especially the couple relationship. The inward and outward social pressures of the young person displaying obvious symptoms of the disorder are examined, but in a much broader interactive context.

A second advantage family therapy has over individual therapy is that it involves other real, significant individuals as a part of the process. There are no surrogate substitutes or "empty chairs" who act as significant people in a client's life. Instead, therapists deal directly with the family members involved. In other words, most family therapy does not depend on role plays or simulations. Therefore, if a young man is having difficulty with his parents or siblings, he is able to address them in person as he strives toward resolution. This type of emphasis usually cuts to the reality of a situation more quickly and more efficiently than indirect methods.

Third, in family therapy, all members of a family are given the same message simultaneously. They are challenged to work on issues together. This approach eliminates "secrets" and essentially makes the covert overt. This results in an increase in openness and communication within the family. If a couple is fighting, the issues over which there is tension are discussed within the family context. Family members become aware of what is involved in the situation. They deal with conflict directly. They also have the opportunity to generate ideas on what might be most helpful in bringing their situation to a successful resolution.

Fourth, family therapy usually takes less time than individual counseling. Many family therapists report that the length of time they are engaged in work with a family can literally be as brief as a few sessions (Fishman, 1988; Gilbert & Shmukler, 1997). Some family therapy approaches, notably those connected with strategic and solution-focused family therapy, emphasize contracting with client families for limited amounts of time (usually no more than 10 sessions). The stress on time is motivational for therapists and families because it tends to maximize their energy and innovation for creating resolutions.

Finally, the approaches utilized in working with families focus on interpersonal instead of primarily intrapersonal factors. This type of difference is comparable with seeing the forest instead of just the trees. The larger scope by which family therapy examines problematic behavior enables practitioners to find more unique ways to address difficulties.

Having examined the reasons for using family therapy as opposed to individual therapy, it is important to understand how it developed. The following sections trace the development of family therapy over time.

Family Therapy Through the Decades

Family therapy is an extension of the attempt by people throughout history to cure emotional suffering. "Over 2,000 years ago the first written accounts of an integrative system of treating mental illness were recorded" (Kottler, 1991, p. 34). Prehistorical records indicate that systematic attempts at helping were prevalent even before that time. Family members throughout history have tried to be of assistance to each other. This help initially took two forms:

1. Elders gave younger members of family clans and tribes advice on interpersonal relationships.
2. Adult members of these social units took care of the very young and the very old (Strong, DeVault, & Sayad, 2005).

Despite this history of care, family therapy is one of the newer methods of professional helping, with its roots in the 20th century.

Even though it is relatively recent in its formal development, multiple events have influenced and shaped the profession of family therapy. Although all of the facts and personalities mentioned here had some impact on the growth of the field, some were more pivotal than others. The exact importance of particulars sometimes changes according to who is recounting events. The order in which these developments occurred, however, can be charted chronologically, and some historical facts and figures stand out regardless of one's historical orientation.

Family Therapy: Before 1940

Inhibitors of the Development of Family Therapy

Prior to the 1940s, family therapy in the United States was almost a nonentity. Three social influences contributed to this phenomenon. The first involved myth and perception. The myth of rugged individualism was the predominant deterrent to the genesis of family therapy. Healthy people were seen as adequate to handle their own problems. Rugged individualism stemmed from the settling of the United States, especially the American West. Individuals were expected to solve their own problems, if they were to survive. Intertwined with this myth was the perception, handed down from the Puritans and other religious groups, that those who prospered were ordained by God (Strong, DeVault, & Sayad, 2005).

To admit one had difficulties, either inside or outside of a family context, was to also admit that one was not among the elect in addition to not being among the strong and rugged individuals upheld by culture.

A second social factor that deterred the development of family therapy was tradition. Historically, people usually confided with clergy, lawyers, and doctors, rather than with mental health professionals, when they discussed their marital and family concerns. These professionals knew the families in question well because they usually lived with them in a shared community over many years. Seeking advice and counsel from these individuals was different from talking to a professional specialist.

A third factor that prevented family therapy from evolving before the 1940s was the theoretical emphases of the times. The major psychological theories in the United States in the early part of the 20th century were **psychoanalysis** and **behaviorism**. Both were philosophically and pragmatically opposed to dealing with more than individual concerns. Proponents of psychoanalysis, for instance, believed that dealing with more than one person at a time in therapy would contaminate the transference process and prevent depth analysis from occurring. Likewise, behaviorists stressed straightforward work with clients, usually in the form of conditioning and counterconditioning. The social and political climate required for family therapy to develop and grow was almost nonexistent.

Catalysts for the Growth of Family Therapy

Despite this inhospitable environment, four factors combined to make family therapy accepted and eventually popular. The first was the growth of the number of women enrolled in colleges and their demand for courses in **family life education** (Broderick & Schrader, 1981). Educators from a number of disciplines responded to this need. Among the most noteworthy was Ernest Groves, who taught courses on parenting and family living at Boston University and the University of North Carolina. Groves later became instrumental in founding the **American Association of Marriage Counselors** in 1942 (Broderick & Schrader, 1991).

The second event that set the stage for the development of family therapy was the initial establishment of **marriage counseling**. In New York City, Abraham and Hannah Stone were among the leading advocates for and practitioners of marriage counseling in the late 1920s and 1930s. Emily Mudd began the Marriage Council of Philadelphia in 1932, which was devoted to a similar endeavor. Meanwhile, in California, Paul Popenoe established the American Institute of Family Relations, which was in essence his private practice. Popenoe introduced the term *marriage counseling* into the English language. He popularized the profession of marriage counseling by writing a monthly article, "Can This Marriage Be Saved?" in the *Ladies Home Journal*—a practice that began in 1945 and continues today (Broderick & Schrader, 1991).

A third impetus to the genesis of family counseling was the founding of the National Council on Family Relations in 1938 and the establishment of its journal, *Marriage and Family Living*, in 1939. This association promoted research-based knowledge about family life throughout the United States. Through its pioneer efforts, and those of the American Home Economics Association, information about aspects of family life were observed, recorded, and presented.

The fourth favorable event that helped launch family therapy as a profession was the work of county home extension agents. These agents began working educationally with families in the 1920s and 1930s and helped those they encountered to better understand the dynamics of their family situations. Some of the ideas and advice offered by agents were advocated by Alfred Adler, who developed a practical approach for working with families that became widespread in the United States in the 1930s (Dinkmeyer, Dinkmeyer, & Sperry, 2000; Sherman, 1999).

Family Therapy: 1940 to 1949

Several important events took place in the 1940s that had a lasting impact on the field of family therapy. One of the most important was the establishment of an association for professionals working with couples. As mentioned earlier, the American Association of Marriage Counselors (AAMC) was formed in 1942 by Ernest Groves and others. Its purpose was to help professionals network with one another in regard to the theory and practice of marriage counseling. It also devised standards for the practice of this specialty.

A second landmark event of the 1940s was the publication of the first account of concurrent marital therapy by Bela Mittleman (1948) of the New York Psychoanalytic Institute. Mittleman's position stressed the importance of object relations in couple relationships. It was a radical departure from the previously held intrapsychic point of view.

A third significant focus during the 1940s was the study of families of individuals suffering from schizophrenia. One of the early pioneers in this area was Theodore Lidz, who published a survey of 50 families. He found that the majority of schizophrenics came from broken homes and/or had seriously disturbed family relationships (Lidz & Lidz, 1949). Lidz later introduced into the family therapy literature the concepts of **schism**, the division of the family into two antagonistic and competing groups, and **skew**, whereby one partner in the marriage dominates the family to a striking degree, as a result of serious personality disorder in at least one of the partners.

The final factor that influenced family counseling in the 1940s was World War II and its aftermath. The events of the war brought considerable stress to millions of families in the United States. Many men were separated from their families because of war duty. Numerous women went to work in factories. Deaths and disabilities of loved ones added further pain and suffering. A need to work with families suffering trauma and change became apparent. To help meet mental health needs, the **National Mental Health Act of 1946** was passed by Congress. "This legislation authorized funds for research, demonstration, training, and assistance to states in the use of the most effective methods of prevention, diagnosis, and treatment of mental health disorders" (Hershenson & Power, 1987, p. 11). Mental health work with families would eventually be funded under this act.

Family Therapy: 1950 to 1959

Some family therapy historians consider the 1950s to be the genesis of the movement (Guerin, 1976). Landmark events in the development of family therapy in the 1950s centered more on individual leaders than on organizations, because of the difficulty of launching this therapeutic approach in the face of well-established opposition groups, such as psychiatrists.

Important Personalities in Family Therapy in the 1950s

A number of professionals contributed to the interdisciplinary underpinnings of family therapy in the 1950s (Shields, Wynne, McDaniel, & Gawinski, 1994). Each, in his or her way, contributed to the conceptual and clinical vitality as well as the growth of the field.

Nathan Ackerman was one of the most significant personalities of the decade. Although he advocated treating the family from a systems perspective as early as the 1930s (Ackerman, 1938), it was not until the 1950s that Ackerman became well-known and prominent. His strong belief in working with families and his persistently high energy influenced leading psychoanalytically trained psychiatrists to explore the area of family therapy. An example of this impact can be seen in Ackerman's book *The Psychodynamics of Family Life* (1958), in which he urged psychiatrists to go beyond understanding the role of family dynamics in the etiology of mental illness and to begin treating client mental disorders in light of family process dynamics. To show that his revolutionary ideas were workable, he set up a practice in New York City, where he could show his ideas had merit through pointing out results in case examples.

Another influential figure was Gregory Bateson in Palo Alto, California. Bateson, like many researchers of the 1950s, was interested in communication patterns in families with individuals who had been diagnosed as schizophrenics. He obtained several government grants for study, and, with Jay Haley, John Weakland, and eventually Don Jackson, Bateson formulated a novel, controversial, and influential theory of dysfunctional communication called the **double-bind** (Bateson, Jackson, Haley, & Weakland, 1956). This theory states that two seemingly contradictory messages may exist on different levels and lead to confusion, if not schizophrenic behavior, on the part of some individuals. For example, a person may receive the message to "act boldly and be careful." Such communication leads to ignoring one message and obeying the other, or to a type of stressful behavioral paralysis in which one does nothing because it is unclear which message to follow and how.

Bateson left the field of family research in the early 1960s, and the Bateson group disbanded in 1962. However, much of the work of this original group was expanded by the Mental Research Institute (MRI), which Don Jackson created in Palo Alto in 1958. Jackson was an innovative thinker and practitioner who helped lead the family therapy field away from a pathology-oriented, individual illness concept of problems to one that was relationship oriented (Ray, 2000). Among the later luminaries to join MRI with Jackson were Virginia Satir and Paul Watzlawick. A unique feature of this group was the treatment of families, which was resisted by Bateson. In fact, the MRI established **brief therapy**, an elaboration of the work of Milton Erickson and one of the first new approaches to family therapy (Haley, 1976).

A third leading professional in the 1950s was Carl Whitaker. Whitaker "risked violating the conventions of traditional psychotherapy" during this time, by including spouses and children in therapy (Broderick & Schrader, 1991, p. 26). As chief of psychiatry at Emory University in Atlanta, Whitaker (1958) published the results of his work in **dual therapy** (conjoint couple therapy). He also set up the first conference on family therapy at Sea Island, Georgia, in 1955.

A fourth key figure of the 1950s was Murray Bowen. Beginning in the mid-1950s, under the sponsorship of the National Institute of Mental Health, Bowen began holding therapy sessions with all family members present, as part of a research project with schizophrenics (Guerin, 1976). Although he was not initially successful in helping family members constructively talk to each other and resolve difficulties, Bowen gained experience that would later help him formulate an elaborate theory on the influence of previous generations on the mental health of families.

Other key figures in family therapy who began their careers in the 1950s were Ivan Boszormenyi-Nagy, at the Eastern Pennsylvania Psychiatric Institute (EPPI), and his associates, including James Framo and Gerald Zuk. The work of this group eventually resulted in the development of Nagy's **contextual therapy**. "At the heart of this approach is the healing of human relationships through trust and commitment, done primarily by developing loyalty, fairness, and reciprocity" (Anderson, Anderson, & Hovestadt, 1993, p. 3).

Family Therapy: 1960 to 1969

The decade of the 1960s was an era of rapid growth in family therapy. The idea of working with families was embraced by more professionals, a number of whom were quite charismatic. Four of the most prominent of these figures were Jay Haley, Salvador Minuchin, Virginia Satir, and Carl Whitaker. Other family therapists who began in the 1950s, such as Nathan Ackerman, John Bell, and Murray Bowen, continued contributing to the concepts and theories in the field. Another factor that made an impact at this time was the widespread introduction of systems theory. Finally, in the 1960s, training centers and academic programs in family therapy were started, strengthened, or proposed.

Major Family Therapists of the 1960s

Numerous family therapists emerged in the 1960s. They came from many interdisciplinary backgrounds and, like their predecessors of the 1950s, most were considered "mavericks" (Framo, 1996). The following therapists are discussed here because of their significant impact in shaping the direction of family therapy.

Jay Haley was probably the most important figure in family therapy in the 1960s. During this time, he had connections with most of the important figures in the field, and through his writings and travels, he kept professionals linked and informed. Haley also began to formulate what would become his own version of strategic family therapy by expanding and elaborating on the work of Milton Erickson (Haley, 1963). He shared with Erickson an emphasis on gaining and maintaining power during treatment. Like Erickson, Haley often gave client families permission to do what they would have done naturally (e.g., to withhold information). Furthermore, Haley used directives, as Erickson had, to get client families to do more within therapy than merely gain insight.

From 1961 to 1969, Jay Haley edited *Family Process*, the first journal in the field of family therapy that helped shape the emerging profession. In the late 1960s, Haley moved from Palo Alto to Philadelphia to join the Child Guidance Clinic, which was under the direction of Salvador Minuchin. His move brought two creative minds together and helped generate new ideas in the minds of both men and the people with whom they worked and trained.

The psychiatrist Salvador Minuchin first began his work with families at the Wiltwyck School for Boys in New York State in the early 1960s. He used his own form of family therapy with urban slum families he encountered because it reduced the recidivism rate for the delinquents who comprised the population of the school. The publication of his account of this work, *Families of the Slums* (Minuchin, Montalvo, Guerney, Rosman, & Schumer, 1967), received much recognition and led to his appointment as director of the Philadelphia Child Guidance Clinic, and to the formulation of a new and influential theory of family therapy: structural family therapy.

Like most pioneers in the field of family therapy (e.g., Whitaker, Haley), Minuchin did not have formal training in how to treat families. He did, however, have an idea of what healthy families should look like in regard to a hierarchy; and he used this mental map as a basis on which to construct his approach to helping families change. Another innovative idea he initiated at the end of the 1960s was the training of indigenous members of the local black community as paraprofessional family therapists. He believed this special effort was needed because cultural differences often made it difficult for white middle-class therapists to understand and relate successfully to urban blacks and Hispanics. Overall, Minuchin began transforming the Philadelphia Child Guidance Clinic from a second-rate and poor facility to the leading center for the training of family therapists on the East Coast of the United States.

Virginia Satir was the most entertaining and exciting family therapist to emerge in the 1960s. Satir, as a social worker in private practice in Chicago, started seeing family members as a group for treatment in the 1950s (Broderick & Schrader, 1991). However, she gained prominence as a family therapist at the Mental Research Institute. There she collaborated with her colleagues and branched out on her own. Satir was unique in being the only woman among the pioneers of family therapy. She had "unbounded optimism about people ... and her empathic abilities were unmatched" (Framo, 1996, p. 311). While her male counterparts concentrated on problems and building conceptual frameworks for theories and power, she touched and nurtured her clients and spoke of the importance of self-esteem, compassion, and congruent expression of feelings.

Satir gained national recognition with the publication of her book *Conjoint Family Therapy* (1964). In this text, she described the importance of seeing both members of a couple together at the same time, and she detailed how such a process could and should occur. Her clear style of writing made this book influential. "Satir's ability to synthesize ideas, combined with her creative development of teaching techniques and general personal charisma, gave her a central position in the field" of family therapy (Guerin, 1976, p. 8).

Carl Whitaker can be described in many ways. He dared to be different and, at his best, was creative as well as wise (Framo, 1996). He was never "conventional." Whitaker, a psychiatrist, became interested in working with families in the 1940s. As already mentioned, he was chair of the psychiatry department of Emory University in the early 1950s. In 1955, he resigned to begin a private practice.

His main influence and renown in the field, however, came following his move to become a professor of psychiatry at the University of Wisconsin in 1965. It was at Wisconsin that Whitaker was able to write and lecture extensively. Beginning in 1965, his affectively based interventions, which were usually spontaneous and sometimes appeared outrageous, gained notoriety in the field of family therapy. In the 1960s, Whitaker also nurtured the field of family therapy by connecting professionals with similar interests.

Continuing Leaders in Family Therapy During the 1960s

Nathan Ackerman continued to be a leader of the family therapy movement throughout the 1960s. In 1961, with Don Jackson, he cofounded *Family Process*, the first journal devoted to family therapy and one that is still preeminent in the field. One of Ackerman's most significant books during this decade was *Treating the Troubled Family* (1966). In this text, he elaborated on how to intervene with families and "tickle the family's defenses" through being involved with them, being confrontive and bringing covert issues out into the open.

John Bell, like Carl Whitaker, began treating families long before he was recognized as a leader in the field of family therapy. Bell's work began in the 1950s when he started using group therapy as a basis for working with families (Gurel, 1999; Kaslow, 1980). He published his ideas about family group therapy a decade later (Bell, 1961) and proposed a structured program of treatment that conceptualized family members as strangers. Members become known to each other in stages similar to those found in groups.

Bell taught his natural family group approach at the University of California, Berkeley, in 1963 in one of the first graduate courses on family therapy ever offered in the United States. From 1968 to 1973, he directed the Mental Research Institute in Palo Alto. It was Bell's belief that "all children 9 years or older and all other adult family members living in the home should be included in family therapy and should be present for all sessions" (Nichols & Everett, 1986, p. 43). Bell's ideas were unique and received considerable criticism, thus generating a good deal of discussion about family therapy (Hines, 1988).

Murray Bowen gained considerable insight into the dynamics and treatment of families during the 1960s. Part of the reason was that he was able to successfully deal with problems within his own family of origin. Another reason was that he began to see a connectedness between working with families that had a family member diagnosed as schizophrenic and working with families that had other problems.

One of his most significant discoveries was the "emotional reactivity" of many troubled families when brought together to solve problems. In these situations, family members had difficulty maintaining their identities and their actions. They would often resemble what Bowen (1961) called an **undifferentiated family ego mass**. In working with these fused families, Bowen found that by being cognitive and detached, he could help them establish appropriate relationship boundaries and avoid projecting (or triangulating) interpersonal dyadic difficulties onto a third person or object (i.e., a scapegoat).

Systems Theory

With the emergence of new ideas came a novel theoretical perspective on which to center these concepts: systems theory (Bertalanffy, 1968). In **systems theory**, a system is a set of elements standing in interaction with one another. Each element in the system is affected by whatever happens to any other element. Thus, the system is only as strong as its weakest part. Likewise, the system is greater than the sum of its parts. Whether the system is a human body or a family, it is organized in a particular manner with boundaries that are more or less open (i.e., permeable) depending on the amount and type of feedback received. Systems can be self-regulating, too, because "the tendency of a system is to seek homeostasis or equilibrium" (Walsh & McGraw, 2002, p. 6).

By viewing the family in this manner, clinicians in the 1960s focused less on **linear causality** (direct cause and effect) and more on **circular causality** (the idea that events are related through a series of interacting loops or repeating cycles). Subsequently, family therapists began to claim their role as specialists within therapy. This position was reinforced in 1963, when the first state licensure law regulating family counselors was passed in California. This legislation was just the beginning of family therapy's increasing prominence.

Institutes and Training Centers

Along with the rise of dynamic figures in family therapy and systems theory in the 1960s, training institutes and centers also came into prominence. In California, the Mental Research Institute in Palo Alto flourished even after Jay Haley's departure for Philadelphia in 1967 and Don Jackson's death in 1968. The Family Institute of New York (headed by Ackerman) thrived during this time, as did the Albert Einstein College of Medicine in New York City and the affiliated Bronx State Hospital (Broderick & Schrader, 1991).

In Philadelphia, the Philadelphia Child Guidance Clinic opened its facilities to surrounding neighborhoods and to aspiring family therapists. Innovative techniques, such as the "**bug in the ear**" form of communication, were devised at the clinic during this time. In 1964, the Family Institute of Philadelphia emerged. This institute was a merger of the EPPI and the Philadelphia Psychiatric Center and fostered such notable practitioner/theorists as Gerald Zuk and Ross Speck (Broderick & Schrader, 1991).

Meanwhile, in Boston, the Boston Family Institute was established in 1969 under the direction of Fred Duhl and David Kantor (Duhl, 1983). This institute focused on expressive and dramatic interventions and originated the technique of family sculpting.

Overseas, the Institute for Family Studies in Milan was formed in 1967. This institute was based on the MRI model and came into prominence in the 1970s with many innovative, short-term approaches to working with families (Selvini Palazzoli, Boscolo, Cecchin, & Prata, 1978).

Family Therapy: 1970 to 1979

The 1970s were marked by several nodal events in regard to family therapy. These events centered around many activities, including a major membership increase in the American Association for Marriage and Family Therapy (AAMFT), the founding of the American Family Therapy Academy (AFTA), the refinement of theories, the influence of foreign therapies and therapists (especially the Milan Group), the growth of family enrichment, and the introduction of feminism into the family therapy field.

Membership in the American Association for Marriage and Family Therapy

In 1970, the membership of the AAMFT stood at 973. By 1979, membership had increased more than 777% to 7,565 (Gurman & Kniskern, 1981). The dynamic growth of the association can be explained in many ways, including that it was recognized by the Department of Health, Education, and Welfare in 1977 as an accrediting body for programs granting degrees in marriage and family therapy. Also, at about the same time, the association changed its name from the American Association of Marriage and Family Counselors to the American Association for Marriage and Family Therapy.

In addition the AAMFT benefited from increased focus placed on families and therapeutic ways of working with them as a result of the upheavals in family life in the 1960s. Furthermore, many of the pioneers of the family therapy movement, such as Virginia Satir, James Framo, Carl Whitaker, Salvador Minuchin, Jay Haley, and Florence Kaslow, began making a greater impact on therapists across the nation with their workshop presentations and writings. To add to this impact, in 1974, the AAMFT began publishing its own professional periodical, the *Journal of Marital and Family Therapy*, with William C. Nichols, Jr., as the first editor, and made plans late in the decade to move its headquarters from Claremont, California to Washington, D.C. (an event that actually transpired in 1982).

Establishment of the American Family Therapy Academy (AFTA)

AFTA was founded in 1977 by a small group of mental health professionals who were active during the early years when the field of family therapy was emerging. Initially, it strove to represent "the interests of systemic family therapists as distinct from psychodynamic marriage counselors" (Sauber, L'Abate, & Weeks, 1985, p. 180). Leaders of AFTA included Murray

Bowen and James Framo. As a "think tank," AFTA's annual meeting brought together professionals to address a variety of clinical, research, and teaching topics.

In 1981, a joint liaison committee made up of AAMFT and AFTA representatives was formed to address the respective roles of the two organizations within the profession. AFTA was identified as an academy of advanced professionals interested in the exchange of ideas; AAMFT retained government recognition for its role in providing credentials to marriage and family therapists. Since that time, AFTA has focused almost exclusively on family therapy clinical and research issues.

Refinement of Family Therapy Theories

The 1970s marked the growth and refinement of family therapy theories outside the psychoanalytical tradition. It is ironic and symbolic that Nathan Ackerman, who carried the banner of psychoanalytical family therapy, died in 1971 (Bloch & Simon, 1982). It is also interesting to note that the works of Salvador Minuchin (structural family therapy), Gerald Patterson (behavioral family therapy), Carl Whitaker (experiential family therapy), and Jay Haley (strategic family therapy) increased in frequency, scope, and influence during this decade. The newness of ideas generated in the 1960s bore fruit in the 1970s.

One major example of this phenomenon was the work of Salvador Minuchin. In a clearly articulated book, *Families and Family Therapy*, Minuchin (1974) outlined a practical guide for conducting structural family therapy. He followed this publication, later in the decade, with a complementary coauthored text entitled *Psychosomatic Families: Anorexia Nervosa in Context* (Minuchin, Rosman, & Baker, 1978), which showcased in a dramatic way the power of the therapy he had created. These writings, combined with his well-staffed training center in Philadelphia, made structural family therapy a major theoretical force in family therapy circles in a relatively brief period of time.

Influence of Foreign Therapies and Therapists

In Europe, in the late 1960s and early 1970s, the development of family therapy grew rapidly. By the mid-1970s, theories and theorists, especially in Italy and Great Britain, became influential in the United States. The influx of non-U.S. family therapists' ideas led many American professionals to question "particular ethnocentric values about what is good and true for families" (Broderick & Schrader, 1991, p. 35).

Particularly influential was the Milan Group in Italy headed by Mara Selvini Palazzoli and staffed by three other psychoanalytically trained psychiatrists: Gianfrano Cecchin, Giulana Prata, and Luigi Boscolo. Their book, *Paradox and Counterparadox* (1978), was influenced by the work of Bateson and Watzlawick in Palo Alto. However, it was original in its emphasis on **circular questioning** (asking questions that highlight differences among family members) and **triadic questioning** (asking a third family member how two others members of the family relate). The Milan approach emphasized developing a hypothesis about the family before their arrival. Furthermore, it prescribed homework assignments that were often ritualistic and difficult.

Two British leaders in the helping profession who influenced the development of family therapy in the United States were R. D. Laing and Robin Skynner. Laing (1965) coined the term **mystification** to describe how some families mask what is going on between family members by giving conflicting and contradictory explanations of events. His complicated but interesting book, *Knots* (1970), further enhanced his status as an original thinker in understanding universal family dynamics in dysfunctional families. Skynner (1981) developed a brief version of psychoanalytic family therapy in the 1970s that helped complement and enrich the work done by Ackerman and Boszormenyi-Nagy.

Feminist Theory and Family Therapy

"Feminist thinking explicitly entered the family therapy field in the 1970s and has increasingly influenced the theory and practice of family therapy" (Framo, 1996, p. 303). As an approach, **feminist family therapy** "is an attitude, a lens, a body of ideas about gender hierarchy and its impact rather than a specific model of therapy or a grab bag of clinical techniques. Feminists recognize the overriding importance of the power structure in any human system" (Carter, 1992, p. 66). They question, among other things, whether or not some concepts in family therapy, such as complementarity, circularity, and neutrality, are oppressive to women (May, 1998). Table 3.1 lists some characteristics of gender-sensitive family therapy.

The challenge to family therapy by feminist theory began in 1978, when an article by Rachel Hare-Mustin entitled "A Feminist Approach to Family Therapy" was published in *Family Process*. Hare-Mustin took the position that family therapy discriminated against women because it basically promoted the status quo that women were unequal in regard to their duties and roles within families.

After Hare-Mustin's paper was published, a number of other pieces on the adequacy of family therapy from a systemic perspective began to be published. Among the most consistently voiced views, from feminist therapists' perspectives, is that historic sexism and structural inequalities cannot be corrected through improving relationships among family members or creating a new family hierarchy. Rather, the goals of working with a family are

Table 3.1
Characteristics of Gender-Sensitive Family Therapy

Nonsexist Counseling	Empowerment/Feminist/ Gender-Aware Counseling
Does not reinforce stereotyped gender roles.	Helps clients recognize the impact of social, cultural, and political factors on their lives.
Encourages clients to consider a wide range of choices, especially in regard to careers.	Helps clients transcend limitations resulting from gender stereotyping.
Avoids allowing gender stereotypes to affect diagnoses.	Recognizes the degree to which individual behaviors may reflect internalization of harmful social standards.
Avoids use of sexist assessment instruments.	Includes gender-role analysis as a component of assessment.
Treats male and female clients equally.	Helps clients develop and integrate traits that are culturally defined as "masculine" and "feminine."
Avoids misuse of power in the counseling relationship.	Develops collaborative counselor–client relationships.

From "Gender Sensitivity and Family Empowerment" by J. Lewis, 1993, *Family Psychology and Counseling, 1,* 1–7. Used with permission of Judith Lewis.

"to facilitate the growth of a strong, competent woman who has enhanced control over resources" and "to increase the ability of women to work together politically to change society and its institutions" (Libow, Raskin, & Caust, 1982, p. 8).

Although feminist family therapists "represent a wide range of theoretical orientations," they are "drawn together by their recognition that sexism limits the psychological well-being of women and men, by their advocacy of equality in relationships and society, and by their refusal to use any counseling methods or explanatory concepts that promote bias" (Enns, 1992, p. 338). Training models developed by feminist family therapists that place gender at the heart of educating family therapists have been and will continue to be developed (e.g., Storm, 1991).

Family Therapy: 1980 to 1989

Several important events marked the emergence of family therapy in the 1980s. One was the retirement or death of leading pioneers in the movement and the emergence of new leaders. A second was the growth in the number of individuals and associations devoted to family therapy. A third was an increase in research in family therapy (Miller, 1986; Sprenkle & Piercy, 2006) and an explosion in publications devoted to family therapy. Finally, further recognition of marriage and family therapy came about on a national level.

Change in Family Therapy Leadership

In the 1980s, new leadership began to emerge in family therapy circles. One reason was the aging of the initial pioneers in the field. Another reason was the maturity of clinicians who studied in the 1960s and 1970s with the founders of the movement. The second and third generations of family therapists had new ideas and abundant energy (Kaslow, 1990). They basically preserved the best of the founders' influences while forging out in different directions. Some of the more established leaders in the field, such as Jay Haley, switched emphases at this time and maintained their leadership roles.

Within the growth of this movement, many women came to the forefront. Among them were Monica McGoldrick, Rachel Hare-Mustin, Carolyn Attneave, Peggy Papp, Peggy Penn, Cloe Madanes, Fromma Walsh, and Betty Carter. These women began to create novel theories and to challenge older ones. Cloe Madanes was especially prolific and creative during the last part of the 1980s. Overall, the work of new women leaders in family therapy contributed much to the profession. Many of these women realized the need to "include women's voices and experiences" within the family therapy field in order to gain a richer and more evenly balanced perspective on family life and to discern what changes are needed in families (Carter, 1992, p. 69). The Women's Project in Family Therapy (Walters, Carter, Papp, & Silverstein, 1988) was a major undertaking of these researchers and practitioners who sought to emphasize the absence of gender in the formation of systems theory. Their presence and prominence altered the view that a professional panel of family therapists consisted of four men and Virginia Satir.

Growth in the Profession of Family Therapy

Family therapy grew significantly as a profession in the 1980s. The membership of the AAMFT, for instance, almost doubled to a total of 14,000 members. At the same time, two new associations devoted to the study and practice of family therapy were formed. The first was the Division of Family Psychology, which was established within the American Psychological Association (APA) in 1984. The division was established because of the desire by some family practitioners to maintain their identity as psychologists (Kaslow, 1990). Such noted individuals as James Alexander, Alan Gurman, Florence Kaslow, Luciano L'Abate, Rachel Hare-Mustin, Duncan Stanton, and Gerald Zuk were among those who became affiliated with this division.

The second new professional association formed in the 1980s was the International Association of Marriage and Family Counselors (IAMFC), which was established initially as an interest group within the American Counseling Association (ACA) in 1986. The IAMFC grew from an initial membership of 143 in 1986 to more than 4,000 in 2001. In 1990, IAMFC became a division of ACA.

The initial goals and purposes of the IAMFC were to enhance marriage and the family through providing educational programs, conducting research, sponsoring conferences, establishing interprofessional contacts, and examining and removing conditions that create barriers to marriages and families. Since its formation, the IAMFC has broadened its vision to include work in promoting ethical practices, setting high-quality training standards, helping families and couples cope successfully, and using counseling knowledge and systemic methods to ameliorate the problems confronting marriages and families (Maynard & Olson, 1987). Overall, the IAMFC provides a base for training, research, collaboration, and support for counselors who work with families (Pietrzak & L'Amoreaux, 1998).

Development of Research Techniques in Family Therapy

Until the 1980s, research techniques and solid research in family therapy were scarce. It was implicitly assumed that other research methodologies could be translated to the family therapy field or that case study reports were sufficient in validating the impact of family therapy. In the 1980s, however, this changed.

A forewarning of the increased emphasis on family research came when a 1982 edition of the *Journal of Marriage and the Family* devoted an entire issue to family research methodologies. A parallel event occurred in the *Journal of Family Issues* in 1984 (Miller, 1986). In addition, a research methods book by Adams and Schvaneveldt (1991) was among the first to use examples involving families. A breakthrough in research in the 1980s came when studies indicated that certain forms of family therapy, e.g., behavioral and systems approaches, were effective in working with families (Gurman, Kniskern, & Pinsof, 1986).

Publications in Family Therapy

The growth in the number of individuals and associations involved in family therapy was paralleled by an increase in publications in this area. Some major publishing houses, such as Guilford Press and Brunner/Mazel, began to specialize in books on family therapy. Almost all publishers of texts in counseling, psychology, and social work added books on marriage and family therapy. In addition, new periodicals were established, and older ones grew in circulation.

The *Family Therapy Networker*, a periodical with a subscription list of over 50,000, was the success story of the 1980s. The success of the *Networker* is attributable to its timely and interesting articles and its journalistic (as opposed to scholarly) form of writing. The magazine format and featured information on professional conferences across the country were undoubtedly additional factors in its success.

National Recognition of Family Therapy

The main national event for family therapy in the 1980s was the listing of the profession as one of the four core mental health professions eligible for mental health traineeships (Shields et al., 1994). This action occurred as a part of the Public Health Service Act, Title III, Section 303(d)(1). It basically placed the profession, in the eyes of the federal government, on a par with psychology, psychiatry, and other professions vying for federal training grants.

Family Therapy: 1990 to 1999

The 1990s proved as much an exciting time in the field as the previous decade. Family therapy became a more global phenomenon and new theories and specialty areas emerged. The number of professionals who primarily identify themselves as family therapists continued to grow—and academic curriculums and experiential components in family therapy were refined. The issues of the 1990s concerned professional recognition, affiliation, accreditation, and licensure, that is, matters related to power and influence. These issues also involved identification and influence specifically regarding whether family therapy would continue to be interdisciplinary or if it would be "marginalized" (Shields et al., 1994).

New Theories and Specialties within Family Therapy

The 1990s saw several new theories of family therapy either emerge or gain added attention. Feminist family therapy, for instance, gained increased recognition as a powerful trend in the field, and issues surrounding the importance of gender grew (Norsworthy, 2000). Family therapy also began concentrating more on examining **"gender-sensitive issues in therapy"** rather than feminine or masculine issues, per se (Smith & Stevens-Smith, 1992). Thus, differences in genders were recognized in a less emotionally or politically volatile way. Solution-focused and narrative theories, developed in the Midwest by Steve deShazer (1988) and Bill O'Hanlon (O'Hanlon & Weiner-Davis, 1989) and in Australia and New Zealand by Michael White and David Epston (1990), respectively, also received much publicity. These theories are characterized by their brevity and creativity and are covered in Chapter 11 of this book.

Other emerging theories for the treatment of families in the 1990s included:

- the **reflecting team approach** of Tom Andersen (1991), a democratic and collaborative model of working with couples and families where clinical observers of a therapeutic session come out from behind a one-way mirror observing room to discuss with the therapist and client couple/family their impressions, so that an open environment is created and the couple/family is made a part of the larger treatment team
- the **therapeutic conversations model** of Harlene Anderson and Harry Goolishian (Anderson, 1994), a postmodern approach where the family therapist relates to the couple or family in a more egalitarian partnership
- the **psychoeducational model** of Carol Anderson (1988), an approach to working with families that have a schizophrenic member, where attention is given to teaching family members about multiple aspects of mental illness in a day-long "Survival Skills Workshop" focusing on boundaries, hierarchy, and maintaining the integrity of subsystems
- the **internal family systems model** of Richard Schwartz (1994), which considers both individual intrapsychic dynamics and family systems

Of these theories, some were considered radically different from their forerunners because they were based on **social constructionism**, a philosophy that states that our experiences are a function of how we think about them instead of objective entities. This viewpoint is different from systemic assumptions and has caused many family therapists to reexamine their basic assumptions (Piercy & Sprenkle, 1990).

Related to these developments in theory and emphasis was the **Basic Family Therapy Skills Project**, which was established in 1987 and focused on determining, defining, and testing "the skills essential for beginning family therapists to master for effective therapy practice" (Figley & Nelson, 1990, p. 225). Four basic family therapy skills research reports were prepared in the 1990s. In these reports, structural, strategic, brief, and transgenerational family therapies were examined from the perspective of distinctive and generic skills critical for beginning therapists (Nelson, Heilbrun, & Figley, 1993). The identified skills generated from this project continue to be researched and refined, as educators, practitioners, and researchers seek to determine what therapeutic interventions are most important and when.

Along with the work in specific theories was an increased emphasis on the **new epistemology**—the idea that the cybernetic approach of Bateson (1972, 1979) and others must be incorporated in its truest sense into family therapy. Among other things, the new epistemology emphasizes **second-order cybernetics**—the **cybernetics of cybernetics**—which stresses the impact of the family therapist's inclusion and participation in family systems (Keeney, 1983) (see Figure 3.1). On its most basic level, second-order cybernetics emphasizes positive feedback in system transformation. It extends first-order cybernetics foci beyond the homeostatic and adaptive properties of family systems, in general. The new epistemology also concentrates on the importance of family belief systems in treatment and on **ontology** (i.e., a view of the world) that stresses the circularity and autonomy of systems (in contrast to linear causality).

Equally pervasive in the 1990s was the redirection of the family therapy education field from a focus on producing narrowly trained, theory-specific clinicians to a focus on training practitioners who know how to work with special types of families (Broderick & Schrader, 1991). With this change has also come a transformation in regard to the way the term *family therapist* is used. It is now better defined in regard to course work, competencies, and clinical experience. Furthermore, there are now a number of well-respected and researched theories that practitioners in the field can claim (Piercy & Sprenkle, 1996). This shift in definition and

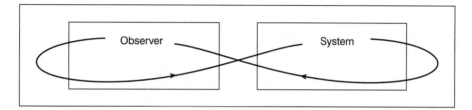

Figure 3.1
Cybernetics of cybernetics.

From Becvar & Becvar, *Family Therapy: A Systemic Integration*, 6e. Published by Allyn and Bacon, Boston, MA. Copyright © 2006 by Pearson Education. Reprinted by permission of the publisher.

scholarship has resulted in a plethora of new books in family therapy and an emphasis on distinct types of family problems and families. For instance, books have been written and specialized courses offered on working with families comprised of individuals who abuse drugs, alcohol, food, or other family members. Literature and academic offerings have also become available for treating single-parent families, remarried families, aging families, as well as intact families who have young children, adolescents, or members with disabilities. Further opportunities for reading about or studying culturally diverse families, as well as gay and lesbian families, have emerged.

Family Therapy: 2000 to the Present

The Global Growth of Family Therapy

Beginning slowly in the 1970s with the growth of family therapy in Italy and England, the growth and influence of the profession have spread around the world. Presently, there are family therapy associations on the continents of Europe, Asia, Africa, Australia, and South America as well as North America (Ng, 2005; Trepper, 2005). New international publications in family therapy continue to spring up, as well. There is now an International Family Therapy Association (IFTA; http://www.ifta-familytherapy.org/home.html), too, that reflects the growing global interest in family therapy. Like the kudzu vine, family therapy has grown fast and taken root in a number of countries.

Impact of Family Therapy Associations and the Number of Marriage and Family Therapists

The major professional associations for family therapists (i.e., AAMFT, IAMFC, AFTA, and Division 43 of APA) continue to have considerable impact on the profession because of their publications, educational emphases, and services. The AAMFT is the largest (more than 23,000 members) and oldest association and it also maintains the most diverse line of services, educational opportunities, and publications. Second in membership is the IAMFC, a division of the American Counseling Association, followed by Division 43 (Family Psychology), which requires American Psychological Association membership. The AFTA, although smaller than any of the three previously mentioned associations, continues to be influential, as well, because of the status and expertise of its members.

Licensing of marriage and family therapists has grown even faster than the influence of professional associations. Under the regulations published in the *Federal Register* (vol. 57, no. 14), marriage and family therapists officially became the fifth "core" mental health profession, along with psychiatrists, psychologists, social workers, and psychiatric nurses (Shields et al., 1994). This regulation has meant that by 2004 there were more than 50,000 state-licensed marriage and family therapists in the United States.

Over 40 states now either license or certify family therapy professionals. The number of states that regulate family therapy is expected to increase in the 21st century until all states require licensure. Such a practice is designed to protect the public from unscrupulous and unqualified practitioners with minimal costs because regulating boards are self-governing.

Accreditation of Family Therapists

Two associations currently accredit programs in family therapy: the AAMFT and IAMFC. Both do so under accrediting commissions that operate independently from their associations.

The AAMFT standards are drawn up and administered by the Commission on Accreditation for Marriage and Family Therapy Education (COAMFTE). Those for IAMFC are similarly handled through the Council for Accreditation of Counseling and Related Educational Programs (CACREP) (Clawson, Henderson, & Schweiger, 2004). A minimum of a master's degree is required as the credential for becoming a marriage and family therapist, although there is debate over the exact content and sequencing of courses.

Both the AAMFT (through COAMFTE) and IAMFC (through CACREP) are working hard in the 21st century to increase the number and quality of programs they accredit. The health reform agenda of the decade has influenced educational programs and the work of family therapists regardless of their professional setting. Being recognized as a core mental health provider is crucial to the well-being of educational programs in family therapy and the profession as a whole. Thus, in many ways training programs have become linked to legislative regulations, and that trend is likely to continue.

Developing Culturally Effective Family-Based Research

A final development in the marriage and family therapy field in the 21st century is more and better research on the effectiveness of family therapy with different cultural groups. Some states, such as California and Texas, have now reached the point where no one cultural group constitutes a majority within that state. Thus, there is renewed interest and renewed efforts to determine what theories and forms work best for what distinct populations under what circumstances and when.

Summary and Conclusion

This chapter examined the rationale for conducting family therapy and the reasons for working with families instead of individuals. It also gave a brief history of family therapy. Both the reasons for working with families and the traditions and methods employed with such groups have expanded with time.

The rationale for conducting family therapy is based on a systems viewpoint of individual, couple, and family functionality. From a systems perspective, people's mental health and difficulties are based more on interpersonal dynamics than on an intrapersonal struggle. Because families, like other living organisms, are only as healthy as their weakest members, it makes logical and empirical sense to treat individuals within a family context, so that the power and resources of families and their members can be supportively maximized. This is a macro, as opposed to a micro, viewpoint of dysfunctionality and one that has an increasing amount of research support.

Parallel to the rationale for family therapy is the history of this movement (outlined in Appendix A), primarily seen in this chapter from the perspective of its development within the United States. Notable events in the development of family therapy have been traced through the decades. Before the 1940s, this form of treatment was virtually nonexistent, because of prevailing beliefs within the culture of the United States that stressed the importance of the individual. A further factor prohibiting the development of family therapy was historic tradition. Individuals in need of assistance in their relationships consulted first with other family members, then with clergy and physicians.

Family therapy grew, however, due to a number of events, such as the growth of the number of women in higher education and increased demand for more courses in family life. Likewise, the founding of associations (e.g., the National Council of Family Relations), the pioneer work in marriage counseling, the growth in the role of county home extension agents, and World War II influenced the formation of the profession.

The 1940s saw the formation of the American Association for Marriage Counselors and initial treatment of individuals with schizophrenia through treating their families. The 1950s saw the emergence of strong personalities who advocated for family therapy, such as Nathan Ackerman, Gregory Bateson, Don Jackson, Carl Whitaker, and Murray Bowen. Their work was expanded in the 1960s, and new important figures that became pioneers at this time were Jay Haley, Salvador Minuchin, Virginia Satir, and John Bell. In retrospect, all of these professionals began their therapeutic journeys in the 1950s, but some came into prominence before others.

In the 1970s, family therapy became more respectable, and the American Association for Marriage and Family Therapy grew rapidly and was recognized by government agencies. New journals and books appeared on a range of family therapy topics. In addition, established family therapies were refined, and practitioners from Great Britain and Italy began to have greater influence on the profession throughout the world. Complementing these developments was an emerging emphasis on marriage and family enrichment, the rise of feminist theory influence in family therapy, and the development of assessment techniques geared to families.

In the 1980s, 1990s, and 2000s, the number of professionals involved in working with couples and families increased. Two new associations were established in the mid-1980s: Division 43 (Family Psychology) of the American Psychological Association and the International Association for Marriage and Family Counselors, a division of the American Counseling Association. There was and continues to be considerable excitement, growth, and governmental recognition and, in some cases, regulation of family therapy.

Overall, family therapy appears to be basically healthy. More women have emerged as leaders, and feminist theory has grown in its influence and impact to make the entire field reexamine itself anew. As in the 1970s, the proliferation of publications in family therapy has increased. New theoretical approaches are also having an impact. Licensure efforts are growing and health care reform has become an issue as well. The outlook for family therapy is promising.

Summary Table

Rationale and History of Family Therapy

Most life difficulties arise and are best addressed in families.

Family therapy is effective in treating a number of disorders.

Client families express satisfaction with family therapy.

Family therapy allows the therapist to see and treat interpersonal dynamics in a systemic and timely way. It is often more effective or appropriate than individual or group therapy.

Family Therapy through the Decades

Before 1940

Cultural beliefs stress the individual, the use of community resources, and psychoanalytic theory.

Ernest Groves, Alfred Adler, and county home extension agents teach family living/parenting skills.

Abraham and Hannah Stone, Emily Mudd, and Paul Popenoe begin marriage counseling.

National Council on Family Relations is founded (1938).

1940 to 1949

The American Association of Marriage Counselors (AAMC) is established (1942).

Milton Erickson develops therapeutic methods that will later be adopted by family therapy.

First account of concurrent marital therapy is published by Bela Mittleman (1948).

Theodore Lidz and Lyman Wynne study dynamics of families with individuals in them who had schizophrenia.

World War II brings stress to families.

The National Mental Health Act of 1946 is passed by Congress.

1950 to 1959

Nathan Ackerman develops a psychoanalytical approach to working with families.

Gregory Bateson's group begins studying patterns of communication in families.

Don Jackson creates the Mental Research Institute (1958).

Carl Whitaker sets up the first conference on family therapy at Sea Island, Georgia (1955).

Murray Bowen begins the National Institute of Mental Health (NIMH) project of studying families with individuals in them who were diagnosed as schizophrenics.

Ivan Boszormenyi-Nagy begins work on contextual therapy.

1960 to 1969

Jay Haley refines and advocates therapeutic approaches of Milton Erickson. He moves from Palo Alto to join the Philadelphia Child Guidance Clinic (1967).

Family Process, the first journal in family therapy, is cofounded by Nathan Ackerman and Don Jackson (1961).

Salvador Minuchin begins development of structural family therapy at Wiltwyck School and continues at the Philadelphia Child Guidance Clinic. He coauthors *Families of the Slums*.

John Bell publishes the first ideas about family group therapy (1961).

Virginia Satir publishes *Conjoint Family Therapy* (1964) and gains a national following.

First state licensure law regulating family counselors is passed in California (1963).

Nathan Ackerman publishes *Treating the Troubled Family* (1966).

Carl Whitaker moves to the University of Wisconsin. He begins to write and lecture extensively.

General systems theory, formulated by Ludwig von Bertalanffy (1934/1968), becomes the basis for most family therapy.

Murray Bowen begins to formulate his own theory.

Training centers and institutes for family therapy are established in New York, Philadelphia, and Boston.

1970 to 1979

Membership in the American Association for Marriage and Family Therapy grows by 777% to 7,565 members.

Nathan Ackerman dies (1971).

The *Journal of Marital and Family Therapy* is founded (1974).

Families and Family Therapy and *Psychosomatic Families* are published by Salvador Minuchin and associates.

The *Family Therapy Networker* is created (1976).

The American Association of Marriage and Family Counselors becomes the American Association for Marriage and Family Therapy (1979). Its degree-granting programs are recognized by the Department of Health, Education, and Welfare.

The American Family Therapy Academy is created (1977).

Paradox and Counterparadox is published by the Milan Group (1978). European family therapists become influential in the United States.

Feminist theorists, led by Rachel Hare-Mustin, begin questioning the premises of family therapy.

Jay Haley publishes *Uncommon Therapy* (1973) and *Problem Solving Therapy* (1976).

1980 to 1989

Membership in the AAMFT grows to 14,000.

Division 43 (Family Psychology) of the American Psychological Association is established (1984).

The International Association of Marriage and Family Counselors within the American Counseling Association is established (1986).

New leaders in family therapy emerge.

Research procedures in family therapy are developed and refined.

Publications in family therapy increase. *Family Therapy Networker* reaches a circulation of 50,000.

Virginia Satir dies (1988).

1990 to 1999

Family therapy becomes more global as an approach to helping others.

Solution-focused family therapies of deShazer and O'Hanlon and narrative approach of White and Epston become popular.

Other new theories are developed for working with couples and families, including constructionist theories. They challenge systems thinking.

The integration and merger of family therapy theories occurs, with less emphasis on specialization.

The new epistemology, which involves second-order cybernetics, emphasizes positive feedback in system transformation.

The Basic Family Therapy Skills Project focuses on determining, defining, and testing the skills necessary for novice therapists to master, generically and specifically.

2000 to the Present

Marriage and family therapy becomes a global phenomenon with professional associations in countries throughout the world.

The influence and impact of professional associations, such as the AAMFT, IAMFC, AFTA, and Division 43 of APA, grows.

Accreditation of programs and licensure efforts increase.

Health care reform and mental health care provider status become increasingly important.

Research on the efficacy of family therapy with different cultural groups increases.

The Process of Family Therapy

— • —

My son, Benjamin, rolls over in his crib
to the applause of his mother and delight of himself
while I catch an afternoon flight to Saint Paul
to conduct a counseling seminar.

These are milestones in our lives
marking steps in family development
as we reach out to touch
and are changed through our behaviors.

At 33,000 feet, I drift in and out of sleep,
aware that in the process, but on a different level,
my wife and child do the same.
In the depth of thought and images
we attempt in special ways
to bridge the gap of distance.

— • —

Gladding, 1988

The process of conducting family therapy is predictable, regardless of one's theoretical approach. All schools of family therapy have a theoretical commitment to working with family interactions. Despite outward appearances, different systems of family therapy are more alike in practice than their theories would suggest. For example, family therapists of all persuasions are concerned with processes involved in clarifying communications among family members, overcoming resistance, and rectifying dysfunctional behaviors. Most see the relationship (not just the individuals within the relationship) as the focus of therapy (Davis & Butler, 2004). Consequently, family therapists have many common concerns and procedures that transcend their different theoretical emphases. In fact, surveys indicate that the dominant theoretical orientation to family therapy is eclectic (e.g., Rait, 1988).

Therefore, it is important for family therapists to be aware of the universal methods of working with families. By being so attuned, they are better able to communicate with a variety of professionals. They are also better able to realize the uniqueness of the theories under which they work. Such knowledge gives them a flexibility and common bond to others in the helping professions.

This chapter covers the importance of the personhood of the therapist in working with families as well as potential problems encountered by family therapists. Along with this material are guidelines for appropriate processes in helping families and expected procedures for the main stages of family therapy. Although this material is targeted toward new family therapists, it is applicable to experienced therapists as well.

The Personhood of Family Therapists

In the process of therapy, the personhood of family therapists is quite important (Aponte, 1992; Satir, 1987). "Research on counseling outcome consistently reports that the beneficial effects of counseling are related more to the personal characteristics of the counselor than to any specific intervention or approach" (Kier & Lawson, 1999, p. 118). Not everyone who is bright, articulate, and attuned to systems theory and the process of change should enter the profession of family therapy. Individuals who have had negative family-of-origin experiences may find that they cannot deal successfully with families or do not wish to work with families (Bowen, 1978; Kier & Lawson, 1999). Persons who treat difficult families must often engage in a considerable amount of therapy for themselves on an individual and family level (Wilcoxon, Walker, & Hovestadt, 1989). Being a family therapist and staying psychologically healthy is not an easy task.

Major stressors for family therapists include increased depression from listening to a client family's problem, less time for one's own family because of work demands, unrealistic expectations of one's own family, and psychological distancing from one's family because of professional status (Duncan & Duerden, 1990; Wetchler & Piercy, 1986).

Not all of the impact from working with families is negative. Enhancers for family therapists include an increased ability to solve one's own family problems, an acceptance of one's part in contributing to family dysfunctions, a deeper appreciation of one's own family, and a greater ability and desire to communicate effectively (Duncan & Duerden, 1990; Wetchler & Piercy, 1986). Being a couples and family therapist is clearly a multifaceted process.

Overall, a couples and family therapist "should be a healer: a human being concerned with engaging other human beings therapeutically, around areas and issues that cause them pain, while always retaining great respect for their values, areas of strength, and esthetic preferences" (Minuchin & Fishman, 1981, p. 1). To achieve the role of a healer requires dedication, awareness, and stable mental health. It is the exceptional person who can achieve this balance. Those who are best suited in nature to be helpers of families most often have artistic qualities; that is, they are intuitive and feeling-oriented in regard to interpersonal relationships (Brammer & MacDonald, 2003). It is these individuals whom some educators recommend for training in the field of family therapy. Regardless, it takes time for people to develop to the point of seeing themselves as competent professionals; often therapists reach such a point only after 5 or 6 years of experience (Kral & Hines, 1999).

Common Problems of Beginning Family Therapists

Several problems are germane and common to family therapists when they are just beginning to work with families. These concerns must be addressed if the therapeutic process is to have a significant impact. Some therapists' downfalls are a result of an overemphasis, while others are the result of an underemphasis.

Overemphasis

Couple and family therapists can overemphasize and try to do too much (Kalima, 2005). The following subsections discuss some common ways in which overemphasis is expressed.

Overemphasis on Details

Two primary components of family therapy are content and process. When families come for treatment, they are usually focused on a content issue, that is, on "what" is being said. For example, a husband may concentrate on why he wants a divorce, a child may talk about the reasons she refuses to go to school, or a wife may describe the ways she is wrestling with depression. **Content** involves details and facts. **Process** focuses on "how" information is dealt with in an interaction. For instance, are couples yelling at each other or are children withdrawing from their parents? Sometimes content is essential to attain. Knowledge of past patterns and the sequencing of family interaction may be helpful in breaking up dysfunctional forms of relating. At other times, facts get in the way of helping couples and families make necessary changes. In such cases, the therapist might be concentrating on the trees instead of the forest. If a couples and family therapist says to a woman, "Tell me about every time your husband has yelled at you in the last few days," the therapist runs the risk of focusing too closely on a specific behavior and not enough on the significance of the behavior. In such a circumstance, the result of the therapeutic intervention is limited.

A good rule to follow in dealing with facts is to ask "how" questions along with "what," "where," and "when" queries. For example, "How does your husband's behavior affect your ability to relate to him?" Such a question helps get to the heart of the relationship between the individuals involved.

Another method that can be useful is **redirection,** where the therapist asks the couple or family to attend to the process of their relationship instead of the content of it. Partners may be instructed to pay attention to the energy in the exchange of their words instead of the words themselves, or to focus on the space between two people rather than just on the individuals themselves. In this kind of maneuver, attention is directed to the feeling that is between people such as tension, excitement, warmth, or coldness (Kalima, 2005).

Overemphasis on Making Everyone Happy

Sometimes family therapists become concerned or overconcerned when families leave their offices in a state of tension. The reason for such disturbance on the part of the therapist is an illogical belief, which essentially purports that if the therapist were competent, the family would be able to resolve its difficulties. While therapists can do a great deal to help families, friction is sometimes unavoidable. Furthermore, friction can be productive. It can motivate individuals to try new behaviors and break out of old patterns.

When clients leave a session in turmoil, the therapist can paradoxically ask them to stay that way until next session or instruct the family to "go slow" in coming to a resolution of the difficulty. The end result in such a case is usually that the family resolves the conflict fairly quickly and either returns to a previous, homeostatic balance or moves on to a more functional set of behaviors. Regardless of whether the family resolves the issue or not, the therapist can use the next session to ask each member of the family what was tried in response to their discomfort. Using this information, the family and the therapist will gain a clearer perspective on the processes the family employs in creating strategies. Then new or varied themes can be explored.

Overemphasis on Verbal Expression

Well-chosen words can have a therapeutic effect on families. For example, if the therapist can verbally assure the family that what they have been through and the strategies they have tried in the past are normal, the family might be open to new ways of working on their present situation. However, in most cases, the exact words said by a therapist are not remembered. A helpful way of understanding the limited impact of a therapist's words is to think about what words or advice you most remember in your life. For the majority of people, the list of such remarks is short, and the people involved are few.

Therapists must work with families in a number of ways. They instruct, comment, and inquire; but they also model behavior, use role plays, and assign homework. In other words, therapists recognize and utilize teachable moments. It is what the family and therapist *do*, as well as what is said, that makes a difference. The timing of such actions is also significant. For example, a therapist could use hand signals like a traffic officer at a crucial time in a family's therapy to indicate who may talk. Although the family might not remember all of what was said, the use of the therapist's nonverbal directions can leave a lasting impression and message about the art of effective communication.

Overemphasis on Coming to an Early or Too Easy Resolution

There is a tendency in therapy for families to "fly into health." After a couple of sessions, a family might report that they are doing better and are ready to terminate therapy. Although this might be true for a few families, most who report feeling better quickly are experiencing the euphoria that often comes out of discussing a situation rather than actually changing it. Flights into health and early or easy resolutions of family problems seldom succeed. Families involved in such processes rarely examine the dynamics in their problems.

From all theoretical perspectives, the conducting of family therapy is an ongoing process. Families need to be initially advised of how long the process of therapy takes and what is expected from them. For example, a brief theory therapist might say: "We will be working together on your situation for ten sessions. It is crucial that you define what you wish to change as soon and as concretely as possible."

Overemphasis on Dealing with One Member of the Family

When family therapists concentrate on just one member of a family, they fall into the same trap that has caused the family difficulty — that is, they **scapegoat** (select one person as the cause of difficulties). Family problems are not linear in nature, and one person does not cause a family to be dysfunctional. It is crucial that beginning family therapists recognize the dynamics within families and the power of homeostasis in keeping families operating at a certain level, even if it is dysfunctional. Only when therapists consider the relationships among everyone in the family can meaningful interventions be made. It is imperative that family therapists periodically remind themselves and their client families about the importance of examining interpersonal dynamics in regard to dysfunctionality.

In working with a couple who brings their adolescent in for breaking curfew, the therapist might say: "While Jane's behavior is of concern, in our sessions we will look at the behaviors of everyone. I have found that when one person in a family is having difficulties, others usually are as well." By alerting the family to this systemic view of family relations, the therapist makes it easier for everyone to become more aware of their actions and how they personally contribute to the family's well-being or lack of it.

Underemphasis

Underemphasis can be as unproductive as overemphasis. By underemphasizing and failing to make an intervention at a strategic time, a therapist might subtly suggest that the family's interaction is adequate when nothing could be further from the truth. Underemphasis takes several forms. Among the most prominent are the following.

Underemphasis on Establishing Structure

If family therapy is to achieve a positive outcome, it helps to start the process properly. The struggle to establish the parameters under which therapy is conducted is referred to as the **battle for structure** (Napier & Whitaker, 1978). This battle must be won by the therapist, otherwise the family members could attempt to run the therapy sessions in the same nonproductive manner in which they conduct their family life.

A key component in winning the battle for structure is for the therapist to delineate the conditions under which treatment will occur. Clients have both a right and a need to know about fees and payment schedules, theoretical frameworks and treatment approaches, rules about appointments, how and when they are allowed to contact you, rules about confidentiality, and your educational background and training (Kaplan & Culkin, 1995; Leslie, 2004a). Much of this information can be provided to families through a **professional self-disclosure statement** (see Figure 4.1) (Gladding, 2004). Such a disclosure statement should be written because verbal statements can be misunderstood or misinterpreted. The statement should be read by the family, and feedback from family members should be solicited, as well. Incorporated into the self-disclosure statement can be an **informed consent brochure** (Kaplan, 2000a). Such a piece includes all the information in a self-disclosure statement, such as the techniques and theories used by the family therapist, the risks of therapy, and the limits of confidentiality (McCurdy & Murray, 2003). However, it goes one step further in that the family signs off that they understand the policies and procedures of therapy and consent to participate. They are given a copy of what they have signed as a reminder.

Professional Disclosure Statement
Dr. Jane Smith
205 Healy Building
Philadelphia, Pennsylvania 16006
814–555–6257

The Nature of Family Therapy

There are many approaches to family therapy, and different clinicians utilize a number of theories and techniques in their practice. Some work only with the individual or couple, while others insist that the whole family be seen. I have prepared this brief professional self-disclosure form to inform you how I conduct sessions.

My Qualifications

I am a graduate of Purdue University's marriage and family therapy doctoral program. I have been in practice for the past 10 years in the Philadelphia area. I am licensed as a marriage and family therapist by the state of Pennsylvania. I am a clinical member of the American Association for Marriage and Family Therapists. I also belong to the International Association of Marriage and Family Counseling and Division 43 (Family Psychology) of the American Psychological Association.

I have done extensive work with families under supervision at the Philadelphia Child Guidance Clinic. I am not a physician and cannot prescribe medicine. However, if medical treatment seems warranted, I consult with a psychiatrist and can make a referral.

Family Therapy as a Process

Family therapy is a process that requires a considerable investment of time. I prefer to work with the entire family, and I realize that this style may make one or more of you uncomfortable. Although each family is unique, there are some common stages you can expect.

The first stage is the beginning session(s) where we will work to clarify your concerns and difficulties. This process will require observation on my part and verbalization/behavior on your parts. My belief is that there is no one single cause of or cure for a family's problems.

The second stage is the working sessions in which we will concentrate on helping you make changes that will work for you and make your relationships and family life better. During this time, I will ask you to be active as problem solvers.

The final stage is termination, in which we will complete the process of change and end our sessions. It is at this time when you may wish to be most reflective.

Length of Family Therapy and Fees

Family therapy sessions are 50 minutes in length once a week. They begin on the hour. The fee is $75 per session and payment is expected at the end of each session. I will work to help you file insurance, if you wish. Although no one can guarantee how many sessions a particular family may need, I have found the range to be between 10 and 30.

Your Rights

As a consumer of therapeutic services, you have a right to be treated with dignity, respect, and in a professional manner. You have the right to ask me questions about your therapeutic concerns at any time.

Emergency

There is someone from the office on call 24 hours a day. Although you will probably not need this service, the number for emergencies is 814–555–8309.

Figure 4.1
Sample professional disclosure statement.

In addition to setting guidelines, the therapist must also physically structure the room so that therapeutic interactions can take place. This includes arranging the furniture so that family members can talk directly with each other. The structure should also be flexible, so the therapist can move family members closer to or farther away from each other.

Underemphasis on Showing Care and Concern

Most families enter counseling with some trepidation. Their anxiety might be increased if family members think they are being treated as objects and not persons, or if they perceive the therapist as rigid and distant. Effective family therapists follow the guidelines of other helping professionals; they are caring, open, sensitive, and concerned; and they are empathetic and show it.

Family therapists can convey this professional care by demonstrating the skills in the acronym **SOLER** (Egan, 2002). The S stands for facing the client or family squarely, either in a metaphorical or literal manner. The O is a reminder to adopt an open posture that is nondefensive, such as avoiding crossing one's arms or legs. The L indicates that the therapist should lean forward in the direction of the client family, to show interest. A therapist can overdo this procedure and must gauge what is appropriate for each family. The E represents good eye contact. One way of letting family members know they are cared about is by looking at them (when appropriate). Finally, R stands for relaxation. Working with families is an intense process, but therapists need to feel comfortable.

Effective family therapists also make brief disclosure statements (when appropriate). For example, in response to a parent who reports having been previously married, a therapist might briefly reveal that he or she is also a stepparent. Therapists might also show concern by using self-effacing humor that indicates to family members their awareness of the difficulties families encounter (Piercy & Lobenz, 1994). For instance, a therapist might briefly recount a time in his or her own family when the family struggled in a futile but serious way, such as trying to make it to church on time the day after daylight savings time ended, with family members waking up late and having to rush, only to find they were hassled, haggled, irreverent, and an hour early!

Underemphasis on Engaging Family Members in the Therapeutic Process

Engaging family members in therapy includes attending to each one personally. For example, shaking hands, bowing, and establishing eye contact are three ways this connection can be made (Olkin, 1993). If a family member feels slighted, chances are increased that this person will overtly refuse to participate or will sabotage the therapeutic process in some subtle manner. Although personally soliciting the participation of all family members takes time, it pays off in the long run.

When therapists meet new families and their members, it is crucial that they spend some time with each person. They should concentrate on the interests and dislikes of each individual for a few moments. Therapists might talk to children about school and to parents about different aspects of work and family life. In so doing, therapists help build rapport and create an atmosphere of cooperation through acknowledging each person's importance to the family.

Underemphasis on Letting the Family Work on Its Problems

Just as the family therapist must win the battle for structure, the family must win the **battle for initiative** (Napier & Whitaker, 1978). This battle centers around the family becoming motivated to make changes. A family that does not see any benefit in altering its behaviors is likely to either drop out of therapy or simply go through the motions. On the opposite side is the effect of initiative on family therapists. When families are not working well, some family therapists mentally take these families home, much to their own distress (Guy, 1987).

Therapists can help families win the battle for initiative by helping them envision how their lives can become healthier collectively and individually. Such a process means that therapists must be enterprising and sell the family a set of possibilities (Holland, 1973). The therapist might ask a family that is constantly fighting these questions:

- "How would it be for you to be able to live in peace with one another?"
- "Think for a moment what you really want from this family. Can you envision some ways that you could settle your differences and get on with your lives?"

Underemphasis on Attending to Nonverbal Family Dynamics

Nonverbal messages are a major part of any therapeutic process (Egan, 2002). These messages are given behaviorally and include eye glances, hands folded across one's body, and even the distancing of people through the arrangement or rearrangement of chairs. The most frequent nonverbal cues are facial. However, facial and other body movements often are combined. For example, when clients are describing feelings about an object or event, they may exhibit increased animation of the face and hands (Cormier & Hackney, 2004).

Family therapists who do not pay attention to the nonverbal aspects of family dynamics only partially decipher what is being conveyed among family members (Brock & Barnard, 1999). The result might be that crucial issues within the family are not addressed and change is limited. If a daughter tells her father she loves him but does so in a trembling voice and with a look of fear, the therapist would be wise to pursue what the relationship between these two family members is really like.

Appropriate Process

The process of family therapy can be conducted in a variety of ways, but some vital aspects of it must be included. If therapists do not plan properly, they are likely to fail. "That is because conceptualizing, planning, and implementing effective interventions with couples and families can be exceedingly more complex given that family dynamics are intertwined with individual dynamics" (Sperry, 2005, p. 71). A keystone of proper planning in working with families encompasses a consideration of ways to conduct sessions based on one's impression of a family, one's theoretical position, and one's clinical skills (Rickert, 1989).

Pre-Session Planning and Tasks

Family therapy "begins the moment of the first interaction" between the family and therapist (Olkin, 1993, p. 32). Initial contact is generally made by a family member's telephone call to a therapist. Also, the individuals who initiate the phone calls are usually "the most interested in change and may be the most open to engaging in therapy" (Weber & Levine, 1995, p. 54). Some calls are handled by an intermediary (i.e., someone other than the therapist, such as a secretary); but the family and the therapist are better served if calls are directed to and handled by the therapist (Brock & Barnard, 1999). One reason is that the therapist can directly answer questions about who should attend the sessions and how the sessions will be structured.

A second reason is that, through the phone conversation, the therapist gains an opportunity to establish rapport and a cooperative alliance with the family member (Weber, McKeever, & McDaniel, 1992). Finally, in answering calls, therapists have an opportunity to demonstrate their own competency and credibility.

Regardless of who answers calls, it is essential during this first contact to obtain certain information and establish a professional but cordial atmosphere (Snider, 1992). Essential information to be gathered includes the name, address, and phone number of the caller. A concise statement of the problem to be addressed is also helpful, even if it is modified or changed later. Other information that is useful includes the referral source, history of previous treatment, and preferred method of payment (if relevant).

The tone and type of speech used by the intermediary or therapist can either help or hinder the decision of the family to engage in the treatment process. If the receiver of the call is supportive, caring, and talks in a manner that conveys respect and receptivity, an appointment is more likely to be made and kept. Whenever possible, the initial appointment should be made within 48 hours of the call. The reason is that most families who call for help are ready to begin the process. Delaying an appointment can cause some members to reconsider their decision to attend or to resist coming.

When evaluating intake information, hypotheses about dynamics within the family should be made, especially if the therapist is operating from a problem-oriented position (Weber et al., 1992). One source to consider in making such speculations is the family life cycle (Duvall, 1977; Carter & McGoldrick, 1999). Therapists need to ask themselves what issues are to be expected from a family in a certain stage of life. Some transitional difficulties are natural, and some are not. The ethnic/cultural background of the family is also a consideration. In some traditional Italian families, for example, an unmarried daughter leaving home might bring about a crisis that would not develop in a traditional British family.

A final pre-session task is to form a preliminary diagnosis of what is happening within the family (Rickert, 1989). Making a preliminary diagnosis of a family is not the same as making a diagnosis of an individual using the *Diagnostic and Statistical Manual (DSM)* of the American Psychiatric Association. The reason is that the *DSM* does not have a nomenclature for diagnosing relational problems except under its so-called **V Codes** and under its **Global Assessment of Relational Functioning Scale (GARF)** (Crews & Hill, 2005). Therefore, in working with families, therapists must be more descriptive and think of how people interact in systemic relationships. In a family where an adolescent male is becoming a delinquent, the therapist might hypothesize that the boy and his father are disengaged and cut off from each other physically as well as psychologically. Similarly, in the case of a child who refuses to attend school, the therapist might hypothesize that the child and the mother are enmeshed and that the child's actions are somehow being reinforced or supported.

Engaging in this diagnostic exercise, which is a hallmark of the Milan approach, requires that the therapist spend time thinking about possible linkages within the family and the development of persons and systems. The payoff for this investment in time is that the therapist can home in on issues more quickly and effectively. Through diagnostic procedures, therapists are more likely to "work within the limits of their training and experience" (Carlson, Hinkle, & Sperry, 1993, p. 309). The therapist is also in a good position to formulate a treatment plan that is communicable to other mental health professionals. Finally, diagnosis is a way for family therapists to comprehend more thoroughly what is happening with family members as well as with the family as a whole.

In the pre-session, therapists, especially those who are theoretically driven, want to ask and answer the following three questions:

- "What happened?" (in order to form an initial diagnosis)
- "Why did it happen?" (in order to formulate a clinical explanation of household dynamics)
- "What can be done about it and how?" (in order to devise a clinical treatment plan) (Sperry, 2005, p. 72)

In doing all of this, family therapists come up with what is known as a **case conceptualization,** which helps them integrate theory with practice and come up with a treatment plan.

Initial Session(s)

Research points out that the first few sessions, not just the first session, are the most critical in terms of successful therapy (Odell & Quinn, 1998). Both **structuring** (e.g., teaching, directing) and **supportive** (e.g., warmth, caring) **behaviors** make a difference in whether client families return. Therefore, in conducting therapy with families, clinicians should realize that the first session is not usually a determinant of whether a family returns for treatment. Rather, most families suspend judgment for a few sessions in order to give the treatment a chance to work and the therapist a chance to prove his or her competence. Nevertheless, therapists should work hard from the beginning to make treatment as effective as possible and set the stage for success.

Before an initial session begins, the therapist should know who is coming; for instance, is just the marital couple coming or the whole family? In some traditions, such as Bowen family therapy, the couple is the unit of treatment, whereas in other schools of family therapy, including strategic, systemic, behavioral, and experiential, children are encouraged to attend treatment and become actively engaged in the therapeutic process (Sweeney & Rocha, 2000). In a study of clinical members of the AAMFT on the inclusion of children in family therapy, Johnson and Thomas (1999) found that "half of the therapists excluded children on the basis of their comfort" with them (p. 117). Children were included most often in sessions where they were prone to be internalizing (i.e., quiet) as opposed to externalizing (i.e., aggressive). Children were also more likely to be seen in family sessions with single-parent (as opposed to two-parent) families and when the presenting problem was child-focused.

During the initial session (or sessions), the therapist must achieve a number of crucial tasks in order to be successful with the family. Some goals must be accomplished simultaneously and others sequentially. As with other stages of family therapy, "timing is everything." The most important tasks in the first session are discussed in the following sections.

Join the Family: Establishing Rapport

The first step in helping a family during the initial session(s) is for therapists to establish a sense of trust between themselves and the members of the family. This stage is referred to as **joining** (Haley, 1976; Minuchin, 1974). It is a crucial component of family therapy and requires therapists to meet, greet, and form a bond with family members in a rapid but relaxed and authentic way. Therapists must make the family comfortable through social exchange with each member.

If a therapist fails to join with a family, its most disengaged members, or the family as a whole, could leave treatment either physically or psychologically. It is usually the least involved member of a family who has the most power in deciding whether the family stays in therapy or not (Mark Worden, personal communication, 1982). A weak alliance with family members is a frequently cited reason for treatment not working (Coleman, 1985).

Inquire About Members' Perceptions of the Family

When making inquiries of family members, family therapists must challenge old perceptions. Individuals within families usually have a problem, person, or situation framed in a certain manner. A **frame,** a concept originated by Bateson (1955), is a perception or opinion that organizes one's interactions so that "at any given time certain events are more likely to occur and certain interpretations of what is going on are more likely to be made" (Coyne, 1985, p. 338).

By challenging the perception (or frame), therapists can get family members to define problems, persons, or situations differently, as well as prompt them to "look for different solutions" (Olkin, 1993, p. 33). Such a change sets up the opportunity for success.

Observe Family Patterns

Families, like individuals, have unique personalities. They come into therapy and display these personalities both in a verbal and nonverbal manner, a phenomenon referred to as the **family dance** (Napier & Whitaker, 1978). Some systematic ways of observing family interactions are helpful for novice and experienced therapists. The following questions are among those that Resnikoff (1981) advised family therapists to ask themselves in regard to how a family functions:

- "What is the outward appearance of the family?" (p. 135) For example, how far do members sit from each other and who sits next to whom?
- "What is the cognitive functioning in the family?" (p. 136) For example, how specifically and straightforwardly do family members communicate? Is there much give and take in the communication patterns?
- "What repetitive, nonproductive sequences do you notice?" (p. 136) For instance, do parents scold or praise their children in certain ways after special behaviors?
- "What is the basic feeling state in the family and who carries it?" (p. 136) All families have a variety of feelings, but often one member conveys the overall affect of the family. For example, a depressed child might indicate a depressed family.
- "What individual roles reinforce family resistances and what are the most prevalent family defenses?" (p. 136) Individuals and families sometimes have characteristic responses to stress, such as anger or denial. It is crucial to recognize these responses and to be sensitive and innovative in responding to them.
- "What subsystems are operative in this family?" (p. 137) Almost all families have **subsystems,** that is, members who because of age or function are logically grouped together, such as parents or siblings. It is important to identify these subsystems and how they function. Some work well, but others end up with someone becoming the scapegoat or **triangulated** (i.e., a person who is focused on as a way of relieving tension between two other family members). It is crucial for the therapists to recognize and work through subsystems so that families can relate in a more open and healthy manner.
- "Who carries the power in the family?" (p. 137) Persons who have power in families make the rules and decisions. They might act in a benign manner, but what they say or do is adhered to by others. For instance, a mother who acts as the family spokesperson

probably has considerable power. Families that operate in a functional way have flexibility in regard to rules and the balance of power.

- "How are the family members differentiated from each other and what are the subgroup boundaries?" (p. 137) In some families, **enmeshment** (overinvolvement physically and/or psychologically) occurs, and in others **distancing** (isolated separateness, physically and/or psychologically) occurs. In healthy families, a balance exists between these two extremes. Therapists need to be aware of family members' degrees of separation and individuation.

- "What part of the family life cycle is the family experiencing and are the problem-solving methods stage appropriate?" (p. 138) For example, is a family treating its 18-year-old like an 8-year-old? Family therapists need to check on how well a family deals with current developmental reality.

- "What are the evaluator's own reactions to the family?" (p. 138) Reactions to families are made on both an emotional and cognitive level. Sometimes, the therapist might see the family in light of his or her own family of origin and confuse the issues to be worked on. Such a perception is not in the service of the family or the therapist. To truly be helpful to a family, a therapist must be aware of the root of his or her reaction and must know how to respond appropriately.

Assess What Needs to Be Done

The family therapist needs to assess what changes should be made or can be made in order to help the family function better (L'Abate & Bagarozzi, 1993). This assessment can mean the employment of specific diagnostic instruments (West, 1988). In most cases, however, this procedure can also be conducted more informally such as through observation. In assessing what needs to be done, family therapists must be aware not only of the family but also of biases they hold because of a client's socio-demographic characteristics. Pals, Piercy, and Miller (1998) found that "a therapist's decision to break confidence appears to depend in part on the therapist's background characteristics" (p. 470). Such may also be the case in assessing what needs to be done, and therapists must be sure they are proceeding in this area as objectively as possible.

Engender Hope for Change and Overcome Resistance

Many family members, and sometimes the family as a whole, need assurance that their situations can get better. Hope motivates them to work and make difficult changes and choices. Essential elements of hope can be given in direct or indirect ways. A family therapist might say: "Your situation did not get this way overnight, and it will not change overnight. But, I think if you work hard it will change." This type of comment directly addresses the family's plight and possibilities. Other less formal statements, such as "I think you might be able to do something more productive," can also be encouraging and foster a positive attitude in family members.

Furthermore, family therapists can engender hope that change can take place within families by helping them identify their assets and strengths. Most families know their liabilities. However, discovering strengths, such as a supportive neighborhood, helps families recognize they have more potential than they might have previously thought.

Regardless of the therapist's words of encouragement or the identified family strengths, almost all families exhibit some form of resistance to treatment (Anderson & Stewart, 1983; Gold & Morris, 2003). **Resistance** comes in many forms, such as "members attempting to control sessions, absent or silent members, refusal of family members to talk to each other in sessions, hostility, and failure to do homework" (Olkin, 1993, p. 33). Other forms of resistance include being late to sessions, denying reality, rationalizing, insisting that one family member is the problem, and challenging the therapist's competence. If treatment is to be successful, family therapists have to understand the nature of resistance and overcome it without alienating family members. "When therapists ... intervene, their choice of a type of intervention, and whether to attempt to overcome, avoid, or use resistance to produce change, will be based on their theoretical orientation and their understanding of where on the compliance/defiance continuum a family or family member is at any given time" (Anderson & Stewart, 1983, p. 38).

One way to overcome resistance is to create **boundaries** for the family (Jaffe, 1991). A therapist may require that all family members must be present for a session to occur, or that there be no name-calling in or outside the therapy sessions. Through the use of boundaries, members and the family as a whole can feel safe and begin opening up to one another. Another strategy is to interpret positively the actions associated with resistance as ways the family copes or protects itself. This is a type of **reframing**: "the art of attributing different meaning to behavior so the behavior will be seen differently by the family" (Constantine, Stone Fish, & Piercy, 1984). Thus, a therapist might commend family members who refuse to participate in a session for being "rightfully cautious" about opening themselves or the family up to new situations. A final way to deal with this phenomenon is to endorse it. The therapist might say, "Go slow." This strategy is called a **paradox,** or a form of treatment in which therapists give families permission to do what they were going to do anyway. This type of directive allows a family to be more flexible in their responses and to deal with matters in a more open manner. Regardless of how accomplished, the family therapist must engage the family in the process of resolving their concerns so that they become, along with the therapist, immersed in finding different ways to function (Mason, 2005).

Make a Return Appointment and Give Assignments

At the end of a first session, some beginning therapists make the mistake of waiting to see if a family wishes to make another appointment. Although it is appropriate to let the family make a decision regarding future sessions, it is equally important that the therapist offer to see the family again. For instance, the therapist can propose that the family come for a set number of additional sessions, say, four. After the additional sessions have taken place, the family can evaluate them and decide what progress has been made. This approach relieves the therapist and the family of the burden of dealing with the question of future sessions after each appointment. However, regardless of whether the number of sessions is agreed to ahead of time or session by session, the therapist needs to take the lead in giving the family options.

If future sessions are agreed to, then the next step in the process is to assign the family **homework** (i.e., tasks to do outside the therapy session), if theoretically appropriate. For example, the structural, strategic, Bowen, and behavioral types of family therapy emphasize working between sessions. Haley (1987) cites three reasons for giving homework. First, it helps families behave and feel differently. Many families need practice in order to be comfortable with new or prescribed ways of interacting. Second, homework assignments intensify the relationship between the therapist and the family. Finally, homework gives the therapist an opportunity to see how family members relate to each other. Homework or directives can be a way to help families help themselves and assist the therapist in deciding what course of action to take next.

In assigning homework, family therapists should make it clear to their families the specifics of what they are to do, as well as when and how often they are to do it (Keim, 2000). A "trial run" should be conducted in the therapist's office, if time allows. For some families, a time should be scheduled to talk over and process what they did; for others, simple action is enough. An example of a homework assignment would be for family members to practice listening to one another, and then for each member to paraphrase what another family member said before making a statement of his or her own.

Record Impressions of Family Session Immediately

Impressions of particular families are fleeting, especially if therapists are busy. The result is that information about a family or a session can become unintentionally distorted over time (Gorden, 1992). Thus, it is crucial that those who work with families record their impressions in the form of **clinical notes** as soon as possible after sessions. Historically, clinical notes have been more content-oriented than process-oriented. However, family therapists have a choice as to what they record and how they do so. A balance between noting the process and the content of sessions probably works best.

In writing clinical notes, therapists accomplish three vital tasks. First, clinical notes can be studied over time in regard to patterns or processes that may evolve. This type of "paper trail" is invaluable because it helps therapists remember nonverbal interactions and occurrences. Clinical notes lend themselves to future use (Gorden, 1992).

Second, clinical notes give therapists the opportunity to be reflective and objective, and to pull away from the seductive power of becoming a family member (Mark Worden, personal communication, 1982). Families are powerful and can easily engulf outsiders into their ways of thinking.

Finally, clinical notes can help therapists probe in a specific way by reminding them of what has been previously said or dealt with. Many families are theme-oriented and talk about behaviors and events in some detail. By referring to notes, therapists can avoid going over the same material twice (Gorden, 1992). They can also see the progress of a family in regard to any treatment plan that has been formulated.

A unique way of recording clinical notes, used by Michael White and other narrative family therapists, is through the practice of writing a letter to the family about what occurred during the session. The letters then become the clinical record—that is, the clinical notes.

Middle Phase of Treatment

If rapport, structure, and initiative have been fostered in the initial sessions of family therapy, the middle phase of treatment can begin. During this phase, family therapists push family members and the family as a whole to make changes and breakthroughs. To do so, the therapist should employ the procedures discussed in the following sections.

Involve Peripheral Family Members

A family is only as productive as its least involved member. Therefore, in most orientations to family therapy, the middle phase of treatment emphasizes making sure that all family members are committed to and working toward a common goal. If a family member is not involved in the process of therapy, the therapist can invite him or her in one or more of three ways (Barker, 2001).

The first way is to invite the uninvolved family member to be an observer of the family. In this role, he or she begins to participate by giving the family feedback on what has transpired in their interaction. He or she acts as a reporter, summarizing what has occurred, at the end of a session.

The second way to get the uninvolved family member to participate is through the Milan therapy technique of **circular questioning.** In this procedure, the detached family member is asked to give his or her impressions about the different interactions of other family members. The therapist might ask: "How does your father act when that happens? How does your mother respond?" The process, in itself, elicits involvement and helps the family recognize the uniqueness of the individuals within it. Circular questioning "can and does trigger therapeutic change" (Tomm, 1987, p. 5).

The third way to entice an uninvolved family member is to use the power of the family group as a whole. This could mean that the uninvolved person is literally carried into the session. Most often it involves physical reassurance and verbal insistence that the reluctant member be present for the session.

Seek to Connect Family Members

A second goal of the middle phase of family therapy is to link members of the family together in an appropriate manner. This objective is especially noticeable in structural family therapy in which boundaries are emphasized (Minuchin & Fishman, 1981). The proper joining and separating of family members in regard to one another is not owned by any theoretical position.

Making sure of linkage between individuals (e.g., siblings) whose generational interests and concerns are common is crucial at this time. Similarly, breaking up inappropriate intergenerational coalitions that are formed against other members of the family, while supporting those that are formed for connection, closeness, and growth, is a must (Milstein & Baldwin, 1997). An example of the former type of coalition occurs when a mother and daughter form an alliance against a father. On the other hand, the latter type of coalition, if considered from a feminist perspective, might be a mother and teenage daughter alliance that provides "strength and a source of comfort during what can be a confusing and painful developmental period" (p. 129).

Establish Contracts and Promote Quid Pro Quo Relations

A third dimension of the middle phase of family therapy is to foster "payoffs" in relationships, especially in newly formed connections. This procedure can be done through the use of contracts, a type of **quid pro quo** (something for something) relationship in which family members begin to benefit from their involvement with each other. For instance, in return for doing chores on Saturday morning, parents make Saturday dinner "pizza time." In such a circumstance, household tasks are completed more easily (a benefit for the parents), and the children enjoy a special treat while also taking on appropriate responsibilities.

Emphasize Some Change Within the Family System

The process of change is difficult for most individuals, let alone families. In helping families consider change, therapists must assist families in understanding what is currently happening in their lives, what options are available, what the consequences are for change, and what new skills they will have to acquire if they change (Snider, 1992). Sometimes change is best approached in small steps. Using this strategy, families can begin to get used to behaving differently. For example, suppose family members have difficulty clearly communicating with one another in the morning because they are so rushed. A small change might be to start getting up 15 minutes earlier and then moving the clock back in 5-minute segments each day until the family arises 30 minutes earlier than before. A similar small change might be a husband and wife who agree to concentrate on listening to each other exclusively for 15 minutes each day.

Emphasizing contracts and small changes is helpful because these procedures are relatively nonthreatening. In addition, they help everyone envision future happenings in a concrete way.

Reinforce Family Members for Trying New Behaviors

Family members and the family as a whole need to be reinforced when they take risks and attempt new behaviors. Such a policy encourages families to try different ways of interacting. For example, when children ask parents if they can have candy instead of just taking it, they should be rewarded (possibly with candy). If a man appropriately asks his estranged spouse if she would sit and talk with him about their relationship, he should be rewarded, especially if he has not engaged in such behavior before.

Family therapists can use many different means to reinforce family members, but probably the most simple and effective, in most cases, is a brief verbal acknowledgment of what has been done. Therapists can say "good" or "nice work" to clients immediately after learning about the risks they have taken. The goal of this procedure is for the therapist's role of giving awards to gradually be taken over by the family members or for the process of reward to become internalized by the family.

Stay Active as a Therapist

Being a family therapist means being mentally, verbally, and behaviorally active (Friedlander, Wildman, Heatherington, & Skowron, 1994). Few approaches to working with families are passive. Therapists are expected to be involved; otherwise, they will probably fail. On the importance of being active, Haley (1969) offers "the Five B's, which guarantee dynamic failure" (p. 61):

- Be passive
- Be inactive
- Be reflective
- Be silent
- Beware

The case for focusing on behavior and action in family therapy is based on the observation that people often do not change even though they understand why and how they should. Individuals may know they need to lose weight, stop smoking or spend time with their children, yet they do not (Nichols & Schwartz, 2004). Promoting insight in people may help them understand themselves better and freely act in their own best interest; but family therapists do not, as a rule, count on this happening. Instead, the therapist invests a great deal in bringing about change in families and does not wait for insight or spontaneous remission of symptoms.

Link Family with Appropriate Outside Systems

Family therapy is limited in time and scope. It is important that families and their members learn to link with outside groups whenever possible. For example, when families are working to overcome problems related to alcohol abuse, it may be helpful if members connect with Alcoholics Anonymous (AA) and Al-Anon. By so doing, they can receive the additional support and knowledge they need in order to cope and change.

Linkage between families and agencies should be made during the middle phase of family therapy. Consequently, family therapists avoid making hasty and often ineffective referrals to outside agencies at the end of treatment. The importance of outside groups to the health and well-being of families is highlighted in the writings of Boszormenyi-Nagy (1987), who stresses that healing and growth for families take place best when the total context in which families operate is included in treatment.

Focus on Process

Family therapy is a continuous process, and when changes are made in families, it is usually because therapists have focused on the process instead of just the content. Those who practice family therapy must realize that just as "one swallow does not a summer make," one change or even several within the family does not indicate that the family is ready to be discharged from treatment. Rather, changes occur over time and tend to be affective, behavioral, and cognitive, with affective changes among family members being especially significant (Friedlander et al., 1994).

In many cases, family members make their easiest adjustments first. Consequently, family therapists must keep unbalancing, or disturbing, the family when it resists dealing with difficulties or focuses on one person instead of on systemic changes. This requires the therapist to engage the family continuously in a therapeutic alliance of collaboration (Friedlander et al., 1994).

Interject Humor When Appropriate

Many families enter therapy with the perception that life is a tragedy. As a result, they struggle, suffer profoundly, and feel alone and unable to change. Although some events and circumstances in life are tragic, most families who seek therapy are not in such a state. It is appropriate at times, especially in the middle phase of family therapy, to help families become more aware of and even enjoy the folly of their existence. In doing so, families might see how they have painted themselves into corners or acted in absurd ways.

Caution must be taken to not make fun of families, but rather to let them have fun and simultaneously gain insight. As Frank Pittman (1995) says: "In my therapy, I don't eschew laughter, but the patients have most of the funny lines" (p. 39). For example, if a mother is obsessed with the fact that her 12-year-old daughter will not pick up her clothes, the therapist might have the mother project the concern into future years and events. In this exercise the mother might imagine her daughter getting married and never being able to have romantic times with her spouse because of her inability to wade through the sea of clothes she has habitually tossed on the floor. Although such an example is absurd, it helps illustrate a point and aids the mother and daughter in sharing a moment of levity. Again, as Pittman (1995) says:

> We can bear far more in comedy than in tragedy, because in comedy we don't have to be perfect, we are not alone in our suffering, and we get to change in time to not die from our hopeless emotional position. If we are fully embedded in our comic perspective then we can bear all the reality life has to offer. (p. 40)

Look for Evidence of Change in the Family

If therapy is going well, it will become evident. Therapists need to closely observe the family system to see if it is accommodating to new experiences and input data from therapy. Many subtle and many blatant signs usually appear to indicate that changes are occurring. Family members might appear to be more relaxed with one another and to talk more directly with one another; or conflict and defensiveness might lessen, and humor and goodwill might increase.

When family therapists discover these changes along with families, it then becomes evident that the work of the middle phase of therapy is winding down. In such cases, families and clinicians move their focus and efforts to termination.

Termination

"Progress in family therapy moves in a circular direction. The potential for reaching new goals depends on the growth that has occurred previously. If one understands systems to be open and changing, it is hard to define the conclusion of family therapy simply in terms of accomplished goals, for the goals themselves may change over the course of therapy" (Nichols & Everett, 1986, p. 266). Nevertheless, family therapy reaches a point in which it is time to end or change the pace of the treatment (Carlson & Ellis, 2004). The family and the therapist are more likely to benefit if termination is handled in a planned and systematic way, rather than in an abrupt manner. If "not properly carried out, the attempt to end therapy can constitute an abandonment" of the client family by the therapist (Leslie, 2004a, p. 46).

Although treatment may be halted by the therapist, the client family, or by mutual agreement, it is usually concluded when:

- "the course of treatment has come to a natural end" and there has been improvement (Leslie, 2004a, p. 46)
- the client couple or family's problem is beyond the competency level of the therapist
- the client couple or family is no longer benefiting
- therapists must leave their employment either temporarily or permanently
- the client family can no longer afford treatment and an alternative arrangement cannot be worked out

Regardless of the circumstances, the termination process has four steps—(1) orientation, (2) summarization, (3) discussion of long-term goals, and (4) follow-up (Epstein & Bishop, 1981)—that are described as follows in more detail:

1. *Orientation:* Just as with other therapeutic processes, the subject of termination is best raised before it is actually implemented. This objective is accomplished in the

orientation step of termination. Orientation commences when therapists realize that families have reached their goals or will be concluding their contracted sessions.

2. *Summarization:* After the family has become oriented to the fact that therapy will be ending, the therapist reviews with the family what has occurred during their sessions together. This process can replace the therapist as chief spokesperson, or it can involve both the therapist and family taking equal responsibility for summarizing their time and experiences together.

3. *Discussion of Long-Term Goals:* The discussion of long-term goals is a means by which families can be helped during termination to anticipate, avoid, or modify potentially troublesome situations. For example, a therapist may ask a family how they are going to avoid yelling at each other when they get tired. In raising such an issue, the therapist and family have an opportunity to identify resources both within and outside the family system that may be helpful to them in the future.

4. *Follow-Up and Relapse Prevention:* The idea behind follow-up and relapse prevention is that family therapy is a never-ending process; it continues long after the therapist and family have finished their formal work. Such a premise considers therapy and termination "open-ended;" that is, the family may need to return in order to receive a boost or avoid regression (Carlson & Ellis, 2004; Nichols & Everett, 1986). It also acknowledges that some families do better over time when they know someone will check up on their progress. In essence, follow-up is a paradox. It is the last step in family therapy, but it can lead to more family therapy.

As far as the mechanics go, one of the simplest ways to achieve termination is to reduce the frequency of sessions. This may be implemented informally or formally over a number of months. There are numerous other procedures as well. One suggestion for bringing family therapy to a close is through a three-session termination process—that is, setting the date, a next-to-the-last session, and the final farewell session (Thomas, 1992). The use of rituals and tasks can be especially meaningful during termination and can remind family members of what they have achieved and of behaviors they need to continue (Imber-Black, Roberts, & Whiting, 1989). For example, in a final session, members of a family can give each other wishes for the future in a written form that can be revisited later. The family can also plan a celebration of who they have become and symbolically lay to rest in a mock funeral the family that originally entered therapy.

The process of termination, like the therapeutic process itself, is more complicated than it seems (Lebow, 1995). If conducted over time and with sensitivity, it can help families and family members recognize their growth and development during treatment. It can also help families and their members recognize and accept their feelings, thoughts, behaviors, failures, and accomplishments. Unfortunately, termination is often premature, and about 40% to 60% of families who begin treatment drop out before therapy is finished (Kazdin, Stolar, & Marciano, 1995). The result is a loss of benefits for families and a lost opportunity for family therapists to work with those in need of mental health services.

Careful attention must always be paid to all aspects of the therapeutic process. Termination should not be treated as the highlight of the therapeutic experience, but it should certainly be a goal (Hackney & Cormier, 2005). Although termination can help bring the therapeutic process to a logical and positive conclusion, it is only one part of the entire system of family therapy. If possible, termination should take into account the family's progress in therapy, including skills they have learned that can be applied later (Lebow, 1995).

Adlerian Family Therapy: An Example of Appropriate Process

Although any of a number of family therapies could be used to illustrate appropriate process, Adler's model is used here for two reasons. First, it is one of the oldest forms of family therapy, having been in use in this way since the 1920s (Sherman, 1999). "Adler was the first to understand and emphasize the importance of a family's influence on an individual's development," as he brought "the focus of family dynamics into the mainstream" (Kaplan, 2000b, p. 1). Second, the model is not easily categorized, although it has a systems and social orientation (LaFountain & Mustaine, 1998). Therefore, it can be employed in a variety of settings.

Background of Adlerian Theory

Adlerian family therapy is an offshoot of the socially oriented and pragmatically focused treatment approach developed by Alfred Adler (1870–1937). It has been perpetuated in the United States by individuals such as Rudolph Driekurs, Don Dinkmeyer, Robert Sherman, Roy Kern, and Thomas Sweeney, as well as organizations such as the Alfred Adler Institute of Chicago and the North American Society of Adlerian Psychology. Some journals, such as the *Journal of Individual Psychology*, are devoted to publishing Adlerian-based research and practice articles.

A major premise of Adlerian theory is that "individuals and social systems are holistic and indivisible in nature, that behavior is purposeful and interactive, and that the individual seeks significance by belonging within a social system" (Walsh & McGraw, 2002, p. 99). The family is seen as the prototype of a social system where each person has a need to belong and seeks a place within (Bitter, 2004).

Another premise of this theory is that perception is subjective, implying that individuals create their own meaning from experiences (Watts, 2003b). The meaning of life and life's roles and responsibilities are influenced by the family atmosphere in which one grows up (Watts, 2000). In the family environment, people formulate their **private logic,** that is, their worldview. A family that is nurturing and democratic may help produce a child with a worldview that is positive and who has a strong self-concept with purposeful and goal-directed behaviors. On the other hand, a family that is authoritarian is more likely to foster a feeling of inferiority in a child that leads to unproductive or even destructive behaviors, such as aggression and violence (Smith, Mullis, Kern, & Brack, 1999).

Birth order, sibling rivalry, and gender roles are also important. A child's **ordinal position** (i.e., birth order in the family, including first, second, middle, youngest, or only) may impact the way that child responds to his or her family and society in general. Firstborns are often achievement-oriented, whereas the youngest are often more socially-oriented. **Sibling rivalry** (the degree of competition between siblings), such as that between first- and second-born children, can also make a difference, with second-born children seeking to pursue roles taken by firstborns and firstborns striving to avoid being "dethroned." In addition, **gender roles** (traditionally prescribed roles for males and females) and the expectations associated with them may either enhance behaviors within a family or lead to conflict. If a boy feels that being sensitive to feelings is "for girls," he may grow up to be brutish and uncaring.

These underlying assumptions are considered by Adlerian family therapists in the preplanning stage of family therapy, because theory is the basis for therapy. Inattention to one or more of these basic assumptions can lead to actions that are incongruent with therapeutic purposes. Overall, "the general goal of Adlerian family counseling is to encourage change in family members, as well as the family as a whole" (LaFountain & Mustaine, 1998, p. 193).

Initial Session(s)

Unlike Adlerian family counseling, which focuses on parent education and prevention, Adlerian family therapy is directed toward changing family interactions (Walsh & McGraw, 2002). It requires that entire families be present in sessions. The first, and for most Adlerians, crucial phase in therapy is focused on building a relationship (Watts, 2003b). Within initial sessions, **joining** and establishing **rapport** with a family are the foci of treatment. An attempt is made to make contact with each family member and listen to his or her concerns. Family dynamics are also directly observed, especially in regard to **power** (i.e., decision making, manipulation, negotiation), **boundaries** (i.e., physical and emotional closeness), **coalitions** (i.e., two or more people joined together for support), **roles** (i.e., behaviors members expect from one another), **rules** (i.e., implicit or explicit guidelines that determine behaviors of family members), and **patterns of communication** (i.e., double messages, withholding information, and overgeneralizing).

In addition to viewing family patterns, an Adlerian family therapist might ask family members to give self-reports about how the family functions. One way of doing this is for family members to talk about a **typical day** in the life of their family. Inventories and assessment techniques, such as the recalling of **early recollections,** are also employed.

With this material in hand, Adlerian family therapists engender hope that change can take place within the family by reframing problems to have more positive connotations and working with the family to formulate appropriate goals. Resistance may be dealt with by renegotiating goals; confronting the family with the fact that it is resisting, thus making them aware of their behaviors; assigning a positive connotation to the resistance to avoid a power struggle; and joining the resistance and even exaggerating it so that resistance requires a level of cooperation between family and therapist (Walsh & McGraw, 2002).

Middle Phase of Treatment

In the middle phase of treatment, Adlerian therapists concentrate on helping family members become more aware of their behaviors (i.e., analysis) and to **reorient** (i.e., change what they are doing). Awareness is increased through such processes as examining individual versus family goals, exploring lifestyles and types of communication between family members, and making explicit the needs and wants of the family as a whole, as well as of its individual members. Through such an understanding, families may become more motivated to want to try new behaviors and ways of interacting.

Reorientation and change can take place by simultaneously addressing several areas of difficulty (Sherman & Dinkmeyer, 1987). Among the most important of these areas are

- changes in perceptions, beliefs, values, and goals
- changes in the structure and organization of the family
- changes in the skills and social behavior of the family through teaching
- changes in the way direct and indirect power are employed in the family

A way to foster these changes is to have client families and their members act **"as if"** they had the qualities and resources they are seeking (Watts, 2003a). Such a stance bypasses "potential resistance to change by neutralizing some of the perceived risk" (Watts, 2003a, p. 73). In addition, families and their members are given an opportunity to try on new roles in a nonthreatening way because they are just acting.

Termination

Termination is initiated in Adlerian family therapy when a family and a therapist agree that change has occurred and that the family is making progress or has made the type of progress initially agreed on. Measuring progress comes through observation of family interactions, self-reports, and various assessment techniques. In initiating termination, the Adlerian family therapist reinforces newly learned skills or ways of behaving. Because Adlerian theory has a strong **teleological** (i.e., goal-oriented) component, a family during termination is encouraged to project ahead to problems that might arise and discuss how they would handle such difficulties.

Finally, during termination, a family's strengths and abilities to continue their success are reiterated by the Adlerian family therapist. The therapist then follows up with the family through a variety of means at a predetermined time. At **follow-up** (an appointed time with the family several weeks or months after formal treatment has ended), the family is again reinforced by the therapist in regard to competencies and ability to maintain or continue change.

Managed Care and the Process of Therapy

In ending this chapter on process, the influence of **managed health care,** or as it is generally referred to, **managed care,** must be considered because of the impact this phenomenon has had and continues to have on family therapy. Managed care began to emerge in the 1980s when businesses perceived the predominantly **fee-for-service health care system,** characterized by overutilization and little accountability, to be hurting them financially. For example, in 1992, General Motors "spent more on employee health care than it did on steel" (Hutchins, 1995, p. 15). Thus, to reduce overall health care costs to their companies, businesses contracted with managed care organizations. In 2000, approximately 60% of Americans enrolled in health care programs were covered by a managed care contract, and that number continues to increase.

The issue of managed care is of importance to family therapists for a number of reasons. For example, it has an impact on private practitioners and agency clinicians in regard to the number of practitioners available to see families, the length of time over which treatment occurs, the type of treatment received, and the compensation received for their services (Adams, 1987). While a "guild" model has arisen in some areas to combat the influence of managed care (Bittner, Blalek, Nathiel, Ringwald, & Tupper, 1999), the fact remains that this type of care is still a dominant force in the health care field.

Managed mental health care (MMHC) is a branch of managed health care that focuses on mental health services, such as family therapy. In MMHC, limits are placed "on the amount and type of services, by monitoring services intensely, and by changing the nature of services" (Foos, Ottens, & Hill, 1991, p. 332). One common component of MMHC is called the **utilization review (UR):**

> UR entails the practitioner submitting a written justification for treatment along with a comprehensive treatment plan. The justification and plan are reviewed by a utilization reviewer, who, if the plan is approved, typically allocates a specific number of sessions; further sessions are subject to reapplication and approval by the reviewer. Only under these conditions can claims be reimbursed. (Huber, 1995, p. 42)

Another emerging managed care method of cutting costs is the **capitated contract** "in which providers ... agree to provide treatment for a population for a per person per year fee. In essence, providers become their own case managers" (Hutchins, 1996, p. 7).

The most prevalent managed care organizations are **preferred provider organizations (PPOs)** and **health maintenance organizations (HMOs)** (Levitan & Conway, 1990). With government, as well as private, interest in the health care field growing, there continues to be a high demand "to minimize the number of sessions available for reimbursement" (West & MohdZain, 2000, p. 293). Therefore, brief family therapy approaches have become quite popular (Fleming & Rickord, 1997). Solution-focused, narrative, and strategic forms of family therapy seem especially well suited for managed health care programs.

Overall, "in a managed care setting, providers must be able to draft a treatment plan, follow it, and provide documentation that it is being followed and, most importantly, that treatment is effective" (Hutchins, 1995, p. 15). Sometimes this process takes the form of **care pathway guidelines** that "delineate specific timelines in which diagnosis and interventions should occur" as well as address the "decision-making process, the clinical services offered, and the potential interactions among multidisciplinary health care professionals" (Miller, Veltkamp, Lane, Bilyeu, & Elzie, 2002, p. 42). A model guideline of a care pathway for abuse is represented in Figure 4.2. Thus, through managed health care, the process as well as the theoretical approaches practiced in family therapy stand to be influenced for years to come.

Summary and Conclusion

This chapter focused on the personhood of the therapist as well as on universal aspects in the process of conducting family therapy. It gave an example of the process of therapy using an Adlerian-based treatment model of a case. It also dealt briefly with the influence of managed care on the practice of family therapy.

What type of person a potential family therapist is becomes crucial to the success of that individual as a clinician. There are certain family-of-origin backgrounds and personal dispositions that are more congruent than others to one becoming a family therapist. Simply being intelligent, articulate, and motivated is not enough.

Specific topics that were addressed in the appropriate process section of the chapter included the initial session(s), the middle phase of therapy, and termination. Within each of these three topics, numerous points were discussed.

During the initial session(s), the task of the therapist is to create a structure in which change can take place. This "battle for structure" process begins on the phone and/or in studying background material. Through such involvement, the family therapist establishes rapport and structure. He or she also hypothesizes what is happening within the family (i.e., makes a diagnosis) from a developmental and systemic frame of reference. It is hoped that during the initial session(s), families will become more motivated and win what has been defined as the "battle for initiative." It is important that families win this battle because the best success in any clinical setting is seen when families are motivated to accomplish goals.

During the middle phase of family therapy, most of the work of therapy takes place. If family therapy is like a play, then the middle phase contains the most action. It is crucial in this phase that clinicians pay as much attention to the processes within families as they do to the content of sessions. It is also important that families be helped or encouraged to make links to support groups and resources within their communities. It is during the middle phase that family therapists are extremely involved in helping families overcome natural and artificial barriers that keep them from achieving their goals.

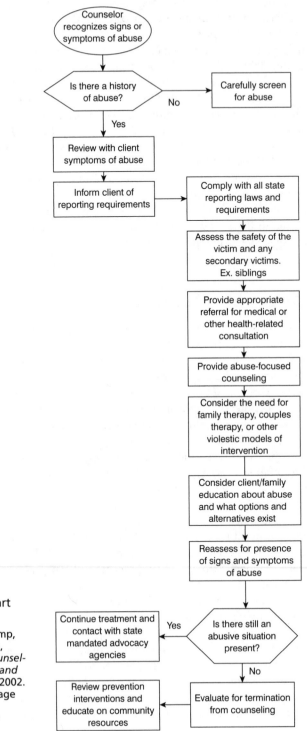

Figure 4.2
Model Guidelines Flowchart
for Abuse.

From T. W. Miller, L. J. Veltkamp,
T. Lane, J. Bilyeu, and N. Elzie,
2002, *The Family Journal: Counsel-
ing and Therapy for Couples and
Families, 10,* p. 42, copyright 2002.
Reprinted by permission of Sage
Publications, Inc.

Finally, the process of termination is the last part of the therapeutic cycle. Termination works best when client families are prepared for it. The results are usually better when both the therapist and family agree to it. Termination is not the highlight of therapy, but if conducted properly, it can help families reflect on what they have accomplished and learned. It can motivate families and their members to continue new behaviors, especially if follow-up is included.

Adlerian family therapy was introduced as an example of how a theory is implemented in the process of working with a family. The Adlerian approach is one of the oldest in the field of family therapy and is socially and pragmatically based. Like other forms of therapy, the Adlerian approach is driven by its theoretical presuppositions about how families function. From the theory, Adlerian family therapists focus on certain aspects of the family in shaping a treatment process that includes initial sessions, a middle or working phase, and then, finally, termination and follow-up.

In the final section of the chapter, the influence of managed health care on the practice of family therapy was discussed. Managed care is a present reality and impacts what treatment will be received by families, what theory will be used, and for how long. While guilds and other alternatives are springing up to challenge managed health care, it continues to dominate the field.

Summary Table

The Process of Family Therapy

The Personhood of Family Therapists

The personhood of family therapists is important to the process of family therapy. Major stressors and enhancers for family therapists continue to be highlighted and evaluated in regard to one's readiness to practice in the profession.

Common Problems of Beginning Family Therapists

Overemphasis

Beginning therapists can overemphasize details.
They can overemphasize making everyone happy.
They can overemphasize verbal expression.
They can overemphasize coming to early or easy resolution.
They can overemphasize dealing with one member of the family.

Underemphasis

Beginning therapists can underemphasize the establishment of structure (use of self-disclosure statements can avoid this problem).
They can underemphasize showing care and concern.
They can underemphasize the engagement of family members in the therapeutic process.
They can underemphasize letting the family work on its problems, that is, win their battle for initiative.
They can underemphasize and, thus, not attend well to nonverbal family dynamics.

Appropriate Process

Pre-Session Planning and Tasks

Establish initial professional relationship with referral source/person.

Collect essential information about the family.

Make arrangements to see the family (within 48 hours if possible).

Hypothesize about dynamics within the family (from family life cycle literature).

Form a preliminary diagnosis (e.g., distancing, cutoffs, enmeshment, disengagement, friction, denial, enabling, unresolved grief).

Initial Session

Make the family comfortable through social exchange with each member; that is, establish rapport and join with the family.

Ask each member for his or her perception of the family.

Observe family patterns, that is, the "family dance" (who speaks to whom and how, what is the outward appearance of the family, what is the family mood, etc.).

Assess what needs to be done (e.g., treatment, referral, testing, and so forth).

Engender hope for change and overcome resistance.

Break dysfunctional patterns through words and actions congruent with one's theoretical perspective (if appropriate).

Make a return appointment and assignments.

Write clinical notes, including impressions of family and progress in the session, immediately after the session ends.

Middle Phase of Treatment

Involve peripheral family members in the therapeutic process (e.g., use circular questioning).

Seek to connect family members with appropriate generational interests and concerns (i.e., break up intergenerational coalitions).

Promote quid pro quo (something for something) relationships so that family members begin to think they are benefiting from the therapeutic process.

Emphasize progress or change within family system however small.

Reinforce family members for taking risks and trying new behaviors.

Stay active as a therapist by continuing to probe, direct, and suggest.

Link family members with appropriate outside support systems if needed.

Focus on process.

Look for evidence of change in the family (i.e., utilize all of the techniques within your approach that are germane to the family with whom you are working).

Termination

Plan with the family for a mutually agreed-on termination.

Consider termination "open-ended" (i.e., the family may need to return).

Reduce the frequency of sessions.

Follow the four-step termination process: (1) orientation, (2) summarization, (3) discussion of long-term goals, and (4) follow-up.

Formally bring family therapy to a close (i.e., discuss what was learned and achieved during family therapy).

Celebrate and/or resolve grief.

Adlerian Family Therapy: An Example of Appropriate Process

Background of Adlerian Theory

The theory was created by Alfred Adler (1870–1937).

Adlerian theory is socially oriented and pragmatically focused.

Social systems are indivisible and holistic; a family is a prototype of a social system.

Perception is subjective; individuals create their own meaning from experiences.

A family atmosphere either promotes or inhibits positive social behaviors.

Birth order, sibling rivalry, and gender roles either enhance or detract from behaviors in families and societies.

Therapists must consider these underlying assumptions of Adlerian theory in the preplanning stage.

Initial Session(s)

The whole family is seen in therapy.

After joining and initial rapport building, the therapist observes family dynamics related to power, boundaries, coalitions, roles, rules, and patterns of communication. Also, self-reports are received.

Adlerian family therapists engender hope for change, reframe problems, and work with family to formulate appropriate goals.

Resistance is dealt with in a number of ways, including confrontation and joining.

Middle Phase of Treatment

Therapist helps families become more aware of their behaviors and to reorient (i.e., make changes).

Individual and family goals are compared and contrasted.

Several areas of change may be addressed at once, for example, perceptions, beliefs, social skills, family structure, and power.

Termination

Termination is initiated when the therapist and family mutually agree concerning progress and goals.

New skills and ways of behaving are reinforced.

Potential future problems are addressed.

Family strengths are reinforced.

A time for follow-up is planned.

Managed Care and the Process of Therapy

Managed care is an attempt to reduce health costs and replaces the fee-for-service model.

Managed health care in the form of PPOs and HMOs is likely to increase in the future and severely impact the services and processes of family therapy.

Briefer forms of family therapy will most likely be more in demand as managed health care becomes even more pervasive.

Guilds and other alternatives to managed health care are being formed.

Couple and Marriage Enrichment and Therapy

All those ancestors who now live in me
through pictures, stories, and memories
Have come to life collectively
as I walk the streets of Arlington.
Some tightly knit together and others estranged
these men and women politely arrange
themselves in different groups in my mind
as I envision
who they were as persons
and who they hoped to be.
In the silence of my stride
I reflect and quietly meet
my heritage in the colorful couples
from whom I am descended.

Gladding, S. T. (2004b)

Becoming a couple is a widespread phenomenon throughout the world. In the United States in 2004, there were over 57 million married couples (Jayson, 2005a) and the prospect was that approximately 90% of people in the nation would pair and eventually marry at least once by age 45 (Everett, Livingston, & Bowen, 2005). The reason pairing is so popular is multidimensional. "In a couple, one can find the deepest experience of intimacy in life. Being a member of a couple can lead to personal growth and self-awareness or the failure of it can cause wounds that take years to heal" (Long & Burnett, 2005, p. 321). In addition, marriage has health benefits for both men and women such as emotional wellness (e.g., less depression), a greater psychological sense of well-being (i.e., self-esteem), physical health, longevity of life, and happiness (Mead, 2002).

It is not surprising that Americans actively seek couple relationships and 93% of Americans rate having a happy marriage as one of the most important objectives of their lives (Waite & Gallagher, 2000). Yet being a couple is not easy, especially in marriage. Epidemiological studies (e.g., Gurman & Fraenkel, 2002) "typically find 20% of the population to be maritally distressed at any moment in time" (Lebow, 2005, p. 38). Couples do break up and approximately 50% of all marriages fail as shown in Figure 5.1. Many of these disintegrations, however, could be avoided which is why couple and marriage counseling services are so important even though only about 3% of the married couples in America use such services every year (Jayson, 2005). Indeed, over 40% of clients who seek psychotherapy of any kind report the reason as marital distress (Gurman & Fraenkel, 2002).

Types of Couple and Marriage Treatments

Couple and marriage therapy can be defined in a number of ways depending on who is in the therapeutic session and the relationship of each individual to the other. A simple way to

Figure 5.1
By the numbers: love and marriage.

From *Counseling Today,* July 2005, p. 3. ACA. Reprinted with permission. No further reproduction authorized without written permission from the American Counseling Association.

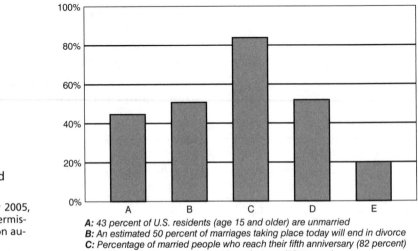

A: 43 percent of U.S. residents (age 15 and older) are unmarried
B: An estimated 50 percent of marriages taking place today will end in divorce
C: Percentage of married people who reach their fifth anniversary (82 percent)
D: Percentage who reach their 15th anniversary (52 percent)
E: Percentage who reach their 35th anniversary (20 percent)

see this phenomenon is to conceptualize it as a process by which a therapist works with two individuals who are in a primary and intimate relationship. Also, couple and marriage therapies differ and are distinct from premarital counseling. **Couple therapy** may be defined as a therapist working with two individuals to improve their relationship as a dyad. The couple may be married or unmarried, gay or straight, white or of color, and have various levels of commitment to each other. **Marriage therapy** is when a therapist works with a couple that is legally married to help them improve their relationship. Marriage therapy is more complicated than couples counseling because of the legal aspects. Both can be intense at times.

In contrast to these two approaches is **premarital counseling,** which is working with a couple to enhance their relationship *before* they get married. Individuals in premarital counseling intend to marry. Obtaining such counseling is increasingly popular, even desirable, because it is seen as preventative by those in their 20s and 30s who are engaged (Bruhn & Hill, 2004; Wolff, 2005). Many premarital programs are centered around either assessment instruments or topics. Among the most popular instruments used in working with couples are PREPARE, FOCUS, and RELATE (Larson, Newell, Topham, & Nichols, 2002). Although all of these inventories have their strengths and weaknesses, "RELATE is the easiest instrument to interpret and the easiest to use in large groups and teaching settings. RELATE is also the most comprehensive and the least expensive if using computer scoring" (p. 237).

At least four topics—communication skills, conflict resolution skills, finances, and parenting—are included in most premarital counseling programs (Murray, 2005). Some states such as Florida even make it easier for couples to marry if they go through an approved premarital program that addresses these four topics. Benefits from such preparation programs include "enhanced conflict management skills, higher dedication to one's mate, greater positivity in marriage, and longitudinally, potentially reduced chances for divorce" (Duncan & Wood, 2003, p. 342). The ideal time for premarital counseling to occur is 4 to 12 months prior to the wedding date in order to maximize learning of the materials (Monarch et al., 2002).

Regardless of whether one is working with couples, families, or those who are engaged to be married, there are a number of similarities. Some of the skills, processes, and techniques involved are the same or similar. Yet when working with a couple, as opposed to a family, there are usually not as many dynamics to which a therapist must attend because there are fewer people and factors involved. Some of the primary ways of dealing with couples regardless of their marital status include preventive approaches, such as marriage education and marriage enrichment, as well as therapeutic treatments involving couples-focused theories such as marriage therapy (DeOlga, 2005), divorce therapy, and mediation.

Preventive Approaches to Working with Couples

"Over the past two decades, there has been an increased emphasis on prevention by professionals who work with couples to help them maintain happy, stable marriages" (Sullivan & Anderson, 2002, p. 388). Indeed, prevention efforts aimed at enhancing family relationships, including couple relations, has been called "the wave of the future" (Fraenkel, Markman, & Stanley, 1997, p. 257).

Preventative work with couples and families seeks to raise protective factors and to lower risk factors (Monarch et al., 2002). It includes three major ways of achieving this goal: (1) universal, (2) selective, and (3) indicated (Murray, 2005). All are aimed at different problems and populations.

Universal prevention focuses on preventing "the development of problems in the general population" (Murray, 2005, p. 29). It might include a media campaign promoting family togetherness. **Selective prevention** focuses on making interventions with at-risk groups in order to prevent problems. An example of such a preventive effort would be parenting classes for parents whose children are having difficulties in school. Finally, there is **indicated prevention** which "focuses on minimizing the harmful impact of serious problems in the early stages of their development" (p. 29). For instance, a therapist might work with a couple whose marriage is coming apart in order to prevent them from doing harm to one another or doing harm to their children.

For all the emphasis in recent years on prevention, preventative services for couples and families are, on the whole, underdeveloped. There are probably a number of reasons why prevention efforts have not progressed quickly. These include a lack of adequate training in prevention modalities, economic barriers, and cultural and family attitudes unsupportive of this approach (Murray, 2005). Two areas that have implemented selective prevention and, to an extent universal prevention, as well, are programs with a marriage education emphasis and those where there is a couple enrichment focus.

Major Theorists for Prevention

The area of prevention has had a number of proponents over the years. Some, such as Rev. Gabriel Calvo of Barcelona, were intuitive and innovative in their work. Others, including many of the premarital program researchers of today such as John Gottman and David Olson, have been more empirical in their approach. David and Vera Mace are highlighted here both because of their early work in the prevention area and the unique fact that they collaborated as a couple.

David and Vera Mace

David and Vera Mace did not initiate the first preparatory and prevention programs centered around marriage enrichment, but they were pioneers in this arena. They also played a major role in moving prevention initiatives forward, especially couple enrichment.

David Mace was British by birth, as was Vera. Both had careers working with youths before their marriage in 1933. Later, David founded and became the executive director of the National Marriage Guidance Council of Great Britain in London in 1942. He and Vera came to the United States in 1949, when David became a professor of human relations at Drew University and Vera earned a master's degree at the same institution. The couple then moved to Philadelphia where David taught at the Pennsylvania School of Medicine. Finally, they moved to the Wake Forest University School of Medicine, where David became a professor of family sociology.

Together the Maces conducted their first marriage-enrichment retreat in Kirkridge, Pennsylvania, in 1962. They were well-known before this time in Quaker and Methodist circles for their work on marriage issues. In the early 1960s, they were searching for ways to prevent marital difficulties and counter the growing divorce rate of the time. They thought that by working with couples who were not in crisis, they could strengthen marriages. They believed that couples wanted to have better marriages and learn skills for living in harmony.

In 1973, on their 40th wedding anniversary, the Maces founded the Association for Couples in Marriage Enrichment (ACME). Their slogan was "To work for better marriages, beginning with our own." They served as presidents of ACME until 1980.

Although David Mace is credited with being the author of many of the couple's books, he and Vera collaborated in their writings. Together they produced 33 books including: *Getting Ready for Marriage, How to Have a Happy Marriage: A Step-By-Step Guide to an Enriched Relationship,* and *Letters to a Retired Couple: Marriage in the Later Years.* As a couple they literally traveled the world together and received a number of honors from professional associations and universities.

David Mace died at age 83, December 12, 1990. Vera Mace was 102 in 2005.

Marriage Education

It is difficult to separate marriage education from marriage enrichment because both strengthen marriages and at times overlap. Marriage education is often more cognitive, whereas marriage enrichment is more experiential. Nevertheless, while they are frequently combined, each is delineated here in order to highlight their uniqueness and contribution to the field of prevention.

In its purest form, **marriage education** includes the use of didactic lectures, visual aids, books, handouts, and interactive discussions. Procedures associated with marriage education are intended to help couples learn more about how relationships work as well as see the rationale behind the strategies employed in helping them relate better to one another. An example of marriage education is research indicating that the difference between happy and dysfunctional couples is not related to the intensity of their disagreements, but to the frequency and types of negative behaviors employed during these times such as criticism, contempt, defensiveness, and stonewalling (Gottman, Coan, Carrere, & Swanson, 1998). Likewise, a study found that decision-making equality between spouses was one of the strongest correlates of husbands' and wives' marital happiness and perceived marital stability (Amato, Johnson, Booth, & Rogers, 2003). Couples who are informed or educated about these matters can try to alter their behaviors and have a better relationship from the beginning of their marriage.

Aside from activities related to research, couples can become better informed on how to deal with potentially problematic behaviors by engaging in **bibliotherapy.** This process may actually be included in premarital programs and enrichment programs. It involves gleaning information by reading books or listening to lectures to learn more about relationship traps and how to avoid them or to repair relationships if necessary. Books that address couple issues include: Allen Fay's (1999) *Making It As a Couple,* John Gottman's (1980) *A Couple's Guide to Communication,* John Gottman and Nan Silver's (2000) *The Seven Principles for Making Marriage Work,* Clifford Notarius and Howard Markman's (1993) *We Can Work It Out: How to Solve Conflicts, Save Your Marriage, and Strengthen Your Love for Each Other,* Susan Page's (1998) *How One of You Can Bring the Two of You Together,* and Jonathan Robinson's (1998) *Communication Miracles for Couples: Easy and Effective Tools to Create More Love and Less Conflict.*

Lazarus (2000) advocates the use of "didactic and pedagogical strategies" (p. 226) in working with couples. His recommendation is espoused by other experts who work with couples from a preventative perspective. The **Smart Marriage** conferences started by Diane Sollee are probably the highest profile events in the marriage education arena.

Marriage Enrichment

A second type of preventative programming aimed at enhancing couple relationships is marriage enrichment. The idea of marriage enrichment is based on the concept that couples stay healthy or get healthier by actively participating in certain activities, usually in connection with other couples (Mace & Mace, 1977). Thus **marriage enrichment** is a proactive, "systematic effort to improve the functioning of marital couples through educational and preventive means" (Sager & Sager, 2005, p. 212). Many forms of this approach use married couples interacting with other couples and specially prepared materials to promote marriage relationships. The idea is for couples to learn from each other and the material at hand so that future marital difficulties may be prevented from developing (Ripley & Worthington, 2002).

Marriage enrichment programs began to emerge in the early 1960s. They were originally generated from faith-based communities to help married couples "become aware of themselves and their partners, explore their partners' feelings and thoughts, encourage empathy and intimacy, and develop effective communication and problem-solving skills" (Bowling, Hill, & Jencius, 2005, p. 87). It is interesting to note that these programs came into existence as faith-based organizations and the government observed an unprecedented increase in the rate of discord, disengagement, divorce, and abuse in couple relations both in the United States and internationally. There are more than two dozen enrichment organizations and programs worldwide today, and the material they offer and participation in them has mushroomed. Now "between one quarter and one third of marrying couples in the United States, Australia, and Britain" attend some form of these seminars (Halford, Markman, Kline, & Stanley, 2003, p. 385).

Although such seminars and marriage enrichment programs are marked by considerable diversity, a part of most marriage enrichment programs involves self-help and couple-help. This type of help is often in the form of couple members participating in structured exercises that theoretically and practically bring them closer together through sharing information and experiences (Calvo, 1975; Guerney, 1977). Such experiences also help couples renew their closeness as well as confront areas of conflict (Eckstein & Jones, 1998). Couples can learn to give and receive nonverbal and verbal messages and reflect on positive times in their life together (Johnson, Fortman, & Brems, 1993). They may also be able to give and receive feedback on important relationship topics of which four of the most important are communication, finances, problem solving, and having children (Sullivan & Anderson, 2002).

A major pioneer in the marriage enrichment movement was a Catholic priest, Fr. Gabriel Calvo. He began leading retreats for married couples in Barcelona, Spain, during the 1950s. His efforts later evolved into the **Marriage Encounter Program** in 1962. The essence of this approach, which is now worldwide, ecumenical, and has reached literally hundreds of thousands of couples, is to have a "team couple" lead a group of husbands and wives during a weekend in exercises that give them the opportunity to share their emotions and thoughts. They are taught how to make effective communication a part of their everyday lives so that what they learn generalizes to their entire relationship.

As discussed earlier in this chapter, David and Vera Mace were also pioneers of the marriage enrichment movement with the establishment of the **Association of Couples for Marriage Enrichment (ACME)** (Mace & Mace, 1977). This program today is nondenominational and national in scope. Like the Marriage Encounter Program, the ACME program is led by a husband and wife team (Mace, 1987). ACME, however, is more than a structured weekend experience. It provides its participants with a long-term support group to help them deal with continued changes in their relationship over time. The ACME process includes the following five stages: (1) security and community building; (2) developing an awareness of the couple's relationship; (3) developing knowledge and skills to help improve the relationship; (4) planning for growth; and (5) celebrating and closure (Williams, 2003). Research has been supportive of the effectiveness of ACME experiences for increasing couple intimacy.

Another program in marriage enrichment is **Relationship Enhancement (RE),** created by Bernard G. Guerney, Jr. (1977) in the 1970s. RE is a skills-building approach that "can be used with married couples as well as engaged couples" (Bowling et al., 2005, p. 88) to enrich their lives together. It is based on "a Rogerian communication model, combining an emphasis on expression of empathic acceptance with instruction in behavioral skills that improve communication" (Monarch et al., 2002, p. 241). Some of the skills taught in RE through coaching, modeling, and positive reinforcement are empathic expression, discussion/negotiation, problem/conflict resolution, facilitation (partner coaching), self-change, other change, transfer generalization, and maintenance.

The strength of RE is that it can be used with distressed and nondistressed couples. It is also adaptable to various formats including weekends and multiweek sessions. Furthermore, RE can be used in counseling with a number of clients such as individuals, groups, and families—not just for working with couples (Accordino, Keat, & Guerney, 2003). Like ACME, Relationship Enhancement has a solid research base (Accordino & Guerney, 2003, 2002).

A fourth well-researched couples relationship program revolves around the **PREPARE/ENRICH inventories** developed by David Olson and associates (Olson & Olson, 2000). These inventories—PREPARE, for engaged couples and ENRICH, for married couples—identify strengths and growth opportunity areas for couples enrolled in the "Growing Together Workshop" that accompanies these instruments. There is a 25-page workbook entitled *Building a Strong Marriage* that each couple is given after they take the inventories (Bowling et al., 2005). This workbook assists couples in dealing with challenges regarding five areas: communication, conflict resolution, family-of-origin topics, financial planning/budgeting, and goal setting. It also helps them identify personal and couple strengths. The research surrounding these instruments is quite strong and has included African-American couples who have been shown to benefit as much from ENRICH as European-American couples (Allen & Olson, 2001).

The **TIME (Training in Marriage Enrichment)** and **PREP (Prevention and Relationship Enhancement Program)** are two other couple enrichment programs that will be discussed. TIME is for married couples and is formatted in a 10-week or weekend period (Dinkmeyer & Carlson, 2003). The program is laid out developmentally and systemically, including a beginning session that focuses on accepting responsibility and final sessions that have a couple resolving an actual conflict based on skills they have learned. PREP is a 12-hour program where couples, either married or unmarried, are taught to become effective communicators and problem solvers while enhancing their commitment to each other (Markham, Stanley, & Blumberg, 2002; Monarch et al., 2002). TIME and PREP research has indicated couples may achieve long-lasting benefit from participating in these programs. PREP has been demonstrated to have a positive effect on couple relationships for up to 5 years following the program (Markman, Renick, Floyd, Stanley, & Clements, 1993).

Other notable couple enrichment programs include:

- the **Couples Communication (CC) Program** (http://www.couplecommunication.com/), which is divided into entry and advanced programs. In CC couples learn about themselves and their partners better. The aim of the program, which is grounded in systems theory, communication theory, and family development theory, is "to help couples develop a greater understanding of their interaction patterns and 'rules' of communication … and to enhance communication skills" (Monarch et al., 2002, p. 243). Participants learn 11 interpersonal skills for effective talking, listening, conflict resolution, and anger management. Embedded within CC is **"Great Start,"** a program that utilizes PREPARE/ENRICH inventories and is designed for premarital and early marital relationships (Miller, Nunnally, & Wackman, 1977, 1979; Miller & Sherrard, 1999).

- **SANCTUS,** a theologically and psychologically based marriage enrichment program based on step-wise process that incorporates building a pattern of love and relationship with God, one's self, and others (Parrott & Parrott, 2003).
- **Practical Application of Intimate Relationship Skills (PAIRS)** (http://www.pairs.com/), a multidimensional marriage enrichment program developed by Lori Gordon. PAIRS seeks to reinvigorate the emotional bond and intimacy between partners (Gordon, Temple, & Adams, 2005). It teaches participants about attitudes, skills, values, emotional understanding, and loving behaviors that nurture and sustain healthy relationships and attachments. The PAIRS program utilizes concepts and techniques from experiential, object relations, communication, behavioral and family systems approaches (DeOlga, 2005; DeOlga & Hannah, 2003). PAIRS has proven to be effective with a number of diverse populations (Gordon et al., 2005).

Marriage and Couple Therapy

Research on couple therapy has repeatedly concluded that "(1) couple therapy effectively reduces conflict and increases marital satisfaction, at least in the short run … ; and (2) for marital problems, conjoint treatment is generally superior to individual treatment" (Beckerman & Sarracco, 2002, p. 24).

Major Theorists

There are a number of theorists that could be highlighted as major proponents of marriage and couples therapy. Among them are Frank Dattilio, Albert Ellis, Robert Liberman, and Richard Stuart. However, Susan Johnson is featured. Her theory is among the newest and most empirically validated.

Susan Johnson

Susan Johnson grew up in a working-class neighborhood in England as an only child. She worked in her parents' pub where she learned a lot early in life about levels of communication, social interaction, fighting, and being pragmatic (Jencius, 2003). Her formal education gave her a love for English literature and opened her eyes to possibilities in relationships. The breakup of her parents' marriage, when she was 11, was a serious disruption in her life and a marker event that led her to wonder how relationships in marriage could be improved.

At 22, Johnson went to Vancouver, Canada, and began work in a treatment center for emotionally disturbed children. In her work there, she learned to be emotionally present. Johnson was initially influenced by Rogerian and Gestalt approaches to therapy, but as she started doing couples work in 1982, she became increasingly attracted to John Bowlby's attachment theory as it applied to adult bonding relationships. She titled her approach **emotionally focused therapy** (EFT) in the mid-1980s as an act of defiance to more behavioral approaches prevalent in the field at the time.

Susan Johnson is now married, a mother of two, and a professor of psychology and psychiatry at Ottawa University and director of the Ottawa Couple and Family Institute.

Therapeutic Approaches for Working with Couples

As important as preventative programs are, the vast majority of family therapists work with couples who are experiencing difficulties in their marriage or relationship and have come seeking help. The good news is that there is clear evidence that couple therapy works (Johnson, 2003; Johnson & Lebow, 2000; Levant, 2003). Moreover, Gottman has found through his research that psychoeducational approaches can be combined with marriage therapy to make a marriage stronger yet (Jenncius & Duba, 2003).

The bad news is that therapists who work with couples from a treatment perspective may help them change what they are doing from a crisis-oriented perspective rather than from a developmental standpoint. While these couples' relationships may get better for awhile, focused as they are on the flashpoint of their relational conflict, they may be more prone to relapse in the long-term. In point of fact, Monarch et al. (2002) have reported that half of all couples participating in therapy eventually return to their original levels of relationship discord. This therapy focus, on highly distressed relational patterns, poses a far greater challenge than those typical of preventative work. Nevertheless, such work is important.

There are a number of reasons couples seek therapy. These include a lack of communication, financial stress, disagreements over priorities, and, one of the most onerous, infidelity (Blow & Hartnett, 2005a,b). Approaches to working with couples who are either married or unmarried are numerous, too. All focus on **marital quality**—that is, how the relationship is functioning and "how partners feel about and are influenced by such functioning" (Young, 2004, p. 159). While it may seem simple to assess couple relationships, there are at least two complicating factors in doing so. One is that "feelings expressed about marriage are greatly affected by the events of the moment and can change considerably over short periods of time. … Additionally, individuals in distressed relationships sometimes do not report themselves distressed" (Lebow, 2005, p. 38).

If distress levels can be gauged, however, there are a number of couple and marital therapies that may be utilized in treatment. All of these approaches require that clinicians establish a therapeutic alliance with the couple and assess what problem(s) they are having. In addition, the therapist must be goal-oriented in de-escalating negative reciprocity (i.e., resolving interpersonal difficulties) and building positive interactions (i.e., promoting intimacy). Monitoring the progress of treatment, including dealing with resistance, noncompliance, and ethical issues must be addressed as well, and a successful termination must be implemented (Lebow, 2005).

All of these challenges are formidable and require that clinicians be attuned to the art and science of the process of therapy. The most prevalent and empirically validated treatment models for working with couples in or outside of marriage are behavioral couple therapy (BCT), cognitive-behavioral couple therapy (CBCT), and emotionally focused therapy.

Behavioral Couple Therapy (BCT)

Premises of the Theory

Behavioral couple therapy (BCT) is "based on an exchange/negotiation model of adult intimacy and focuses on negotiating pleasing behaviors and teaching problem solving and communication skills" (Johnson, 2003, p. 366). BCT "evolved from a focus on behavioral exchange contracts into an approach that combined problem solving and communication skills with behavioral contracting" (Johnson & Lebow, 2000, p. 25). The preliminary efforts in behavioral couple therapy were initiated by Robert Liberman (1970) and Richard Stuart (1969).

Treatment Techniques

Many of the techniques used in behavioral marital/couple therapy were originated by Liberman and Stuart. They are discussed here with more recent contributions.

Liberman expressed his approach to couples in the language of behavioral analysis and worked with couples to define specific behavioral goals. His initial efforts to help couples were based on **operant conditioning** and included such techniques as **positive reinforcement, shaping,** and **modeling.** Later, he and his colleagues devised a more sophisticated behavioral approach that included aspects of **social learning theory** and **communications theory** (Liberman, Wheeler, deVisser, Kuehnel, & Kuehnel, 1980). This more refined focus helped couples recognize and increase their positive interactions while eliminating negative interactions. The approach also focused on problem solving, building communication skills, and teaching couples how to use **contingency contracts** in order to negotiate the resolution of persistent problems.

Stuart's early initiatives in couple therapy were described as an **operant interpersonal approach.** He assumed that, as in **exchange theory** (Thibaut & Kelley, 1959), the interactions between spouses at any one time were the most rewarding of alternative possibilities. He also believed, like Don Jackson, that successful relationships were based on a **quid pro quo** formula (i.e., something for something). To take advantage of the positive basis of relationships, Stuart proposed that couples make explicit reinforcement contracts with each other that were of a positive nature. He later refined his theory to include an eight-step model designed to accelerate positive behavioral change (Stuart, 1980, 1998).

Among the most creative of Stuart's techniques to increase consistent pleasure within marriages is one called **caring days.** In this procedure, one or both marital partners act as if they care about their spouse regardless of the other's action(s). This type of technique, which is at the heart of Stuart's approach, embodies the idea of a **positive risk,** which is a unilateral action that is not dependent on another for success. Stuart has been quite detailed in describing his behavioral theory and methods in couple treatment, as indicated by the "caring days" contract shown in Figure 5.2.

Process and Outcome

Overall, behavioral couple therapy typically includes four basic components (Hahlweg, Baucom, & Markman, 1988):

1. A **behavioral analysis** of the couple's marital distress. This analysis is based on interviewing, administering self-report questionnaires, and making behavioral observations.
2. The establishment of **positive reciprocity,** that is, a mutual or cooperative exchange of rewarding and valued behaviors between partners. This type of action is generated through techniques such as "caring days" and contingency contracts.
3. **Communication skills training.** Here couples learn to use **"I" statements** to express their feelings. They also learn to stick to here-and-now problems, rather than dwell on the past. Furthermore, they begin to describe their spouse's specific behavior

Bill	Agreements	Jocelyn
9/3 9/4 9/6 9/7 9/8 9/9	Ask how I spent the day.	9/3 9/4 9/6 9/7 9/8 9/9
9/10 9/11 9/12 9/14		9/10 9/12 9/14 9/16
9/17 9/20 9/21		9/20 9/21 9/23
9/3 9/4 9/9	Offer to get the cream or sugar for me.	9/4 9/9
9/10 9/14 9/16		9/12 9/15
9/20 9/21 9/22 9/23		9/23
9/3 9/7 9/9	Listen to "mood music" when we set the clock radio to go to sleep.	9/3 9/7 9/9
9/15		9/15
9/21 9/23		9/21 9/23
9/7 9/8	Hold my hand when we go for walks.	9/7 9/8
9/11		9/11 9/16
9/19		9/19 9/21 9/23
9/9	Put down the paper or your book and look at me when we converse.	9/4 9/6 9/7 9/8
9/14 9/16		9/10 9/13 9/14 9/16
9/23		9/18 9/20 9/21 9/22 9/24
9/4 9/7	Rub my back.	9/5 9/8
9/11 9/12 9/14 9/16		9/10 9/14 9/15
9/21 9/23		9/19
9/3 9/4 9/5 9/7 9/8	Tuck in the sheets and blankets before we go to bed.	9/6 9/9
9/11 9/16		
9/19		9/23
9/3 9/8	Call me during the day.	9/5 9/6 9/7 9/8 9/9
9/15		9/11 9/13 9/14 9/16
9/17		9/18 9/20 9/21 9/22 9/23
9/4 9/6	Offer to play short games with the children when my friends drop in for a few minutes.	9/8
9/13		9/12 9/15
		9/21
9/7	Offer to read the rough drafts of my reports and offer comments.	9/9
9/11 9/16		
9/23		9/20
9/5 9/7 9/8 9/9	Sit down with me when I have coffee even if you don't want any, just for the company.	9/7
9/11 9/14 9/17		9/10 9/13
9/18 9/21		9/23
9/7	Call my folks just to say "hello."	9/9
9/12		
9/20 9/23		9/23
9/6 9/7	Fold the laundry.	9/9
9/15		9/10 9/14 9/15
9/18 9/20 9/23		9/20
9/4 9/7 9/9	Buy me a $1 present.	9/8 9/9
9/13		9/12 9/14
9/18		9/21 9/23

Figure 5.2
Caring days agreement.

From *Helping Couples Change: A Social Learning Approach to Marital Therapy* (p. 200) by R. B. Stuart, 1980, New York: Guilford. Reprinted with permission of the publisher.

rather than apply a label to it, such as "lazy," "aloof," or "frigid." Finally, in communication skills training, couples are taught how to provide positive feedback to their significant other in response to similar behavior from that person.

4. Training in **problem solving.** This component of behavioral couple therapy helps equip couples with new problem-solving skills, such as specifying what they want, negotiating for it, and making a contract.

Unique Aspects of Behavioral Couple Therapy

BCT is one of the most well-researched forms of working with couples (Shadish & Baldwin, 2005). Couples who receive this type of therapy do much better than those who receive no treatment.

John Gottman has stated that behavior marital therapy works best with young couples who do not have a long history of marriage. The reason is that often such couples do not know how to build their relationship in a positive way. Behavior marriage therapy gives them structure and a way of negotiating conflict. It also helps them come to some agreements and have loving and caring days (Young, 2005).

Behavioral couple therapy has also been found to be clearly more effective than individual treatment in working with alcoholics and has been shown, with this population, to reduce social costs, domestic violence, and emotional problems of the couple's children (O'Farell & Fals-Stewart, 2003).

Overall, behavioral couple therapy has been found "to be efficacious for treating **marital distress**" in which marriage partners experience communication and problem-solving difficulties to the point that they find it hard to work together and have difficulty accepting each other's differences (Mead, 2002, p. 307). It has not only been used in the United States but in a number of other cultural settings, including Belgium, Great Britain, Germany, and the Netherlands.

Comparison with Other Theories

Behavioral couple therapy is a very skills-based approach and is specific and precise in doing so. For instance, BCT therapists work with couples to learn positive social relationship enhancement behaviors, such as greeting and calling the partner by name, talking to the partner about common events, praising the partner, sharing memories, doing things together, and providing appropriate feedback (Shumway & Wampler, 2002).

When compared to other approaches, behavioral couple therapy is more linear than systemic. It examines cause and effect to a greater extent than most other couple therapies and tries to change antecedent behaviors so that consequential behaviors will be more positive.

Offshoots of Behavioral Couple Therapy

A more recent form of behavioral couple therapy is **integrative behavioral couple therapy (IBCT),** which adds promotion acceptance to the traditional focus of behavioral couple therapy on overt behavioral change (Cordova, Jacobson, & Christensen, 1998). The idea is "that not all aspects of a couple's relationship are amenable to negotiated change. … In general, promoting acceptance helps couples identify those aspects of their relationship that are unlikely to change [unresolvable problems] and coaches them in ways of coming to terms with those problems" (p. 439). In addition to acceptance, IBCT emphasizes "the reframing of harder emotions (e.g., hostility) in terms of softer emotions (e.g., sadness) and using insight into lessons learned about intimacy in families of origin to frame present behavior" (Johnson & Lebow, 2000, p. 26). Initial findings show that IBCT, when compared to BCT, results in more nonblaming descriptions of problems and more **soft emotions** such as hurt, loneliness, insecurity, and fear that reveal personal vulnerability. Consequently, more empathy is generated from one's partner, emotional closeness is created, and adjusted emotional reactions become more resistant to change (Christensen et al., 2004; Gilbert, 2005).

Cognitive-Behavioral Couple Therapy (CBCT)

Cognitive-behavioral couple therapy (CBCT) provides several strong approaches to working with couples. These "grew out of the behavioral approach, first as a supplemental component and later as a more comprehensive system of intervention" (Dattilio, 2001, p. 6). As a group, cognitive-behavioral theories are empirically supported, highly effective, and short-term in nature. Yet cognitive-behavioral couple therapy is underutilized because of both its historical tradition of being a linear model and because of the popularity of noted influential practitioners who have advocated for other marital and family therapies (Dattilio, 2001).

"CBCT is not a singular model; it draws upon psychodynamic constructs as well as cognitive and behavioral principles and may also incorporate humanistic approaches" (Patterson, 2005, p. 119). A version of what is now a part of cognitive-behavioral couple therapy was first introduced by Albert Ellis, using what was then **rational emotive therapy (RET),** and nowadays called **rational emotive behavior therapy (REBT),** to help couples dispute irrational thoughts they have about themselves, their spouses, or their marriages (Ellis, 1977, 1978, 1993; Ellis & Harper, 1961). In this approach, Ellis employed an **ABC procedure,** with *A* standing for an event, *B* standing for a thought, and *C* standing for an emotion. In addition to the sequential ABC schema, which postulates that emotions are derived from thoughts, Ellis stated that individuals and couples had four choices in regard to what they thought. They could think and therefore feel positive, negative, neutral, or mixed.

Thus an event such as forgetting a spouse's request to get something from the store could result in four different scenarios. For example, one member of the couple might react negatively and think, "He doesn't love me anymore." This could lead to depression or other unhealthy emotions and hurtful words or behavior. Through disputation, the therapist could help the spouse and the couple to learn to think about an event of this type neutrally (e.g., "He did not bring home what I requested."), positively (e.g., "Because my spouse did not get what I requested, I can now ask for more, and I am sure he/she will be more sensitive this time."), or in a mixed way ("Well, he did not bring home the bacon, and that is an inconvenience and frustrating. However, I now have a chance to talk to him about our relationship, which I think might do some good.").

In summing up the research on forms of cognition that have implications in couple distress, Dattilio and Epstein (2005, p. 9) have found the five most lethal are:

1. selective perceptions about the events occurring in couple interactions
2. distorted attributions about causes of positive and negative relationship events
3. inaccurate expectations or predictions about events that may occur in the relationship
4. inappropriate or inaccurate assumptions or general beliefs about the characteristics of people and their intimate relationships
5. extreme or unrealistic standards to which individuals hold relationships and their members

These types of cognitions have to be cleared up if couples are going to relate in healthy ways. Besides the REBT approach, there are several other methods cognitive-behavioral family therapists use with couples.

One of them is to teach the couple **cognitive distraction** (thinking of something other than negative aspects). Another is **self-control strategies** such as how to employ rational coping statements. A particular type of self-control strategy is known as **relapse prevention (RP)**. This cognitive-behavioral approach "enables clients to learn self-control strategies to prevent relapse" and has been applied to the areas of substance abuse, sex offenders, and anger as well as family therapy (Curich & Stone, 1998, p. 328). **Psychoeducational methods** as mentioned earlier, such as reading books, attending workshops, and listening to audiovisual material are also used (Ellis, 1993, 2000; Lazarus, 2000). In the psychoeducational methods, individuals are taught to be more aware of their relationship-related cognitions and the benefits and deficits of these thoughts. This strategy shows promise in reducing the divorce rate for participants (Gottman & Silver, 2000; O'Leary & Smith, 1991). It also could have a favorable effect on other family units (Schwebel & Fine, 1994).

Emotionally Focused Therapy (EFT)

Premises of the Theory

Emotionally focused therapy (EFT) is a systemic approach to therapy based on an assimilative integration of experiential psychotherapy with structural family therapy (Simon, 2004). It focuses on "**intrapsychic processes** (i.e., how partners process their emotional experiences) and **interpersonal processes** (i.e., how partners organize their interactions into patterns and cycles)" (Kowal, Johnson, & Lee, 2003, p. 303).

The roots of the approach are based in attachment theory first posited by John Bowlby (Hollist & Miller, 2005). This theory is considered by many "to be the most cogent theoretical model for understanding adult relationships" with "the most basic elements of an adult-adult love relationship [being] ... emotional accessibility and responsiveness (Naaman, Pappas, Makinen, Zuccarini, & Johnson-Douglas, 2005, p. 56). Secure attachment is related to higher self-esteem, internal locus of control, extroversion, and openness to experience (Simms, 2002; Van Alstine, 2002). In addition, during conflict, adults with secure models of attachment "exhibit more positive behaviors, such as validation, empathy, interest and humor, than do their insecure counterparts" (Bailey, 2002, p. 90).

EFT strives to foster the development of more secure attachment styles in couples by seeing emotions "as a positive force for change in couple therapy" rather than "something to be overcome and replaced with rationality. ... Emotion is the music of the attachment dance; changing the music rapidly reorganizes the partners' interactional dance" (Johnson, 1998, p. 451).

Insecure attachment is often rooted in family-of-origin issues and is expressed in a couple relationship in the form of put-downs, belligerence, lecturing, stonewalling, and anger (Bailey, 2002). Since such styles negatively impact couples' relationships, EFT seeks to establish secure attachment bonds (Johnson, 2002). "A secure attachment bond is an active, affectionate, reciprocal relationship marked by emotional closeness, comfort, and security" (Beckerman & Sarracco, 2002, p. 24).

To promote such styles and bonding, interventions use both experiential and structural techniques, with the structural techniques such as enactment and complementary being modified to fit into the experiential framework of therapy (Johnson & Lebow, 2000; Simon, 2004). As in Rogerian theory, emotionally focused marriage therapists listen to individuals in couple relationships and follow their emotions and experiences (Young, 2005). The idea is to help partners "soften" or modify their intense, heightened emotions—anger, resentment, bitterness, and other distancing feelings—into sensations that help build attachment and connectedness such as communication of loss, sadness, fear, or grief (Croyle & Walz, 2002; Johnson, 2004). There is also an existential element to this process in regard to couples finding meaningfulness in their relationship with one another and in their lives.

Treatment Techniques

Treatment in EFT focuses on helping couples feel better about themselves and their partners. Thus, techniques in this approach concentrate on disclosure of feelings. There are several ways feelings are mined. One technique is for the therapist to probe and ask partners to acknowledge immediate feelings, such as anger, and to be accepting of that emotion. Therapists may also interrupt couples' arguments and disagreements. In doing so, they reflect with each member of the couple and defuse hostility. In addition, EFT therapists explore the perceptions that underlie partners' emotional responses which, up to that point in time, they have kept hidden. If members of the couple begin to express feelings, they may benefit from the release of emotions—a **catharsis**—while at the same time becoming more self-aware. Both catharsis and self-awareness are encouraged. During this process, the partner receiving the emotional response is provided with "the opportunity to become aware of the other's viewpoint and to develop empathic closeness" (Young & Long, 1998, p. 131). If such understanding is achieved, empathy becomes instrumental in the couple relationship.

EFT clinicians can also use techniques from psychodrama and gestalt therapy, such as having one member of the couple be the alter ego for the other or using an empty chair technique.

Role of the Therapist

The role of the therapist in emotionally focused therapy is to provide a safe environment for the release of positive and negative emotions (Young & Long, 1998). As such, the therapist is an encourager of emotional expression and a protector of the couple as individuals and as partners.

Process and Outcome

EFT is a three-stage interaction process with nine steps. The first stage is **cycle de-escalation.** Steps 1 through 4 are involved in this stage during which time couples are helped to uncover negative or hard feelings that lie beneath their defensive expressions of hurt, anger, and withdrawal. In this stage "the escalation of negative cycles and reactive secondary emotions, like a reactive anger or a numbing out" surface (Kowal et al., 2003).

In the second stage, **restructuring interactional positions,** steps 5 through 7 are implemented. Step 5 is the most individually oriented step in the EFT process. In it the therapist "explores the intrapsychic processing of attachment-related affect with more experiential detail" (Bradley & Johnson, 2005, p. 186). The focus is on one partner within the couple relationship, and the therapist works with that person to create a new interactive pattern which helps "withdrawn partners become more engaged and more blaming-coercive partners soften and engage in interactions where they can ask for their attachment needs to be met in a soft way that pulls their partner toward them" (Kowal et al., 2003). In this stage, specifically in step 6, the therapist switches focus and engages the opposite partner in a step 5 process. Finally, in step 7, the couple talks about their needs and fears together, and each member starts to soothe the other. This process is achieved by externalizing their conflict so that it is not the problem of one or both individuals but a difficulty that has evolved in the relationship and is a common enemy. EFT clinicians assist couples in understanding how their feelings play out in their relationship (Johnson, 1998). Therefore, they can face and attack this difficulty together (Kowal et al., 2003).

Finally, in the third stage, **consolidation/integration,** the therapist reviews the accomplishments of the couple by contrasting their initial negative interactional cycle with their new positive interactional cycle (Bradley & Johnson, 2005). The focus is on creating secure bonding interactions by reinforcing it (Jencius, 2003, p. 430). In this stage the therapist helps couples continue to restructure their interaction patterns more positively (Beckman & Sarracco, 2002). The focus of EFT is on meeting the longings that individuals have for secure relationships as opposed to a focus on finding fault with a spouse. EFT helps partners create positive interactions that produce bonding.

Unique Aspects of Emotionally Focused Therapy

EFT has a strong empirical base. It is very process-research-oriented and focuses on key elements of change (Greenberg & Johnson, 1986). In sync with John Gottman's research on how the importance of positive and negative interaction ratios affect a relationship, Johnson has found that it is not enough to have only a 5 to 1 ratio of positive to negative interaction; the timing of these interactions is also crucial. When a couple ends the day with a negative interaction, it is usually detrimental.

Because attachment and emotions are universal and cut across cultures, EFT is appropriate to use with couples from all backgrounds, although it may need to be modified to accommodate certain cultural groups.

Outside of distinct cultural groups, EFT has been found applicable in working with such diverse populations as individuals with post-traumatic stress disorder (Beckerman, 2004), moderately distressed couples (Bailey, 2002), families with a bulimic child, couples suffering from trauma, couples with depression and chronic illnesses, as well as older and gay couples (Bradley & Johnson, 2005).

In addition, EFT has started focusing on forgiveness and reconciliation as well as dealing with attachment injuries and relationship traumas. Research on EFT shows around a 70% recovery rate for distressed couples and around a 90% significant improvement rate for all couples with whom it is used (Jencius, 2003).

Comparison with Other Theories

EFT differs from most theories in its emphasis on the place of emotion in couple relationships and its simultaneous insistence that its techniques and procedures be empirically validated. Most experiential theories have not been researched very well.

Unlike some couple theories, EFT has been found to demonstrate efficacy apart from the originators of the approach (Bradley & Johnson, 2005).

EFT focuses on emotion and the inclusion of the concept of self, which makes it different from more pure systematic models. "The idea of emotion, often thought of as a 'within' phenomenon, being a leading or organizing element in interactional cycles is not addressed in traditional versions of systems theory" (Bradley & Johnson, 2005, p. 182).

-------------------- **CASE EXAMPLE OF EFT THERAPY** --------------------

THE KAPLANOVICS

Family Background

Boris and Olga Kaplanovic were married young. She was 19, and he was 21. They had dated in high school and had somehow drifted into a marriage about which they were unsure, even though it made their families excited and proud. Both families were first-generation Russian immigrants in the United States and had worked hard to make sure that their children had more opportunities and a better environment than they had.

Now married five years, Boris and Olga have started having difficulty in their relationship. He works construction. Recently, he has been coming home late. He seems more interested in watching television and having a beer than he does in interacting with his wife. She is clearly frustrated with his behavior and wants to talk with him and tell him about her day as an assistant to a financial analyst. Lately, they have said little to each other for fear of fighting. She fears he is hiding something from her.

Conceptualization of the Couple Relationship

This couple is still relatively young and, although they have had passionate fights, they have settled into a pattern of neither helping nor hurting each other at this point. They are basically going through the motions of being married.

Even though they see their extended families often, the couple has not received much support from them. One reason is that they have simply pretended everything in their relationship is fine. However, recently Olga has talked to her mother about Boris's behavior. She is very upset with the way he is acting and with their marriage.

Process of Treatment: Emotionally Focused Therapy

There are several approaches that could be effectively used with this couple. Behavioral couple therapy and emotionally focused therapy are two of the prime candidates. Both would work because the couple has not had a long time to build up negative interaction cycles. However, because the couple, especially Olga, is emotionally stirred up about the relationship that they share, emotionally focused therapy is used.

In this approach, the therapist first works with the couple to uncover the harsh feelings that have been generated. It is discovered that Boris is uncomfortable with emotional closeness, so he withdraws to avoid it. He feels that his mother smothered him with too much closeness and emotion when he was a child. This behavior made him angry and inhibited his relationships with other people, especially men. He drifted into his marriage because he found Olga physically attractive. However, he would rather look at her from a distance than talk with her up close. Olga, on the other hand, states that she has idealized marriage ever since she was young. She was unsure about marrying Boris but thought he would "come around" after they became a couple. The fact that he has not makes her resentful, and she blames him for not trying to do more to get to know her.

After the hard feelings of anger, resentment, and blame come out, the therapist moves the couple individually and then together into exploring the emotions behind what they have disclosed. The process begins with Olga who expresses frustration that her dreams of marriage have not materialized. She acknowledges that many of her reactive emotions now come from not living her fantasy. Still she feels hurt while at the same time wanting to have a real relationship with her husband. Boris talks about being scared to get too close to Olga for fear that she will become just like his mother and hold him back. He has chosen construction work to make sure he is able to be around other men. He states that he feels a bit "helpless" as to how to do anything different than what he is doing now. Together, the couple recognizes the hurt and helplessness in each other, and they begin to comfort each other.

In the final phase of EFT, the therapist works with the couple on how they can be different as a couple and get their emotional needs taken care of. Olga feels she can give Boris "more space" to be by himself or with other men when he needs to, while Boris proposes that he would feel comfortable in talking with Olga more if he could give her a signal as to when he felt "uncomfortable" and be able to disengage from the conversation then. Olga and Boris agree that they can help each other and the relationship through this initial plan. Later, with the help of the therapist, the couple makes other plans on how they can interact and emotionally get their needs met.

Divorce Therapy and Mediation

There is no such thing as a conflict-free marriage. The stress and strain of daily living, along with individually held values and opinions, get expressed in couple relationships and sometimes lead to disagreements, arguments, and a desire by one or both members in the relationship to leave. The result is that many couples seek a divorce. Given the inherent difficulties of marriage, it is surprising how relatively few couples seek assistance in saving their marriage. Only about one fourth of couples who seek divorce report seeking professional help of any kind, and those who do seek help wait an average of 6 years after a serious problem develops (Doss, Simpson, & Christensen, 2004).

There are a number of reasons for seeking a divorce. They are similar to those for seeking marriage or couples therapy, except that in the case of divorce, they are usually long-term in nature or have been exacerbated to the point that one or both partners in the relationship wish to terminate it. Marital stress can intensify or lead to such psychological disorders as anxiety, depression, substance abuse, and health difficulties (Doss, Atkins, & Christensen, 2003). These difficulties can lead to general unhappiness and negativity and in some cases can escalate to more serious problems, of which physical assault from one's spouse is the most grave. Such assaults are estimated to affect 16% of couples in the United States in any one year (Loy, Machen, Beaulieu, & Greif, 2005). Yet most couples who are discontent and seek marital therapy—or a divorce—do not report a specific problem. Rather, they simply note that they are having interpersonal or communication difficulties. Studies have shown that, at the time of an intake interview with a counselor, only about 6% of wives report suffering abuse from their spouses, even though researchers have estimated that some 50% to 60% of couples who seek therapy are dealing with the effects of domestic violence (Lawson, 2003). Therapists must take great care in assessing whether their efforts will help salvage a relationship or assist in its dissolution.

There are at least two ways couples can accomplish the task of breaking up: divorce therapy and mediation.

Divorce Therapy

Divorce therapy is a part of marital therapy and, as such, seeks to help couples separate from each other physically, psychologically, and/or legally. Therapists who work with divorce situations need to have theoretical tools and practical clinical strategies to help clients deal with and get through difficult personal and familial problems and challenges associated with divorces (Rice, 2005). Goals of divorce therapy include:

- accepting the end of the marriage
- achieving a functional postdivorce relationship with an ex-spouse
- achieving a reasonable emotional adjustment and finding emotional support
- coping with religious or spiritual angst (Murray, 2002)
- realizing the part one played in the dissolving of the marriage
- helping the children from the marriage (if there are any) adjust to the loss
- using the crisis of the divorce as opportunity to learn about oneself and to grow
- negotiating a reasonably equitable legal settlement
- developing healthy habits (Sprenkel, 1990)

As pointed out, couples use a number of means to strengthen their relationships and avoid divorce. Marriage counselors, who work with couples considering divorce, use a number of procedures that have both theoretical and atheoretical roots. These include having individuals look at their own family of origin and the issues that remain unresolved from their family. A wife may feel that her opinions were never valued growing up. Therefore, when her spouse does not listen carefully to what she is saying, she feels devalued and becomes upset. Recognizing this fact is a beginning step in breaking a pattern of pain as well as beginning to set up a new productive type of interaction which will serve the couple well, whether they ultimately choose to remain married or divorce.

Couples can work with therapists to deal with divorce-related issues in their marriage in a number of ways, but again one of them is through reading, reflecting, and participating in structured exercises. Such books as Michele Weiner Davis's *Divorce Busting: A Step-by-step Approach to Making Your Marriage Loving Again* (1993) and *The Divorce Remedy: The Proven 7-Step Program for Saving Your Marriage* (2003) are appropriate for such times with some couples.

Some other techniques marriage therapists use in helping couples who are considering divorce help themselves include:

1. listening for feelings in conversations rather than facts because feelings reflect an individual's values
2. placing a moratorium on the use of the word "you" because it tends to put individuals on the defensive and can be accusatory
3. setting aside time to discuss troublesome issues in couple relationships because these issues remain if left unattended or neglected
4. attending fully to one's partner during times of conflict and not interrupting
5. preventing the practice of "gunnysacking" or "dumping" where past unresolved issues or examples of behavior are brought up
6. using "I statements" to own one's thoughts and feelings about the subject in question

7. refraining from physical actions and/or advice giving
8. postponing resolution, if needed, so that the situation can be revisited again when both parties are fresher and have had time to think

Family Mediation

Family mediation is the process of helping couples and families settle disputes or dissolve their marriages in a nonadversarial way. Mediation is an increasingly utilized alternative to court action (Gladding et al., 2001). As a family mediator, family therapists are specially trained to function in a legally related role as an impartial, cognitive, neutral third party to facilitate negotiation between disputing parties, often a husband and wife. The objective is to help those involved make an informed and mutually agreed on decision that resolves differences between them in a practical and fair manner (Ferstenberg, 1992; Waxman & Press, 1991). "Mediation involves the resolution of conflict, not merely the cessation of it" (Huber, Mascari, & Sanders-Mascari, 1991, p. 117).

Steps involved in the mediation procedure include the mediator obtaining a brief history of the couple/family, including information about children. The family members also disclose to the mediator their assets, incomes, liabilities, and goals, whenever appropriate. They prioritize their most important issues. Where necessary, the mediator may involve or consult with other professionals, such as accountants. However, information, ideas, and decisions are generally limited to the parties involved and the mediator.

In contrast to divorce proceedings, mediation is less time-consuming, less costly, less hostile and stressful, and more productive (Ferstenberg, 1992). It protects clients and their records from public scrutiny and helps them problem-solve and reconstruct their lives in a reasonable and settled manner. There is an external deadline, and mediation concludes with a negotiated written agreement. The important point is that family therapists who function as mediators must remember that they have to help the parties involved learn how to bargain and come to a fair agreement. In doing so, they function in a role quite apart from that of a family therapist, let alone an attorney.

Organizations that family therapists can consult in finding out more about mediation include the Academy of Family Mediators in Lexington, Massachusetts, www.mediationa-dr.net/index.htm; the Association of Family and Conciliation Courts in Madison, Wisconsin, http://www.afccnet.org/; and the Association for Conflict Resolution, Washington, D.C., http://www.acrnet.org/ .

Summary and Conclusion

Couple and marital therapy is comprised of a number of approaches ranging from those that are primarily preventative, such as psychoeducational and enrichment experiences, to those that are treatment-oriented, such as cognitive-behavioral therapy, emotionally focused therapy, divorce therapy, and mediation. Meta-analysis of prevention and treatment studies supports the "efficacy of marital and family therapy for distressed couples, and marital and family enrichment" (Shadish & Baldwin, 2003, p. 547).

When working with couples, it is imperative that the therapist engage both individuals in the treatment process whenever possible. In regard to therapies, "cognitive-behavioral couple therapy has been subjected to more controlled outcome studies than has any other therapeutic modality" (Dattilio & Epstein, 2005, p. 7). However, emotionally focused therapy is process-research-oriented and has accumulated a wealth of data on its effectiveness with couples (Jencius & Duba, 2003).

Summary Table

Types of Couple and Marriage Treatments

Couple therapy is defined as a therapist working with two individuals to improve their relationship as a dyad.

Marriage therapy is when a therapist works with a couple that is legally married to help them improve their relationship.

Premarital counseling is when a professional works with a couple to enhance their relationship before they get married and helps them acquire skills and realistic expectations.

When working with couples, there are not as many dynamics for a therapist to attend to as when working with a family.

Major Theorists for Prevention

David and Vera Mace, Fr. Gabriel Calvo, Bernard Guerney, David Olson, and Lori Gordon.

Preventive Approaches to Working with Couples

Universal prevention focuses on preventing the development of problems in the general population such as promoting family togetherness.

Selective prevention focuses on making interventions with at-risk groups in order to prevent problems, e.g., conducting parenting classes.

Indicated prevention focuses on minimizing the harmful impact of serious problems in the early stages of their development such as working with a divorced couple in order to prevent them from doing harm to their children.

Preventive approaches are undeveloped as a group due to a lack of training in these modalities, economic barriers, and unsupportive cultural and family attitudes.

Psychoeducation, such as marriage education, a preventive approach, includes the use of didactic lectures, visual aids, handouts and interactive discussions. It includes bibliotherapy and conferences, such as Smart Marriage.

Marriage enrichment, a preventive approach, is a proactive systematic effort to improve the functioning of marital couples through a variety of means, such as structured exercises. There are more than two dozen enrichment organizations and programs worldwide.

Some of the better-known marriage enrichment programs are Marriage Encounter; Association of Couples for Marriage Enrichment (ACME); Relationship Enhancement; PREPARE/ENRICH; Training in Marriage Enrichment (TIME); Prevention and Relationship Enhancement Program (PREP); Couples Communication Program; SANCTUS; and Practical Application of Intimate Relationship Skills (PAIRS).

Marriage and Couples Therapy

Major Theorists

Susan Johnson, John Gottman, Richard Stuart, Frank Dattilio, Albert Ellis, and Robert Liberman.

Therapeutic Approaches for Working with Couples

Research indicates that couples therapy works. However, couples who come for therapy are doing so from a crisis rather than a developmental standpoint.

Primary reasons couples seek therapy are: a lack of communication, financial stress, disagreement over priorities, and infidelity.

All approaches to working with couples focus on marital quality—that is, how the relationship is functioning and how partners feel about that functioning.

Assessing couple relationships is complicated. Therapies seek to not only assess but to de-escalate negative reciprocity and build positive interactions.

Behavioral couple therapy (BCT) is based on the exchange/negotiation model of adult intimacy and focuses on increasing pleasing behaviors and teaching prosocial skills.

BCT is strongly researched.

Robert Liberman, a BCT practitioner, bases his approach on operant conditioning, social learning, and communication theory.

Richard Stuart's couples therapy is based on an operant interpersonal approach and a quid pro quo formula. He utilizes contracts, caring days, positive risks, positive reciprocity, communication skills training, and problem-solving skills.

BCT works best with young couples who do not have a long history of marriage.

Integrative behavioral couple therapy (IBCT) is a more recent form of behavioral couple therapy. It promotes acceptance of unresolvable problems, as well as change.

Cognitive-behavioral couple therapy (CBCT) is seen as more linear and is therefore underutilized more than any other couple therapy.

Albert Ellis's rational emotive behavior therapy (REBT) is an example of such a cognitive-behavioral approach.

Besides Ellis's theory, other CBCT approaches teach couples cognitive distraction, self-control strategies, and relapse prevention.

Emotionally focused therapy (EFT) is a systematic approach to working with couples based on experiential and structural family therapy. It is based on attachment theory and seeks to foster the development of secure attachment styles in couples.

EFT seeks to soften harsh emotions. It has a strong empirical base.

Divorce Therapy and Mediation

Only about one in four couples who seek a divorce seek professional help, and these couples tend to wait an average of 6 years after serious problems develop.

There are a number of reasons for seeking a divorce but most couples do not report a specific problem.

Divorce Therapy

Divorce therapy is a part of marital therapy but with an emphasis on helping couples separate from each other physically, psychologically, and legally.

Goals of divorce therapy include accepting the end of marriage, achieving a functional relationship with an ex-spouse, achieving reasonable emotional adjustment, helping children from the marriage adjust, realizing one's part in the divorce, using the crisis as an opportunity to learn, negotiating a reasonable legal settlement, and developing healthy habits.

Those divorcing should examine their families of origin and read appropriate literature.

Techniques that are universally used in divorce situations are listening for feelings, placing a moratorium on the word "you," setting aside time to discuss troublesome issues, preventing the practice of bringing up the past, and using "I statements."

Family Mediation

Mediation is the process of helping couples/families settle disputes or dissolve relationships in a nonadversarial way.

Skills associated with mediation include abilities to be cognitive, neutral, impartial, practical, and fair-minded.

Steps in the mediation process include taking a brief history of the couple/family and obtaining disclosure of assets, incomes, liabilities, and goals. Prioritizing choices is essential.

Overall, mediation is less time-consuming, costly, hostile, and stressful than legal divorce proceedings. It is also more productive and protects clients and their records from public scrutiny.

Mediation concludes with a negotiated written agreement.

There are a number of associations to which family mediators belong.

CHAPTER 6

Psychodynamic and Bowen Family Therapies

———————————————— • ————————————————

I walk thoughtfully down Beecher Road
at the end of a summer of too little growth,
the autumn wind stirring around me
orange remnants of once green leaves.

I am the son of a fourth-grade teacher
and a man who excelled in business,
a descendant of Virginia farmers
and open-minded Baptists,
the husband of a Connecticut woman,
the father of hazel-eyed children.

Youngest of three, I am a trinity:
counselor, teacher, writer.
Amid the cold, I approach home,
midlife is full of surprises!

———————————————— • ————————————————

Gladding, 1993

P sychodynamic and Bowen family therapies began developing in the 1950s. Their founders, Nathan Ackerman and Murray Bowen respectively, were known for their strong personalities and loyal followings. They originally were educated to utilize Freud's (1940) psychoanalytic theory with individual clients. Indeed, the tenets of psychoanalysis are a shared source from which psychodynamic and Bowen family therapies sprang. However, Ackerman and Bowen, because of their interests and circumstances, took liberties to apply Freud's theory to families and stressed the development of interpersonal as well as intrapersonal relationships.

This chapter examines the main aspects of psychodynamic and Bowen family therapies. In identifying themselves as either psychodynamic or Bowen family therapists, clinicians are distinct in emphasizing specific theoretical techniques and factors associated with each theory (e.g., who they are working with, as well as how and when treatment occurs). At the heart of treatment, from both viewpoints, is a belief that changes in families and their members occur best when the family is examined in the context of its history and development. Conscious and unconscious processes are collectively and individually the focus of therapeutic interventions.

On the surface, psychodynamic and Bowen family therapies have much in common. This is particularly true in regard to numerous premises and beliefs. For instance, psychodynamic and Bowen family treatments are based on conceptual models that are comprehensive in scope. They also have applied techniques that have developed from both research and practice (e.g., Papero, 1990; Titelman, 1987).

Another unifying feature that psychodynamic and Bowen family therapies share is the belief that in family therapy an emphasis should be placed on the fact that "the past is active in the present" (Smith, 1991, p. 24). These two approaches stress the importance of social and historical data in the lives of families. For example, early childhood experiences (i.e., the past), whether consciously maintained, can have an impact on an individual and a family now (i.e., the present) and for years to come. Initial experience associated with bonding and connectedness are particularly relevant. The memories and patterns of interaction established during these moments continue to influence present levels of functioning in multiple ways (Gibson & Donigian, 1993). For example, a couple's struggle over emotional and physical closeness might be a renewal of difficulties each had in forming relationships early in life.

A further common denominator of these theories is their focus on how intrapersonal and interpersonal aspects of life impact on each other. Basically, the way people relate to themselves influences how they interact with others. Similarly, the way in which people have been reacted to by others in the past affects how they perceive and treat themselves. For instance, an 11-year-old girl who withdraws from social activities may be expressing her feelings about her inadequacy in a family and minimizing her risk of being ridiculed.

Those associated with psychodynamic and Bowen family therapies have created their own specific descriptors of interactions as well. A number of phrases from each theory characterize family dynamics. Psychodynamic theorists have coined terms such as *marital schism, marital skew* (Lidz, Cornelison, Fleck, & Terry, 1957), and *pseudomutuality* (Wynne, Ryckoff, Day, & Hirsh, 1958) to describe dysfunctional relationships within families. Bowen family therapists have crafted other words or phrases such as *differentiation, fusion*, and *emotional cutoff* (Kerr & Bowen, 1988).

A final premise these two theories share is their view that change is usually gradual and requires hard work with a heavy investment of time and resources. Bowen and Ackerman, as psychodynamically trained psychiatrists, did not let their theories stray far from an in-depth treatment perspective. Although Bowen family therapy may sometimes achieve good results in as few as 5 or 10 sessions, families using either of these two approaches generally require as many as 20 to 40 sessions (Bowen, 1975). Members within families usually examine their relationships in regard to themselves and others before they risk trying new patterns of behavior.

Psychodynamic Family Therapy

Psychodynamic family therapy encompasses more than traditional psychoanalytic theory applied to families. Rather, it is composed of a number of approaches, such as object relations theory, that are offshoots of Freud's basic tenets.

Major Theorists

The most prominent professionals associated with psychodynamic family therapy are Nathan Ackerman, Ivan Boszormenyi-Nagy, James Framo, Theodore Lidz, Norman Paul, Donald Williamson, Robin Skynner, and Lyman Wynne. However, Ackerman is generally credited as the founder of psychodynamic family therapy.

Nathan Ackerman

Nathan Ackerman (1908–1971) became a family therapist over an extended period of time. Initially, he was educated as a child psychiatrist and followed the traditional psychoanalytic approach of seeing one patient at a time. However, in the 1930s, Ackerman became interested in families and their influence on mental health and illness (Ackerman, 1937). This interest was sparked by his observations about the effect of unemployment on men and their families in a mining town in western Pennsylvania and about how families seemed to change more rapidly when all members were interviewed together (Broderick & Schrader, 1991). In his initial clinical work at the Menninger Clinic in Topeka, Kansas, he began treating whole families and sending his staff on home visits (Guerin, 1976). He was especially interested in the psychosocial dynamics of family life and in applying psychoanalytical principles to family units.

In the 1950s and 1960s, Ackerman was even more heavily involved in his work with families and, consequently, became the leading family therapist on the East Coast. He opened the Family Mental Health Clinic at Jewish Family Services in New York in 1957 and established the Family Institute in New York in 1960. In 1961, he became the cofounder of *Family Process*, the first journal in family therapy (Kaplan, 2000). This publication, along with Ackerman's earlier landmark text, *The Psychodynamics of Family Life* (1958), gave credibility and credence to the field of family therapy. Ackerman remained staunchly psychodynamic in outlook throughout his professional career.

Ackerman made many contributions to the field of family therapy. His overall success as a therapist is especially noteworthy. Ackerman documented many of his sessions with families by publishing transcripts of them (Kaplan, 2000). He was also an excellent theorist who made unique contributions to the literature in the field of family therapy through articulating arguments that were based on principles and filled with passion. His writings and practice documented the principles by which he operated. Finally, Ackerman had a strong, charismatic personality, which helped attract interest in what he was doing (Bloch & Simon, 1982). He was a fighter for what he believed in. "Innumerable minor skirmishes and border wars" that Ackerman engaged in "were never chronicled but clung to the man's reputation like the leathery scars of an old warrior chief" (Bloch & Simon, 1982, pp. xv–xvi). He has been described as feisty, brilliant, charming—and a gadfly.

Ackerman influenced many psychodynamically oriented practitioners, as well as other professionals, to treat individuals and families together as a system. He did so in a variety of ways, one of which was to hypothesize that underneath the outward unity of a family "they are emotionally split into competing factions" (Nichols & Schwartz, 2005, p. 34). Ackerman also helped open the field of psychoanalysis to nonmedical specialists by establishing the American Academy of Psychoanalysis in 1955.

Ackerman defined the difference between family psychotherapy and psychoanalysis (Ackerman, 1962). His conceptualizations of families and presentations about them were creative and thought provoking. Ackerman published transcripts of family therapy sessions that contained interpretive comments in the margins such as "Therapist contrasts father's quiet way with Alice's noisy aggressiveness" (Ackerman, Beatman, & Sherman, 1961, p. 139). Ackerman is recognized as being the initiator of, or at least the one who emphasized, such concepts as scapegoat, **tickling of defenses** (i.e., provoking family members to open up and say what was on their mind), complementarity, focus on strengths, and interlocking pathology.

Nathan Ackerman was a leading pioneer in family therapy. His work ethic and sense of responsibility to the field of family therapy advanced the field considerably. Unfortunately, his early death, at the age of 63, deprived the field of a crusader and innovative thinker.

Premises of the Theory

Psychodynamic family therapy is based on the classic work of Sigmund Freud, as interpreted, modified, and applied to family life. Freud viewed human nature as one based on drives (e.g., sexuality and aggression). Mental conflict arises when children learn—and mislearn—that expressing these basic impulses will lead to punishment. Conflict is signaled by unpleasant affect: anxiety or depression. In other words, to resolve conflict one of two actions must occur: There must be (1) a strengthening of defenses against a conflicted wish or (2) defenses must be relaxed sufficiently to permit some gratification.

In addition to Ackerman, several other theorists and practitioners helped apply Freud's individually focused approach to families, including Heinz Kohut (1977), James Framo (1981), and Ivan Boszormenyi-Nagy (1987). However, Ackerman took the lead by setting up a training and treatment center for this purpose, the Family Institute—now known as the **Ackerman Institute for the Family** in New York City (http://www.ackerman.org/). This facility provided a place where professionals could come and observe his work. He also wrote prolifically on the diagnosis and treatment of families (e.g., Ackerman, 1958). As a psychodynamically oriented therapist, he initiated a new way of thinking about individuals and families and advocated that an accurate understanding of an individual's unconscious requires an understanding of its context. One of the primary contexts is the reality of family interactions. The importance of context in the treatment of families has continued to be stressed by Boszormenyi-Nagy (1987).

Ackerman (1956) connected family context and the unconscious in interlocking patholo-gy, which explains how families and certain of their members stay dysfunctional. In an **interlocking pathology**, an unconscious process takes place between family members that keeps them together. If members violate the unwritten family rules, then the members either make a conscious decision to leave the family and become healthier, or they are drawn back into the familiar family pattern by other members and continue to function in a less than ideal manner. For example, a young adult who has not adequately separated from his or her parents may move into an apartment. If the young adult gets an adequate job and makes new friends in his or her age group, he or she may avoid being pulled back into the family and may begin to establish a new identity and way of life. Otherwise, the inadequate sepa-ration will influence him or her to return to the parents physically, psychologically, or both!

A more recent focus of psychodynamic theory is object relations theory (Kohut, 1977; Scharff, 1989; Slipp, 1988). **Object relations theory** is the bridge between classical Freudian theory, with its emphasis on individual drives, and family therapy, with its emphasis on social relationships. An **object** is something that is loved, usually a person. The term **object relations** means "rela-tions between persons involved in ardent emotional attachments. These attachments can exist in the outer world of reality or as residues of the past—that is, inner presences, often uncon-scious, that remain vigorous and very much alive within us" (Scarf, 1995, p. xxxvii).

Through object relations theory, relationships across generations can be explained. Ac-cording to this theory, human beings have a fundamental motivation to seek objects (i.e., people in relationships) starting at birth (Fairbairn, 1954; Klein, 1948). In this case, an object is a significant other (e.g., a mother during infancy) with whom children form an interac-tional, emotional bond. As they grow, children often internalize (interject) good and bad characteristics of these objects within themselves. These interjections over time form the basis for how individuals interact and evaluate their interpersonal relationships with others, especially those with whom they are close.

This process of evaluation occurs at its lowest level through an unconscious procedure known as splitting (Kernberg, 1976). In **splitting**, object representations are either all good or all bad. The result is a projection of good and bad qualities onto persons within one's environment. Through splitting, people are able to control their anxiety and even the objects (i.e., persons within their environment) by making them predictable. However, the drawback to splitting is that it distorts reality. When splitting occurs, children (and later their adult counterparts) fail to integrate their feelings about an object (a person) into a realistic view (Hafner, 1986). For exam-ple, in a couple relationship each spouse might project unrealistic patterns of behavior onto the other. In addition to distorting the relationship, this type of projection causes conflict and con-fusion. Individuals who operate in this way have trouble dealing with the complexity of human relationships and may be immature in their interactions (Kernberg, 1976; Kohut, 1971).

The importance of object relations theory in family therapy is that it provides a way for psy-chodynamic clinicians to explain reasons for marital choices and family interaction patterns (Dicks, 1963). It stresses the value of working with unconscious forces in individuals and fami-lies beyond Freud's metaphorical concepts of id, ego, and superego. Unconscious and unre-solved early object relations that adults may bring into their marriage relationships can result in the development of dysfunctional patterns in which persons cling to each other desperately and dependently (Ackerman, 1956; Napier & Whitaker, 1978). These patterns keep repeating them-selves until one or both spouses (or in some cases their children) become more aware, take ac-tions to differentiate themselves from past objects, and learn to act in new and productive ways.

Treatment Techniques

In psychodynamic family therapy, considerable emphasis is placed on the unconscious, early memories and on object relations. The therapeutic techniques used include transference, dream and daydream analysis, confrontation, focusing on strengths, life history, and complementarity.

Transference

Transference is the projection onto a therapist of feelings, attitudes, or desires. This technique is employed in individual analysis to help clients work through their feelings by viewing the therapist as a significant other with whom relationships are unresolved (Ellis, 2000). Transference is utilized in family therapy in order to understand dominant feelings within a family unit and delineate which emotions are being directed toward what people.

In cases where transference occurs, clients in the family form a bond with the therapist and act toward the therapist as they would toward people with whom they are having difficulties. Thus, they benefit through the expression of pent-up emotion (i.e., catharsis) and through self-discovery, insight, and the learning of new ways to interact. Family members who are angry with each other and frustrated with social service agencies might say to a family therapist such words as:

- "I don't see what good you are going to do us."
- "What's the use of talking to you."
- "I'm really mad that this family is going down the tubes and all we are doing is talking to you. When are we going to get some real help?"

By treating these sentences in a nondefensive and understanding way, the family therapist can help a family get through dealing with unproductive emotions and move toward the task of working on important issues in their lives.

Dream and Daydream Analysis

The objective of having family members discuss their dreams or daydreams is to analyze what needs within the family are not being met. If a father has a recurring dream of being abandoned on a desert island, he may be expressing a need for greater affiliation with family members. Strategies are then developed to meet members' deficits. In the case of the father, family outings or dinners could be planned to help tie the father closer to other members in a pleasant way.

Dream and daydream analysis may be quite useful for some families in helping them see areas that need attention. However, dream analysis can become problematic and difficult to handle if the number of family members participating is large.

Confrontation

In confrontation procedures, the therapist points out to families how their behaviors contradict or conflict with their expressed wishes (Ackerman, 1966). A father who protests that he wishes to spend more time with his wife and children, yet who continues to work late at his office on a consistent basis, may be confronted by the therapist as follows:

> George, I see you voluntarily working at your business all hours of the night and day. Yet, I hear you want to spend more time with your family. Help me understand what you are doing to get what you say you want.

The idea behind confrontation is to help family members become more aware of what they are doing and to change their strategies for coping and becoming functional.

Focusing on Strengths

As with other therapeutic endeavors, psychodynamic family therapists are aware that most families come to treatment because they are focused on perceiving and dealing with weaknesses in themselves and their families. By concentrating on strengths, family therapists help change the family's focus. The therapist may point out to a family that they all seem quite willing and capable of breaking past patterns of interaction by saying:

> I have heard from each of you how you would like for your family to work. Bill, I am impressed with your strong commitment to doing whatever it takes. Sue, I am equally struck by the fact that you have stated you are willing to make any sacrifice necessary for the family to run more smoothly. Likewise, Chip, even though you are only fourteen years old, I am aware that you are mature and willing to work with your parents to bring about needed changes.

As a consequence of focusing on strengths, structured activities can be designed to promote cooperation and break dysfunctional patterns of behaving. For example, a family can be asked to plan an event that will utilize the abilities of all family members.

Life History

By taking and assessing a family's life history, psychodynamic family therapists can report present and past patterns of interaction within the family. This process also affirms to family members that they are valued and accepted regardless of their backgrounds. Taking a family life history promotes trust in the therapist and also provides family members with insight. The history can be written in a narrative or an abbreviated form.

Complementarity

Complementarity is the degree of harmony in the meshing of family roles. For example, if a husband and wife agree that her role should be planning the family budget and his should be balancing the checkbook, they have established a complementarity relationship in regard to financial roles. When roles dovetail, as in the previous example, family life is likely to be satisfactory. One task of the therapist is to help family members provide and receive satisfaction from their relationships. It may mean asking members what they want and what they are willing to do in return.

Role of the Therapist

In psychodynamic treatment, the therapist plays several roles. One is that of a teacher. It is crucial that family members understand that influences in their past, especially unconscious ones, have an impact on them now. Therefore, it is essential that family members learn basic psychoanalytic terms and how these terms apply on a personal and interpersonal basis.

A second role the therapist might play is that of a good enough mother (Winnicott, 1965). A **good enough mother** is one whose infant feels loved and cared for and is able to develop trust and a true sense of self. This role might call for the therapist to actually nurture the family member by providing encouraging behaviors that were absent at earlier developmental stages. In this role, the therapist might involve family members in interactions with one another that help them make up for past deficits. This behavior could take the form of anything from pats on the back to the giving of compliments.

A final role the psychodynamic therapist might play is that of a **catalyst** who moves into the "living space" of the family and stirs up interactions. Ackerman (1966) was a master of engaging families in this manner. The result was that families in treatment would often have a meaningful emotional exchange. In the role of a catalyst, the therapist activates, challenges, confronts, sometimes interprets, and helps integrate family processes. Such a role requires high energy and stamina.

In fulfilling any of these roles, but especially the last one, the therapist must be careful to emphasize family as well as individual interactions. It is crucial that family members have extensive and free-flowing interchanges and that the therapist does not become overly involved or central in the process. Such a stance is easier to describe than to implement.

Process and Outcome

A major goal of psychodynamic family therapy is to free family members of unconscious restrictions. This outcome is sometimes achieved through the therapist's interpretation of events and insight on the part of family members regarding events. Interpretation is best offered by the therapist on a preconscious level, that is, on material that family members are almost aware of. When insights are achieved in such an endeavor, they must be worked through, that is, translated into new and more productive ways of behaving and interacting.

Once unconscious restrictions are worked through, family members are able to interact with one another as whole, healthy persons on the basis of current realities rather than unconscious images of the past. When this goal is achieved, the results are usually manifested in changes that are described by the term **differentiation**. The idea behind differentiation is that individuals have reached a level of maturity in which they can balance their rational and emotional selves and in which they can separate themselves from others in a nonanxious way. When this dynamic occurs, family members can interact thoughtfully as persons. They can participate in the family fully and can also be themselves. Furthermore, they do not get caught up in dysfunctional interactions with other family members.

Sometimes the achievement of differentiation is not possible. Professionals can then opt for **crisis resolution**, which is similar to that of other treatment modalities and basically involves a reduction in symptoms. Therapists focus more on supporting defenses and clarifying communication than on analyzing defenses and uncovering repressed needs and impulses.

Unique Aspects of Psychodynamic Family Therapy

Emphases

A major emphasis of psychodynamic family therapy is that it concentrates on the potency of the unconscious in influencing human behavior. How the unconscious influences interpersonal and intrapersonal relationships, such as those found in marital and family living, is a focus. This method of treatment can increase family members' awareness of how forces within themselves and others, such as **invisible loyalties** to their parents, either bring them closer to each other or influence their distancing (Boszormenyi-Nagy & Spark, 1973).

The psychodynamic approach examines basic defense mechanisms and the part they play in family relationships. This is a unique contribution to the literature on family dynamics and helps make interactions among some family members more understandable (Skynner, 1981). For example, abused children who stay loyal to their parents may be seen from this perspective as employing the Freudian defense mechanism of identification with the aggressor (see Table 6.1).

A third novel aspect of psychodynamic family therapy is its emphasis on historical origins of dysfunctions and the treatment of persons and families so affected. By working with a family or an individual, therapists get to the roots of problems formulated in childhood. They can then help families resolve troublesome issues by exploring past ways the family, as a unit, acted during troublesome times.

Finally, psychodynamic family theory, especially object relations, helps explain how persons form attachments and how family members function as a result. This emphasis on the genesis of family relationships is something no other approach to working with families explores in as much depth.

Comparison with Other Theories

As opposed to most family therapies, psychodynamic-oriented family therapy is linear—it focuses on cause-and-effect interactions. This quality of the theory has resulted in criticism. Although Ackerman and others attempted to make psychodynamic theory applicable to

Table 6.1
Basic Psychoanalytic Defense Mechanisms

Repression	The most basic of the defense mechanisms, repression is the unconscious exclusion of distressing or painful thoughts and memories. All other defense mechanisms make some use of repression.
Denial	In this process, a person refuses to see or accept any problem or troublesome aspect of life. Denial operates at the preconscious or conscious level.
Regression	When individuals are under stress, they often return to a less mature way of behaving.
Projection	Instead of stating what a person really thinks or feels, he or she attributes an unacceptable thought, feeling, or motive onto another.
Rationalization	This defense mechanism involves giving an "intellectual reason" to justify doing a certain action. The reason and the action are only connected in the person's mind after the behavior has been completed.
Reaction Formation	When an individual behaves in a manner that is just the opposite of how he or she feels, it is known as a "reaction formation." This type of behavior is usually quite exaggerated, such as acting especially nice to someone whom one dislikes intensely.
Displacement	This defense is a redirection of an emotional response onto a "safe target." The substitute person or object receives the feeling instead of the person directly connected with it.

From *Group Work: A Counseling Specialty* (3rd ed., p. 344) by S. T. Gladding, © 1991. Reprinted by permission of Prentice-Hall, Inc., Upper Saddle River, NJ.

family systems, they only partially succeeded. Too often this type of treatment is either limited to an individual or not broadened to family life (Perosa, 1996).

A second comparison of psychodynamic family therapy to other approaches is its expense in regard to financial and time commitments. Psychodynamic-based approaches are demanding in the investment they require of their participants. Individuals and families must be prepared to explore the roots of their difficulties, including early childhood/parent interactions. Most cannot afford to take the time or pay the price.

A third comparison that can be made between psychodynamic family therapy and other approaches is that psychodynamic treatment generally requires higher than average intellectual ability. Psychodynamic theory may not be appropriate for families that are concrete in handling situations or become impatient with the abstract. These families want immediate results and cannot cope well with abstract concepts, such as the unconscious.

Compared with most family therapy approaches, especially recently developed ones, psychodynamic treatment lacks empirical research (Shields, Wynne, McDaniel, & Gawinski, 1994). Instead, psychoanalysis has a strong preference for nonempirical and nonquantitative studies such as case examples. This emphasis "has contributed to the near demise of psychoanalysis as a recommended therapy" (Shields et al., 1994, p. 121).

CASE ILLUSTRATION

THE CASA FAMILY

Family Background

Maria Casa is a 39-year-old single parent with a 13-year-old daughter, Gloria, and an 11-year-old son, Juan. She has been divorced for 5 years, but before her divorce was married for 10 years. Her husband, Roberto, kept in touch with the children for about 2 years after the divorce, but then moved to a distant city and last year quietly remarried. The children hear from him only at Christmas, when he sends them each a present and a card.

Maria works as an executive assistant to a vice president of a major local employer. Earlier, she had been on the company assembly line, so she appreciates her position because of its greater benefits and flexibility. Yet, she resents having to dress well for the job and occasionally stay late at the office to finish reports. She feels she is losing touch with her children because of her work responsibilities.

Recently, Juan has started using profanity and being disrespectful to his mother and sister. He does a poor job on family chores such as cutting the grass. He has begun to hang out after school with a group of boys Maria considers undesirable. Gloria, on the other hand, is making good grades in school and working especially hard to please her mother by doing extra tasks Maria does not have time for, such as sweeping the walk. Maria is angry at Juan and proud of Gloria. She is worried that both children may get stuck in patterns that will ultimately not benefit them. She is particularly concerned about Juan.

Conceptualization of Family: Psychodynamic Perspective

On an unconscious level, this family appears to be enacting roles that are noncomplementary. Maria and Gloria are acting out heroine roles; Juan is the rebel. Underneath all of their public behaviors are feelings, most likely anger, about their life condition and the desertion of their father, Roberto. Juan is playing the role of the scapegoat to bring the family into treatment. Interestingly, all members of the family are seeking some social interaction, either with other family members (e.g., Gloria and Maria) or with a group (e.g., Juan and his gang). Defense mechanisms, such as sublimation by Gloria, are also evident.

Process of Treatment: Psychodynamic Family Therapy

To help the family, a psychodynamic therapist need not bring all members of the present family into treatment. However, to understand the family thoroughly, it would be beneficial to have all members present, including Roberto if he would agree to come. After taking time to join with the family, a therapist should take a history of the family up to and after the time of the mother–father divorce. Nodal points in the family's history before and after that time should be assessed. In taking the family history, the therapist should observe the similarities and discrepancies voiced by the members of the family and the feelings associated with particular events, people, and times.

From this point on, a psychodynamic therapist has several choices. First, the therapist can try to get family members to engage in transference and ventilate their feelings about their situation and themselves. Through such a collective process, catharsis could be promoted. Second, the therapist can look for and utilize opportunities to confront family members in regard to their present behaviors and the behaviors they claim they want. This type of confrontation may be especially helpful to Juan because of the nature of his aggressive actions. Such a confrontation starts with the therapist saying: "Juan, I hear you really want to be close to others, such as your mother and sister. Yet, I notice you are cursing at them and staying away from them. Help me understand how what you are doing is helping you."

A third option for the therapist is to examine cultural and unique family/individual patterns related to the current crisis. Psychodynamic theory is not culturally specific, but a therapist should view a family in light of its cultural background regardless of the theory being utilized. The Casas are Hispanic/Latino, and, as pointed out in a later chapter, there are general cultural influences that impact on family life from this tradition.

A fourth option that may come up immediately, later, or concurrently through treatment is exploring the unconscious. It is the task of a psychodynamic-oriented family therapist to help family members delve into themselves intrapersonally as well as interpersonally. Unconscious material may surface and can be handled through dream analysis or through dealing with memories. The idea is that through handling aspects of the unconscious, family members will gain insight into themselves and others. They can then use this knowledge to change their behavior.

Overall, a psychodynamic therapist's work with families, such as the Casas, is to identify and utilize individual and family unit strengths. It is hoped that, through the therapeutic process, unconscious aspects of family life that keep members apart will surface and be resolved.

———————————— ● ————————————

Bowen Family Therapy

Bowen family therapy has the distinction of being among the first, if not the first, systemically based approaches for working with families. It has a historical overtone and at times has been referred to as **transgenerational family therapy**. Despite its emphasis on family history, it is simultaneously geared toward the present.

Major Theorists

Murray Bowen and Michael Kerr have been the chief architects and advocates of Bowen family therapy. However, the major originator of this approach was Murray Bowen. Bowen formulated the ideas that resulted in a distinct theory of family therapy. The theory and its techniques have been popularized by authors such as McGoldrick, Gerson, and Shellenberger (1999) (*Genograms: Assessment and Intervention*) and Friedman (1985) (*Generation to Generation: Family Process in Church and Synagogue*).

Murray Bowen

The oldest of five children, Murray Bowen (1913–1990) grew up in a tightly knit family that for several generations resided in a small town in Pennsylvania. As an adult, Bowen moved away and kept a formal distance from his parents. He maintained family relations on a comfortable but superficial level. Bowen, like Nathan Ackerman, was a psychiatrist who became interested in working with families while employed at the Menninger Clinic. As early as 1951, he began to require that mothers of disturbed children live in the same hospital setting as their offspring (Guerin, 1976). From this experience, he became interested in studying "mother–patient symbiosis," the intense bond that develops between a parent and child that does not allow either person to differentiate him- or herself from the other (Bowen, 1960, 1961).

In 1954, Bowen moved to join Lyman Wynne at the National Institute of Mental Health (NIMH) in Bethesda, Maryland, where he continued to be involved in studying the dynamics of families with schizophrenic children. As a part of the treatment, Bowen worked with the research team at NIMH on a pilot project to hospitalize and treat all members of such families. He recognized during this time that the characteristics exhibited by a schizophrenic family were similar to symptoms in many dysfunctional families. A few years later, he moved to Georgetown University in Washington, D.C., where he researched family dynamics and developed his therapeutic approach until his death.

During his years at Georgetown, especially in the 1970s, Bowen completed his most productive personal and professional work. Personally, he detriangulated himself from his parents by returning home and reacting cognitively and neutrally to a number of emotional issues family members presented to him (Anonymous, 1972). Professionally, he clarified his theory (Bowen, 1978); began the Georgetown Family Center Symposium; expanded the Georgetown Family Center to new, off-campus quarters; and initiated the founding of the **American Family Therapy Association (AFTA)**, "in order to restore a serious research effort in family therapy" (Wylie, 1991, p. 77).

Premises of the Theory

For Bowen, therapy and theory are part of the same fabric and cannot be separated without doing a disservice to each. Bowen preferred to think of himself as a theorist. He saw himself as one who stood alone in conceptualizing "the family as a natural system . . . which could only be fully understood in terms of the fluid but predictable processes between members" (Wylie, 1991, p. 26). Bowen was a scientist in search of universal truths. "Bowen theory constantly strives to make continuous what other theories dichotomize" (e.g., nature/nurture, male/female, and physical illness/emotional illness) (Friedman, 1991, p. 136). However, sometimes

Bowen's writings about the continuity and connection between theory and therapy are criticized for their complex and convoluted nature (Kaplan, 2000).

Bowen was influenced by events in his own life history, especially his difficulties with his family of origin. Thus, his personal situation had a major impact on what he proposed (Anonymous, 1972; Papero, 1991). Basically, Bowen stated that unless individuals examine and rectify patterns passed down from previous generations, they are likely to repeat these behaviors in their own families (Kerr, 1988, 2003). The possibility of repeating certain behaviors in interpersonal relations is particularly likely if family members, especially between the generations, are characteristically either emotionally overinvolved (i.e., **fused**) with each other or emotionally cut off (psychologically or physically) from each other. Bowen concerned himself with the family's emotional system.

A key element of Bowen family therapy is "that there is a chronic anxiety in all of life that comes with the territory of living" (Friedman, 1991, p. 139). This anxiety is both emotional and physical and is shared by all protoplasm. Some individuals are more affected than others by this anxiety "because of the way previous generations in their families have channeled the transmission" of it to them (Friedman, 1991, p. 140).

If anxiety remains low, few problems exist for people or families. In such cases, the family emotional system is undisturbed. However, in the midst of anxiety, some predictable patterns occur. According to Greene, Hamilton, and Rolling (1986, p. 189):

> Lower scale [undifferentiated] people are vulnerable to stress and are much more prone to illness, including physical and social illness, and their dysfunction is more likely to become chronic when it does occur. Higher scale people can recover emotional equilibrium quickly after the stress passes.

To address chronic anxiety and emotional processes in families and society, Bowen emphasized eight basic concepts that are interrelated and logically connected. Through understanding these concepts, a therapist understands and successfully treats a family. These basic concepts are (Bowen, 1978; Kerr, 1981, 2003):

- differentiation
- emotional system
- multigenerational transmission process
- nuclear family emotional system
- family projection process
- triangles
- sibling position
- societal regression

Differentiation refers to the ability of persons to distinguish themselves from their family of origin on an emotional and intellectual level as well as to balance the intrapsychic and interpersonal dimensions of the self (Bowen, 1978). There are two counterbalancing life forces: togetherness and individuality. People vary as to the level of self-differentiation that they achieve at any one time, and the concept itself denotes a process (Bowen, 1965). Bowen hypothesized that most people do not reach a true differentiation of self until at least age 25 (Kerr & Bowen, 1988). Regardless, the level of differentiation is on a continuum, from **autonomy** at one end (which signals an ability to think through a situation clearly) to **undifferentiated** on the other end (which implies an emotional dependency on one's family members, even if living away from them). This relationship is described as being **fused** or as an **undifferentiated family ego mass** (Bowen, 1965).

"Theoretically, at least four factors influence a person's level of differentiation: emotional reactivity, emotional cutoff, fusion with others, and the ability to take an 'I-position'" (Tuason & Friedlander, 2000, p. 27). It is through the process of differentiation that families and the individuals in them change (see Figure 6.1).

In a fused situation, family members may exhibit dysfunctional behaviors such as bulimia. In these cases, family therapists should try to help family members (usually young women) increase their degree of self-differentiation. Procedures that are sometimes used include assertiveness training, building healthier family boundaries, enhancing cognitive communication skills, and finding new coping behaviors for stress (Levy & Hadley, 1998).

Coping strategies and patterns of coping with stress tend to be passed on from generation to generation, a phenomenon known as the **multigenerational transmission process**. Families who present a problem have had the forces of several generations shaping and carrying the symptom. Bowen (1976) theorized that in marriage people tend to select partners at their own level of differentiation (Bowen, 1976). His hypothesis has been supported as a number of studies have found "a strong, positive relationship between differentiation and marital quality" (Miller, Anderson, & Keala, 2004, p. 457). In these unions, a nuclear family emotional system evolves.

Spouses with equally high levels of identity are able to establish and maintain clear individuality "and at the same time to have an intense, mature, nonthreatening, emotional closeness" (Bowen, 1965, p. 220). Research shows that couples who are less reactive, cutoff, or fused and are able to relate from an I-position "experience the greatest levels of marital satisfaction" (Skowron, 2000, p. 233). Such is particularly true if the male partner remains emotionally present and available. On the other hand, spouses with equally low levels of differentiation have difficulty establishing intimacy because they have developed only **pseudoselves**, that is, "pretend" selves (Kerr, 1988, p. 43). The pseudoselves fluctuate according to situations and usually result in the fusion of these selves into a "common self with obliteration of ego boundaries between them and loss of individuality to the common

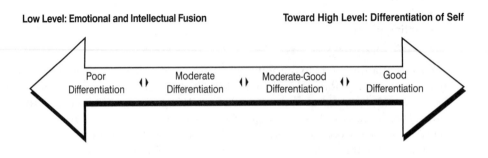

Figure 6.1
Bowen's continuum of self-differentiation.

self" (Bowen, 1965, p. 221). Couples tend to produce offspring at the same level of differentiation as themselves, a process Bowen describes as **family projection** (Kilpatrick, 1980).

To rid themselves of anxiety, spouses who are low on differentiation of self keep an emotional distance from each other. When distance cannot be kept and anxiety becomes too great, it is frequently manifested in one of four ways: (1) marital conflict, (2) physical or emotional illness in one spouse, (3) projection of the problem to the children, or (4) a combination of these (David, 1979).

Bowen family therapists look for triangles when working with couples. Triangles can occur between people or between people and things. They consist of a state of calm between a comfortable twosome and an outsider (Anonymous, 1972). A **triangle** is "the basic building block of any emotional system and the smallest stable relationship system" (Kilpatrick, 1980, p. 168). Some triangles are healthy, others are not. In the latter case, triangles are a frequent way of dealing with anxiety in which tension between two persons is projected onto another object (Bowen Center, 2004, http://www.thebowencenter.org/pages/concepttri. html). The original triangle is between a child and parents. In stressful situations, anxiety spreads from one central triangle within the family to interlocking triangles outside the family, especially in work and social systems (Kerr, 1988).

Given this background, it is understandable why Bowen family therapists work to help people, especially couples, separate their feelings from their intellect and, in the process, **detriangulate**. They do this through asking questions about thoughts and constructing a type of family tree (which is explained later) called a **multigenerational genogram** (McGoldrick et al., 1999). They also give homework assignments that require individuals to visit their families in order to learn through questioning (Bowen, 1976). Furthermore, Bowen therapists examine sibling positions; people can develop fixed personality characteristics based on their functional birth order in the family (Toman, 1961). The more closely a marriage replicates a couples' sibling positions in the family of origin, the better the chance for success. If a youngest son marries an oldest daughter, both have much to gain from the arrangement because the youngest son will most likely enjoy "being taken care of," and the oldest daughter will probably enjoy "taking care of" someone.

By examining the processes just mentioned, family members gain insight and understanding into the past and are freed to choose how they will behave in the present. Similarly, Bowen family therapists may lead family members into gaining a perspective on how well society as a whole is doing. If a society is under too much stress (e.g., population growth, economic decline), **societal regression** will occur, because of too many toxic forces countering the tendency to achieve differentiation.

Treatment Techniques

Bowen family therapy focuses on the promotion of differentiation (in regard to self/family and intellect/emotion). This approach is not technique-oriented, because of the tendency to get caught up and overpowered by particular techniques at particular times. However, among those techniques most often employed are genograms, going home again, detriangulation, person-to-person relationships, differentiation of self, and asking questions.

Genograms

A genogram is a visual representation of a person's family tree depicted in geometric figures, lines, and words (Sherman, 1993) (see Figure 6.2). Genograms include information related to

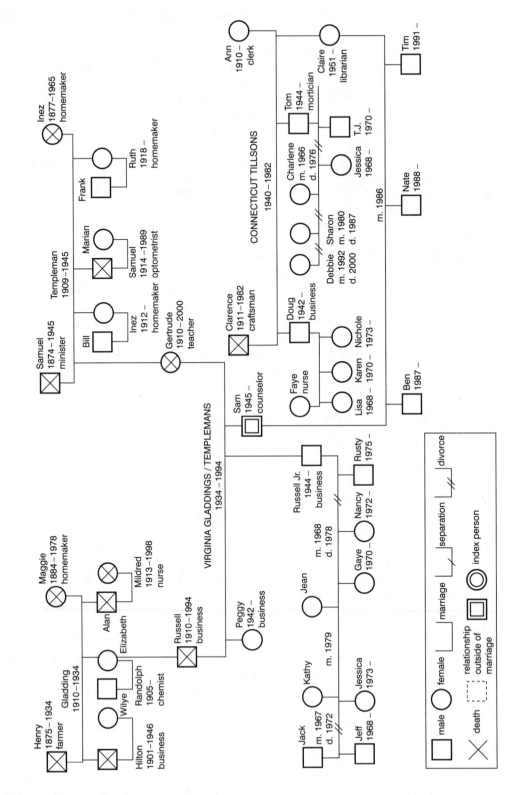

Figure 6.2
Gladding family genogram.

at least three generations of a family and its members' relationships with each other. A genogram helps people gather information, hypothesize, and track relationship changes in the context of historic and contemporary events (Dunn & Levitt, 2000). "From this simple diagram, counselors and clients alike are able to view simultaneously family composition, gender, age, ethnicity, dates of birth, marriages, divorces, deaths, and other important family events" (Frame, 2000, p. 69).

The tangibility and nonthreatening nature of making a genogram helps family clinicians gather a large amount of information in a relatively short period of time. Furthermore, genograms can increase "mutual trust and tolerance" among all involved in their construction (Sherman, 1993, p. 91). Bowen family therapy "advises people to go 'back, back, back; and up, up, up' their family tree to look for patterns, 'recycling,' getting not just information but a feel for the context and milieu that existed during each person's formative years" (White, 1978, p. 25–26). This process promotes the shift from emotional reactivity to clear cognitions.

Genograms can be color coded to indicate everything from substance abuse to forms of spirituality (Frame, 2000). They can also be multicultural in nature and include an assessment of worldview and cultural factors that influence the behaviors of family members (Thomas, 1998). Data in a genogram is scanned for:

1. "repetitive patterns," such as triangles, cutoffs, and coalitions
2. "coincidences," such as the death of members or the age of symptom onset
3. "the impact of change and untimely life cycle transitions," such as **off-schedule events** (i.e., major life events, such as marriage, death, and the birth of children, occurring at different times than is the norm) (McGoldrick et al., 1999)

Contemporary clinicians have combined genograms with other approaches. Practitioners now use genograms in order to examine intimacy, to treat alcoholism, to work with stepfamilies, to help families resolve issues related to loss, to identify solutions and family strengths, to work with older clients, to work with children and adolescents, to supplement individual counseling with client self-help, and to explore sources of influence and values in career counseling (Magnuson & Shaw, 2003). A popular program for constructing genograms on the Internet is GenoPro, http://www.genopro.com/.

Going Home Again

In going home again, the family therapist instructs the individual client or family members to return home in order to get to know their family of origin better (Bowen, 1976). The idea behind this technique is that with this type of information, individuals can differentiate themselves more clearly. Such a process allows persons to operate more fully within all family contexts of which they are a part. Before returning home, clients may need to practice learning how to remain calm (Bowen, 1976).

Detriangulation

The concept of detriangulation involves "the process of being in contact and emotionally separate" (Kerr, 1988, p. 55). It operates on at least two levels. On one level, a person resolves his or her anxiety over family situations and does not project feelings on to another. At a second level, Bowen therapists help individuals separate themselves from becoming a focus when tension or anxiety arises in the family. Through this procedure, persons do not become targets or scapegoats for others who may be overcome with anxiety. If a person who is usually triangled stays rational during times of emotional stress, he or she seldom becomes the attention of two other people (Bowen, 1972). On both levels, families and their individual members are free to voice their concerns and try out new ways of acting.

Person-to-Person Relationships

In the person-to-person relationships, two family members "relate personally to each other about each other; that is, they do not talk about others (triangling) and do not talk about impersonal issues" (Piercy & Sprenkle, 1986, p. 11). For instance, a father may say to his son: "Your actions remind me of myself when I was your age." In return the son may say: "I really don't know much about you when you were a boy. Tell me about what you did and how you felt when you were my age." Such a process helps promote individuation (autonomy) and intimacy.

Differentiation of Self

"Differentiation of self has to do with the degree to which a person is able to distinguish between the subjective feeling process and the more objective intellectual (thinking) process" (Gibson & Donigian, 1993, p. 28). This procedure may involve all of the preceding techniques plus some confrontation between family members and the therapist.

A failure to differentiate results in **fusion** in which "people are dominated by their automatic emotional system." In fusion, individuals have "less flexibility, less adaptability, and are more emotionally dependent on those around them" (Sauber, L'Abate, & Weeks, 1985, p. 43). They do not have a clear sense of self and others. They are uncomfortable with autonomy in relationships, wish to psychologically merge with another, and have difficulty tolerating differences of opinion (Skowron & Platt, 2005). In close relationships, they "fear being overwhelmed, controlled, or abandoned" (LaSala, 2002, p. 335). Sometimes fused family members move excessive distances from each other or cut off from each other in an attempt to separate. Neither strategy works. Unfortunately, individuals who do not resolve their emotional issues within their families of origin often project such issues onto spouses, resulting in marital distress (Kerr & Bowen, 1988). Over generations, children most involved in family fusion move toward a lower level of differentiation of self (Bowen, 1972).

Asking Questions

In each of the techniques in Bowen family theory, an underlying aspect is to ask questions. From this perspective, asking questions is deemed the "magic bullet" and is a main tool of Bowen therapists. Nodal events, such as deaths, births, and marriages, have an impact on families. For instance, death of family members disturbs the equilibrium of a family, and "emotional shock waves" can be expected as a result (Bowen, 1976). By asking questions, people involved in Bowen family therapy learn to understand the reactions of those in their families better.

Role of the Therapist

In the Bowen model, the differentiation of the therapist is crucial. The Bowen family therapist must maintain a calm presence and be differentiated from his or her family of origin (Friedman, 1991). Objectivity and neutrality are important behavioral characteristics for therapists to display. To be able to work with families, the therapist must first undergo an emotional change (Kerr, 1981). The idea is that, if those who do treatment do not first undergo changes important in family therapy, those they work with will not experience healthy shifts either.

As someone who has personally resolved family-of-origin concerns, the Bowen therapist is usually involved in coaching and teaching (Kerr, 2003). These activities occur on more cognitive levels, initially with family members, primarily individuals or couples, talking to the therapist or to one another through the therapist so that emotional issues do not cloud communication messages.

According to Bowen, therapists should not encourage people to wallow in emotionalism and confusion, but teach them to transcend it by setting examples as reasonable, neutral, self-controlled adults. Therapy should be, in fact, just like a Socratic dialogue, with the teacher or "coach" calmly asking questions, until the student learns to think for him- or herself (Wylie, 1991, p. 27).

In the process of therapy, there is concern with boundary and differentiation issues from an historical perspective. The therapist instructs individuals to search for "clues" as to where the various pressures on the family have been expressed and how effectively the family has adapted to stress since its inception. One way of obtaining this information is for individuals to draw a genogram or to visit their family of origin. Through examining the dynamics in these experiences, therapists become interpreters with their clients in assessing and working through multigenerational patterns of fusion and cutoffs. Unresolved areas of difficulty become resolved.

Process and Outcome

One of the primary outcomes of successful treatment with families from a Bowen standpoint is that family members will understand intergenerational patterns and gain insight into historical circumstances that have influenced the ways they currently interact (Learner, 1983). Furthermore, it is expected that accompanying this knowledge is a focus on changing "intergenerational inferences operating with the current family" (Smith, 1991, p. 25). Changes such as these occur when therapists help family members differentiate from each other and become more diverse and fluid in their interactions (Bowen, 1978). At the end of treatment, issues related to fusion and unconscious relationship patterns should be cleared up. Individuals should be able to relate on an autonomous, cognitive level, and projective patterns of blame should be changed (Kerr & Bowen, 1988). There should be a greater self-differentiation among nuclear family members.

In Bowen family therapy, the chief focus and place where change is emphasized is the individual or couple. The whole family is usually not seen. Instead, individuals are often targeted for treatment, even though the emphasis in this approach is systemic. "A theoretical system that thinks in terms of family, with a therapeutic method that works toward improvement of the family system, is 'family' regardless of the number of people in the sessions" (Kerr, 1981, p. 232). Therefore, by changing one person, a family may be directly influenced for the better.

"Since the two spouses are the two family members most involved in the family ego mass, the most rapid family change occurs when the spouses are able to work as a team in family psychotherapy" (Bowen, 1965, p. 220). The family can improve its functioning when spouses become more cognitively based, although in this process, the therapist may work "with all involved family members present, with any combination of family members present, or with only one family member present" (Bowen, 1965, p. 220).

Unique Aspects of the Bowen Family Therapy Approach

Emphases

Bowen family theory calls attention to family history and the importance of noticing and dealing with past patterns in order to avoid repeating these behaviors in interpersonal relationships. The use of the genogram in plotting historical linkages is a specific tool developed for this purpose. The genogram is increasingly being used by theorists of all persuasions in assessing their client families.

The theory and the therapy of Murray Bowen are extensive, complex, and intertwined. The theory is a blueprint for therapy. Therefore, therapy is consistent with and inseparable from theory. Family therapists are indebted to Bowen for intertwining these two aspects of his approach. He was also insightful and detailed in suggesting the course of working with families. The Georgetown Family Center in Washington, D.C. (http://www.thebowencenter.org/), which he established for educating practitioners in his method, ensures the Bowen approach continues to be learned, used, and refined.

Bowen family therapy is systemic in nature, controlled in focus, and cognitive in practice, thereby giving clinicians and their clients a way of concretely evaluating progress (Bowen, 1975). Unlike many other systemic family approaches, Bowen family therapy can be used extensively with individuals or couples—and it is considered "the most comprehensive theory of individual functioning from a family systems perspective" (Skowron & Platt, 2005, p. 281).

Comparison with Other Theories

Bowen family therapy is a well-established and heuristically appealing approach. Its strong emphasis on theory and its practical nature make it attractive. "Empirical research supports many of the theoretical ideas of Bowen theory" (Miller et al., 2004, p. 462). The theory is not entirely supported, and some feminists criticize the approach for being too male-oriented and politically conservative (Horne & Hicks, 2002). There is also "a lack of research testing Bowen's claim that his theory is universal" (p. 463). In regard to Bowen's intergenerational hypothesis, evidence exists that differentiation is a concept applicable on a multicultural level, for example, with Filipinos and North Americans. However, "psychological well-being in adulthood may well be affected by factors outside of the family, such as peer relationships, employment, or societal influences" (Tuason & Friedlander, 2000, p. 33). Bowen's stress on the importance of the past encourages some families or family members to examine their history rather than deal immediately with present circumstances. Such a process promotes insight before action. Client families in which there are severe dysfunctions or low differentiation of self may benefit most from this emphasis.

Another aspect of Bowen family therapy that makes it unique compared with other approaches is that the theory underlying the approach is its own paradigm (Friedman, 1991). Thus, setting up research questions to refute or verify this way of working with families is a challenging task of the highest order. One way theoretical research is being conducted is by exploring the significance of family-of-origin experiences (Hovestadt, Anderson, Piercy, Cochran, & Fine, 1985).

A final unique angle in regard to Bowen family therapy is the time and, consequently, the money it requires of its clients. Most people cannot afford to invest as heavily in this process as is necessary. As with psychodynamic-oriented therapy, the number of people who can benefit from this approach is limited.

─────────────────── **CASE ILLUSTRATION** ───────────────────

THE COBB FAMILY

Family Background

The Cobb family is a three-generational family composed of the father, David, age 45; mother, Juanita, age 42; son, James, age 16; daughter, Anita, age 12; and maternal grandmother, Lilly, age 65. The maternal grandfather, John, a farmer, died 3 years ago of a heart attack. The paternal grandparents, Dan, a retired banker, age 70, and Ruth, a homemaker, age 68, live in a nearby city. The couple, David and Juanita, have been married for 20 years. Like his father, David is emotionally withdrawn from his family and overinvolved with his job.

In terms of family background, David comes from a middle-class background. He has an older sister, Daisy, who is 3 years his senior. His father has a history of high blood pressure, but his mother is in good health. Juanita was an only child. After 20 years of marriage, her mother, Lilly, almost divorced her father when Juanita was 13 years old. Juanita and her mother have had a close but conflictual relationship since that time, with Lilly coming to live with her daughter after the death of John. At present, Juanita and Lilly take care of the house and children, and David works as a salesperson for a cleaning supply company.

The problem for which the Cobb family has requested help centers around James. Instead of doing well academically and socially, James is failing all his subjects and staying out late at night. He has been arrested once for vagrancy, and David and Juanita suspect he is drinking alcohol and doing drugs. Money from Juanita's purse has been stolen twice in recent weeks. Lilly has written James off as a delinquent. Interestingly enough, he has the same first name as her former lover, who almost ended her marriage. Anita simply ignores James whenever possible. Although she is a good student, her relationship with her mother is conflictual.

Conceptualization of Family: Bowen Perspective

The Cobb family is notable from a Bowen family perspective for several reasons. For one, there is a repeated pattern of mother/daughter conflict over the generations. For another, there is a tendency for men in the family to be emotionally cut off from other family members through withdrawing or rebelling. It is also striking that James has the same name as his maternal grandmother's lover, who almost broke up her marriage of 20 years when Juanita was 13 years old. It appears to be more than coincidental that, during the 20th year of Juanita's marriage, another James has created turmoil in the family's life.

Process of Treatment: Bowen Family Therapy

Treatment of any family from a Bowen family therapy perspective usually involves either an individual or a couple. In the case of the Cobbs, initially, the therapist might help the marital unit make a genogram (see Figure 6.3). The genogram would then be examined by the therapist and the family to denote patterns such as those mentioned previously.

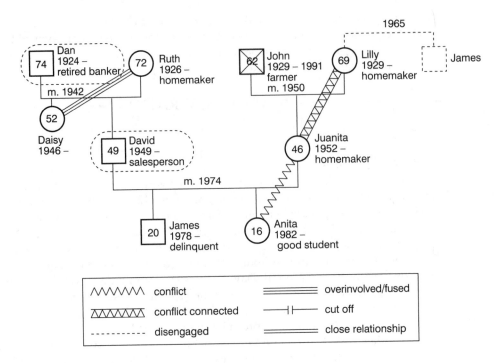

Figure 6.3
Cobb family genogram.

After analysis of family life patterns, the therapist might concentrate with the couple on issues involving detriangulation. For instance, there is a triangle between Lilly, Juanita, and James that works in a dysfunctional way. Likewise, the issues of emotional disengagement would be addressed, such as the ones Dan and David have exemplified. Their lack of involvement in the family has created a parenting void. It is most likely associated with James's present rebellious behavior. Therefore, parenting skills and ways of interacting in parent/child relationships might be stressed, especially as they relate to previous family-of-origin patterns.

To help the Cobb family break out of its present condition, the therapist could have the couple engage in person-to-person conversations on a dyadic basis. This might begin with David and Juanita talking to each other about their marriage. Other person-to-person relationships might be conducted outside of the treatment sessions, with James and Juanita, or Lilly and Juanita, talking with each other. In these exchanges, the asking of cognitively based questions would be encouraged, especially about topics not discussed previously, such as Lilly's affair.

Through these procedures, the family would begin to engage in new behaviors that were less blaming, conflictual, or withdrawn. Appropriate ways of interrelating could then be set in motion, with family members interacting from a position of differentiation.

Summary and Conclusion

Psychodynamic and Bowen family therapies are two of the most established approaches to working with families. Psychodynamic family therapy was first developed by Nathan Ackerman, who applied the principles of individual psychoanalysis to families. In doing so, he made the treatment of families more respectable and prevalent among psychiatrists. Murray Bowen, a psychoanalytically trained psychiatrist, devised his own approach to working with families, especially couples, based in part on his life experiences and in part on psychoanalytic theory.

Both psychodynamic theory and Bowen theory emphasize the importance of unconscious forces in family life. Psychodynamically oriented family therapy, however, is an eclectic mix of psychoanalysis and systems concepts that sometimes make it more linear in its stress on working with individuals in families. Bowen theory is systemic, although its primary clients are individuals and couples. It emphasizes the importance of looking at historical intergenerational patterns. Moreover, the Bowen approach uses a cognitive strategy to help couples and family members differentiate; psychodynamic family therapy is insight-oriented. In both approaches, the therapist acts as a coach, a teacher, and a catalyst, although the content and unit of treatment, as well as final end results, differ.

Overall, both approaches are in-depth and concentrate on long-term results. They emphasize the unconscious and require a considerable investment of time and resources. Bowen theory is concrete in outcome and gives its clients a way to recognize dysfunctional patterns transmitted across generations (i.e., a genogram). On the other hand, psychodynamic theory provides its recipients with a way to work through issues that frees them from relying on defense mechanisms. Each theory can be beneficially utilized by some client families/individuals.

Summary Table

Psychodynamic and Bowen Family Therapies

Common Characteristics of Psychodynamic and Bowen Theories

Both theories are conceptual and comprehensive. They emphasize the importance of historical, social, and childhood experiences and stress the significance of unconscious forces in the lives of families.

The founders of the two approaches were trained as psychoanalytical therapists.

Each theory has developed its own terminology.

Both treatments may be long-term (over 20 sessions).

Psychodynamic Family Therapy

Major Theorists

Sigmund Freud, Nathan Ackerman, Ivan Boszormenyi-Nagy, James Framo, Theodore Lidz, Donald Williamson, Norman Paul, Lyman Wynne, and A. C. Robin Skynner.

Premises of the Theory

Unconscious processes link family members and influence individuals in the decisions about whom they marry. Objects, significant others in one's life, are identified with or rejected.

Unconscious forces must be worked through, and "interlocking pathologies" must be broken up.

Treatment Techniques

The individual or the individuals within a family are the units of treatment.

The goals of treatment are to break dysfunctional interactions within the family based on unconscious processes and to resolve individual dysfunctionality.

The therapeutic techniques include transference, dream analysis, confrontation, focusing on strengths, and life history.

Role of the Therapist

The therapist is the teacher (especially of terms), "good enough mother" (or "parent"), and interpreter of experience.

Process and Outcome

Help family members work through unconscious restrictions and insights.
Assist family members to interact on the basis of current realities.

Unique Aspects of Psychodynamic Family Therapy

The psychodynamic approach emphasizes:
- the potency of the unconscious in influencing human behavior
- defense mechanisms and the part they play in family relations
- an in-depth historical perspective on the development of problems and a treatment of dysfunctionality that is thorough
- an attachment of people to objects (i.e., other people)

Comparison with Other Theories

Compared with other approaches, psychodynamic therapy:
- offers a treatment that is primarily linear and limited more to individuals than families
- offers a treatment that is costly in regard to both time and money
- is not appropriate for concrete thinkers or those who want immediate results
- lacks traditional empirical research and is reliant on case history reports

Bowen Family Therapy

Major Theorists

Murray Bowen, Michael Kerr, and Ed Friedman.

Premises of the Theory

Theory and therapy are the same.
Family patterns are likely to repeat.

It is important to differentiate oneself from one's family of origin.

Uncontrolled anxiety results in family dysfunctionality.

The formation of triangles is a key manifestation of uncontrolled anxiety.

Treatment Techniques

The individual or the couple is the unit of treatment.

The goals of treatment are to prevent triangulation and help couples and individuals relate more on a cognitive, as opposed to an emotional, level, and to stop dysfunctional, repetitive, intergenerational patterns of family relations.

The therapeutic techniques include genograms, going home again, detriangulation, person-to-person relationships, differentiation of self, and asking questions.

Role of the Therapist

The therapist is a differentiated person who acts as a coach and teacher and concentrates on boundary and differentiation issues.

Process and Outcome

Help family members to become more differentiated and fluid in their interactions.

Assist family members in therapy to be more cognitive and understand intergenerational patterns better.

Unique Aspects of the Bowen Family Therapy Approach

The Bowen approach emphasizes:
- intergenerational relationships and the nature of repeating patterns
- an in-depth theory of family relationships
- a systemic and cognitive theory that provides a concrete evaluation of progress

Comparison with Other Theories

Compared with other approaches, Bowen therapy:
- stresses the importance of the past, thereby encouraging some families or family members to examine history and not deal with present circumstances
- is difficult to research
- requires a high degree of investment in time and money

Experiential Family Therapy

———————●———————

My father tells me
my mother is slowing down.
He talks deliberately and with deep feelings
as stoop-shouldered he walks to his garden
behind the garage.

My mother informs me
about my father's failing health.
"Not as robust as before," she explains,
"Lower energy than in his 50s."
Her concerns arise
as she kneads dough for biscuits.

Both express their fears to me
as we view the present from the past.
In love, and with measured anxiety,
I move with them into new patterns.

———————●———————

Gladding, 1992b

he experiential branch of family therapy emerged out of the humanistic-existential psychology movement of the 1960s—and was most popular when it was new. Some of its proponents and creators drew heavily from Gestalt therapy, psychodrama, client-centered therapy, and the encounter-group movement of the time. The emphasis is on immediate, here-and-now, intrapsychic experiences of people as opposed to historical information. Concepts such as encounter, process, growth, spontaneity, and action are emphasized. Theory and abstract factors are minimized. The quality of ongoing experiences in the family is the criterion for measuring psychological health and for deciding whether or not to make therapeutic interventions.

Experiential family therapy, which has a number of forms, emphasizes **affect**, that is, emotions. Awareness and expression of feelings are considered the means to both personal and family fulfillment. Professionals who operate from this perspective consider the expression of affect to be a universal medium in which all can share. The expression of feelings in a clear and effective way is encouraged (Kane, 1994). A healthy family is a family where people openly experience life with each other in a lively manner. Such a family supports and encourages a wide range of emotions and personal encounters. In contrast, dysfunctional families resist taking affective risks, and members are rigid in their interactions. They do not know how to empathize with one another and reflect feelings.

Major Theorists

A number of professionals have contributed significantly to the development of experiential family therapy. Among the most notable are David Kantor, Frank Duhl, Bunny Duhl, Virginia Satir, Carl Whitaker, Bernard Guerney, Louise Guerney, Walter Kempler, Augustus Napier, Leslie Greenberg, Susan Johnson, and David Keith. Virginia Satir and Carl Whitaker are examined here as representatives of this approach.

Virginia Satir

Virginia Satir (1916–1988) was born and raised on a Wisconsin farm. She was extraordinarily different from others even at an early age. At 3, she had learned to read, and "by the time she was 11, she had reached her adult height of nearly six feet" (Simon, 1989, p. 37). Although she was sickly and missed a lot of school, she was a good student and began her college experience after only 7.5 years of formal education. Her initial goal, which she achieved, was to become a schoolteacher. "Growing up a big, awkward, sickly child, Satir drew from her experience of being an outsider" and developed an acute sensitivity for others (Simon, 1989, p. 37). This quality eventually led her from the classroom to social work with families.

Satir entered private practice as a social worker in 1951 in Chicago. This venture came after 6 years of teaching school and 9 years of clinical work in an agency. Her unique approach to working with families evolved from her treatment of a schizophrenic young woman whose mother threatened to sue her when the young woman improved. Instead of becoming defensive, Satir invited the mother to join the therapy and worked with them until they reached communication congruence (Satir, 1986). She then invited the father and oldest son into treatment until the family had achieved a balance.

Satir was influenced by Murray Bowen's and Don Jackson's work with schizophrenic families, and in 1959 she was invited by Jackson and his colleagues to help set up the Mental Research Institute (MRI) in Palo Alto, California. From her clinical work and interaction with other professionals there, she refined her approach to working with families, which was simultaneously folksy and complex. "Satir was the archetypal nurturing therapist in a field enamored of abstract concepts and strategic maneuvers. Her warmth and genuineness gave her a tremendous appeal" (Nichols & Schwartz, 2004, p. 205). At the core of Satir's approach was "her unshakable conviction about people's potential for growth and the respectful role helpers need to assume in the process of change" (Simon, 1989, p. 38).

Satir gained international attention in 1964 with the publication of her first book, *Conjoint Family Therapy*. The clarity of her writing made the text a classic and put Satir in demand as a workshop presenter. She continued to write and demonstrate her "process model of therapy" (Satir, 1982) until her death. Among her many contributions were a strong, charismatic leadership (Beels & Ferber, 1969); a simple but eloquent view of effective and ineffective communication patterns (Satir, 1972; Satir & Baldwin, 1983); and a humanistic concern about building self-worth and self-esteem in all people. "She also pioneered the concept of actively engaging couples and families in exercises during and between sessions" (Kaplan, 2000, p. 6). She conducted much of her work using structured experiential exercises (Woods & Martin, 1984).

Satir is often described as a master of communication and even as an originator of family **communications theory** (an approach that focuses on clarifying transactions among family members). During her lifetime she worked with more than 5,000 families, often in **group family therapy** where she saw a number of unrelated families at one time in a joint family session. She also demonstrated her skills and her approach before hundreds of audiences (Satir & Bitter, 2000). She genuinely believed that healthy families are able to be reciprocal and open in their sharing of feelings and affection. Satir died in 1988 at the age of 72. Today her model of working with families is often referred to as **communication/validation family therapy**.

Carl Whitaker

Carl Whitaker (1912–1995) grew up on a dairy farm in upstate New York. With few exceptions, his nuclear family was his "entire social existence" (Simon, 1985, p. 32). He was shy, and when his family moved to Syracuse in 1925, he felt awkward and out of place. He attributed his ability to stay sane and adjust to two "cotherapists"—two fellow students with whom he made friends, one the smartest and the other the most popular student in the school (Whitaker, 1989).

Whitaker entered medical school in 1932, penniless but with a sound work ethic and a bent toward public service. He had originally planned to specialize in obstetrics and gynecology, but a tragic operation on a patient who died, even though his surgery was perfect, proved to be a turning point in Whitaker's life. It influenced him to switch to psychiatry during the last year of his residency and to concentrate his attention on working with schizophrenics. Toward the end of his medical training in 1937, Whitaker married and he and his wife raised six children over the years.

Whitaker developed the essence of his approach to therapy while assigned to Oak Ridge, Tennessee, during World War II (Whitaker, 1990). There he saw as many as 12 patients a day in half-hour sessions. He did not have any mentors and basically taught himself psychiatric procedures. From his experience, he realized he needed a cotherapist in order to be effective. He also experimented during this time with the technique of using the spontaneous unconscious in therapy (Whitaker & Keith, 1981).

"The turning point in Whitaker's career came in 1946 when he was named chairman of the Department of Psychiatry at Emory University" at age 34 (Simon, 1985, p. 33). It was at

Emory in Atlanta, Georgia, that Whitaker hired supportive colleagues, increased his work with schizophrenic patients, and began developing his own freewheeling style. He was dismissed from Emory in 1956 and went into private practice with his colleagues in Atlanta. In 1965, he accepted a faculty position at the University of Wisconsin's Department of Psychiatry, where he stayed until his retirement in 1982. During the Wisconsin years, Whitaker devoted his efforts almost entirely to families and served as a mentor to young practitioners, such as Augustus Napier, who coauthored with him one of the best-selling books in the field of family therapy, *The Family Crucible* (1978). Also during this time, Whitaker traveled extensively, giving workshops on family therapy.

"More than with most well-known therapists, it is difficult to separate Whitaker's therapeutic approach from his personality" (Simon, 1985, p. 34). As a family therapist, Whitaker was quite intuitive, spontaneous, and unstructured. His surname, derived from *Witakarlege* (meaning a wizard or witch), has prompted at least one writer (Keith, 1987) to put Whitaker in a class of his own. Yet Whitaker focused on some therapeutic elements that are universal. His main contribution to family therapy was in the uninhibited and emotional way he worked with families by teasing them "to be in contact with their absurdity" (Simon, 1984, p. 28). He used the term **absurdity** to refer to half-truthful statements that are silly if followed out to their natural conclusion (Whitaker, 1975). He likened the use of absurdity to the Leaning Tower of Pisa, which, if built high enough, would eventually fall.

Whitaker accomplished his tasks in family therapy by being spontaneous, especially in dealing with the unconscious, and by highlighting the absurd. He influenced family members to interact with each other in unique and new ways. For example, Whitaker once encouraged a boy and his father, who were having a dispute over who had the most control in the family, to arm wrestle, with the winner of the match becoming the winner of the argument. Obviously, the flaw in such a method, that is, its absurdity, was crucial to Whitaker in helping the family gain insight and tolerance.

Regardless of what he suggested on the spur of the moment, Whitaker refused to become involved in giving families overt directives for bringing about change. He was a "Don Quixote" who challenged people to examine their own view of reality and the idea that they can be in control of their lives apart from others in the family (Simon, 1984, p. 28).

In general, Whitaker (1989) emphasized uncovering and utilizing the unconscious life of the family. He related to some of the psychoanalytic dimensions of other family therapy pioneers. However, in contrast to this connection, Whitaker focused on helping the family live more fully in the present. Since 1988 his approach has been labeled **symbolic-experiential family therapy**. In this position, he assumed that experience, not education, changes families. The main function of the cerebral cortex is inhibition. Thus, most of our experience goes on outside of our consciousness. We gain best access to it symbolically. For us "symbolic" implies that some thing or some process has more than one meaning. While education can be immensely helpful, the covert process of the family is the one that contains the most power for potential changing (Keith & Whitaker, 1982, p. 43).

Whitaker died at age 83 on April 21, 1995, after an illness of 2 years.

Premises of the Theory

The underlying premise of the experiential approach is that individuals in families are not aware of their emotions, or if they are aware of their emotions, they suppress them. Because of this tendency not to feel or express feelings, a climate of emotional deadness is created which results in the expression of symptoms within one or more family members. In this type of atmosphere, family members avoid each other and occupy themselves with work and other nonfamily activities (Satir, 1972). These types of behaviors perpetuate the dysfunctionality of the family further in a downward spiral.

The resolution to this situation is to emphasize sensitivity and feeling-expression among family members and within the family itself. This type of expression can come verbally, but often it is expressed in an affective or behavioral nonverbal manner. For instance, family members in therapy may represent the distance they wish to maintain between themselves and other family members by using role play, mime, or even arranging physical objects, such as furniture, in a particular way.

Regardless of how relationships are enacted or represented, it is crucial that emphasis be placed on the present. The experiential family therapy approach concentrates on increasing self-awareness among family members "through action in the here-and-now" (Costa, 1991, p. 122). Interpersonal skills are also taught directly and indirectly. The theoretical roots of this treatment are humanistic and phenomenological in origin. Moreover, even though it is usually not acknowledged, **attachment theory** is a major component of the experiential approach, especially in regard to Satir's understanding of interactional behavior and deficits in self-esteem (Simon, 2004).

Treatment Techniques

Experiential family therapists "can be divided into two groups in regard to therapeutic techniques" (Costa, 1991, p. 121). A few clinicians (e.g., Carl Whitaker) rely more "on their own personality, spontaneity, and creativity" (Costa, 1991, p. 121). The effectiveness of experiential family therapy depends on the personhood of the therapist (Kempler, 1968). However, the majority of experiential therapists (e.g., Virginia Satir, Peggy Papp, Frank and Bunny Duhl, Bernard and Louise Guerney) employ highly structured activities such as sculpting and choreography. Experiential family therapists who use techniques usually find procedures that are congruent with or extensions of their personalities.

Therapists Who Use Few Techniques: Carl Whitaker

Experiential family therapists who do not consider techniques important may advocate at least a few of these processes in conjunction with the use of their personality. Carl Whitaker advocates seven different active interventions that aid the therapeutic process (Keith & Whitaker, 1982):

1. *Redefine symptoms as efforts for growth:* The experientialists, especially Satir, believe that all behavior is oriented toward growth, even though it may look otherwise (Walsh & McGraw, 2002). By viewing symptoms in this way, therapists help families see previously unproductive behaviors as meaningful. Families and therapists are able to evaluate symptoms as ways families have tried to develop more fully.

2. *Model fantasy alternatives to real-life stress:* Sometimes change is fostered by going outside the realm of the expected or conventional. Modeling fantasy alternatives is one way of assessing whether or not client families' ideas will work. The modeling may be done through role play by either therapists or families.

3. *Separate interpersonal stress and intrapersonal stress:* **Interpersonal stress** is generated between two or more family members. **Intrapersonal stress** is developed from

within an individual. Both types of stresses may be present in families, but it is important to distinguish between them, because there are often different ways of resolving them (e.g., face-to-face interactions versus muscle relaxation exercises).

4. *Add practical bits of intervention:* Sometimes family members need practical or concrete information to make needed changes. Adolescents may find it beneficial to know that their fathers struggled in achieving their own identity. Such information helps teenagers who are confused feel more "normal." They may be further assisted through finding that there are career tests they can take to help them sort out their preferences.

5. *Augment the despair of a family member:* Augmenting the despair of a family member means to enlarge or magnify his or her feelings so that other family members, and the family as a whole, understand them better. When families have difficulties, they often deny that any of their members are in pain. In addition, family members may suppress their feelings. Augmenting despair prevents the occurrence of such denial or suppression.

6. *Promote affective confrontation:* As mentioned earlier, a major premise of the experiential approach and those associated with it is its emphasis on the primacy of emotion. Therefore, in confronting, therapists often direct family members to examine their feelings before exploring their behaviors.

7. *Treat children like children and not like peers:* A major emphasis of the experiential approach is to play with children and treat them in an age-appropriate manner. Although children are valued as a part of the therapeutic process, they are treated differently from the rest of a family.

Therapists Who Use Structured Techniques: Virginia Satir

Among the most widely used structured therapeutic responses are those that were originated by Virginia Satir. They include modeling of effective communication using "I" messages, sculpting, choreography, humor, touch, props, and family reconstruction (Satir, Stachowiak, & Taschman, 1975). These techniques are frequently employed in order to increase family members' awareness and to alter their relationships (Duhl, Kantor, & Duhl, 1973; Jefferson, 1978).

Modeling of Effective Communication Using "I" Messages

In dysfunctional families, members often speak in the first-person plural (i.e., "we"); give unclear and nonspecific messages; and tend to respond to others with monologues (Stoltz-Loike, 1992). In response to her daughter, a mother might drone on about her daughter's behavior by saying: "Someone is going to get angry unless you do something good quickly."

To combat such ineffective and indirect communication patterns, experiential family therapists insist that family members take "I" positions when expressing their feelings. In response to the situation just given, a mother might say to her daughter: "I feel discouraged when you do not respond to my requests."

"I" statements involve the expression of feelings in a personal and responsible way and encourage others to express their opinions. This type of communication also promotes **leveling** or congruent communication, in which straight, genuine, and real expressions of one's feelings and wishes are made in an appropriate context. When leveling and congruence occur, communication increases, stereotyping decreases, and self-esteem and self-worth improve (Satir,

1972). When leveling does not occur, Satir states that people adopt four other roles: blamer, placater, distractor, and computer (or rational analyzer). These four roles are used by most individuals at one time or another. They can be helpful in some situations, but when they become a consistent way of interacting, they become problematic and dysfunctional.

Blamer

A **blamer** is one who attempts to place the focus on others and not take responsibility for what is happening. This style of communication is often done from a self-righteous stance and is loud and tyrannical. A blamer might make this type of statement: "Now, see what you made me do!" or "It's your fault." In blaming, a person may also point his or her finger in a scolding and lecturing position.

Placater

A **placater** is one who avoids conflict at the cost of his or her integrity. This type of stance is one that is self-effacing and apologetic. It originates out of timidity and an eagerness to please. A placater might say in response to something with which he or she disagrees, "That's fine," or "It's okay."

Distractor

A **distractor** is one who says and makes irrelevant statements "that direct attention away from the issues under discussion" (O'Halloran & Weiner, 2005, p. 183). This type of person tries to be evasive and elusive and does not seem to be in contact with anything that is going on. For instance, when a family is talking about the importance of saving money and being thrifty, a distractor might try to tell a joke, say something flippant, or even walk around looking out the windows and calling the family over to look at a stray cat or a passing car.

Computer (or Rational Analyzer)

A **computer** (or **rational analyzer**) is one who interacts only on a cognitive or intellectual level and acts in a super-reasonable way. This type of person avoids becoming emotional and stays detached. In a situation where the person playing this role is asked how he or she feels, the response might be: "Different people have different feelings about this circumstance. I think it is difficult to say how one feels without first looking at what one's thoughts are."

To help family members level and become congruent, Satir (1988) sometimes incorporated a technique known as the **communication stance**. In this procedure, family members are asked to exaggerate the physical positions of their perspective roles. A blamer may be asked to make an angry face, bend over as in scolding, and point a finger at the person he or she is attacking. This process promotes an increase in awareness of what is being done and how it is being conveyed. Feelings may surface in the process. The result may be a conversation on alternative ways of interacting, which could lead to practicing new ways of opening up.

Sculpting

In **sculpting**, "family members are molded during the therapy session into positions symbolizing their actual relationships as seen by one or more members of the family" (Sauber, L'Abate, & Weeks, 1985, p. 147). Past events and patterns that affect the family now are perceptually set up. The idea is to expose outgrown family rules and clarify early misconceptions so that family members and the family, as a whole, can get on with life. For example, a historic scene of a father's involvement with a television program and his neglect of his son might be shown through having the father sit close to an imaginary television and the son sit isolated in a corner. The point is that, in this still-life portrait of time, family members and the therapist gain a clearer view of family relationships. Often the therapist plays the part of the person setting up the scene. Sculpting consists of four steps and their accompanying roles (Duhl et al., 1973; Moreno & Elefthery, 1975):

1. *Setting the scene:* The therapist helps the sculptor identify a scene to explore.
2. *Choosing role players:* Individuals are chosen to portray family members.
3. *Creating a sculpture:* The sculptor places each person in a specific metaphorical position spatially.
4. *Processing the sculpture:* The sculptor and other participants derole and debrief about experiences and insights acquired through engaging in this exercise.

Choreography

In **choreography**, family members are asked to symbolically enact a pattern or a sequence in their relationship to one another. This process is similar to mime or a "silent movie." Through it, family members come to see and feel alliances and distances that are not obvious through merely discussing problem situations (Papp, 1976).

In a family with an overinvolved mother and an underinvolved father, members may be asked to act out a typical scene showing this dynamic at a certain time of the day such as breakfast. Each family member then takes a turn positioning other family members in certain spatial relationships to one another. A daughter might have her father turn the pages of a newspaper and sit away from her while her mother heaps cereal into the daughter's bowl and/or straightens the daughter's hair or dress. At the same time, the daughter may lean toward her father and push away her mother.

Such scenes should be reenacted three or four times so that family members get a good feeling for what certain experiences are like from the perspectives of other family members. Then, the family and the therapist can sit down and discuss what has occurred and what family members would like to have happen. In many cases, new scenes are created and acted out (Papp, 1976).

Humor

Creating **humor** within a family therapy session is a risky proposition. If successful, humor can reduce tension and promote insight. Laughter and the confusion that goes with it create an open environment for change to take place (Whitaker & Keith, 1981). If unsuccessful, attempts at humor may alienate the family or some of its members. Therefore, creating humor is an art form that is carefully employed by some experiential family therapists.

Humor is often initiated with families by pointing out the absurdity of their rigid positions or relabeling a situation to make it seem less serious (Carter & McGoldrick-Orfanidis, 1976). In regard to absurdity, a mother might say to a therapist, for example, that she "will die" if her daughter is late for curfew again. A humorous response by the family therapist might be: "Take it easy on your mother. Just paralyze her arm next time."

If the therapist is really into acting out the absurdity, he or she might then ask the daughter to show how she would go about paralyzing her mother's arm. In the interaction following such a strange request, the therapist would probably even engage the mother to help her daughter in such a process. The idea behind this request is to help everyone recognize the distorted power given up by the mother to her daughter. If such insight into this absurdity is developed, a more functional mother/daughter relationship can be formed.

Touch

Virginia Satir, Carl Whitaker, and Walter Kempler are the best known practitioners, among prominent historical experiential therapists, for their use of **touch** as a communicative tool in family therapy. Touch may be putting one's arms around another, patting a person on the shoulder, shaking hands, or even, in an extreme case, wrestling (Napier & Whitaker, 1978). In using touch, experiential family therapists are careful not to violate the personal boundaries of their clients. Physical touch is representative of caring and concern. It loses its potency if it is employed inappropriately or if it is overused.

Props

Props are materials used to represent behaviors or to illustrate the impact of actions. Virginia Satir was well-known for using props, such as ropes and blindfolds, in her work with families (Satir & Baldwin, 1983). Props may be metaphorical, as well as literal. A rope may represent how family members are connected to each other. In her work with the family, Satir sometimes tied ends of the rope around all members' waists and selectively asked them to move. This way the entire family could experience being tied to one other. They also got a feel for how the movement of one family member influenced the rest of the family (Murray & Rotter, 2002).

After the props are used, the therapist might ask the family to process the experience and then relate how the experience is similar to and/or different from the dynamics in their present family relationship.

Family Reconstruction

Family reconstruction is a therapeutic innovation developed by Satir in the late 1960s. The purpose of family reconstruction is to help family members discover dysfunctional patterns in their lives stemming from their families of origin. It concentrates on (1) revealing to family members the sources of their old learning, (2) enabling family members to develop a more realistic picture of who their parents are as persons, and (3) setting up ways for family members to discover their own personhood.

Family reconstruction begins with a "**star**" or "**explorer**" (i.e., a central character) who maps his or her family of origin in visually representative ways (Nerin, 1986; Satir, Bitter, & Krestensen, 1988). A **guide** (usually the therapist) can help the star or explorer chart a chronological account of significant family events from paternal, maternal, and family-of-origin histories. The process of family reconstruction attempts to uncover facts about the origin of distorted learning, about parents as people, and about the person as a separate self. "Family maps, the family life fact chronology, and the wheel of influence (Satir & Baldwin, 1983) are the points of entry, the tools, for a family reconstruction" (Satir et al., 1988, p. 202).

1. *Family map:* As shown in Figure 7.1, a **family map** is "a visual representation of the structure of three generations of the star's family" (Satir et al., 1988, p. 202), with adjectives to describe each family member's personality. Circles represent people on the map and lines suggest relationships within the family.

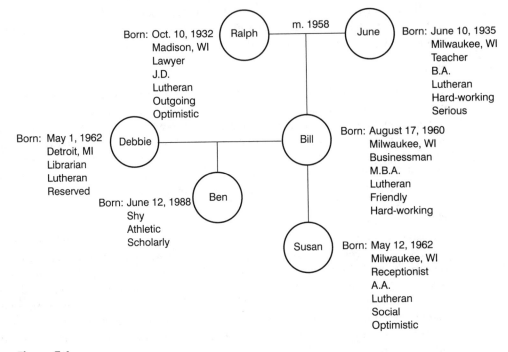

Figure 7.1
Basic family map of a star.

From "Family Reconstruction: The Family Within-a-Group Experience" by V. Satir, J. R. Bitter, and K. K. Krestensen, 1988, *Journal for Specialists in Group Work, 13*, p. 202. © ACA. Reprinted with permission. No further reproduction authorized without written permission of the American Counseling Association.

2. *Family life fact chronology:* The **family life fact chronology** is the next tool employed in family reconstruction (see Figure 7.2).

    The star creates the chronology by listing all significant events in his or her life and that of the extended family. Chronologies begin with the births of each set of grandparents. All events having an impact on the people in the family, including all significant comings and goings, are then listed in order. "The family life fact chronology includes the demographic information already on the family map as well as a record of such events as illnesses, geographical moves from one place to another, a father going off to war, a sister's teenage pregnancy, or the long-term alcoholism of a family member. When appropriate, historical events associated with given dates are noted to ground the event in time and place" (Satir et al., 1988, p. 203).

3. *Wheel or circle of influence:* A **wheel** or **circle of influence** representing those who have been important to the star or explorer is the final tool employed in family reconstruction (see Figure 7.3). The star is shown in the middle of those who have had either positive or negative impacts on him or her. A spoke is drawn for every relationship important to the star. The thicker the line, the more important or closer the relationship. "When completed, the wheel of influence displays the star's internalized strengths and weaknesses, the resources on which he or she may rely for new and, it is hoped, more effective ways of coping" (Satir et al., 1988, p. 205).

Date	Event	Relation	Location
Paternal			
1–1–1918	John S. born	Star's paternal grandfather	Hastings, MN
2–27–1921	Martha R. born to rich family	Star's paternal grandmother	Minneapolis, MN
1941	John S. is 4F	Star's paternal grandfather	Minnesota draft board
1944?	John S. courts & wins rich man's daughter; married Martha R.	Star's paternal grandparents	Minneapolis, MN war in Europe
8–8–1946	Thomas born	Star's father	Minneapolis, MN
10–1–1946	John S. goes to work for father-in-law	Star's paternal grandfather	Minneapolis, MN
4–18–1949	Sam S. born	Star's paternal uncle	Minneapolis, MN
Maternal			
12–4–1918	Hugh G. born	Star's maternal grandfather	Homer, NY
10–9–1930	Emma B. born	Star's maternal grandmother	Oshkosh, WI
1943	Hugh seriously wounded in war & returns home	Star's maternal grandfather	Homer, NY
12–1–1947	Janice born out of wedlock	Star's mother	Milwaukee, WI
5–1–1948	Hugh moves to start sales job; meets Emma 1st day	Star's maternal grandfather	Oshkosh, WI
9–9–1948	Hugh marries Emma	Star's maternal grandparents	Milwaukee, WI
1949?	Hugh, Emma, & Janice move to escape gossip	Star's mother's family	Saint Paul, MN
Family of Origin			
9–22–1961	Thomas & Jan meet and fall in love	Star's parents	Minneapolis, MN
9–22–1968	Thomas & Jan marry	Star's parents	Minneapolis, MN
3–9–1970	Annie is born	Star	Mankato, MN
2–3–1979	Thomas & Jan divorce	Star's parents	Mankato, MN
1–1–1982	Thomas dies of sudden heart attack	Star's father	Mankato, MN
9–5–1987	Annie enters college; lives at home with mom	Star	Mankato, MN

Figure 7.2
Reconstruction of the star's family.

From "Family Reconstruction: The Family Within-a-Group Experience" by V. Satir, J. R. Bitter, and K. K. Krestensen, 1988, *Journal for Specialists in Group Work, 13,* p. 204. © ACA. Reprinted with permission. No further reproduction authorized without written permission of the American Counseling Association.

Figure 7.3
Wheel of influence.

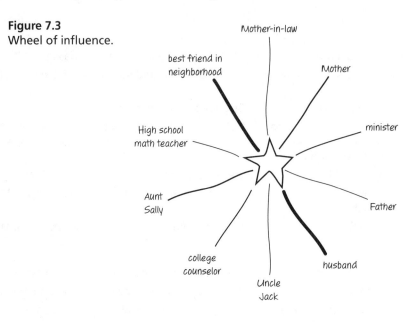

The final aspect of family reconstruction is to have the star or explorer give life to the events that he or she has discovered. This is done by working with a group of at least 10 people, aided by a leader guide (i.e., a therapist), to enact important family scenes. Members of the group play key figures in the star's life or the life of his or her family. The idea behind this procedure is to help the star or explorer gain a new perspective on family characteristics and patterns. "It is a time when significant questions can receive straight answers, when old, distorted messages can be cleared up, and when understanding can replace judgment and blame" (Satir et al., 1988, p. 207).

Other Experiential Techniques

In addition to Whitaker's procedures and Satir's techniques, experiential family therapists may use other ways of working with families. These include play therapy, filial therapy, family drawings (Bing, 1970) and family puppet interviews (Duhl et al., 1973).

Play Therapy

Play therapy is a general term for a variety of therapeutic interventions that use play media as the basis for communicating and working with children (Johnson, Bruhn, Winek, Krepps, & Wiley, 1999). In child-centered play therapy, which is based on the humanistic theory of Carl Rogers, the therapist accepts the child unconditionally and allows the child complete freedom of expression. In this process, the child explores feelings and relationships with the therapist and comes to resolution of troubling matters in his or her life over time. In experiential family therapy, play therapy is usually done within the context of a family session.

Filial Therapy

Filial therapy is a unique approach used by therapists trained in play therapy "to train parents to be therapeutic agents with their own children through a format of didactic instruction, demonstration play sessions, required at-home laboratory play sessions and supervision" (Watts & Broaddus, 2002, p. 372). As such, filial therapy is a hybrid form of child-centered play therapy in which parents (or other primary caregivers) engage in play therapy with their own children (Guerney & Guerney, 1994). The aim of filial therapy is to address the child's problems in the context of the parent–child relationship, effecting changes in parent–child interactions (Johnson et al., 1999). In filial therapy, the family therapist can work with parents in groups where parents can give and receive feedback and suggestions (Guerney, 1991), or they can work with individual families (VanFleet, 1994).

Research on filial therapy shows that it is effective in training parents to "acquire reflective listening skills, to allow children self-direction, to demonstrate involvement in children's emotional expression and behavior" and to maintain these positive changes long term (Johnson et al., 1999, p. 171). Generally, filial therapy equips parents to handle emotional expression and problems with their children better and to reduce parenting stress for couples. It focuses on building "the kind of relationship where the child feels safe enough to play out problems … and to express … emotions fully through symbolic expression" (Watts & Broaddus, 2002, p. 374).

Family Drawings

Experiential family therapists have at their disposal many variations on the technique of family drawings. One is the joint family scribble in which each family member makes a brief scribble. After these scribbles have been made, the whole family incorporates their scribbles collectively into a unified picture (Kwiatkowska, 1967). In this procedure, family members get a feel for what it is to work both individually and together. The advantages and disadvantages of each can be talked about, as well as what was produced in each case.

Another drawing approach is known as conjoint family drawing. In this procedure, families are given the instruction to "draw a picture as you see yourself as a family" (Bing, 1970). Each member of the family makes such a drawing and then shares through discussion the perceptions that emerge. A younger son might see his older brother as being closer to their parents. His drawing would reflect this spatial difference. On the other hand, a parent in the same family might see all the family members as being equally close to one another and portray that perception in his or her drawing.

Still another type of family drawing is the **symbolic drawing of family life space** (Geddes & Medway, 1977). In this projective technique, the therapist draws a large circle and instructs family members to include within the circle everything that represents the family and to place outside of the circle those people and institutions that are not a part of the family. After this series of drawings, the family is asked to symbolically arrange themselves, through drawing, within a large circle, according to how they relate to one another. An example of symbolic drawing of family life space is shown in Figure 7.4.

Discussion should follow all of these types of drawing techniques. Family members can discuss what was drawn and why, as well as the dynamics of their life, as seen from the perspective of the individual members and the family as a whole. Different ways of interacting can be explored with the therapist and illustrated in another drawing.

Puppet Interviews

In this procedure, the therapist asks one of the family members to make up a story using puppets (Irwin & Malloy, 1975). The idea is that family difficulties can be displayed in the story, and the therapist can gain valuable insight in an indirect manner. In the case, for example, of

Figure 7.4
Symbolic drawing of family life space.

a 4-year-old girl who is having nightmares, the story might be one of a child who is taken by a witch to a land of dragons, where she is constantly threatened and helpless. Actual circumstances could relate to the child's day-care arrangement in which personnel are scaring children into behaving. Through acting out the scene with puppets, the child can begin to feel safe enough to talk about what is happening in real life.

Family therapists who utilize this process need to be sure they have a variety of puppets for family members to use—and this technique is limited in actual practice. Adults may resist expressing themselves through puppets because they prefer verbal interaction. Children may make up stories that have little or no relationship to what is occurring in their actual lives. A puppet technique, however, can be employed effectively in situations in which young children, shy children, or selectively mute children are being treated who will not or cannot relate much about family dynamics in other ways.

Role of the Therapist

From the less structured tradition, an experiential family therapist assumes the role of active participant, a whole person—not a director or teacher. To be effective in this capacity, the therapist can use a cotherapist. According to Whitaker and other symbolic-experiential therapists, the presence of a cotherapist allows greater utilization of intuition (Napier & Whitaker, 1978).

Experiential family therapists who follow Whitaker's lead at times engage in spontaneous and absurd activities, such as falling asleep in a therapy session or having a dream about a family and reporting back to the family what they dreamed. This use of the absurd can result in raised emotions, anxiety, and, often, insight (Keeney, 1986). It can also break down rational defenses.

The role of the experiential family therapist from the more structured tradition is best described as that of being a facilitator and resource person. In these roles, therapists help family members understand themselves and others better. Furthermore, they help families discover their innate abilities and help promote clear communication (Simon, 1989). The therapist makes use of himself or herself in interacting with the family (Mitten & Connell, 2004). Thus, "the therapist enters into relationship with each of the family members, uses his or her feelings as guides toward intervention, and models effective interactional styles" (Kane, 1994, p. 256). More structured experiential family therapists use props or other objects, too, as representations or illustrations of distances and interaction patterns between people in families (Satir & Baldwin, 1983).

Generally, experiential therapists try to assist family members in discovering their individuality and in finding fulfilling roles for themselves. They do this by establishing an environment that communicates warmth, acceptance, respect, hope, and an orientation toward improvement and change (Woods & Martin, 1984). A warm environment promotes a willingness to take risks and open up. In such a setting, therapists help families take the first step toward change by verbalizing presuppositions of hope that the family has. They also help family members to clarify their goals and to use their natural abilities.

In addition to creating an atmosphere that encourages change, experiential family therapists promote growth through stimulating experiences that provide opportunities for personal existential encounters (Mitten & Connell, 2004). Through these encounters, it is hoped that awareness and authenticity will increase and lead "to a reintegration of repressed or disowned parts of the self" (Costa, 1991, p. 122).

Experiential family therapists are likely to behave as real, authentic people. In contrast to psychoanalytic therapists, they do not encourage projection or act as blank screens for their families. The more involved, energetic, and creative experiential family therapists are, the greater chance they have of making a major impact on the families with whom they work. Experiential family therapy is an approach to working with families that helps both the families and the therapists gain self-awareness and growth. It requires not only commitment but also active risk-taking to be an effective experiential family therapist. Experiential family therapists must ask their client families to try new ways of interacting without knowing the ultimate effect of these behaviors.

Process and Outcome

During experiential family therapy, family members should become more aware of their own needs and feelings. They should share these impressions with each other. This illustrates the inside-out process of change promoted by experiential therapists (Duhl, 1983). Through therapy, family members become more attuned to their emotions and more capable of autonomy and real intimacy. Treatment is generally designed to help individual family members find fulfilling roles for themselves, without an overriding concern for the needs of the family as a whole. However, as in filial therapy, systemic changes occur (Johnson et al., 1999).

Many experiential family therapists concentrate on whoever comes to therapy. Others insist on having the whole family in treatment. They request that three generations be present during each session (Whitaker, 1976). Even though the entire family is present, most experiential family therapists usually do not treat the family as a systemic unit. Instead, the emphasis is on the impact of what the therapist and other members of the family do in the sessions. Therapists believe this knowledge is more powerful when shared with everyone present than when it is conveyed to others in the family indirectly.

The process of family therapy differs for each experiential family therapist. Whitaker described family therapy as a process that "begins with a blind date and ends with an empty nest" (Whitaker & Bumberry, 1988, p. 53). For Whitaker, therapy occurred in three phases: (1) engagement, (2) involvement, and (3) disentanglement. During these phases, the therapist increases, in a caring way, the family's anxiety. The idea is to escalate pressure in order to produce a breakdown and breakthrough, both among family members and in the functioning of the family itself. Therapists use themselves, as well as planned and spontaneous actions, to intensify the sane and crazy elements within the family (Whitaker & Keith, 1981). Through these means, they get the family to move toward change.

Engagement consists of therapists becoming personally involved with their families through the sharing of feelings, fantasies, and personal stories. During this time, therapists encourage families to become invested in making needed changes within a structured environment. If all goes smoothly, therapists are able to demonstrate their caring attitude to client families. Next, during the **involvement** stage, therapists concentrate on helping families try new ways of relating through the use of playfulness, humor, and confrontation. The emphasis in this stage is on families' broadening their horizons and trying new behaviors. Once constructive action is taken and roles and rules are modified, therapists disengage from families and become their consultants.

Similarly, Satir's approach has three phases of intervention. In Satir's Human Validation Process Model, the three stages are (1) making contact, (2) chaos, and (3) integration. These phases are present in each interview and in the therapy as a whole. In the first stage, making contact, Satir would shake each person's hand and focus her attention on that person, in an attempt to raise the level of the person's self-worth (i.e., self-esteem). Satir (1988) compared **self-worth** with a pot. When the pot of self-worth is "high," people are vitally alive and have faith in themselves. The opposite is true when the pot of self-worth is "low." The establishment of trust and hope takes place during this first 45- to 60-minute nonjudgmental session, as well. Family members would be asked what they hoped would come out of the therapy. Then through active techniques, Satir would begin to make interventions.

During the second stage, chaos and disorder among family members are prevalent. Individuals are engaged in tasks, take risks, and share their hurt and pain. This stage is unpredictable, as family members open up and work on issues in a random order.

In the last stage, integration and closure are worked on in regard to issues raised in the second stage. The third stage is often an emotional one. Satir, however, would interject cognitive information at this time to help members understand themselves and issues more thoroughly. She might have said to a man grieving the loss of his father with whom he was always distant: "You now understand through your hurt how your father kept all people, including you, from getting close to him."

The family is terminated when transactions can be completed and when family members can see themselves as others do. It is vital that family members be able to share with each other honestly. It is a positive sign when members can argue, disagree, and make choices by taking responsibility for outcomes. The sending and receiving of clear communication is a further indicator that the family is ready to end treatment (Satir, 1964). If family members can tell each other that they would rather go somewhere different on vacation than back to the same beach they visited last year, progress has been made.

Regardless of the techniques and procedures employed in the experiential approach, the primary goal of therapy is growth, especially in the areas of sensitivity and the sharing of feelings. Therapists and families focus on growing. Growth is usually accomplished through the therapist's work of winning the battle for structure and the client family's work of winning the battle for initiative (Napier & Whitaker, 1978). In the **battle for structure**, the therapist sets up the conditions (e.g., the length of sessions and/or the order of speaking) under which the family will proceed. In the **battle for initiative**, the family becomes actively involved and responsible for making changes that help them as individuals and as a family (e.g., several family members express a desire to work through a disagreement that has continued to keep them angry and apart). If the battle for structure is won, chances are improved that the battle for initiative will go well. An ideal outcome for experiential family therapists is to help individuals gain congruence between their inner experiences and outward behaviors.

Unique Aspects of Experiential Family Therapy

Emphases

The unique qualities of the experiential approach are found on several levels that involve both people and processes. A major uniqueness developed by Virginia Satir and by Bernard and Louise Guerney is the training programs set up to educate others in their approaches to family therapy. The Avanta Network (http://www.avanta.net/) now carries on the interdisciplinary work of training therapists in Satir's methods. The Guerneys' training program in filial therapy is known as the National Institute of Relationship Enhancement (http://www.nire.org/) and carries out regular training sessions in this approach.

A second novel element of the experiential approach relates to research. "Experiential therapies are difficult to operationalize" (Mitten & Connell, 2004, p. 467). Nevertheless, there has been some work in this area. Satir gave consent for her model and methods to be used in one research project. This study (Winter, 1989), which compared her work with that of Bowen and Haley, produced very favorable results on both a multiple-family group level and with individual family units. These results, plus her own demonstration of work before large audiences of professionals, have given Satir's approach, and the experiential school of therapy in general, credibility, with the possibility that more will be gained in the future through the generation of data (Satir & Bitter, 2000). Likewise, the filial therapy approach of the Guerneys has distinguished itself in regard to research (Johnson et al., 1999).

Whitaker, on the other hand, was unique in his stance that empirical research, just like theory, can get in the way of helping a family. Whitaker reported numerous examples of how he conducted family therapy. He insisted that because each family is different, each treatment plan should be different and, therefore, cannot really be used for research. In essence, Whitaker is impossible to imitate, as are his therapeutic sessions (Framo, 1996).

The length of treatment and the focus of therapists practicing experiential family therapy represent a third unique aspect of it. Experiential family therapy focuses on immediate experiences and the uniqueness of every family. Treatment tends to be of shorter duration and often more direct than with historical-based approaches.

A fourth quality of experiential family therapy is that it calls attention to emphasizing people as well as structures within the change process. As a theory, experiential family therapy places a great deal of attention on persons within families. It emphasizes that families are composed of individuals. For family systems to change, those who are a part of them must alter their behaviors (Duhl, 1983).

Comparison with Other Theories

Experiential family therapy is often seen as hard to conceptualize and therefore hard to compare with other approaches. However, experiential approaches can be contrasted with other types of family therapy both directly and indirectly.

One comparative aspect of many of the experiential approaches is their dependence on sensitive and charismatic therapists. Virginia Satir and Carl Whitaker, pioneers in the family therapy movement, both fit this profile. Additionally, they were both rather large framed. They encouraged family members to participate physically in activities (e.g., using props in the case of Satir) and by using their person (e.g., arm wrestling contests in the case of Whitaker). Both had a spontaneous theatrical style that was uniquely their own and made them difficult to emulate. Whitaker especially has been hard to model, partly because of his encouragement of intuitive action by a therapist and partly because of the need for a therapist to do an apprenticeship with him in order to really learn his approach (Sugarman, 1987).

Unlike psychodynamic or Bowen family treatment, experiential family therapies focus on the present rather than on the past. Such an emphasis can keep therapists and families from dealing with historical patterns or events. By neglecting historical information, therapists could miss data that shed light on patterns that, if properly understood, could be altered and, thereby, help alleviate problems. In this last respect, however, experiential and most other family therapies are the same.

Furthermore, experiential family therapies promote individual growth and intrapersonal change as opposed to family growth and interpersonal change. Although personal development is an admirable and noteworthy goal, it may not be sufficient in some cases to help families alter their dysfunctional behaviors. Individual members who have become healthier during treatment may leave the family, or, if the family stays together, more dysfunctional family members may work hard to return the family to the way it was before therapy.

Finally, experiential approaches emphasize dealing with feelings in the here and now rather than concentrating on guidance for now and the future. Some theorists criticize making therapeutic interventions without offering family members education about how to help themselves in the future. This critique of the experiential therapies, however, has not altered the overall emphasis of the approach (Duhl & Duhl, 1981).

———————— CASE ILLUSTRATION ————————

THE STEINHAUER FAMILY

Family Background

When Frank first bumped into Heather, it was literally in a car. The accident was minor, but the mutual interest between the divorced man and the widow soon grew. In 6 months, Frank had proposed, and the wedding took place on the anniversary of their collision.

Frank's 16-year-old son, David, was reluctantly his father's best man; and Heather's 8- and 9-year-old daughters, Ruth and Sarah, respectively, were her bridesmaids.

Heather's daughters quickly accepted Frank as their new father. (Their biological father had died of cancer when they were 4 and 5.) David was not as accepting and told Heather prior to the wedding ceremony that he already had a mother, Judy. Judy and his father had divorced in a nasty civil suit 2 years previously.

Although David has been disrespectful to Heather in subtle ways since, Heather worries more about her daughters' behavior in regard to Frank. They frequently manipulate him into buying them clothes and toys that the family budget cannot afford. Frank reassures Heather that his behavior with respect to the girls is temporary, but she thinks otherwise. Frank is 40, the oldest sibling in his family of origin, which was composed of him, his 32-year-old sister, Emily, and his parents, both hardworking schoolteachers. Heather thinks he should be wiser and more appropriate in his interactions with her daughters. Lately, Heather has started scolding Frank and then withdrawing into silence. According to Frank, she is acting more like a 3-year-old than like the 33-year-old woman that she is.

Conceptualization of Family: Experiential Perspective

As a remarried family, the Steinhauers are encountering difficulties in becoming a functioning unit. Some of it is on a conscious, overt level; and some of it appears unconscious and covert. David is openly withdrawn from his stepmother, and Heather has begun an emotional withdrawal from Frank. At the same time, Frank is being drawn into a relationship with Heather's daughters, who are manipulating him into buying them things they want. Frank is treating them well on the surface, but it is difficult to tell whether he has anything more than a superficial interaction with them. Furthermore, it is interesting to note that Frank has continued his behavior with Heather's daughters despite her disapproval.

There is stress in the marital unit, as well as between the generations. It appears individual members of the family are having problems, too. Clear communication is lacking. Family members seem to hurt themselves and others when they try to make a point (e.g., by giving one another the "cold shoulder").

Process of Treatment: Experiential Family Therapy

To help the Steinhauers become a more functional family, an experiential family therapist would go through three phases of treatment and, most likely, would use a number of procedures. If the therapist followed Whitaker's symbolic-experiential approach, he or she might initially show care and concern for the family through expressing feelings about individual family members. In this process, the therapist would address remarks to one member of the family at a time. However, it is the manner in which the therapist's remarks are conveyed that establishes trust among all members.

The therapist following Satir's model would likewise focus initially on making contact with family members on a personal level. In such a scenario, the therapist would use "I" statements: for example, "Heather, I really hear that you are feeling hurt and angry about Frank's behavior." The emphasis in such a first session would be on making sure family members felt validated and affirmed as members of the family unit.

After this preliminary engagement/contact, the therapist would move the family into involvement. For a therapist following Whitaker's symbolic-experiential approach, involvement is getting the family to win the battle for initiative by working on problematic areas. In the case of the Steinhauers, these behaviors range from the proper expression of affection to the expression of anger. To make the family more aware of the importance of the issues involved, a symbolic-experiential therapist might do something absurd, such as sharing a daydream with the family about their situation. Through such a process, some unconscious aspects of the family's life would become more obvious. The therapist would also try to get individuals talking to one another about their feelings and how they have handled them previous to this family situation. An opportunity would then be given for family members to try new behaviors.

In the Satir model, the middle part of the therapeutic process might involve chaos, out of which would come clarity. This middle phase would involve such procedures as sculpting, choreography, or art, in which members would get an opportunity to express their feelings in direct and indirect ways. Props might be used in these situations to enhance the quality of the affect that is generated. There would be an emphasis at this stage on exploring, through activities, concerns such as individual self-worth and their family life together (Satir, 1972).

In the final stage of the experiential process, a symbolic-experiential therapist would disengage from the Steinhauer family by encouraging family members to speak more to each other. Likewise, in the Satir model, the therapist would help the Steinhauer family integrate what they learned through their enactments and come to closure. A more cognitive focus would eventually be emphasized by Satir, after emotions concerning the therapeutic experience were expressed.

Summary and Conclusion

Experiential family therapy grew out of the humanistic-existential psychology movement of the 1960s. Its original founders were involved with experimental and experiential forms of treatment. They concentrated on immediate personal interactions and sometimes conducted their family sessions like a group by treating all members of the family as equals. Above all, they stressed the importance of taking risks and expressing emotions.

Some of the initial practitioners within this theoretical camp, such as Carl Whitaker, relied more on their personality, creativity, and spontaneity to help them make timely and effective interventions with families. Other founders of this approach, such as Virginia Satir, developed highly structured treatment methods, such as using "I" messages, sculpting, and family reconstruction. Most clinicians who favor this approach today lean toward this latter method of treatment and have specific techniques and procedures that they employ.

Some of the major roles of experiential family therapists are to act as facilitators and resource persons. Therapists encourage change and set up a warm and accepting environment in which such a process is possible. Most experiential family therapists use a wide variety of techniques that are both concrete and metaphorical. They act as models of clear communication in the hope of promoting intimacy and autonomy. It is assumed that, if individuals within families find proper roles for themselves, the family as a whole will function well.

Some of the pioneers of family therapy, such as Virginia Satir and Carl Whitaker, are among the best-known experiential family therapists. Although the therapy they helped develop is valued for its emphasis on stressing the importance of affect in families, it is perceived as weak from a traditional research perspective, except in the area of filial therapy. Furthermore, focusing on persons within the family, instead of on the family as a whole, can make systemic change difficult. Complicating the matter still further is the emphasis from the experiential perspective of concentrating on the here and now at the expense of teaching families how to work better in the future.

Many forms of experiential family therapy are seen as less viable today than previously because of the accountability that is linked with therapeutic treatment. However, this approach continues to be attractive to many practitioners, and the institutes set up by Satir and the Guerneys hold promise for its continued development and growth.

Summary Table
Experiential Family Therapy

Major Theorists

Virginia Satir	Peggy Papp	Susan Johnson
Bunny Duhl	Carl Whitaker	Frank Duhl
Walter Kempler	Bernard Guerney	Louise Guerney
Leslie Greenberg	Augustus Napier	David Keith

Premises of the Theory

Family problems are rooted in suppression of feelings, rigidity, denial of impulses, lack of awareness, emotional deadness, and overuse of defense mechanisms.

Treatment Techniques

The focus is on individuals and couple dyads, except for Whitaker, who often concentrated on three-generational families. It is assumed that families will benefit if the individuals within them receive help.

The goals of treatment are:

- to promote growth, change, creativity, flexibility, spontaneity, and playfulness
- to make the covert overt
- to increase emotional closeness of spouses and disrupt rigidity
- to unlock defenses, enhance self-esteem, and recover potential for experiencing

To accomplish these objectives:

- The therapist must win the battle for structure, and the family must win the battle for initiative.
- The therapist makes suggestions and gives directives; therapists such as Carl Whitaker use the power of their personalities as a technique to bring about change.
- They disregard theory and emphasize intuitive spontaneity.
- They share feelings and create an emotionally intense atmosphere.

Other clinicians, such as Virginia Satir, use more metaphorical and concrete techniques such as:

- Modeling and teaching clear communication skills
- Sculpting
- Choreography
- Humor
- Role playing
- Reconstruction

Other experiential therapy techniques include:

- Play therapy
- Filial therapy
- Puppet interviews
- Art therapy

Role of the Therapist

Therapists use their own personalities.

Therapists must be open, spontaneous, empathic, sensitive, and demonstrate caring and acceptance.

They must be willing to share and risk, be genuine, and increase stress within the family and its members.

They must deal with regression therapeutically and teach family members new skills in clearly communicating their feelings.

Process and Outcome

Family members become more aware of their needs and feelings.

Therapy for Satir occurs in three stages: making contact, chaos, and integration.

Therapy for Whitaker occurs in three phases: engagement, involvement, and disentanglement.

Therapists and families focus on growing and winning the battles for structure and initiative respectfully.

Unique Aspects of Experiential Family Therapy

Experiential family therapy emphasizes:

- creativity and spontaneity in families
- changing roles and increased understanding of self and others
- treating all members of the family as equal in status
- increasing awareness of feelings within and among family members
- breaking down defenses within the family and among family members through structured exercises
- growth

Comparison with Other Theories

In experiential family therapy, with the exception of filial therapy, there is little interest in research or data on results of using the theory.

Much of the practice of experiential family therapy is not systems-oriented.

The experiential approach can overemphasize emotion.

Experiential family therapy may be too advice-oriented and individualistic.

Experiential family therapists use a lot of borrowed techniques.

Much of the effectiveness of experiential family therapy depends on the spontaneity, creativity, and timing of the therapist.

CHAPTER

Behavioral and Cognitive-Behavioral Family Therapies

---•---

They trade insults and accusations like children
afraid to be vulnerable and scared not to be.
Underneath all the words and bravado
is a backlog of bitter emotion
dormant so long that like dry kindling
it burst into flames when sparked.
Through the dark and heated fights
points are made that leave a mark.

In the early morning, she cries silently
into black coffee grown cold with age
while he sits behind a mahogany desk
and experiences the loneliness of depression.

---•---

Gladding, 1991b

Behaviorism is one of the oldest traditions in the helping professions. It developed from the research and writings of Ivan Pavlov, John B. Watson, and B. F. Skinner. Initially, it focused on observable behavior and concentrated on assisting individuals modify dysfunctional behaviors. Since the 1970s, the impact of **cognitions** (i.e., thoughts) has become incorporated into behaviorism, an approach known as cognitive-behavioral therapy.

Behavioral family therapy (BFT) is a fairly recent treatment methodology that had its origins in research involving the modification of children's actions by parents (Horne & Sayger, 2000). The initial work in this area was conducted at the Oregon Social Learning Center under the direction of Gerald Patterson and John Reid in the mid-1960s. It involved training parents and significant adults in a child's environment to be agents of change (Patterson, 1975; Patterson & Gullion, 1971). Treatment procedures were based on **social learning theory** (Bandura & Walters, 1963), which stressed the importance of modeling new behaviors. Techniques included "the use of rewards such as candy, but quickly moved toward using basic point systems, modeling, time-out, and contingent attention" (Horne & Sayger, 2000, p. 457). The emphasis in this program gradually shifted toward working with families in their natural settings.

From this rather structured beginning, in which observers recorded family problems on a checklist that was linear in nature (i.e., "A" caused "B"), behavioral family therapy grew to embrace a more interactional style of explaining family behavior patterns and treating family behavior problems (Falloon, 1988). A type of behavioral family therapy that is basically systemic is **functional family therapy** (Alexander & Parsons, 1982; Barton & Alexander, 1981).

Likewise, **cognitive-behavioral family therapy** is a fairly new treatment, although the importance of thoughts has been stressed throughout history. "It appears that cognitive restructuring and inducing behavioral change is much of what therapists attempt to do regardless of the modality that they espouse" (Dattilio, 2001, p. 6). Cognitive-behavioral theorists postulate that "cognitions such as irrational beliefs, arbitrary inference, dichotomous reasoning, and overgeneralization can be primary factors in causing, or at least maintaining, maladaptive behaviors and psychological disorders in individuals" (Sullivan & Schwebel, 1995, p. 298). Since the 1970s a concerted effort has been made to apply cognitive-behavioral theory and procedures to couples and families (e.g., Baucom & Epstein, 1990; Beck, 1976; Dattilio & Bevilacqua, 2000; Ellis, 2000; Schwebel & Fine, 1994). Cognitive-behavioral approaches to working with families now appear to be fully developed and even "conducted against the backdrop of a systems approach" (Dattilio, 2001, p. 7). Some of the leading proponents of cognitive-behavioral marital and family therapy are Aaron Beck, Frank Dattilio, Albert Ellis, Norman Epstein, and Andrew Schwebel.

This chapter examines the major forms of behavioral and cognitive-behavioral family therapy. Both have been found "to be equally effective or more effective than comparison family treatments" (Northey, Wells, Silverman, & Bailey, 2003, p. 537).

Major Theorists

There are many well-known behavior and cognitive-behavioral theorists. Early pioneers in this area were John B. Watson, Mary Cover Jones, and Ivan Pavlov. It was not, however, until the emergence of B. F. Skinner that behaviorism gained national prominence. Skinner was the first to use the term *behavior therapy*. He argued convincingly that behavior problems can be dealt with directly, not simply as symptoms of underlying psychic conflict. Skinner was also the originator and a proponent of **operant conditioning**. This viewpoint says that people learn through rewards and punishments to respond behaviorally to their environments in certain ways. For instance, if a man smiles at a woman and she smiles back, he may voluntarily approach and talk with her because his initial action was reinforced. Skinner publicized his ideas on operant conditioning in such scholarly texts as *Science and Human Behavior* (1953) and in popular books such as *Walden Two* (1948).

It is on the work of Skinner, combined with that of Joseph Wolpe and Albert Bandura, that much of behavioral family therapy and cognitive-behavioral family therapy were built. Other significant contributions in this area have come from Gerald Patterson, Richard Stuart, Norman Epstein, Neil Jacobson, John Gottman, Walter Mischel, Robert Weiss, Ed Katkin, Gayola Margolin, Michael Crowe, Albert Ellis, Aaron Beck, Frank Dattilio, David Burns, and Donald Meichenbaum. Gerald Patterson and Neil Jacobson are highlighted here as representatives of this approach.

Gerald Patterson

Gerald Patterson is often credited as being the primary theorist who began the practice of applying behavioral theory to family problems in the 1960s. His work at the Oregon Social Learning Center, especially in training parents to act as agents of change in their children's environment, led to the identification of a number of behavior problems and corrective interventions. Among the interventions utilized in helping parents and children are primary rewards, such as the use of candy, and innovative techniques involving modeling, point systems, time-out, and contingent attention (Patterson & Brodsky, 1966; Patterson, Jones, Whittier, & Wright, 1965; Patterson, McNeal, Hawkins, & Phelps, 1967). Patterson and his associates developed a family observational coding system to use in assessing dysfunctional behaviors through their observations of parents and children in laboratories and natural environments (such as homes, neighborhoods, and schools).

Patterson (1975) has also been instrumental in writing programmed workbooks for parents to employ in helping their children, and ultimately their families, modify behaviors. He is credited with playing a critical role in the extension of learning principles and techniques to family and marital problems. His practical application of social learning theory has had a major impact on family therapy. He has influenced other behaviorists to work from a systemic perspective in dealing with families.

Neil Jacobson

Neil Jacobson, like a number of prominent theorists in behavioral family therapy, began his work in the 1970s. As a graduate student in psychology at the University of North Carolina in 1972, he initially intended to be a psychoanalytic and humanistic-oriented clinician. However, he "became a born-again behavior therapist" (Hines, 1998, p. 244) after reading Albert Bandura's (1969) *Principles of Behavior Modification*. The appeal of behaviorism according to Jacobson was not the theory itself but the accountability, empiricism, and methodologies associated with the theory. Jacobson pursued behaviorism with a passion, reading books and articles by Albert Bandura, Walter Mischel, Richard Stuart, Gerald Patterson, and Bob Weiss and arranging to meet some of these individuals at the conferences of the Association for the Advancement of Behavior Therapy (Wood & Jacobson, 1990).

After completing his doctorate, Jacobson settled into an academic career at the University of Washington in 1979. There he developed a clinical practice based on research. His practice helped refine his theoretical contributions to behavioral marital therapy and domestic violence. His graduate students also kept him focused on theory and challenged him to advance it. According to Jacobson, while behaviorism is at the base of his theory, the clinical application of his approach is more eclectic (Hines, 1998). Jacobson crusaded to bridge the gap between "academic statistical research and in-the-trenches, clinical-outcome research" (Wylie, 1999, p. 16).

Jacobson, until his untimely death on June 2, 1999, was on the leading edge of the family therapy field. He was involved in longitudinal research on couples and was constantly making discoveries, some of which were controversial. For example, Jacobson and his colleagues found that 20% of male batterers, whom he designated as Type I or "cobras," have lower (i.e., decelerated) heart rates during times of physical assault, not higher as previously thought (Jacobson, Gottman, & Wu Shortt, 1995). Jacobson, along with his research team, also found that **acceptance**—loving your partner as a complete person and not focusing on differences—may lead to an ability to overcome fights that continuously focus on the same topic (Christensen & Jacobson, 2000). Such a strategy may promote change.

Jacobson's findings and insights have challenged marital and family therapy practitioners to be more innovative and effective in their work. His nearly 200 research papers and articles as well as his nine books are still widely cited and emulated as standards of scholarly and pragmatic writing (Wylie, 1999). Overall, Jacobson's research is a legacy that has contributed greatly to clinicians' understanding of couple interactions and ways of promoting positive family relationships.

Premises of the Theory

In its simplest forms, behavioral family therapy is based on the theoretical foundations of **behavioral therapy** in general. An assumption underlying this premise is that all behavior is learned and that people, including families, act according to how they have been previously reinforced. Behavior is maintained by its consequences and will continue unless more rewarding consequences result from new behaviors (Patterson, 1975).

A second major principle of this approach is that maladaptive behaviors, and not underlying causes, should be the targets of change. The primary concern of behaviorists is with changing present behavior, not dealing with historical developments. Ineffective behaviors can be extinguished and replaced with new sequences of behavior patterns. To do this, continuous assessment of treatment is recommended. Tangible behavior changes in the present are the focus of behaviorally based family therapists.

A third premise behind behavioral family therapy is the belief that not everyone in the family has to be treated for change to occur. Many behavioral family therapists work with only one member of a couple or family. In most reported cases involving one individual, the targeted person is the wife. The reason is that women have traditionally been more open to therapy and therapeutic interventions than men. Regardless, in the therapeutic process, behaviorists teach this person new, appropriate, and functional skills, such as **assertiveness** (i.e., asking for what one wants) and **desensitization** (i.e., overcoming unnecessary and debilitating anxiety associated with a particular event) (Goldiamond, 1965; Lazarus, 1968).

Behavioral family therapists who are more systemic concentrate on dyadic relationships, such as a parent and child or the couple system (Dattilio, 1998; Gordon & Davidson, 1981; Stuart, 1980, 1998). The idea behind this procedure is that the correction of dysfunctional behaviors in key members of a family results in significant, measurable, positive changes in the family as a whole.

Because of its focus on identifiable, overt behavioral changes with individuals sometimes apart from the family as a unit, the behavioral approach is not usually considered a systemic approach to working with families in the fullest sense of the term. Behaviorism does share with systems theory an emphasis on the importance of "family rules and patterned communication processes, as well as a functional approach to outcome" (Walsh, 1982, p. 17). Furthermore, a number of behaviorally based family therapists, known as functional family therapists, operate from a systemic perspective (e.g., Alexander & Parsons, 1982; Barton & Alexander, 1981).

Regardless of its degree of systems orientation, behavioral family therapy emphasizes the major techniques within a behavioral theory approach, such as stimulus, reinforcement, shaping, and modeling. Some practitioners of this approach incorporate **social exchange theory** (Thibaut & Kelley, 1959), which stresses the rewards and costs of relationships in family life according to a behavioral economy. For example, individuals stay in marital relationships because the rewards they receive are equal to or greater than the cost to them in time, effort, and resources. Otherwise, they leave. A major focus behind the idea of social exchange is mutual reciprocity, for example, pleasantness begets pleasantness.

Many behavioral therapists also emphasize cognitive aspects of treatment (Dattilio & Bevilacqua, 2000; DiGuiseppe, 1988; Epstein, Schlesinger, & Dryden, 1988). In the cognitive-behavioral approach, attention focuses on what family members are thinking, as well as how they are feeling and behaving. Cognitive-behaviorists believe it is important to gain insight into how cognitions influence a problem (Watts, 2001). The premise behind **cognitive-behavioral theory** is that "the relationship-related cognitions individuals hold, shape how they think, feel, and behave in couple and family relationships" (Sullivan & Schwebel, 1995, p. 298). Relationship-related cognitions contain assumptions about how relationships work and the roles people play in them; expectations and perceptions regarding what particular events occur in relationships; and standards about how individuals in relationships should behave and how relationships ought to work.

In cognitive-behavioral family therapy, there are health-promoting, relationship-related cognitions that promote growth and negative relationship-related cognitions that lead to distress and conflict. In healthy relationships, partners might believe, for example, that it takes work to build a relationship; that both partners' needs are important; and that relationships are not always going to be free of conflict. Conversely, partners in unhealthy relations might believe that they do not have to work at relationships; that one partner's needs are more important than the other's; and that good relationships are free of conflict.

In addition, therapists must deal with irrational beliefs on the part of resistant family members. Examples of such irrational beliefs (Ellis, 1985, p. 32) include:

- "I must do well at changing myself, and I'm an incompetent, hopeless client if I don't."
- "You [the therapist and others] must help me change, and you're rotten people if you don't."
- "Changing myself must occur quickly and easily, and it's horrible if it doesn't."

Types of Behavioral and Cognitive-Behavioral Family Therapies

Behaviorism (with or without a cognitive component) has more specific forms of treatment than any other form of family therapy, with the exception of strategic family therapy. Three of the most prevalent forms of behavioral and cognitive-behavioral family therapy are behavioral parent training, functional family therapy, and behavioral treatment of sexual dysfunctions.

Behavioral Parent Training

Parenting behaviors are those that are used to socialize and manage children. Some are more effective than others because of what they are and how they are administered. Behavioral parent training is sometimes referred to as **parent-skills training**. In this model, the therapist serves as a social learning educator whose prime responsibility is to change parents' responses to a child or children, both through thoughts and actions. By effecting such a change in parents, children's behavior is altered. This type of treatment is linear in nature, and therapists who utilize it are precise and direct in following a set procedure.

For example, one of the initial and main tasks of the therapist is to define a specific problem behavior. The behavior is monitored in regard to its antecedents and consequences. The parents are then trained in social learning theory (Bandura, 1969). Parent-training procedures usually include verbal and performance methods. Verbal methods involve didactic instruction as well as written materials. The aim is to influence thoughts and messages. Performance training methods may involve role playing, modeling, behavioral rehearsal, and prompting. Their focus is on improving parent/child interactions. Regardless of the form of the training, parents are asked to chart the problem behavior over the course of treatment. Successful efforts are rewarded through encouragement and compliments by the therapist.

A psychoeducational parenting program that is essentially cognitive-behavioral in approach has been found to be especially effective as an intervention for at-risk parenting behavior (Nicholson, Anderson, Fox, & Brenner, 2002). This type of program has demonstrated significant gains among low-income parents, who are at more risk for child abuse. Among these parents measures of stress, anger, child behavior problems, and corporal punishment fell as a result of their participation in this course. "Children also made observable changes by increasing their positive behaviors and decreasing their negative behaviors" (Nicholson et al., 2002, p. 369).

Functional Family Therapy

For functional family therapists, all behavior is adaptive and serves a function. Behaviors represent an effort by the family to meet needs in personal and interpersonal relationships. Ultimately, behaviors help family members achieve one of three interpersonal states (Alexander & Parsons, 1982):

1. Contact/closeness (merging). In the contact/closeness state, family members are drawn together (e.g., in their concern over the delinquent behavior of a juvenile).
2. Distance/independence (separating). In separating, family members learn to stay away from each other for fear of fighting.
3. A combination of 1 and 2 (midpointing). In this situation, family members fluctuate in their emotional reactions to each other so that individuals are both drawn toward and repelled from each other.

Functional family therapy, which is systemic, is a three-stage process. In the first stage, assessment, the focus is on the function that the behavioral sequences serve. The question is "Do behavioral sequences promote closeness, create distances, or help the family achieve a task?" The therapist determines this through gathering information about the family both by asking questions and by observing.

The second stage of therapy involves change. The purpose is to help the family become more functional. It is carried out by:

- clarifying relationship dynamics
- interrelating thoughts, feelings, and behaviors of family members
- interpreting the functions of current family behavior
- relabeling behavior so as to alleviate blame
- discussing how the removal of a behavior will affect the family
- shifting the treatment from one individual to the entire family

The third and final stage of functional family therapy, maintenance, focuses on educating the family and training them in skills that will be useful in dealing with future difficulties. Specific skills taught during this stage of therapy are those dealing with effective communication, team building, and behavioral management (e.g., contracting).

Behavioral Treatment of Sexual Dysfunctions

In addition to working with couples on communication issues, behavioral approaches to marital and couple therapy also include behavioral treatment of sexual dysfunctions. Such treatment may seem passé in light of pharmaceuticals that now enhance men's abilities to have and maintain an erection. Yet, sexual functioning is much more than having intercourse. It is a physical as well as a psychological experience comprised of intimacy, relationship satisfaction, self-esteem, and family life (Bridges, Lease, & Ellison, 2004, p. 158).

Masters and Johnson pioneered the cognitive-behavior approach to working with couples in the late 1960s and early 1970s with the publication of *Human Sexual Response* (1966) and *Human Sexual Inadequacy* (1970). Prior to these publications "people with sexual dysfunctions relied primarily on folk cures or saw psychodynamically oriented therapists, who offered long-term insight-oriented treatment with questionable results" (Piercy & Sprenkle, 1986, p. 94).

Masters and Johnson (1970) were not original in all of their contributions, but from their research and clinical observations, they delineated **four phases of sexual responsiveness**: excitement, plateau, orgasm, and resolution. They also discovered the importance of learning and behavioral techniques in the remediation of sexual dysfunctions. In their approach to the treatment of sexual dysfunctions, techniques are tailored to specific problems. In almost all cases, however, couples are taught to relax and enjoy touching and being touched. Then, through in vivo desensitization, they learn how to gradually become more intimate with one another and how to feel comfortable either asking for sex or refusing it. For couples who have specific problems, specialized treatments are used. For example, in treating premature ejaculation, the **squeeze technique** (in which the woman learns to stimulate and stop the ejaculation urge in a man through physically stroking and firmly grasping his penis) is used. Other treatments, such as the **teasing technique** (in which a woman starts and stops stimulating a man) are also employed to overcome performance anxiety.

Masters and Johnson (1970) stressed the conjoint treatment of couples using a dual-sex therapy team. A basic assumption in the Masters and Johnson approach is that there is no such thing as an uninvolved partner in a relationship in which some form of sexual inadequacy exists. To tailor a treatment plan for a couple, Masters and Johnson took an extensive sexual history on each partner, a practice that is still followed. Their work from beginning to end is systemic.

In addition to Masters and Johnson, Helen Singer Kaplan (1974) developed direct behavioral treatment strategies to work with couples and combined this approach with psychoanalytic techniques. Unlike Masters and Johnson, Kaplan's approach employs an outpatient treatment practice. According to Kaplan, couple sexual dysfunctions can result from one force or a combination of forces such as intrapsychic conflict (e.g., guilt, trauma, or shame), interpersonal couple conflict (e.g., marital discord, distrust), and anxiety (e.g., pressure to please, fear of failure).

Joseph LoPiccolo (1978, 2002, 2004) and associates have also reported success with behavioral sex therapy techniques. In analyzing the success of heterosexual couples in behavioral sex therapy, Heiman, LoPiccolo, and LoPiccolo (1981) reported that behavioral approaches had the following elements in common:

- the reduction of performance anxiety
- sex education including the use of sexual techniques
- skill training in communications
- attitude change methodologies

Overall, behavioral-oriented therapy for sexual dysfunctions has been found to produce excellent outcomes (Miller & Ullery, 2002).

Cognitive-Behavioral Family Therapy

In cognitive-behavioral family therapy, the same principles and techniques used in **cognitive-behavioral marital therapy** (CBMT) are employed, except on a broader and more extensive basis. The cognitive component of the therapy places a heavy emphasis on modifying personal or collective core beliefs, i.e., **schema**. It is especially important to help change stable, entrenched, and long-standing beliefs that family members have about family life, like parenting, especially if such beliefs are not factual or functional (Azar, Nix, & Makin-Byrd, 2005; Dattilio, 2005).

A major emphasis in CBFT is to teach families how to think for themselves and to think differently when it is helpful. When schemata are modified, the "behavioral component of CBFT focuses on several aspects of family members' actions. These include:

1. excess negative interaction and deficits in pleasing behaviors exchanged by family members
2. expressive and listening skills used in communication
3. problem solving skills
4. negotiation and behavior change skills" (Dattilio, 2001, p. 11)

Treatment Techniques

As a rule, behavioral and cognitive-behavioral family therapists use a variety of learning theory techniques to bring about change in families. Originally devised for treating individuals, these techniques are modified and applied to problems encountered by couples and families.

Among the most well-known of these procedures are positive reinforcement, extinction, shaping, desensitization, contingency contracts, and cognitive/behavior modification. These techniques and others are described in the following sections. They are usually applied in combination so that family members learn individually and collectively how to give recognition and approval for desired behavior, instead of rewarding maladaptive actions.

General Behavioral and Cognitive-Behavioral Approaches

A review of behavioral-family-therapy practice reveals that a relatively small number of interventions tend to form the basis for most therapeutic plans across a broad range of settings. They include education, communication and problem-solving training, operant conditioning approaches, and contingency management (Falloon, 1991, p. 81).

Education

Education includes a wide variety of methods intended to help family members learn more about how relationships work. The aim is to help them relate to one another better. Thus, families may be encouraged to attend lectures, read books together, view videos as a group, and even have discussions based on what they have heard, read, or seen.

Communication and Problem-Solving Strategies

Communication and problem-solving strategies and techniques are intended to help families develop mutually enhancing social exchanges. "Instruction, modeling, and positive reinforcement (e.g., praise) are used to enhance communication skills until a level of competence has been achieved that satisfies the family and therapist" (Falloon, 1991, p. 82). Problem solving is directed at the resolution of conflict within the family.

Operant Conditioning

Operant conditioning is employed mostly in parent/child relationships. "The most common approach involves teaching parents to use shaping and time out procedures to increase the desirable behavior patterns in children" (Falloon, 1991, p. 83).

Contracting

Contracting is used when family interactions have reached a severe level of hostility. Contracts build in rewards for behaving in a certain manner. A token economy is one type of contract; but in many cases, more sophisticated ways of earning points and reinforcing appropriate behavior are used.

Specific Behavioral and Cognitive-Behavioral Techniques

The following sections highlight more specific techniques used in the behavioral and cognitive-behavioral family therapy approaches. Almost all of these techniques are used frequently. They have the common characteristics of being operationally definable, precise, and measurable. They are applicable to psychological and, in some cases, sexual situations. Furthermore, they foster change through having clients try new forms of acting. Overall, they are able to bring about fairly significant change in a short period of time. (Meichenbaum's self-instructional training and stress inoculation techniques are particularly suited for children.)

Classical Conditioning

Classical conditioning is the oldest form of behaviorism. In it, a stimulus that is originally neutral is paired up with another event to elicit certain emotions through association. In the case of Pavlov's dogs, the ringing of a bell was paired with the presenting of food so that the sound of the bell elicited a salutary response in the dogs. In families, classical conditioning is used to associate a person with a gratifying behavior, such as a pat on the back or a kind word. For instance, when a preschool child gets dressed, a parent might gently touch and praise him or her immediately after the task is completed. Through such a timely and rewarding interaction, the child may come to view the parent in a different and more positive way, that is, one that represents a pleasant association. Therefore, the relationship becomes more valued.

Coaching

In coaching, a therapist helps individuals, couples, and families make appropriate responses by giving them verbal instructions. The therapist might say: "Sally, when you want John to make eye contact with you and he is looking around, gently touch him on the knee. John, that will be your signal to look directly at Sally." Just as athletes excel through coaching, individuals, couples, and families do best when they are informed about what to do and then have an opportunity to practice their new responses.

Contingency Contracting

In contingency contracting (see Figure 8.1), "a specific, usually written schedule or contract [describes] the terms for the trading or exchange of behaviors and reinforcers between two or more individuals" (Sauber, L'Abate, & Weeks, 1985, p. 34). One action is contingent, or dependent, on another. For example, a child and her parent may write up an agreement whereby the daughter will receive an allowance of 5 dollars a week upon taking the garbage out every day after supper. The way this type of contract is assessed is known as contingency management.

Extinction

Extinction is the process by which previous reinforcers of an action are withdrawn so that behavior returns to its original level. For example, a child is ignored by a parent when having a

Contingency Contract
week one
(must earn 5 points for a reward)

	make bed	clean room	hang up clothes	pick up toys	set table	read a book	Goal
George	✓	✓		✓	✓	✓	Pizza
Will		✓		✓			Baseball game
Ann	✓	✓	✓	✓	✓	✓	Spend-the-night party

Figure 8.1
Contingency contract.

temper tantrum. Similarly, a spouse may not be rewarded by his mate for saying unkind remarks. In almost all cases of extinction, it is important that a replacement behavior be positively reinforced to take the place of the behavior that is being extinguished. In the case of the child or the spouse just mentioned, attention should be given to appropriate or pleasing behaviors.

Positive Reinforcement

A positive reinforcer is usually a material (e.g., food, money, or medals) or a social action (e.g., a smile or praise) that increases desired behaviors. For a reinforcer to be positive, the person involved must be willing to work for it. Children, for example, are often willing to perform certain actions when the reward is money, candy, or tokens. Adults may be prone to work for verbal or physical recognitions such as praise or smiles.

Quid Pro Quo

Literally translated, the Latin phrase *quid pro quo* means "something for something." Behavioral marital contracts are often based on quid pro quo—that is, a spouse agrees to do something as long as the other spouse does something comparable. In maintaining a house, one spouse may agree to do the dishes if the other does the laundry. In a quid pro quo arrangement, everyone wins. When quid pro quo arrangements are in written form, they often take the shape of contingency contracts.

Reciprocity

The concept of reciprocity involves "the likelihood that two people will reinforce each other at approximately equitable rates over time" (Piercy & Sprenkle, 1986, p. 76). Many marital behavior therapists view marriage as based on this principle (Stuart, 1969). When spouses are not reinforced reciprocally, one of them will often leave the relationship either emotionally or physically. If a spouse feels he or she is doing most of the couple's work, such as paying the bills and keeping the house, but is not receiving adequate appreciation, he or she may stop taking care of these duties.

Shaping

The process of learning in small, gradual steps is called shaping. It is often referred to as **successive approximation** (Bandura, 1969). For example, during potty training, children are reinforced in small steps from "running to the potty," to "pulling down their pants," to "sitting on the potty," to "having a bowel movement in the potty." Gradually, children put all of these actions together. In a similar fashion, couples learn to speak and act in routine ways that help them bond. He fixes breakfast in the morning while she takes a shower and gets dressed; then they share a meal and conversation together; then she fixes his lunch and starts the car while he gets dressed; and, finally, they leave for work together.

Systematic Desensitization

The process of systematic desensitization is one in which a person's dysfunctional anxiety is reduced or eliminated through pairing it with incompatible behavior such as muscular or mental relaxation. This is a gradual procedure in which progressively higher levels of anxiety are treated one step at a time (Wolpe, 1969). This treatment is one of the main approaches to several forms of sexual disorders, such as vaginismus. It may also be used to help individuals

Targeted Behavior: Speaking to others without being anxious	
Event	*Anxiety Rating*
Speaking in public to a large audience (20 people or more)	100%
Speaking in public to a small audience (e.g., my scout troop)	90%
Speaking with a group of strangers	80%
Speaking casually with someone in a public place	70%
Speaking to someone at a social event	55%
Speaking casually with someone when we are alone	40%
Speaking with my friends when I have an idea	30%
Speaking with my friends in casual conversation	15%
Speaking with my family	5%
Being alone	0%

Figure 8.2
Hierarchy of troublesome behavior.

feel less anxious about stating what they need from other members of the family. In all such instances, a hierarchy of troublesome behaviors is set up and worked through (see Figure 8.2).

Time-Out

The process of time-out involves the removal of persons (most often children) from an environment in which they have been reinforced for certain actions. Isolation, or time-out, from reinforcement for a limited amount of time (approximately 5 minutes) results in the cessation of the targeted action. For example, a child who is biting his sibling during play has to sit down in a separate room and face a wall for 5 minutes each time it happens.

Time-outs can be used to shape the behaviors of normal children as well as the maladaptive behaviors of problem children. Time-outs are best accompanied by a retraining program in which rewards are given when the undesirable behavior is absent for an agreed-upon period of time, or if a competing, new, desirable behavior occurs several times a day (Thomas, 1992, p. 288).

Job Card Grounding

Job card grounding is a behavior modification technique that is used with preadolescents and adolescents (ages 11–18). It is more age-appropriate than the continuous use of time-out. In this procedure, parents make a list of small jobs that take 15 to 20 minutes to complete and that are not a part of the adolescent's regular chores. These jobs are written on index cards, and materials to complete them are kept readily available. When a problem behavior begins and the adolescent does not heed a warning behavior, he or she is given one of the jobs to complete and is grounded until the job is finished successfully (Eaves, Sheperis, Blanchard, Baylot, & Doggett, 2005).

Grounding

Grounding is a disciplinary technique used primarily with adolescents where the individual is removed from stimuli, thus limiting his or her reinforcement from the environment.

"Specifically, grounding means that the adolescent is required to attend school, perform regular chores, follow house rules, and stay in his or her room unless eating meals, conducting chores, or attending school. Grounding further means that the adolescent is not allowed to (1) use the telephone; (2) watch television; (3) have access to the computer (other than schoolwork); (4) have visitors; or (5) engage in other reinforcing activities until the job is completed" (Eaves, Sheperis, Blanchard, Baylot, & Doggett, 2005, p. 256).

Charting

The procedure of charting involves asking a client or clients to keep an accurate record of the problematic behavior (Katkin, 1978). The idea is to get the family member to establish a **baseline**—that is, a recording of the occurrence of targeted behaviors before an intervention is made. From this baseline, modifications can be made to reduce problem behaviors. A couple might be asked to make a chart of the number of fights they have a day and the type of fights that occur. Similarly, a child may be asked to keep a chart of the number of fights he or she has with parents and when they occur.

Premack Principle

The Premack principle is a behavioral intervention in which family members must first do less pleasant tasks before they are allowed to engage in pleasurable activities (Premack, 1965). For example, a child having problems with schoolwork would be required to do his or her homework before going outside to play. This technique may have, as a by-product, closer parent/child relationships because parents serve as reinforcers for their children's task accomplishment.

Disputing Irrational Thoughts

Disputing irrational thoughts through the use of an ABC format (*A* stands for the event, *B* stands for the thought, and *C* stands for the emotion) was discussed previously. It is crucial to realize that, in disputing (for example, with couples), the absurdity of irrational thoughts is often stressed by cognitive-behavioral family therapists with remarks such as "Where is it written that you should have all your needs filled in marriage?" (Ellis et al., 1989). It is hoped that through disputing, couples and families will develop more rational thoughts and behaviors.

Thought Stopping

The technique of thought stopping is used when a family member unproductively obsesses about an event or person. The therapist teaches the individual, or even in unusual cases the whole family, how to stop this repetitive and unhealthy behavior. This is done through inviting the person or persons involved to begin ruminating on a certain thought, for example, "My life is unfair." In the midst of this rumination, the therapist yells, "Stop!" This unexpected response disrupts the person's or family's thought process. Instruction is then given to those involved on how to move from an external disruption like the one they just had to an internal process. As in the case of disputation, neutral or healthy thoughts are substituted for those that have been nonproductive or unhealthy.

Self-Instructional Training

Self-instructional training is a form of self-management that focuses on people instructing themselves (Meichenbaum, 1977). It is assumed that self-instruction affects behavior and behavioral change. Thus, problems may be based on maladaptive self-statements. In self-instructional training, a self-statement can serve as a practical clue in recalling a desirable behavioral sequence, or it can interrupt automatic behaviors or cognitive thought chains and thereby encourage more adaptive coping strategies. In families, spouses can use this approach in dealing with each other; however, it is more often employed in helping impulsive children "modulate their impulsivity through deliberate and task-oriented 'self-talk'" (Schwebel & Fine, 1994, p. 26).

Modeling and Role Playing

Modeling and role playing can take many forms (Bandura, 1977). In certain situations, family members might be asked to act "as if" they were the person they wanted to be ideally. In other cases, family members might practice a number of behaviors to see which work best. Feedback and corrective action, which are a part of modeling and role playing, can be given by the therapist or by other family members.

Shame attack, a process within role playing, occurs when a family member does something he or she has previously dreaded (Ellis, 2000), for example, asking for an allowance. Individuals who use this technique find that when they do not get what they asked for, they are not worse off for having asked. Similarly, family members may steel themselves for what lies ahead through a **stress inoculation** (Meichenbaum, 1985). Here members break down potentially stressful events into manageable units that they can think about and handle through problem-solving techniques. Then the units are linked together so that the entire possible event can be envisioned and handled appropriately.

Role of the Therapist

In behavioral and cognitive-behavioral family therapies, the therapist is the expert, teacher, collaborator, and coach (Dattilio, 2001; Dattilio & Epstein, 2005; Schwebel & Fine, 1992). He or she helps families identify dysfunctional behaviors and thoughts and then works with these families to set up behavioral and cognitive-behavioral management programs that will assist them in bringing about change. Part of the process of teaching new behaviors to families includes modeling, giving corrective feedback, and learning how to assess behavioral and cognitive modification.

To be effective, the therapist has to learn to play many roles and be flexible. In the cognitive-behavioral approach, "the therapist assists family members in identifying how emotions commonly are linked with specific cognitions and helps family members explore the appropriateness and variety of cognitions that are associated with negative emotions" (Dattilio, 2005, p. 20). The process of working for change from a behavioral and cognitive-behavioral perspective has been described as the **Anatomy of Intervention Model (AIM)** (Alexander, 1988). AIM delineates five phases in therapy: (1) introduction, (2) assessment, (3) motivation, (4) behavior change, and (5) termination. "Each phase has different goals, central tasks, needed skills of the therapist, and therapeutic activities or techniques" (Thomas, 1992, p. 289). In addition to utilizing structural skills to achieve the goals of each phase, a therapist must also be able to exhibit relationship skills such as warmth, humor, nonblaming, and self-disclosure. From a behavioral and cognitive-behavioral perspective, the effective treatment of a family is complex.

Cognitive-behavioral family therapists, in particular, concentrate on modifying or changing family members' cognitions as well as their interactions (Dattilio & Bevilacqua, 2000;

Schwebel & Fine, 1992). "CBFT is grounded in cognitive mediation of individual functioning which purports that an individual's emotional and behavioral reactions to life events are shaped by the particular interpretations that the individual makes of the events, rather than solely on objective characteristics of the events themselves" (Dattilio, 2001, p. 7). For instance, a negative thought by a son about his father might be "He cares more about his work than he does me." Such a cognition might be modified to "He cares about me, but he has to work long hours and sometimes cannot give me the type of attention I want." To make changes in thoughts and consequently behaviors, cognitive-behavioral family therapists spend more time discussing issues with family members than do strictly behavioral family therapists.

Being a behavioral or cognitive-behavioral family therapist means taking an active part in designing and implementing specific strategies to help families. Such a process can help members eliminate dysfunctional behaviors and replace them with more effective ways of relating. Behavioral and cognitive-behavioral family therapists must have persistence, patience, knowledge of learning theory, and specificity in working with family members. Therapeutic interventions require a great deal of energy and investment.

Process and Outcome

If behavioral family therapy is successful, family members learn how to modify, change, or increase certain behaviors in order to function better. In successful cognitive-behavioral family therapy, dealing constructively with the cognitions of each family member is crucial. In both approaches, family members learn how to eliminate or decrease maladaptive or undesirable behaviors and, in cognitive-behavioral family therapy, negative thoughts as well (Dattilio, 2005). Behavioral and cognitive-behavioral family therapies stress the employment of specific techniques aimed at particularly important actions. A behavioral approach used in family therapy might concentrate on communication skills in which family members are taught to listen, to make requests using "I" statements, to give positive feedback, to use immediate reinforcement, and to clarify through questioning the meaning of verbal and nonverbal behaviors (Stuart, 1980).

Behavioral family therapy focuses in particular on increasing parenting skills, facilitating positive family interactions, and improving sexual behaviors. Cognitive-behavioral family therapy is most powerful in helping families deal with stress (Freeman & Zaken-Greenberg, 1989), addiction (Schlesinger, 1988), and adult sexual dysfunctions (Walen & Perlmutter, 1988). In practice, blending of the behavioral and cognitive-behavioral techniques often occurs.

By the end of treatment, couples and individuals should be able to modify their own maladaptive behaviors and/or cognitions. They should also be able to lower their anxieties about troublesome situations by using relaxation procedures, such as desensitization or thought stopping.

Unique Aspects of Behavioral and Cognitive-Behavioral Approaches

Behavioral and cognitive-behavioral family therapies, like other therapeutic approaches, have both unique and universal points. Practitioners who are considering using these approaches need to be sure they are aware of the commonalties and differences imbedded in their theory and practice. In this way, they can ensure themselves and others of the best possible outcome.

Emphases

One unique characteristic of behavioral and cognitive-behavioral family therapies involves the theory behind these approaches. The behavioral and cognitive-behavioral approaches utilize learning theory, which is a well-formulated and highly researched way of working with people. Learning theory focuses on pinpointing problem behaviors and making use of behavioral and cognitive techniques, such as setting up contingency contracts, reinforcement, punishment, and extinction.

Another emphasis of behavioral and cognitive-behavioral family therapies approaches is research. The results of applying learning theory to families indicate that such a process gives parents a management tool that works at home and has a carryover effect at school. Behavioral family therapy aimed at one child's dysfunctional behavior seems to generalize in many cases so as to positively influence interactions with other children, especially siblings. Parental self-esteem and the family's ability to function seem to improve adequately as well (Gurman, Kniskern, & Pinsof, 1985).

A third aspect of these approaches involves continued evolution. Behavioral family therapy has evolved from a focus on parent management to a focus on the family as a system (i.e., functional family therapy). In addition, behavioral family therapy has incorporated many ideas from cognitive approaches in its handling of families (Falloon, 1988). Because of their considerable flexibility, behavioral and cognitive-behavioral family therapies are able to focus on a variety of problems and concerns, from promoting changes within individuals in families to altering family interaction styles. Likewise, the procedures and processes within behavioral and cognitive-behavioral family therapies have influenced other approaches, such as the structural family therapists in their treatment of anorexia nervosa (Minuchin, Rosman, & Baker, 1978).

A fourth unique quality of behavioral and cognitive-behavioral family therapies is that treatment is short-term. Therapists who work from these perspectives "take presenting problems seriously and examine them in their interpersonal context" (Fish, 1988, p. 15). Thus, on a more microscopic level, the therapist is able to break down the problem into definable parts and then target strategies to either teach skills or extinguish behaviors associated with difficulties.

A fifth emphasis of behavioral and cognitive-behavioral family therapies is that they reject the medical model of abnormal behavior. "Behavior therapists believe many problems result from inadequate personal, social, or work-related skills ... [and that] inadequately skilled clients need training" (Fish, 1988, p. 15). Time is not spent on looking for biological or chemical causes of behavior or cognition, nor is time spent on examining the history of the client. Because of an immediate focus, problems can be addressed more directly and efficiently without labeling (Atwood, 1992).

Behavioral family therapy is a robust treatment approach with demonstrated effects, such as "specific benefits in the treatment of conduct disorders of childhood and adolescence" (Falloon, 1991, p. 88). Combined with cognitive processes, it is useful in the management of many adult mental disorders, such as depression. On the whole, behavioral and cognitive-behavioral family therapies can be useful on a number of levels as long as they are employed as part of a comprehensive treatment plan that takes into account the uniqueness of families.

Comparison with Other Theories

Compared with other ways of working with families, behavioral and cognitive-behavioral family therapies are less systemic. The orientation of learning theory, on which these approaches are based, is to bring about linear changes in individuals or subunits of the family. Such a perspective often hinders the introduction of a complete family change process. In behavior parent training, a child may be viewed as "the problem" that the therapist needs "to fix." With such a view, modification of behaviors and/or cognitions that would benefit everyone in the family, such as learning to communicate more clearly, may not be addressed.

Another distinction of behavioral family therapy is that some behavioral family therapists do not focus on the affective components of behavior, such as feelings. Instead, they look primarily at behaviors and secondarily at thoughts (i.e., cognitive-behaviors) (Piercy & Sprenkle, 1986). Some family members who have been through this type of treatment may act properly but not feel or think differently. The operational procedures are successful, but a price is paid in regard to helping the recipients of the services access their emotions and thoughts.

A third distinct aspect of behavioral and cognitive-behavioral family therapies compared with others is their preciseness. Some therapists who use these approaches think they need to be rigid in their application. Their lack of spontaneity and dependence on techniques may result in their losing rapport with families. Both the family and therapist end up becoming frustrated, and the therapy is not as effective as it might be otherwise (Wood & Jacobson, 1990).

A fourth aspect of behavioral and cognitive-behavioral family therapies compared with other approaches is the consideration of historical data. Although it is true that, as behaviorists, Masters and Johnson (1970) emphasize the importance of sexual histories, their approach is more the exception than the rule. By not attending to the past, users of behavioral and cognitive-behavioral family theory may misunderstand family patterns and dynamics. Once a symptomatic behavior is eliminated, another one may appear out of habit or tradition. Alcoholism, for example, may be brought under control while workaholism emerges.

A fifth comparable dimension of the behavioral and cognitive-behavioral perspective in family therapy is that these approaches generally stress family action over family insight. As a result, too much emphasis may be given to the employment of methods that facilitate change without ensuring family members' comprehension. In a situation in which a child has been acting out, parents might learn to use behavioral techniques, such as time-out; but they might not comprehend the dynamics that led to the child's misbehavior in the first place.

Finally, a promising aspect of comparison with other theories is that cognitive-behavioral family therapy has "integrated concepts and methods from so many other approaches" (Dattilio, 2005, p. 28). Therefore, "cognitive-behavioral strategies may be worth considering as an effective adjunct to treatment" when another theoretical approach is employed (Dattilio, 2005, p. 28).

--- **CASE ILLUSTRATION** ---

THE BROWN FAMILY

Family Background

Bob Brown, age 50, has reached a stalemate with his wife, Amy, age 47. They are a dual-career couple and have been highly successful financially. Yet Bob is tired of being on the road three nights a week and wants to take an early retirement. Amy, who loves her in-home computer job, cannot imagine such a situation. Bob, a former football athlete, has always had plenty of energy and drive. His early retirement would mean he would be around the house more and probably interfere with her business and routine. As an only child, Amy values her space and privacy. Now that Bob, Jr., age 17, is ready to go to college, she thinks that her husband should "stick it out" for at least 4 or 5 more years for the good of the family.

Bob disagrees. He has a history of heart trouble, and his father died of a heart attack at age 62 during Bob's senior year of college. He wants to quit his job now. He believes that if he stays on much longer, he will become very unhappy and distressed. Open fights that last late into the night began about a month ago. No one in the family is saying anything constructive to anyone else. The tension is as thick as an early morning fog.

Conceptualization of Family: Behavioral and Cognitive-Behavioral Perspective

The Browns both have strong beliefs about what should occur. Yet they lack the proper skills to negotiate and settle their dispute. Bob thinks he has worked hard and deserves a rest. He also thinks he will endanger his health by continuing in his present position. Amy thinks if he quits now, he will get in her way and, in addition, not be able to help their son through college. Neither one is reinforcing the other. The result is disruptive behavior and fights that are growing in intensity.

Process of Treatment: Behavioral and Cognitive-Behavioral Family Therapies

To help the Browns, a behavioral or cognitive-behavioral family therapist would work with the couple and the family to set up quid pro quo relationships. This would most likely mean drawing up a contingency contract that would describe the terms for exchanging behaviors and reinforcers. If Bob is going to give up his job, he might agree to do it gradually, instead of all at once. Regardless of the manner in which he quits his job, he would come to an agreement with Amy as to how much time per day he would spend around the house and with her. On Amy's part, she would be explicit about what time she would like to have Bob at home. Beliefs as well as wishes would be aired.

Once decisions regarding Bob's job and time together were settled, the couple and the family would concentrate with the therapist on the extinction of negative behaviors, such as fights and irrational thoughts. They might use thought stopping or disputation to deal with the underlying cognitions that led to their conflict. At the same time, the couple would work on the establishment of reinforcing behaviors, for example, establishing enough time alone for Amy and adequate time together for Bob. Specific rewards could be built into the contingency contract, and the contract itself could be prominently displayed on the refrigerator or some other mutually agreed on setting.

To help the couple and the family as a whole, the therapist might need to help shape their behaviors toward one another and give them a means to disengage from negative interactions, such as the use of time-out. Through all of this action, the couple and therapist would chart the behaviors displayed and refine the process of working with each other on a weekly basis.

Summary and Conclusion

Behavioral and cognitive-behavioral family therapies are relatively recent phenomena that are based on one of the most thoroughly researched approaches in the helping professions—learning theory. The origin of the theory can be traced back to the beginning of the 20th century. It included such luminaries as Ivan Pavlov, John B. Watson, and B. F. Skinner.

Behavioral family therapy has three basic forms: behavioral parent training, treatment of sexual dysfunctions, and functional family therapy. These emphases often utilize cognitive-behavioral methods. All except the last approach are linear and stress individual or dyadic relationships. Many of the interventions used in behavioral and cognitive-behavioral family therapies are the same as those employed in individual treatment. Reinforcement, shaping, modeling, role playing, thought stopping, and extinction are common. However, aspects of behavioral and cognitive-behavioral family therapies also include novel implementations, such as contingency contracts and behaviors based on the principle of quid pro quo.

In their therapeutic role, both the behaviorists and cognitive-behaviorists are the experts, teachers, and trainers. The instructions of the therapist are usually carried out by an individual, a couple, or a family, and are carefully monitored. It is the therapist, however, who is most powerful and rewards positive behaviors and thoughts as often as possible. In his or her central role, the therapist helps clients learn how to reinforce themselves as well.

If all goes well during the treatment process, the results will be measurable. Traditionally, this has included the emergence of overt behaviors such as parent/child interactions. In more recent times, treatment has focused on the modification of cognitive processes as well, such as the elimination of negative self-statements.

At their best, behavioral and cognitive-behavioral family therapies are concrete and readily applicable to helping parents, couples, and families change. A branch of this approach, functional family therapy, is systemic. The basic concepts on which treatment is based have been well-researched. Of all the family therapies, behavioral and cognitive-behavioral family approaches are the most rigorously measured.

On the other hand, behavioral and cognitive-behavioral family therapies, for the most part, still continue to rely heavily on a linear and limited view of families. These approaches assume that if treatment is applied to one unit in the family and to this unit's symptomatic behavior, the other aspects of the family will change.

Summary Table
Behavioral and Cognitive-Behavioral Family Therapies

Major Theorists

Richard Stuart	Neil Jacobson	Norman Epstein
Gerald Patterson	Robert Weiss	Gayola Margolin
Albert Ellis	Albert Bandura	Walter Mischel
William Masters	Virginia Johnson	Frank Dattilio
John Gottman	Joseph Wolpe	Donald Meichenbaum
Ed Katkin	Aaron Beck	Helen Singer Kaplan

Premises of the Theory

Behavior is maintained or eliminated by consequences.

Maladaptive behaviors can be unlearned or modified. Adaptive behaviors can be learned.

Likewise, cognitions are either rational or irrational. They can be modified and, as a result, bring about a change in couple or family behaviors and interactions.

Treatment Techniques

In behavioral family therapy, the focus is on parent training, interpersonal family functioning, and the treatment of sexual dysfunctions. Cognitive-behavioral family therapy also emphasizes working with those under stress but emphasizes thoughts and behaviors.

Dyads and individuals are seen more than families with both approaches. The emphasis is on dyadic interactions, except in functional family therapy.

In behavioral family therapy, the emphasis is to bring about behavioral changes by modifying the antecedents or consequences of an action. Special attention is paid to modifying the consequences. Emphasis is on elimination of undesirable behavior and acceleration of positive behavior. Teaching social skills and preventing problems from recurring are stressed, too. Promoting competence and fostering an understanding of the dynamics of behavior are highlighted.

In cognitive-behavioral family therapy, the focus is on modifying irrational or unproductive beliefs and the behaviors that go with them.

Behaviorists and cognitive-behaviorists rely primarily on:

- Operant conditioning
- Classical conditioning
- Social learning theory
- Cognitive-behavioral strategies

General Behavioral and Cognitive-Behavioral Approaches include:

- Education
- Communication and Problem-Solving Strategies
- Operant Conditioning
- Contracting

Specific Techniques include but are not limited to:

- Classical conditioning
- Coaching
- Extinction
- Positive Reinforcement
- Quid Pro Quo
- Reciprocity
- Shaping
- Systematic Desensitization
- Time-out
- Job Card Grounding
- Grounding
- Charting
- Premack principle
- Disputing irrational thoughts
- Thought stopping

- Self-instructional training
- Modeling and Role Playing

Role of the Therapist

The therapist is a teacher, collaborator, coach and an expert. Presenting problems are the focus. Modeling, corrective feedback, and learning new behaviors are a part of the process.

There is an Anatomy of Intervention Model (AIM) that delineates five phases in therapy: introduction, assessment, motivation, behavior change, and termination.

Cognitive-behavioral family therapists concentrate on modifying family members' cognitions as well as their interactions.

Therapists are active in designing and implementing specific strategies to help families.

Process and Outcome

Family members learn to modify, change, or increase/decrease certain behaviors and/or thoughts in order to function more effectively. They increase their skills in specific areas such as parenting, interpersonal functioning, and improving sexual behaviors.

Family members eventually are able to modify their own behaviors and cognitions without the aid of a therapist.

Unique Aspects of Behavioral and Cognitive-Behavioral Approaches

Behavioral and cognitive-behavioral family therapies emphasize:

- use of learning theory and research
- straightforwardness with attention paid to observations, measurements, and use of the scientific theory
- teaching new social skills and cognitions while eliminating dysfunctional ones
- short-term treatment and rejection of the medical model
- with regard to behaviorism: a simple and pragmatic intervention with a variety of workable techniques, such as use of contracts; with regard to cognitive-behaviorism: a straightforward approach that can be pragmatically employed
- the treatment of a variety of presenting symptoms and problems

Comparison with Other Theories

Some behaviorists operate from a linear perspective and work on individual rather than system concerns. The exceptions are functional family therapy and cognitive-behavioral therapy which are more systemic.

Behaviorism and cognitive-behaviorism disregard the use of historical data in the treatment of families.

Some behavioral and cognitive-behavioral procedures may be at times more mechanical than experiential in practice.

Some critics of behavioral and cognitive-behavioral family therapies claim there is too much emphasis on action in these approaches and not enough attention to family dynamics.

Behaviorism does not focus attention on affective responses or deal with emotional problems. Cognitive-behaviorism is more attuned to affect and emotion but emphasizes that affect is dependent on thoughts.

CHAPTER 9

Structural Family Therapy

———————————•———————————

She flips through a magazine on the blue-striped couch
sometimes entertained but often bored,
while he gulps down popcorn and televised football,
feeling occasionally excited yet often empty.

At midnight when the lights go off
and the news of the day and the games are decided,
She lays in anticipation, but without hope, of his touch
while he tackles fullbacks in his sleep
and ignores inner needs.

Alone, they together form a couple,
together, all alone, they long for a relationship.

———————————•———————————

Gladding, 1991c

Structural family therapy was initially based on the experiences of Salvador Minuchin and his colleagues at the Wiltwyck School, a residential facility in New York for inner-city delinquents. The treatment was created out of necessity. Long-term, passive, and historically based approaches to working with the families of these children proved unsuccessful (Piercy, Sprenkle, & Wetchler, 1997). The active and often aggressive nature of family members at the Wiltwyck School and their tendencies to blame others and react immediately meant therapists had to be powerful and quick. Minuchin soon discovered that dramatic and active interventions were necessary to be effective.

Since its conception, structural family therapy has grown in popularity and use. It was refined at the Philadelphia Child Guidance Clinic in the 1960s and 1970s. Today, its numerous practitioners are found in many mental health settings. Structural family therapy's major thesis is that an individual's symptoms are best understood when examined in the context of family interactional patterns (Minuchin & Nichols, 1998). A change in the family's organization or structure must take place before symptoms can be relieved. This idea about the impact of family structure and change on the lives of individuals has continued to be influential in the current practice of many family therapists, even those outside of a structural family therapy orientation.

Major Theorists

There are several prominent theorists in structural family therapy, including Braulio Montalvo, Bernice Rosman, Harry Aponte, and Charles Fishman. The best known, however, is the founder of the theory, Salvador Minuchin.

Salvador Minuchin

Salvador Minuchin was born in 1921 to Russian Jewish emigrants in Argentina. He never felt total allegiance to Argentina, but he did learn the rituals of Latin pride and ways of defending his honor against anti-Semitic remarks (Minuchin & Nichols, 1998; Simon, 1984). He completed a medical degree in Argentina and, in 1948, he joined the Israeli army as a doctor and spent the next 18 months in this position. In 1950, Minuchin came to the United States with the intention of studying with Bruno Bettelheim in Chicago. However, he met Nathan Ackerman in New York and chose to stay there. After another 2 years in Israel, Minuchin returned to the United States for good. In 1954, he began studying psychoanalysis; a few years later, he took the position of medical director of the Wiltwyck School.

Through his experiences at Wiltwyck, Minuchin became a systems therapist and, along with Dick Auerswald and Charles King in 1959, began developing a three-stage approach to working with low-socioeconomic-level black families. As time progressed, the Minuchin team "developed a language for describing family structure and methods for getting families to directly alter their organization" (Simon, 1984, p. 24). It was his innovative work at Wiltwyck that first gained Minuchin widespread recognition. The essence of the method used was published in *Families of the Slums* (Minuchin, Montalvo, Guerney, Rosman, & Schumer, 1967).

In 1965, Minuchin became the director of the Philadelphia Child Guidance Clinic. He transformed the clinic into a family therapy center. There he gained a reputation as a tough and demanding administrator. Minuchin was always creating ideas. One of the most innovative of these was the **Institute for Family Counseling**, a training program for community paraprofessionals that proved to be highly effective in providing mental health services to the poor.

Minuchin worked closely in Philadelphia with Braulio Montalvo and Jay Haley, whom he hired from California. "Probably Minuchin's most lauded achievement at the Clinic was his development of treatment techniques with psychosomatic families, particularly those of anorectics" (Simons, 1984, p. 24). In 1974, Minuchin published *Families and Family Therapy*, one of the most clearly written and popular books in the family therapy field. This work propelled Minuchin into widespread notoriety. In 1975, he stepped down as director of the clinic, but he remained its head of training until 1981.

Since 1981, Minuchin has written several plays and books, including *Mastering Family Therapy: Journeys of Growth and Transformation*, which he coauthored with nine of his supervisees. He set up the Family Studies Institute in New York City, which was renamed the Minuchin Center for the Family when he retired in 1996. Minuchin continues to give workshops and to train therapists from all over the world, including consulting with the Massachusetts Department of Mental Health on home-based therapy. He remains an expert on working with families from diverse cultures and settings. He is passionately committed to social justice. Overall, even in retirement, Minuchin remains a force in the field of family therapy. He now lives with his wife, Patricia, in Boston.

Premises of the Theory

The structural approach as a theory is quite pragmatic. Minuchin's theoretical conceptualization was influenced by the philosophy of Ortega y Gasset, who emphasized individuals interacting with their environment.

One of the primary premises underlying structural family therapy is that every family has a **family structure**, an "invisible set of functional demands that organizes the ways in which family members interact" (Minuchin, 1974, p. 51). This structure is revealed only when the family is in action. In other words, it is impossible to tell what a family's structure is unless the family is active and one is able to observe repeated interaction patterns between family members.

Structure influences families for better or worse. In some families, structure is well organized in a hierarchical pattern, and members easily relate to each other. In others, there is little structure and few arrangements are provided by which family members can easily and meaningfully interact. In both cases, developmental or situational events increase family stress, rigidity, chaos, and dysfunctionality, throwing the family into crisis (Minuchin, 1974). Families that have an open and appropriate structure, however, recover more quickly and function better in the long term than families without such an arrangement.

The structural approach emphasizes the family as a whole, as well as the interactions between subunits of family members. In some dysfunctional families, coalitions arise (Minuchin, Rosman, & Baker, 1978). A **coalition** is an alliance between specific family members against a third member. A **stable coalition** is a fixed and inflexible union (such as a mother and son) that becomes a dominant part of the family's everyday functioning. A **detouring coalition** is one in which the pair holds a third family member responsible for their difficulties or conflicts with one another, thus decreasing the stress on themselves or their relationship.

Furthermore, a major thesis of structural theory is that a person's symptoms are best understood as rooted in the context of family transaction patterns. The family is seen as the client. The hope is that through structuring or restructuring the system all members of the family and the family itself will become stronger (Minuchin, 1974). Families are conceptualized from this perspective as living systems. They operate in an ever-changing environment in which communication and feedback are important (Friedlander, Wildman, & Heatherington, 1991). Consequently, lasting change is dependent on altering the balance and alliances in the family so that new ways of interacting become realities.

Subsystems are another important aspect of the theory. **Subsystems** are smaller units of the system as a whole. They exist to carry out various family tasks. Without subsystems, the overall family system would not function. They are best defined by the boundaries and rules connected with them. Subsystems are formed when family members join together to perform various functions. Some of these functions are temporary, such as painting a room. Others are more permanent, such as parenting a child. Of particular significance are the spousal, parental, and sibling subsystems (Minuchin & Fishman, 1981).

The **spousal subsystem** is composed of the marriage partners. In families where there are two such individuals, the way they support and nurture each other has a lot to do with how well structured the family is and how functionally it runs. Spousal subsystems work best when there is **complementarity** of functions. In such circumstances, there are "reciprocal role relationships that typically constitute an important element in family organization" (Simon, 2004, p. 260). For example, a husband and wife may operate as a team, with one being more responsible for inside house chores and the other for outside house chores, but both accepting the influence they have on each other and their interdependency.

The **parental subsystem** is made up of those responsible for the care, protection, and socialization of children. "A universal tenet of structural family theory is the belief that a cohesive, collaborative parental subsystem is critical for healthy family functioning" (Madden-Derdich, Estrada, Updegraff, & Leonard, 2002, p. 242). As with the spousal subsystem, the parental subsystem is considered healthy if it does not function in a cross-generational way. A **cross-generational alliance** in a family contains members of two different generations within it. If a parent and child collude to obtain certain objectives or needs, such as love or power, they have entered into a cross-generational alliance. Parental subsystems must change as children grow. The rules that are applicable to children, for example, at age 8 do not work at age 18. Therefore, parents are constantly challenged to define appropriate, clear, and permeable boundaries that help family members gain access to each other without becoming fused or distanced.

The **sibling subsystem** is that unit within the family whose members are of the same generation. For example, brothers and sisters are considered to be a sibling subsystem. In some families, the sibling subsystem is composed of those born of the same parents. In other families, such as in remarried arrangements (i.e., stepfamilies), the sibling subsystem is made up of unrelated children. Age differences may affect how well sibling subsystems function. Subsystems of siblings are often composed of those children who are relatively close to each other in age, for example, 2 or 3 years apart. They are generally closer to one another psychologically because of their opportunities to interact together. The larger the age gap between siblings, the less likely they will become allies (i.e., a subsystem).

A third major aspect of structural family therapy is the issue of boundaries. Basically, **boundaries** are the physical and psychological factors that separate people from one another and organize them. "For proper family functioning, the boundaries of subsystems must be clear" (Minuchin, 1974, p. 54). The strength of boundaries is represented in structural family mapping systems by broken, solid, and dotted lines. There are three major types of boundaries:

- clear, represented by a broken horizontal line: -----
- rigid, represented by a solid line: ———
- diffuse, represented by a dotted line: ·····

Clear boundaries consist of rules and habits that allow family members to enhance their communication and relationships with one another because they encourage dialogue. In families with clear boundaries, members freely exchange information and give and receive corrective feedback. For example, in such a family, only one person talks at a time. With clear boundaries, negotiation and accommodation can successfully occur in families. These processes facilitate change, but still maintain the stability of the family. Parents and children feel a sense of belonging, but nevertheless individuate. For a functional, two-parent family with children, clear boundaries might be represented as shown in Figure 9.1(a).

Rigid boundaries are inflexible and keep people separated from each other. In families with rigid boundaries, members experience difficulty relating in an intimate way to one another, and, therefore, individuals become emotionally detached or cut off from other family members. For example, a family in which a husband and wife are detached from each other is represented in Figure 9.1(b).

In the case of **diffuse boundaries**, there is not enough separation between family members. In this arrangement, some family members are said to be "fused." Instead of creating independence and autonomy within individuals, as with clear boundaries, diffused boundaries encourage dependence. A two-parent family with children in which diffused boundaries exist is represented in Figure 9.1(c).

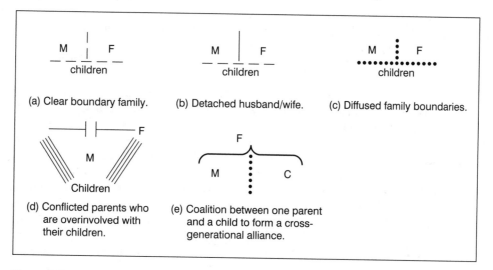

Figure 9.1
Types of family boundaries.

Figure 9.2
Symbols representing how families relate.

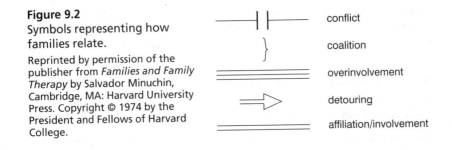

conflict

coalition

overinvolvement

detouring

affiliation/involvement

Reprinted by permission of the publisher from *Families and Family Therapy* by Salvador Minuchin, Cambridge, MA: Harvard University Press. Copyright © 1974 by the President and Fellows of Harvard College.

Other symbols are also used to show how families relate. Among the most common are shown in Figure 9.2.

A two-parent family with children in which there is conflict and overinvolvement is represented in Figure 9.1(d). In such families, **triangulating** exists, and the relationships between the parents and children become closer as the conflict between the parents intensifies. Another family in which a coalition between a parent and children exists is represented in Figure 9.1(e). In this situation, a child becomes **parentified**, as the parents disengage from one another. A **parentified child** is one who is given privileges and responsibilities that exceed what would be considered developmentally consistent with his or her age (Minuchin, 1974).

In the development of families, boundaries and the structure of the family may change regardless of the type of family. Families are not static and new developments or challenges may bring a family closer together or draw it further apart (Pistole & Marson, 2005). It is crucial not to mistake normal family development and growing pains for pathological patterns (Minuchin, 1974). It is also important to realize that, during the course of family life over time, alignments are formed. **Alignments** are the ways family members join together or oppose one another in carrying out a family activity.

In addition to structure, subsystems, and boundaries, structural family therapy is based also on (1) roles, (2) rules, and (3) power (Figley & Nelson, 1990). In regard to **roles**, therapists need to understand the positions under which families are operating (Kaplan, 2000). Families experiencing difficulties have members who relate to each other according to certain expectations that are either outdated or ineffective. The inefficiency of these families includes "little or no expectations that anyone will hear or be affected by what they say [and] little or no expectation of reward for appropriate behaviors" (McWhirter & McWhirter, 1989, p. 23). For instance, the youngest member of such a family may constantly be placed in the role of "the baby" and never be taken seriously by anyone.

Similarly, **rules** that the family first developed may be adhered to regardless of the changes that have occurred in the family's lifestyle or outside circumstances. A family in which the chief wage earner is laid off may still insist on buying clothes at expensive stores. Such a rule, when adhered to, is to the detriment of the family as a functioning unit. Generally, rules in families "may be explicit or implicit." More functional families have more explicit rules. Rules "provide the family ... with structure"—an organized pattern that becomes predictable and manifests itself in repeated patterns (Friesen, 1985, p. 7).

Power is the ability to get something done. In families, power is related to both authority and responsibility (or the one who makes and the one who carries out the decisions). Structural family therapists observe that, in dysfunctional families, power is vested in only a few members. The ability of family members to provide input in the decision-making process that governs the family is limited. Disenfranchised family members may cut themselves off from the family, become enmeshed with stronger members, or battle to gain some control in an overt or covert way. The structural family therapist, after noting how power is distributed in the family, will often use his or her skills to unbalance the family and help them learn new ways of dealing with situations that are power based.

Treatment Techniques

Structural family therapy is sometimes referred to as a way of looking at families. According to Minuchin (1974), dysfunctions result from the development of dysfunctional sets. **Dysfunctional sets** are the family reactions, developed in response to stress, that are repeated without modification whenever there is family conflict. For example, one spouse might verbally attack the other, bringing charges and countercharges, until the fight escalates into physical violence or the couple withdraws from each other.

A number of procedures are associated with the structural family therapy approach (Friesen, 1985; Minuchin & Fishman, 1981). These techniques are sometimes employed in a sequential manner, or they may be combined. They are basically divided into those "that are primarily used in the formation of a therapeutic system," that is, techniques for joining, and those that are "more directly aimed at provoking disequilibrium and change" (Colapinto, 2000, p. 152). The most frequently used structural treatment methods are highlighted in the following sections.

Joining

Joining is defined as "the process of 'coupling' that occurs between the therapist and the family, leading to the development of the therapeutic system" (Sauber, L'Abate, & Weeks, 1985, p. 95). "In this process, the therapist adjusts to the communication style and perceptions of the family members" (Carlson & Ellis, 2004, p. 353). To do so, the therapist makes contact with each family member. In the process, the therapist allies with family members through expressing interest in them as individuals and working with and for them (Minuchin & Fishman, 1981). In this leadership role, the therapist helps initiate the treatment process. Joining is considered one of the most important prerequisites to restructuring. It is a contextual process that is continuous. It is particularly important to join powerful family members, as well as angry ones. Special care and attention must be taken to accept the point of view of the father, who thinks therapy is a waste of time and money, or of the angry teenager, who feels victimized. It is also important to reconnect with such people at frequent intervals during the therapy, particularly during times of overt tension or anger.

The structural family therapy approach joins families in one of four ways. The first is by tracking. In **tracking**, the therapist follows the content of the family (i.e., the facts). For instance, the therapist might say to a woman: "So as I understand this situation, you and your husband were married last May and had your first child this past March. You do not think you had enough time to establish a relationship with your spouse before you were required to start one with your baby."

During tracking, judgments are not made by the therapist (at least not overtly). Rather, information is gathered by means of open-ended questions to inquire about the interests and concerns of family members. Tracking is best exemplified when the therapist gives a family feedback.

The second way of joining is through mimesis. In **mimesis**, the therapist becomes like the family "in the manner or content of their communications, for example, joking with a jovial family, or talking slowly or sparsely with a slow-talking family" (Sauber et al., 1985, p. 107). Or, if a family frequently uses road metaphors to describe what is occurring between its members, a therapist would do likewise by stating: "I want to help you find a highway you can travel that leads somewhere and that everyone enjoys."

A third way of joining is through confirmation. **Confirmation** of a family member involves using an affective word to reflect an expressed or unexpressed feeling of that family member. It may also be accomplished through a nonjudgmental description of the behavior of the individual. For example, a therapist might say to a daughter who stares at the floor when addressing her father: "I sense that your looking at the floor when you talk to your father is connected with some depression you feel inside."

The final way to join with a family is by accommodation. In **accommodation**, the therapist makes personal adjustments in order to achieve a therapeutic alliance. For example, the therapist would remove his or her coat if the family came to the session in shirtsleeves (Minuchin, 1974).

Disequilibrium Techniques

As indicated earlier, disequilibrium techniques are interventions that are aimed at changing a system. "Some of them, like enactment and boundary making, are primarily employed in the creation of a different sequence of events, whereas others, like reframing, punctuation, and unbalancing, tend to foster a different perception of reality" (Colapinto, 2000, p. 154).

Reframing

The technique of reframing involves changing a perception by explaining a situation from a different context. In this activity, the facts of an event do not change, but the meaning of the situation is examined from a new perspective (Kim, 2003; Sherman & Fredman, 1986). For instance, at the birth of our third child, my wife looked up at me and said: "The honeymoon is not over. There are simply more people on it." Through the reframing process, even a negative situation can sometimes be viewed in a more favorable light. This type of change is crucial to the promotion of movement in family therapy. For example, if disruptive behavior is reframed by the therapist as being "naughty" instead of "incorrigible," family members can find ways to modify their attitudes toward the "naughty" person and even help him or her make changes.

Punctuation

Punctuation is a universal phenomenon and is characteristic of all human interaction. It is the way a person describes a situation, that is, begins and ends a sentence, due to a selective perspective or emotional involvement in an event. In structural family therapy, punctuation is "the selective description of a transaction in accordance with a therapist's goals" (Colapinto, 2000, p. 158). If a therapist is trying to show that a mother has competence in controlling the behavior of her children, the therapist may declare her competent when she corrects or disciplines a child. By punctuating a particular situation at a specific moment in time, the perception of everyone involved is changed. Punctuation enhances possibilities for new competencies and behaviors in the future.

Unbalancing

Unbalancing (or allying with a subsystem) is a procedure wherein the therapist supports an individual or subsystem against the rest of the family. A therapist may sit next to a daughter who is being accused of not living up to the family's tradition. In this position, the therapist can also take up for the daughter against the family and give reasons why it is important for the daughter to create new ways of behaving. Family members, individually and as a group, are then forced to act differently with the person or subsystem. They have to expand their roles and functions. When this technique is used to support an underdog in the family system (as it usually is), a chance for change within the total hierarchical relationship is fostered (Sauber et al., 1985).

Enactment

The process of enactment is when the therapist "invites client-system members to interact directly with each other" (Simon, 2004, p. 260). It consists of families bringing problematic behavioral sequences into treatment by showing them to the therapist in a demonstrative transaction. Such a process redirects communication between the therapist and the family so that communications and resulting changes in behaviors occur "among family members instead of between the family and the therapist" (Kim, 2003, p. 390). In other words, enactment uses the relationship between family members as an agent or mechanism of change while it simultaneously and directly facilitates change within the relationship (Davis & Butler, 2004).

A family that frequently argues about how they are going to spend their Saturdays may be asked by the therapist to have a heated argument in front of him or her instead of describing the fight or waiting for the fight to occur at another time. The idea is to see how family members interact with one another and to challenge their existing patterns and rules. This method can also be used to help family members gain control over behaviors they insist are beyond their control. It puts an end to members' claims that they are helpless in controlling their actions, thoughts, and feelings. The result is that family members experience their own transactions with heightened awareness (Minuchin, 1974). In examining their roles, members hopefully discover more functional ways of behaving.

Working with Spontaneous Interaction

Working with spontaneous interaction is similar to being a lighting expert, who focuses the spotlight of attention on some particular behavior. It occurs whenever families display actions in sessions that are disruptive or dysfunctional, such as members yelling at one another or parents withdrawing from their children. In these cases, therapists can see firsthand the dynamics within a family's interactions. On such occasions, therapists can point out the dynamics and sequencing of behaviors. The focus is on process, not content. It is crucial that therapists use such occasions to help families recognize patterns of interaction and what changes they might make to bring about modification.

Boundary Making

A boundary is an invisible line that separates people or subsystems from each other psychologically (Minuchin, 1974). To function effectively, families need different types of boundaries at distinct times of stage development. "Each stage brings demands, forcing the family members to accommodate to new needs as family members grow up or age, and circumstances change" (Minuchin, 1993, p. 40). Families may need more rigid boundaries during stages when children are young, in order to make sure that everyone is taken care of, and more flexible boundaries during the time when there are teenagers in the house, in order to meet the demands of different schedules. "Part of the therapeutic task is to help the family define, redefine, or change the boundaries within the family. The therapist also helps the family to either strengthen or loosen boundaries, depending upon the family's situation" (Sauber et al., 1985, p. 16).

Intensity

Intensity is the structural method of changing maladaptive transactions by using strong affect, repeated intervention, or prolonged pressure. The tone, volume, pacing, and choice of words used by a therapist can raise the affective intensity of statements. For example, intensity is manifested if a therapist keeps forcefully telling a family to "do something different" (Minuchin & Fishman, 1981). The persistence employed in this technique breaks down family patterns of equilibrium and challenges the family's perception of reality. Intensity works best if therapists know what they want to say and do so in a direct, unapologetic manner that is goal specific.

Restructuring

The procedure of restructuring is at the heart of the structural approach. The goal of this approach to family therapy is structural change. Restructuring involves changing the structure of the family. The rationale behind restructuring is to make the family more functional by altering the existing hierarchy and interaction patterns so that problems are not maintained. It is accomplished through the use of enactment, unbalancing, directives, and boundary formation.

If a father dominates to the point where children feel intimidated, the therapist may ask the family to enact a "father-dominated scenario." As it occurs, the therapist may instruct the rest of the family members to behave in a certain way, for example, uniformly refusing to do what the father requests without getting something in return. If these instructions are carried out, the family behaves differently and change becomes possible. If change occurs, members generally feel more enfranchised and invested in the family.

Shaping Competence

In the process of shaping competence, structural family therapists help families and family members become more functional by highlighting positive behaviors. Therapists may reinforce parents who make their children behave, even if the parents succeed only momentarily in accomplishing this feat. In effect, shaping competence is a matter of therapists not acting as experts all of the time. They should instead reinforce family members for doing things right or making their own appropriate decisions (Minuchin, Lee, & Simon, 1997). As a result, positive abilities are highlighted and appropriate alternative ways of working with problems are produced.

Diagnosing

One of the main tasks of structural family therapists is to diagnose the family in such a way as to describe the systemic interrelationships of all family members. This type of mapping, as shown in Figure 9.1, allows therapists to see what needs to be modified or changed if the family is going to improve. For example, therapists may note disruptive coalitions or triangles among family members (see Figure 9.1(d) and (e)).

Diagnosing is done early in the therapeutic process before the family can induct the therapist as a part of their system. By diagnosing interactions, therapists become proactive, instead of reactive, in promoting structural interventions.

Adding Cognitive Constructions

Although structural family therapy is primarily action-oriented, it does include verbal components in the form of words to help families help themselves. The multiple aspects of the technique of adding cognitive constructions include advice, information, pragmatic fictions, and paradox. *Advice* and *information* are derived from experience and knowledge of families in therapy. They are used to calm anxious family members and to reassure them about certain actions. They may occasionally include explanations about structure within the family. If a family member says, "I'll bet you've never seen a family as messed up as we are," the therapist might reply, "Your family is unique in quite a few ways, but many of your concerns and behaviors are common among families I see."

Pragmatic fictions are pronouncements that help families and family members change. For instance, therapists may occasionally tell children that they are acting younger than their years. These pronouncements help children gain a greater grasp of reality. **Paradox**, on the other hand, is a confusing message meant to frustrate or confuse families and motivate them to search for alternatives. For example, a family that is resistant to instructions and change may be told not to follow the therapist's instructions and not to change. Given this permission to do as they wish, families may defy the therapist and become better, or they may explore reasons why their behaviors are as they are and make changes in the ways they interact.

Role of the Therapist

The structural family therapist is both an observer and an expert who is active, like a theater director, in making interventions to modify and change the underlying structure of the family (Simon, 2004). Successful structural family therapists require high energy and precise timing so that in-session interactions among client-families result in new family organization (Minuchin et al., 1967).

The therapist's role changes over the course of therapy (Minuchin, 1974). In the first phase of treatment, the therapist joins the family and takes a leadership position. In phase two, the therapist mentally maps out the family's underlying structure. In the final phase, the therapist helps transform family structure. Thus, during treatment the therapist watches "the family 'dance' and then enters ('joins') and leaves the interactional field at will in order to transform it therapeutically" (Friedlander et al., 1991, p. 397).

The therapist uses a number of techniques to accomplish the goal of change, including unbalancing (e.g., siding with one member of the family), praise, challenges, direct orders, and judgments (Fishman, 1988; Minuchin & Fishman, 1981). An implicit, if not explicit, assumption is that the therapist has a "correct" interpretation of what is happening within the family and powerful tools for helping the family construct and maintain a more functional system.

"Like a theatrical director, the therapist assumes responsibility for setting up" dramatic scenes, "designating which family members will be involved, what they will talk about, and how they will talk about it" (Simon, 2004, p. 260). Once the scene is set in motion, the "therapist remains on the periphery of the enactment, observing. Should the enactment bog down, or revert to old dysfunctional patterns, the therapist enters as a 'critic,' sometimes even a harsh one, challenging client-family members to renounce apparent self-interest … " (Simon, 2004, p. 260).

In some cases, the therapist acts dramatically (if this is the only way to get the attention of the family) (Simon, 1984). As a critic, the therapist may say to a withdrawn or denying family member: "Admit it, through your actions and passivity you are playing a major role in how this family operates. You are being selfish and the family is suffering as a result." At other times, the therapist is low-key and notices repetitive interactions, such as a young girl clinging to her mother. On such occasions, the therapist may or may not mention the actions. Regardless, the therapist is never a "player" in any of the family scenes and thus operates in what may be called a "'middle-distance'—as opposed to proximal—position vis-à-vis the client system" (Simon, 2004, p. 260). Thus the therapist works to change the structure of the family at crucial times, without becoming a part of it, so that the family collectively can unite in a healthy and productive way.

Process and Outcome

The process of change within structural family therapy is probably best described as gradual but steady. It is geared to the cultural context of the family but follows some general patterns. When successful, this approach results in symptom resolution and structural changes. Usually, significant changes occur after a few sessions because the therapist uses specific techniques to help family members interact in new ways. These techniques are often used in an overlapping manner in order to help the family to become less homeostatic. The idea is to emphasize action over insight. Family members are given **homework** (i.e., activities to do outside of the session) in addition to the work they do within their therapeutic time.

In successful treatment, the overall structure of the family is altered and reorganized. This change in structure enables family members to relate to one another in a more functional and productive manner. As a part of this process, dated and outgrown rules are replaced by those more related to the family's current realities. In addition, parents are in charge of their children, and a differentiation between distinct subsystems emerges (Piercy et al., 1997).

Unique Aspects of Structural Family Therapy

Emphases

One strong aspect of structural family therapy is its versatility. The structural approach has proven successful in treating families experiencing difficulties with juvenile delinquents, alcoholics, and anorexics (Fishman, 1988). It is as appropriate for low-socioeconomic-level families (Minuchin, Colapinto, & Minuchin, 1999) as for high-income families. It can be adapted for use with minority and cross-cultural populations as well (Boyd-Franklin, 1987; Jung, 1984). Its concepts, for example, such as hierarchy and advocacy for a parental-executive system, boundaries, and subsystems, "make it ideal for and compatible with Asian-American cultural and family values" (Kim, 2003, p. 391). In essence, structural family therapy is suitable for a wide variety of client-families. It is sensitive to the effect of culture on families.

A second characteristic of this approach is its emphasis on terminology and ease of application. Basically, structural family therapy has clearly defined terms and procedures. Treatment methods and techniques are described in such a way that novice therapists can easily conceptualize what they are to do and when to do it (Minuchin & Fishman, 1981). The process is clear because of the clarity of the theory.

A third attribute of structural therapy is that it helped make family therapy as a whole acceptable to medicine in general and psychiatry in particular (Simon, 1984). As a psychiatrist, Minuchin was able to make a case with the medical community for his approach and for family therapy treatment. Without this recognition and implicit endorsement, family therapy would be more of an intellectual exercise and a mystery.

A fourth aspect of the structural approach is its emphasis on symptom removal and reorganization of the family. "Changes in family structure contribute to changes in behavior and the inner psychic processes of the members of the system" (Minuchin, 1974, p. 9). Families have a different emphasis as a result of treatment and are able to cope better. Members experience their families in new and positive ways.

A fifth dimension of structural family therapy is its pragmatic, problem-solving emphasis. Therapists are active in bringing about change (Colapinto, 2000). By using reframing, for example, a structural family therapist can help a family conceptualize a situation as being "depressive" rather than "hopeless." By seeing the difficulty in this way, the family can take steps to cope with or address depression and thereby gain greater control over themselves and their environment. In essence, structural family therapy was born out of necessity. It has not deviated from its origins.

Comparison with Other Theories

Structural family therapy is a well-developed, action-oriented, and pragmatic approach to working with families. It has been as well articulated and illustrated as any other family therapy. However, critics charge that the theory is not complex or profound enough to address the complexity of family life to any great extent.

A second point of comparison is based on the accusation by some clinicians that the focus of the theory lends itself to reinforcing sexism and sexual stereotypes (Simon, 1984). These critics stress that Minuchin encourages husbands to take on executive roles and wives to take on expressive roles in the family so that everyone does not suffer (Luepnitz, 1988). They contend that mothers should be encouraged and supported to become more effective. In fairness, it must be said that Minuchin developed his theory with low-income families in which husbands had hidden or indirect power and would undermine the efforts of their spouses.

A third distinction of the structural approach is that it focuses on the present. Past patterns and history are not emphasized (Minuchin, 1974). Structural family therapy basically ignores historical data. For example, structuralists mentally map the present configuration of the family rather than pay attention to the historic or developmental landmarks of the family over time.

A fourth aspect of structural family therapy is that it is sometimes hard to distinguish from strategic family therapy (Friesen, 1985; Stanton, 1981). In both approaches, there is a pragmatic emphasis on identifying and blocking present behaviors that are destructive and repetitive. There is also a focus on the process, as opposed to the content, of sessions. The therapist takes a great deal of responsibility for initiating change through such techniques as enactments or homework assignments. In both approaches, the time frame for treatment is relatively short-term—less than 6 months.

A final distinction of structural family therapy is that families may not become as empowered because the therapist is active and in control of the process (Friesen, 1985). This aspect of treatment may be helpful to families who would not have taken any initiative by themselves, but for others it may hinder the speed of progress.

CASE ILLUSTRATION

THE JOHNSON FAMILY

Family Background

Melinda Johnson, age 28, is the mother of four children: Bill, age 12, Sally, age 8, Holly Jean, age 5, and Michael, age 2. Her common-law husband, George, lives with the family on occasion but usually stays away because he fears Melinda's social worker will cut off government support if he is discovered in her apartment. Because of George's frequent absence and his financial inability to contribute to the family, Melinda and her children often go without needed food and medical care. Their apartment in "the projects" is in serious disrepair.

Melinda recently told her social worker that Bill has been sneaking out late at night. She is unable to control him, and the social worker is considering removing him from the family. Melinda fears the effects of such a process and is equally distressed at the thought that Bill may become part of a gang and endanger her and the younger children. Her social worker wants specific detailed information on what Bill is doing. Melinda's mother, age 45, who lives nearby, is urging Melinda to "do something and do it quickly."

Conceptualization of Family: Structural Perspective

From a structural perspective, the Johnson family is unorganized and problematic. It lacks resources. Melinda does not have a supportive relationship with either George or her mother. The fact that Bill is beginning to act out is indicative of this lack of a hierarchy and the effects of poverty. Power is being usurped by Bill because the boundaries within the family unit are diffused. If the family structure is not strengthened soon, Bill will most likely become triangulated.

Process of Treatment: Structural Family Therapy

To help the Johnsons, a structural family therapist would first join with all members of the family that come for treatment. The therapist would then urge all members of the family, including George and Melinda's mother, to attend most, if not all, sessions. The therapist would next mentally map the family after they are seated and notice who sits next to whom and the verbal interactions that take place. Then, to help the family begin to help itself, the therapist would move members around until natural subsystems within the family are grouped together, such as parents and children. With the Johnsons, the therapist would concentrate also on mimesis and match the family's feeling mood, most likely hopelessness.

After the therapist "joins" and "accommodates" the family, he or she would begin to take a leadership role in the family. First, he or she would unbalance the family by allying with the parent subsystem. By doing so, the therapist emphasizes the importance of a strong couple subsystem, that is, both Melinda and George. The therapist might then work with spontaneous interactions within the session itself. If Melinda and George ask Bill to sit down and he does not, the therapist might insist through the use of an intensity method of repetition and would keep trying until successful. Then, even if only momentarily, the therapist would note the success and in doing so would shape competence. The therapist might also use reframing and state that Melinda's mother, through her overinvolvement in pressuring her daughter to act, is "quite concerned" about her daughter and the family's well-being.

In this approach, the therapist would always begin an intervention with the parent subsystem in order to clarify and emphasize boundaries. As treatment progresses each session, the therapist would seek to put less attention on Bill and more on family dynamics and processes as influenced by structure. Bill would lose his status as the identified patient and the family would become the treated unit. As boundaries and structure are changed, power would regress to the parent subsystem. At this time, the therapist would share with Melinda and George some pragmatic and cognitive knowledge to help them stay on top of the family situation.

Summary and Conclusion

Structural family therapy was formed out of necessity in the 1960s by Salvador Minuchin and his colleagues at the Wiltwyck School in New York. It was begun because traditional methods of treatment, especially psychoanalysis, were not effective in serving the needs of inner-city ghetto boys from low-income families, who were the primary residents of this facility. It was refined at the Philadelphia Child Guidance Clinic in the 1970s and 1980s. It continues to be a major theoretical approach to helping families change.

Like most systems theorists, the structural family therapists are interested in how the components of a system interact, how balance or homeostasis is achieved, how family feedback mechanisms operate, and how dysfunctional communication patterns develop and are sustained. A particular emphasis of the structural approach is that all families have structures that are revealed through member interactions. Some family structures are more functional than others. Families that have a hierarchy that is well organized adjust better to their environment and crises than families that are not set up in this manner. Of special interest to structural family therapists are spouse, parent, and sibling subsystems and the clearness of boundaries between them. In addition, roles, rules, and power within the family are emphasized.

A number of innovative techniques and procedures have come from structural family therapy. Among the best known and most effective are joining, reframing, unbalancing, enacting, working with spontaneous interaction, boundary formation, intensity, restructuring, shaping competence, and adding cognitive constructions. Like an artist, structural family therapists time the intensity and emphasis of their inputs. On some occasions, they "map" family interactions; on others, they intervene in dramatic fashion. This unpredictability can be a powerful feature of the approach.

If all works well, families leave structural family treatment with more functional ways by which members can interact and with clearer boundaries. Families may not have insight into their new behaviors, but they have new ways of relating. Structural family therapy is versatile in the types of families with which it can be used. It is also easily combined with other family therapy approaches, such as strategic family therapy. Critics of the approach claim it concentrates too much on surface issues and that it may be implicitly sexist. Nevertheless, structural family therapy remains popular as a treatment methodology.

Summary Table

Structural Family Therapy

Major Theorists

Salvador Minuchin

Bernie Rosman

Thomas Todd

Braulio Montalvo

Harry Aponte

Charles Fishman

Duncan Stanton

Premises of the Theory

Family functioning involves family structure, subsystems, and boundaries.

Overt and covert rules, hierarchies, and interpersonal accommodation must be understood and changed, if necessary, to keep the family flexible and adjusted to new situations.

Treatment Techniques

The family is treated as a system or a subsystem. However, individual needs are not ignored.

One goal of treatment is to bring problematic behaviors out in the open so therapists can observe and help change them.

Another goal is to bring about structural changes within families, such as organizational patterns, hierarchies, and sequences.

Therapeutic techniques include the following:

- Joining
- Accommodating
- Restructuring
- Working with interaction (enactment, spontaneous behaviors)
- Intensifying messages
- Unbalancing
- Reframing
- Shaping competence
- Making boundaries

Role of the Therapist

Therapists mentally "map" their families and work actively in counseling sessions. They instruct families to interact through enactments and spontaneous sequences. Therapists are like theater directors.

Process and Outcome

Action is emphasized over insight with the therapist using specific techniques to help family members interact in new ways.

Family members are given homework to do outside of therapy sessions. The overall structure of the family is altered and reorganized.

Unique Aspects of Structural Family Therapy

Structural family therapy emphasizes the following:

- The approach was the first developed for low-socioeconomic-level families and is very pragmatic.
- It was one of the first developed exclusively for families.
- It was influential in getting the profession of psychiatry to respect family therapy as an approach to treatment.
- The tenets and techniques of the therapy are clearly stated by Minuchin, Fishman, Stanton, and others.
- Treatment has proven effective in working with families of addicts, eating disorders, and suicidals.
- The therapy is well-researched, systemic, problem-focused in the present, and relatively short-term (generally less than 6 months).
- Therapists and families are active during the sessions.
- Homework is sometimes assigned in between sessions.

Comparison with Other Theories

The theory is as well-developed and well-articulated as any approach in the family therapy field.

Some feminists believe the theory promotes gender stereotypes by emphasizing traditional paternal roles, but that is not Minuchin's focus.

The theory is not as strong in explaining family dynamics and development as the practice of this approach is in fostering change.

The therapist must be active and creative. He or she is highly influential in the change process and may inadvertently prevent maximum family interaction and employment.

Structural family theory and strategic family theory are sometimes conceptualized as one in the same, which makes it hard for some therapists to discern the unique aspects of each. The result is often a failure to appreciate the contributions of structural family therapy or to use it appropriately.

CHAPTER 10

Strategic and Systemic Family Therapies

---•---

After giving birth to Nathaniel
you asked for a Wendy's shake and fries.
I can still remember as if yesterday
the words that broke the silence
surrounding the miracle of new life:
"I'm hungry."

Walking from your room still dazed,
through the Sunday streets of Birmingham,
I brought you back your first request from labor.
That cold November morning is now a treasure in my mind
as are you and the child that you delivered.

---•---

Gladding, 1993b

Strategic and systemic family therapies are method-oriented and brief in duration. In this chapter, the essence of these theories is examined and compared. Strategic and systemic therapies are indebted to the work of Milton Erickson, whose work influenced their founders. Erickson's goal in treatment was change. He believed in utilizing the resources of his clients and designing a "strategy for each specific problem" (Madanes, 1991, p. 396). Erickson then worked with his clients to help them become active in assisting themselves. He did so through giving them directives and indirect suggestions. He did not care if people gained insight as long as their actions produced beneficial results. "If Freud was a philosopher-priest from Vienna, Erickson was a samurai warrior from Wisconsin" (Wylie, 1990, p. 28).

Despite sharing a common heritage—both obtained ideas from Erickson and used some of the same methods (e.g., seeing families for a limited period of time)—strategic and systemic family therapies are distinct. The differences between these approaches have been articulated by theorists representing:

- the strategic family therapists of the Mental Research Institute (MRI) (http://www.mri.org/)
- the strategic family therapists of the Family Therapy Institute, specifically, Jay Haley (http://www.jay-haley-on-therapy.com/) and Cloe Madanes (http://www.cloemadanes.com/index.htm)
- the systemic family therapists of the Milan Systems Group

The MRI form of strategic family therapy is the oldest of these therapeutic approaches. It is a descendent of the Bateson communications studies group, which was conducted in Palo Alto from 1952 to 1962. Among the most active modern proponents of this approach are Paul Watzlawick and John Weakland. Other figures connected with this branch of strategic family therapy are Lynn Hoffman, Peggy Penn, and Richard Rabkin.

A second type of strategic family therapy is that articulated by the cofounders of the Family Therapy Institute of Washington, most notably Jay Haley and Cloe Madanes. This school of thought was organized in the mid-1970s although the institute Haley and Madanes established is now defunct (Keim, 2000). Nevertheless, Haley, Madanes, and their followers continue to have an influence on other theories, theorists, and teams of researchers, including those in the MRI Palo Alto group.

The third group of theorists considered here was from Milan, Italy. The genesis of this branch of family therapy, usually referred to as **systemic family therapy**, was formulated by a team of practitioners whose members originally included Mara Selvini Palazzoli, Luigi Boscolo, Gianfranco Cecchin, and Guiliana Prata (Campbell, Draper, & Crutchley, 1991). The team leader of this effort was Selvini Palazzoli. In 1967, she established the Milan Center for the Study of the Family. Previous to this landmark event, Selvini Palazzoli had devoted her life to the study and treatment of anorexia nervosa, with limited success (Selvini Palazzoli, 1974). Systemic family therapy is characterized as **long brief therapy** because of the amount of time that lapses between sessions (usually a month) and the duration of treatment (up to a year) (Tomm, 1984a).

The format of this chapter consists of discussions of the underlying principles of strategic and systemic theories as unique but related approaches. Included in this examination is a brief description of major professionals involved in formulating these theories. The primary assumptions and underpinning techniques of these positions are highlighted. The foci of therapists using these orientations are then discussed. Finally, the process and outcome of these theories are described along with their unique contributions to the field of family therapy.

Strategic Family Therapy

The strategic family therapy approaches have a history that is both long and distinguished. Jay Haley (1963, 1973) coined the term **strategic therapy** to describe the work of Milton Erickson. Erickson conducted therapy by paying extreme attention to details of the symptoms his clients presented. His focus, like that of most present-day strategic therapists, was to change behavior by manipulating it and not to instill insight into those with whom he worked.

Erickson achieved his objectives in therapy by:

- accepting and emphasizing the positive (i.e., he framed all symptoms and maladaptive behaviors as helpful)
- using indirect and ambiguously worded directives
- encouraging or directing routine behaviors so that resistance is shown through change and not through normal and continuous actions (Haley, 1963)

Major Theorists

The strategic family therapy approaches have many well-known practitioners, such as Paul Watzlawick, John Weakland, and Cloe Madanes. However, as a representative of these approaches, the background of Jay Haley is highlighted here.

Jay Haley

Jay Haley is considered to be one of the first generation of family therapists. His theoretical writings and techniques have had a powerful impact on the development of family therapy worldwide, especially the Milan systems approach originated by Selvini Palazzoli. He has served as an effective communicator between people and groups and has been a strong advocate of family therapy in public and professional settings. Haley's development is unique among family therapists. He learned from and with the three people who had the most influence on the evolution of family therapy: Milton Erickson, Gregory Bateson, and Salvador Minuchin.

Haley began his career with Gregory Bateson in 1952. Because he had a master's degree in communications, his chief responsibility in the research team Bateson assembled was to take a lead in diagnosing communication patterns in schizophrenic families. As a result of his work, Haley became interested in studying the hypnotherapy communication process of Milton Erickson. He learned hypnosis from Erickson in 1953 and later taught and practiced it (Simon, 1982). He incorporated much of Erickson's ideas into his own concepts about how to do therapy. Erickson supervised him as he learned to become a therapist. Basically, he adopted and modified Erickson's individual emphasis so that it would work with families.

In 1962, after the Bateson team dissolved, Haley joined the Mental Research Institute staff, where he worked until 1967. It was at this time that he stopped doing therapy and became primarily involved in "family research and the observation of therapy" (Simon, 1982, p. 20). He also became the first editor of the initial journal in the field of family therapy, *Family Process*, a position he held from 1962 to 1969. Haley became even more involved in supervision when he moved east to join Salvador Minuchin at the Philadelphia Child Guidance Center in 1967. With Minuchin, he organized "the **Institute for Family**

Counseling (IFC), a project training people from the Philadelphia ghetto, who had no formal education beyond high school, to be family therapists" (Simon, 1982, p. 20). This process further established his prominence.

In 1974, he moved to the Washington, D.C., area to establish the Family Therapy Institute with Cloe Madanes. After this move, he published two of his most influential books, *Problem Solving Therapy* (1976) and *Leaving Home* (1980). These books spelled out the essence of strategic family therapy as Haley views it, an approach that distinguishes itself by its emphasis on power and hierarchy. He is described as having the skills of a power broker and a military strategist and having made these skills "respectable therapeutic techniques" (Wylie, 1990, p. 28). Haley retired in 1995 and currently lives in La Jolla, California.

Premises of the Theory

As a group, strategic family therapies follow many of Milton Erickson's principles. They emphasize short-term treatment of about 10 sessions. Often strategic therapies are characterized as brief therapies. The term *brief*, used in this way, is misleading. **Brief therapy** has to do more with the clarity about what needs to be changed rather than with time. "A central principle of brief therapy is that one evaluates which solutions have so far been attempted for the patient's problem" (Priebe & Pommerien, 1992, p. 433). After the evaluation, different solutions in therapy are tried. These solutions are often the opposite of what has already been attempted (Watzlawick, 1978).

For instance, if parents have begged a daughter to make good grades, treatment might focus on having the parents ask the daughter to show them how she manages to do so poorly in school. They may even instruct her to continue what she has been doing. "Brief therapists hold in common the belief that therapy must be specifically goal-directed, problem-focused, well-defined, and, first and foremost, aimed at relieving the client's presenting complaint" (Wylie, 1990, p. 29).

In general, strategic family therapists concentrate on the following dimensions of family life:

- **Family rules**: the overt and covert rules families use to govern themselves, such as "you must only speak when spoken to"
- **Family homeostasis**: the tendency of the family to remain in its same pattern of functioning unless challenged to do otherwise, for example, getting up and going to bed at the same time
- **Quid pro quo**: the responsiveness of family members to treating others in the way they are treated, that is, something for something
- **Redundancy principle**: the fact that a family interacts within a limited range of repetitive behavioral sequences
- **Punctuation**: the idea that people in a transaction believe that what they say is caused by what others say
- **Symmetrical relationships** and **complementary relationships**: the fact that relationships within a family are both among equals (symmetrical) and unequals (complementary)
- **Circular causality**: the idea that one event does not "cause" another but that events are interconnected and that the factors behind a behavior, such as a kiss or a slap, are multiple

Treatment Techniques

As a group, strategic family therapists are very innovative. They believe that telling people what they are doing wrong is not helpful. The same is true concerning the encouragement of catharsis (Haley, 1976). If families are going to change, alterations in the ways their members act must precede new perceptions and feelings. This goal can be accomplished in an almost endless number of ways. Some problems can be resolved by not treating them as problems, for example, such as not becoming overly concerned when a 2-year-old throws a temper tantrum because that is typical behavior at that age.

Each intervention in strategic therapy is tailored to the idiosyncrasies of persons and problems. The customization makes strategic therapies some of the most technique-driven of all family therapies. Among the various schools of strategic family therapy, different concepts and methods are highlighted here. In general, strategic family therapists emphasize reframing, directive, paradox, ordeals, pretend, and positioning techniques.

Reframing

Reframing involves the use of language to induce a cognitive shift within family members and alter the perception of a situation. In reframing, a different interpretation is given to a family's situation or behavior. In this process, a circumstance is given new meaning and, as a consequence, other ways of behaving are explored. Reframing does not change a situation, but "the alteration of meaning invites the possibility of change" (Piercy & Sprenkle, 1986, p. 35). "Depression" may be conceptualized as "irresponsibility" or "stubbornness."

Reframing helps establish rapport between the therapist and the family and breaks down resistance. Through the use of reframing, what was once seen as out-of-control behavior may become voluntary and open to change.

Directive

A directive is an instruction from a family therapist for a family to behave differently. "The directive is to strategic therapy what the interpretation is to psychoanalysis. It is the basic tool of the approach" (Madanes, 1991, p. 397). Many types of directives can be given in strategic therapy, including **nonverbal messages** (e.g., silence, voice tone, and posture), **direct and indirect suggestions** (e.g., "go fast" or "you may not want to change too quickly"), and **assigned behaviors** (e.g., when you think you won't sleep, force yourself to stay up all night). The purpose of these "outside of therapy" assignments is to help people to behave differently so that they can have different subjective experiences. Directives also increase the influence of the therapist in the change process and give the therapist information about how family members react to suggested changes.

An example of a directive is to tell a family to "go slow" in working to bring about change. In this situation, their resistance to change may dissolve as they attempt to disobey the directive. On the other hand, if they follow the directive, the therapist can gain more influence in their lives.

Paradox

One of the most controversial and powerful techniques in strategic family therapy is paradox (Sexton & Montgomery, 1994). Although fine distinctions can be made between them, this process is very similar to **prescribing the symptom**. It gives client-families and their members permission to do something they are already doing and is intended to lower or eliminate resistance. Jay Haley (1976) is one of the best-known proponents of this technique. Paradox takes many forms, including the use of restraining, prescribing, and redefining:

1. In **restraining**, the therapist tells the client-family that they are incapable of doing anything other than what they are doing. A therapist might say: "In considering change, I am not sure you can do anything other than what you are presently doing."
2. In **prescribing**, family members are instructed to enact a troublesome dysfunctional behavior in front of the therapist. Parents may be asked to show how they argue with their 16-year-old about when he will be allowed to get a driver's license. They are to continue the argument for about the same amount of time the argument usually takes and to come up with the same impasses.
3. **Redefining** is attributing positive connotations to symptomatic or troublesome actions. The idea is that symptoms have meaning for those who display them whether such meaning is logical or not. In the case of a school-phobic child, the therapist might redefine her behavior as an attempt to keep her parents together in the marriage through focusing their attention on her.

It should be noted, especially by novice therapists, that a paradox is never used when a more straightforward approach, like a directive, can be implemented effectively.

Ordeals

The ordeals technique involves helping the client to give up symptoms that are more troublesome to maintain than they are worth (Haley, 1984). In this method, the therapist assigns a family or family member(s) the task of performing an ordeal in order to eliminate a symptom. The ordeal is a constructive or neutral behavior that must be performed before engaging in the undesirable behavior. For example, an ordeal might be to exercise before the onset of depression or to give a present to a despised person or group. In essence, the ordeal is always healthy, but is not an activity that those directed to do it want to engage in. The hope is that those involved will give up the symptom in order to avoid performing the constructive behavior.

Pretend

The pretend technique is a gentler and less confrontive technique than most of the other procedures used in strategic family therapy. Cloe Madanes (1981, 1984) is identified as the creator of this concept. Basically, the therapist asks family members to pretend to engage in a troublesome behavior, such as having a fight. The act of pretending to fight helps individuals change through experiencing control of a previously involuntary action.

Positioning

The act of positioning by the therapist is one that involves acceptance and exaggeration of what family members are saying (Piercy & Sprenkle, 1986). If conducted properly, it helps the family see the absurdity of what they are doing. They are thereby freed to do something else. For example, if a family member states that her relationship with her father is "difficult," the therapist might respond: "No, it is hopeless" (Watzlawick, 1983).

Role of the Therapist

The roles of strategic therapists differ among their subschools. However, those who work within this methodology share a belief in being active and flexible with their family clients. It is the therapist's responsibility in these family therapy approaches to plan strategies to resolve family problems. Therapists often proceed quickly and specifically in their focus on resolving presenting problems and virtually ignore family histories and personal diagnoses (Wylie, 1990). "They are symptom focused and behaviorally oriented" (Snider, 1992, p. 20).

"The first task of the therapist is to define a presenting problem in such a way that it can be solved" (Madanes, 1991, p. 396). Although the problem can be conceptualized in a number of ways, the therapist usually tries to define it as one that the family has voluntary control over and that involves a power struggle. In defining the problem in such a manner, the therapist sets out to help family members make changes that alter the family dynamics from a competitive stance (in which there are winners and losers) to a cooperative position (in which everyone wins) (Watzlawick, 1983).

Most strategic therapists are overtly active. Haley (1990) believes it is essential to make changes in people and families within the first three sessions. He works hard at reframing client's perceptions and presenting complaints and strives to come up with a unique innovative method to use in each case. He tailors his approach for each family in the same way as Milton Erickson, one of his mentors, and in the same way a surgeon would plan an operation.

Strategic family therapists try to use presenting problems as ways to bring about change in families by giving them tasks that are usually carried out between sessions, that is, **homework**. "Therapists also use structural interventions such as attempting to unbalance family systems by joining with one or more members on a conflictual point, fortifying generational boundaries, and supporting members at particular times to accomplish a specific objective" (Snider, 1992, p. 20).

Process and Outcome

The goal of strategic family therapy is to resolve, remove, or ameliorate the problem the family agreed to work on (Snider, 1992). The family must learn, at least indirectly, how to address other problems in a constructive manner. Often, resolving family difficulties involves a multitude of interventions or steps. Four common procedures for ensuring a successful outcome include:

1. defining a problem clearly and concisely
2. investigating all solutions that have previously been tried
3. defining a clear and concrete change to be achieved
4. formulating and implementing a strategy for change (Watzlawick, 1978)

The emphasis in strategic therapy (as in systemic family therapy) is on process rather than content. The methods used in bringing about change focus on breaking up **vicious cycles** of interaction and replacing them with **virtuous cycles** that highlight alternative ways of acting (Friesen, 1985).

Unique Aspects of Strategic Family Therapy

Emphases

A major emphasis of strategic family therapy is its flexibility as a viable means of working with a variety of client-families. This approach has been successfully used in treating families and their members who display such dysfunctional behaviors as enmeshment, eating disorders, and substance abuse (Haley, 1980; Stanton, Todd, & Associates, 1982).

A second characteristic of this approach is that, with the exception of a few true believers, most therapists who use it "now concede that real change is possible at the individual and dyadic level—that the entire system need not always be involved in lower-order change" (Fish, 1988, p. 15). Because significant change can be brought about without having the entire family involved in treatment sessions, the chances of obtaining a desirable outcome are increased.

A third emphasis of strategic family therapy is its focus on innovation and creativity. As previously mentioned, strategic therapists trace their lineage to Milton Erickson, who was especially potent in devising novel ways to help his clients. Many strategic family therapy practitioners, especially Cloe Madanes (1990), are a part of this tradition. Madanes has devised a 16-step procedure for working with sex offenders and their victims. This approach is notable for its concreteness in obtaining clear facts, its linkage in connecting sexuality with spirituality, and its power in persuading the offender to seek forgiveness from the victim on his knees.

As a group, strategic family clinicians view the major goal of therapy as changing the perception and, hence, the interaction of families. Through their "introduction of the novel or unexpected, a frame of reference is broken and the structure of reality is rearranged" (Papp, 1984, p. 22).

A fourth quality of strategic family therapy is the way it can be employed with a number of other therapies, particularly the behavioral and structural family therapy schools of thought (Alexander & Parsons, 1982; Fish, 1988; Haley, 1976; Steinberg, Sayger, & Szykula, 1997). One reason this quality is so prevalent in strategic therapy is that one of its codevelopers, Jay Haley, worked at the Philadelphia Child Guidance Clinic in a structural setting and incorporated parts of that theory into his version of strategic treatment. Another reason is that behavioral family therapy focuses on defining, clarifying, and changing specific interactional patterns in a parallel manner to the strategic approach (Fish, 1988). A final reason is that many influential therapists have a historical or personal connection with strategic therapy. Consequently, they continue to be influenced in their thoughts and actions by dialogue and debate among and with strategic family therapists.

Comparison with Other Theories

One aspect of strategic family therapy, especially of the MRI group, which set it apart from other family therapies early in its development, is that it concentrates on one problem. Basically, a strategic family therapist focuses on one problem and helps families marshal their resources in dealing with an identified difficulty quickly and efficiently (Snider, 1992).

A second point of comparison is based on the accusation that strategic family therapy is too "cookbookish" and "mechanical" (Simon, 1984). This charge is the result of prescribed methods of treatment by the MRI and Jay Haley. In fairness, however, there is considerable flexibility among therapists who embrace this theory.

A third comparable quality associated with strategic family therapy is the controversial view about schizophrenia proposed by one of its leading proponents, Jay Haley. Haley, in essence, denies the existence of schizophrenia.

A fourth comparative feature of strategic family therapy involves the skill necessary to implement some of its methods. For example, the use of paradox can be powerful in the hands of a skilled clinician, but its use can be a catastrophe if employed in a naive way (Friesen, 1985). Some strategic family therapy approaches demand considerable training of practitioners before they can be implemented properly.

A fifth comparative factor of strategic family therapy concerns time and emphasis. All subschools within this orientation restrict the number of therapeutic sessions. Although this format motivates families to work, it is limiting. For example, the seriousness or extent of problems may not be dealt with adequately (Wylie, 1992). It is hoped that by resolving one specific situation, families will learn problem-solving skills. Although this is the case for some families, it is not universal.

A final comparable quality of strategic family therapy is its lack of collaborative input from client-families. Some strategic family therapy models, such as those devised by Haley, emphasize power techniques and the expertness of the therapist. All stress the creativeness of the therapist to find a solution for the family. Much like a physician, the strategic therapist who does not produce the desired results in clients usually takes the blame. This type of procedure is the antithesis of most other forms of family therapy.

A comparison between strategic and structural family therapies is shown in Figure 10.1. In some instances, the two approaches are so compatible that theorist Duncan Stanton (1981) has suggested they be integrated into a single approach. (Stanton's idea is not universally shared.) Although some professionals experience confusion over the differences between the two therapies, rules and guidelines are available to help either combine the two approaches or sequence them in a complementary manner. A general rule is that when structural interventions fail, therapists should try strategic methods because these methods were developed on more highly resistant clients (Friesen, 1985).

Systemic (Milan) Family Therapy

Systemic (Milan) family therapy is sometimes confused with the overall concept of "systemic" as an approach to family therapy. Systemic as a general term is inclusive and encompassing. It describes a therapeutic approach with interrelated elements. Systemic family therapy, also known as the Milan approach, stresses the interconnectedness of family members while also emphasizing the importance of second-order change in families (Tomm, 1984a, 1984b).

Major Theorists

Mara Selvini Palazzoli

Like many well-known therapists in the family therapy field, Mara Selvini Palazzoli was initially trained as a psychoanalyst. In her native Italy, she specialized in working with patients who had eating disorders, but she became increasingly frustrated with the results (Selvini Palazzoli, 1974). In 1967, she became the leader of a group of eight psychiatrists who were the forerunners in applying psychoanalytic ideas to working with families. Later

Common View of the Family

- People are seen as interacting within a context that they influence and are influenced by.
- The family life cycle and developmental stages are important in the assessment of families and their members.
- Symptoms are system maintained and maintain the system.
- The family can change its behavior if the overall context in which they live is changed.

Overlap in Therapy Process

- Treatment is viewed from a pragmatic perspective, although structural family therapy follows a more detailed plan of action in providing services than strategic family therapy.
- The emphasis is on the present, not the past.
- Repetitive and destructive patterns of behavior are focused on as targets of change.
- The emphasis of intervention is on family process not content.
- Both structural and strategic family therapies are symptom oriented.
- The family therapist is active in helping families change and often directs the process.
- Contracts for change are negotiated between the family and the therapist and are aimed at presenting problems and goals of treatment.
- Reframing is emphasized, not insight.
- Considerable effort is made by the therapist in "joining" the family and establishing rapport.
- The therapist assigns homework and tasks to be completed outside of the therapy sessions.
- The total time of treatment is relatively short, about 6 months.

Distinctions Between Strategic and Structural Family Therapies

- "Structuralists emphasize the importance of system role relationships . . . whereas strategists emphasize mainly function or process" (Fraser, 1982, p. 14). In essence, the structuralists strive to help a family member change his or her position; the strategic family therapists concentrate on breaking up or changing dysfunctional repetitive patterns.
- "Structural views are centered around negative feedback cycles and breaking homeostatic bonds, whereas strategic views focus on positive feedback cycles and interrupting vicious cycles to create virtuous ones" (Fraser, 1982, p. 14). A negative feedback loop is one that maintains homeostasis. Structural family therapists try to break the status quo through restructuring, for example, by helping the family create new rules for an adolescent because rules that worked for him or her as a child are no longer appropriate. On the other hand, strategic family therapists seek to help families do less, not more, of a particular activity, for example, arguing. In the beginning of a family's history, arguing may have resolved some issues, so arguing continued (a positive feedback loop) with the expectation that more issues would be resolved. However, the results were negative (a vicious cycle). In strategic family therapy, attention is paid to positive deviations that are adaptable (a virtuous cycle).
- "The unit of intervention in structural therapy is the entire family unit and its subunits as they function now. . . . The Strategic unit of intervention may be with a subsystem of the family system" including an individual (Fraser, 1982, p. 14).

Figure 10.1
Distinctions and similarities in strategic and structural family therapy.

Adapted from "Structural and Strategic Family Therapy: A Basis for Marriage, or Grounds for Divorce?" by J. S. Fraser, 1982, *Journal of Marital and Family Therapy, 8*(2), 13–22. Copyright 1982, American Association for Marriage and Family Therapy. Reprinted by permission; and "An Integrated Structural/Strategic Approach to Family Therapy" by M. D. Stanton, 1981, *Journal of Marital and Family Therapy, 7*(4), 427–439. Copyright 1981, American Association for Marriage and Family Therapy. Reprinted by permission.

they discovered the ideas of Bateson, Haley, Watzlawick, and others and began to modify their approach. By 1971, there was a systemic faction of the group. Selvini Palazzoli, Boscolo, Cecchin, and Prata formed the Center for the Study of the Family in Milan, where they developed the Milan model (Wylie & Cooper, 2000).

The Milan team split up in 1980. Selvini Palazzoli and Prata continued to do family systems research until 1982. At that time, Selvini Palazzoli formed a new group to work with families of schizophrenics and anorectics (Selvini, 1988). Simultaneously, her conceptual ideas underwent change, and she began to describe her client-families as engaged in a series of **games**. When families are engaged in games, the children and parents stabilize around disturbed behaviors in an attempt to benefit from them. To break up these games, family therapists must first meet with families and then with parents separately to give them an invariant or variant prescription (explained later in the techniques section) that is designed to produce a clear and stable boundary between generations.

Palazzoli died June 21, 1999, in Milan, Italy, at the age of 83. She was one of the family therapy field's "most unconventional and charismatic personalities" (Wylie & Cooper, 2000, p. 11).

Premises of the Theory

Systemic family therapy is premised on the idea that therapists will take a systemic (circular) view of problem maintenance and a strategic (planned) orientation to change. Symptoms serve a purpose. Individual distress, anguish, or acting out is seen as the "thermometer of family functioning" (Snider, 1992, p. 13). Aberrant behaviors by one member of the family suggest a disturbance within the entire family. Therefore, systemic therapies concentrate on the consequences of family communication patterns and conflict between competing hierarchies. They shy away from doing anything more than accepting the symptoms as described by the family or family members.

The concept of **neutrality** is one of the main pillars underlying the Milan family systems approach (Selvini Palazzoli, Boscolo, Cecchin, & Prata, 1980). It is referred to as **therapeutic neutrality**. It keeps the therapist from being drawn into family coalitions and disputes and gives the therapist time to assess the dynamics within the family. This type of neutrality also encourages family members to generate solutions to their own problems (Boscolo, Cecchin, Hoffman, & Penn, 1987).

Treatment Techniques

Systemic (Milan) therapists have created and utilized a number of therapeutic treatment techniques. In addition to paradox (described earlier) these five techniques are widely utilized: hypothesizing, positive connotation, circular questioning, invariant/variant prescriptions, and rituals.

Hypothesizing

Hypothesizing is central to the Milan approach. It involves a meeting of treatment team members before the arrival of a family in order to formulate and discuss aspects of the family's situation that could be generating a symptom. During this pre-session, the team members attempt to prepare themselves for treating the family. Their belief is that they must come up with ideas about how a particular family operates, or the family will define the problem and treatment in a faulty way. Hypotheses are modified as treatment continues. Circularity throughout the family system is stressed.

Positive Connotation

A positive connotation is a type of reframing in which each family member's behavior is labeled as benevolent and motivated by good intentions. If a mother is overinvolved with her daughter, the therapist might label her behavior as one of concern. By giving positive connotations to behaviors, therapists simultaneously reduce resistance to treatment by the family and establish rapport.

Circular Questioning

Circular questioning originated with the Milan team (Selvini Palazzoli et al., 1980). It focuses attention on family connections through framing every question so that it addresses differences in perception by family members about events or relationships. Each family member might be asked to state how he or she perceived the family dealing with a crisis situation. The intent is to highlight information, differences, and circular processes within the family system. It gives the family clear information while breaking down the idea of individual causes and helping family members raise questions.

Invariant/Variant Prescriptions

An **invariant prescription** involves a specific kind of ritual, and it is given to parents with children who are psychotic or anorexic in an attempt to break up the family's **dirty game** (i.e., power struggle between generations sustained by symptomatic behaviors) (Selvini Palazzoli, 1986; Simon, 1987). The invariant prescription requires parents to unite so that children cannot manipulate them or stereotype them as "winners" or "losers" and thereby side with them.

The essence of this technique is that parents tell their symptomatic children that they have a secret, but they never reveal what the secret is. In addition, they record the reactions of family members to the fact that the parents have a secret. They then go out together for varying periods of time (some of them quite long) without telling their children where they are going or when they will return. This mysterious type of behavior allies parents in a new way and gives them an opportunity to observe and discuss the family's reactions. In the process, changes within the parents themselves and the family as a whole are noted. Constructive changes are preserved.

A **variant prescription** is given for the same purpose as an invariant one. The difference is that a variant prescription is tailored to a particular family and considers unique aspects of that family.

Rituals

The assignment of rituals is an attempt to break up dysfunctional rules in the family (Selvini Palazzoli, Cecchin, Prata, & Boscolo, 1978). In essence, **rituals** are specialized directives that are meant to dramatize positive aspects of problem situations (Boscolo et al., 1987). Rituals occur daily at mealtime, bedtime, and during chores. They can occur, for example, when sitting down to a meal together or when saying "goodnight" to everyone before bed. They include five components essential to family health: membership, belief expression, identity, healing, and celebration (Imber-Black, 1988, 1989, 1999). In essence, a ritual is a type of prescription that directs the members of the family to change their behavior under certain circumstances. By changing the actions of the family members, the therapist hopes to change the cognitive map or meaning of the behavior. When prescribing a ritual, the therapist should state a specific time when the ritual is to be carried out.

Effective rituals are specific in describing what is to be done, who is to do it, and how it is to be done. An anorexic girl might be given the assignment of saying to her dying grandmother every night: "I love you so much that I did not want my parents to feel much pain about your impending death, so I am starving myself to cause them to worry about me." The grandmother would respond: "Thank you, but your parents are strong enough to handle my situation and still love you."

Role of the Therapist

In the Milan family systems approach, the therapist is both an expert and "a co-creator of the constantly evolving family system" (Friedlander, Wildman, & Heatherington, 1991, p. 397). The therapist in these roles takes a nonblaming stance, gives directives, and is neutral to the point of even avoiding the use of the verb "to be" (Boscolo et al., 1987). Thus, the Milan family systems therapist does not usually try overtly to challenge or change families. Instead, the therapist takes a paradoxical position of being a change agent who argues against change (Simon, 1987). As such, the therapist uses circular questioning and other indirect forms of intervention to bring about family transformation. The therapist stresses the positive connotations of a behavior and explains to the family how even the most troublesome symptom is "ultimately in the service of family harmony" (Simon, 1987, p. 19).

Process and Outcome

When successful, systemic family therapy results in symptom resolution in a relatively short period of time (10 or fewer sessions). In addition, family dynamics change. The family experiences how family members are interlinked. The connection between what family members do and how the health of every member influences the others becomes evident. In addition, one member of the family stops being the focus of the family's problems, that is, the scapegoat. Further, nonproductive interactions and "games" change. As the family evolves and discards the **old epistemology**, or dated ideas, that do not fit their current situation, more productive and appropriate behaviors emerge (Tomm, 1984a). Perhaps most importantly, families make changes that are directed to their particular circumstance. For example, a family that was centered around eating problems can now become focused on affirmation of one another and clear communication.

If the therapy is successful, the process of growth within families continues after they formally terminate therapy. Growth continues because the family has experienced a pattern of change on which they can build; they have moved from a vicious to a virtuous cycle of interaction with renewed energy and focus.

Unique Aspects of Systemic Therapy

Emphases

One characteristic of systemic family therapy is its flexibility in being a viable means of working with a variety of client-families. This approach has been successfully used in treating families and their members who display such dysfunctional behaviors as enmeshment, eating disorders, and substance abuse (Selvini Palazzoli, 1981).

A second aspect of systemic (Milan) family therapy is that therapists work in teams to help families solve problems. With few exceptions, systemic family therapists work with some team members present with the family and others behind a one-way mirror (Simon, 1986). The team approach is monetarily expensive, but it is effective. The team concept has been borrowed and modified by a number of other schools of family therapy and has proven especially popular as a format to use in educating novice family therapists.

The team approach is especially powerful in the hands of skilled clinicians, such as Peggy Papp (1980), who has devised a form of it known as the **Greek chorus**. In this format, observers of a family treatment session (i.e., the team) may do such things as debate the merits of what a therapist is doing to bring about change. Families are helped to acknowledge and feel their ambivalence.

A third aspect of systemic therapy is its concentration on one problem over a short period of time. In so doing, systemic therapy helps families marshal their resources in dealing with an identified difficulty (Snider, 1992). Therapists who follow this approach might help a family find ways to share free time together so that members are not in competition with one another. Once that problem has been resolved, the family and therapist might spend their time and resources in more productive ways.

Comparison with Other Theories

A major contrast of the Milan school with other theories is its "European bias toward nonintervention" (Simon, 1984, p. 28). The roots of the nonintervention approach, according to Salvador Minuchin, come from the European experience of Hitler and Nazi Germany. "In Europe, there is a great respect for people's individual boundaries" (Simon, 1984, p. 28). This same type of view is not shared worldwide, and the mentality of this approach is not universal. Therefore, the Milan systemic approach is not widely used in most countries outside of Europe.

A second comparable quality associated with systemic family therapy is the controversial view about schizophrenia proposed by one of its leading proponents, Mara Selvini Palazzoli. It is Selvini Palazzoli's contention that "schizophrenia always begins as a child's attempt to take sides in the stalemated relationship between . . . parents" (Simon, 1987, p. 19). Although Selvini Palazzoli's view is not exactly the same as that of Jay Haley in this matter, it is interesting that Selvini Palazzoli, who was influenced by Haley, holds such a view because, as previously discussed, Haley's position on schizophrenia is controversial.

A final comparative feature of the Milan systemic approach is that, similar to strategic family therapy, there is an attempt in this treatment to tailor interventions to the specifics of a family. Therapists working as a team are responsible for creating innovative treatment plans. Like strategic and structural family therapies, systemic family therapy takes on some of the most outwardly difficult families with which to work.

———————————— **CASE ILLUSTRATION** ————————————

THE WILSON FAMILY

Family Background

Bo and Harriet Wilson have been married for 15 years and are the parents of Rich, age 12, and Ryan, age 11. Rich has a learning disability and is in a special school. He also has a physical handicap, having been born with dislocated hips. He requires frequent medical attention from physicians and is described as "a source of worry" by his parents. He wears braces. Ryan, on the other hand, is bright, attractive, and full of energy. He loves sports and is a member of a number of youth teams, including soccer, basketball, and baseball. He seems to have little interest in his brother's condition and is quite demanding on his parents, insisting that they "take him" to games and play with him.

Bo is a painter and his work is seasonal. During the winter months, he has more time for his family and himself. He has tended to drink heavily during the winter months, but during the past 3 years, he has begun drinking heavily all year round. As a result, he misses work, gets fired from jobs, and is not paid regularly. He has lost the medical benefits he once had. Harriet is a waitress. She initially worked only during the lunch shift, but during the past year, she has begun working breakfast and dinner shifts as well. She is physically drained at the end of the day but has to do housework when she is home. She is concerned that none of the males in her life is doing well and that the family is "falling apart." She made the call for the therapy appointment.

Conceptualization of Family: Strategic and Systemic Perspective

The Wilsons are disengaged interpersonally and are under a lot of financial and physical stress. They are displaying a number of repetitive patterns such as excessive drinking and overwork that are not benefiting family members individually or the family as a whole. The children are demanding physically and psychologically. Harriet is overfunctioning; Bo is underfunctioning.

Process of Treatment: Strategic and Systemic Therapies

To treat the Wilsons, strategic and systemic family therapists would convey to them initially that treatment would consist of a limited number of sessions, say, 10. The family would be asked before treatment began to define their problem/concern in a solvable format "to decrease the amount of friction, that is, the number of fights/arguments, between family members." Removal of the problem/concern would be seen as an index of change (Bodin, 1981). Regardless of what the problem/concern was, it would be accepted and seen by the therapist as serving some useful function.

In treatment, it would be ideal if the whole family could be seen. The therapist, in any of these approaches, would initiate actions and interventions and would clearly be in charge. The therapist would first gather information through such procedures as circular questioning or direct observations of nonverbal behaviors. During this process, the problem of friction would be reframed as behaviors associated with concern by family members for the well-being of the family as a whole. Attention would be focused on creating a specific approach that would help the Wilson family make needed transitions and second-order change. Some of the initial interventions of strategic and systemic family therapists might go as follows:

1. In the MRI form of strategic therapy, a directive might initially be given to break up the family's homeostasis: "Spend an hour with each other doing a mutually decided activity, such as playing board games like checkers and monopoly." The rules of the game, as well as the rules of the family (e.g., how decisions are made to play games), would be discussed when the family returned for its next appointment.
2. In the Washington School (i.e., Haley/Madanes) form of strategic therapy, the use of pretend might be employed. This would require members of the family to pretend

to care for each other in some specific way, such as giving one another imaginary gifts of traits/characteristics (e.g., bravery, assertion) or needed necessities. Activity would take place in the presence of the therapist. If such an approach were not utilized, an ordeal might be employed. For example, a son might be required to give his mother money before he would be allowed to argue with her.

3. In the Milan format, the therapist along with the observation/treatment team might have the family engage in a ritual, such as eating dinner together in silence, for an extended period of time. At the conclusion of the meal, each member of the family would have to convey to the rest of the family how isolated and lonely he or she felt, and the others would simply acknowledge what they heard.

Regardless of their initial intervention, strategic and systemic family therapists would be active in sessions with this family and look for ways to bring about rapid change. With the Wilsons, a focus might be to get the parents more involved with each other and with their children. This might mean further treatment for the alcoholism and workaholism in Bo and Harriet, respectively. It might also mean finding ways for Rich and Ryan to cooperate with each other and with their parents. Ryan, for instance, might be able to focus some of his attention on tutoring Rich academically and athletically; Rich could concentrate on encouraging and supporting Ryan in his practices and games.

———————————————————— ● ————————————————————

Summary and Conclusion

Strategic and systemic family therapies are among the most popular approaches to working with families. They are short-term, specific, positive, and appealing to families that have difficulty with organization and development. Inherent in their techniques are directives designed to change behaviors and thoughts, which are often overlooked by other therapeutic approaches (Perry, 1992).

The Mental Research Institute, following the creative genius of Milton Erickson, formulated the innovative foundation of the strategic therapy model in the 1960s. Members of this Palo Alto institute limited to ten the number of sessions they would agree to see families. They also consented to accept for treatment the problems families wished to work on, as long as they were clearly definable. Instead of trying to change families as they saw fit, these pioneers in family therapy focused on working with symptomatic behavior(s) and viewed dysfunctional behavior as having an underlying positive and beneficial basis. The MRI version of strategic family therapy has stood the test of time and is still being both refined and utilized.

The MRI therapeutic approach was later modified by Jay Haley, one of its initial participants. Haley's particular contributions include his ways of working with young adults and their families who conspire to keep them from leaving home. Later, he partnered with Cloe Madanes at their Washington Family Therapy institute. Madanes' creativity added significantly to this form of strategic family therapy. Both the MRI and Haley/Madanes versions of strategic family therapy have similarities and differences related to structural family therapy. They have influenced a wide variety of therapeutic approaches.

Strategic family therapy, particularly the MRI approach, was one of the influences in the original Milan, Italy, systemic family therapy treatment team. The Milan group originally concentrated on treating eating disorders, but from its study of strategic family therapy, it broadened its base.

Systemic family therapy has been both praised and criticized for its treatment procedures. Some of the techniques employed in strategic and systemic family therapies—hypothesizing, utilization of teams, invariant prescriptions, circular questioning, and the use of paradox—are among the most innovative ever formulated. These therapeutic approaches appear to be strong. They are applauded for making necessary and sufficient changes that help families work better. However, these brief-oriented family therapies are criticized for not dealing extensively enough with family problems. Overall, strategic and systemic family therapies are well-defined, specific, and goal-directed treatments that employ a variety of techniques.

Summary Table
Strategic and Systemic Family Therapies

Major Theorists

Strategic Family Therapy

Milton Erickson	Paul Watzlawick	John Weakland
Richard Fisch	Jay Haley	Cloe Madanes
James Keim		

Systemic (Milan) Family Therapy

Mara Selvini Palazzoli	Luigi Boscolo	Gianfranco Cecchin
Guiliana Pata	Karl Tomm	Lynn Hoffman
Peggy Papp	Olga Silverstein	Peggy Penn
Richard Rabkin	Joel Bergman	Carlos Sluzki
James Coyne		

Premises of the Theory

Strategic Family Therapy

Treatment should be pragmatic and short-term.
Insight and history are not a part of treatment.
Family rules, homeostasis, quid pro quo, the redundancy principle, punctuation, symmetrical and complementary relationships, along with circular causality underlie behavior.

Systemic (Milan) Therapy

A circular view of the problem maintenance is taken.
There is a planned orientation to change.
Symptoms are seen as serving a purpose and they are accepted.
Therapeutic neutrality is taken to avoid being drawn into family problems.

Treatment Techniques

Although these approaches can be selectively used with dyads and individuals, the family is treated as a system.

The focus of treatment is on resolving present problems and bringing about change. Definable behavioral goals are targeted. Insight is minimized.

Strategic therapeutic techniques include the following:

- Reframing
- Using directives
- Paradox compliance-based and defiance-based
- Ordeals
- Pretend
- Positioning

Systemic (Milan) therapeutic techniques include the following:

- Hypothesizing
- Positive connotation
- Circular questioning
- Invariant and variant prescriptions (to disrupt dirty games)
- Rituals

Role of the Therapist

Strategic Family Therapy

Therapist is active and flexible, designs strategies to resolve family problems.
Therapist helps family members change from a competitive to a cooperative stance.
Therapist helps bring about change by giving tasks and homework.

Systemic (Milan) Therapy

Therapist is a nonblaming, neutral expert, and cocreator.
Therapist gives directives and uses circular questioning.
Therapist stresses the positive.
Therapist hypothesizes and develops strategies for helping families change.

Process and Outcome

Strategic Family Therapy

Family is helped to resolve and remove problem they agreed to work on.
Four common procedures used: defining a problem clearly, investigating all solutions previously tried, defining concrete change, and implementing a strategy for change.
Emphasis is on process not content.

Systemic (Milan) Family Therapy

Family symptoms are removed and family members experience how they are interlinked.
Family members give up dated ideas.
Change focuses on breaking up vicious cycles of interaction and replacing them with virtuous cycles.

Unique Aspects of Strategic and Systemic Family Therapies

Strategic and systemic therapies emphasize

- seeing symptoms in a positive way
- short-term treatment (usually 10 or fewer sessions)
- changing present problematic behavior
- tailor-made techniques for each family
- innovative treatments
- flexible, evolving, and creative approaches (that combine easily with other theories)

Comparison with Other Theories

Historical patterns of family interaction are ignored.

The medical model, that is, expertise, is emphasized.

The use of teams, such as in the Milan approach, is featured.

The employment of paradox is widely used.

Families can change in treatment but not understand why.

Some confusion exists about the differences between strategic and structural family therapy.

Solution-Focused and Narrative Family Therapies

He changed
giving her small compliments at breakfast such as:
"I like the way your hair looks" or
"Nice dress."
She wondered:
"What is he doing?"
but she also knew she liked his words.
So as the days continued
she responded
and acts of kindness became more common.

He changed
She changed
They changed
And it was for the better.

Gladding, 1996

The most recent theoretical development in the field of family therapy is the creation of solution-focused and narrative family therapies. Solution-focused family therapy grew out of strategic therapy, particularly the MRI model. It also represents a departure from that tradition by concentrating on finding solutions instead of dealing with problems. Narrative family therapy originated in Australia and New Zealand and focuses on helping families solve difficulties by depersonalizing them and rewriting family stories.

The two most experienced and elegant spokespersons for solution-focused family therapy are Steve deShazer and Bill O'Hanlon, both of whom studied with Milton Erickson. The model appeared in its earliest form in the writings of Steve deShazer and his associates at their Brief Family Therapy Center in Milwaukee, Wisconsin (deShazer, 1982, 1985, 1988, 1991). The writings and work of Bill O'Hanlon and his associates also are solution-focused (O'Hanlon & Weiner-Davis, 1989; O'Hanlon & Wilk, 1987). Present advocates of the solution-focused theoretical position include Patricia O'Hanlon Hudson (Hudson & O'Hanlon, 1991), Michele Weiner-Davis, Alan Gurman, Eve Lipchik, and Scott Miller.

Michael White and David Epston (1990) formulated narrative therapy. While the focus of this approach is on engaging families in solution-oriented therapeutic processes, it is distinct from the approaches of deShazer and O'Hanlon in its origin, having been derived from the research and writings of Gregory Bateson, Edward Bruner, and Michel Foucault (Monk, 1998). Difficulties are externalized and families are asked to work together as a team to develop strategies for overcoming problems. Just as solution-focused therapy has a Midwest origin with a worldwide application, so narrative family therapy has a Pacific Rim genesis with a global usefulness.

In this chapter, solution-focused family therapy is examined first, followed by an examination of narrative family therapy.

Solution-Focused Family Therapy

Major Theorists

Many of the major figures in solution-focused therapy originally worked with one another at the Brief Family Therapy Center in Milwaukee. Notables attached to the center at one time or another include the husband and wife team of Steve deShazer and Insoo Kim Berg as well as Michele Weiner-Davis and Eve Lipchik. Even though Bill O'Hanlon was never a part of this group, he has been influenced by the Brief Family Therapy Center at least indirectly in his collaborative writing with Weiner-Davis. DeShazer and O'Hanlon are highlighted here.

Steve deShazer

Steve deShazer began his career by working at the Mental Research Institute in the mid-1970s. In the late 1970s, deShazer and a group of individuals in Milwaukee established the Brief Family Therapy Center. He first gained national attention as director of the center and began to emerge and gain recognition as a major theorist in family therapy in the 1980s. Initially, deShazer was considered to be a strategic family therapist who was influenced by the work of not only Milton Erickson but also Gregory Bateson, and the staff of the

MRI. From the 1980s onward, however, the writings and presentations of deShazer and Berg became distinct.

DeShazer (1982) identified his theory as brief family therapy, sometimes called just **brief therapy**, and described it as an ecosystemic approach. His approach, like that of the Milan Group, employs a team whenever possible. The team, collectively known as **consultants**, observes from behind a one-way mirror and transmits messages to the therapist at a designated break time in the session. Thus, the family in treatment can be the beneficiary of multiple inputs. As with any theory, deShazer devised special terms to describe what made his approach unique.

DeShazer died unexpectedly September 11, 2005, in Vienna, Austria, with his wife, Insoo Kim Berg by his side.

Bill O'Hanlon

Bill O'Hanlon entered family therapy because of his interest in his own life experiences. As an adolescent, he was unhappy and shy. As a college student, he was isolated and uncomfortable in the world. He reports that he felt "like all exposed nerve—no skin—everything hurt" (Krauth, 1995, p. 24). He experimented with drugs and noticed that "the reality we all take for granted could be changed by a couple of micrograms of something introduced into one's body" (Bubenzer & West, 1993, p. 366). He also contemplated suicide, but changed his mind when a friend offered him hope by promising him a lifetime of free rent on a Nebraska farm if he would stay alive. That possibility changed his outlook on life and led to his interest in therapeutic work beyond repairing damage or dealing with pathology.

Later, after earning a tailor-made master's degree from Arizona State University in family therapy, he went on to receive special tutelage under Milton Erickson in exchange for being Erickson's gardener. The influence of Erickson on O'Hanlon was profound and shifted his attention to focusing on solutions. O'Hanlon was also influenced by the work done at the Mental Research Institute.

In 1980, O'Hanlon set out to become a major proponent of solution-focused therapy, which he now prefers to call **possibility therapy** (Bubenzer & West, 1993; Krauth, 1995). His motivation was to shift the focus of family therapy from problems to solutions. He characterizes his approach as one that is pragmatic and full of Midwest values.

Premises of the Theory

Solution-focused family therapy is built on the philosophy of **social constructionism**. This theory states that knowledge is time- and culture-bound. It also emphasizes that language influences the way people view the world. Therapeutic treatment of families or persons must include their social, historic, and cultural context. Furthermore, the philosophy underlying this position states that reality is not an objective entity, but a reflection of observation and experience (Maturana & Varela, 1987; Simon, Stierlin, & Wynne, 1985). In other words, the social constructionist paradigm emphasizes that meaning is constructed in certain cultural conversations and context and it challenges the notion of objective knowledge or absolute truth otherwise (Sinclair & Monk, 2004).

In addition to this underlying idea, solution-focused therapy shares some of the same premises about families as the MRI strategic and Milan systemic approaches. At the foundation of this approach is the belief that dysfunctional families get "stuck" in dealing with problems (deShazer, 1985). These families basically use an unsatisfactory method to solve their difficulties, that is, they rely on patterns that do not work (Bubenzer & West, 1993). Solution-focused family therapy is aimed toward breaking such repetitive, nonproductive behavioral patterns by deliberately setting up situations in which families take a more positive view of troublesome situations and actively participate in doing something different. "It is not necessary to know the cause of the complaint or even very much about the complaint itself in order to resolve it" (Cleveland & Lindsey, 1995, p. 145). Rather, the presenting problem is seen as the problem for which a solution needs to be worked out (Kaplan, 2000). There is no need for extensive analysis.

Identifying what is a problem versus what is a nonproblem or exception is a key component in the solution-focused perspective (deShazer, 1988). Exceptions to general ways of behaving and viewing situations are emphasized (O'Hanlon & Wilk, 1987). The aim is to help families unlock their set views, to be creative, and to generate novel approaches that may be applicable in a number of circumstances. It is believed that all families have resources and strengths with which to resolve complaints (Cleveland & Lindsey, 1995). The task is simply getting them to use the abilities they already have. The focus is on solutions, not problems. To increase motivation and expectation, solution-focused family therapy, like strategic and systemic therapy, emphasizes short-term treatment, between 5 and 10 sessions.

As a theory, solution-focused family therapy does not focus on a detailed family history of problems. Such a process is believed to be unhelpful (deShazer, 1985; O'Hanlon & Weiner-Davis, 1989). A foundational belief of this approach is that causal understanding is unnecessary. To stress this point, O'Hanlon and Wilk (1987) state that every psychotherapy office should have a couch for therapists, instead of clients, because "every now and then, in the course of a session, a hypothesis might accidentally enter the therapist's head, and the best remedy for it is to lie down until it goes away" (p. 98).

Another premise of solution-focused family therapy is that families really want to change. As a way of underscoring this idea, deShazer (1984) has declared the death of resistance as a concept. Thus, when families do not follow therapists' directions, they are "cooperating" by teaching therapists the best way to help them.

A final concept underlying solution-focused family therapy is that only a small amount of change is necessary. An analogy that is used to illustrate this point is that a one-degree error in flying across the United States will result in a plane being considerably off course in the end (deShazer, 1985). Small amounts of change can also be reinforcing to families in helping them realize they can make progress. It boosts confidence and optimism and, in effect, creates a "ripple effect" (Spiegel & Linn, 1969).

Treatment Techniques

Solution-focused therapy constructs solutions in collaboration with the client (Kiser, Piercy, & Lipchik, 1993). One subtle but primary treatment technique is to cocreate a problem with a family. For the therapeutic process to be productive, initially, an agreement must be made as to which problem they want to solve. A therapist and a family, for example, must agree that a family's failure to discipline a child properly is the difficulty that needs to be addressed.

A second key component in treatment is to ask a family for a hypothetical solution to their situation. This process is often achieved by asking the **miracle question**—such as, "If a miracle happened tonight and you woke up tomorrow and the problem was solved, what would you do differently?" (Walter & Peller, 1993, p. 80). A question like this invites family members to suspend their present frames of reference and enter a reality that they wish to achieve. A miracle question is asked only after the therapist has gained enough background information on a family and the family itself has demonstrated its ability to respond positively to treatment and to notice exceptions to its complaints.

Another novel technique in solution-focused therapy related to the first two emphases is to focus on **exceptions**, that is, to look for "negative" or "positive" space (or time when a family goal may be happening) (Krauth, 1995). "In a practical sense, exceptions do not exist in the real world of clients; they must be cooperatively invented or constructed by both the client and the therapist while exploring what happens when the problem does not occur" (Fleming & Rickord, 1997, p. 289). A family that is quarrelling a lot might find that they are peaceful whenever they sit down to eat. At such times, they may agree to disagree and actually have civil conversations with one another. By examining the dynamics of the family at this time, members may learn something about themselves and the dynamics of their relationship and in the process become different. "Inventing exceptions to problems deconstructs the client's frame: I am this way, or it always happens that way" (Fleming & Rickord, 1997, p. 289).

Solution-focused family therapists following deShazer and Berg's approach use the technique of scaling, too. In **scaling**, questions are asked using a scale of 1 (low) to 10 (high) to help move clients toward their goals. The therapist might say: "On a scale of one to ten, how far do you think you have come in solving your problem?" If the client-family replies "six," the therapist would then challenge them to think what it would take to move to a "seven." By answering the question, the client-family could reach a new understanding in regard to their goal and what immediate, realistic, and measurable steps they would have to take to get there (Fleming & Rickord, 1997).

A fifth emphasis in this approach involves **second-order (qualitative) change** or a qualitatively different way of doing something. The goal is to change the family's organization and structure. This change can be accomplished through planning interventions in accordance with the order of events within a family's life or by altering the frequency and duration of a dysfunction (O'Hanlon, 1987). For example, a family that has been having long fights at dinner might agree to finish their meal before arguing and then limit their disagreement time to 15 minutes. This type of change in the structure and length of events is likely to alter family dynamics.

Another intervention is to give the family a compliment. For solution-focused therapists, especially deShazer (1982), a **compliment** is a written message designed to praise a family for its strengths and build a "yes set" within it. A compliment consists of a positive statement with which all members of a family can agree. The therapist might say: "I am impressed with your hard work to bring about change and the way all of you are discussing what needs to happen next." A compliment is always planned as a lead-in to giving a family a task or assignment.

A seventh major technique is to provide the family with a **clue**, or an intervention that mirrors the usual behavior of a family. It is intended to alert a family to the idea that some behavior is likely to continue (deShazer, 1982). The intervention of the therapist might be: "Don't worry about working too hard in trying to spend time together talking, because conversation is something that regularly occurs in your environment and you can do it naturally." The idea behind clueing is "to build mutual support and momentum for carrying out later interventions" (Sauber, L'Abate, & Weeks, 1985, p. 23).

A final treatment intervention is to use procedures that have worked before and that have a universal application. These **skeleton keys** will help families unlock a variety of problems (deShazer, 1985). For instance, deShazer has refined five interventions that have been useful to him in a number of situations (deShazer, 1985; deShazer & Molnar, 1984):

1. "Between now and next time we meet, we (I) want you to observe, so that you can tell us (me) next time, what happens in your (life, marriage, family, or relationship) that you want to continue to happen" (deShazer, 1985, p. 298). Such a request encourages a client-family to look at the stability of the problems on which they wish to work.

2. "Do something different" (p. 300). This type of request encourages individuals and the family to explore the range of possibilities they have, rather than to continue to do what they believe is correct. deShazer gives an example of a woman who complained that her husband, a police detective, was staying out late every night with his friends. The message she received from the deShazer team was that her husband might want more mysterious behavior from her. Therefore, one night she hired a babysitter, rented a motel room, and stayed out until 5 A.M. Her husband came in at 2 A.M. Nothing was said, but her husband began staying home at night.

3. "Pay attention to what you do when you overcome the temptation or urge to ... perform the symptom or some behavior associated with the complaint" (p. 302). This instruction helps families to realize that symptoms are under their control.

4. "A lot of people in your situation would have ... " (p. 302). This type of statement again helps family members realize they may have options other than those they are exercising. Through such awareness, they can begin to make needed changes.

5. "Write, read, and burn your thoughts." This experience consists of writing about past times, such as times spent with an ex-spouse, and then reading and burning the writings the next day.

Overall, solution-focused therapy interventions help the client-family to view their situation differently. These interventions can also give them hope, thereby assisting clients in powerful ways (Bubenzer & West, 1993). To use the words of deShazer and Molnar (1984): "It now appears to us that the therapists' ability to see change and to help the clients to do so as well, constitutes a most potent clinical skill" (p. 304). Families become more empowered as a result of participating in solution-focused therapy.

Role of the Therapist

One of the first roles of a solution-focused therapist is to determine how active a client-family will be in the process of change. Clients usually fall into one of three categories: visitors, complainants, or customers:

- **Visitors** are not involved in the problem, are not motivated to make changes, and are not part of the solution. In other words, they do not wish to participate in therapy and they do not wish to work on anything. The therapist's best stance with visitors is to respect them, try to establish rapport with them, and hope that they will eventually become customers.

- **Complainants**, as their name implies, complain about situations but can be observant and describe problems even if they are not invested in solving them. A good role for a therapist to take with complainants is to assign them activities whereby they focus on exceptions to complaints. When therapists respect complainants and do not push them, complainants become open to becoming customers.
- Finally, **customers** are individuals who are not only able to describe a problem and how they are involved in it, but are willing to work to solve it. With customers, a therapist's role is to engage the person in solution-oriented conversations, "compliment the client, and cocreate assignments to reproduce those behaviors that are exceptions to the problem" (Crethar, Snow, & Carlson, 2005, p. 152). If a therapist is working with customers or can help visitors and complainants evolve into customers, intervention strategies can be developed (Fleming & Rickord, 1997).

In the process of helping the client-family become involved in therapy, a solution-focused family therapist becomes a "facilitator of change, one who helps clients access the resources and strengths they already have but are not aware of or are not utilizing" (Cleveland & Lindsey, 1995, p. 145). To do so, solution-focused practitioners focus attention on complaints that families want to change and work with families in helping them gain a different perspective on a problem. They accomplish this goal partly through their words.

Language becomes important (West, Bubenzer, Smith, & Hamm, 1997). Positive assumptions about change are constantly conveyed by the therapist. For example, the therapist might ask a **presuppositional question** such as "What good thing happened since our last session?" "By selecting a specific verb tense, or implying the occurrence of a particular event, the family is led to believe that a solution will be achieved" (Gale, 1991, p. 43). Likewise, when an improvement occurs, therapists use "positive blame" and recognition of competence through such questions as "How did you make that happen?" (Fleming & Rickord, 1997).

Solution-focused family therapists believe that it is important to "fit" therapeutic interventions into the context of family behavior. The fit of a solution has been particularly articulated by deShazer (1985). He contends that a solution does not have to be as complex as the presenting problem and need not include everyone in the family. He uses the metaphor of locks and keys to illustrate what he means. Locks may be complex, but opening them does not require a similar complexity of keys. In fact, several keys may fit the lock (or problem) well enough to open the door to change. **Skeleton keys** (i.e., standardized therapeutic techniques) can be helpful in dealing with most locks regardless of complexity.

To obtain a proper solution fit for a family, deShazer (1985) uses a team to begin mapping or sketching out the course of successful intervention. From the mapping experience, multiple perspectives about the family's problem are given. It is up to the family to define what they wish to achieve; the therapist then helps them define clear, specific goals that can be conceptualized concretely (deShazer, 1985; O'Hanlon & Weiner-Davis, 1989). It is through this process that families and therapists begin to create **solutions**, that is, desired behaviors. "Therapy is over when the agreed upon outcome has been reached" (O'Hanlon & Wilk, 1987, p. 109).

Solution-focused family therapists encourage families to make small changes and to do so rapidly (deShazer, 1985; O'Hanlon & Weiner-Davis, 1989). The therapist encourages the family to focus on changes in their behaviors, changes in their perceptions, and the recognition and use of family resources/strengths that can be brought to bear on a problematic situation (Cleveland & Lindsey, 1995). Indeed, the solution-focused approach "holds change as a central component" (Murray & Murray, 2004, p. 351). One way of making such change is through a "gender solution-focused genogram to help clients identify the beliefs and behaviors related to their presenting problems" especially those involving gender role messages from the past that have negatively influenced their present behaviors (Softas-Nall, Baldo, & Tiedemann, 1999, p. 179). Regardless of the method used, once small change is achieved, the therapist gets out of the way and lets the "beneficial difference amplify itself naturally" (Fleming & Rickord, 1997, p. 289).

In solution-focused family therapy, the therapist does not distinguish between short-term and long-term problems, because such a difference is irrelevant. Some problematic behaviors endure longer than others because often the right solutions have not been tried. Solution-focused therapists are always challenging families to envision a "future that has possibilities of change" (Bubenzer & West, 1993, p. 372). This type of focusing on how things will be different in the future "provides hope and expands the options for solutions" (Erdman, 2000, p. 100).

Process and Outcome

Solution-focused family therapy concentrates on encouraging client-families to seek solutions and tap internal resources. It encourages, challenges, and sets up expectations for change. The concept of pathology does not play a part in the treatment process. Rather, solution-focused therapists see client-families as cooperative. They frequently commend the family on an aspect of a member's behavior, even if the behavior seems negative to the family. Solution-focused therapy takes the Milton Erickson position that change is inevitable; it is only a matter of when it will happen. This type of therapy is oriented toward the future and helps client-families change their focus and reframe their situations positively. By stressing that the family can change, finding incidents where the family acts differently than usual, asking optimistic questions, and reinforcing small but specific movement, solution-focused family therapy helps its families resolve difficulties and make needed changes.

Unique Aspects of Solution-Focused Family Therapy

Emphases

As a group, solution-focused family therapies concentrate on and are directed by a family's theory (i.e., their story). Before any attempt is made to help families change, their experiences are accepted. O'Hanlon compares this type of approach with the person-centered concept of first listening attentively to how people are feeling before trying to implement change (Bubenzer & West, 1993).

A second characteristic of solution-focused therapy is that therapists assist families in defining their situations clearly, precisely, and with possibilities. "The defined problem should be achievable" (Todd, 1992, p. 174). Sometimes success is measured in the elimination of problems. Often, therapy is significant if the family changes its perception of a situation or discovers exceptions to troublesome times. Regardless, whatever the family brings to therapy is examined from a broad context. The past is not emphasized, except when it calls attention to the present.

A third emphasis is that solution-focused therapy does not focus on clinical understanding of the family situation by the family or the therapist. Rather, the focus is on change. The therapist's job is to produce change by helping the family to focus on what they see as solutions to the problems they have reported. That is, families should look at exceptions to behaviors. Therapists also produce changes in families by challenging their worldview, by asking them appropriate questions, and by giving them skeleton keys, which are, as discussed earlier, universal tasks that have the power to help families find ways to unlock their potential.

A fourth quality of solution-focused family therapy is that it is empowering and meant to assist families in assessing and utilizing their resources. Formula tasks, such as "Do something different," and awareness exercises, such as "Find times when symptoms do not occur," help families help themselves. Families "are encouraged to imagine a future without the problem(s) so that they can identify what they will be doing (solutions)" (Kok & Leskela, 1996, p. 398).

Finally, achievable goals are emphasized, such as small changes in behavior. These changes are seen as the basis for larger systemic changes. Therapists encourage and reinforce any type of family change. The idea is that once change starts, it will continue. "Solution-focused brief therapy further asserts that change is inevitable and that clients want to change" (Kok & Leskela, 1996, p. 398).

Comparison with Other Theories

Unlike Bowen or psychoanalytic theory, virtually no attention is paid to history with solution-focused therapy. Rather, perception and minimal change are the focus. If families change their views on situations, they behave differently or more functionally (Bubenzer & West, 1993). Likewise, if a family begins to interact differently, they begin to see their situation from a new perspective.

As with strategic and systemic family therapy, solution-focused family therapy is brief in regard to the situation focused on and the amount of time allotted to it. Structuring the sessions in a way that emphasizes the therapist's expectations regarding doing something differently encourages rapid change. Difficulties lose their potency. Sometimes this results in a one-session treatment. However, deShazer (1989, 1991) has found that most clients (80.37%) meet their goals or make significant progress in an average of 4.5 sessions. Milton Erickson's influence on rapid changes is an obvious factor in all solution-focused approaches.

Therapy ends when an agreed-on behavioral goal is reached, rather than when a hypothetical therapeutic issue is discussed (O'Hanlon & Wilk, 1987). If there is no complaint or objective, there is no need for treatment. In this respect, solution-focused family therapy is similar to many forms of behavioral family therapy, in that it concentrates on resolving a concrete objective.

Like systemic (Milan) family therapy, some proponents of solution-focused therapy, mainly deShazer and Berg, use a team in helping the family help itself. The expense of treatment may be high even though there are generally fewer sessions than in some other approaches, such as psychoanalytic therapy.

Like MRI strategic therapy, solution-focused therapy aims to help client-families change their thoughts or actions so that they become more satisfied with their lives. However, solution-focused therapists trust and utilize family resources more than MRI strategic therapists.

Finally, like a few other couple and family therapies, solution-focused therapy is being used as an adjunct to conventional medical treatment. Currently, it has been used in the treatment of migraines but the therapy holds promise for being an effective approach for other types of headache symptoms (Gutterman, Mecias, & Ainbinder, 2005).

——————————————— **CASE ILLUSTRATION** ———————————————

THE ROBERTS FAMILY

Family Background

After 25 years of marriage and the raising of two children, Don and Kathy Roberts are contemplating a divorce. This crisis has led them to family therapy. Since the children left home 2 years ago, they have been drifting apart. Both Don, a computer analyst, and Kathy, a school superintendent, think they have little in common anymore. They work long hours, take separate vacations, spend the weekends with friends or by themselves, and basically just share space in their house. The couple is saddened by the fact that their marriage is no longer vibrant, but they are proud of their children and what they accomplished while the children were young.

Conceptualization of Family: Solution-Focused Perspective

Don and Kathy are at a critical stage in their personal, professional, and couple life. They have focused on their children and activities outside the marriage to the extent that they have failed to cultivate common interests and activities. Both seem to have taken a fatalistic view that their marriage is over. Yet, by coming to therapy, they have some hope that perhaps their relationship can be saved.

There is a long history on which to build in working with this couple. Finding patterns and exceptions are real possibilities. The couple has some motivation and considerable ability given their jobs and past successes. A drawback to this situation is that the couple may be operating in the cognitive domain. Also, the spouses are presently detached from each other.

Process of Treatment: Solution-Focused Therapy

In working with the Roberts, a solution-focused family therapist would first listen to their concerns. In this case, a lack of closeness and common interests would most likely surface. From the first session, the therapist would begin to discuss with the Roberts exceptions to their complaint, that is, times when they were close and shared common interests. They may have both shared a love for knowledge at the beginning of their marriage and throughout the time of raising their children.

In the deShazer model of solution-focused therapy, the therapist might take a break after listening to the complaints and exceptions. At the break, the therapist would either consult with a team of other professionals watching the session or think alone about setting up a homework assignment for the Roberts. When the therapist returned, he or she would lead off with a compliment to build a "yes set" and then give the homework assignment. In the O'Hanlon model, this structure (especially the break and the possible use of a team) would not be implemented. Instead, the therapist would focus on giving the couple a task to either make a small change (e.g., talk together for 5 minutes) or increase what they have been doing less of (i.e., make a second-order change, such as talking about what they might do in the future together).

In either form of solution-oriented therapy, the emphasis would be on working with the couple to do something different. In the deShazer version of this model, the couple would be asked on return appointments to check on clues (i.e., "What is different this week from last week?"). There would also be an emphasis on scaling (i.e., ranking the concern on a scale of

1 [bad] to 10 [good]). The idea behind this method would be to get the Roberts to become increasingly aware of their improvement in therapy and to give them hope that their situation could be better. In both forms of solution-focused therapy, considerable emphasis would be placed on the strengths of the Roberts—their intelligence, hardworking spirit, motivation, and past success. Considerable talk would also revolve around change. In the de-Shazer model, the therapist might employ the miracle question to encourage more thought about change and elicit solution-focused information, if the therapeutic process did not proceed smoothly or efficiently.

The total number of sessions needed to work with the Roberts or a typical client-family would be between five and six. By the end of therapy, the Roberts should have made changes in their lifestyle and have skills to take with them should they drift apart again.

Narrative Family Therapy

Major Theorists

The most prominent professionals associated with narrative family therapy are Michael White—who is highlighted here—the codirector of the Dulwich Centre in Adelaide, South Australia, and David Epston, the codirector of the Family Therapy Centre in Auckland, New Zealand. Other professionals include associates of White and Epston such as Michael Durrant and Gerald Monk.

Michael White

Michael White began his work as a family therapist in the 1970s in Australia. He was initially attracted to the work of Gregory Bateson and Bateson's explanatory model of systems analysis, but later, almost by accident, he discovered Edward Bruner's ethnographic work in library research (Monk, 1998). From Bruner, White took the idea that stories are not just descriptive but are constitutive as well. Furthermore, lived experiences, that is, **narratives**, may be overshadowed by dominant problem-saturated stories. The task of therapists is to coconstruct with a client an alternative, more favored storyline.

White then discovered the writings of Michel Foucault (1980, 1982, 1984), a French intellectual who formulated theories of knowledge and power. "Foucault described how people are constantly evaluating their worth in relation to widely accepted societal norms" (Monk, 1998, p. 3). This act of subjecting oneself or others to comparison and evaluation becomes the source of many problems in life. Problems can thus be addressed when a culture's values and ideas are questioned or challenged. White has read extensively outside the field of family therapy and has drawn heavily from literary theory, anthropology, and critical theory. He has also been influenced by feminist theory (Bubenzer, West, & Boughner, 1994).

In recent years, White has increasingly turned toward the narrative metaphor and away from systems thinking. He sees people's problems as related to the stories they have about themselves, which in turn often reflect oppressive cultural practices. A unique feature about White's narrative approach, compared with others based on social constructivism, is that White does not see one description of reality as better than any other. Instead, values play a role in actions, such as action against abuses of power, against neglect, against cruelty, and against injustice (White, 1993).

Premises of the Theory

Narrative family therapy is a nonsystemic approach to working with individuals and families based on a liberation philosophy consistent with postmodernism and social constructionism. It eschews attempts to formulate universal, generic principles. Indeed, the creators of this theory base much of their approach on the writings of Michel Foucault (1965, 1980), who asserts that human sciences (including social sciences like family therapy) generally characterize, classify, and specialize along a scale that objectifies people. As such, human sciences repress personal experiences and stories. The result is that people internalize and judge themselves in a logical and normative way that limits their options.

Thus, the narrative therapy approach distinguishes between **logico-scientific reasoning**, which is characterized by empiricism and logic, and **narrative reasoning**, which is characterized by stories, substories, meaningfulness, and liveliness. The narrative therapy perspective is that "people live their lives by stories" (Kurtz & Tandy, 1995, p. 177) and "families are formed, perpetuated, and transformed through the stories they share" (Ponzetti, 2005, p. 132). The emphasis in the narrative approach is towards a storyline way of conceptualizing and interpreting the world. Narrative therapy emphasizes empowering client-families to develop their own unique and alternative stories about themselves in the hope that they will come up with novel options and strategies for living. By **reauthoring** their lives, families are enabled to change in ways not possible before (Bubenzer et al., 1994; Hodas, 1994; White, 1995).

In the process of changing their lives by changing their stories, client-families are urged to externalize problems in order to solve them. Externalization breaks the habitual reading and retelling of the complaint-saturated story as residing in the person. In **externalization** "the problem becomes a separate entity" (White & Epston, 1990, p. 38). A characteristic such as envy is no longer seen as something that is personal to one or more members of the family but rather it is now seen as a problem the family needs to solve because of the negative ways it impacts their relationships. Thus, family members reduce their arguments about who owns a problem and ideally form a team and enter into dialogue about problem solving.

Treatment Techniques

Narrative therapy is a process-oriented as opposed to a technique-driven approach. However, many narrative family treatment techniques are quite innovative. The most prevalent are highlighted here.

Externalization of the Problem

As previously stated, through externalization, therapists seek to separate problems from people. The result is usually (1) a decrease in unproductive conflict between persons; (2) a lessening of the sense of failure an unresolved problem has on persons; (3) an increase of cooperation among family members to problem-solve and dialogue with each other; (4) an opening up of new possibilities for action; and (5) a freeing of persons to be more effective and less stressed in approaching problems (White & Epston, 1990).

In externalization, the problem is the problem. As such, it becomes objective and can be addressed in unique ways (White, 1991). In some cases, the problem can be described in such a way that it takes on a personality of its own, such as *encopresis* (lack of bowel control) being given the name "Sneaky Poo" (White, 1989). In situations like this, all family members can relate to what is facing them. They may then become consultants to the therapist helping to solve the problem and not themselves defined by the problem itself (Bitter, 2000).

Influence (Effect) of the Problem on the Person

The goal of asking how a problem has influenced a person is to increase the person's awareness and objectivity. This type of awareness can best be generated by the therapist asking each family member to give a detailed, no-holds-barred account of how the problem has affected him or her (e.g., dominated his or her life). A typical question in this process might be: "How has the problem influenced you and your life and your relationships?"

Influence (Effect) of the Person on the Problem

The purpose of asking family members how they have influenced a problem is twofold. First, it makes them increasingly aware of their response to a problem. Second, it helps them realize their strengths or potential in facing such a situation. In essence, this technique is the opposite of the influence of the problem on the person (see preceding section). Again, this type of treatment breaks a fixed perception or behavior pattern and creates a new possible way to combat or stand up against a problem.

Raising Dilemmas

The effect of raising dilemmas is to get client-families to examine possible aspects of a problem before the need arises. For instance, parents might be asked in relation to their misbehaving son how they would cope with "Worry" if the son's behavior became better, worsened, or remained the same. They might also be asked to consider how they would handle "Worry" if their youngest sibling began misbehaving as well.

Predicting Setbacks

Setbacks in family therapy are almost inevitable. Narrative family therapy takes the approach that setbacks are best dealt with when they are planned for or anticipated (White, 1986). By doing so, families can decide ahead of time how they will act in the face of adversity. For instance, in regard to "Worry," narrative therapists might ask a family what they would do if, once they appear to have resolved their problem, "Worry" reappeared. In other words, would they give up and let "Worry" reenter their lives or would they fight back and drive "Worry" away?

Using Questions

Through the use of questions, therapists can challenge families to examine the nature of the difficulties they bring to therapy and what resources they have and can use to handle their problems. Questions can take a variety of forms but two of the most prevalent types are those that explore exceptions and those that deal with significance.

Exceptions questions are directed toward finding instances when a situation reported to be a problem was not true. If a family reports they are in chaos, an exceptions question would be aimed at finding examples of times when the family was not chaotic. The idea behind such questions is to challenge the family's view of the world and to offer them hope that their lives can be different because some change has already taken place. Most exceptions questions begin with *when* or *what*. Research on exceptions questions reveals that blaming statements decrease and positive statements increase during exceptions questions conditions (Meidonis & Bry, 1995).

Significance questions are "unique redescription questions, they search for and reveal the meanings, significance, and importance of the exceptions" (Kurtz & Tandy, 1995, p. 189). A family might be asked: "Now that you are more aware of how you acted in this situation, to what do you attribute that behavior?"

Letters

Writing letters to families after therapy sessions is an important part of narrative therapy. According to Epston (1994), "words in a letter don't fade or disappear the way a conversation does. … A client can hold a letter in hand, reading and rereading it days, months, and years after the session" (p. 31). Thus, letters can serve as a medium for continuation of the dialogue between the therapist and family members and as a reminder of what has occurred in the therapy session. For Epston, letters are case notes. Through them, he attempts to be transparent and congruent in his statements to families while they are in therapy.

Celebrations and Certificates

Celebrations and certificates are a unique and important part of narrative therapy and are used to bring closure to therapy. They serve as tangible affirmations of the defeat of a problem. They also mark the beginning of a new description of a family (White & Epston, 1990). Celebrations can and should take on a festive air and include cakes, cookies, punch, and other goodies that signify a victory or an achievement.

Certificates (see Figure 11.1) can and should be tailored for the family and the situation they have faced. Certificates are best when printed and affixed with a logo. For instance, in regard to a family that has defeated "Apathy," a certificate might read:

> This certificate is awarded to the Fong Family in recognition of their conquest of Apathy and its insidious effect upon their lives. Family members are commended for their persistence in the face of inertia and their ability to mobilize their energy to do something about troublesome situations rather than wait for them to go away.

Role of the Therapist

The narrative family therapist works in a number of ways but is primarily a collaborator who assumes the role of a nonexpert. Like therapists in other traditions, narrative family therapists engage their clients and use the basic relationship skills of attending, paraphrasing, clarifying, summarizing, and checking to make sure they hear the client's story or problem correctly (Monk, 1998). The therapist does not assume that symptoms serve a function for families. Just the opposite is true. Problems are seen as oppressive for families. They need to be addressed and eliminated as rapidly as possible. Therefore, the narrative therapist is a questioner who works to find unique outcomes or exceptions when families experience problems. The therapist is also notable for examining the meaning of situations for families.

CERTIFICATE OF ACCOMPLISHMENT

This award is presented to

JOHN AND JANE DRIVER

FOR CONQUERING JEALOUSY IN THEIR MARRIAGE

"A Goal Without a Plan Is a Dream." — Anonymous

You planned well and achieved your goal — Congratulations!

Kevin Kennorgel
Signature

April 9, 2006
Date

Figure 11.1
Sample certificate of accomplishment.

To help families, the therapist assists them in separating themselves from old, problem-saturated stories by constructing new stories in which they, instead of their problems, are in control. This procedure is called **reauthoring** (White, 1992, 1995). It involves the redefining of lives and relationships in a new narrative. "During the reauthoring phase of the story, counselors help new stories emerge by looking for unique outcomes. **Unique outcomes** are defined as clients' storied experiences that do not fit the problem-saturated story" that they have already told the therapist (Molina et al., 2004, p. 144). Sometimes this process can be accomplished creatively such as through the use of music and verse (Hodas, 1994). At other times, it is accomplished through a series of questions and the careful use of language. Regardless, "memory is central to the process of restorying and reinterpreting" (Tootle, 2003, p. 186). Family members and families as a whole are successful when they organize to help themselves and escape the power of oppressive influences.

Process and Outcome

The process of narrative family therapy is one in which individuals and families are aided in learning to value their own life experiences and stories. It consists of three phases: (1) deconstructing the dominant cultural narrative, (2) externalizing the problem, and (3) reauthoring the story (Molina et al., 2004, p. 144). In **deconstruction**, individuals and families are challenged to examine exceptions to problems they bring in. They are then asked to change their behaviors so that they collectively address difficulties by externalizing them. Finally, in reauthoring they are taught that the history of a problem is not as important as making the effort to reconstruct or reauthor a story so that problems are less dominant and significant in a family's life.

In this final phase, questions are raised that are aimed at finding exceptions to the dominant influence of problems. The externalization of the problem unites the family in attacking it and, thus, helps the family to avoid scapegoating. By marshaling family resources, expecting setbacks, and raising dilemmas, narrative family therapists help families construct new stories and meaning in their lives without falling into old and unproductive patterns of perception and behavior.

Narrative family therapy has been applied to the following problems: couple relationships, substance abuse, adolescent sexual offenders, schizophrenia, post-traumatic stress disorder (PTSD), AIDS, learning disabilities, temper problems within a family, anorexia/bulimia, and grief. Most of the outcome studies on its effectiveness have been in the form of case reports [for an example, see Merscham (2000)].

Overall, narrative therapy is a social constructionism approach that is eclectic and uses the literary metaphors of storytelling and writing. Therapeutic relationships are collaborative. It emphasizes cocreating differences, new stories, and new realities. Problems are investigated in terms of exceptions and meaning rather than causes. There is a focus on societal influences on people.

Unique Aspects of Narrative Family Therapy

Emphases

Narrative family therapy emphasizes the reauthoring by families of their life stories. According to White (1992), a key component of family therapy is a deconstruction, which involves "procedures that subvert taken-for-granted realities and practices" (p. 121).

Using questions is one way of employing deconstruction as a therapeutic tool. For instance, the therapist might ask: "Does this problem or situation invite you to react in certain ways?" or "What ideas do you have about _____ that explain why you acted that way?" (Monk, 1998, p. 5). Through deconstruction, the client is helped to move beyond symptom-maintaining myths to create a more vital story. Family problems are externalized to increase cooperation among family members to problem-solve and create new possibilities for action.

In narrative family therapy, the individuals and families are asked to look for exceptions to the difficult situations they are experiencing. The idea is to focus on solutions, which are the exceptions, rather than problems, which are the rule. Questions are used extensively.

The expectation of setbacks and the raising of dilemmas are built into narrative family therapy so that the people involved can realize ahead of time some of the problems they might have in creating new lifestyles. Expecting setbacks may be especially helpful in lowering resistance to making changes.

Letters are sent to families about their progress. Celebrations are held and personalized certificates are issued when goals are achieved.

Comparison with Other Theories

Both solution-focused and narrative family therapies are based on postmodern, social constructionist points of view (Freedman & Combs, 1996). As such they are among the most cerebral and intellectual of any of the family therapy approaches. From a narrative family therapy perspective, there is no normative family pattern that should be achieved. Instead, meaning, purposefulness, and health are determined by each family based on their own life history and culture.

Narrative family therapy pays particular attention to the use of language. "The power of language and its ability to shape reality are key to narrative family therapy" (Walsh & McGraw, 2002, p. 129). Thus, while other family therapy approaches put an emphasis on the importance of verbal behavior, narrative therapy is especially centered on the use of and influence of language.

Little attention is paid in narrative family therapy to the history of the concern (or complaint) brought by the family. In this regard, narrative family therapy is similar to solution-focused, strategic, systemic, and behavioral therapies in its focus on the present rather than the past. Like systemic family therapy, the origins of narrative family therapy began outside the United States. Narrative family therapy focuses on collaborative therapeutic relationships, which is similar to solution-focused and systemic family approaches. However, narrative family therapy is not a systems-oriented approach to working with families. Gus Napier sees the narrative approach "as falling into the individual model" both conceptually and in the way it is practiced (Disque & Morrow, 2002, p. 114).

In general, narrative therapy takes:

> a strong stand against the functionalist elements of both family systems and psychoanalytic models that led therapists to believe that problems are inherent in individuals (as psychoanalysis would have it) or in families (as family systems would have it). Instead, they believe that problems arise because people are induced by our culture into subscribing to narrow and self-defeating views of themselves and the world. (Schwartz, 1999, p. 264)

——————————— **CASE ILLUSTRATION** ———————————

THE BEARCLAW FAMILY

Family Background

David Bearclaw married Claire Standback in a civil ceremony after a whirlwind courtship lasting 3 months. David, age 23, was new to city life and missed the comfort of friends and family on the reservation where he grew up. Claire, age 22, was away from her family for the first time. The couple shared a high hope for their marriage and a physical attraction for one another, but their cultural backgrounds were different as were their expectations for the relationship. David expected to be a good provider and to head the household. Claire, although not opposed to these roles, expected to have a say in the way the family functioned, especially after the birth of their daughter, Rose, now age 5, and their son, Hunter, now age 3. The trouble was that David worked construction and was often between jobs. During these times, he would insist that Claire not work and that she use the money they had saved to pay the bills and keep creditors from bothering them. David also would isolate himself from Claire during these times of unemployment and would leave home to meditate. Claire became depressed but continued going to church and nurturing her children.

Conceptualization of Family: Narrative Perspective

The 6-year-old marriage of David and Claire is stressed due to economic concerns, a lack of common strategies for problem solving, the stress of preschool children, and other external and internal pressures. The couple has had time to get to know one another, but it appears they do not. They live according to rigid and passive gender roles that do not serve them or their family well. Their lack of outside social support and their tendency to retreat from talking with each other during times of heightened stress contribute to their difficulties.

Process of Treatment: Narrative Therapy

To help the Bearclaws, narrative family therapists would first listen to their story and help them rank the difficulties they face. In this case, financial stress would be rated number one and the therapist would then work with the Bearclaws to externalize the problem and give it a name, such as "Money." After externalizing the problem, the Bearclaws would be asked by the therapist to state how the problem has affected them and how they have influenced the problem as well.

The therapist would then use questions to help the Bearclaws find times when there were exceptions to their present way of acting and how that behavior impacted on them. For instance, the therapist would compliment the Bearclaws on their ability to buy necessary items on sale and on their agreement to make and keep a budget that allowed for some savings during times of employment. The therapist would make case notes in a letter to the Bearclaws on these exceptions and their work on the troublesome problem of "Money." The therapist would raise dilemmas during treatment on aspects of "Money" the Bearclaws may not have considered and would predict setbacks in the Bearclaws solving their "Money" trouble, too.

Through all of the sessions, the narrative therapist would encourage the Bearclaws to create a new story of their lives, such as switching roles when David is out of work and letting Claire bring home "Money" by working for a temporary employment agency while David takes care of the children. In such a story, the Bearclaws could be more united and less concerned about "Money." The result should lead to a celebration and new strategies for living as a family.

Summary and Conclusion

In the 1980s, but especially in the 1990s, the work of deShazer and O'Hanlon brought national attention to solution-focused therapy. This approach concentrates on bringing change to a wider range of client-family problems. It is short-term, specific, positive, and concentrates on bringing about small changes in the process of facilitating larger ones. Both deShazer and O'Hanlon have been greatly influenced by Milton Erickson.

In the 1990s, narrative family therapy emerged as another strong approach that continues today. Like solution-focused therapy, it is based on a postmodern, social constructionist view of the world that emphasizes the subjective nature of reality and the importance of families making their own meaning in the world by creating stories that are not problem-centered. In this approach, difficulties are externalized and, like solution-focused therapies, exceptions to problems are noted and utilized to help families change their behaviors for the better.

Both solution-focused and narrative family therapies are concerned with changing present behaviors, not examining past histories. They both stress that families have untapped resources that can and should be marshaled in helping them help themselves. Likewise, these therapies are creative in innovative ways that go beyond traditional forms of family therapy, such as emphasizing that change is inevitable. Together, solution-focused and narrative family therapies represent the best of the dynamic family therapy approaches that continue to develop.

Summary Table
Solution-Focused and Narrative Family Therapies

Solution-Focused Therapy
Major Theorists

Steve deShazer	Insoo Kim Berg	Bill O'Hanlon
Eve Lipchik	Alan Gurman	Michele Weiner-Davis
Scott Miller	Patricia O'Hanlon Hudson	

Premises of the Theory

Reality is seen as a reflection of observation and experience, not as objective reality.
Focus is on exceptions to dysfunctionality, hypothetical solutions, and small changes.
Exceptions to patterns are highlighted.
The present is emphasized.
The family is viewed as an ally that wants to change.

Treatment Techniques

The unit of treatment is the family as a system, although solution-focused approaches can be selectively used to help dyads and individuals make changes.

The goals of treatment are:

- to help the family to seek solutions and tap internal resources
- to help the family perceive the world differently, especially in regard to the inevitability of change and the importance of making small changes

The therapeutic techniques include:

- Joining
- Listening and accepting
- Noting of patterns and exceptions
- Awareness exercises
- Hypothetical solutions, particularly the "miracle question"
- Making small changes
- Skeleton keys
- Task assignments
- Compliments
- Scaling
- Clues
- Mapping

Role of the Therapist

The solution-oriented family therapist initially determines the motivation of families and their members; that is, are they visitors, complainants, or customers? Then the therapist works as a facilitator with families, asking them questions and talking to them about expectations of change. Simple and universal solutions are emphasized by the therapist whenever possible.

Process and Outcome

Families are presented with the Ericksonian position that change is inevitable.
Families are asked optimistic questions and reinforced for small but specific movement.
Families are encouraged to seek solutions and tap internal resources.

Unique Aspects of Solution-Focused Therapy

Unique aspects of solution-focused therapy include:

- the acceptance of a family's situation through listening
- an emphasis on the present and clear definition of a family's situation
- the noting of exceptions to family patterns and raising of awareness (including family resources)
- a focus on small changes through completion of an assigned task or through observation within the family

Comparison with Other Theories

Unlike Bowen or psychoanalytic approaches, no attention is paid to history.
Like strategic and systemic family therapies, solution-focused therapy is brief (usually five to six sessions).

Like behavioral therapy, treatment ends when goals are achieved. However, universal solutions may be utilized in the process of fostering change.

Like systemic family therapy, a team is sometimes used in treatment (deShazer).

Like MRI strategic therapy, solution-focused therapy is aimed at helping families think and act differently.

Narrative Family Therapy

Major Theorists

Michael White	David Epston	Michael Durrant
Gerald Monk	Associates of White and Epston	

Premises of the Theory

Narrative therapy is based on a postmodern and social constructionist perspective that rejects classification systems based on empiricism and promotes empowering persons and families through emphasizing their stories.

Problems are seen as external to persons and families.

Problems should be attacked in a cooperative manner by families who work as teams and utilize their resources.

Treatment Techniques

Narrative therapy treats family units, subunits, and individuals.

The goal of treatment is on helping families reauthor their lives and bring about change so that they and not their problems dominate.

Narrative therapy treatment techniques include:
- Externalization of the problem
- Influence (effect) of the problem on the person
- Influence (effect) of the person on the problem
- Raising dilemmas
- Predicting setbacks
- Use of questions (exceptions and significance questions)
- Letters
- Celebrations and certificates

Role of the Therapist

The therapist views problems as oppressive to families and in need of elimination.

The therapist works to find unique outcomes, that is, exceptions, to families' problems.

The therapist uses questions and helps families create new stories where they, and not their problems, are in control.

Process and Outcome

Individuals and families are challenged to reconstruct and reauthor their lives.

Problems are externalized and attacked by the whole family.

Problems are investigated in terms of meaning and exceptions rather than causes.

Unique Aspects of Narrative Family Therapy

Unique aspects of narrative family therapy include:

- families learn to value their own life experience and stories and to reauthor their lives
- families learn to find exceptions to their regular patterns of living
- problems are externalized and worked on cooperatively
- expectations of setbacks and the raising of dilemmas help lower resistance
- letters to families by their therapists are sent regarding their progress
- celebrations by families and therapists are held when goals are reached

Comparison with Other Theories

Narrative therapy is postmodern and based on a social constructionist viewpoint like solution-focused therapy.

The theory originally developed outside of the United States, like that of systemic therapy.

The emphasis of therapy is on the present as compared with the historical emphasis of Bowen and psychoanalytic approaches.

The focus of the approach is on collaborative effort of families and therapists, like strategic and solution-focused family therapies.

Special Populations in Family Therapy

Working with Single-Parent Families

She talks about her unborn
as three small children noisily play
in the dusty red dirt around her cluttered yard
with hand-me-down toys
from their richer peers in Buena Vista.
Amid the chaos and bleakness,
I wonder how she survives summer's heat
or manages a smile in the face of stress
as her bills pile up like unwashed clothes
in a house without running water.
But in the silence,
as the noise of that scene fades in my mind,
at the end of a day filled with mental struggles
I hear the strength of resolve in her voice,
remember her caring eyes and toughness,
and in it all I know, though pained,
she will prevail.

Gladding, 1993b

Single-parent families are those either headed by a mother or a father, a sole parent, responsible for taking care of herself or himself and a child or children (Walsh, 1991). The term has been applied to a number of different family forms. The families covered under this designation include those created as a result of divorce, death, abandonment, unwed pregnancy, adoption, and uncontrollable circumstances, such as receiving a military assignment into a combat zone. They differ in regard to dynamics and vary in their interactions depending on the number of people within the family unit, the background and resources of the members, and the stage of the individual and family life cycle at the time the unit was formed. There is no prototype of a single-parent family.

The number of single-parent families in the United States has increased sharply in recent years (Kleist, 1999). There are now over 90,000 single mothers and fathers in the armed forces, up from almost 48,000 in 1992 (Piore, 2004). Single parents are increasingly common across all socioeconomic groups and life circumstance (Coates, 1996). Prior to 1970, about one family in ten (10%) was headed by a single parent, usually the mother (Seward, 1978). By the turn of the 21st century, however, "almost one third of the 35 million households with children in the United States" were headed by a single parent (Krauth, 1995, p. 14) with about one-quarter of children in the United States living in such families (Parke, 2004). All cultural groups in the United States have changed in regard to the number of single-parent households within their subpopulations.

Historically, most single-parent families had been created by the death or desertion of a spouse. In the 1950s, a new trend began: The percentage of single-parent families created by divorce started to exceed those created by death (Levitan & Conway, 1990). Further, the decision of many unmarried women to bear and raise children by themselves, which began in the 1970s, also increased the number of single-parent families. The number of births "to unmarried mothers hit a record high in 1990 of 1,165,384." Approximately "20 percent of white births, 37 percent of Hispanic births, and 67 percent of black births" were to unmarried women (Associated Press, 1993a, p. 2). While this trend has subsided in recent years, more than half a million children are born out of wedlock each year.

This chapter examines four distinct single-parent family lifestyles: those created by divorce, death, choice, and temporary circumstances (i.e., where one parent in a two-parent household may be absent for a substantial time such as being deployed in the military). It also examines the dynamics underlying and affecting these types of single-parent families, as well as single-parent families in general. The common strengths and challenges associated with the single-parent family lifestyles are highlighted. Finally, therapeutic approaches for working with single-parent families that experience difficulties are discussed from selected theoretical and self-help perspectives. The role of the family therapist and expected outcomes are highlighted.

Types of Single-Parent Families

Single-parent families vary greatly. Whether they are planned or unplanned, the formation of these types of single-parent families occurs over time. No one type of single-parent family works best in all situations. Also, time lines must be kept flexible when considering single-parent family development. Different circumstances within each type of family require adjustment considerations that are unique. Two years after the family first develops, however, reality (as opposed to idealization) should be present in all of these types of families (Freeman, 1985).

Four major types of single-parent families are those that develop as a result of divorce, death, choice, and temporary circumstances. A common dimension of all single-parent families is that the process in their development is one that has definable stages, although these stages are more nebulous in those families created by choice and because of temporary circumstances.

Single Parenthood as a Result of Divorce

There are approximately a million divorces each year in the United States. The underlying factors contributing to divorce are complex. They range from infidelity to incompatibility. Regardless of the reasons, however, "divorce does not end family life, although it changes its shape" (Barnes, 1999, p. 436) for a divorce does not just uncouple incompatible partners, it "changes the structure of the entire family system" (Goldenberg & Goldenberg, 2002, p. 107). Therapists who successfully help families deal with divorce situations assist them in establishing a functional binuclear family, which in turn continues with the most important task of the family—namely, the socialization of their children (Sholevar & Schwoeri, 2003).

In the United States "two of every three divorces are now initiated by women" (Silverstein & Levant, 1996, p. 18). Despite who initiates the action, when single-parent families begin as a result of divorce, two subunits are formed (except in some cases of **joint custody** arrangements). One subunit involves the **custodial parent**, with whom the child resides, and his or her interactions with the ex-spouse and child(ren). The other subunit includes the **noncustodial parent** and his or her relationships with the ex-spouse and child(ren) (Carter & McGoldrick, 1988). In such a situation, both parents have the same rights in regard to the child or children involved unless there is a court order expressly stating otherwise (Stone, 2005).

Both parental/child arrangements for single-parent families of divorce experience stresses and rewards (Blaisure & Geasler, 2000). For custodial parents in such situations, stressors include rebuilding financial resources and social networks, with the most stressful time for these families being during their first 3 years (Morrison, 1995). A major benefit for successful custodial parents is a renewed sense of confidence in themselves. For the noncustodial parent in such a family, stressors include finding ways to continue to be involved with one's children as a parent and the rebuilding of social networks. When successful, noncustodial parents experience rewards. The rewards include devising creative problem-solving methods and gaining renewed self-confidence. Carter and McGoldrick (1988, p. 22) conceptualize the stages of single-parent families formed through divorce as shown in Table 12.1.

Single Parenthood as a Result of Death

In single-parent families that begin as a result of death, the stages of development have not been as specifically delineated as in those single-parent families resulting from divorce. However, it is clear that death has an overall impact on family life and that reestablishment of one's life and the restructuring of the family are major tasks (Brown, 1988; Moody & Moody, 1991; Pulleyblank, 1996).

The family's development may involve three stages, as shown in Table 12.2. The first stage is mourning, which takes time and cannot be forced (Rotter, 2000). It is vital in the **mourning stage** for surviving family members to release both positive and negative feelings about the deceased because "death ends a life, not a relationship" (Albom, 1997, p. 174). This

Table 12.1

Dislocations of the Family Life Cycle Requiring Additional Steps to Restabilize and Proceed Developmentally

Phase	Emotional Process of Transition Prerequisite Attitude	Developmental Issues
Divorce		
1. The decision to divorce	Acceptance of inability to resolve marital tensions sufficiently to continue relationship	Acceptance of one's own part in the failure of the marriage
2. Planning the breakup of the system	Supporting viable arrangements for all parts of the system	a. Working cooperatively on problems of custody, visitation, and finances b. Dealing with extended family about the divorce
3. Separation	a. Willingness to continue cooperative coparental relationship and joint financial support of children b. Work on resolution of attachment to spouse	a. Mourning loss of intact family b. Restructuring marital and parent–child relationships and finances; adaptation to living apart c. Realignment of relationships with extended family; staying connected with spouse's extended family
4. The divorce	More work on emotional divorce: Overcoming hurt, anger, guilt, etc.	a. Mourning loss of intact family: giving up fantasies of reunion b. Retrieval of hopes, dreams, expectations from the marriage c. Staying connected with extended families
Post-divorce family		
1. Single-parent (custodial household or primary residence)	Willingness to maintain financial responsibilities, continue parental contact with ex-spouse, and support contact of children with ex-spouse and his or her family	a. Making flexible visitation arrangements with ex-spouse and spouse's family b. Rebuilding own financial resources c. Rebuilding own social network
2. Single-parent (noncustodial)	Willingness to maintain parental contact with ex-spouse and support custodial parent's relationship with children	a. Finding ways to continue effective parenting relationship with children b. Maintaining financial responsibilities to ex-spouse and children c. Rebuilding own social network

From Carter, B & McGoldrick, M. *The Expanded Family Life Cycle*, 3/e. © 1999. Published by Allyn and Bacon, Boston, MA. Copyright © 1999 by Pearson Education. Reprinted by permission of the publisher.

Table 12.2
Single-Parent Families Created by Death

Stage	Task	Result
Mourning	Emotional catharsis	Resolution of past relationship
Readjustment	Learning/dropping of duties	Performance of essential duties
Renewal and accomplishment	Personal and family development	Acquiring new skills and interests

type of catharsis makes it possible to move to the second stage—readjustment. The **readjustment stage** involves learning to do new tasks, dropping old tasks, and/or reassigning duties previously done by the ex-spouse to other members of the family (Murdock, 1980). When this stage is completed, the family can move into a final phase—the **renewal and accomplishment stage**—in which family members, and the family as a whole, can concentrate on finding and engaging in new growth opportunities. This last stage, which may or may not be achieved, results in new collective and individual identities and relationships.

Single Parenthood by Choice

A third way in which single-parent families begin involves choice and intentionality. The actions associated with intent are (1) purposefulness in conceiving a child out of wedlock; (2) deciding to carry a child to term after accidentally becoming pregnant out of wedlock; or (3) adopting a child as a single adult. The unique aspect of this type of single-parent family is that the parent has time to prepare before the child arrives. Furthermore, it is clear to the parent in these situations that there will usually be no other support outside of the parent's resources. In these cases, single-parent families go through the stages, processes, and outcomes listed in Table 12.3.

Single Parenthood as a Result of Temporary Circumstances

In addition to single-parent families formed through divorce, death, or choice, there is also the single-parent family formed out of uncontrollable circumstances, such as a war or a job

Table 12.3
Single-Parent Families Created by Intention

Stage	Task	Result
Planning	Preparing for the arrival of the child	Marshaling of resources; Mental expectation of change
Arrival	Creating a parent and child relationship	Physical and emotional bonding
Adjustment and achievement	Resolving situational and development needs	Growth of family and individual

change that involves one parent making an immediate move while the family stays behind. These types of single-parent families are often temporary lasting anywhere from a few weeks to, in extreme cases, several years. Regardless, family members face stress because of the suddenness and oftentimes the seriousness of a situation that separates a parent from a family and leaves the other parent (if there is one) behind.

The military family is a good example of the latter type of circumstance with "most army families" experiencing "annual duty-related separations, one third for more than a total of 17 weeks" (Drummet, Coleman, & Cable, 2003, p. 281). With approximately 1.4 million active-service members in the United States armed forces, the number of families affected directly and indirectly is quite large.

Dynamics Associated with the Formation of Single-Parent Families

In defining how single-parent families are formed, the roots from which they spring need to be examined. Divorce, death, choice, and temporary circumstance all present different dynamics. By understanding the factors underlying these diverse ways of establishing single-parent families, therapists can make better decisions in formulating treatment strategies.

Dynamics of Single-Parent Families Formed through Divorce

"Ten to fifteen percent of couples separate in the first four years of marriage and only 70% make it through the first decade of marriage" (Lebow, 2005, p. 38). Numerous factors influence the decision for couples to divorce. Among the top three considerations affecting the dissolution of marriages are social, personal, and relationship issues (Bornstein & Bornstein, 1986).

On a social level, the pace of American life has changed rapidly, especially since World War II (Levitan & Conway, 1990). Major changes include new technology, more alternatives, less stability, and the opportunity for greater frustration, fulfillment, and alienation. Women's roles have changed; and the alliance between men and their work has weakened. In addition, the mobility of society has contributed to an acceptance of options, transitions, and a new openness to mores and laws. Divorce is more acceptable today (Bumpass, 1990).

A second reason for not staying married involves personal issues. People marry at different levels of psychological maturity and with varied expectations. If they are immature, their decisions and actions will most likely reflect it (Bowen, 1978). Some relationships are doomed to failure before they even begin because of the personalities of those involved. In these marriages, the individuals involved are probably best served when the relationship dissolves, especially if they seek help in becoming more autonomous and mature.

Interpersonal issues are a third variable related to divorce. Marriage and family life involve give-and-take interactions (i.e., a quid pro quo, or something for something). People often do not stay married when they perceive that they are giving more than they are receiving (Klagsbrun, 1985). There are ways to rectify such situations, but frequently couples do not seek help or seek it too late. The result is the splitting of a relationship.

In all of these situations, men or women who become single parents following divorce and separation deal with the following issues (Garfield, 1982):

- resolution of the loss of the marriage
- acceptance of new roles and responsibilities

- renegotiation and redefinement of relationships with family and friends
- establishment of a satisfactory arrangement with one's ex-spouse

The transition is not easy. In fact, "divorce is much more devastating than people who go into the process anticipate" (Moody, 1992, p. 171). It may be especially miserable for couples with children (Hetherington, 2004). For example, "most divorced families with children experience enormous drops in income, which lessen somewhat over time but remain significant for years" (Parke, 2004, p. 111). Individuals who have ample resources in the form of psychological or financial aid/support find the difficulties less intense but still formidable. "Loss is an issue of great significance with regard to how adults and children experience divorce" regardless of financial or psychological support (Arditti & Prouty, 1999, p. 63). Added to these difficulties is the fact that society still disapproves of and stigmatizes those who divorce. Little wonder then that at least 10% of individuals who experience marital separation or divorce see a therapist or counselor (Sweet, Bumpass, & Call, 1988).

Dynamics of Single-Parent Families Formed through Death

Death is a shock even when it is expected. This reaction is especially prevalent if a person is survived by a spouse and child(ren). "About 800,000 spouses ... die every year" (McGoldrick, 1986, p. 30), leaving behind millions of immediate family members to mourn the loss. It is important that survivors of these deaths properly grieve. Such a process may be difficult because of the lack of mourning rituals in modern society. Yet if family members, especially widows and widowers, do not appropriately grieve for their former spouses, their chances of reestablishing themselves or establishing a healthy single-parent family are greatly lessened.

It is crucial that family members talk to one another and others, such as neighbors, extended kin, or counselors, after the death of a spouse/parent. By doing so, they release their feelings and are able to see the dead person as mortal instead of superhuman. Such a perspective helps family members deal with their feelings and external demands productively and realistically.

Dynamics of Single-Parent Families Formed through Choice

The number of people, especially women, who raise a family by themselves is large and growing. It cuts across racial, social, and economic divisions in American society (Associated Press, 1993b). Some reasons for this pattern are due to tradition, some to change and acceptance by society, and some to choice.

Historical tradition is one factor that helps explain why certain groups of women have children out of wedlock. In certain subcultures, a maternally oriented society has evolved in which children have been raised by single-parent mothers. Here many young women and men are inclined to avoid marriage and to follow the pattern they grew up in, especially if they are not exposed to other role models. The socioeconomic milieu in such cases has a strong influence that can prove detrimental to the subculture and simultaneously give it a distinction and even, ironically, pride. Racism, ignorance, and socioeconomic crises also contribute to such a pattern of maternal single-parenting and make it hard to break the cycle (Strong, DeVault, & Cohen, 2005).

Acceptance is a second reason women elect to have children out of wedlock. The upheavals in American society following World War II helped break down stigmas and taboos.

The turbulence of the 1960s further eroded some traditional norms and patterns, such as ostracizing women who bore children out of wedlock. According to figures kept by the National Center for Health Statistics there has been an increase in the number of women who have elected to have children out of wedlock since the 1970s (National Center for Health Statistics, 2005). For example, in 2002, the percentage of women aged 15 to 44 giving birth outside of marriage was 34% which resulted in the production of 1,365,966 children (National Center for Health Statistics, 2005). "Society is not frowning on them any more" (Associated Press, 1993b, p. 2).

A final factor that has influenced the increased number of women bearing children out of wedlock is choice. A small percentage of women who thoughtfully decide to bear and raise children by themselves are well educated; about 33% are high school graduates; and over 8% hold a managerial or professional position (Associated Press, 1993b). In addition, the number of prominent older women who thoughtfully decided to raise a baby by themselves increased beginning in the 1980s. Two well-publicized examples are Mia Farrow and Goldie Hawn (Erbe, 1993).

Furthermore, the dramatization of the lives of fictitious women who choose parenthood outside of marriage as seen in movies, such as *The Big Chill*, or television programs, such as "Murphy Brown," has been extensive. Whether one agrees or disagrees with their decisions, the fact is that more mothers over age 25 are deciding to have babies outside of marriage; "about one quarter in 1980 compared with about one third in 1988," with no slowdown in the trend expected (Bray, 1993, p. 95).

Although not a complete parallel, the reasons for unmarried women choosing to adopt babies have some similarity to those who become pregnant (Pavao, 1998). It is more socially acceptable for unwed women to adopt babies than it was in the past. Furthermore, because of resources and desire, many professional women are electing to adopt and raise children by themselves. Two major differences between single women who adopt and those who elect to biologically have a baby are timing and resources. Women who adopt can more precisely pick the time when they wish to become a parent. Many of the women are affluent. Like other single women, they are not encumbered by the demands of a marital relationship and can therefore give more time and nurturance to their child(ren) (Groze, 1991).

Dynamics of Single-Parent Families Formed through Temporary Circumstances

Families formed through temporary circumstances go through a number of transitions but depending on the conditions end up disorganized and stressed for a time. Military and corporate families, in which one parent or the only parent is deployed or sent on assignment, must cope with the stressors of relocation, separation, and reunion (Drummet et al., 2003). Here the institutions involved seek exclusive and undivided loyalty and the parent involved usually does not have a choice.

In such circumstances, the parent left in charge of the household duties finds himself or herself in an overload position with extra duties and no additional resources. That parent must decide what tasks are essential, what obligations can be postponed, and what activities can be dropped. This readjustment is usually not one that occurs through thoughtful planning but rather it is one that emerges out of necessity. Food shopping, for example, is not something that can be postponed. Planning a weekend outing is.

Despite the best efforts of the parent left to cope as a single parent, stress surfaces. Single-parent households formed through temporary circumstances face the same type of challenges as those that occur due to death or divorce. The difference is that the time period for functioning in this way is limited.

Single-Parent Mothers and Fathers

Gender issues can have an impact on how single-parent families function. To understand the life and needs of these families, it is necessary to be aware of how they differ according to who is parentally in charge. Although single-parent families are formed in a number of different temporary and permanent ways, they are ultimately headed by either a mother or father (Hill, 1986).

Families of Single-Parent Mothers

Historically, between 85% and 90% of children in single-parent households live with their mothers (Glick, 1988; Krauth, 1995). This figure varies from year to year and in some subgroups it is higher than others. For instance, about 45% of African-American families (or 3.8 million households) were led by women without partners present in 1999, while approximately 13% of European-American families in the same year were headed by women alone (Associated Press, 2000).

In regard to single-parent mothers and finances, research shows contrasts. Children whose single-parent mothers engage in full-time, paid work report "more positive self-esteem and daily affect and arousal" than those whose mothers do not engage in paid work (Duckett & Richards, 1995, p. 427). Employment has been found to contribute to single-mothers' health. However, because women are paid, on average, lower wages than men, these single-parent mothers and their children generally have fewer resources than most families in the United States. For instance, the median income for all households in the United States in 2004 was $44,389, as compared with a single-parent father's income of $44,923 and a single-parent mother's income of $29,826 (U.S. Census Bureau, 2005, p. 11). Although the figures for such families continue to change, the pattern has not: single-parent mothers as a group are still poorer than their counterparts, single-parent fathers, and are five times as likely to be poor when compared to two-parent families (Parke, 2004).

Single-parent mothers who have been married may potentially collect either insurance or child support. However, "nearly 70 percent of noncustodial fathers become delinquent within a few years of child support" (Levitan & Conway, 1990, p. 18). When there is regular child support, it does not usually come without some restrictions. Noncustodial fathers who pay support often wish and have the right to be involved in decisions made regarding the welfare of their children (Melli, 1986). Unwed mothers, particularly if they are adolescents themselves, find it difficult to obtain enough financial support to make ends meet. Violence and abuse are unfortunately associated with mother-only homes at the poverty level (Gelles, 1989, 1997).

In addition to limited financial assets and the drawbacks that come with them, single-parent mothers may also be pressed for time (Murdock, 1980). Often they sacrifice time in personal-care activities, including sleep and rest, in order to take care of their families (Sanik & Mauldin, 1986). They also have new time demands to take care of, such as work duties or school obligations. For some there is the difficulty of dealing with a former spouse's family. These families may want to visit with the child(ren) on occasions, regardless of whether it is convenient for the custodial parent. This type of time demand may interfere with the welfare of the single-parent family as a whole, but it may especially affect the mother.

Furthermore, there is the problem of identity or establishing a different identity. Young single-parent mothers are frequently in need of care, support, and guidance. As a group, they usually have low self-esteem and little work experience and education (Levitan & Conway, 1990). Besides the difficulties of identity and functioning, the parent within these households frequently lacks knowledge about how to obtain medical and psychological services. Women over 40, especially if they have mainly worked inside the home, have a hard time rebuilding their lives socially, psychologically, and economically (Wallerstein, 1986).

The health and well-being of households headed by single-parent mothers depends on the age and stage of the parent and her children, as well as her level of education, income, and social support. Conditions are often perilous. Children raised by single-parent mothers, for example, "drop out of high school twice as often as children from two-parent households, and their daughters are twice as likely to become teen mothers" (Krauth, 1995, p. 14). Despite numerous difficulties, there are many mother-headed single-parent families that function quite well.

Families of Single-Parent Fathers

The historical trend for single-parent families headed by men has been between 10% and 15%. However, in recent years an increasing number of men are seeking and gaining custody of their children (Bumpass & Sweet, 1989; Davis & Borns, 1999). Single-parent families headed by fathers are growing fast numerically and may well increase as a percentage of all single-parent families.

One advantage fathers have as single parents is that they usually have access to more than twice the financial resources of women (Elias, 1992). This monetary strength allows them flexibility in what they do with their children. It also enables them to hire more caretakers as a group than single-parent women and to take much needed breaks from the duties of raising children. These parents can afford to choose when to be close to their children and be good role models for them. What they give up, though, is time with their offspring. Quality time alone seldom brings closeness to a relationship the way that a combination of qualitative and quantitative time does. In addition, children of single-parent fathers who hire domestic help to take care of them may find that their children have incorporated the caretaker's value system into their lives.

A characteristic of single-parent fathers in general is that most feel comfortable and competent as single parents (Riseman, 1986). This quality seems to hold true regardless of the reason for custody or the father's financial status. However, societal norms and personal traditions dictate that men should generally place work responsibilities above parenting duties. This means single-parent fathers may be absent from their children more than single-parent mothers. Otherwise, they have to take less desirable and demanding jobs, which reduces their financial resources and stops or regresses their career advancement.

A final factor associated with single-parent families headed by fathers involves time and social life. Like single-parent mothers, single-parent fathers are frequently pressed for time and may experience exhaustion at the end of the day, with no relief from others. Socially and parentally, single-parent fathers are sometimes hindered by fatigue (Davis & Borns, 1999). The plight of Dustin Hoffman as a single-parent father in the movie *Kramer vs. Kramer* is a good example of all the factors and dilemmas facing men who opt for such a lifestyle.

Effects of Divorce or Death on Children in Single-Parent Households

Estimates have been made that approximately 50% of all children under age 18 will spend some time growing up in a single-parent household (Casto & Bumpass, 1989). Most of the children will live in single-parent households created by divorce and death. Their adjustment will vary but is strongly influenced by the functioning of the family and the children before the divorce or death, experiences surrounding the creation of the single-parent household, and the resources available to children afterward.

Children Who Lose a Parent by Divorce

Children whose parents divorce tend to do best if their mothers and fathers continue or resume their parenting roles, manage to put differences aside, and allow children to have a continuing relationship with both of them (Barnes, 1999; Wallerstein, 1992). "Children who experience a positive relationship with their parents show fewer behavioral problems regardless of family structure" (Duckett & Richards, 1995, p. 419). Good sibling relationships, social support from adults outside the immediate family, such as teachers, positive friendships, and someone to openly talk to and confide in are most helpful also (Barnes, 1999). Unfortunately, many children do not experience such an atmosphere. These children suffer mental and emotional anguish long after their parents divorce and may act out behaviorally. Among the difficulties they may have are those related to externalizing and internalizing behavior problems, poor academic achievement, and physiological troubles (Doss, Atkins, & Christensen, 2003).

In a 15-year follow-up of children whose parents divorced, Wallerstein (1990) found that children had vivid memories of their parents' separation. Ironically, those who were most distressed during the time of the breakup, preschoolers, were best adjusted as a group at the time of follow-up. Those who were adolescents during the time of divorce were the most pained as a group at the time of follow-up, when they were young adults. They felt physically and emotionally abandoned. Wallerstein concluded that "divorce is not an event that stands alone in children's or adults' experience. It is a continuum" (1992, p. 167). Children from families disrupted by divorce are less likely to do well educationally including applying to, being admitted to, and enrolling at more select colleges (Gose, 1996). They are also less prone to form strong adult attachment bonds in later life, a finding that cuts across racial/ethnic groups (Lopez, Melendez, & Rice, 2000).

One of the primary tasks for society in the years ahead is to strengthen families, not by turning back the clock, but by helping children feel as socially, economically, and emotionally secure as possible. Otherwise, children who emerge from particularly conflicted divorces may become what Nurse (1996, p. 22) calls "**cardboard kids** ... good surface, but nobody knows the depth, or if in fact there is any depth, or authentic self." Suggestions from Glang and Betis (1993) for helping children through the divorce process include:

- having both parents tell the children about the divorce with care and concern
- giving children advanced warning before a parent moves out
- ensuring that children do not feel they are being divorced from either parent
- explaining divorce to children in words they understand
- giving children space of their own both physically and psychologically
- helping children look forward to the visit of a noncustodial parent (which includes realizing and accepting the fact that children often wish their parents to reconcile)

In addition, it is important for children in the long term to have continued contact with noncustodial parents, which in most cases is usually the father. Children who do best after the actual event of a divorce perceive their fathers as accepting, supportive, and trustworthy regardless of marital status (Arditti & Prouty, 1999). They sense that their fathers will be there for them as well as financially provide for them. Noncustodial fathers, in order to be a good parent and helpful, often have to work through their grief involving the termination of their marriage and their new, less intimate, relationship with their children (Spillman, Deschamps, & Crews, 2004).

Children Who Lose a Parent by Death

Children who experience death within the family, especially of a parent, express a number of emotions and behaviors depending on their age and attachment to the deceased. They may become anxious, hope for a reunion, blame themselves or others, and become overly active (Olowu, 1990). To cope, they need to be given accurate information on what happened and the support of the surviving parent. These children usually go through three distinct stages of bereavement: protest, despair, and detachment.

Adolescents have some of the same reactions to the death of a parent as younger children. Support from the surviving parent and peers is generally helpful to them (Gray, 1988, 1989). Their grief and response are influenced by their adjustment prior to the parent's death and their religious beliefs (Gray, 1987).

Strengths and Challenges Connected with Single-Parent Families

Embedded within the structure of single-parent families are inherent strengths and challenges. Sometimes these two aspects of family life are ironically the same. For example, the freedom that single-parent families have to interact with a wide variety of people can also be a detriment to them because of the resources such types of relationships demand. Despite this irony, some unique aspects of single-parent families are mainly positive or negative.

Strengths of Single-Parent Families

A strength of single-parent families as a whole is that they tend to be more democratic than most family types (Wallerstein & Kelly, 1980; Weiss, 1979). An informal style of relating to each other is developed out of necessity. This aspect of family life often helps children and their parents interact in unique ways. When decisions have to be made, the needs of all parties, parent and child(ren), are usually taken into consideration.

A second strength of single-parent families relates to roles and rules. Because of limited resources, many single-parent families are flexible in regard to which members will perform what tasks. In single-parent families, any member can wash dishes, sweep the floor, or work in the garden. Adjustability in regard to members' responsibilities is essential and usually occurs.

A third unique quality of single-parent families is the pace at which members go through developmental stages. In single-parent families, children often learn how to take responsibility for their actions at an early age (Wallerstein & Kelly, 1980). They also learn essential skills, such as finding a bargain or saving money, faster than most children. This behavior often endears these individuals to the parent with whom they live and gives them a certain maturity beyond their years in relating to adults.

The final area in regard to assets of single-parent families is the matter of resources. On the positive side, the children of single parents, and the adults themselves, often are creative in locating and utilizing needed materials for their overall well-being. They learn to survive through being frugal as well as innovative. Single-parent family members realize quite realistically the value of commodities, such as money and time, that other families take for granted (Ahrons & Rodgers, 1987).

Challenges of Single-Parent Families

A challenge of single-parent families involves the defining or refining of boundaries and roles (Glenwick & Mowrey, 1986). Troublesome areas include boundary disputes between former spouses, absent spouses, and between children and their custodial parent or joint custody parents. Boundary issues with former spouses involve everything from visitation situations to sexuality (Goldsmith, 1982). Within single-parent families, the democratic nature of these families may blur needed boundary distinctions between a parent and child. In either of these cases, if boundaries are not clear and enforced, chaotic and confusing interactions may result and children may get out of control (Glenwick & Mowrey, 1986). Unfortunately, children who grow up in single-parent households often exhibit behavior problems as a result of boundary issues. They are more than twice as likely to have emotional and behavioral problems as those who grow up in intact families (Blaisure & Geasler, 2000).

Role delineation is likewise a hurdle that must be overcome. Although role flexibility may prove useful and valuable in helping single-parent families accomplish tasks, it may add stress and work onto select members of these families. They in turn may experience role reversal or role overload (Weiss, 1979). Fatigue and burnout on the part of one or more members of the family unit are often the outcome of this type of open operating procedure.

Another challenge for single-parent families, especially when they result from divorce, is educational achievement. Children have noticeable academic difficulties during the first 18 months of their parent's divorce (Benedek & Benedek, 1979). These effects may be long lasting. For instance, children reared in single-parent families, especially boys, are likely to receive reduced schooling (Krein, 1986). "On the average, children of divorced parents are less educated than others their age and are less likely to graduate from high school than are children of similar backgrounds who grow up in intact families" (Carlson & Sperry, 1993, p. 6).

A third challenge for single-parent families is connected with identity. Many children, especially those who have been raised in a single-parent family as a result of divorce, have difficulty establishing a clear and strong identity and relating to others of the opposite gender. "Children of divorce leave home earlier than others, but not to form families of their own. They are far more likely than their peers to cohabit before they marry, and when they do marry, they also are more likely to divorce" (Carlson & Sperry, 1993, p. 6). They may not experience childhood to the fullest. In adulthood they may come to resent growing up so fast and may consciously or unconsciously display less personal maturity.

A fourth potential problem for single-parent families is poverty. As a group, single-parent families are financially less well-off than other family forms. For instance, they are five to six times as likely to be poor when compared with nuclear families (Urschel, 1993). Part of the disparity in income is due to the disproportionate number of female-headed single-parent families. Approximately 85% to 90% of these families are led by women who, as mentioned earlier, earn less than men as a group. In addition to generally lower wages earned by women, the lack of child support has further strained the financial resources of these families. Overall, 50% of children living in single-parent households live below the poverty line (Walsh, 1991).

A final challenge that a single-parent family usually faces relates to emotions. The psychological feelings expressed by parents and children in these families include helplessness, hopelessness, frustration, despair, guilt, depression, and ambivalence (Baruth & Burgraff, 1991; Goldsmith, 1982; Murdock, 1980). These feelings come with the awareness that one has not resolved matters with a significant other, such as a former spouse or parent. These feelings are complicated when one does not have ready access to the needed person. With time, these feelings increase and stress intensifies. They keep the person within the single-parent family "hooked" emotionally to historical times and situations. It usually takes 2 or more years for single-parent family members to resolve their plethora of emotions and to form into a functional unit (Goldenberg & Goldenberg, 2002).

Approaches for Treating Single-Parent Families

Several family therapy approaches work well with single-parent families (Westcot & Dries, 1990). Most are dependent on therapists taking the time and effort to get to know the unique aspects of each family. Assessment of the unique as well as universal aspects of a single-parent family always precedes therapeutic interventions. To treat single-parent families effectively, therapists must help them work together as a team systematically and in some cases must work with individuals within the family.

Prevention Approaches

One preventive measure families may take has to do with the couple relationship. If a couple suspects they may not have control over a number of their circumstances when they establish a family, they are wise to receive premarital counseling. The reason is that such a preventive approach seems to be beneficial to them when they are separated from each other. So, military families and some families from large corporations where spouses are asked to travel a great deal do better when they receive premarital counseling. The evidence comes from a worldwide, stratified probability sample of more than 20,000 officers and enlisted servicemen and women (Schumm, Stillman, & Bell, 2000). The authors of this study found couples who received premarital counseling were more likely to seek marriage therapy more often and had lower levels of stress than those who did not. These couples also tended to benefit more from marriage therapy than couples who sought marriage therapy without premarital counseling.

In addition to preventive measures before marriage, programs that help a spouse after a traumatic separation may also be extremely beneficial. For instance, the United States Armed Forces now has a mandatory Deployment Cycle Support Program which helps ease the transition of troops home after service in a war zone (Davey, 2004). The program involves 10 days of counseling and helps soldiers returning to their spouses and families deal with such matters as post-traumatic stress, thus easing the job of reunion and going home for both the service person and his or her family.

Family Theory Approaches

Family therapy is also an option for single-parent families regardless of circumstances. Six family theories most often employed with single-parent families are (1) structural, (2) strategic, (3) solution-focused, (4) Bowen, (5) experiential, and (6) narrative.

Structural family therapy appears to be popular because it deals with common concerns of single-parent families such as structure, boundaries, and power (Minuchin & Fishman, 1981). The interventions of structural family therapists seek to restructure or redefine family systems (Minuchin, 1974). This approach is designed to put the parent in charge of the way the family functions. The family moves from being a system in which there is a parentified child or an equalized relationship among parents and children to one in which power is vested in a custodial parent.

Strategic family therapies are utilized frequently with single-parent families because they focus on immediate problem solving in connection with a particular problem, such as acting out behavior (Westcot & Dries, 1990). The interventions of these approaches may be direct, but often they are more subtle, for example, as in reframing, the use of paradox, and prescribing symptoms. One strategic method that may be particularly effective is reframing. A reframe may be used to describe a child's behavior as "depressed" instead of "hostile." In such a case, single-parent family members can rally around the child rather than make accusations and continually argue about the child's behavior.

Solution-focused therapy may be particularly helpful to single-parent families because it helps them focus on new aspects of their lives by finding exceptions to difficult situations and doing something different (deShazer, 1991; O'Hanlon & Weiner-Davis, 1989). The emphasis on making small changes is ideally suited to the beginning developmental phase of single-parent family life in which there is much unrest, and the ability to participate in therapeutic work is limited because of demands and fatigue. When family members perceive they are in harmony with each other, even for a short period, they can focus their energy and efforts on cultivating these exceptional times and in the process make significant and healthy changes.

Bowen family therapy is employed because of its emphasis on resolving the past and examining historical family patterns (Bowen, 1978). Through the construction of a genogram, single-parent families may come to notice and deal with the absent person or persons that have influenced them positively or negatively previously. A solo parent may realize that he is still trying to live up to the words of his mother who admonished him to "stay married at all costs" and "always put your children's needs before your own." In the process of constructing a genogram, such "ghosts" from the past lose their power to interfere with the family's present interactions because they are recognized as historical figures over which one has control.

Experiential family therapy, especially as advocated by Virginia Satir (1967), is useful for single-parent families in helping their members enact metaphorically—through sculpting and choreography—troublesome and unresolved situations. The feelings that arise in connection with these symbolic experiences often help family members work through emotions and experience affective relief from circumstances they can no longer influence or control.

Finally, narrative family therapy can be helpful to single-parent families both at the initial time of forming the family, especially if through divorce, and in resolving other routine and special difficulties associated with being a single-parent family. If the family is formed due to a divorce, the narrative technique of externalizing the problem may be useful

(White & Epston, 1990). Such a process helps family members pull together and combat emotions such as fear, anger, and anxiety that might otherwise take a toll on them individually. Future stories created by children or the parent(s) involved in a single-parent household can also be therapeutic and provide hope and direction for the family in regard to relationships, meaning, and development (Arditti & Prouty, 1999).

Regardless of what theoretical approach is employed with single-parent families, therapists should keep in mind that a number of children and parents in these units have already formed opinions about treatment. The reason is that "children in single-parent families are twice as likely to have behavior problems and undergo professional help for these problems than are children in nuclear families" (Bray, 1993, p. 95). Although these families are in need, they may have mixed feelings—ranging from prejudice to negative expectations—about entering treatment. If complicating and detrimental factors are not addressed, families may not be helped.

Other Approaches for Treating Single-Parent Families

Several other strategies work well in helping single-parent families. These non-theory strategies are especially useful if they are employed simultaneously.

One approach is to help family members communicate clearly and frequently with each other. Clear family communication patterns are associated with the well-being of single-parent families (Hanson, 1986). A forum family therapists can use in this way is the Adlerian concept of a weekly family conference (Baruth & Burgraff, 1991). This type of meeting in which all members are present and talk about their concerns encourages families to resolve problems and plan for the future.

A second way of working with single-parent families involves linking family members and the family as a whole to needed sources of social support. The work of Nagy, which emphasized community connectedness, is the underpinning for this functional approach (Boszormenyi-Nagy, 1987). For example, Parents Without Partners is a national organization that helps single parents and their children deal with the realities of single-parent family life in educational and experiential ways (Murdock, 1980). Single parents also need the positive involvement and care of extended family and friends whenever possible (Gladow & Ray, 1986).

A third non-theory way of working with single-parent families involves assisting them in getting their financial matters resolved. As a general rule, most single-parent families have economic problems (Norton & Glick, 1986). Financial counseling through, for example, United Way agencies or volunteers can be quite beneficial for these families. Job training and educational opportunities connected with advancement also can help. Through these types of assistance, family members can best utilize their resources.

A final approach to working with single-parent families is through educational methods, such as providing them with reading resources (Blaisure & Geasler, 2000). One particularly helpful means of working with these families is through bibliotherapy (Gladding, 2005a; Pardeck & Pardeck, 1997). Bibliotherapy involves the reading by a family or members of a family of literature and the processing of the reading experience with the therapist. A number of appropriate books written for all members of single-parent families and for the families themselves can help individuals involved realize they are not alone in what they are experiencing. *This Is Me and My Single Parent* (Evans, 1989) is a discovery type of workbook that children (ages 4 to 12) and single parents can work on together. In addition, even a simple newsletter that provides educational information and emotional support can make a difference in the adjustment and well-being of single-parent families (Nelson, 1986).

Role of the Therapist

The role of family therapists in working with single-parent families parallels in some ways their role in helping other types of families. Therapists must deal with issues related to boundaries, hierarchies, and engagement/detachment. However, both subtle and obvious differences exist that must be taken into consideration when treating single-parent families. These distinctions are related to the uniqueness of these families as well as their commonness with other families. As a general rule, family therapists "should not be guided by the intact family model and attempt to replicate a two-parent household" (Walsh, 1991, p. 533). Single-parent families are socially, psychologically, and economically unique.

In working with single-parent families, therapists must lay aside personal prejudices and biases. The ability to avoid making judgments and criticisms is especially difficult if therapists have not resolved their own personal problems (e.g., a divorce) that might involve the issue of a single-parent family. To be effective, family therapists must deal directly with people, hierarchies, and circumstances of these families, not myths (Bray, 1993). They must assist single-parent families in giving up any negative stereotypes of themselves.

A second area family therapists must address, especially with those who have become single parents due to divorce, involves emotional volatility. "Interactional conflict between former spouses is the norm" (Walsh, 1991, p. 532). Therapists must help their clients "distinguish between emotional divorce issues and legal divorce issues and to understand that the emotional issues must be set aside at times in order to make mature and reasonable legal decisions" (Oliver, 1992, p. 41). Getting single parents to separate their feelings from their functions is at best difficult. It requires that therapists stay focused and balanced in their interactions with family members.

A third role of family therapists in working with single-parent families is to help members and the family as a whole tap their own inner resources as well as utilize support groups (Juhnke, 1993). Many single-parent families are caught up in their problems and biased against themselves. In these situations, members become discouraged and unable to perceive successful problem-solving methods. A single-parent mother may find through treatment that she is better at achieving results with her children when she listens to them instead of yelling at them. The talent to tap this resource may go unused if the family therapist does not help the parent discover and utilize it. Similarly, in assisting the family, the therapist needs to be aware of both formal and informal support groups, such as friends in the neighborhood. Through such groups, parents and children may find encouragement, relief from each other, and renewal through interacting with different people and ideas.

Process and Outcome

Single-parent families that are successful in family therapy show a variety of improvements. Four of the most important are highlighted here, with the realization that other changes may be unique to particular families.

First, as a result of therapeutic interventions, single-parent families manifest more confidence and competence in themselves (Baruth & Burgraff, 1991). Often single-parent families and their members lose self-esteem and exhibit dependence, helplessness, and hopelessness. Single-parent mothers may feel especially overloaded in performing their executive tasks as head of these families (Weltner, 1982). If treatment has been beneficial, family members rely more on themselves and extended networks of family and friends. They function with greater efficiency. They also have a better knowledge of a number of agencies or networks from which they can get the help they need. Furthermore, these families as units experience fewer behavior problems and less stress, and they see an increase in relationship skills, especially between parent and child(ren) (Soehner, Zastowny, Hammond, & Taylor, 1988).

A second expected outcome of family treatment with single-parent families is that members within these units are helped to have clear and functional boundaries (Westcot & Dries, 1990). Single-parent families are frequently enmeshed with cross-generational alliances and nonproductive structures (Glenwick & Mowrey, 1986). When a family breaks up, the custodial parent must help himself or herself, as well as any children involved, adjust to a new hierarchy. Ideally, this type of structure allows for the interaction between the new single-parent family and others (Minuchin & Fishman, 1981). In the case of divorce, an amiable relationship between children and both former marriage partners is needed whether or not there is joint custody.

When these outcomes do not occur, children and adults are forced to operate in inappropriate ways (Juhnke, 1993). For example, when single-parent families are enmeshed, a child, usually the oldest, is often "parentified" (Minuchin, Montalvo, Guerney, Rosman, & Schumer, 1967). **Parentified children** are forced to give up their childhoods and act like adult parents even though they lack the necessary knowledge and skills. When freed from intergenerational enmeshment, the parentified child's role is no longer necessary and can be given up. If all goes well in family therapy, members of single-parent families gain a clearer perspective on their lives, the dynamics of their families, and appropriate behaviors.

A third area of improvement involves the ability to make informed decisions regarding remarriage. Research shows there is a strong tendency for single parents to move into new marital relationships too quickly. This tendency is especially true when single parenthood is the result of a divorce. The majority of single parents in this category are single for less than 5 years. Yet, remarriage is a move that "often compounds problems rather than leading to resolution" (Carlson & Sperry, 1993, p. 6). Remarriages have a higher probability of dissolving than first marriages (Levine, 1990). Counseling can help single parents and their children examine more thoroughly the pros and cons of remarriage options. Through such a process, single parents can make better decisions, and children can work through their feelings before instead of after the marriage.

Lastly, families can utilize resources in the community better and make use of their own resources to the fullest. Improvements are seen in financial and personal management areas. Negative feelings accumulated through past experiences begin to dissipate, and, the development of friends, the tapping of family, and the pulling together of family members within the single-parent family unit should occur.

Summary and Conclusion

Single-parent families have a lifestyle that is both temporary and permanent. Although there have always been single-parent families, the growth in their number within the United States has increased drastically since World War II. The reasons for the quantitative rise are varied and complex but include such factors as history, choice, and detrimental circumstances, such as death, divorce, or unavoidable temporary assignments. In the 1950s, divorce became the leading cause of the formation of single-parent families. It continues to be a driving force, along with death of a spouse, choice, and temporary assignments that take one parent away for an extended period of time.

Single-parent families come in many forms. They include at least one parent who is biologically related to the child (or the children) or who has assumed such a role through adoption. Because of the structure of single-parent households, a less structured and more democratic setup is created. This type of atmosphere may promote psychological bonding but may also blur needed boundary lines and lead to some confusion and frustration. As a group, single-parent families are less affluent than other family forms, and the majority of them are headed by women.

The possibilities and problems of single-parent families are numerous. As a group, single-parent families may find it easier to relate to a variety of family types and individuals. Most of these families are flexible in their form and functionality. On the other hand, finding resources to support themselves and finding time together (or alone) to enjoy each other (or themselves) is difficult. Many single-parent families live in or close to poverty. They are often adversely affected by such environments.

Through therapeutic interventions, family therapists can help these families maximize their potential and minimize their problems. In working with single-parent families, therapists utilize mainstream theories, such as structural, strategic, solution-focused, Bowen, experiential, and narrative family therapies. They also employ communication procedures, bibliotherapy, and linkage with relevant outside groups, such as Parents Without Partners and financial counselors. The role of the family therapist is to be an advocate for these families in finding resources within themselves and others. To do so, therapists must lay aside prejudices and deal with volatile emotions.

If therapy is successful, single-parent families should show a number of improvements. These improvements include more confidence and competence, better efficiency, clear and functional boundaries and structures, and better decision-making ability in regard to considerations such as remarriage and finances.

Summary Table
Working with Single-Parent Families

The term *single-parent families* is applied to a number of different family forms such as those created by divorce, death, abandonment, unwed pregnancy, adoption, and even extended temporary assignments.

A common thread of single parenthood is that one parent is primarily responsible for him-self/herself and a child or children.

Single-parent families compose over 30% of today's families with children.

Historically most single-parent families were created by death or divorce.

One reason single-parent families are increasing is that many single women are choosing to bear and raise children themselves.

Types of Single-Parent Families

Single-parent families that form as a result of divorce contain both custodial and noncustodial parents. Each parent faces challenges individually and in connection with her or his child(ren).

Single-parent families that form as a result of death face the task of having all members go through the stages of mourning, readjustment, and achievement.

Single-parent families formed as a result of choice must deal with planning, arrival, and adjustment stages of development.

Single-parent families created because of uncontrollable temporary assignments such as a call-up to military action or a transfer by a corporation to overseas duties have to adjust to a rapid change of roles, rules, and duties in addition to the departure and reentry of a parent.

Generally, all types of single-parent families require time (about 2 years) to form into functional units.

Dynamics Associated with Single-Parent Families

By understanding the dynamics underlying the formation of single-parent families, therapists can best help them.

Single-parent families that form as a result of divorce have spouses who have generally been influenced by rapid change, personality compatibility factors, and unequal distribution of power.

Members must deal with the loss of the marriage, new roles, redefinement of relationships, and establishment of a satisfactory arrangement with the ex-spouse or noncustodial parent.

Single-parent families formed as a result of the death of a spouse must deal with shock, grief, a new family reality, and internal/external demands.

Single-parent families that form as a result of choice must successfully combat societal pressures. Furthermore, they must justify their decision, and marshal their resources.

Single-parent families that are formed as a result of extended temporary assignments face immediate task overloads and must make adjustments, including reassigning or dropping jobs. They must constantly adjust and readjust when a parent leaves or reenters the family.

Single-Parent Mothers and Fathers

Families headed by single-parent mothers make up between 85% and 90% of all single-parent households. They face problems associated with finances, role overload, extended family or ex-spouse interference, and parental identity. Conditions are often perilous.

Families headed by single-parent fathers make up between 10% and 15% of all single-parent households. They are usually more affluent than those of single-parent mothers. In addition, confidence and competence in single-parent fathers are high. Negatives of these families are job/career limitations, social restrictions, and physical fatigue.

Effects of Divorce and Death on Children

Children's reactions to divorce or death in a family setting are sometimes delayed or inhibited.

Children of divorce do best if their custodial parents allow relationships with both parents to continue and put aside differences.

Regardless of adjustment, children whose parents divorce have memories of it. Their later reactions depend on their ages at the time of separation and the support they receive in working through their feelings about the divorce.

Children who face the death of a parent must deal with their grief through proper mourning and not become overanxious, blameful, or overactive. Detachment is the final stage of the grief process after bereavement and despair. Surviving parents and peer support groups are most helpful.

Strengths and Challenges Connected with Single-Parent Families

Single-parent families often have the following strengths:

- They are more democratic.
- They have flexible roles and rules.
- The children mature and take responsibility earlier.
- They are creative in locating needed resources.

Single-parent families often face the following challenges:

- They have unclear or undefined boundaries and roles.
- Their children, especially boys, may not achieve to the same extent as children from other types of families. This is particularly true if the single-parent family is a result of divorce.
- The children contend with identity confusion.
- The children may have difficulty relating to the opposite gender.
- They live in or near the poverty level.
- They must cope with depression and other negative emotional residue.

Approaches for Treating Single-Parent Families

Prevention work such as premarital counseling helps single-parent families make better adjustments when a spouse is away especially temporarily.

Theories that work with single-parent families are:

structural	strategic	solution-focused
Bowen	experiential (Satir)	narrative

In addition to theories, family therapists can utilize:

- communication methods (e.g., Adlerian family council)
- social support groups (e.g., Parents Without Partners)
- financial counseling services
- bibliotherapy

Role of the Therapist

The role of the family therapist includes dealing with boundaries, hierarchies, and engagement/detachment.

Family therapists must lay aside personal biases/prejudices.

Family therapists must deal with emotional volatility of the family.

Family therapists must help foster inner resources and support groups for family members.

Process and Outcome

If single-parent family therapy is successful, families should

- manifest more competence in dealing with the external environment and be more confident interpersonally and intrapersonally
- have clear and functional boundaries
- make better financial and remarriage decisions
- utilize their own and community resources more fully

CHAPTER 13

Working with Remarried Families

They were a trio,
a mother and young children
scared and scarred.
Learning to sing songs without a bass
while opening jars and opportunities
through the strength of sheer persistence.

He became a part of them,
breaking through boundaries with clumsy actions
while exposing his feelings with caring words.
Slowly, through chaos, a family emerged
as a group, like a jazz quartet.
Through improvisation
they developed a syncopated rhythm.
In an atmosphere of hope,
came the sounds of harmony.

Gladding, 1992c

Many terms are used to describe remarried families such as stepfamilies, reconstituted families, recoupled families, merged families, patched families, and blended families. Regardless of the terminology used, these families "consist of two adults and step-, adoptive, or foster children" (Pearson, 1993, p. 51). Although most prevalent among European Americans because of their high divorce and remarriage rate, remarried families are found among all cultural groups within the United States. They have become a norm in American society (Howell, Weers, & Kleist, 1998).

Remarried families have always been a part of American family life. The way they are formed has changed, and their numbers have increased dramatically in recent years. In the 1880s, the divorce rate for first marriages was only 7%, and the most prevalent reason for forming remarried families was due to the death or desertion of a spouse (Martin & Bumpass, 1989). These figures shifted in the decades that followed. After World War II, the divorce rate in the United States began to rise rapidly. The 1960s and the 1970s saw divorce reach an unprecedented height quantitatively, with approximately 50% of all marriages ending in divorce (Levitan & Conway, 1990). These decades also marked the beginning of a large remarriage movement (Braver et al., 1993).

By the beginning of the 21st century, 1 million of the 2 million marriages in the United States each year involved at least one formerly married person. Reasons for the growth of this type of family are associated with the fact that approximately 3 out of every 4 people who divorce eventually remarry (Carter & McGoldrick, 1999). In addition, more than 40 million adults had been or were stepparents by this time. Furthermore, it was estimated that "about a third of all Americans" would "remarry at least once in their lives" (Levine, 1990, p. 50).

As a result of the remarried family trend, approximately 40% of all children born in the 1980s and 1990s have lived in such an arrangement before reaching the age of 18 (Glick, 1989). Indeed, the growth of remarried families is one of the major reasons that during the last half of the twentieth century the perception of what was "normal" or "common" in family life changed and divorce came to be seen by many as a point and process in the family development cycle (Sholevar & Schwoeri, 2003).

This chapter examines the dynamics and life cycle of remarried families. These families share unique and universal qualities with other types of families. It is important to delineate and address the issues faced by these families if therapists are going to work with them effectively. By understanding the nature of remarried families, family therapists can assess areas of distinction and commonness (Hayes & Hayes, 1991). "One of the difficulties" of remarried families is that they are fairly new as a common entity and "we have neither terminology to discuss [them] nor do we have research that explains [their] complex nature" (Pearson, 1993, p. 51). In addition, there is still too little information in the professional literature about clinically working with remarried families (Darden & Zimmerman, 1992). Remarried families are a professional challenge. The issues surrounding them, however, are understandable.

Forming Remarried Families

Many possible configurations of remarried families exist. Compared with "first-marriage families, the structures are more complex" (Bray, 1994, p. 67). Remarried families are most commonly formed when a person whose previous marriage ended in death, divorce, or abandonment marries either another previously married person or someone who has never been married. The result is a new combination of people, histories, issues, and interactions that are unique to that particular relationship. Unique opportunities arise from this complex joining of personalities and families. However, in this section an emphasis is placed on the most common concerns of remarried families, because they are the issues therapists deal with frequently.

Common Concerns of Remarried Families

Establishing a remarried family is a more complicated process than creating a nuclear family (Visher & Visher, 1993). Remarried families face many situational and developmental tasks that are quite different from those found in other family lifestyles. They must systemically deal with complex kinship networks, define ill-defined goals, develop patterns of interaction that assist them in being cohesive, and reach consensual goals (Bernstein & Collins, 1985; Roberts & Price, 1986). As a way of understanding remarried families and the issues they encounter, Carter and McGoldrick (1988) have formulated a table (see Table 13.1) that outlines the stages, prerequisite attitude, and developmental issues of these family forms.

Dealing with the Death of a Parent

Before the 20th century, one out of every two adults died before age 50 and life expectancy was 47 years (Coontz, 2000). "Families had to face the possibility that neither parent would survive to raise children to maturity. Not more than a third of the population had a single marriage last more than 10 years. Fifty percent of the time, children lost a parent before reaching maturity" (McGoldrick, 1986, p. 30). "The fundamental uncertainty of life was much harder for families to avoid" (McGoldrick, 1986, p. 29). Life-shortening events included women dying in childbirth and men dying in accidents. The result was a blending of families and kinship networks. Another consequence of such times was that families developed rituals, such as wearing black for a year and visiting a grave on anniversaries, to deal with death and move on with life.

Today, a death is denied or covered up in many families. Death often occurs in hospitals away from all family members. Funeral services frequently include a closed coffin, and those who have died are often described in vague expressions (e.g., "departed" or "passed on") that fail to adequately describe the realities of death. This type of experience with death is particularly true of American families of European descent but much less true for other groups such as African-American families. Therefore, forming a remarried family after the death of a spouse is more difficult for some cultural groups than others because grief may not have been adequately expressed or processed. In these cases, "family members may refuse to accept a new member who is seen as replacing the deceased" (McGoldrick & Walsh, 1999, p. 187). The situation is further complicated by the fact that there are no established guidelines for couples and their offspring to follow in coming together. Indeed, "new roles and rules need to be worked out, relationships developed and maintained, and a working relationship created between households" (Visher & Visher, 1994, p. 208). The process differs in kind and degree from establishing such a family after a divorce (Visher & Visher, 1988).

Dealing with the Divorce of a Couple

Divorce has become a common experience in American culture (Hetherington & Kelly, 2003). As mentioned previously, more than 50% of first marriages end in divorce and

Table 13.1
Remarried Family Formation: A Developmental Outline

Steps	Prerequisite Attitude	Developmental Issues
1. Entering the new relationship	Recovery from loss of first marriage (adequate "emotional divorce")	Recommitment to marriage and to forming a family with readiness to deal with the complexity and ambiguity
2. Conceptualizing and planning new marriage and family	Accepting one's own fears and those of new spouse and children about remarriage and forming a stepfamily Accepting need for time and patience for adjustment to complexity and ambiguity of: 1. Multiple new roles 2. Boundaries: space, time, membership, and authority 3. Affective issues: guilt, loyalty conflicts, desire for mutuality, unresolvable past hurts	a. Work on openness in the new relationships to avoid pseudomutuality b. Plan for maintenance of cooperative coparental relationships with ex-spouses c. Plan to help children deal with fears, loyalty conflicts, and membership in two systems d. Realignment of relationships with extended family to include new spouse and children e. Plan maintenance of connections for children with extended family of ex-spouse(s)
3. Remarriage and reconstitution of family	Final resolution of attachment to previous spouse and ideal of "intact" family; acceptance of a different model of family with permeable boundaries	a. Restructuring family boundaries to allow for inclusion of new spouse—stepparent b. Realignment of relationships throughout subsystems to permit interweaving of several systems c. Making room for relationships of all children with biological (noncustodial) parents, grandparents, and other extended family d. Sharing memories and histories to enhance stepfamily integration

From Carter, B & McGoldrick, M. *The Expanded Family Life Cycle*, 3/e. © 1999. Published by Allyn and Bacon, Boston, MA. Copyright © 1999 by Pearson Education. Reprinted by permission of the publisher.

some demographers argue that the actual divorce rate is greater than 50% (Castro-Martin & Bumpass, 1989; McGoldrick & Carter, 1999a). This rate has held steady since the late 1980s. It is estimated that if you include couples who separate but never file for divorce, the number of first marriages that end in divorce or separation may be as high as 66% (Walker, 1990).

Divorces occur for numerous reasons, including affairs and conflicting role expectations. Gottman and Carrere (Peterson, 2000d) have found through longitudinal research of couples that there are several key predictors of couples most likely to divorce. These predictors include "a husband's unwillingness to be influenced by his wife, who is often the one trying to solve marital problems; and the wife starting quarrels 'harshly' and with hostility" (p. A1). A dynamic of this type tends to escalate into bigger conflicts and ultimately the dissolution of the marriage.

Interestingly, two thirds of divorces occur in the first 10 years of marriage with the median duration of marriages in the United States that end in divorce being between 7.8 and 7.9 years (Divorce Magazine.com, http://www.divorcemag.com/statistics/statsUS.shtml, p. 1, 2005b). There are two vulnerable times for divorce: during the first seven years and the time period of 16 to 24 years after marriage (Gottman, 1999). Breakups also frequently occur if newlyweds cannot adjust to each other and decide that the relationship they have entered is not working; and after the birth of a child, when the couple becomes unsettled and stressed as new routines are established and disrupted because of infant needs. The ages of men and women who divorce for the first time have risen slightly since the 1970s. However, these figures are more a reflection of later first marriages than increased marriage/family stability (Divorce Magazine.com, http://www.divorcemag.com/statistics/statsUS.shtm, p.1; Mullins, 1993).

Another factor associated with the dissolution of a marriage is that most people who go through this experience eventually remarry (Marano, 2004). Approximately "two thirds of divorced women and three fourths of divorced men" marry again (Bray & Hetherington, 1993, p. 3). The divorce rate among divorcees is slightly higher than for couples that have never been married (i.e., approximately 60% versus 50%). Remarried couples that do best have extended family that approve or accept the new union, with those who do second best having extended family that disapprove of the remarriage (McGoldrick & Carter, 1999a). Indifference or being cut off from one's extended family is the worst thing that can happen.

A final phenomenon associated with marriage breakup is that ethnic groups experience the consequences of this activity differently. When compared with European Americans, African-American couples are more likely to separate and stay separated longer before obtaining a divorce. They are also less likely to remarry once separated (Cherlin, 1992). A greater percentage of African-American children (75%), as opposed to European-American children (40%), will experience their parents' divorce or separation by age 16 (Bumpass & Sweet, 1989).

An outcome of marital dissolvement is that contact between nonresidential parents and their children declines over the years (Bray, 1994; Hetherington & Kelly, 2003; Seltzer, 1991). Noncustodial mothers (about 10% to 15% of nonresidential parents) maintain better contact with their children than do nonresidential fathers (Furstenberg, 1990). Boys are particularly impacted in a negative way when their nonresidential fathers fail to maintain contact with them (Depner & Bray, 1993; Hetherington, 1990; Weiss, 1979). As a group, they become less competent and exhibit more behavioral problems than do children in other types of family arrangements.

Making Healthy Adjustments in Remarried Families

Making healthy adjustments in remarried families is easier to conceptualize than to achieve. It takes dedication and work. If remarried families are to achieve a sense of harmony and stability, family members must concentrate on taking care of their own individual issues, as well as family issues (Roberts & Price, 1986). They must learn to relate productively to others with whom they now interact in a manner that connects them as a system. The two subunits that must make this systemic change are children and parents (Bray, 1993).

Transitions for Children in Remarried Families

Issues for children who are making the adjustment to remarried families revolve around liabilities and benefits that result from such arrangements. Resolving issues surrounding the death of a parent takes time. It is a loss in which the normal grief period is from 6 to 36 months. Divorce for children also takes time. Divorce is a psychological death, as opposed to a physical death, of an intimate relationship. "The ways in which children perceive and respond to their parents' divorce vary by age, gender, parental conflict, pre- and postseparation, caretaking arrangements, individual resiliency characteristics, and the availability of emotional support" (Schwartz, 1992, p. 324). Liabilities for children may include losing the closeness of a previous parent relationship, losing one's ordinal position from a previous family experience (especially seniority), moving into a new house and/or neighborhood, and having to relate to stepsiblings and a stepparent (Wald, 1981; Wallerstein & Kelly, 1980).

Despite the loss of a family member, benefits for children in remarried families may be significant. Children may gain closeness with their biological parents as well as their stepparent. They may also be the recipients of increased positive attention from known and new relatives and relations. A third advantage for children in remarried families is they may find areas of common interest among their new stepsiblings and develop lasting friendships. Finally, moving (if it occurs) may provide children in remarried families with the opportunity to establish a different identity that is more congruent with whom they wish to become (Kitson & Holmes, 1992; Visher & Visher, 1988).

Transitions for Parents and Stepparents in Remarried Families

Parenting and stepparenting have drawbacks and attractions associated with them. One unattractive aspect of stepparenting is uncertainty. "There are no accepted social roles for stepparents" (Bray, 1994). In the case of a new stepparent, he or she may find that his or her new spouse and stepchildren have established routines that are difficult to modify or break. Therefore, a previously unmarried parent may have to work especially hard to make a place for himself or herself within the family system. In the process, these individuals may alienate or create friction among the ones with whom they are trying to relate (Bray, 1993).

For previously married spouses, the difficulties of forming a remarried family involve expectations and realities. These individuals may expect their reformed family to act similarly to their previous one. The reality may be quite different and a source of consternation. Previously married spouses may have unpleasant memories, or unpleasant present encounters, involving an ex-spouse. These types of situations can magnify the stress under which formerly married spouses operate in reestablishing themselves in a new family (Visher & Visher, 1985). The nature of the relationship between ex-spouses is a significant predictor of intimacy in the remarried spouses (Gold, Bubenzer, & West, 1993). It has an impact on their children too with those children who do best having parents who form an ongoing parental alliance (Whiteside, 1998).

Dynamics Associated with Remarried Families

It is sometimes said that remarried families are born out of loss and hope. As previously indicated, most adults and children who form this type of union have experienced a divorce, abandonment, or death. They wish, as well as expect, the remarried family to be a different and better experience. A characteristic of remarried family members is that they often carry a positive fantasy with them about what family life can be like (Schulman, 1972). Adults who form a remarried family believe marriage and family life can be good. Most children who come into these relationships share a similar belief (Visher & Visher, 1993).

Before a remarriage can develop, however, previous experiences in life, especially those associated with a former family, must be resolved. Adults and children of these former unions are often in mourning and must work through their feelings before they can emotionally join a new family. The extent to which loss is resolved or hope fulfilled makes a major difference in how the people in such arrangements adjust (Pill, 1990).

Another factor that influences the dynamics of remarried families is structure. Remarried families have structural characteristics that make them unique (Galvin & Brommel, 1986; Visher & Visher, 1979). Structural distinctions of remarried families include:

- a biological parent elsewhere
- a relationship in the family between an adult (parent) and at least one child that pre-dates the present family structure
- at least one child who is a member of more than one household
- a parent who is not legally related to at least one child
- a couple that begins other than simply as a dyad
- a complex extended family network

The structure of most remarried families initially is "a weak couple subsystem, a tightly bonded parent–child alliance, and potential 'interference'" (Martin & Martin, 1992, p. 23).

A third dynamic characterizing remarried families is that they are binuclear—two inter-related family households that comprise one family system (Ahrons, 1979; Piercy & Sprenkle, 1986). As a remarried (REM) family form, these families have multiple subsystems that include an entourage of adults, children, and legally related persons such as cousins and stepgrandparents (Sager et al., 1983). They have **quasi kin** who are a "formerly married person's ex-spouse, the ex-spouse's new husband or wife, and his or her blood kin" (Ihinger-Tallman & Pasley, 1987, p. 43). These people are a part of the extended kin network of remarried spouses' families. They make communications and relations among family members difficult.

Issues Within Remarried Families

Many issues arise in remarried families. Because each family is unique, the importance of these concerns varies. Among the most prominent that surface, according to Carter and McGoldrick (1988), are those that center around:

- resolving the past
- alleviating fears and concerns about stepfamily life
- establishing or reestablishing trust
- fostering a realistic attitude
- becoming emotionally/psychologically attached to others

A major issue in remarried families is finding time to consolidate the couple relationship (Pill, 1990). Research shows that children below the age of 9 accept a stepparent more readily than those above this age (Hetherington, Cox, & Cox, 1981). At the same time, young children are more physically demanding on parents than older children. They may keep the new couple from adequately bonding. The presence of older children may also complicate the bonding process because of the need of adolescents to establish identities through interactions, which often take the form of rebellion or disruption (Schwartzberg, 1987). Less cohesion in remarried families is more common during the early years of a family's formation (Bray, 1994).

A second factor that becomes an issue in reconstituting a remarried family is that of feelings. The life circumstances surrounding the dissolution of the previous marriage and the adjustment and life experiences of present family members since that time must be worked through. Romantic and negative feelings must be sorted out in a timely and appropriate way. Sometimes partners in a remarried family do not think through the feelings they bring into the relationship until after it is formed (Pill, 1990). What they expect in regard to closeness may be shattered. Likewise, when members of a newly formed family are still mourning the loss of a previous relationship, they may not be adaptable or open to changes. In either of these cases, the past relationships and present realities are issues that inhibit or facilitate the adjustment and satisfaction of these families as units (Pill, 1990).

A third issue that occurs in remarried families is the integration of members into a cohesive family unit. "Cohesion and adaptability represent two pivotal dimensions of family behavior related to family function" (Pill, 1990, p. 186). In the professional literature, "stepfamilies are described as less cohesive, more problematic, and more stressful than first-marriage families" (Bray & Hetherington, 1993, p. 5). Both stepparent/child and sibling relationships are characterized as less warm and intimate than those in first-marriage families. Most members of remarried families have to work harder than those in nuclear or extended families to create interpersonal connectedness and rapport with other family members. The process of relating in remarried families is often troubled in stepfather/daughter interactions, especially when the arrangement involves preadolescent children (Hetherington, 1991). Many other arrangements of children and stepfathers are also bothersome (Ahrons, 1996; Grove & Haley, 1993; Stern, 1978; Visher & Visher, 1978). A relatively high percentage of stepchildren have behavioral problems in remarried families during the first 6 months of the new union (Bray, 1988).

On average it takes approximately 2 to 5 years for stepparents to form an in-depth relationship with stepchildren and to achieve the role of being a primary parent (Dahl, Cowgill, & Asmundsson, 1987). This 2- to 5-year forming period parallels that of the first stage of the newly married couple (DuVall, 1977). According to Visher and Visher (1986), the eight tasks listed in Figure 13.1 must be completed in order to develop a stepfamily identity.

Strengths and Challenges of Remarried Families

Remarried families come in many forms. They share some universal qualities, but they also have unique situational and developmental factors that either help or hinder them in their total functioning and interpersonal relationships.

Strengths of Remarried Families

The strengths of blended families are important to the stability and survival of these units. Sometimes they are overlooked. However, if utilized, remarried families grow stronger in both their relationships and their overall functioning.

1. Dealing with losses and changes
2. Negotiating different developmental needs
3. Establishing new traditions
4. Developing a solid couple bond
5. Forming new relationships
6. Creating a "parenting coalition"
7. Accepting continual shifts in household composition
8. Risking involvement despite little societal support

1. Dealing with losses and changes
   - Identifying/recognize losses for all individuals
   - Support expressions of sadness
   - Help children talk and not act out feelings
   - Read stepfamily books
   - Make changes gradually
   - See that everyone gets a turn
   - Inform children of plans involving them
   - Accept the insecurity of change
2. Negotiating different developmental needs
   - Take a child development and/or parenting class
   - Accept validity of the different life-cycle phases
   - Communicate individual needs clearly
   - Negotiate incompatible needs
   - Develop tolerance and flexibility
3. Establishing new traditions
   - Recognize ways are *different*, not right or wrong
   - Concentrate on important situations only
   - Stepparents take on discipline enforcement slowly
   - Use family meetings for problem solving and giving appreciation
   - Shift "givens" slowly whenever possible
   - Retain/combine appropriate rituals
   - Enrich with new creative traditions
4. Developing a solid couple bond
   - Accept couple as primary long-term relationship
   - Nourish couple relationship
   - Plan for couple "alone time"
   - Decide general household rules as a couple
   - Support one another with the children
   - Expect and accept different parent–child and stepparent–stepchild feelings
   - Work out money matters together

(Continued)

Figure 13.1
Tasks that must be completed to develop a stepfamily identity.

5. Forming new relationships
   - Fill in past histories
   - Make stepparent–stepchild one-to-one time
   - Make parent–child one-to-one time
   - Parent make space for stepparent–stepchild relationship
   - Do not expect instant love and adjustment
   - Be fair to stepchildren even when caring not developed
   - Follow children's lead in what to call stepparent
   - Do fun things together

6. Creating a "parenting coalition"
   - Deal directly with parenting adults in other household
   - Keep children out of the middle of parental disagreements
   - Do not talk negatively about adults in other household
   - Control what you can and accept limitations
   - Avoid power struggles between households
   - Respect parenting skills of former spouse
   - Contribute own "specialness" to children
   - Communicate between households in most effective manner

7. Accepting continual shifts in household composition
   - Allow children to enjoy their households
   - Give children time to adjust to household transitions
   - Avoid asking children to be messengers or spies
   - Consider teenager's serious desire to change residence
   - Respect privacy (boundaries) of all households
   - Set consequences that affect own household only
   - Provide personal place for nonresident children
   - Plan special times for various household constellations

8. Risking involvement despite little societal support
   - Include stepparents in school, religious, sports activities
   - Give legal permission for stepparent to act when necessary
   - Continue stepparent–stepchild relationships after death or divorce of parent when caring has developed
   - Stepparent includes self in stepchild's activities
   - Find groups supportive of stepfamilies
   - Remember that all relationships involve risk

Figure 13.1 (Continued)

From *Stepfamily Workshop Manual* (pp. 235–236) by E. B. Visher and J. S. Visher, 1986, Baltimore, MD: Stepfamily Association of America. Reprinted with permission of the publisher.

Life Experience

One of the strongest assets of remarried family members is their life experience. Sometimes a stepparent can offer a new spouse or stepchildren something that was not there before, such as a common interest or opportunity unavailable in the original family of origin (Marino, 1996). In addition, both adults and children who form blended families have survived a number of critical incidents that have usually taught them something about themselves and others (Hetherington, 1991). This life knowledge can help them understand their environments in different and potentially healthy ways. It can assist members in being empathic toward new family members, and it can influence individual and family resilience in adverse situations.

Kin and Quasi-Kin Networks

A second strength of remarried families is the kin and quasi-kin networks that they establish. Remarried couples and families are sometimes isolated and frustrated when dealing with societal events, such as father/son or mother/daughter events in community clubs, associations, or educational institutions (Martin & Martin, 1992). Through kin and quasi-kin networks, remarried family members can help one another in a variety of ways, such as offering moral support, guidance, or physical comfort.

Creativity and Innovativeness

A third positive facet of remarried families is their creativity and innovation. Sometimes remarried family members are able to generate new ideas, perceptions, and possibilities because they realize that what they have tried before has not worked. As in Gestalt therapy, remarried families who develop these abilities are able to see and act on their perceptions of relationships involving present situations (i.e., figure) and less important present situations or those in the future (i.e., ground) (Papernow, 1993). A stepmother and daughter in a remarried family might decide to throw a surprise birthday party for their husband/father, rather than doing routine shopping. By doing so, they create a memory of a shared experience that strengthens the relationship bonds between them. The result may be a synergistic flow of energy and enthusiasm that lasts a lifetime.

Appreciation and Respect for Differences

A further strength of remarried families is their ability to appreciate and respect differences in people and ways of living (Crohn, Sager, Brown, Rodstein, & Walker, 1982). Through experiencing stepparents and new siblings, children especially can benefit. They learn that mothering or fathering can take on several forms. In the process of obtaining this insight, they pick up new habits from their stepsiblings that may benefit them. Remarriage makes it possible for individuals to observe a richer variety of models for emulating than they may have typically experienced.

Making the Most of Situations

Still another strength of remarried families is their ability to make the most of situations and in the process teach other families how to have fulfilling relationships (Martin & Martin, 1992). Not all remarried families and their members learn how to cope with difficulties, such as loss, or how to promote care and open communication within a new context.

However, in remarried families that develop these abilities, the insight they bring to other families in distress can be rewarding and enabling. It is a dynamic that therapists and educators must utilize whenever possible.

Challenges of Remarried Families

Challenges and potential problems exist in remarried families that need to be resolved. Some of these difficulties revolve around psychological phenomena, such as competing for attention; others center on physical realities, such as the fact that remarried families move three times as often as dual-parent households (Krauth, 1995).

Loss of an Important Member

One challenge almost all remarried families face is the loss of an important member(s) of the former family. For example, even though a noncustodial parent may be physically absent from a household, such a person may retain a "tremendous impact," both directly and indirectly, on the remaining family members (Braver et al., 1993, p. 9). The loss of significant others is complicated when difficulties arise concerning feelings about these individuals who are unavailable. The result is a ripple effect throughout the family. All members of the family can be affected by one individual's unresolved personal issues related to loss.

Establishment of a Hierarchy

Another significant challenge for remarried families is the establishment of a hierarchy. Children may have difficulty in this area because they can lose status in regard to their ordinal position in the family. A sibling can become the middle child instead of the oldest, and in the process lose his or her leadership role and privileges. This loss of place and power may be complicated even further if the children involved do not particularly like their new stepsiblings or stepparent. Because working out relationships among children takes time and is not always amiable, newly formed remarried families with children are vulnerable to disruption and volatile outbreaks of emotional, if not physical, struggle (White & Booth, 1985). Adults must give up myths and unrealistic expectations in order to rectify this potential problem area (Bray, 1994).

Boundary Difficulties

A third challenge sometimes endemic to remarried families concerns boundaries. "Unlike biological families in which family membership is defined sanguinely, legally, and spatially and is characterized by explicit boundaries, the structure of a stepfamily is less clear" (Pasley, Rhoden, Visher, & Visher, 1996, p. 344). The result is that children who are a part of two families may experience boundary ambiguity, which results in loyalty conflicts and feelings of guilt about belonging simultaneously to two households. Overall, boundary difficulties include issues of:

1. Membership (Who are the "real" members of the family?)
2. Space (What space is mine? Where do I really belong?)
3. Authority (Who is really in charge? Of discipline? Of money? Of decisions? etc.)
4. Time (Who gets how much of my time and how much do I get of theirs?) (McGoldrick & Carter, 1988, pp. 406–407)

Often, stepfamily members who have boundary problems characterize their relationships as chaotic (Pill, 1990). They are unsure of who and what is involved in making their lives adaptable. To resolve issues around the confusion in boundaries, most remarried families need time, flexibility, and commitment (Ihinger-Tallman & Pasley, 1987). They must deal with issues in a straightforward manner, including those involving sexuality between unrelated siblings or parents and siblings. Members can and should discuss and negotiate how they would like their blended family to function.

Resolving Feelings

The fourth challenging area remarried families must address is related to feelings. In some remarried families, especially those in which members have been in denial, emotions remain unresolved. These emotions include guilt, loyalty, and anger. A typical response for some remarried family members is to suppress their emotions when they begin to recognize that such affect is related to unresolved feelings. A teenage boy might deny his anger toward his stepmother especially if he still has unresolved anger toward his mother. An equally destructive way of handling these emotions is to project them onto others. Some remarried family members may act in this manner so that stepsiblings or stepparents become negatively characterized or stereotyped (Marino, 1996). In such a situation, a stepmother might be seen as a "witch."

Economic Problems

Another potential challenge remarried families encounter is economic. As a group, blended families are less affluent than other family types except single-parent families. The lack of money adds additional stress to family members and the family as a whole (Coleman & Ganong, 1989). Furthermore, many remarried families have expenses, such as child support or the cost of maintaining two residences, that other families do not have. Such families may have a difficult time making ends meet.

Blending finances requires a number of unromantic, pragmatic steps. They include reevaluating insurance needs, updating financial documents, creating and sticking to a budget, rethinking asset allocations, and developing a will or a living will (Nance-Nash, 2005).

Approaches for Treating Remarried Families

"Many stepfamilies seek therapy when emotional tensions are high, integration seems impossible, and the family is functioning in ways that increase rather than reduce stress" (Pasley et al., 1996, p. 344). Fortunately, a number of approaches work when helping remarried families. These approaches range from educational to theoretical interventions (Visher & Visher, 1994; Woestendiek, 1992).

Guidance in Retaining Old Loyalties

Remarried family members must first be helped to recognize that they do not have to give up old loyalties in order to form new ties (Visher & Visher, 1988). Too often individuals, especially children, believe that they must not think or talk about their past lives. This type of repression is likely to lead to resentment, exclusion, isolation, and depression rather than adjustment and growth. Often the new stepparent is treated like an "outsider." This situation can cause the stepparent to feel angry and frustrated, which in turn can lead to complete withdrawal or violence. The important thing is that family members learn through interaction with the therapist to be inclusive rather than exclusive. This may mean that the therapist draws instructional diagrams for the family of how they are operating and also challenges them to participate in cooperative interactive events, such as picnics or board games.

Focus on Parental Involvement

Another way of helping remarried families is to focus on parental involvement. Stepparents need to maintain a balance in their involvement with their natural children (if any), new children (if any), former spouse (where applicable), and present spouse. The more children and spouses in one's past, the harder this task is to accomplish. Therefore, before and after their wedding, stepparents should spend time discussing the impact of past relationships on new relationships (Martin & Martin, 1992). They can then work with a family therapist to overcome unresolved issues and, thus, learn to contribute to the well-being of all family members.

Provide Education

Education is one of the best ways to help remarried families to adapt, adjust, and grow. For example, remarried family members need to understand the differences between a stepfamily and a nonstepfamily system (Pasley et al., 1996). Learning what to expect and having guidelines for handling typical situations is rated high by remarried families (Visher & Visher, 1994). Stepparents are often unsure, for example, of how to discipline the other spouse's children (Woestendiek, 1992). Likewise, children brought into remarried families are frequently confused about how to relate to their new parent and stepsiblings.

A number of popular books and pamphlets are available for individuals in newly created blended families to read and discuss with members of their new family. The Stepfamily Association of America (http://www.saafamilies.org/) both publishes and recommends materials that are helpful in developing effective stepparenting skills (Larson, Anderson, & Morgan, 1984; Nance-Nash, 2005).

Numerous books that can be utilized in a bibliotherapeutic way are available for children (Pardeck & Pardeck, 1987). An example is a book authored by Richard Gardner (1971) entitled *The Boys and Girls Book About Stepfamilies*. It is a work meant to be read and responded to verbally by stepparents and children (Gardner, 1984). *This Is Me and My Two Families* (Evans, 1988) is an engaging and therapeutically oriented scrapbook/journal for children ages 4 to 12 living in remarried families. Similarly, *The Stepkin Stories: Helping Children Cope with Divorce and Adjust to Stepfamilies* (Lumpkin, 1999) is an anthology that features short stories about divorce and stepfamilies that can be read in 10 minutes and are suitable for children aged 4 to 8.

Assist in the Creation of Family Traditions and Rituals

A fourth therapeutic method of working with remarried families is through assisting them in devising their own traditions and rituals (Coale, 1994). Rituals facilitate "developmental transitions, maintenance of stability and continuity; healing processes; and connectedness. . . . Healthy ritual life can also serve to buffer families from toxic effects of stress and pathology" (Giblin, 1995, p. 37). The use of rituals has also been found to be powerful in assisting remarried families in thinking through their definition of what makes a family (Peterson, 1992; Whiteside, 1989). Traditions and rituals include ways of celebrating nodal events, such as birthdays and anniversaries. They also include mundane daily transactions such as when to go to bed, when to get up, and who will do what chores. When these situations are worked out, new and predictable ways of interacting are established that give family members predictability and stability—and provide time for fun while allowing family members to experience security.

In addition to their celebration and enjoyment functions, rituals may facilitate:

- the forming of relationships
- the resolution of ambiguous boundaries
- the healing of loss
- the settling of hierarchy and power struggles
- the creating of beliefs
- the beginnings of changes (Coale, 1994; Roberts & Imber-Black, 1992; Viere, 2005)

By gathering all members of a new family together once a week for "game night," a step-mother may help family members learn more about each other and develop friendships. The overall impact is one that is likely to result in the building of trust and care.

Apply Structural Family Therapy

A particularly effective theoretical approach for working with remarried families is structural family therapy. The reason is that structural family therapy concentrates on setting up a clear hierarchy within the family and on establishing boundaries (Minuchin, 1974). If remarried families do not structurally readjust boundaries after the new family unit is formed, the family may experience conflict that is prone to escalation in negative outcomes such as anger or abuse (Friesen, 1985).

In working from a structural perspective, it is crucial that the family be encouraged to set up an **open system** "with permeable boundaries between current and former spouses and their families" (Goldenberg & Goldenberg, 2002, p. 187). The reason for such an arrangement is that it facilitates coparenting relationships and prevents children from exerting a type of inappropriate power to decide important parental prerogatives such as remarriage, custody, or visitation.

Apply Experiential Family Therapy

Another approach for helping remarried families is experiential family therapy. Some of the methods associated with the work of Virginia Satir may be especially useful (Satir, Banmen, Gerber, & Gomori, 1991). Sculpting and choreography may help family members see the closeness or distance of relationships and the interrelatedness of certain actions. Role playing also may assist family members to become sensitized to the real and imagined restraints that keep them in dysfunctional patterns. Such information helps them become aware of how they can break out of vicious cycles and make progress in their personal and interpersonal lives.

Do Transgenerational Work

A final theoretical perspective that is pertinent for remarried families is transgenerational work, especially Bowen family therapy (Bowen, 1981; Visher & Visher, 1996). In this approach, the use of a three-generational genogram helps families detect patterns that can both inform and assist them in forming a new family unit. By examining the past through a genogram, remarried families can plan for a productive future and avoid previous mistakes. This process is the same as that for other family types.

Role of the Therapist

Therapists who work with remarried families wear many hats. They must deal with a variety of dynamics and complexities that are more complicated than those found in nuclear families (Visher & Visher, 1996). For example, they must deal with issues involving separation and custody; they must be concerned with the developmental dilemmas that can arise within newly formed families (Bray & Berger, 1992); and they must concentrate on fostering a strong and healthy parental coalition (Visher & Visher, 1994):

> Because stepfamily issues and needs are diverse and often emotionally charged, the ability to be active, to take charge of intensely emotional sessions, and to be flexible and resourceful in the use of different therapeutic modalities contributes to therapists' effectiveness in working with families. (Pasley et al., 1996, p. 347)

In working with remarried families in regard to separation and custody issues, children within the family system must be given special consideration. "Child clients may experience confusion, fear, and depression as they become aware that they are the focal point in a custody, visitation, or child support dispute" (Oliver, 1992, p. 41). To alleviate undue anxiety and distress, family therapists need to be well-informed about legal processes as well as psychological ones. For example, they should be aware of legal precedence concerning custody decisions. Family therapists who are knowledgeable about such aspects of family jurisprudence can help all members of families make better decisions. They are enabled and empowered by such legal insight to work in helping the family process information on an emotional and intellectual level so that everyone in the family, including small children, understands what is happening or can happen (Oliver, 1992).

Family therapists must also work with the family in arranging predictable and mutually satisfactory arrangements between former parents and their child or children (if the family was formed as a result of divorce). The continuity and quality of children's relationships with their parents following a divorce is a major factor in determining the children's healthy development (Wallerstein, 1990). Therefore, in some cases, counseling sessions may include the noncustodial parent, as well as the reconstituted family. In these situations, family therapists must focus their attention on helping families negotiate arrangements that will benefit everyone involved.

Fostering strong and healthy parental coalitions means helping stepparents work together to nurture one another and find ways for them to work together to be effective parents. Such a task may involve the couple spending select time together, working with former spouses (if present) to be supportive of them, and finding ways for children in the new family to care for one another physically and psychologically (Visher & Visher, 1994).

Hayes and Hayes (1986) mention four more issues that must be dealt with:

1. Family members must be encouraged to relinquish personal myths they have carried into the new family relationship. These myths may take many forms, but often they involve seeing former relationships as idyllic and viewing other people as either saints or devils.
2. Family members must learn effective ways of communicating with each other. Effective communication skills used in remarried families are the same as those used in facilitating other counseling relationships. They include paying attention to verbal and nonverbal messages, the use of "I" messages, and concreteness.

3. Family members need structured programs of parent training and reading lists of materials that are germane to their situation in the new family structure. Material provided in this bibliotherapeutic process should include research, especially for the adults in the relationship, as well as other books or pamphlets that are more simply formatted.
4. Family members, especially children, need a forum within the therapeutic setting in which they can mourn the loss of previous relationships and develop relationships in the reconstituted family.

The family therapist working with remarried families must focus on external and internal factors that tend to unbalance the family system. Although family therapists dealing with traditional two-parent families concentrate on some of these same factors, the degree and complexity of the dynamics are not the same. Remarried families have more emotional, historical, and internal issues that must be settled.

To be effective, family therapists who work with remarried families must devote large amounts of energy and effort to bring about multiple-person resolutions. They must join with members of the family in order to understand the frustrations inherent in each person's role while seeking to bring about resolutions to real and potential problems within the family system as a whole. It is not an easy or simple task.

Process and Outcome

If therapy is successful with remarried families, these families come to understand themselves better as systems. This goal is often disruptive and stressful because remarried families are "an evolving family system in which each member reciprocally influences and is influenced by other family members" (Bray, 1993, p. 272). Yet the process of better understanding the unity of the family can be achieved in several ways.

One systemic-based way of helping remarried families come to terms with themselves is by supporting the new parent and sibling subunits. This type of support stresses the importance of the couple and children learning to work, play, and make mistakes together. If successful, remarried families become aware of themselves as family units composed of subsystems. They begin to gel in age- and stage-appropriate ways. Children within remarried families may unite to ask for special privileges or a raise in their allowance. Similarly, parents may present a unified front as to behaviors that are and are not acceptable.

Effective therapy also helps family members become tolerant of and deal realistically with one another and family life events. This means that persons within reconstituted families must avoid projection and distortions. "[T]he entrance of a new parent figure is a ... unique experience" for children who may "displace their anger" onto this person (Walsh, 1991, p. 521). Likewise, all involved in a remarried family must give up romanticizing or idealizing those who are now outside the formal structure of the family, such as a parent who no longer lives with his or her children (Everett & Volgy, 1991).

On a developmental level, effective therapy helps family members find their place in the new family as it is now. In some remarried families, congruence between individual and family developmental issues exist, such as in remarried families with young children. In this case, both parents and children seek cohesion. In other remarried families, divergence between the goals of individuals and families exists, such as in a remarried family with adolescents. Here the new couple might be developmentally prone to closeness while the teenagers are ready to separate (Bray, 1993). When family therapy is successful, members become aware that they are in an environment in which novel roles can be explored (Martin & Martin, 1992). Such an environment is one in which family members are safe, and the overall atmosphere is one in which members can deal with their losses, gains, aspirations, and/or regrets.

A fourth dimension of process and outcome involves fostering new traditions, including those dealing with both responsibility and celebrations (Imber-Black, 1988b). Many rituals in American society are inadequate as ways of terminating relationships (Everett & Volgy, 1991). Likewise, few models are available for joining family members from different backgrounds (Imber-Black, 1988b). Family therapy helps remarried families create new and lasting ways of humanizing relationships. New traditions can be built around a commonly shared meal, such as dinner, in which everyone is given space and time to relate. Holiday periods can become opportunities for family members to celebrate old and new traditions.

In working with remarried families, therapists must help them develop a healthy self-concept of themselves as a family. The mass media and even some scholarly journals generally portray remarried families in a negative way. Whitehead (1993) states that research has found "stepfamilies disrupt established loyalties, create new uncertainties, provoke deep anxieties, and sometimes threaten a child's physical safety as well as emotional security" (p. 71). To do well, remarried families must first find internal strength, in order to deal with the external pressures and stereotypes that are less than healthy (or accurate).

Summary and Conclusion

Working with remarried families is a challenging process because of the multitude of variables and personalities involved. Family therapists who work with such families need to realize that remarried families have unique as well as universal characteristics. Remarried families have a particular life cycle of their own. They are binuclear in their structure. Many members of remarried families are dealing with loss and grief because their previous relationships ended in death, abandonment, or divorce. The expression of feelings is probably higher than in traditional nuclear families.

On the other hand, like other family forms, members of remarried families must deal with the universal aspects of parent/children and sibling relationships. Members must balance concerns so that neither the individual nor the family suffers or is ignored.

Helping remarried families means that therapists must be sensitive to their own biases and perceptions and flexible in their theoretical approaches. Structural, experiential, and transgenerational (i.e., Bowen) family therapies are three ways to assist these families in resolving the issues and tasks before them. The use of rituals from a strategic family therapy point of view is also an important therapeutic tool that can be employed. Remarried families need to formulate and practice new traditions in a ritualistic manner. Such behavior helps them bond and overcome physical and psychological barriers that would otherwise hinder them. Bibliotherapy and psychoeducational processes are yet other possible ways to help.

Family therapists who work with remarried families need energy and imagination. They are called on to engage family members in ways that are complex and taxing. At times therapists may need to see significant others in the family outside of those living under one roof. Just as being a successful remarried family requires negotiation skills from members, the same is demanded of family therapists. With the number of remarried families growing, it is doubtful one can be a family therapist without acquiring skills in regard to this population. The challenge is to continuously learn about common elements special to remarried families while treating each new remarried family as a one-of-a-kind phenomenon.

Summary Table

Working with Remarried Families

A remarried family consists of two adults and step-, adoptive, or foster children. They are most prevalent among European Americans, although they are found among all cultural groups.

Historically, remarried families have always been part of American family life, although their numbers have increased dramatically in recent years.

It is predicted that up to 40% of children born in the 1980s will spend part of their life in a remarried family.

The growth of remarried families is a major reason the perception of what is "normal" in family life has changed.

One of the problems of treating remarried families is that there is no terminology to discuss the complex dynamics within them.

Forming Remarried Families

A remarried family is most commonly formed when a person from a previous marriage remarries someone who is single or previously married. One or both of the marriage partners comes into this arrangement with children.

Prior to the 1950s, death was the most frequent reason for the ending of a marriage. Rituals helped survivors deal with death. About 800,000 spouses die each year. Many do not mourn their loss appropriately.

More than 1 million divorces occur each year. The actual divorce rate is between 50% and 66%. About two thirds of divorces occur in the first 10 years of marriage. Most who divorce eventually remarry. Ethnic groups experience divorce differently. After divorce, contact between a child and a noncustodial parent, especially child/father contact, frequently declines.

Making Healthy Adjustments in Remarried Families

Healthy adjustment in remarried families depends on members working on both individual and family issues.

Children must deal with real and perceived losses such as parental closeness, seniority privileges, moving, and adjustment to new stepsiblings and a stepparent.

Benefits for children in remarried families include closeness to a new adult parent figure, increased attention, new friendships, and the opportunity to establish a different identity.

Drawbacks for new stepparents include breaking into or modifying established routines, adjusting to expectations and realities, and managing the stress of different relationships.

Dynamics Associated with Remarried Families

Remarried families are born out of loss and hope.

Most children and adults who become part of a remarried family can have a good experience, but first they must resolve past experiences and modify unrealistic fantasies.

Remarried families have structures that both help and inhibit bonding and alliances. These
structures are different from those of nuclear families.

Many remarried families are binuclear and involve the interrelating of two or more households.

Issues Within Remarried Families

Remarried families face situational and developmental tasks that are different from those
of other families. They must resolve the past, alleviate fears, deal with trust, be realistic,
and become psychologically/physically attached.

The ages and stages of children and parents influence how many issues remarried families
face and how they are resolved.

Integrating members into remarried families is difficult and takes at least 2 years. Some
relationships, such as that between children and stepfathers, are bothersome.

Strengths and Challenges Connected with Remarried Families

Assets remarried family members bring to each other include:
- different life experiences
- kin and quasi-kin networks
- creativity and innovation
- appreciation and respect for differences in living styles
- the ability to make the most of situations and model appropriate coping strategies for
  other families

Challenges that remarried families must deal with include:
- the loss of an important member (or members) of the former family
- the establishment of a workable family hierarchy
- boundary difficulties
- unresolved emotions
- economic concerns and financial difficulties

Approaches for Treating Remarried Families

To deal effectively with remarried families, therapists should:
- help families to recognize and deal appropriately with old loyalties and new ties
- help families become involved constructively with significant others, such as a
  former spouse or new children
- provide families with educational materials
- help families to develop their own rituals and traditions
- apply structural, strategic, Bowen, and experiential family therapy to deal with issues
  such as history, boundaries, structure, and feelings

Role of the Therapist

Therapists who work with remarried families wear many hats. They must help remarrieds
deal with separation/custody issues rationally and psychologically.

Therapists must help remarried families to arrange predictable and mutually satisfactory
interactional patterns, including relinquishing personal myths, teaching communication
skills, offering parent training, and providing a forum for the airing of common and
unique concerns.

In general, family therapists must work with a variety of internal and external issues that tend to unbalance remarried families.

Process and Outcome

As a result of effective family therapy interventions, remarried families are:
- able to understand personal and systemic issues related to this arrangement
- aware of subunits within their families and more tolerant and realistic with each other
- able to find their place within these families and deal effectively with individual and family developmental issues
- able to understand the importance of integrating family members into a working system through creating unique family ways of operating and traditions
- stronger internally and able to withstand negative portrayals of remarried families in the popular press

CHAPTER 14

Working with Culturally Diverse Families

---•---

She works cleaning clothes and ironing sheets,
a person of color in a bland and bleached world
where there is little emotion amid the routine
as the days fade like memories into each other.

He struggles trimming hedges and mowing grass,
a solitary white man surrounded by people
whose skin is darker than his.

Sometime when discouraged she struggles
to stop her dreams from slipping away,
like the fresh steam from her always hot iron,
by giving them vividness in her mind
and calling her hopes by name.

He too concentrates on the future
amid the tedium of routine and long hours
as he imagines scenes of those who love him
and conjures up pictures of home.

---•---

Gladding, 1992d

D istinct cultures and culturally diverse families have been a part of American society since its inception. Since the 1970s and 1980s, however, there has been a focus on **multiculturalism**, a term used to refer to the cultural groups within a region or nation. There are various reasons for this neglect. One is the assumption that conceptual, theoretical, and methodological frameworks already developed would be appropriate for persons of color regardless of their background (Turner, Wieling, & Allen, 2004). That supposition translated into benign neglect in regard to research, theory, and practice. A second reason for the delay in addressing the needs of multiple cultures was that until the 1980s the number of and percentage of people in the United States who identify themselves as other than "White" was relatively small. Now in the 21st century, the number of people whose origins are non-European is growing exponentially in the U.S. population. Furthermore, the estimated number of foreign-born people in the United States is increasing rapidly (Lee & Ramsey, 2006).

Not only are distinctive U.S. Census Bureau groups such as Asian Americans and African Americans flourishing, but marriages across racial and ethnic lines are also increasing at a phenomenal rate. **Intercultural couples** are becoming more prevalent. More "than 80% of Italians and more than 40% of Hispanics, respectively, choose mates outside their own cultural groups [and] the rates of marriages between African Americans and European Americans has tripled" since 1980 (Molina, Estrada, & Burnett, 2004, p. 139). Overall, 1 in 15 marriages in the United States in 2005 was between people of different races or ethnicities versus 1 in 23 in 1990—a 65% increase (El Nasser & Grant, 2005b).

While these interethnic, interfaith, and interracial couples provide individuals with enrichment and challenges to their **worldview,** they also complicate interpersonal relationships both inside and outside the couple and family. Even though all marriages are cultural intermarriages to a degree (McGoldrick & Giordano, 1996), overt changes in the population makeup has called attention to the increased importance of understanding culture and multiculturalism in couple and married relationships. Thus "openness to diversity and cultural competence when providing family therapy is essential" (Lee & Mjelde-Mossey, 2004, p. 497).

Professionals who would work with families must gain knowledge about different family types and develop skills in treating them. Increasingly, family therapists are "finding themselves working with families in multicultural context" (Goldberg, 1993, p. 1). The "families of today—postmodern families—are characterized by diversity, not only diversity of structure but also diversity along class, ethnic, culture, and gender lines" (Ahrons, 1992, p. 3). Therapists are now striving to understand individuals and families "in the context of the family's culture" and the culture at large (Gushue, 1993, p. 489). In short, they are seeking **cultural competency,** which is a sensitivity to such factors as race, gender, ethnicity, socioeconomic status, and sexual orientation as well as the ability to respond appropriately in a therapeutic manner to persons whose cultural background differs from their own.

Working with culturally diverse families is not simple or easy. Situations that encompass the life span, from dealing with health to reacting to death, are treated differently by distinct cultural groups (Brown, 1988; Hines, Preto, McGoldrick, Almeida, & Weltman, 1999; Jencius & Duba, 2002). In working with families, therapists must take into account how different cultures instill in family members attitudes and actions, such as social and communication patterns and how these values play out in intracultural and intercultural couples and families as well (Goldenberg & Goldenberg, 1993; Thomas, 1998). Some of the best research in the field has been done by Jose Szapocznik and associates, which is discussed in Chapter 17.

Regardless, when family therapists do not comprehend the values and characteristics of specific cultures and their families, the behaviors associated with these beliefs and traditions are likely to be undervalued, misunderstood, and/or pathologized (Billingsley, 1968; McGoldrick & Giordano, 1996). This misunderstanding is associated with cultural prejudices, flaws in collecting data about minorities, stereotyping, and unrecognized economic differences (Hampson, Beavers, & Hulgus, 1990; Ma, 2005).

Culturally diverse families need to be seen in regard to their strengths and liabilities both collectively and individually. One way to do this is to study culturally diverse families from the perspective of their competencies, social class, honored behaviors, customs, typical behaviors, and observed family styles (Billingsley, 1992; Hampson et al., 1990; Lee & Mjelde-Mossey, 2004). This type of approach makes it more likely that significant differences and similarities of families from various backgrounds will be reported accurately and fairly.

This chapter discusses numerous aspects of culturally diverse families. The emphasis is on the dynamics that are common to a broad range of families. Issues involved in working from a multicultural point of view are stressed. Special aspects of conducting family therapy with culturally diverse families are also highlighted. Matters pertaining to working with gay and lesbian families are addressed first because this kind of family is found to some extent within all cultures and, until recently, has been "invisible." Issues in working with more identifiable cultural groups—African-American, Asian-American, Hispanic/Latino American, Native American, Arab American, and European-American families—are dealt with next. In discussing cultural groups, it must be stressed that it is easy to stereotype groups according to cultures and that therapists must take extreme care not to get caught in this trap. They must realize that within-group differences are greater than outside differences in cultures. Furthermore, they must be open to working with the uniqueness that is every family.

What Is a Culture?

To tackle the issues involved in multicultural family therapy, we must first define culture and distinguish it from race and ethnicity. Such a procedure helps clarify concepts and the interrelatedness of terms. It is a difficult process and one for which there is no universal agreement.

Culture can be defined in numerous ways, but it is generally considered to be "the customary beliefs, social forms, and material traits of a racial, religious, or social group" (Webster's, 1989, p. 314). This broad definition implies that culture is a multidimensional concept that encompasses the collective realities of a group of people (Lee & Ramsey, 2006). As such, culture is made up of behaviors and traditions that have been cultivated over a long period of time. It may be a conscious aspect of a family's identity, such as taking pride in ancestry, or it may consist of unconscious practices that family members perform and never question. Both conscious and unconscious practices of culture involve seeing and being in the world through a persistence to continue to live a certain way despite information to the contrary (Watzlawick, 1976).

A culture includes diverse groups of people who may differ in regard to race, religion, or social status but who identify themselves collectively in a particular way. For instance, it is possible to speak about Jewish, Christian, Buddhist, Hindu, or Muslim cultures that encompass people from a wide range of social classes. It is also appropriate to talk about specific countries and their cultures, such as Japanese, Egyptian, Kenyan, or Indian. Culture may be spoken of in regard to those who are racially in either the majority or the minority. The point is that cultures operate on many levels, that is, inclusive and exclusive, specific and general. Many cultures are open to people of various backgrounds who identify with them and act in accordance with their traditions and values. Some are closed. In a pluralistic society such as the United States, "a complex mélange of cultural influences" exists that impacts families and their members (Szapocznik & Kurtines, 1993). "Cultural values define behaviors and therefore establish norms for attitudes and behaviors within families" (Thomas, 1998, p. 24).

Racial groups and ethnicity are not so broadly defined. A **racial group** is "a family, tribe, people, or nation belonging to the same stock" (Webster's, 1989, p. 969). It may include an ethnic group, but "race is primarily a biological term" (Lee, 1991, p. 12). **Ethnic groups** are "large groups of people classed according to common racial, national, tribal, linguistic, or cultural origin or background" (Webster's, 1989, p. 427). Ethnic identity "is anything but homogenous" (Giordano & Carini-Giordano, 1995, p. 352). In describing ethnic groups, the term *ethnicity* is used to reflect a sociological concept (Lee, 1991). "Ethnicity … influences the kinds of messages that people learn … for example, Scandinavian patterns for expressions of intimacy may differ greatly from Italian and Greek messages" (Mason, 1991, p. 481). Therefore, ethnic family customs influence a group's "fit" within an overall culture, just as race does.

Although race and ethnicity may be used synonymously at times to refer to people who share similar traits or characteristics, they differ when employed in their most precise form. The term *culture* is more widely utilized when discussing a group of people with similar backgrounds, beliefs, and behaviors. The broadness of culture is the primary reason it is employed in this chapter as a modifier of family diversity.

Dynamics Associated with Culturally Diverse Families

Culturally diverse families are affected by the same social pressures that impact other families. These families must learn to cope with the stressors associated with money, work, children, aging, death, success, and leisure (Turner, 1993). However, the ways in which families from different cultural backgrounds view and respond to life events differ. For example, some general and striking characteristics of Jewish families are to marry within the group, to encourage children, to value education, and to use guilt as a way of shaping behavior. Some Italian families, to use another example, place importance on expressiveness, personal connectedness, enjoyment of food and good times, and traditional sex roles (McGoldrick & Rohrbaugh, 1987). These point to how minority culture families are affected both quantitatively and qualitatively in regard to life experiences in ways that members of majority families are not (Sue & Sue, 2002). "Certain moments in the family life cycle will represent greater crisis for one culture than for another" (Gushue, 1993, p. 489). In Irish families, "death is generally considered the most significant life cycle transition and members will go to great lengths not to miss a wake or a funeral" (McGoldrick, 1986, p. 31). On the other hand, "because of the stress on interdependence in Puerto Rican culture, the loss of a family member is experienced as an especially profound threat to the family's future and often touches off reactions of extreme anxiety" (Garcia-Preto, 1986, p. 33).

Culturally diverse families who are in the minority must also contend with overt as well as covert criticism of their patterns of family interaction that may not be universally accepted (Tseng & Hsu, 1991). If women are treated by certain families as inferior or subservient, these families and their culture may be taken to task by others. Likewise, a majority culture may ignore important civic or religious holidays in particular cultural groups and both directly and indirectly convey to members of these groups their disinterest or disdain in them as people.

Another difficulty for culturally diverse families is appearance. Members of some families may be recognized by their distinct skin color, physical features, or dress. They must deal with subtle and blatant prejudice and discrimination on an almost continuous basis (Ho, 1987). As a result of discrimination or hatred based on outward appearance, some families are faced with the task of nurturing and protecting each other in ways unknown to majority culture families.

A fourth dynamic that affects culturally diverse families involves their access to mental health services (Sue & Sue, 2002). The location of mental health services, their formality, and the way they advertise their services is often a turnoff for culturally diverse families. Native Americans may have to drive miles for treatment and then find that the clinic operation hours are not convenient to their lifestyle. This kind of situation is known as an **institutional barrier.** Other institutional barriers include the use of a language not understood by minority families and the lack of culturally diverse practitioners.

A final factor influencing culturally diverse families involves economics (Arnold & Allen, 1995). To function well in society, families must have one or more persons earning wages that make it possible to live beyond a survival level. Minority cultures are often excluded from certain jobs and their employment opportunities can be limited by events in society such as the rise of technology and service industries and the shrinkage of the working class in the United States. These events have resulted in many heads of minority households being cut out of employment opportunities that paid good wages and falling into the ranks of the working poor and underclass.

Issues Within Culturally Diverse Families

A number of critical issues are involved in working with culturally diverse families. These issues center around attitudes, skill, and knowledge. Many family therapists are at an initial disadvantage in dealing with culturally diverse families considering the fact that as a field marriage and family therapy "reflects a bias toward the dominant European American culture in its history, theories, and membership" (McDowell et al., 2003, p. 179). While virtually no family therapist can be an expert on all cultures (Hines et al., 1999), most family therapists can acquire general abilities that enable them to be effective in helping a wide variety of families. In acquiring cultural knowledge, such factors as sensitivity, experience, acceptance, ingenuity, specificity, and intervention often determine whether family therapists are successful or not.

Sensitivity

The issue of sensitivity is one with which all helping professionals must deal. "Sensitivity and respect for the beliefs and world view of the client/family is crucial" (Santisteban & Szapocznik, 1994, p. 22). If family therapists are not sensitive to the similarities and differences between themselves and the families they work with, they may make assumptions that are incorrect and unhelpful (Boynton, 1987). Professionals who are insensitive have been described as **culturally encapsulated counselors** (Wrenn, 1962, 1985). They tend to treat everyone the same, and in so doing, make mistakes. For example, every Native American Indian family differs in regard to its makeup and the strategies members use to resolve problems. If therapists are not sensitive to this fact, they may try the same methods with all Native American Indian families and get mixed results.

Experience

The issue of experience refers to that of the family therapists as well as that of the families they treat. Professionally, a family therapist may find it hard to work with a family of a diverse background if the therapist has not had some life experiences with members of that culture. A therapist from a socially isolated, homogeneous, middle-class background may become lost when trying to help a poor, newly immigrated family resolve family conflict.

Also important is the specific experience of culturally diverse families. Specific cultural backgrounds are often influenced by a family's experiences in the larger society. If a family of Hispanic/Latino descent has a history of affluence and acceptance within mainstream society, a family therapist needs to recognize and respect the socioeconomic factors that influence that family. Such families and their members often find themselves in conflict because of their inheritance of two different cultural traditions (Ho, 1987; Sue & Sue, 2002).

Acceptance

The issue of **acceptance** encompasses therapists' personal and professional comfortableness with a family. If therapists cannot openly accept culturally diverse families, they are likely to display overt or covert prejudice that negatively impacts the therapeutic process. Therefore, it is of utmost importance that therapists assess their thoughts and feelings about the families that are before them. The question of racism must be raised early if the family and therapist are of different racial backgrounds (Franklin, 1993). Social, behavioral, and economic differences need to be examined also to assess whether the family and therapist are a good match. Models for examining therapists' values in regard to families and self have been developed by Ho (1987) (see Table 14.1).

Table 14.1

Cultural Value Preferences of Middle-Class White Americans and Ethnic Minorities: A Comparative Summary

Area of Relationships	Middle-Class White Americans	Asian/Pacific Americans	American Indian, Alaskan Native	African Americans	Hispanic Americans
Man to nature/ environment	Mastery over	Harmony with	Harmony with	Harmony with	Harmony with
Time orientation	Future	Past-present	Present	Present	Past-present
Relations with people	Individual	Collateral	Collateral	Collateral	Collateral
Preferred mode of activity	Doing	Doing	Being-in-becoming	Doing	Being-in-becoming
Nature of man	Good and bad	Good	Good	Good and bad	Good

From *Family Therapy with Ethnic Minorities* (p. 232) by M. K. Ho, 1987, Newbury Park, CA: Sage. Copyright © 1987 by Sage Publications, Inc. Reprinted by permission of Sage Publications, Inc.

Ingenuity

To be effective in treating culturally diverse families, therapists must use their ingenuity. Most cultural settings provide natural help-giving networks (Sue & Sue, 2002). Effective family therapists utilize these networks and are innovative as well. Instead of trying to treat some families within the confines of an office, therapists act as consultants to agencies and persons who can best work with certain families. In the African-American community, for example, churches and ministers have traditionally been a source of strength and help (Richardson & June, 2006). Therapists may act in conjunction with and in direct and open collaboration with these sources in treating a family in context (Boszormenyi-Nagy, 1987). On the other hand, with traditional Asian Americans, subtlety and indirectness may be called for rather than direct confrontation and interpretation (Sue & Sue, 2002).

Specificity

Specificity is necessary because each family is unique and must be treated differently. Family therapists must assess the strengths and weaknesses of individual families and design and implement specific procedures for each. In "families that expect therapy to be a growth experience … the therapy must be presented in this light. Conversely, in families that expect a no-non-sense, problem-solving approach, therapy should be presented as having concrete, attainable, short-term goals" (Santisteban & Szapocznik, 1994, p. 22). Although strategic family therapy (Haley, 1973, 1976) and solution-focused therapy (deShazer, 1988) pride themselves on devising approaches that address the needs of specific families, other family therapy models also modify their goals, guidelines, and interventions, depending on the particular families they are treating.

In practical terms, family therapists must realize that the needs and issues of first-generation families differ from those of more acculturated families. Contrary to popular belief, as families become acculturated, they do not drop former cultural ways but instead add new ones and synthesize "both the new and the old in a creative manner" (Newlon & Arciniega, 1991, p. 202). The issue of specificity is a reminder that the application of treatment needs to be congruent with and tailored to families' experiences.

Intervention

A final aspect of being an effective counselor with culturally diverse families involves the challenge of intolerance within systems. Such a goal of working productively with families in the face of intolerance is accomplished when a counselor assumes the role of a **systematic change agent** (Lee, Armstrong, & Brydges, 1996). In this role, a therapist tries to intervene on behalf of families in unhealthy and intolerant systems. There are two types of unhealthy systems. One involves a "passive insensitivity to diversity" (Lee et al., 1996, p. 5), that is, the plight of people outside one's culture is simply ignored. The other intolerant system is "one characterized by an active and intentional insensitivity to diversity" (Lee et al., 1996, p. 5). This latter type of system fosters active discrimination that is easier to identify. Bringing about change in either type of system takes courage, persistence, and time.

Approaches for Treating Culturally Diverse Families

Culturally diverse families have several characteristics in common. The importance and influence of the extended family and kinship ties are almost universal (Johnson, 1995). However, all families have unique characteristics that must be considered when working with them. Therapists should consider that "the definition of family, as well as the timing of life cycle phases and the importance of different transitions, varies depending on a family's cultural background" (Carter & McGoldrick, 1988, p. 25). With this in mind, the following sections highlight some common aspects of and therapeutic issues surrounding the "invisible family" form composed of gays and lesbians and six distinct culturally diverse family groups in the United States: African Americans, Asian Americans, Hispanic/Latino Americans, Native Americans, Arab Americans, and European Americans.

Gay and Lesbian Families

Family therapists are seeing increasing numbers of gay and lesbian couples and families (Chen-Hayes, 1997; Laird, 1993). It is reported that approximately 1 out of every 10 cases in marriage and family therapy involves lesbians or gay men (Alonzo, 2005). As a rule such couples "are more likely than heterosexual couples to avail themselves of professional services to address problems in their current relationship" (Means-Christensen, Snyder, & Negy, 2003, p. 80). By understanding the dynamics surrounding these relationships, family therapists can overcome negative and detrimental stereotypes associated with this population and at the same time be able to provide proper and needed services.

Until recently there has not been much research on gay and lesbian families (Alonzo, 2005). The gay and lesbian family form has been all but "invisible" in family therapy research and this population has been mainly studied in regard to individuals (Laird, 1993; Means-Christensen et al., 2003). However, a number of facts are known about gay and lesbian families.

First, as a group, gay and lesbian families are intergenerational. "Each partner, child, and other family member is influenced by and must come to terms with the specific history and culture of his or her own family of origin in its sociocultural context" (Laird, 1993, p. 285).

Second, there is a cycle to gay and lesbian family life, and issues at each stage are crucial to understand if these families are to be understood. In becoming a couple, gays and lesbians, like other men and women, wish to have parental approval (LaSala, 2002). Throughout their lives together, gay and lesbian families "must decide who will do what, when, where, and how in order to meet the particular needs of the family as a whole and of individual family members, whose interests at times may conflict or compete" (Laird, 1993, p. 308).

Third, gay and lesbian families are varied within as a group. There is no "typical" gay or lesbian family form any more than there is a typical family form for any other cultural group.

Finally, as much as any minority group, gay and lesbian families have mixed levels of satisfaction in their relationships. Research indicates that lesbian and gay couples have relationships that are as satisfying as those of heterosexuals and sometimes even better for lesbian couples (Stabb, 2005). However, many gay and lesbian couples and families suffered from a lack of affirming role models and social support. They still face discrimination on all levels and are stigmatized within society in general (Janson & Steigerwald, 2002; Sayger, Homrich, & Horne, 2000). This type of treatment adds additional stress to their lives and makes dealing with daily issues, let alone crises, more difficult (Robertson, 2004).

Therapeutic Treatment of Gay and Lesbian Families

The place most family therapists need to start when working therapeutically with gay and lesbian families is with themselves, especially in sorting out their feelings in regard to this population (May, 1994). Most family therapists are heterosexuals and carry conscious and unconscious negative thoughts and feelings about those who are not. To be effective with gay and lesbian families, family therapists need to stay open, aware, and acknowledging of their beliefs and biases as well as studious regarding current scientific knowledge and clinical issues regarding gay and lesbian lifestyles (Alonzo, 2005; Sayger et al., 2000).

After working on themselves and sharpening their clinical abilities to be therapeutic with members of this population, family therapists must address both external and internal issues associated with being a gay or lesbian couple or family. Externally, gay and lesbian families face a world of obstacles including cultural and societal homophobia. Therefore, family therapists need to be familiar with "local, state, and national laws" affecting gays and lesbians, "as well as community and psychoeducative resources" available to them and their families of origin (Sayger et al., 2000, p. 34).

Another external issue is that some parents and relatives of gays and lesbians have difficulty accepting the sexual orientation and lifestyle of their kin. Therapeutic treatment may involve working with the extended family members of this population so that at least an understanding, if not an acceptance, of the gay and lesbian family can be gained. Bowen family therapy is a good approach in these cases.

A challenge that is continuous for family therapists is dealing with the diversity of gay and lesbian family lifestyles and subcultures (Snead, 1993). Treatment for gay and lesbian families that may be appropriate in one case may not be appropriate in another. Some forms of these families have "fluid boundaries and flexible composition" (Patten, 1992, p. 34) while others do not. Abuse may be present in some situations, while in others it is moot.

Family therapists face the challenge of helping these families relate positively to themselves, their partners, and society. In some cases, there is **commitment ambiguity** in which "one partner is not sure about his or her place in the relationship" (Alonzo, 2005, p. 375). In others, an assessment of internalized beliefs needs to be gathered. Regardless, thoughts and matters related to feelings clients have about themselves and their partners need to be clarified. In working with gay and lesbian families, therapists often have to work with society at large and its institutions, too, in order to deal with matters of prejudice and discrimination (May, 1994). All of these processes take time, support, and creativity.

African-American Families

African Americans are the second largest minority group in the United States. There were approximately 35 million African Americans in the United States or 13% of the total population in 2000 with a projected growth in this population of 45 million by 2020 (U. S. Bureau of the Census, 2000). Families of African Americans are diverse in regard to background and traditions. However, they have much in common—many of their ancestors were brought to the Americas as slaves and their black skin color differentiates them from the majority of people in the United States. These two characteristics have kept African Americans and their families at an extreme disadvantage in acculturating and being accepted in society (Walsh, 1982).

As a result, they have had to face continuous racism, poverty, and discrimination. African Americans have thus encountered many socioeconomic disadvantages and a great deal of stress (Kazdin, Stolar, & Marciano, 1995). Because of this prejudice, the family unit has been an essential institution for survival in the African-American community. It has been especially supportive for the most vulnerable. Interestingly, on popular television shows and in films, African Americans have been depicted in a number of sometimes contradictory ways such as wise and witty (e.g., *The Cosby Show*), middle-class (e.g., *Laurel Avenue*), violent and unruly (e.g., *Boyz N the Hood*), and heroic (e.g., *Passenger 57*). What is true is that African-American families vary just like other types of families.

In regard to strengths, African-American families are known for being "strong" in the areas of kinship bonds. Most African-American families "are embedded in a complex kinship and social network" that includes both blood relatives and close friends (Lambie & Daniels-Mohring, 1993, p. 74). Another strength of African-American families is their religious orientation and spirituality. They often utilize the resources of their clergy and churches (Richardson & June, 2006). Cooperation, strong motivation to achieve, caring parenting, and work orientation are other positive characteristics that describe African Americans (Hill, 1972; Olson, 2000). Finally, African Americans are "adaptable" in their family roles. Members of such families are less likely to stereotype each other into roles based on gender (Ericksen, Yancey, & Ericksen, 1979).

Despite their strengths, African-American families face a number of negatives. Internally, African-American male–female relationships have "become more problematic, conflictual, and destructive" (Willis, 1990, p. 139). The reasons for this phenomenon are complex and relate to factors—such as mistrust, insecurity, unemployment, socialization, and rage—that are the conscious and unconscious legacies of slavery and a changing society. For example, black men have traditionally been denied the role of provider, which along with the roles of protection and procreation, has been one of the three traditional roles for men in society (Levant, 2003). Thus, "census figures show that while 35% of Americans between 24 and 34 have never married, the figure is 54% for African Americans" (Peterson, 2000c). Regardless of the underlying dynamics, the result is that despite their belief in the institution of marriage and an increase in affluence, fewer African Americans marry today than at any time in history (Cherlin, 1992; Waller & McLanahan, 2005) and out-of-wedlock births account for two out of three first births to African-American women under age 35 (Ingrassia, 1993).

African-American families must deal with outside pressures such as racism, prejudice, poverty, and discrimination (Lee, 1995). The social and economic turmoil surrounding the civil rights movement, the women's movement, and the Vietnam War changed the overall makeup of African-American families. Two of the best aspects of change that occurred in African-American families in the 1970s were financial and social upward mobility. Employment and educational opportunities, previously closed because of racial barriers, opened. Housing and social options became more available. The opposite side of the upward mobility movement was the poverty and hopelessness of the African Americans left behind, especially in inner-city ghettos. These African Americans tended to be poorer and less educated, and to have less opportunity to advance. Unemployment rose in general among African-American men from the late 1950s on because of the elimination of many working-class jobs (Gaston, 1996). The consequence was that a large economic underclass of African Americans developed. Within this class was a loosening of family ties because of the stress and strain associated with single parenting, high unemployment, and living in or near the poverty level.

These external factors influence the inner realities affecting family dynamics today (Franklin, 1993). Such stress within any group takes its toll on family life and individuals within these families.

Therapeutic Treatment of African-American Families

Although African Americans have high utilization rates for individual therapy, the concept of family therapy is still relatively new to most of them (Willis, 1988; Wilson & Stith, 1991). "African Americans are often strangers in an alien land of therapists, many of whom have not received or are not invested in training about African-American cultural realities" (Burton, Winn, Stevenson, & Clark, 2004, p. 405). Traditionally, African Americans have relied on extended family networks to take care of their needs. African-American men have, as a group, been particularly reluctant to share their most intimate thoughts and feelings because of socialization patterns that have taught them not to share pain and frustration (Peterson, 2000c).

Yet, many African-American families may benefit from time-specific therapy approaches that are problem-focused or multigenerational in nature (Boyd-Franklin, 1993). Structural, Bowen, and strategic family therapy theories have been found appropriate in working with African-American families (Boyd-Franklin, 1987). Psychoeducation, especially with single-parent African-American women, can be effective (Lee, 1995). However, in treating African-American families, there is "no prescriptive approach" that can be applied universally in the helping process (Newlon & Arciniega, 1991, p. 192).

Furthermore, family therapists, regardless of their cultural heritage, must be attuned to African-American experiences and perceptions. To be successful, family therapists need to understand the historical and social background of African-American families in the United States. They must also appreciate the issue of trust that arises between African-American families and non-African-American family therapists (Willis, 1988). An important point for family therapists to comprehend is that many African-American families first need to perceive treatment as a form of social support that can benefit them. Then they can more readily accept it.

Working with African-American families requires that therapists have an understanding of multigenerational family systems (Hines, Garcia-Preto, McGoldrick, Almeida, & Weltman, 1992). Therapists must also be sensitive to the importance of respect for elderly family members. Often family therapy is begun by African-American families because therapists have emphasized to older family members that therapy can be of value.

Therapists must assure African-American families that through the therapeutic process they can learn how to handle many of their own problems. Through "education about various issues (e.g., parental rights in educational systems) and concrete skills training," confidence and competence may be enhanced in African-American families so they can advocate on their own behalf (McGoldrick, Preto, Hines, & Lee, 1991, p. 561). Lee (1995) describes how single African-American mothers may be empowered to effectively deal with their children and extreme environmental hardships through helping these women foster a positive culture identity in their children. In addition, these women can be assisted by helping them appreciate parenthood from an Afrocentric perspective.

Furthermore, in working with African-American families, therapists need to address social and institutional issues that have adversely affected African Americans. These include working in an outreach fashion to marshal support of institutions, such as governments and churches, which can lend support to African-American families and help change detrimental policies affecting these families. The presentation of positive role models of African-American families can also make a difference (Stovall, 2000).

Other guidelines besides those given above for conducting family therapy with African-American families include: addressing the family's concern about having a non-African-American therapist (if that is the case); not assuming familiarity with the family in first sessions; joining with the family before gathering sensitive information; conducting home visits if needed; acknowledging strengths, successes and resources; and using appropriate metaphors and scriptural references when warranted (Bean, Perry, & Bedell, 2002).

Asian-American Families

In 2004, Asian Americans constituted about 4% of the population of the United States or 11 million people (Kim, Bean, & Harper, 2004). By 2020, they are projected to be about 20 million. Asian Americans trace their cultural heritages to countries such as China, Japan, Vietnam, Cambodia, India, Korea, the Philippines, and the Pacific islands. The backgrounds of Asian Americans are diverse, "with as many as 32 different Asian ethnic groups now identified in the U.S." (Cheng, 1996, p. 8). They differ in regard to language, history, and socioeconomic factors. Yet Asian Americans share many cultural values, such as a respect and reverence for the elderly, extended family support, family loyalty, and a high value on education (Olson, 2000). They also place a strong emphasis on self-discipline, order, social etiquette, and hierarchy (Hong, 1989; London & Devore, 1992).

"Traditional Asian/Pacific values governing family life have been heavily influenced by Confucian philosophy and ethics, which strongly emphasizes specific roles and proper relationships among people in those roles" (Ho, 1987, p. 25). Three main relationship roles that are stressed within the family are father/son, husband/wife, and elder/younger siblings (Keyes, 1977). In these relationships, there are feelings of obligation and shame. If a member of a family behaves improperly, the whole family loses face. Buddhist values also are prevalent in many Asian-American families. These values stress harmonious living and involve "compassion, a respect for life, and moderation of behavior; self-discipline, patience, modesty, and friendliness" (Ho, 1987, p. 25).

As Asian-American families have moved into mainstream American society, they have had to contend with a number of problems that are both unique and universal to other families. For instance, like other families, Asian-American families have had to face the fact that geographically and emotionally, families are moving further apart. This is a trend in American society that places more emphasis on the individual than the family (Sue & Morishima, 1982). Substance abuse, once rare among some Asian-American populations, is on the rise (Mercado, 2000). Unique to Asian-American family culture is the reality that "parents can no longer expect complete obedience, as families become more democratic and move away from the patriarchal system of the past" (London & Devore, 1992, p. 368). In many ways, Asian-American families and other U.S. families appear to be similar, but the dynamics underlying them differ substantially.

Therapeutic Treatment of Asian-American Families

In working with Asian-American families, therapists must take acculturation into account. First-generation Asian-American families, for instance, may need assistance from family therapists in learning how to interrelate properly to other families and societal institutions. They may likewise face problems involving social isolation, adjustment difficulties to a particular location, and language barriers (Hong, 1989). The role of the therapist in such cases is primarily educational and avocational rather than remedial. It is directed toward outreach efforts (Cheng, 1996).

On the other hand, many established Asian-American families need help in resolving intrafamily difficulties, such as intergenerational conflicts, role confusion, and couple relationships (McGoldrick et al., 1991). There may be an **acculturation gap** (i.e., different rates of acculturation) between immigrant parents and U.S.-raised children that "complicates the normal generation gap, resulting in greater misunderstandings, miscommunications, and eventual conflicts among family members" (Lee, Choe, Kim, & Ngo, 2000, p. 211). In these cases, therapists work according to both specific cultural norms as well as universal treatment model procedures.

Like African-American families, Asian-American families seem to do best in family therapy when the focus of sessions is problem- or solution-oriented and when the family is empowered to help itself through its own and community resources. Most Asian-American families are reluctant to initiate family therapy; and if therapists are to be of assistance to these families, they must do the following:

- orient them and educate them to the value of therapy
- establish rapport quickly through the use of compassion and self-disclosure
- emphasize specific techniques families can use in improving their relationships and resolving their problems

Problematic to Asian-American families, and all recognizable ethnic minority families, is **racism,** which may disrupt their internal family dynamics as well as outside relationships (Sue & Morishima, 1982). In such situations, family therapists not only work to address societal changes but also focus with family members on assessing the values and skills within the family for dealing with prejudice and discrimination. This type of work utilizes family cultural strengths and family therapy strengths.

In working with families of Asian origin, therapists need to recognize that they may be most effective if they are knowledgeable about Asian philosophers, such as Lao Tzu and Confucius. They are also usually at their best when they seek "to create a safe and nurturing environment that mirrors a supportive and caring family and where each participant is respected, and without fear, can explore relevant problems and concerns" (Cheng, 1996, p. 8). Kim et al. (2004) also lays out other guidelines for working with Asian-American families in general and Korean Americans in particular. Among these are: assess support available to the family, assess past history of immigration, establish professional credibility, be problem-focused/present-focused, be directive in guiding the therapy process, and provide positive reframes that encourage the family.

Hispanic/Latino American Families

"The term **Hispanic,** or **Latino,** refers to people who were born in any of the Spanish-speaking countries of the Americas (Latin America), from Puerto Rico, or from the United States who trace their ancestry to either Latin America or to Hispanic people from U.S. territories that were once Spanish or Mexican" (Cohen, 1993, p. 13). One in every 7 residents of the United States is of Hispanic/Latino origin, with a combined population of 41.3 million. Data from the 2004 Census (El Nasser & Grant, 2005a) indicate that Hispanics have become the nation's largest minority and are growing rapidly especially among the younger generations. Almost 22% of children under the age of 5 were Hispanic in 2004 (El Nasser & Grant, 2005b, p. 4A). Regardless of age, the majority (76%) of Hispanic/Latino American families trace their ancestry to Mexico, Cuba, or Puerto Rico.

Considerable diversity exists among Hispanics/Latinos and the families they create. Most wish to be in the mainstream of society in the United States, and a majority do not support "traditional" roles for women (Benedetto, 1992). As a group, Hispanics/Latinos also tend to be family-oriented with children being at the center of the family and parents "typically assuming complementary roles in the disciplining (i.e., fathers) and nurturing (i.e., mothers) of their children" (Madden-Derdich, Estrada, Updegraff, & Leonard, 2002, p. 251). Differences in distinct groups of Hispanics/Latinos, however, mean that each family is unique, sharing both common and special qualities when compared with others.

As a group, Hispanic/Latino families have the following difficulties (Puente, 1993; Usdansky, 1993):

- They have a higher unemployment rate than non-Hispanic/Latinos.
- They live below the poverty line at over twice the rate of non-Hispanic/Latinos.
- They lag behind non-Hispanic/Latinos in earning high school diplomas and college degrees.

Hispanic/Latino families have a number of assets and strengths. "Hispanics come to the United States from collectivistic cultures" which "view their accomplishments as being dependent on the outcomes of others" (Carlson, Kurato, Ruiz, Ng, & Yang, 2004, p. 114). Among these are cultural values and scripts such as *dignidad* (dignity), *orgullo* (pride and self-reliance), *confianza* (trust and intimacy), and *respecto* (respect)" (Johnson, 1995, p. 319) as well as "*simpatia* (smooth, pleasant relationships), *personalismo* (individualized self-worth)… *familismo* (family relations), *marianismo* (female self-sacrifice), and *machismo* (male self-respect and responsibility)" (Carlson et al., 2004, p. 114).

Therapeutic Treatment of Hispanic/Latino Families

In working with Hispanic/Latino families, it is helpful for family therapists to develop a basic knowledge about cultural traditions before attempting to employ treatment modalities. Traditional rituals, such as religious festivities, Quinceanos (when a daughter is presented to society as a woman), engagements, weddings, and funerals, are highly valued in Hispanic/Latino culture and bring families together (Ponce, 1995, p. 7). Hispanic/Latino individuals are also "interested in getting to know someone as a person rather than assessing a person based on external factors such as occupational or socioeconomic status" (Cooper & Costas, 1994, p. 32). As a group, Hispanics/Latinos tend to be "physically expressive, such as gesturing with their hands and face (e.g., eyes/eyebrows and mouth) while they talk" (Ponce, 1995, p. 7).

This type of cultural information can be obtained through specific academic courses as well as through direct observation, interactions with Hispanics/Latinos, and continuing education opportunities. Educational information helps therapists learn as well as, if not better than, case-by-case supervision (Inclan, 1990). No matter what kind of approach the family therapist employs, several unique factors must be taken into consideration when helping Hispanic/Latino families.

The first factor is external. A disproportionate number of Hispanic/Latino families live at or below the poverty level (Facundo, 1990). More than 40% of Hispanic/Latino children live in poverty, with the proportion of Puerto Rican children especially high (57%) (Usdansky, 1993). Stress related to economic factors and working conditions often contributes to intrafamily difficulties. Serving as an advocate and a resource is a crucial role family therapists sometimes need to play in helping poor Hispanic/Latino families help themselves.

Another area that family therapists need to address with Hispanic/Latino families relates to **acculturation,** for they seek to fit into the larger U.S. culture as rapidly as possible (LeVine & Padilla, 1980; Olson, 2000). However, family members may do so at different rates. For instance, school-age children may become "Americanized" at a faster and easier rate than grandparents. The older Hispanic/Latino family members may fear the loss of their children and traditions to a new culture and, hence, may become isolated and depressed because of rapid changes and loss (Baptiste, 1987). In working with Hispanic/Latino families, therapists should consider how the pressure for acculturation may contribute to family turmoil, especially as it relates to family loyalty (Hines et al., 1992). Language factors, especially bilingualism, must also be explored (Sciarra & Ponterotto, 1991).

Another consideration in treating Hispanic/Latino families involves outside sources and internal beliefs. An institution that encompasses both of these helpful dimensions is the Catholic Church, especially for Mexican Americans and Puerto Ricans (Johnson, 1995). Historically, the Catholic Church has provided social, economic, and emotional support to Hispanic/Latino families when few other community services were available.

A fourth area that needs to be addressed in Hispanic/Latino families is the family hierarchy and roles. "By accepting therapy, the Hispanic father may feel … humiliated and shown to be ineffective" (Santisteban & Szapocznik, 1994, p. 21). From the point of first contact, the therapist "must send the message that the father is a central figure in the family" (p. 21). Similarly, Hispanic/Latino women may present themselves as self-sacrificing and victims of other family members. The therapist will do best not to immediately challenge this assumption but rather to redirect this behavior "to fit the needs … of getting other family members into therapy" (p. 22).

The length of therapy and its focus must be considered when working with Hispanics/Latinos. Because Hispanic/Latino families are accustomed to being treated by physicians, they generally expect mental health services to be similar. Family therapists therefore need to be active and employ direct and short-term theories. Two family therapy approaches that appear to be best suited for use with this population are behavioral family therapy and structural family therapy (Canino & Canino, 1982; Juarez, 1985; Madden-Derdich et al., 2002; Ponterotto, 1987). Structural family therapy can be especially useful in addressing problems of extreme enmeshment—that is, "when several generations live in the same household, causing problems like lack of privacy, undefined boundaries in the family structures, and confusion as to who gives the discipline at home" (Ponce, 1995, p. 11).

Native American Families

Approximately 2.4 million Native American Indians, Eskimos, and Aleuts live in the United States (U.S. Bureau of the Census, 2000). They are an extremely diverse group belonging to 557 federally recognized and several hundred state-recognized nations (Garrett, 2006; Herring,

1991). Collectively, Native American life has been built around cultures that emphasize harmony, acceptance, cooperation, sharing, and a respect for nature and family. "Family, including extended family, is of major importance, and the tribe and family to which one belongs provide significant meaning" (Newlon & Arciniega, 1991, p. 196).

Difficulties within this population vary. Because the extended family is important in most Native American cultures, one prevalent problem is the breakup or dysfunctionality of these families (Herring, 1989). Some historical practices of the U.S. government have resulted in "between 25% and 55% of all Native American children" being separated from their family of origin "and placed in non-Native American foster homes, adoption homes, boarding homes, or other institutions" (Herring, 1991, pp. 39–40). Many Native Americans who have had such experiences suffered both a confusion about their identity and trauma in their relationships with others (Garrett, 2006). Families have likewise been negatively affected.

Another problematic family concern centers on geography and culture. Many Native Americans are torn between living with their families on a reservation or trying to adjust to life in the dominant culture of the United States. Cultural connectedness with other like-minded individuals is important to Native Americans, as is a relationship with the land. Yet there are more Native Americans living in urban areas than on reservations. Urban life is stressful and is often not conducive to maintaining good mental health. For Native American Indian families as a group, isolation from their roots presents multiple difficulties in terms of functionality.

A final problem of Native American families involves substance abuse, particularly alcoholism (Hill, 1989). In some family groups, drinking is encouraged as a form of socialization (Manson, Tatum, & Dinges, 1982). The results are manifest in higher death and disorder rates. Suicide, cirrhosis of the liver, and fetal alcohol syndrome are three examples of alcohol-related problems within Native American families.

Therapeutic Treatment of Native American Families

Treating Native American families requires sensitivity, cultural knowledge, and innovation. Outsiders, including family therapists, do not gain entrance into the family easily (Ho, 1987). To be accepted and be effective with Native Americans, therapists who treat these families should recognize that some techniques work better than others. For example, indirect forms of questioning and open-ended questions lead to responses. Direct forms of questioning and closed-ended questions do not (Tafoya, 1994).

Therapists should also know and utilize certain symbols. The circle is considered sacred and represents unity and reciprocal relationships (Tafoya, 1994). This symbol, and others like it, can be used metaphorically as models for relationships (Tafoya, 1989). Finally, the admission by therapists that they may make mistakes in treatment because of cultural ignorance can go a long way toward establishing rapport and trust (Tafoya, 1989).

One approach for working with Native American families is to use **home-based therapy** (Schacht, Tafoya, & Mirabla, 1989). This method requires that family therapists be with a family before attempting to help them. Thus, therapists spend more time than usual with families and may actually do chores with them before discussing troublesome areas of family life. From a pragmatic point of view, this approach does not appear to be the most efficient use of time. However, by devoting one's self to home-based therapy, essential services can be offered to families who would not otherwise receive them.

Another approach to working with Native American families is to combine structural family therapy with traditional healing modalities. In both structuralism and traditional healing, the concepts of spontaneity, joining, and complementarity are utilized (Napoliello & Sweet, 1992). Family therapists can therefore employ concepts that transcend two cultures in order to promote change and resolution. This type of family therapy recognizes the importance of the fit between a therapeutic ideology and a family/cultural tradition (Hodges, 1989).

The "importance of visual mode should be noted—for a number of Native American languages, the verb 'to learn' is a combination of the verbs 'to see' and 'to remember'" (Tafoya, 1994, p. 28). Therefore, concrete and active behavior, rather than insight, is stressed in traditional Native American healing. In working with Native American families, therapists would be wise to use therapeutic approaches that are directive but open-ended, such as those that are strategically oriented.

Arab Americans

Arab Americans are a fast growing and mosaic group with a population that is over three quarters immigrant. Most Arab Americans come from Asia, Africa, and the Middle East and make up the largest cohort of Muslims in the United States which is estimated to be between 6 and 8 million people (Al-Krenawi & Graham, 2005). In actual numbers, however, Arab Americans are estimated to be about 1.2 million people (U.S. Census Bureau, 2000).

Arab cultures tend to be of a high context rather than of a low context such as in North American society. Therefore, Arab Americans as a group usually differ significantly from traditional Americans in that they emphasize social stability and "the collective over the individual" as well as a "slower pace of social change" (p. 301).

The family is also the most significant element in most Arab American subcultures with the individual's life dominated by family and family relations. As such, "people rely on family connections for influence, power, position, and security" (p. 304). Overall, there is a patriarchal structure, with husbands the undisputed head of the household and husbands subordinate to their own fathers who in turn defer to the authority of the head of the clan.

Therapeutic Treatment of Arab Americans

When working with Arab Americans, especially immigrants, it is crucial for family therapists to remember that there is a sharp delineation of gender roles in such families. Furthermore, patriarchal patterns of authority, conservative sexual standards, and the importance of self-sacrifice for the greater good of the family prevail. There is also an emphasis on the importance of honor and shame since people in Arab cultures only seek outside help from so-called helpers or doctors as a last resort (Abudabbeth & Aseel, 1999; Al-Krenawi & Graham, 2005). Complicating matters even more is the fallout, tension, and distrust from September 11, 2001 (Beitin & Allen. 2005).

Clinical recommendations for working with such families include:

- being aware of the cultural context in which the family operates
- being mindful of the issue of leadership and the importance that authority figures play in the life of the family
- being attentive to the part that the family, especially the extended family, plays in decision making

- being sensitive to the large part culture plays as "an active and tangible coparticipant in treatment" (Al-Krenawi & Graham, 2005, p. 308)
- being conscious of the fact that a strength-based approach to treatment is both desirable and works better
- being active as a therapist and balancing the role so as not to be seen as a rescuer or a threat

From conducting extensive qualitative interviews with Arab Americans, Beitin and Allen (2005) suggest specific ways of helping Arab American couples and their families. The first of their interventions focuses on exploring identity, especially creating a new meaning that includes being both Arab and American instead of getting trapped into thinking that the choice is an either/or decision. In focusing on identity, a genogram can be used to assess couple and family strengths both in the present and ancestrally.

In addition, Beitin and Allen (2005) propose that therapists concentrate on couple dynamics which is difficult to do because of contrasting sex roles. Nevertheless, in deftly looking at the couple relationship, the therapist can help each spouse find needed support.

Finally, family therapists can help Arab American couples by helping them access religious and other groups where they can find support and become members of a larger community that is dealing with issues of acculturation as they are.

European Americans

European Americans are sometimes referred to under the category of "**White**" due to their skin color. "In the past and even today, having white skin is assumed to grant an individual membership into a privileged group" (Alessandria, 2002, p. 57). However, what most people equate with White is White Anglo-Saxon Protestant (**WASP**) ideals. Yet, all Whites are not WASPs, nor do they all have the same value system. European Americans are diverse, just like other groups, and come from various countries and cultures such as France, Germany, Italy, Sweden, Hungary, Ireland, and Greece. Some groups of European Americans, such as Italian, Slavic, and Irish immigrant groups have even experienced racist treatment from other European-American groups (Hartigan, 1997).

While the popular assumption is that most European Americans embrace WASP values such as rugged individualism, mastery over nature, competitiveness, and Christianity, that is not necessarily the case. "Italian and Irish cultures are more collectivistic than the WASP culture" and "are expressive, though in different ways, which is different from the WASP value of self-restraint" (Alessandria, 2002, p. 58). In addition to the differences within European-American cultures, there are "similarities between European American groups and other groups. Vontress, Johnson, and Epp (1999) provided the example of a middle-class African American and a middle-class European American being more alike than a middle-class European American and a middle-class Russian-born White American" (Alessandria, 2002, p. 58).

Therapeutic Treatment of European Americans

Given within-group differences of European Americans, no one family therapy approach fits them best. Rather, like other cultural groups, client-families need to be worked with in the context of their lives. Vontress et al. (1999) recommend an existential approach with all families since it focuses on their uniqueness. Patterson (1996) takes a more Rogerian and experiential stand and espouses universal qualities such as genuineness, empathic understanding, and structuring be employed.

However, different approaches may work for select groups better than others. Some European-American families may be more comfortable with Bowen therapy or Narrative therapy since both focus a good deal on individuals and are cognitive more than affective. Seeing beyond the stereotype of "whiteness" to what treatment is best for the family is as demanding with this cultural group as with any other.

Guidelines for Selecting Treatment Approaches in Working with Culturally Diverse Families

Two main approaches are used in working with culturally diverse families. The first is the culture-specific model; the second is the universal perspective model. The **culture-specific model** emphasizes the values, beliefs, and orientation of different ethnic cultural groups (Sue, 1994). Most courses offered in higher education reflect this model. In such an approach, students memorize cultural variations among groups. Although this knowledge may be extremely valuable for therapists working with some families, it has its drawbacks. Basically, the culture-specific model may become unwieldy and may lead to stereotyping in which group characteristics, instead of unique characteristics, are singled out.

The **universal perspective model** is more general. It assumes that counseling approaches already developed can be applied with minor changes to different cultural groups. Cultural differences are recognized from a family systems perspective. This approach also attempts to "identify human processes that are similar, regardless of ethnicity or cultural backgrounds" (Sue, 1994, p. 19). The only problem is that this way of working with culturally diverse families may be too general to be of any real use to a therapist.

The task of finding one approach that is always useful in working with culturally diverse families is next to impossible. However, a number of general guidelines can help family therapists choose an appropriate approach for working with specific families.

A broad guideline for therapists to use in selecting an intervention strategy is to assess whether the family's difficulties are mainly internal or external. If the problems are primarily internal, such as a failure to communicate effectively, well-established theoretical approaches may be employed. On the other hand, if the concerns are external, such as racism, the therapist may need to shift to a culture-specific way of helping.

Another guideline is to determine the family's degree of acculturation. Families that are more "Americanized" are generally open to a wider range of theoretical approaches than are the families of those who are new immigrants or only second-generation.

A third guideline to use in working with culturally diverse families is to explore their knowledge of family therapy and their commitment to resolving their problems or finding solutions. If the family is unsophisticated about mental health services and pressed for time, the therapist is wise to use both educational and/or direct, brief theory-driven treatments, such as behavioral family therapy, solution-focused therapy, or structural family therapy. Otherwise, a culture-specific approach may be employed.

A fourth guideline for choosing an approach for culturally diverse families is to find out what has been tried and what is preferred. By determining what has been tried, therapists can devise methods that are appropriate and that overcome resistance. Preference is important to the establishment of rapport and effectiveness of treatment. "There are certain culture-preferred patterns for families to cope with problems" (Tseng & Hsu, 1991, p. 107). Upwardly mobile African-American families, for example, gravitate toward dependence on extended family members during times of high stress (McAdoo, 1982). In working with these families, therapists should include extended family members.

Role of the Therapist

For family therapists to be competent in working with culturally diverse families, they must examine their own biases and values (Ma, 2005). This examination must be conducted on both an intellectual and an emotional level (Sue & Sue, 2002). Research indicates that some majority-culture therapists may minimize or avoid the impact of societal expectations on cultural minority families (Rowe, Bennett, & Atkinson, 1994). Therefore, it is crucial for these family therapists to examine their thinking and feelings in regard to families whose cultural heritage differs from theirs. In general, culturally skilled family therapists are:

- aware and sensitive to their own cultural heritage and to valuing and respecting differences
- comfortable with differences that exist between themselves and their clients in terms of race and beliefs
- sensitive to circumstances (personal biases, stage of ethnic identity, sociopolitical influences, etc.) that may dictate referral of a family
- knowledgeable of their own racist attitudes, beliefs, and feelings (Sue & Sue, 2002)

After family therapists have dealt constructively with themselves, they are then able to fulfill vital roles in working with culturally diverse families.

> One obvious question is how different styles of family therapy (e.g., more or less active, directive, collaborative, strategic, interpretive, etc.) intersect with the cultural or ethnic values that families bring to the therapy room. It is reasonable to expect that cultural values differentially affect family members' expectations for the therapist's behavior, their communication patterns in the session, and their perceptions of the therapeutic alliance. (Friedlander, Wildman, Heatherington, & Skowron, 1994, p. 411)

An initially important role of family therapists is to be concurrently culturally sensitive and open to themselves and to the families with whom they work (Franklin, 1993). If family therapists are not attuned and responsive to specific aspects of families, stereotyping may occur to the detriment of everyone involved (Tseng & Hsu, 1991). A lack of openness restricts the topics that can be discussed and the good that can be achieved through family therapy.

A second role of family therapists is to help culturally diverse families acknowledge and deal with their thoughts and emotions. For example, many of these families suppress anger and manifest depression. Although white, Anglo-Saxon, Protestant (WASP) families are most known for the suppression of thoughts and feelings, other cultural groups, such as Asian Americans, also utilize this approach (Tseng & Hsu, 1991). It is important that where and when appropriate, cognitions and emotions are expressed and therapeutically dealt with.

A third role of family therapists is to help culturally diverse families acknowledge and celebrate their heritages. "It is essential for clinicians to consider how ethnicity intersects with the life cycle and to encourage families to take active responsibility for carrying out the rituals in their ethnic or religious group(s) to mark each phase" (Carter & McGoldrick, 1988, p. 25). By being true and loyal to their pasts, culturally diverse families can deal better with the present.

A fourth role of family therapists is to help culturally diverse families move through and adjust to family life stages in the healthiest way possible. This means helping them become aware of, accept, and function in new family life cycle roles, whether in a nuclear or extended family.

To be effective with culturally diverse families, family therapists would do well to remember the acronym **ESCAPE** (Boynton, 1987). This symbolic word stands for four major investments therapists must make: (1) engagement with families and process, (2) sensitivity to culture, (3) awareness of family potential, and (4) knowledge of the environment.

Process and Outcome

The process of family therapy with culturally diverse families is one that takes into consideration the uniqueness and common components of each family and culture. Process has an impact on outcome. Similarly, cultural patterns and traditions have an impact on families, and families have an influence on cultures (Tseng & Hsu, 1991).

Initial Phase of Working with Culturally Diverse Families

Working with culturally diverse families requires that the family therapist first establish rapport. This may be done in a number of ways, but it could be problematic because many "ethnic minority Americans find it difficult to trust a family therapist who represents the majority system" (Ho, 1987, p. 255). One way to broach this barrier is for family therapists to define their roles clearly and early in the initial session. By so doing, they set the stage for future relationships.

A second way to establish rapport is through office furnishings and decorations. If family therapists show they have a broad knowledge and appreciation for cultural differences, families who exemplify these characteristics will feel much more comfortable. They are also likely to be more trusting.

A third way of helping culturally diverse families is for family therapists to respect the family hierarchy (Minuchin, 1974). This means talking to the person of highest status first, usually the husband/father, and then to others in the family. Such a procedure demonstrates an appropriate personal/family interest.

A final way to help culturally diverse families become a part of the therapeutic process is for therapists to set the rules of operation (Napier & Whitaker, 1978). This type of action alleviates anxiety and gives families an indication of where therapy will lead.

Middle Phase of Working with Culturally Diverse Families

After family therapists have earned the respect, trust, and faith of culturally diverse families, they can begin to help these families deal with their problems. This middle phase of the process involves setting a mutually agreed on focus and goal for families. This process usually involves families and therapists working together in a consensual manner. In this phase, therapists must be patient and help family members be as specific as possible.

A number of techniques can be employed at this time to help families reach a productive outcome, for example, stressing family values, using reframing, or even employing a therapist-helper, such as a grandparent or family friend (Ho, 1987). All of these techniques are meant to utilize resources within families for promoting change without violating their cultural heritage.

Final Phase of Working with Culturally Diverse Families

In the last phase of process and outcome, family therapists evaluate with culturally diverse families what has been achieved and what still needs to be accomplished. This phase focuses on the abilities that family members have to work in harmony with each other to accomplish a task. It draws families closer together through formal or informal celebrations. The ways in which families made their changes are highlighted so that the model of interacting can be utilized again.

Summary and Conclusion

The multidimensional aspects of working with culturally diverse families were covered in this chapter. As the United States has become a country of increased diversity, family therapists are finding it critical and demanding to become competent in helping families from many backgrounds. This does not mean that family therapists must learn specific information about all cultures, for cultures are broad-based entities and have many subtle differences. However, it does mean that therapists must be aware that the treatment of families and their concerns are often culture specific. Approaches that may be applicable to one society may not be appropriate in another (Ma, 2005). Thus family therapists must know where to find suitable information and what guidelines they should follow if they are to be of assistance to families that clearly differ from those they have previously known.

While culturally diverse families, especially those that are minorities, face most of the same life situations other families encounter, they generally differ in their stress levels. These families often encounter barriers, such as prejudice or limited access to services, in resolving problems and dilemmas. Thus, the dynamics affecting culturally diverse families differ from those that other families face.

In working with culturally diverse families, therapists must be sensitive to their own backgrounds and those of their client-families. Furthermore, they must become innovative and experienced in applying theories to specific situations. They should obtain supervision and specialized educational training when needed. Family therapists must also be accepting of themselves and others. Otherwise, culturally diverse families are labeled pathological and are not helped. Successful treatment of most culturally diverse families depends on their ability to tap nontraditional centers of help. Using extended family members or institutions, such as the church or a club, may provide families with a sense of empowerment and connectedness as well as assistance. Finally, therapists need to be guided by specificity so that they make appropriate cultural interventions.

Gay and lesbian families are emerging from being invisible to being families therapists will work with and help. The gay and lesbian culture is imbedded in most other family cultures. African-American, Asian-American, Hispanic/Latino, Native American, Arab

American, and European-American families are visible cultural families that all share common and unique concerns. In selecting approaches to employ with these families, therapists need to consider the degree of acculturation, the individual/family life stages, and the level of understanding and commitment to family therapy.

The role of the therapist is to be sensitive and sensible when working with culturally diverse families. Also, family therapists need to realize that the process of assisting these types of families is a process that has a beginning, middle, and final phase in which some interventions are more appropriate than others in achieving a positive outcome. Overall, "family therapy has a great deal of promise in working with ethnic minority families, but it needs to be modified to include a comprehensive understanding of the diverse entities we call families" (Sue, 1994, p. 21).

Summary Table

Working with Culturally Diverse Families

Culturally diverse families have always been a part of American society, but often they have been cut off physically and psychologically from mainstream society.

As American culture becomes more diverse, family therapists must learn to work with families within their cultural context.

When culture is ignored families are misunderstood or pathologized.

What Is a Culture?

Culture is a broadly defined term referring to the customary beliefs, social forms, and traits of a group.

Race is more narrowly defined as primarily a biological term.

Ethnicity is a sociological concept that is used to classify people according to a common origin or background.

Dynamics Associated with Culturally Diverse Families

Culturally diverse families face the same pressures as other families, but they are affected in qualitatively and quantitatively different ways.

Certain family life cycle events have more impact on some families than others.

Unique traditions, distinctions in appearance, and access to mental health services can adversely affect culturally diverse families.

Issues within Culturally Diverse Families

Family therapists cannot become experts in all cultures. Instead they must acquire more general abilities to work with culturally diverse families. The following factors determine the effectiveness of family therapists:

- sensitivity (i.e., the ability to be open, rather than "culturally encapsulated")
- experience (i.e., social life experience with and knowledge of specific cultural backgrounds)
- acceptance (i.e., personal/professional comfortableness)

- ingenuity (i.e., the willingness to try innovative methods)
- specificity (i.e., the ability to assess the strengths/weaknesses of a particular family)
- intervention (i.e., the active involvement of challenging intolerance with systems)

Approaches for Treating Culturally Diverse Families

Gay and Lesbian Families

Gay and lesbian families are becoming increasingly visible in American society.

These families must overcome negative and detrimental stereotypes.

Until recently not much research had been conducted on these families.

As a group, gay and lesbian families are intergenerational. There is also a cycle to gay and lesbian family life.

Gay and lesbian families vary greatly and, as with other minority-culture groups, these families suffer from a lack of affirmative role models and social support.

Therapy with gay and lesbian families must start with therapists examining themselves in regard to conscious and unconscious thoughts and feelings about these families since most therapists are heterosexual.

Externally, family therapists should help gay and lesbian families deal with homophobia and restrictive laws as well as their family networks.

Internally, family therapists should help family members explore their relationships and community resources.

Overall, family therapists must be flexible and work on multiple levels, including societal, in treating gay and lesbian families.

African-American Families

Commonalities among African-American families include slave history, skin color, and past discrimination treatment (i.e., racism).

Strengths associated with African-American families include kinship bonds, social networks, religion/spirituality, cooperation, work orientation, and adaptability.

Weaknesses associated with African-American families include internal stresses (e.g., male–female relationships) and external pressures (e.g., discrimination, poverty, single-parenting, less education, high unemployment).

The weaknesses associated with African-American families have a negative systemic impact on these families as a whole and increase prejudice.

African-American families generally benefit when treatment is time-specific, problem-focused, and multigenerational.

Structural, Bowen, and strategic family therapies are often used with African-American families, but there is no prescriptive approach.

Developing trust, understanding African-American culture (including the importance of extended families), and assuring families that therapy is useful in self-help are keys to successful treatment.

Asian-American Families

Asian-American families come from diverse cultural heritages with different languages, histories, and values.

Most of these families have reverence for the family and the elderly.

Confucian and Buddhist philosophies influence roles and relationships.

Family strengths include an emphasis on self-discipline, patience, modesty, and friendliness.

Acculturation into mainstream society is associated with problems in Asian-American families, including issues of loyalty.

Therapy with Asian-American families must take into consideration problems associated with acculturation, such as intergenerational conflict and role confusion. Racism must also be addressed.

Asian-American families usually respond best to treatment when it is problem-focused and empowering.

Family therapists do best when they orient themselves to Asian-American values, establish rapport quickly, and emphasize relationship enhancement and problem-solving therapies.

Hispanic/Latino Families

Hispanic/Latino families, the largest minority group in the United States, trace their roots to Spanish-speaking countries.

Hispanic/Latino families wish to acculturate, do not support traditional roles for women, and are family-oriented.

Weaknesses associated with Hispanic/Latino families include high unemployment, poverty, and low educational attainment.

Strengths associated with Hispanic/Latino families include family loyalty and parent/child dedication.

The treatment of Hispanic/Latino families includes developing knowledge about their culture, assessing the relationship between financial factors and intrafamily difficulties, and addressing acculturation.

Family therapists work best with Hispanic/Latino families when they are active and direct, and therapy is short-term. Structural and behavioral family therapies are usually appropriately employed.

Native American Families

Native American families are diverse, belonging to 557 federally recognized nations and several hundred state-recognized tribes.

Strengths of these families include an emphasis on harmony, acceptance, cooperation, sharing, and respect for nature/family.

Weaknesses include alcoholism and dysfunctional families as a result of government policies regarding the removal of children.

Successful treatment of Native American families requires sensitivity, cultural knowledge, innovation, and use of certain symbols, for example, the circle.

Indirect questions work best with Native American families. Home-based approaches and a variation of structural family therapy and native healing modalities have also been utilized.

Arab American Families

Arab Americans are a fast growing and mosaic group with a population that is over three quarters immigrant.

Arab cultures tend to be of a high context with an emphasis on social stability, the collective over the individual, and the family.

In general, people rely on family connections for influence, power, position, and security. There is a patriarchal structure to most households.

When working with Arab Americans, especially immigrants, it is crucial for family therapists to remember that there is a sharp delineation of gender roles and an emphasis on the importance of honor and shame.

Interventions focus on exploring identity and finding support both inside and outside the therapeutic setting.

The therapist should be active and play to Arab American culture strengths such as its family system.

European-American Families

European Americans are sometimes referred to under the category of "White" due to their skin color but this group, like others, is quite diverse and even of different hues, religions, and worldviews in regard to individualism and collectivism.

Given within-group differences of European Americans, no one family therapy approach fits them best. Families must be worked with in context.

Existential and experiential approaches work well with many European-American families as do Bowen and Narrative therapies.

Seeing beyond the stereotype to what treatment is best for the family is as demanding with this cultural group as with any other.

Guidelines for Selecting Treatment Approaches in Working with Culturally Diverse Families

Specific approaches for working with culturally diverse families include those that are culture-specific and those that are based on a universal perspective. Other general guidelines family therapists need to master include:

- determining if difficulties are primarily internal or external
- determining the degree of a family's acculturation
- exploring a family's knowledge of family therapy and commitment to problem
- finding out what has been tried

Role of the Therapist

Family therapists must examine their own biases and values before beginning to work with culturally diverse families.

Effective family therapists are aware of their own heritage, comfortable with differences, sensitive to circumstances, and knowledgeable of feelings/attitudes.

Family therapists must be open to themselves and to families to avoid stereotyping.

Family therapists must help families acknowledge their emotions when appropriate.

Family therapists must help families celebrate their cultural heritage.

Family therapists must assist families in dealing successfully with events in the family life cycle.

Process and Outcome

Process has an impact on outcome, just as culture has an influence on families.

In the initial phase of the therapy process, the therapist establishes rapport, builds trust, defines his or her role clearly, makes the family comfortable, shows respect for the family hierarchy, and sets the rules for operation.

In the middle phase of the therapy process, the therapist helps the family focus on goals and achievement of a productive outcome through the use of specific family therapy techniques that are mainstream and innovative.

In the final phase of the therapy process, the therapist helps the family evaluate achievements and celebrate changes.

CHAPTER 15

Working with Substance-Related Disorders, Domestic Violence, Child Abuse, and Infidelity

As an old dog, he has survived
the marriage of his master to a Nutmeg woman,
the first clumsy steps of sandy-haired toddlers,
and the crises of moves around eastern states.

So in the gentle first light of morning
he rolls leisurely in piles of yesterday's clothes
left over from last night's baths by little boys,
an act of independence.

Then slowly, with a slight limp,
he enters his daily routine,
approaching the kitchen at the breakfast rush hour
to quietly consume spilled cereal
and dodge congested foot traffic.

Sure of his place in a system of change
he lays down to sleep by an air vent.
A family grows around him.

Gladding, 1991d

buse of any kind within a family is tragic. Like a plague that cripples and kills, abuse has been pervasive through time and cultures. It has affected families in different life cycles and in distinct ways. It has taken a number of forms—substance, mental, and physical—and has involved a variety of people—spouses, siblings, the elderly, and children—in different relationships and stages of life. The impact of abuse on lives is long-lasting. The results are multiple and may be manifested in behavioral, psychological, sexual, or even economical ways. Domestic violence costs U.S. employers approximately $100 million a year in lost wages, sick leave, absenteeism, and nonproductivity (Chronister & McWhirter, 2003).

For some families abuse is an entity from which they never recover. For other families, the healing process is painful and the memory is permanent. In short, abuse is a blight that stains and puts a strain on a family even after actions that were abusive have outwardly disappeared. In this chapter three forms of abuse, substance-related, domestic violence, and child abuse, are examined, along with infidelity, in regard to the nature and appropriate treatment of each. Substance-related disorders provide a context for an overall model in this chapter of how to engage families into therapy. However, in treating abuse or infidelity, each case, like every family, is unique.

Substance-Related Disorders and Families

Substance-related disorders are "disorders related to the taking of a drug of abuse (including alcohol), to the side effects of medication, and to toxin exposure" (American Psychiatric Association, 1994, p. 175). For diagnostic purposes, substances are grouped into 11 classes: "alcohol; amphetamines or similar acting sympathomimetics; caffeine; cannabis; cocaine; hallucinogens; inhalants; nicotine; opioids; phencyclidine (PCP) … and sedatives, hypnotics, or anxiolytics" (p. 175).

Substance-related disorders due to the side effects of medication and to toxin exposure will not be covered here because problems regarding substances for most families tend to be associated with the taking of a drug of abuse. Nearly 60% of the world's production of illegal drugs and a substantial percentage of legal alcohol products are consumed in the United States. Approximately 1 in 11 Americans suffers from severe addictive problems, and "one third of all American families are affected by alcohol problems" (Daw, 1995, p. 19). The rate of illicit drug use is 12.3 percent among American Indians or Alaska Natives, 9.3 percent among African Americans, 7.2 percent among Hispanics (all races), 8.1 percent among Caucasians, and 3.1 percent among Asian Americans (2004 National Survey on Drug Use & Health: Overview, http://www.oas.samhsa.gov/nsduh/2k4nsduh/2k4overview/2k4overview.htm#ch2).

In the particular area of alcohol problems there are two general levels or forms of alcohol use disorders. The first is **alcohol abuse**, "a problem pattern where the drinking interferes with work, school, or home life" in addition to other difficulties with the law and society (Stanton, 1999, p. 1). The second is **alcohol dependency** where the person is unable to control the drinking even after trying.

Regardless of the level or form, as a group substance-related disorders are considered to be family based and supported with individuals in families abusing various substances for a variety of reasons, for example, as a way of coping with crisis or connecting with one another (Schroeder, 1989). The literature shows that the family plays a role in the development and maintenance of substance abuse (Slesnick & Prestopnik, 2004). Tragically, instead of helping family members relate, substance-related disorders have a profound negative effect on individual, couple, and family life cycles. Developmental stages are altered significantly. For example, young adults going off to college may find they are unable to assimilate into the academic and social environment and make necessary adjustments (Cutler & Radford, 1999).

Similarly, families of addicts are often stuck in a lifestyle that promotes dependency of the young and a false sense of identity known as **pseudo-individuation**. Young people in such circumstances lack basic coping skills and fail to achieve real identity. As a result, they become "competent within a framework of incompetence" (Stanton et al., 1982, p. 19). They become marginalized in society and noncontributors to it. As the research shows, "alcohol and other substance abuse is the cause of more deaths, illnesses, and disabilities than any other preventable health condition, and consequently undermines family life, the economy, and public safety" (Chan, 2003, p. 129).

Manifestation of Substance-Related Disorders

Substance-related disorders impact couples, families, and the individuals within them as well as society in general. While the over 14 million persons in the United States (6.3% of the population) with a substance-related disorder may think that taking a substance is only an intrapersonal problem, they are wrong (Rowe & Liddle, 2003). The behaviors that go with substance abuse or dependence permeate and penetrate into other relationships and impact the actions of everyone who comes in contact with the person who has the disorder. "Estimates of the economic costs of mental and substance abuse disorders in the United States are in excess of $200 billion per year" (Evans et al., 2005, p. 621).

Couple and Family Manifestations

Couples and families deal with substance-related disorders in a number of ways. Unhealthy or dysfunctional methods of working with the situation and person(s) involved are usually tried initially and are displayed through various strategies (Elkin, 1984).

One way couples and families may deal detrimentally with substance-related disorders is to have the nonabusing members of the couple or family shield the substance-related abuser from the negative consequences of his or her actions. By doing so, the abuser does not get a true picture of the seriousness of his or her actions (Meyers, Apodaca, Flicker, & Slesnick, 2002).

Another way couples and families deal unsuccessfully with the seriousness of a substance-related disorder problem is through denial. In such a scenario, the couple or family pretends that the existence of the disorder is not present in their household. A spouse may make excuses for his or her mate by saying that the substance abuser's actions were due to other circumstances, such as fatigue or frivolity. This strategy is somewhat akin to not acknowledging an elephant in one's living room and is similar to shielding the abuser from the consequences of his or her actions.

A third way couples and families deal inappropriately with the existence of a substance-related disorder is through the expression of negative feelings. Members of the couple or family, except for the abuser(s), experience a plethora of unpleasant emotions such as fear, anger, shame, guilt, resentment, insecurity, confusion, and rejection. When a couple or family is caught up in such a whirlwind of affect, they relate to each other and to the outside world in a despondent and anxious manner.

Still a fourth way for couples and families to maladaptively cope with a substance-related disorder is for members to assume roles that allow them and others to survive. Among these roles, according to Murphy (1984) are:

- the **enabler**, a spouse or other family member on whom the substance abuser is most dependent and who allows a substance abuser to continue and become worse
- the **family hero**, an adult or oldest child who functions to provide self-worth for the family
- the **scapegoat**, often a child who attempts to distract the family focus away from the substance abuser by acting out in a disruptive manner and being blamed for the family's problems
- the **lost child**, usually a child in the family who suffers from rejection and loneliness and who offers a substance-abuser family relief
- the **family clown**, who is often the youngest member of the family and whose function is to provide the family with humor and thus reduce tension

A fifth way for couples and families to disastrously cope with substance-related disorders is for the couple or family itself to deteriorate. In these cases, members of couples and families do such things as drink or take drugs together. This type of behavior is not common but it does occur especially as children in families grow into adolescents. Usually, within a couple or family the consumption of a harmful substance is centered around an adult or adults as in the play *Who's Afraid of Virginia Woolf.*

Another pattern that highlights a bad strategy for handling a substance-related disorder is for couples and families to focus all of their energy on the substance abuser. In this type of reaction, the individuals and families as a whole may spend the majority of their time begging, pleading, blaming, or shaming a substance-abusing or dependent family member for all of their problems. A son might spend countless hours trying to help his father stay sober in the belief that the family would become a warm and loving entity if that happened.

A final unfortunate way a substance-related disorder may be handled by couples or families is for individuals in such relationships to misuse or abuse not only the substance in question but also the family resources. Everyone suffers physically because of a lack of money and effort to purchase essential necessities. A popular book of the late 1990s, *Angela's Ashes* (McCourt, 1996), describes the impact of such a substance abuse system, in this case alcohol. *Angela's Ashes* and other literature reveal that family members, especially children, can be severely affected in multiple ways because of substance-related disorders.

Individual Manifestations

In addition to couples and families showing the effects of substance-related disorders, individuals within families also display manifestations. Children may behave confused about their self-identity and self-worth. As a result, they may become controlling in their interpersonal relationships as a way of gaining security (Schroeder, 1989). Children who live in an environment where at least one parent is an abuser of alcohol are twice as likely as their counterparts to develop "social and emotional problems," such as low school achievement and trouble with the law (Lawson, 1994, p. 213). They may also feel less attached and bonded to others and therefore have more difficulties than most people in intimate relationships such as marriage.

Adults, having grown up in families where there was a substance-related disorder, may also spend considerable time and energy attempting to resolve issues related to the dysfunctional nature of their families of origin. Many adults, for example, coming from an alcohol abuse family environment struggle in dealing with feelings of numbness, a sense of guilt, confusion, denial, and compulsive behavior (Black, 1990). Their intrapersonal relations with themselves and interpersonal dynamics with others are affected and again they may be unable to form long-lasting and intimate relationships.

Engaging Substance-Related Disorder Families in Treatment

Family-based treatments are currently recognized as among the most effective approaches for treating substance abuse (Meyers et al., 2002; Rowe & Liddle, 2003). However, even though family therapy is one of the preferred methods of working with families who have substance-related problems, especially where alcohol is the primary drug (Edwards & Steinglass, 1995), only a small percentage of family therapists report treating such families (Northey, 2002). When such treatment is employed, it is usually effective—and when family therapy is appropriately applied, research shows that episodes of harmful drug use are significantly reduced (Whittinghill, 2002). On the other hand, when treatment is not forthcoming the results are almost always negative. The "consequences of not treating a family that has become dysfunctional by the substance abuse of a family member can be disastrous for the family, the chemically dependent individual, or both" (Murphy, 1984, p. 106).

Getting the family to agree to therapy is often a challenge. "The task of engaging an entire family unit from the onset is a very difficult, yet critical component of the family therapy process." This undertaking "may be particularly true when working with minority families because cultural factors can create unique family dynamics that become intertwined with the complex issue of engagement" (Santisteban & Szapocznik, 1994, pp. 9–10).

One way to get the family engaged is to involve **concerned significant others (CSOs)** in the process of treatment. CSOs can be spouses, relatives, or children of the substance abuser or dependent person. It used to be that CSOs would meet with a substance abuser in a surprise meeting known as "the intervention." Here the abuser would be confronted by the CSOs about all of the problems his or her behaviors caused. In place of that approach, many CSOs now meet with therapists to learn behavioral skills designed to influence the substance abuser's use of substances, with the ultimate goal of getting the abuser to enter treatment (Meyers et al., 2002). The success of the CSO strategy has proven to be effective in engaging initially unmotivated problem drinkers in treatment (Miller, Meyers, & Tonigan, 1999). Rates of success for such an approach are high (64%) and have proved to be better than interventions from other professional groups. Treatment engagement rates are higher for CSOs who are parents than for spouses.

Another way to engage families in the process of treatment is to widen "the focus of attention from providing therapy once a family brings itself to the clinic to considering that the treatment begins prior to the first clinic visit" (Santisteban & Szapocznik, 1994, pp. 11–12). With this emphasis, the interaction between the therapist and the family is included in the formation of a therapeutic system. A de-emphasis is placed on the therapist as the ally of the family member who made the initial call. Instead, issues in diagnosing potential obstacles to engaging the family include those involving the family system (e.g., characteristics and/or interactional patterns of the family) and issues involving the therapeutic system (e.g., the interface/interaction between the family system and the therapist).

The developmental issue that may present itself most blatantly in this early stage of treatment is the status of the identified patient in the family system. The **identified patient (IP)** is usually an extremely powerful member of the family whose development has been arrested and who is generally resistant to therapy because to engage in the process is to agree to someone else's agenda and weaken one's own position of power. If such families are going to be brought successfully into family therapy, especially if the IP is an adolescent, the therapist must contact the identified patient directly and immediately. In this contact, the therapist makes it clear that he or she "would like to explore the IP's goals" (Santisteban & Szapoczik, 1994, p. 16).

To engage a substance-related disorder family to the fullest, the family therapist may also call the person in the family who is most disengaged, often a father, or another family member who is "allegedly unwilling" to enter family therapy. A direct conversation may be persuasive in helping such a family member realize that he or she has much to contribute to the therapeutic process. Likewise, if a family is fearful or suspicious of where therapy will lead, the therapist must reframe the process so that the family is in agreement as to the specific nature of what will be worked on so they will feel more in control.

Approaches for Treating Substance-Related Disorder Families After Engagement

Individuals and families who are engaged in substance-related activities are often difficult to treat. Many have a high degree of resistance to therapy, and relapse may be frequent with up to 90% having one relapse during the first 4 years following treatment (Diamond, 2000). To help rehabilitate these individuals and their families once they have been engaged, therapists are wise to use systems and resources in the community in which these people live and to realize that recovery is a matter of "phasing" in treatment to fit the developmental readiness of the family (Berenson, 1992). This **community reinforcement approach (CRA)** is among the top five treatments for substance abuse when examined empirically (Meyers et al., 2002). Recovery in the CRA model is a process that occurs in and with systems support and in stages.

Areas that must be addressed within couples and families are issues dealing with physical, emotional, social, and vocational impairments. All of these areas influence each other systematically. For example, physical factors, such as excessive drinking and the behaviors that accompany it, such as undue disorderliness, spill over and impact emotional, social, and vocational arenas of the family. The reverse occurs too. Fortunately, there are a number of ways to address these family dynamics (Lewis, 1994).

Probably the most important dimension to initially address in families who are in treatment for substance-related problems is "environmental influences" (Lawson, 1994, p. 213). **Environmental influences** include the physical aspects of a family's life, such as getting the substance abuse behavior stopped. An example would be getting the alcoholic "dry." This process may involve a detoxification center where the abuser is helped physically and psychologically to give up the substance he or she has been abusing. The theoretical base that is used from this perspective is a **multisystemic framework of therapy**. This approach is based on social ecology "in which individuals are viewed as being nested within a complex of interconnected systems that encompass individual, family, and extrafamilial (peer, school, neighborhood) factors. Behavior is seen as the product of the reciprocal interplay between the family and these systems and the relations of the systems with each other. Multisystemic treatments are based on the recognition that substance use and other related problem behavior derive commonly from many sources of influence and occur in the context of multiple systems" (Slesnick & Prestopik, 2004, p. 244).

Once substance-related behavior, such as abuse, stops, then the family can enter a new phase of treatment such as determining when and where they interact as well as how they engage in activities both within and outside the environment in which they live. These physical influences can be manipulated more easily early on in the therapeutic process and can help the family realize the power of simple change such as rearranging times when tasks are done or assigning different individuals to complete essential jobs needed to keep the family functioning.

In addition to making environmental changes, clinicians must help spouses and individual family members, as well as the family, with emotional, social, and vocational issues. In situations where an adolescent is the identified patient, a primary role of the family therapist is to make an assessment and decision about the use of the substance an adolescent may be abusing. That task is required for members of this population because drug consumption can take three forms with adolescents: experimenting, dependence, or addiction (Schroeder, 1989). If the adolescent is merely experimenting, issues surrounding consumption can be addressed in an easier and more straightforward manner than if the adolescent has become dependent on or addicted to a substance. In the case of dependence and addiction, dysfunctional behaviors in families arise and professional intervention is both warranted and needed.

Among other issues that must be highlighted in addressing families where there are substance-related problems are feelings (e.g., anger, intimacy), defense mechanisms (e.g., denial, projection), and work by individuals in these families. In the process, therapists help the family and its members take responsibility for behaviors that before have been minimized, excused, or enabled (Krestan & Bepko, 1988; Meyers et al., 2002). They help the family get back on track as a functional system by getting "involved in the treatment process" and "helping the abusing member overcome … addiction, rather than serving as a force that maintains it" (Van Deusen, Stanton, Scott, Todd, & Mowatt, 1982, p. 39).

Ways in which therapists assist families are often tied to specific family theories (Todd & Selekman, 1991). Among the most prominent approaches that have been used with substance-related disorder families are structural-strategic, Bowen, behavioral, Adlerian, and multifamily therapies. Increased emphasis has also been placed on preventive efforts that involve marshaling community resources as well (Bry, 1994).

Structural-Strategic Family Therapy

Early in its history, family therapy addressed the problem of substance abuse as a family systems problem. The documentation of the effectiveness of family therapy forms of treatment for drug abuse and addiction was particularly well demonstrated in the structural/strategic emphasis of Stanton et al. (1982) and Todd and Selekman (1991). The meticulous work of these researchers underscores the importance of family dynamics in such situations, and the crucial nature of involving the entire family in treatment.

Among the recommended models for treatment and prevention of substance-related family disorders from a structural-strategic approach are the following. Treatment should initially address excessive drinking or other forms of substance abuse in order to get it stopped. Such a process might mean getting inpatient detoxification, enrolling appropriate family members in Alcoholics Anonymous (AA) or Al-Anon, and mobilizing support networks. After the abuse of substances has come to an end, then treatment based on clear thinking and a drug-free mind can begin, using a combination of structural/strategic family therapy methods.

Structural family therapy may be used just by itself as well. In working with a multigenerational Hispanic stepfamily experiencing alcohol dependence, Wycoff and Cameron (2000) found that "because structural family therapy is action oriented … and encourages active participation by the counselor, it lends itself nicely to the educative and supportive facilitation process needed during the early recovery period for the alcohol dependent family" (p. 52). Family mapping, searching for family strengths, the use of praise, and respecting as well as working within cultural traditions produced needed results in the modification of the family structure.

Bowen Family Therapy

Effective therapy for alcohol-abuse families may also take a Bowen family therapy approach (Bowen, 1974). Bowen theory is especially helpful as a component in implementing a program that deals with codependency treatment (Gibson & Donigian, 1993). In **codependency,** there is a dynamic in a family of overresponsibility (the codependent family member, usually a spouse) and underresponsibility (the substance abuser) (Morgan, 1998). However, in the Bowen model of family therapy, emphasis is placed on the differentiation of oneself and achieving an interplay between two counterbalancing life forces—individuality and togetherness. The family therapist works with both the substance-related abuser and codependent in the family to help them and the family become balanced. This process is often worked out by toning down the functioning of the overresponsible member (i.e., the codependent), since it is easier to do so than to boost up the behavior of the underresponsible member of the family.

In reaching a balanced state of being, individuals, especially those with low self-esteem such as codependents, learn to distinguish between subjective feelings and objective thoughts. They become more flexible, adaptable, and independent. Through the use of genograms, "I" position statements, and reconnections of emotional cutoffs, codependents gain a greater awareness and understanding of how family patterns developed and have been maintained (Gibson & Donigian, 1993). They gain a greater freedom to change how they relate to all family members and to stop behaving in ways that either make them dependent or that enable someone in the family to be a substance-related abuser.

Behavioral Family Therapy

Behavioral therapies have produced good results in treating couples and families with a substance-related problem, particularly alcohol abuse (Chan, 2003; Meyers et al., 2002). A number of behaviors can be specified and modified in behaviorally oriented approaches to treatment by incorporating basic behavioral methods such as reinforcement, modeling, rehearsal, and extinction.

Written behavioral contracts may be particularly effective. These contracts have a number of common elements that make them useful. In these documents the drinking behavior goal is made explicit. Furthermore, specific behaviors that each spouse can incorporate to help achieve this goal are detailed. The contract provides alternative behaviors to negative interactions about drinking, too. "Finally, the agreement decreases the nonalcoholic spouse's anxiety and need to control the alcoholic and his or her drinking" (O'Farrell, 1996, p. 106).

Adlerian Therapy

The Adlerian approach to working with substance-related abusers in families is premised on the idea that members of such families are discouraged. Treatment then is designed to increase the social interest of family members, particularly those who may be most affected by the abuse (Odom, Snow, & Kern, 1999). The problem of substance-related abuse is reframed also from one that is disease focused to one that is socially focused.

One way to increase social interest and consequently the health and functioning of the family is to work with the parents and children in multiple ways. A major avenue of intervention from this perspective is to get parents involved in a group that helps increase their self-esteem as well as their skills. **Systematic Training for Effective Parenting (STEP)** is such a group that can help parents increase their understanding of family relations as well as improve their communications with their children (Dinkmeyer & McKay, 1989). A child who may have been parentified because of the dysfunctioning of the family system may also be used and can serve as a cofacilitator in family therapy. The child can both role play situations in the STEP program and otherwise educate or reeducate parents about what works in family relations (Odom et al., 1999).

Multifamily Therapy

Another way of working with families who have individuals who are substance-related abusers is through **multifamily therapy**. The idea behind multifamily therapy is to treat several families at the same time (Laqueur, 1976). Such treatment is not only cost-effective but is also reported to have a high success rate. In these settings, according to Carl Whitaker, a person may experience his or her dynamics in other families, "whereas the same dynamics could be overwhelming to address in the context of one's own family" (Boylin, Doucette, & Jean, 1997, p. 400).

One of the prime beneficiaries of multifamily therapy are women who often feel more pressure to leave treatment before they are ready because of family obligations. "By attending multifamily therapy, the family gives the client permission to stay in treatment and demonstrates that its members are managing at home without the client" (Boylin et al., 1997, p. 45).

Use of Community Resources and Prevention

Outside community resources are often essential in helping a substance-related abuse family help itself. These resources can be informative as well as supportive of the family as it wrestles with overcoming substance-related abuse. Family members, especially those who may be religiously inclined, can participate in Alcoholics Anonymous (AA), Narcotics Anonymous (NA), and Al-Anon, which complement almost any therapeutic approach (Berenson, 1992; Morgan, 1998). By participating in such groups, family members gain insight into themselves and how their behaviors affect family functioning. They learn from others who have similar experiences and backgrounds how they are coping with substance-related abuse and what works for them.

Prevention from substance-related abuse is a critical element in treatment as well. Prevention is dependent on both keeping a person or family from engaging in the habitual activity of taking substances and on making other activities with reliable positive outcomes (e.g., art, athletics, hobbies, meaningful work) available and central to their lives (Bry, 1994). At its best, prevention involves the substance-related abuse couple or family in community activities. In such an environment, the family becomes more consistent in its effort and sustains it better. Present policies in the United States do not encourage prevention on such a level and, for this reason, more individualized and piecemeal programs prevail. In regard to teen alcohol abuse, forms of prevention that are recommended include:

- giving kids accurate information about alcohol use in an objective way
- presenting information through a 'teen-respected' source

- helping kids say yes to life, not just no to drugs
- parent networking
- setting strict rules about drinking with kids
- continued pressure to "take back the communities" (Daw, 1995, p. 19)

While some of these preventive efforts involve networking and the setting up of structure, such as making rules, they are not usually tied to specific organizations. Until or unless more community resources are made available to help "people from outside the family to support parents' efforts to reduce their adolescents' substance abuse," it is doubtful that the preventive efforts under way for primary prevention in this arena will have more than scattered success (Bry, 1994, p. 21).

Secondary and tertiary prevention for family members of substance-related abusers and substance-related abusers themselves may be more successful. Recovery and prevention programs such as 12-step programs are aimed at keeping substance-related abusers free from the resumption of the habits that harmed their family lives. In addition, family programs, such as Al-Anon, assist family members in both understanding the dynamics involved in substance-related abuse and ways of not enabling the abuser to resume his or her past destructive behavior. Other self-help groups, such as Rational Recovery or Women for Sobriety, can also provide assistance in offering support for substance-related abusers and their families (Lawson, 1994).

Domestic Violence and Families

Domestic violence refers to "aggression that takes place in intimate relationships, usually between adults" (Kemp, 1998, p. 225). It is an attempt by one to "control the thoughts, beliefs, or behaviors of an intimate partner or to punish the partner for resisting one's control" (Peterman & Dixon, 2003, p. 41). The topic is referred to in a number of ways, including "spousal abuse," "partner abuse," and "marital violence." Domestic violence can take many forms, including physical, sexual, psychological, and economic (see Figure 15.1) (Schecter & Ganley, 1995). It is not confined to any economic class, family structure, sexual orientation, race/culture, or social status in society (Lawson, 2003; Peterman & Dixon, 2003; Weitzman, 2000). While there are a number of common forms of domestic violence, such as grabbing, slapping, pushing, and throwing things at one another (O'Leary & Murphy, 1999), the worst form is referred to as **battering**—"violence which includes severe physical assault or risk of serious injury" (Kemp, 1998, p. 225).

Increasing attention is being given to domestic violence in the United States. The reason is that "approximately one-third of all married couples experience physical aggression" (Crespi & Howe, 2000, p. 6). Although some men are the victims of abuse and violence by their mates, the large majority of those assaulted each year are women with between 11% to 16% of women in the United States reporting violent aggression by their partners each year (Lawson, 2003). Those who batter come in "all shapes, sizes, classes, races, and sexual orientation" (Almeida, 2000, p. 23). John Gottman has found, however, that there are basically two types of batterers. The first is violent only within the relationship and is so afraid of abandonment that he monitors his partner's independence and is jealous of her every move, especially any move toward independence, such as getting a job. The second type of batterer is violent with just about everyone. This type of batterer is very belligerent, provocative, and angry (Jencius & Duba, 2003).

Regardless of the type of batterer, about 13% of all murders involve husbands killing their wives, and at least 1.6 million wives are severely beaten by their husbands each year (Gottman

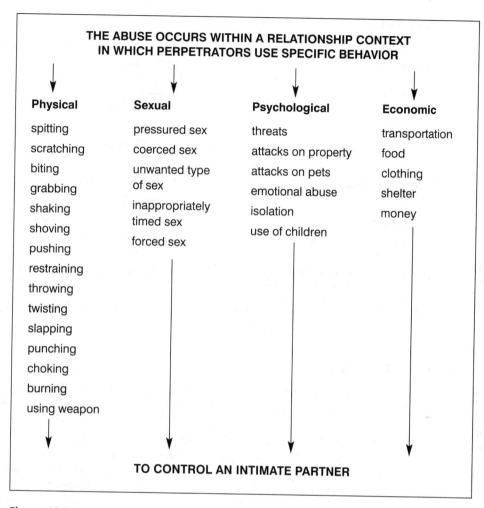

**THE ABUSE OCCURS WITHIN A RELATIONSHIP CONTEXT
IN WHICH PERPETRATORS USE SPECIFIC BEHAVIOR**

Physical	Sexual	Psychological	Economic
spitting	pressured sex	threats	transportation
scratching	coerced sex	attacks on property	food
biting	unwanted type of sex	attacks on pets	clothing
grabbing		emotional abuse	shelter
shaking	inappropriately timed sex	isolation	money
shoving		use of children	
pushing	forced sex		
restraining			
throwing			
twisting			
slapping			
punching			
choking			
burning			
using weapon			

TO CONTROL AN INTIMATE PARTNER

Figure 15.1
Graphic representation of Schecter and Ganley's definition model.

This material was adapted from "Understanding Domestic Violence," by S. Schecter and A. Ganley, in *Domestic Violence: A National Curriculum for Family Preservation Practitioners,* written by Susan Schecter, M.S.W., and Anne L. Ganley, PhD. Copyright © 1995 Family Violence Prevention Fund.

et al., 1995). Even premarital rates of physical violence are high—about 36% (McLaughlin, Leonard, & Senchak, 1992). "Not surprisingly, there is a well-documented association between alcohol intoxication and battering, that is, intoxication accompanies violence." Research indicates "a 60% to 70% rate of alcohol abuse among men who batter" (Wycoff & Cameron, 2000, p. 53). In addition, in a temporal study of alcohol consumption and violence, Fals-Stewart (2003) found severe aggression was 19 times higher when a male partner in a heterosexual relationship had become intoxicated. Other factors that raise the risk of domestic violence are a multigenerational pattern of abuse and a family constellation that reflects a victim-victimization spectrum (Miller, Veltkamp, Lane, Bilyeu, & Elzie, 2002) (see Table 15.1).

Table 15.1
Victim–Victimizer Spectrum

Victim	Victimizer
Isolation from others	History of multigenerational abuse
Feeling of helplessness	Learned violent behavior
Vulnerable	Unstable
Secrecy	Low self-esteem
Indecision	Impulsive
Poor self-confidence	Impaired judgment
Low self-esteem	Narcissistic
Fear, anxiety, depression	Alcohol and/or substance abuse
Impaired ability to judge trustworthiness in others	Control and power seeking
Accommodation to the victimization	Perpetuates continued forms of victimization

From "Care Pathway Guidelines for Assessment and Counseling for Domestic Violence" by T. W. Miller, L. J. Veltkamp, T. Lane, J. Bilyeu, and N. Elzie, 2002, *The Family Journal: Counseling and Therapy for Couples and Families, 10,* p. 44. Reprinted by permission of Sage Publications, Inc.

Assessment of Domestic Violence

Several barriers impede the assessment of the degree of domestic violence that couples and families experience. These barriers include those that are legal, such as court orders that mandate separation of family members from one another, and those that are psychological, such as the stigma that surrounds abuse of this nature.

In assessing domestic violence, one of the first things to realize is that "determining the level and prevalence of violence within the family is extremely difficult," yet important and essential (Rotter & Houston, 1999, p. 59). The reason is that without this knowledge, the therapist will not know how best to work with the family. Yet violent families will go to almost any lengths to keep this family secret hidden. There is a tendency in these families to minimize the amount of violence and its impact on the family and relationships.

Assessing the level of violence may be done in a number of ways. Determining the power imbalance within the family is one place to start. This assessment helps individuals make the transition from violent to nonviolent behavior and assists them in learning what each is. Pence and Paymar (1993) have created two wheels to illustrate the difference: a "power and control wheel" (Figure 15.2), aimed particularly at men, and an "equality wheel" (Figure 15.3), aimed at promoting positive behaviors such as mutuality, respect, and egalitarianism.

Assessment when conducted in an open manner usually results in obtaining the most information. An **open assessment** is one where blame is not a primary emphasis and also one where the therapist emphasizes that the expression of violence in the family hurts the entire family rather than just one person (Almeida, 2000). Therefore, the focus of the assessment centers around dynamics within the family associated with family relationships, such as emotional expression, handling of money, sexuality, and social connections. It is

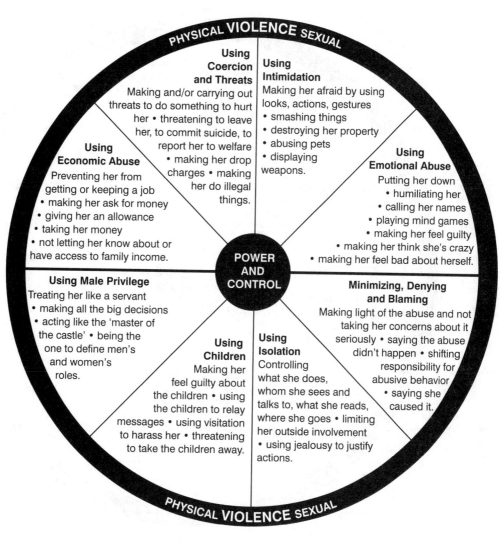

Figure 15.2
Power and control wheel.

From *Education Groups for Men Who Batter,* by E. Pence and M. Paymar. Copyright © 1993 Springer Publishing Company, Inc., New York, 10036. Used by permission.

the interconnection of these aspects of interpersonal life that signals whether there is a harmful power imbalance in the family and therefore gives clues as to what can or should be changed and to what degree.

Approaches for Treating Domestic Violence

Once an assessment of domestic violence is made, various treatment options are available, including those that are individually, group, educationally, and family systems focused.

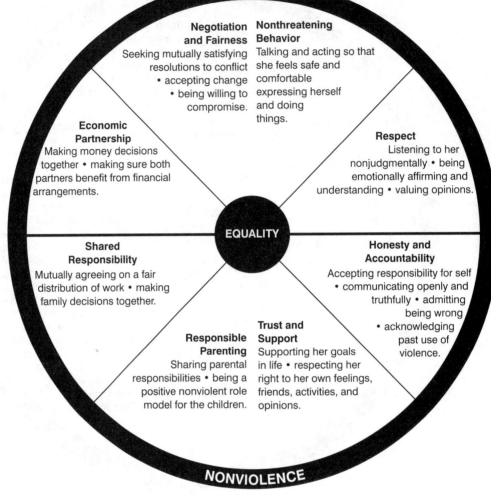

Figure 15.3
Equality wheel.

From *Education Groups for Men Who Batter,* by E. Pence and M. Paymar. Copyright © 1993 Springer Publishing Company, Inc., New York, 10036. Used by permission.

No one approach to treatment addresses all dimensions of partner violence—both developmental and stratified approaches may be used (Lawson, 2003).

In family therapy "two positions have typified popular ideas about responsibility and domestic violence: (1) both parties are equally responsible for the violence; and (2) the perpetuator is unilaterally responsible" (Bograd, 1999, p. 284). The position that a family therapist takes in regard to responsibility influences the type of treatment option chosen.

If the therapist assumes both parties have equal responsibility in spousal abuse and domestic violence cases, then traditional conjoint or couples therapy may be used in some cases. This controversial approach is usually done with "carefully screened couples and appears to be at least as effective as gender-specific treatment approaches" (Stith, Rosen, & McCollum, 2003, p. 418). On the other hand, if the perpetuator is seen as having unilateral responsibility, then an intimate justice theory may be employed that is based on an ethics of accountability from the abuser and is employed on an individual and couple level (Jory & Anderson, 2000; Rotter & Houston, 1999). In the intimate justice approach, it is up to the abuser to recognize that abuse and accountability are related and to thereby make needed changes. In this approach, gender-specific treatment is used often in the form of groups (Stith et al., 2003). The benefits and limitations of both approaches are discussed here.

Conjoint or Couples Therapy

Conjoint therapy involves seeing the couple together. "A primary concern about the wisdom of couples therapy is the woman's safety" (Bograd & Mederos, 1999, p. 293). This concern requires an assessment of safety issues. According to Bograd and Mederos (1999) three conditions must be satisfied to ensure safety:

- the man's participation must be voluntary
- "special agreements about confidentiality must be established," that is, material on domestic violence will not be disclosed by the woman or the therapist until the woman is ready
- "an optimal therapeutic stance must be achieved" (p. 294), that is, the therapist must be able to "create a context of self-protection" (p. 296) because working with domestic violence is often emotionally disturbing, dehumanizing, and intimidating.

In such circumstances couple therapy may work if the following criteria are met:

- There has been only a history of minor and infrequent psychological violence or abuse.
- There are no risk factors for lethality, such as prior use or threat of weapons.
- The man admits to and takes responsibility for abusive behavior and also demonstrates an ongoing commitment to contain his explosive feelings without blaming others or acting them out (Bograd & Mederos, 1999).

In this approach, the couple talks about their wishes as well as the dynamics currently present in their relationships. Through such communication, agreement can be reached as to new or altered ways of behaving and relating (Stith et al., 2003). For couples who have a history of mild-to-moderate partner violence and who freely choose to stay together this approach can be safe and productive (Stith, Rosen, McCollum, & Thomsen, 2004).

Intimate Justice

Intimate justice theory "includes the ethical context of abuse and violence in intimate relationships" (Rotter & Houston, 1999, p. 60). "Intimate justice theory encompasses three ethical dimensions and nine ethical concepts" shown in Figures 15.4 and 15.5 (Jory & Anderson, 1999, p. 350). This theory "encourages therapists to confront, challenge, explore, and educate clients about abuse of power in emotional systems" (p. 350).

Intimate justice theory is akin to solution-based approaches and confronts disempowerment and abuses of power in a partnership while challenging internalized beliefs about how one should treat one's partner (Jory, Anderson, & Greer, 1997). The approach also explores experiences with empowerment, disempowerment, and abuses of power in one's family of

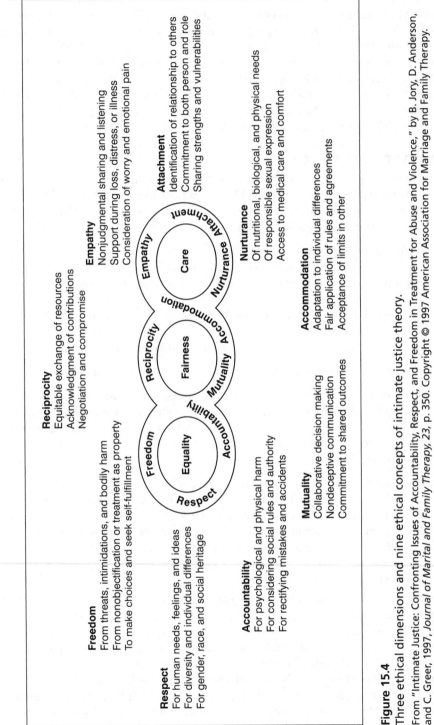

Figure 15.4

Three ethical dimensions and nine ethical concepts of intimate justice theory.

From "Intimate Justice: Confronting Issues of Accountability, Respect, and Freedom in Treatment for Abuse and Violence," by B. Jory, D. Anderson, and C. Greer, 1997, *Journal of Marital and Family Therapy, 23*, p. 350. Copyright © 1997 American Association for Marriage and Family Therapy. Reprinted with permission.

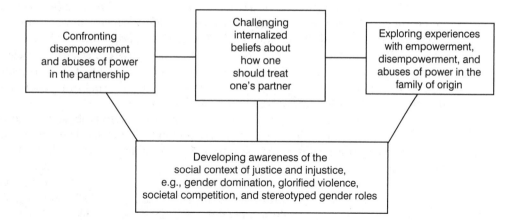

Figure 15.5
Confronting, challenging, and educating clients about abuses of power in emotional systems.

From "Intimate Justice: Confronting Issues of Accountability, Respect, and Freedom in Treatment for Abuse and Violence," by B. Jory, D. Anderson, and C. Greer, 1997, *Journal of Marital and Family Therapy, 23*, p. 350. Copyright © 1997 American Association for Marriage and Family Therapy. Reprinted with permission.

origin. It has been found to be effective as a treatment for abuse in couples who voluntarily enter therapy (Jory & Anderson, 2000). Through knowledge and insight, both behavioral attitudes and behaviors in couples may be modified.

Educational Treatment

Educationally, programs based on intimate justice theory and cognitive behavior theory have also been employed with domestic violence families. One such is the **Duluth model**, which is a cognitive-behavioral model of treatment (Pence & Paymar, 1993). The premise of this model is that people learn violent behaviors because of being reinforced for them in cultural and social circles. They can therefore unlearn these behaviors and learn new ones through cognitive-behavioral means, such as education.

Almeida (2000) argues that social and educational programs that are based on cognitive-behavioral principles are effective in producing rehabilitation in perpetrators if they are long-lasting. The term long-lasting, according to Almeida, means a time span of at least a year. Participants must be held accountable for their actions, too.

Child Abuse and Neglect in Families

With the lifestyle changes that have occurred in the forms and behaviors of American families in recent years, concern has increased over the welfare and well-being of children (Popenoe, 1993). Children face a number of problems in families. Among them are "delinquency and crime (including an alarming juvenile homicide rate), drug and alcohol abuse, suicide, depression, eating disorders, and the growing number of children in poverty" (Popenoe, 1993, p. A48).

   Child abuse (which involves acts of commission) and **child neglect** (which involves acts of omission) are major concerns in American family life. Each year more than 1 million children are victims of child abuse (Skowron & Platt, 2005; U.S. Department of Health and Human Services, 2004). Included in this category of abuse are physical, sexual, and psychological abuse, as well as neglect and abandonment. It should be stressed that abuse is seldom of one type and that families who engage in abuse are usually chaotic in nature and have relationship deficits (Mullen, Martin, Anderson, Romans, & Herbison, 1995).

   The effects of child abuse, especially emotional and psychological abuse, include aggression, delinquency, suicide, as well as cognitive, academic and psychological impairment in children (McWey, 2004). Such treatment may also have a powerful influence on adult behavior that is lifelong (Elam & Kleist, 1999). Adults who were abused as children are less satisfied with their lives and prone to suffer from a number of disorders, including those that are behavioral, cognitive, and affective such as depression and low self-esteem (May, 2005). However, there is not a causal relationship between abuse and adult symptomatology (Mullen et al., 1995).

   Child physical abuse resides on a continuum from physical contact that is mild to that which is severe (Kemp, 1998). Severe physical child abuse is manifested in everything from skin injuries and physical traumas—such as broken bones, soft-tissue swelling, and bleeding—to death. In addition to physical marks, psychological consequences result from physical abuse that range from fearfulness of others to post-traumatic stress responses. Many children who are physically abused become distrustful of others, delinquent, and even depressed. A number of these children have difficulty forming close, lasting relationships with peers, let alone adults. Also, physical child abuse can lead to serious cognitive problems including cognitive impairment, poor school performance, and later substance abuse (Skowron & Platt, 2005).

   Besides physical abuse, one of the most insidious forms of child abuse is **childhood sexual abuse (CSA).** This type of abuse includes unwanted touching (i.e., fondling), making sexual remarks, voyeurism, intercourse, oral sex, and pornography (Cobia, Sobansky, & Ingram, 2004; Elam & Kleist, 1999). "It is generally believed that sexual abuse of all children is significantly underreported, with sexual abuse of boys being reported least" (Tomes, 1996, p. 55). In sexual abuse situations, "most abuse of boys is done by perpetrators outside the family; girls' abuse is predominantly intrafamilial" (Hutchins, 1995, p. 21). Almost 1 in 3 girls is sexually abused by age 18 (Crespi & Howe, 2000) and 12% to 18% of boys are sexually abused during childhood or adolescence (Cobia et al., 2004; Tomes, 1996).

   Child abuse of either a physical or sexual nature has become prominent news, from notorious cases to lesser known court trials (Shapiro, 1993). Such abuse is traumatic and has long-term psychological, physiological, and interpersonal consequences (Cobia et al., 2004). Yet the most long-range type of abuse is psychological abuse or emotional neglect. It is both more constant in nature and more damaging throughout life (Elam & Kleist, 1999).

   The National Clearinghouse on Child Abuse and Neglect Information (http://www.calib.com/nccanch/index.htm) provides current updates and background on abuse and neglect problems. Still, child abuse and neglect are pervasive problems and ones most family therapists must obtain clinical skills in if they are to confront them effectively.

Approaches for Treating Child Abuse and Neglect

   Treatment of child abuse and neglect is complicated because it involves legal, developmental, and psychological issues (Gladding, Remley, & Huber, 2001; Pistorello & Follette, 1998). All states require mental health workers and other professional helpers to report child abuse and neglect. "Failure to report child abuse usually constitutes unprofessional conduct that can lead to disciplinary action by a regulation board, possible conviction of a crime, and a civil lawsuit for damages" (Leslie, 2004b, p. 48). Before treatment can begin in most cases, legal issues must be resolved. Developmental and psychological matters must be dealt with as well. For example, when child sexual abuse occurs early in a person's life, the child may blame herself or himself for the abuse just as children of divorce often first find themselves at fault before they come to realize they have been victimized. In addition, child sexual abuse is often not treated until adulthood when other complications, such as couple intimacy, overlay the original problems.

Family therapists must deal with a plethora of current and historical issues in working with child abuse. Anger and feelings of betrayal on the part of the abuser must often be dealt with before working with the family as a whole in correcting the problem and preventing it from happening again. Because of legal issues involved, the abuser in the family may be separated from the family, which makes the job of working with the family even more difficult and challenging.

Nevertheless, when family therapists encounter child abuse cases of any type, they "should not attempt to take the focus off the abuser, as this approach serves only to lead family members and community service agencies to believe that the therapist is excusing the violent acts" (Fenell & Weinhold, 1996, p. 5). Rather, they should concentrate on (1) assisting the abuser in learning how to delay acting impulsively and (2) helping the abuser and the abused family members to recognize and select alternatives other than violence. Motivation for achieving these goals is greatest immediately following abusive behavior, when the family is in crisis and the abuser is usually feeling bad about what has happened.

In working with adult survivors of abuse, clinicians must be able to treat not only issues these individuals have from childhood but also "the specific adult behaviors that may be associated with the history" (Elam & Kleist, 1999, p. 159). In this double emphasis, the clinician needs to understand the context in which the abuse occurred, for instance, in a family that had other relationship deficits, and also needs to realize that children are rarely abused in only one way. The process of treatment in these cases can vary from Bowen-based family-of-origin work, which explores the dynamics associated with the abuse, to behavioral interventions, which help the client and his or her family modify or change behaviors triggered by memories of the abuse.

Children who have been abused physically or sexually likewise do not have one treatment modality that works best in helping them resolve the traumas of their experiences and make adequate and necessary adjustments (Hyde, Bentovim, & Monck, 1995; Oates & Bross, 1995). Rather, a variety of treatments have been used with members of this population and follow-up studies have, for the most part, not taken place or been inconclusive (Greenwalt, Sklare, & Portes, 1998).

Knowledge is scarce on what treatment works best with survivors of child abuse. It does appear that children and their mothers who attend groups with peers in addition to family/ network meetings alone benefit in regard to increased self-esteem and outcome (Hyde et al., 1995). Group work may be an added component that helps children and parents face and talk through problems and possibilities they do not do when in a family context.

Infidelity

Infidelity is defined in a myriad of ways and can comprise a number of activities including: "'Having an affair,' 'extramarital relationships,' 'cheating,' 'sexual intercourse,' 'oral sex,' 'kissing,' 'fondling,' 'emotional connections that are beyond friendships,' 'friendships,' 'internet relationships,' 'pornography use,' and others" (Blow & Hartnett, 2005b, p. 186).

Regardless of its form unfaithfulness in marriage is common in American society. Research indicates that approximately 25% of men and 10% of women have affairs sometime during their marriage and many more engage in other forms of infidelity (Olson, Russell, Higgins-Kessler, & Miller, 2002). Risk factors associated with infidelity include gender as can be seen from the statistic above, as well as race, "with African Americans being most at risk, and age, with younger couples more at risk. … Other risk factors include employment status, with those working outside the home being more at risk, infrequent church attendance, and low marital satisfaction" (p. 425).

There are a number of typologies of affairs including conflict-avoidance marriage, sexual addiction, and empty-nest affairs. Several descriptors of extramarital sex also exist such as accidental infidelity, philandering, romantic affairs, and marital arrangements (Pittman & Wagers, 1995). Underneath all of the categories for such behavior lie hurt and a sense of betrayal. Infidelity is a major marital stressor (Cano, Christian-Herman, O'Leary, & Avery-Leaf, 2002).

Approaches for Treating Infidelity

Therapists need to take couples' cultures into account when working on the issues of infidelity for culture may define how a couple views unfaithfulness (Penn, Hernandez, & Bermudez, 1997). For most cultural groups, "infidelity is not just another problem that couples bring into therapy … infidelity couples are notably and reliably more distressed than their noninfidelity peers at pretreatment" (Atkins, Eldridge, Baucom, & Christensen, 2005, p. 147). Therefore, couple and marriage therapists consider infidelity, especially affairs, to be one of the most damaging problems couples face and one of the most difficult problems to treat (Gordon, Baucom, & Snyder, 2004). The hurt and complexity surrounding infidelity may explain why "treatment for couples experiencing infidelity is relatively undeveloped" (Mamalaskis, 2001, p. 41).

Yet, there is a pattern surrounding some forms of infidelity that can inform treatment. Spouses who are seeking to recover after an extramarital affair appear to go through three stages: (1) an emotional roller coaster of emotions, (2) a moratorium, and (3) trust building (Olson, Russell, Higgins-Kessler, & Miller, 2002). While these stages may be sequential, they are not without their regressive moments and the recovery process is often uneven. Therapists should take note.

One of the factors in the progress of the couple after infidelity has occurred is whether the act of infidelity should be revealed and how much should be told. There are two lines of thought on this matter. One is a model of therapy that requires no disclosure and respects self-determination (Scheinkman, 2005). This view is more prevalent in countries outside of the United States. It basically allows couples to share with the therapist and with the other spouse what they will and when they will in conjoint and individual sessions. The second model in working with couples where there has been infidelity is to make sure the noninvolved spouse is aware of the affair, if it has not been disclosed before therapy begins. The reason for such disclosure is the belief that if an affair is kept secret, it cannot be treated. Thus the "disclosure of infidelity is an … essential component of healing" for couples so affected (Blow & Hartnett, 2005b, p. 229).

The next step, especially if the infidelity is revealed, is to find an appropriate treatment. Behavioral couple therapy has been found to facilitate significant gains in overall levels of distress for couples when the act of infidelity is addressed in therapy (Atkins et al., 2005).

Likewise, a cognitive-behavioral approach, with an emphasis on forgiveness, which sees forgiveness as a willful, cognitive act of "letting go of resentment, bitterness, and need for vengeance" has been found to be empowering and preventative (DiBlasio, 2000, p. 150). Forgiveness keeps couples from getting caught in a downward cycle of punishing and retaliatory behaviors (Weeks, Gambescia, & Jenkins, 2003). In the DiBlasio (2000) approach, the actual forgiveness session is lengthy and comes at the beginning of therapy so that couples have more choice of how they participate in the process.

Regardless of the treatment chosen, therapists need to lend hope to the couple that they can make it to the other side of the pain they are feeling and rekindle an atmosphere of love. Such a task is easier said than done and in many cases couples separate and divorce rather than trying to go on with their lives together.

Summary and Conclusion

This chapter has dealt with three types of abuse: substance-related, domestic violence, and child abuse, as well as with the major marital stressor of infidelity. Unfortunately, all three types of abuse are found in a number of American families and a significant minority of the population participates in infidelity. These dysfunctional behaviors manifest themselves in many ways such as abuse of alcohol, narcotics, battering, inappropriate usurping of power, neglect, and betrayal of trust and responsibility. They are all "tragic and inexcusable and every effort must be made by couples and family therapists to intervene with the family to stop the abuse and help the family become more supportive" (Elam & Kleist, 1999, p. 159).

To treat any of these maladies, family therapists must first assess what is occurring and then find treatment strategies that have proven effective. Working with just the abuser or the betrayer is usually futile because these behaviors are a systemic problem that has both their origins and solutions within a family and societal context.

In the treatment of substance-related disorders, family therapists have two choices. First, they can work with the family in order to confront the problem that is being experienced with substance-related abuse or dependence. Second they can work with the family once the abuser is "dry" and more motivated. In some cases, the therapist will work with the family in both ways. Regardless, therapists must realize that those with substance-related disorders have power within a family. If they as clinicians are to help the family, they will have to engage the person with the substance-related disorder as well as the family in treatment.

Once the substance-related problem family enters therapy, a number of approaches can be used to help them. Theoretical methods of helping include structural-strategic, Bowen, behavioral, Adlerian, and multifamily. An emphasis on the use of community resources for both the prevention and treatment of substance-related disordered families is also necessary.

Families that are engaged in domestic violence and child abuse/neglect provide equally difficult challenges for family therapists to handle. In these cases, families may use a number of defense mechanisms, for instance, denial, in order to minimize or excuse their behaviors. Complicating both situations from the standpoint of treatment is the fact that legal and psychological barriers must be addressed and worked through often before any therapeutic action can be taken.

In domestic violence, power issues have to be confronted and modified. In child abuse and neglect, power issues also prevail as well as those connected with trust. Family therapists can help families in these circumstances by assisting them in learning alternatives to the actions they are currently taking. Changing the dynamics that underlie such behaviors may involve a gamut of treatment strategies from those that explore the family of origin to those that are behaviorally based.

Infidelity is complex and complicated. Infidelity can encompass a variety of behaviors from kissing to sexual intercourse. Certain groups are more at risk for engaging in extramarital affairs and other forms of infidelity. The cultural context of such actions must be considered. However, couples are usually very distressed when infidelity occurs. Treatment is a process with most therapists taking the position that whatever has occurred must be revealed. Behavioral and cognitive-behavioral approaches with an emphasis on new behaviors and the cognitive act of forgiveness have proven to have the best results. In all such cases, therapists must offer hope as well as direction in assisting couples as they work through the situation.

Summary Table
Working with Substance-Related Disorders, Domestic Violence, Child Abuse, and Infidelity

Substance-Related Disorders and Families

Substance-related disorders are "related to the taking of a drug of abuse (including alcohol), to the side effects of medication, and to toxin exposure" (APA, 1994, p. 175).

Substance-related disorders that involve taking a drug of abuse were dealt with in this chapter since many families are affected by them and they are a family systems problem.

Manifestation of Substance-Related Disorders

Families and individuals manifest substance-related disorders in a number of ways such as denial, expression of negative feelings, assumption of roles, deterioration, scapegoating, misuse of resources, confusion about self-worth, and expenditure of time/energy resolving past issues.

Engaging Substance-Related Disorder Families in Treatment

Engaging the family in the therapeutic process involves having the therapist contact the least engaged as well as the most engaged member(s) of the family.

Use of significant others, such as parents and siblings, and widening the focus of therapy are helpful.

Approaches for Treating Substance-Related Disorder Families After Engagement

Treatment for substance-related disorder families must address issues such as relapse, the environment, and intrapersonal (i.e., emotions) and interpersonal (i.e., social) relations.

Prominent approaches to working with substance-related disorder families consist of a number of proven approaches. Among these are structural-strategic family therapy, Bowen family therapy, behavioral family therapy, Adlerian family therapy, and multifamily therapy.

Community resources, such as AA and Al-Anon, and prevention activities are a part of treatment too.

Domestic Violence and Families

Violence against spouses, primarily women, takes many forms: physical, sexual, psychological, and economic.

Violence in families stems from a power imbalance.

Assessment of Domestic Violence

Assessment of domestic violence is complicated by legal and psychological barriers.

Assessment of domestic violence is best done in an open manner where emphasis is on how the family is hurt rather than who is to blame.

Approaches for Treating Domestic Violence

Family therapists primarily use conjoint family therapy, intimate justice theory, and educational methods such as cognitive-behavioral theory, in working with families involved in domestic violence.

Child Abuse and Neglect in Families

Child abuse and neglect first became a major concern in American society in the 1960s.

Included in child abuse are physical, sexual, and psychological abuse as well as neglect and abandonment.

Emotional/psychological abuse is the most long-lasting and damaging.

Approaches for Treating Child Abuse and Neglect

Treatment of child abuse is complicated because it involves legal, developmental, and psychological issues.

All states require reporting of child abuse and neglect cases.

Treatment of child abuse and neglect may focus on historical as well as current issues. Bowen and behavioral family treatments are used as well as peer groups of children and parents.

Infidelity

Infidelity is defined in a myriad of ways and can comprise a number of activities.

Regardless of its form unfaithfulness in marriage is common in American society, i.e., about 25% of men and 10% of women.

Risk factors associated with infidelity include gender, ethnicity, age, employment status, church attendance, and marital satisfaction.

Underneath all of the categories of infidelity lie hurt and a sense of betrayal.

Approaches for Treating Infidelity

Couples' cultures must be taken into account when working on the issues of infidelity.

Treatment for couples experiencing infidelity is relatively undeveloped.

Spouses who are seeking to recover after an extramarital affair appear to go through three stages: (1) an emotional roller coaster of emotions, (2) a moratorium, and (3) trust building.

There is debate about whether infidelity should be disclosed with most therapists believing it should.

Behavioral and cognitive-behavioral therapies that focus on new actions and the willful act of forgiveness appear to be effective in addressing issues surrounding infidelity.

In working with couples where there has been infidelity, a therapist must always offer a couple hope that they can make it again as an entity.

Professional Issues and Research in Family Therapy

CHAPTER 16

Ethical, Legal, and Professional Issues in Family Therapy

—————————————— • ——————————————

Like veneer on the surface of chairs
how you appear is not who you are;
you pretend you are solid
instead of looking at what lies beneath.
I have seen such attempts before
from actors on stage
blowing up words by giving them air
while posturing in the hope of gaining depth.
But this off-stage production is packed with new scenes
full of action and direction
your life need not be ingrained
like furniture waiting for inspection.

—————————————— • ——————————————

Gladding, 2005

Professional issues in family therapy very much pertain to ethics, law, and identity. In the process of helping families, there is a link between the selection of treatment procedures and the consideration of professional issues (Gladding, Remley, & Huber, 2001). Therapeutic interventions must be based on ethical and legal factors. Nevertheless, professional issues receive less attention than therapeutic ones. This is because professional matters are so basic. They are discussed in more mechanical and less appealing ways than those related to what we find interesting in treatment. Ethical guidelines, legal standards, and association bylaws are, indeed, prosaic. They are not inviting to read—and are not always clear. Yet the codes, guidelines, and associations that make up family therapy are at the heart of the profession. It is crucial that the issues surrounding the work of family therapy be well understood by clinicians and the public.

Family therapists should be vigilant in their pursuit and knowledge regarding ethical, legal, and professional identity issues. If they are not, the result may be clinical or personal actions that are harmful though well-intended. Just as the family is a system, so the field of family therapy is systemic. For family clinicians to stay healthy, they and their colleagues must abide in harmony with ethical codes and legal statutes and practice according to the highest standards possible. They must form a strong identity as family therapists. Membership in an association that nourishes and enriches them professionally is necessary. For the sake of colleagues, and themselves, family therapists must deal with professional issues (Wendorf & Wendorf, 1992).

This chapter examines issues connected with ethics, the law, and family therapists' identities. Ignorance can get practitioners into serious trouble, cost them time and money, and even their careers.

Overview of Ethics in Families and Family Therapy

Human experience is a moral enterprise (Doherty, 1995). **Ethics** are moral principles from which individuals and social groups, such as families, determine rules for right conduct. Families and society are governed by **relationship ethics.** These ethics are based on two main principles:

1. **equitability** or the proposition "that everyone is entitled to have his or her welfare interests considered in a way that is fair from a multilateral perspective" (Boszormenyi-Nagy & Ulrich, 1981, p. 160)
2. **caring** or the idea that moral development and principles are centered in the social context of relationships and interdependency (McGoldrick & Carter, 1999)

Family therapy initially grew up in an atmosphere in which practitioners believed that the theories and practices involved in working with families were "value free" (Krasner & Houts, 1984). The resulting **neutrality** stance meant that ethical principles for working with families were rarely discussed by family therapists on a formal or informal basis until the mid-1960s (Grosser & Paul, 1964; Hurvitz, 1967). Then and later, the feminist critique of family therapy, especially in regard to responsibility in family violence, shook up the field in regard to being complacent or noncommittal about values and ethics (Walters, Carter, Papp, & Silverstein, 1988). Practitioners began to realize that every stand, whether of an absolute or relative nature, was related to values—that is, therapeutic decisions were not and could not be ethically neutral (Janson & Steigerwald, 2002).

Knowing that values and ethics are related has only been helpful up to a point. There is still a great deal of uncertainty about ethical decision making in family therapy. That is because ethical decision making is not easy. When faced with an ethical dilemma, the therapist usually has "two or more good reasons to make two or more reasonable decisions" (Burkemper, 2002, p. 203). If the dilemma is complex, many clinicians are quite sure they will be making a big mistake regardless of what path they choose (Hundert, 1987).

Despite this historical conflict and present reality, the domain of ethics is part and parcel of the total fabric of family treatment. It needs to be considered thoughtfully "for there is an inherent ethical dimension in all forms of therapy" (Melito, 2003, p. 3). To complicate matters more, family therapists probably face more ethical conflicts than any other type of therapist (Morrison, Layton, & Newman, 1982). For instance, in family therapy the relationship between family members is usually considered to be the client. Of course, there is more than one person in the relationship, and in order to proceed with therapy, the therapist must obtain the informed consent from multiple individuals, some of whom may have divided loyalties and distinct needs that are different from the majority (Haslam & Harris, 2004).

Thus to be an ethical and effective family therapist, clinicians must be aware and knowledgeable of the values within the theories they embrace and the families they serve. They must be up-to-date on current codes of ethics for the profession. Being actively engaged in making suggestions for revisions of these codes is part of the process, too (Jordan & Stevens, 1999). In essence, clinicians must be thoughtful and flexible in all that they do.

Ethics and Values

Ethical decision making is based on an awareness and understanding of values. A **value** is "the ranking of an ordered set of choices from the most to the least preferable" (Spiegel, 1971, p. 53). Basically, there are four domains of values: personal, family, political/social, and ultimate. Each has an impact on the other (Thomas K. Hearn, March 23, 1993, personal communication). Family therapy, theoretically and clinically, is a profession that now acknowledges it is based on multiple sets of values (Gladding et al., 2001).

Effective therapists realize the therapeutic process is influenced by the complexity of personal values, client-family values, and theoretical values (Melito, 2003). They examine their own values first. These "are influenced by a therapist's age; marital status; gender; ... and ethnic, religious, and socio-cultural background" (Aponte, 1992, p. 273). For example, a young, single, Catholic Hispanic/Latino male family therapist from an affluent background may have values different from an older, divorced, Native American who is the parent of two adolescents and has lived in poverty most of her life.

A way of ferreting out personal values and understanding one's style in ethical decision making is to construct an ethical genogram (Peluso, 2003). This type of genogram focuses on how a person's family of origin attended to making tough ethical decisions. Parents of a therapist may have been slack or they may have been rigid in their interpretation of right and wrong behavior. Such stances may well still play a part, for better or worse, in how the therapist now makes decisions regarding ethical situations. Some of the questions for ethical genograms are laid out in Table 16.1. Once family therapists are aware of their values, how they came to "own" them, and how they are different and similar to others, they are likely to work with families more effectively and ethically.

Table 16.1
Questions for Ethical Genogram

1.	How did your father (or any parental figure in your youth) make tough decisions? Describe his style in two or three words.
2.	How did your mother (or any parental figure in your youth) make tough decisions? Describe her style in two or three words.
3.	Do you remember a particular instance where a tough moral or ethical decision had to be made? What do you remember about it? Who made it: mother or father?
4.	Do you remember a particular instance where a tough moral or ethical decision should have been made but was not? What do you remember about it? Who was involved: mother or father? Do you know what the reasons were?
5.	From where did your father's style come? What were his parents' styles of ethical decision making? Do you remember any particular stories or incidents that demonstrate this style?
6.	From where did your mother's style come? What were her parents' styles of ethical decision making? Do you remember any particular stories or incidents that demonstrate this style?
7.	Was there conflict or disagreement between your mother and father when it came to making difficult or ethical decisions? Who usually prevailed? Why?
8.	Is there anyone else who influenced your ethical decision making? Siblings, friends, teachers, or mentors? How did they influence you? Describe in two or three words their styles as they influenced you.
9.	Were there additional influences on your ethical decision making style? Cultural, religious, philosophical, and so forth? How were you influenced by these, positively and/or negatively?
10.	Did you ever break any rules or the law in your youth? Were you caught? How did your parents deal with it?
11.	In general, how was punishment for infractions dealt with by your parents? Harshly or leniently, consistently or inconsistently?

From "The Ethical Genogram: A Tool for Helping Therapists Understand Their Ethical Decision-Making Styles" by Paul R. Peduso, 2003, *The Family Journal: Counseling and Therapy for Couples and Families, 11*, p. 288. Reprinted by permission of Sage Publications, Inc.

Next, therapists look at the values of their client-families. "Research indicates that diversity in family values, particularly among different cultures is normative" (Pistole & Marson, 2005, p. 16). In families, personal and political/social values of members make an impact in multiple ways. Inherited values within the family also have an influence (McGoldrick, Gerson, & Shellenberger, 1998). In working with families, their values must be examined from a systemic point of view—that is, how family members' values affect the family as a whole. Such a perspective complicates the matter of dealing with values; but simultaneously, it puts values into a realistic framework and makes the study of them a dynamic enterprise. If therapists and their client-families are far apart in regard to espoused core values, negotiations between them or a referral may be needed.

Finally, therapists explore values connected to the theories, processes, and outcomes they embrace (Giblin, 1993). In this last arena, ethical issues in family therapy are seen in relationship to which values in families need to be kept, emphasized, and reinforced, and which ones should be changed (Carter, 1986). Some family therapists center their treatment on helping families remove symptoms. Others focus on establishing a new structure or boundaries. Still others concentrate on helping individuals differentiate from their families of origin or find new solutions.

Uninformed practitioners may try to deny the nature or even importance of values. Others may attempt to "use therapy as a means to campaign for the revisions [of values] they favor" (Wendorf & Wendorf, 1992, p. 316). Both approaches are filled with flaws and possible danger. In the long run, values and respect for the values of others are the driving forces behind ethical behavior and the conduct of family therapy.

How Do Values Influence Ethical Practice?

Values influence ethics in the sense that, as beliefs and preferences, they "undergird the ethical decisions made by individuals and groups. In other words, all ethical issues involve values as grounds for decision making, and all values that deal with social rights and obligations inevitably surface in ethical decisions" (Doherty & Boss, 1991, p. 610). Jacobson (1994) admonished those studying family violence to concentrate on **action-oriented research,** which focuses on finding solutions to this problem, because he believed that such a focus was the only ethical way to investigate a phenomenon where people were being abused.

In family therapy, some therapists work from an individual therapeutic approach in the presence of the family, or they work with family members individually. This type of treatment raises a value and an ethical question because problems of the family in such an arrangement are not being viewed from their "context as a whole" (Fishman, 1988, p. 5). The result is that recommendations for modifications in the family's way of interacting do not consider the overall complexity of the situation. Because such an approach is limited, it is of little or no value. It may even be unethical because research has shown a correlation between individual therapy for married persons and the disturbance of the marital relationship (Haslam & Harris, 2004).

Family therapists are "ethically bound to be honest and forthright with … clients, clearly informing them of their choices, [the therapist's] biases, and … professional judgments" (Wendorf & Wendorf, 1992, p. 317). The values that family therapists embrace directly affect their clinical practices and outcomes.

Guidelines for Making Ethical Decisions

To guard against making unethical decisions, family therapists can use a number of models and resources, once they are aware of what values are involved (Cottone & Claus, 2000). Five of the most prevalent and useful means of making ethical decisions are association codes of ethics, educational resources, professional consultation, interactions with colleagues and supervisors, and consideration of metaethical principles.

Codes of Ethics

Primary resources for family therapists to use in ethical decision making are association codes of ethics. "Ethical codes are set up not to prevent what will happen, but to prevent what might happen" (Kaplan & Culkin, 1995, p. 337). Both the American Association for

Marriage and Family Therapy (see Appendix B) and the International Association of Marriage and Family Counselors (see Appendix C) have codes of ethics that address issues confronting family therapists.

Topics covered include confidentiality, responsibility to clients, professional competence, integrity, assessment, financial arrangements, research and publications, supervision, and public statements. In these areas and others family therapists face a number of ethical dilemmas (Green & Hansen, 1989). Many of the most common ethical concerns are those that involve treating the entire family, being current on new family therapy developments, seeing one family member without the others present, and sharing values with clients (Green & Hansen, 1986).

Unfortunately, there are few specific behavioral guidelines in codes of ethics that direct family therapists on what to do and how. As a result, family therapists will sometimes make unethical decisions because they use rationalization or hearsay, such as "other practitioners do this or that" (Pope & Vasquez, 1998). The limitations of ethical codes may become especially pronounced when attempts are made to deal with complicated issues such as **dual or multiple relationships,** which are not built on mutuality and where a therapist assumes a second role as a friend, business associate, and so on (Leslie, 2004a; Ryder & Hepworth, 1990). Determining the best course of action from simply reading an ethical code may be difficult for experienced, as well as beginning, therapists.

Educational Resources

A second source family therapists can utilize in making informed ethical decisions is educational material. One of the best educational resources is found in the form of case histories related specifically to dilemmas in family therapy. Peggy Papp (1977), Frank Dattilio (1998), and Larry Golden (2004) have all edited books of case studies to which family therapists can refer. Briefer in format is the *User's Guide to the AAMFT Code of Ethics* (American Association for Marriage and Family Therapy, 2001) and columns in *The Family Journal: Counseling and Therapy for Couples and Families,* which feature case consultations from a particular theoretical view. Such educational cases need to be studied on a systematic basis. Knowledge of how family therapists made decisions in the past can be useful to current practitioners.

Case studies can also help family therapists reason through the steps needed in making ethically appropriate choices. In ethical decision making, step-by-step processes have been established (Corey, Corey, & Callanan, 2002). These processes emphasize generating a continuum of alternative actions that therapists can take for the good of the family's welfare and to meet their own professional responsibilities. Therapists then evaluate and weigh the consequences of these alternatives. From this process, they make a tentative decision and implement that decision, after they have double-checked it with supervisors, consultants, or colleagues if they are in doubt. The final step involves documenting what has been done (Mitchell, 1991). Documenting should be based on customary practices or reputable suggested practices that are defensible ethically and legally (Wilcoxon, 1993).

Professional Consultation

A third resource for making ethical decisions is professional consultation. Professional **consultation** is the use of experts in an area, such as family therapy ethics, to enhance one's own knowledge and abilities (Kurpius & Fuqua, 1993). Consultation can take many forms. For example, consultation can be internally or externally oriented, process- or outcome-focused, and formal or informal.

Internal consultation can take the form of talking with an expert where one works about an ethical matter concerning a family. **Outside consultation** would involve conversation with a professional outside one's agency or setting. **Process consultation** refers to conferring with an expert about the ethics of methods one is using with a family, whereas **outcome-focused consultation** would be centered on the ethics of what the therapist and/or family hopes to accomplish. **Formal consultation** is input gained from an expert through an appointment or structured meeting, whereas **informal consultation** may well take the form of talking with an expert in the hallways at a professional therapy conference or some less structured way of interacting.

Whatever the form, the idea is that through consultation services, family therapists can gain a broader view of the principles and case histories associated with specific aspects of ethical codes. In consultation encounters, therapists become consumers of services that are aimed toward prevention, enlightenment, and change.

Interaction with Colleagues and Supervisors

A fourth source of support in making ethical decisions involves associating with colleagues and supervisors. Family therapists need to interact with their peers for many reasons, but mainly to share in the collected wisdom and opinions of these individuals when it comes to matters of ethical conduct. Peers are usually more accessible than consultants and educational materials. Furthermore, the cost of using peers, such as in peer supervision, is inexpensive or free and may actually pay psychological dividends both in knowledge and support. In addition, colleagues can often inform professionals of new trends.

Direct supervision of one's work by noncolleagues is also effective and recommended, especially as professionals begin their careers (Cobia & Boes, 2000). Unlike individual supervision, **family therapy supervision** is systemic and includes a focus on interpersonal as well as intrapersonal issues (Gladding, Wilcoxon, Semon, & Myers, 1992). Furthermore, family therapy supervision places an emphasis on the critiquing of videotapes as well as the use of one-way mirrors for live observation and intervention (Schwartz, Liddle, & Breunlin, 1988). By using various forms of supervisory interaction—such as a supervision team behind a one-way mirror or a **bug-in-the-ear supervision method** (in which the therapist receives messages from a supervisor through a telephone hookup device)—family therapists are less likely to make ethical mistakes through omitting data or avoiding personal/professional issues.

Meta-ethical Principles

Meta-ethical principles are high-level standards that guide clinicians as they make their decisions (Bukemper, 2002). These principles are especially useful in resolving ethical and moral dilemmas. All five of these principles are considered in interaction with one another:

- **autonomy:** the right of individuals to make decisions and choices
- **nonmaleficence:** the avoidance of doing possible harm to a client through one's actions
- **beneficence:** doing good and promoting the welfare of the client
- **fidelity:** being trustworthy, loyal, and keeping one's promises
- **justice:** treating people equally

The principle that most family therapists keep uppermost in mind when interacting with couples and families is nonmaleficence, that is, first do no harm. That principle, while not always easy to follow, is less complicated in some ways than the other principles. Fidelity in family therapy deals with being loyal to the family, its members, and the relationships they have. Attention is required to all three of these areas and they must be kept in mind when making decisions. Nevertheless, when family therapists realize the complexity of what, as well as who, they are working with, they are usually more thoughtful, careful, and, in the end, more competent.

Common Ethical Concerns

Some conduct in family therapy is considered unethical regardless of the experience of the professional involved. However, some practices are not as clearly defined. Common ethical concerns are examined here.

Confidentiality

Confidentiality is "the ethical duty to fulfill a contract or promise to clients that the information revealed during therapy will be protected from unauthorized disclosure" (Arthur & Swanson, 1993, p. 7). In addition to its ethical focus, confidentiality is a legal matter, as well. In a 1996 U.S. Supreme Court decision (*Jaffe v. Redmond*), the high court upheld that a therapist could not be forced to testify about confidential communications in treatment settings (Seppa, 1996). However, if confidentiality is broken during treatment, it may become an ethical and/or legal nightmare. Therefore, family therapists need to take precautions ahead of time.

One of the best strategies for family therapists to initiate is to inform all family members in the initial session that the family relationship is the client, and that no one will be scapegoated or treated as "the problem." This process can be done verbally, but it, and other philosophical and professional tenets, should be conveyed in writing through the use of a **professional self-disclosure statement.** This statement, which contains essential information about therapy and the mutual rights and responsibilities of all involved, is signed by the family and returned to the therapist. A copy is then given to all members of the family and retained by the therapist (see Chapter 4 for an example of a professional self-disclosure statement).

By informing the family that the relationship is the client and using a professional disclosure statement to do this, family members are concretely informed about the parameters of therapy, including confidentiality. They are discouraged from seeking individual sessions with therapists unless appropriate. They are also informed that they should not try to persuade therapists to keep their secrets from other family members. This approach basically reinforces a systems perspective; that is, the family is an interrelated unit and what affects one member has an impact on the entire family.

At times, family therapists may have to break confidentiality. These times involve when the therapist sees that someone in the family may inflict harm to self or others, or when the physical or mental health of a client is called into question (Filaccio, 2005). Therapist decisions at these times are dictated by ethical and legal considerations regarding the well-being of the family (Kaplan & Allison, 1993b). In these situations, the question of privileged communication comes to the forefront. **Privileged communication** is "a client's legal right, guaranteed by statute, that confidences originating in a therapeutic relationship will be safeguarded" (Arthur & Swanson, 1993, p. 7). While both the client and therapist hold the privilege, only the client can waive it under normal circumstances (Filaccio, 2005). However, if it becomes clear during a session that, for example, a child or older adult in the family is being abused, the therapist has a legal and ethical obligation to report the abuse to an agency responsible for dealing with it, usually a department of social services (Welfel, Danzinger, & Santoro, 2000). All states grant immunity from criminal or civic liability to professionals who report child abuse (Gladding et al., 2001). Family therapists need to check their state regulations and seek advice from colleagues, professional association and ethical guidelines, supervisors, and attorneys, if there is ever a question of what they should reveal professionally or legally.

Confidentiality broken through carelessness is another matter. Carelessness can involve an impropriety such as talking about a case in public. It can also be more innocent, such as using a cellular phone to call a client or an insurance agency. Electronic communication tools (including e-mail and fax) provide no guarantee that information will be received by the person for whom it is intended without being intercepted or read by someone else (O'Malley, 1995). Such situations constitute an ethical violation, and it is possible that a civil suit will follow (Woody, 1988). "Office personnel may need to be trained to think preventively about possible violations of confidentiality that may occur with a computer system" (O'Malley, 1995, p. 9). This type of protection would include placing the computer in a discrete position so that only office staff can view it. Family therapists who use computers to type progress notes must also take care with computer access and display. Client notes and records that are typed on computer disks must be protected in the same way as hardcopy notes. Proper precautions must be used when employing electronic devices.

Gender Issues

Gender can be an important ethical issue in conducting family therapy. "Gender is not just a set of behaviors and expectations but rather a principal of social organization that structures relations, especially the power relations, between men and women" (Smith & Stevens-Smith, 1992, p. 436). The genders of the therapist and of those in the family play a part in what issues are addressed during treatment and how they are addressed (Walsh, 1993). In its early years, family therapy was male-focused (Weiner & Boss, 1985). Social and system issues involving women were, as a result, ignored or glossed over (Costa & Sorenson, 1993).

Since the 1980s, gender issues have been dealt with extensively in family therapy (Hare-Mustin, 1987). The status of core inequality among individual members within the family, especially women, has been focused on (Carter, 1992; Walters, Carter, Papp, & Silverstein, 1992). Nevertheless, the conduct of many families and that of family therapy have changed only slightly. Males and females who did not grow up in a nonstereotyped environment tend to act and react in the same manner as their caretakers. This behavior has ethical implications because traditional roles have sometimes inhibited the growth, change, and healthy functioning of both genders. Women may be shortchanged in therapy if they assume that, because of their gender, they must be cooperative and make concessions regardless of cost (Nixon, 1993). Men raised in stereotyped ways may think they cannot make concessions within the family without losing face or power.

In working with whole families, therapists must be attuned to such ethical and practical issues as:

- the balance of power between a husband and wife both financially and physically
- the rules and roles played by members of different genders and how these are rewarded
- what a shift in a family's way of operating will mean to the functionality of the family as a whole (McGoldrick, 1999)

A balanced perspective needs to be maintained in regard to gender and change. Urging or implementing change in gender-prescribed behaviors within a family solely because a therapist believes it is right may be quite costly to all involved (Wendorf & Wendorf, 1992). On the other hand, condoning through silence emotional abuse or intimidation that is lethal to the life and functioning of the family is irresponsible, too. Ethical and systemic considerations need to be addressed when discussing gender issues in family therapy (Bograd, 1992). This is especially true when changes in relationship patterns are being contemplated or implemented.

Sex Between a Therapist and a Family Member

One of the most important ethical taboos in professional family therapy is for a therapist to become sexually involved with a client. Unfortunately, in the history of mental health treatment, blatant cases are seen of sexual affairs between therapists and those they have treated. Movies from *Spellbound* to *The Prince of Tides* have portrayed forbidden intimacy within the confines of analysis (Ansen & Springen, 1992). In the annals of therapeutic history, two publicized cases of sexual involvement with clients are those documented between Carl Jung and a couple of the women he treated who became his mistresses, and Otto Rank, who had a long love affair with one of his patients (Beck, Springen, & Foote, 1992).

Noted practitioners in the mental health field have warned against such liaisons. Furthermore, sexual relations between a therapist and client are forbidden in the codes of ethics of all family therapy associations. Unfortunately, the practice clearly goes on even though "fewer therapists admit to indiscretions these days even in anonymous surveys" (Beck et al., 1992, p. 54).

When it is discovered that this type of conduct is probably occurring, the person receiving the news should confront the accused professional with the evidence in order to verify its truthfulness. If there is a conflict of information between the therapist and client, a written report of the incident by the client should be made. After the complaint is made, the national ethics board that governs the mental health discipline under which the person in question is a member (e.g., AAMFT, American Counseling Association, or American Psychological Association) has the authority to gather evidence, to hear testimony if necessary, and, then, to make a decision.

Theoretical Techniques

Some theoretical techniques are controversial and should only be used as a last resort and with discretion. For instance, the use of conscious deceit or paradox as applied in strategic family therapy is not recommended when a straightforward approach would work just as well (Henderson, 1987; Solovey & Duncan, 1992). Similarly, the strategic stance of neutrality is of questionable ethical use when violence between family members is occurring. Family therapists who practice from the strategic point of view should concentrate on actively bringing the violence within the family to cessation and initiate a contract between members for nonviolence (Willbach, 1989). Only by working with the family in such a way can therapists hope to bring about stability and change. Again, legal as well as ethical factors may need to be considered in deciding on a course of action.

Multicultural Therapy Issues

Another area in which ethical issues commonly arise is in the multicultural domain (Saba, Karrer, & Hardy, 1996). Multicultural competence is necessary to ensure that "a therapist is not imposing his or her values" in the assessment, diagnosis, and conceptualization of family and couple issues (Hill & Crews, 2005, p.179). In working with minority-culture families, Pedersen (1996) proposes that there are three serious errors, all of which have ethical implications that should be avoided. These errors are a tendency to

1. overemphasize similarities
2. overemphasize differences
3. make assumptions that either similarities or differences must be emphasized

Instead, family therapists need to take a "culturally relevant perspective that attempts to identify cultural significance from the family's own perspective rather than a prescribed set of cultural characteristics that may or may not be relevant to a family" (Kurilla, 1998, p. 210). Such situations may be difficult to handle, and supervision and/or consultation are recommended as ways to keep perspective and act ethically. For example, family therapists generally avoid touching clients. Yet Hispanic/Latino family members may openly touch or hug therapists, especially in greeting them (Cooper & Costas, 1994). In a situation where the therapist was with a Hispanic/Latino family where touch was frequent, he or she would face the ethical dilemma of respecting cultural tradition, while at the same time making sure that ethical codes regarding intimacy between the therapist and the family were not violated.

Use of the Internet for On-Line Therapy

The World Wide Web has opened up possibilities and problems regarding its ethical and legal use as a tool in therapy (Caudill, 2000; Hohenshil, 2000). The Internet is already used by some practitioners to communicate with clients both around their community and around the world (Frame, 1998; Hannon, 1996). In some setups, clients, regardless of where they live, "e-mail a question of no more than 200 words to a counselor who then e-mails a response within 24 to 72 hours" (Frame, 1998, p. 328). A prepayment is required, usually by credit card.

A related use of the Internet is in working with families who are hearing-impaired or in remote areas where the physical presence of a therapist is not possible. Clinicians working with special populations or in rural and isolated regions may use this means to help families for whom services would not otherwise be available. The length of questions and payment will vary.

In yet a third kind of setup, family therapists simply communicate with families or members of families between regular therapy sessions. Such a practice may provide guidance, clarify issues, or lower anxiety.

The ethical dilemmas associated with the use of the Internet are numerous. They include a lack of security, possible breaches of confidentiality, an inability on the therapist's part to fulfill the duty to either protect the client or warn others of potential danger, and the inability of the therapist to read nonverbal responses and clues. Clients may also misunderstand written communications and are vulnerable to incompetent practice.

To complicate matters even further, there are few ethical guidelines and virtually no existing laws about the use of technology, specifically the Internet, in conducting marriage and family therapy. One factor does seem clear. The use of Internet and long-distance therapy will increase, and there are risks of malpractice associated with it (Caudill, 2000).

Addressing Unethical Behavior

By reading codes of ethics, consulting with colleagues, studying cases, operating from a theoretical position, developing policies and strategies beforehand, and receiving supervision or peer consultation, family therapists can usually avoid making unethical decisions (Brendel & Nelson, 1999; Gladding et al., 2001). At times therapists may notice unethical actions in fellow professionals. When such behavior comes to the attention of a therapist, he or she should address it. The first step in such a process is to discuss the violation directly with the professional in whom it was observed or who allegedly acted in an unethical way.

If the situation is not resolved on this level, the family therapist should report it to an appropriate professional association, such as the AAMFT or IAMFC, as well as inform licensure or certification boards regulating the practice of family counseling. When reported to such agencies, a formal investigation will almost always take place. "If found guilty, professionals under the jurisdiction of these agencies are usually admonished and expelled" (Kaplan & Culkin, 1995, p. 337).

Addressing unethical behavior in fellow professionals becomes more difficult when the information is conveyed through a client that the therapist is seeing. The question of confidentiality arises. It then becomes the responsibility of the therapist to check with an attorney or ethics case manager in the profession in which he or she practices to determine whether or not his or her duty to report overrides the duty to maintain confidentiality. If there is a clear violation, then there are at least three options: "encourage your client to file an ethics complaint with her [or his] professional association or licensure board; file a complaint yourself; or do nothing, if your professional code doesn't require you to report" (Piercy, 2000, p. 21). Each option involves risks and it can be a traumatic experience for a client to come forward against a therapist.

Legal Issues in Family Therapy

"Ethics and law frequently overlap" (Wilcoxon, 1993, p. 3). If a family requests that they be billed for individual counseling, rather than for the couple therapy that they are receiving, and a family therapist complies, the parties involved are not only violating sections of the AAMFT and IAMFC codes of ethics but are also committing insurance fraud (Kaplan & Allison, 1993a; Stevens-Smith & Hughes, 1993). If such a complaint is raised against a therapist, it may be handled by an ethics committee, a state regulatory commission, or a court of law (Woody, 1988).

Because of the interrelatedness of family ethics and law and the prevalence of law in governing interpersonal relationships, family therapists need to be aware of legal issues affecting therapy. Family therapists are not exempt from dealing with the legal system anymore than they are exempt from being involved in ethical decision making. It is important that family therapists "be aware of legislative decisions, legal precedents, and professional practices" connected with the law (Wilcoxon, 1993, p. 3) in case they are called on to participate in the legal system.

The Legal System

The term **legal** refers to "law or the state of being lawful"; the term **law** refers to "a body of rules recognized by a state or community as binding on its members" (Shertzer & Stone,

1980, p. 386). A **liability,** on the other hand, is a legal term dealing with obligation and responsibility one person has to another, such as a therapist to a client-family. It can take one of three forms:

> **Civil liability** usually results from a lawsuit by a client against the therapist for professional malpractice (negligence) or gross negligence. **Criminal liability** usually results from the commission of a crime by the therapist, such as failing to report child abuse, engaging in sexual relations with a patient, or insurance fraud. **Administrative liability** means that the therapist's license to practice is threatened by an investigation from the licensing board, which has the power to suspend a license. (Leslie, 2004b, p. 46)

The "law is not cut and dried, definite and certain, or clear and precise" (Van Hoose & Kottler, 1985, p. 44); and most family therapists are not familiar with American jurisprudence in more than a superficial way. They do not realize the fluidity within the legal system. The reason is largely because the law is a specialty that requires years of study and practice for one to become proficient in its use. However, without becoming an expert in law, family therapists must master certain aspects of the legal system in order to be effective within this domain.

Interesting similarities exist between the legal and therapy communities. Both are concerned with setting up healthy relationships between people. Both handle cases that involve drama and resolution. Also, coincidentally, professionals in both fields are sometimes referred to as "counselors." Yet the differences between the legal and the therapeutic systems are greater than their areas of overlap. A few of these differences are quite noticeable. The legal system is concerned with gathering evidence based on facts; therapy is more interested in processes and making changes. Attorneys therefore spend more time gathering information and concentrating on content than therapists do. Another distinction is that the legal system relies on adversity (Gladding et al., 2001); the therapeutic system relies on cooperation. Although some legal decisions may involve compromises, attorneys focus on "winning" cases for their clients. Lawyers engage in discrediting or disproving other evidence that contradicts their cases. For attorneys, their clients' well-being and rights are based on representation that is singularly focused. And while attorneys represent families as a whole in some legal cases, they do not deal with whole families when there are internal disputes. In the legal system, each family member involved in a dispute is represented by a different legal counselor. In such situations, the focused outcome is on a just settlement rather than family change and resolution.

In recognition of the growing need for marriage and family therapists to have affordable, regular, and up-to-date information about managing legal risks in their practices, the American Association for Marriage and Family Therapy established a legal and risk management plan in 1995 for its members. Under the plan, clinical members can receive "one free legal consultation per quarter with the AAMFT in-house attorney" (Jester, 1995, p. 6).

Types of Law

Family therapists should be familiar with several types of law. Some of the most important of these types of law have been defined by Gladding et al. (2001). They are common law, statutory law, administrative (regulatory) law, case law (court decisions), and civil and criminal law.

Common Law

Common law is law derived from tradition and usage. The common law of the United States has its roots in England and the tradition of accepting customs passed down from antiquity. The idea behind common law is that all law does not need to be derived from written sources. For instance, there are common law family matters, such as common law marriages.

Statutory Law

In contrast to common law, statutory law consists of those laws passed by legislative bodies, such as state and national legislatures, and signed by an authorized source, such as a governor or the president. Statutory laws are only valid in the jurisdiction in which they are passed. Some states have laws, for instance, addressing marital rape, and other states do not. In 2005, most states regulated the practice of marriage and family therapy through statutory laws regarding licensure. Unfortunately, becoming licensed or certified as a family therapist in one state does not guarantee recognition of that license or certification by another state.

Administrative (Regulatory) Law

Administrative (regulatory) law consists of specialized regulations passed by authorized government agencies that pertain to certain specialty areas. Laws governing the use of federal land are often made under this arrangement. Some regulations in regard to families, such as those dealing with abuse cases, may also fall in this category.

Case Law (Court Decisions)

As the name implies, case law is the type of law decided by decisions of courts at all levels from state to federal. Cases are decided in regard to legal statutes, but many nuances enter the process. Even a minor change in the facts can change the decision of the court. Matters pertaining to child support, for example, may be decided by case law.

Civil Law Versus Criminal Law

Civil law pertains to acts offensive to individuals, **criminal law** to acts offensive to society in general. Most of the law involving family therapists falls into the civil law classification (Hopkins & Anderson, 1990). One of the primary civil legal issues confronting some family therapists is divorce. Therapists who are familiar "with the legal issues facing families in transition can be effective in helping those clients make informed, rational, and realistic decisions" (Oliver, 1992, p. 41). The essential element at such times is being knowledgeable about therapeutic and legal issues.

Some incidents in family therapy involve issues that are legally criminal in scope. Therapists must be aware of what their duties and responsibilities are and what roles they need to play professionally. Two examples of criminal actions within families are spousal abuse and child abuse. In both cases, family therapists have a duty to take actions that are not usually within their domains, such as reporting their knowledge to a legally responsible agency.

Legal Situations that Involve Family Therapists

Family therapists can encounter any number of legal situations. Most of these occur on the state or local level. Some of the most common legal issues that come up in family therapy "revolve around state laws focusing on the reporting of child abuse, maltreatment, and neglect of minors" (Kaplan & Culkin, 1995, p. 337). Therefore, it behooves family therapists to become familiar with their state's legal system and even the courts and judges in their area (Stevens-Smith & Hughes, 1993). After all, "it is difficult to uphold state laws if you don't know what they are" (Kaplan & Culkin, 1995, p. 337).

Therapists may be called on to participate in some legal and legally related situations in the following capacities: expert witness, child custody evaluator, reporter of abuse, and court-ordered witness.

Expert Witness

As an expert witness, family therapists are asked to give testimony about probable causes and recommendations in regard to family members, such as juveniles who are acting out behaviorally. Because courts are adversarial, therapists must prepare themselves before their appearance. They must stay objective and establish their credibility by presenting their credentials and qualifications. They must speak from authoritative sources and be specific. This type of preparation can help them increase their confidence and competence.

Child Custody Evaluator

As a child custody evaluator, family therapists are asked to determine what is in the best interest of a child in custody arrangements. In these cases, "the child custody evaluator represents the children and the courts, not the parents" (Stevens-Smith & Hughes, 1993, p. 27). The evaluation of a child includes home visits, testing, and conversations with the child involved. It requires that the family therapists involved have a background and experience in child development, family systems, parenting skills, psychometrics, counseling, and witness testimony (Remley & Miranti, 1992).

Reporter of Abuse

As a reporter of abuse, family therapists must break confidentiality. In doing so, therapists are following the *Child Abuse Prevention and Treatment Act of 1974*, which mandates the reporting of such situations for the greater good of society. Abuse includes all forms of maltreatment whether physical, sexual, or emotional. It is recommended that family therapists advise families when they are obligated to report abuse and explain to these families how the reporting process works (Stevens-Smith & Hughes, 1993).

Court-Ordered Witness

As a court-ordered witness, family therapists must appear before a court to testify on behalf of or against a family or family member. If given a choice, most family therapists "would prefer to refuse to testify because they see problems as being systemic and no one is to blame" (Green & Hansen, 1989, p. 156). However, in cases in which they are subpoenaed, family therapists can help themselves and the persons involved by preparing ahead of time. One way they may do this is by essentially doing nothing even though they may be pressured by select clients or their attorneys to write a letter or make a declaration in favor of one party in the family (Leslie, 2004b). By doing nothing until they seek the advice of an attorney, therapists keep themselves out of possible penalty and perjury situations (Remley, 1991). Instead through consultation with an attorney and by learning about trial procedures and role playing possible situations, family therapists come to understand courts of law as they do other systems. Thus, they are able to function more effectively.

Issues of Law in Family Therapy

Legal issues in family therapy are usually in the background, as opposed to the foreground, of a clinician's practice. Most involve matters germane to the question of **malpractice,** which is defined as "the failure to fulfill the requisite standard of care" (Woody, 1988, p. 2). Malpractice can occur because of "omission (what should have been done, but was not done) or commission (doing something that should not have been done)" (Woody, 1988, p. 2). In both cases, negligence must be proved for a malpractice suit to be brought forward. Such an incidence may happen if the family therapist either fails to report criminal activities [*Missouri v. Beatty*, 770 S.W.2d 387 (Mo. Ct. App. 1989)] or does not inform a family or some of its members that they are in grave danger [*Tarasoff v. Regents of the University of California*, 551 P.2d 334 (Cal. 1976)].

Two other frequent situations that relate to malpractice involve advertising and record keeping. In regard to advertising, most states "place legal limits" on what family practitioners can do to advertise their skills and services (Bullis, 1993, p. 15). These limits take the form of protecting a title. Thus, only professionals who have met the necessary criteria can call themselves "licensed marriage and family therapists." Because state laws vary, family therapists need to become informed of their state's general statutes before they advertise. They must also check professional ethics codes. For instance, the AAMFT has an extensive section in their code of ethics on advertising.

Records may be thought of as remembrances. They are the written notes from sessions with couples and families and are important for treatment purposes and as a defense for therapists if they are accused of wrongdoing (Leslie, 2004b). In the matter of record keeping, clinical notes should be carefully worded, kept "accurately and professionally," and be housed "separately" from any required business transactions (Hopkins & Anderson, 1990, p. 18). Accuracy encompasses the sequential and cogent nature of what was written. In maintaining accuracy, therapists should "indicate any addendum to records and sign and date such additions. All changes to diagnoses or treatment plans must be made as separate entries" (Marine, 1995, p. 11).

Professionalism deals with the legibility and protection of records, too. "Therapists must always know where their records are and who is responsible for them. Failure to produce records reflects poorly on malpractice litigation" (Marine, 1995, p. 11). Family therapists are advised to keep their records locked in file cabinets that are then secured in locked storage areas. In addition, most states require therapists to keep client records and have stipulations as to the length of time records must be kept. "Because family therapy has a long maturation process for claims (sometimes 10, 15, or 20 years after treatment is terminated), maintaining records is a primary risk management technique" (Marine, 1995, p. 11). If there is a question in a legal proceeding, such as a custody case, about the relevance of material in therapists' records, therapists and their attorneys may request what is known as a **"camera review"** where an impartial party, usually a judge, reviews the records and releases only those portions that are relevant to the situation at hand (Filaccio, 2005).

Family therapists can help themselves and their client-families by being current on acceptable practices and codes within the family therapy field and by making referrals to other more skilled clinicians when they are beyond their level of competence (Hopkins & Anderson,

1990). Carrying professional **liability insurance** is a must and being uninsured for any period of time is dangerous (Bullis, 1993; Leslie, 2004b). Such insurance protects therapists financially from legal claims that they have mishandled family needs or members. The responsibility for legally and ethically protecting client-families lies squarely on the shoulders of family therapy professionals.

Professional Identification as a Family Therapist

In addition to ethical and legal questions in the practice of family therapy, there is at least one other professional issue: professional identification. Identifying oneself as a marriage and family therapist is a developmental process. It does not occur overnight anymore than skill building does.

Demographics: Who Are Marriage and Family Therapists?

William F. Northey, Jr., the professional development research specialist for the American Association for Marriage and Family Therapy (AAMFT), published an article on the demographics of marriage and family therapists from surveys conducted between 1986 and 2004 from various research projects (Northey, Jr., 2004b). He found that in 2004 there were over 50,000 professionals who identified themselves as marriage and family therapists by having obtained a state license to practice as an independent clinician treating couples and families. At the same time, there were another 30,000 individuals who were classified as "trainees" in the discipline. These individuals did not have the credentials to obtain a license and were working under supervision or were completing coursework.

Two-thirds of the licensed group had master's degrees. The remainder had doctorates. Half of these professionals worked "exclusively in private practice settings," one-quarter worked "in institutional or organizational settings," and another quarter worked "in both" (p. 11). In addition, two-thirds of marriage and family therapists worked "full time and 21% part time." The vast majority of marriage and family therapists saw "clients during normal business hours," while 73% saw "clients in the evenings," as well, and one-third saw "clients on the weekends" (p. 11).

The mean salary for marriage and family therapists in 2004 was $46,573, "almost identical to that of the general population at a little over $43,000" (p. 13). Their income, however, varied greatly because of the diverse settings in which they worked as well as other factors such as experience.

In regard to age, gender, and ethnicity, "the mean age of marriage and family therapists in 2004 was 54. Approximately 60% of licensed clinicians were women, and the profession was predominantly white—91%. "African Americans, Hispanics, Native Americans, Asians and 'others' represent[ed] 3%, 2.1%, 1.5%, 1.4%, and 2.2% respectively" (p. 10).

As far as who seeks marriage and family therapy, Northey (2004a) reported in another article that the majority were women, but the ethnic distribution was much more similar to the population of the United States as a whole. Specifically, 80% were White, 9% were Black, 10% were Hispanic, 4% were Asian, 1% were Native American, and 10% were other. Children were overrepresented in MFT case loads.

On the average marriage and family therapists "spent 59 minutes with clients for each session," and two-thirds of clients "were in therapy for less than a year" (Northey, 2004a, p. 16).

Favorite theoretical approaches used by therapists were "cognitive-behavioral (33%), Multi-Systemic/Systems (10%), Psychodynamic (6%), Bowen Family Systems (5%), and Solution-Focused (5%)" (p. 17). Interestingly, the most common presenting problems reported by marriage and family therapists were "1) mood disorders, 2) couple relationship problems, 3) family relationship problems, 4) anxiety disorders and 5) adjustment disorders" (p. 16).

Organizations Associated with Family Therapy

Professional associations exist for a number of reasons such as establishing standards for their members to follow. They also offer a means for those within the public domain to address grievances or concerns related to a practitioner or the profession in general. Belonging to a professional association, as well as being licensed, helps clinicians and the public relate to one another on a higher plane and in a better way than would otherwise be possible.

Before the 1980s, the four major associations dealing with issues connected with family therapy were the American Association for Marriage and Family Therapy (AAMFT), the American Family Therapy Academy (AFTA), and the National Council on Family Relations (NCFR). Of the three, the AAMFT was dominant in regard to membership and influence.

However, in the 1980s, two new family therapy associations were established. The first was Division 43 (Family Psychology), which was formed within the American Psychological Association in 1984. The second fledgling group, established in 1986, was the International Association of Marriage and Family Counselors (IAMFC). The IAMFC has been connected with the American Counseling Association from its beginning.

American Association for Marriage and Family Therapy (AAMFT)

The American Association for Marriage and Family Therapy (http://www.aamft.org/) is the oldest and largest (23,000 members) professional family therapy organization in the world (Nichols, 1992; Northey, 2004b). It was initially established in 1942 as the American Association of Marriage Counselors (AAMC). The driving force behind the forming of this group was Lester Dearborn of Boston, who organized the AAMC like a private club. Some of the most prominent names in the field of marriage counseling were charter members of the AAMC including Emily Mudd, Ernest Groves, and Abraham Stone. (See Chapter 3 on the history of family therapy for more details on the establishment of the AAMFT.) From 1942 to 1967, the AAMC was "an elite interest group" that struggled in regard to both its identity and its financial stability (Nichols, 1992, p. 5).

In 1970, the AAMC became the American Association of Marriage and Family Counselors (AAMFC). At the same time, membership standards were lowered and membership (and revenue) increased. It changed its name to the American Association for Marriage and Family Therapy in 1979 and moved its headquarters to Washington, D.C., in 1982.

The AAMFT and its affiliate organizations concentrate on accrediting educational programs that meet prescribed standards and advocating for licensure for family therapists on the state level. The AAMFT also produces videos on family therapy and publishes professional literature, including the *Journal of Marital and Family Therapy* and the *Family Therapy News*. It also holds an annual convention. In addition, the AAMFT lobbies for passage of select federal legislation that is in the interest of family therapy, including the recognition of family therapists as "core" mental health providers.

Overall, the AAMFT is a multifaceted, multidisciplinary professional association that is active in positively impacting the health care delivery system in the United States as it affects families.

American Family Therapy Academy

The American Family Therapy Academy (AFTA)(http://www.afta.org/) was founded by Murray Bowen in 1977. Its stated objectives include:

- advancing theories and therapies that regard the entire family as a unit
- promoting research and professional education in family therapy and allied fields
- making information about family therapy available to practitioners in other fields of knowledge and to the public
- fostering the cooperation of all who are concerned with the medical, psychological, social, legal, and other needs of the family
- promoting the science and practice of family therapy

The five categories of AFTA membership are charter, clinical-teacher, research, distinguished, and foreign. Academy members represent a wide variety of disciplines. Membership requirements are essentially a terminal professional degree, 5 years of post-degree clinical experience with families, and 5 years of teaching family therapy or performing significant research in the family field. The membership numbers approximately 1,000 family therapy teachers and researchers who meet once a year to share ideas and develop common interests (Kaslow, 1990).

Division 43 of the American Psychological Association: Family Psychology

Division 43 (Family Psychology) of the American Psychological Association (APA) (http://www.apa.org/divisions/div43/about.html) was established to enable psychologists who worked with families to keep their identity as psychologists (Kaslow, 1990). As a division, Family Psychology includes approximately 3,000 practitioners and academicians who are concerned with the science, practice, public interest, and education of psychologists who work with families. Family psychologists are involved in premarital, marital, divorce, and remarriage counseling. They focus on family abuse and violence, pediatrics, geriatrics, and governmental policies connected with family issues.

To become a division member, a professional must hold membership in the APA. Like the AAMFT and AFTA, the Division of Family Psychology sponsors a number of programs in which members may participate, including the annual APA convention. It has established task forces and committees that members may join. A bulletin, *The Family Psychologist*, is published regularly by the division, and many Division 43 members contribute to the APA periodical *Journal of Family Psychology*.

According to L'Abate (1992), family psychology differs from family therapy in three areas. First, "family psychology is interested in the whole functionality-dysfunctionality continuum, while family therapy is mainly concerned with dysfunctionality" (p. 3). Second, "while family psychology focuses reductionistically on the relationship of the individual within the family, family therapy focuses holistically on the family as a whole unit or system" (p. 3). Third, "family psychology stresses objective evaluation and primary and secondary prevention approaches" (p. 3). Family therapy, on the other hand, "stresses the subjective understanding of the family and sees therapy as one type of tertiary prevention" (p. 3). Not all family therapists agree with L'Abate, and the debate about the identity of family psychology continues.

International Association of Marriage and Family Counselors

The International Association of Marriage and Family Counselors (IAMFC) (http://www.iamfc.com/) is a division of the American Counseling Association (ACA). IAMFC membership is interdisciplinary. The major elements common to the approximately 4,000 members include professional training in marriage and family counseling/therapy and an interest/involvement in working with couples and families directly or tangentially. Members participate in regional and national conferences sponsored by the IAMFC and the ACA. In addition, the IAMFC has developed national training standards accepted by its membership and the Council for Accreditation of Counseling and Related Educational Programs (CACREP).

The IAMFC publishes the *IAMFC Newsletter*, which is devoted to examining current issues related to marriage and family counseling, and *The Family Journal: Counseling and Therapy for Couples and Families*, a quarterly periodical. It also produces videos and publishes books related to family therapy—and it is involved in credentialing marriage and family counselors/therapists. The IAMFC is helping to upgrade ethical standards within the ACA on marriage and family counseling/therapy, but maintains its own standards as well.

National Council on Family Relations

The National Council on Family Relations (NCFR) (http://www.ncfr.org/) is the oldest professional association dedicated to working with families. It was established in 1939, and many of its members helped to create and support the AAMFT (Nichols, 1992). Throughout its history, the NCFR has concentrated on education. Its membership is interdisciplinary and includes family life educators, sociologists, family researchers, and family therapists.

A specialty of the NCFR is delineating information about family history, family forms and functions, and family life in a variety of settings. It publishes a variety of publications including the *Journal of Marriage and the Family* and *Family Relations: Interdisciplinary Journal of Applied Family Studies*. It also sponsors annual conventions in which professionals from a wide variety of settings can exchange ideas. One of its major subspecialty groups is devoted to family therapy.

Education of Family Therapists

Part of professional identity is one's education. The educational programs of family therapists are conducted in collaboration with learned societies and associations. The formal process of education is overseen by representatives from a number of associations, such as the Commission on Accreditation for Marriage and Family Therapy Education (COAMFTE) or the Council for Accreditation of Counseling and Related Educational Programs (CACREP).

In recent years the curriculums for graduating master's degree family therapists have been similar in accredited AAMFT and CACREP programs. Table 16.2 shows the required coursework areas for these two programs.

Table 16.2

Example of Coursework Areas Required for a Master's Degree in AAMFT-Accredited and CACREP-Accredited Programs

CACREP Curriculum	AAMFT Curriculum
Human Growth & Development	Introduction Family/Child Dev.
Social and Cultural Foundations	Marital & Family Systems
Helping Relationships	Intro. Family/Child Development
Groups	Dysfunctions in Marriage/Family
Lifestyle & Career Development	Advanced Child Development
Appraisal/Assessment	Assessment in Marital/Family
Research and Evaluation	Research Methods Child/Family
Professional Orientation	Professional Issues Family
Theoretical Foundation MFT	Theories of MFT
Techniques/Treatment MFT	Marriage/Family Pre-Practicum
Clinical Practicum/Internship	Clinical Practicum
Substance Abuse Treatment	Human Sexual Behavior
Human Sexuality	Thesis
Electives	Electives

From "The Training of Marriage and Family Counselors/Therapists: A 'Systemic' Controversy among Disciplines" by Michael Baltimore, 1993, *Alabama Counseling Association Journal, 19,* 40. Copyright 1993, Alabama Counseling Association. Reprinted with permission.

Numerous problems are associated with current educational programs in family therapy. For example, among professional association groups, there is considerable in-fighting for recognition that one method of educating family therapists is superior to others. This type of "turfism" is sometimes conducted in a blind fashion, with some professional groups refusing to recognize other similar groups (Baltimore, 1993).

A second weakness in family therapy education programs as they are presently structured is that "they tend to ignore issues that are controversial and difficult to teach" (Smith & Stevens-Smith, 1992, p. 438). Areas that arouse emotion in regard to therapeutic content and process need to be examined. Divorce, substance abuse, homelessness, teen pregnancies, extramarital affairs, and the impact of AIDS on family life are but a handful of these subjects. They may require specialized courses or they may be explored in different regular course offerings.

Issues in Professional Identification

As is evident from this overview of professional family therapy associations, practitioners have a wide choice regarding which group or groups with which they will align. Each association has unique aspects or foci. For instance, educational groups, such as the National Council on

Family Relations, are most concerned with training and the distribution of information (i.e., secondary intervention). The other associations, such as the AAMFT, concentrate on the therapeutic treatment of dysfunctionality (i.e., tertiary intervention). Each of these associations sponsors programs and speakers that address the issues involved in prevention and education, too. They all like to think of themselves as holistic in their approaches, and indeed the case can be strongly made that the AAMFT, IAMFC, AFTA, and Division 43 of APA do follow such a comprehensive model.

Emphasis aside, friction exists among associations that are dedicated to family therapy. In all likelihood, turf issues surrounding this uneasiness will continue in the foreseeable future.

Summary and Conclusion

Ethical, legal, and professional identity issues are of major importance to family therapists. Ignorance of codes, standards, and associations is no excuse for acting unethically, illegally, and/or unprofessionally.

Family and societal conduct is based on relationship ethics. Thus, family therapy is not value free. When faced with a dilemma, family therapists must know their own values, the values on which ethical codes are based, and the values of the families with whom they work. They can then make informed ethical decisions. Four of the most useful tools they can use in this process are codes of ethics, educational resources, professional consultation, interaction with colleagues, including supervisors, and meta-ethical principles. Common ethical concerns are related to confidentiality, gender inequality, sexual relationships, therapeutic techniques, multicultural therapy issues, and use of the Internet to provide therapy.

Legal issues often overlap with ethical matters. The law and therapy share some common concerns regarding relationships between people. They differ in their emphases on facts/process and adversarial/cooperative approaches. The most common type of law most family therapists are concerned with is civil law (acts offensive to individuals). However, it is important that therapists know other types of law and local/state statutes related to families. Family therapists are most likely to participate in legal situations as expert witnesses, child custody evaluators, reporters of abuse, and court-ordered witnesses. They must actively protect themselves against malpractice by adhering to commonly accepted and legal ways of handling family therapy cases. Furthermore, they must carry malpractice insurance.

In regard to identity, family therapists generally belong to one or more professional associations, including the AAMFT, AFTA, Family Psychology (APA), IAMFC, and NCFR. All of these groups have much to offer that can positively influence the careers of family therapists; however, they sometimes quarrel.

Summary Table
Ethical, Legal, and Professional Issues in Family Therapy

Ethics, law, and identity are of major concern to family therapists.
It is crucial for family therapists to be knowledgeable about issues in ethics, law, and identity if they are to practice according to high standards and avoid serious trouble.

Overview of Ethics in Families and Family Therapy

Families and societies are governed by relationship ethics based on the principle of equitability.

Family therapy is also governed by principles of ethics that have been codified.

Ethics are a part of the total system of family therapy.

Family therapists face more ethical conflicts than other therapists.

Ethics and Values

Ethical decision making is based on an awareness and understanding of values. A value is a choice that is more or less preferable.

Effective therapists are aware of their own values and those of the families with whom they work. Values have an impact on families and are the source from which ethical decisions emerge.

Ethical dilemmas in family therapy are related to deciding which values to keep and which to discard. Emphasis of values is of concern.

How Do Values Influence Ethical Practice?

All ethical issues involve values as grounds for decision making.

The values family therapists embrace directly affect their clinical practice.

Guidelines for Making Ethical Decisions

Five prevalent resources family therapists use in ethical decision making are:
- codes of ethics
- educational resources
- professional consultation
- interactions with colleagues, including supervision
- meta-ethical principles

Both the AAMFT and the IAMFC have developed codes of ethics.

Ethical codes are sometimes limited by the complexity of issues.

Educational resources include case studies and columns on family therapy ethics. Ethical decision making is a step-by-step process.

Professional consultation involves the use of experts to enhance one's knowledge and abilities.

Interactions with peers, including supervision, help family therapists draw on the wisdom and opinions of others in a systemic manner.

Common Ethical Concerns

Among the most common ethical concerns are those involving:
- confidentiality (i.e., the revealing to others of information revealed in a therapy session)
- gender issues (e.g., inequality of men and women)
- sex between a therapist and a client
- use of some theoretical techniques (e.g., conscious deceit or neutrality)
- multicultural therapy issues
- use of the Internet for therapy

Addressing Unethical Behavior

Addressing unethical behavior with fellow professionals accused of violations is the first step in resolving it.

Reporting to professional associations/organizations is a second step.

Complaints by clients to a licensure board is a third step.

Legal Issues in Family Therapy

Ethics and law frequently overlap, such as with cases involving intentional misdiagnosis.

Family therapists are not immune to dealing with the legal system and must be aware of legal decisions, precedents, and practices.

The Legal System

Legal refers to "law or being lawful." Law refers to a body of rules, made on a variety of levels, such as state or federal, that are binding in certain locales and under specific situations.

The legal and therapeutic systems are similar in that they both are concerned with setting up healthy relationships, and both handle cases that involve drama and resolution.

Differences between legal and therapeutic systems also exist. The legal system is concerned with gathering evidence based on facts, and the therapeutic system is more interested in process and change. In addition, the legal system relies on adversity, and the therapeutic system relies on cooperation.

Types of Law

The most common types of law are:

- common law (law derived from tradition)
- statutory law (rules passed by legislative bodies)
- administrative law (rules made by government agencies)
- case law (court decisions)
- civil versus criminal law (offenses against individuals versus those against society in general)

Therapists who are knowledgeable about the law can help themselves and their client-families.

Legal Situations that Involve Family Therapists

Family therapists may be called on to participate in some legal and legally related situations in the following capacities:

- expert witness (one who gives testimony in the form of recommendations about a family or family member)
- child custody evaluator (one who determines the best interest of a child in a custody hearing)
- reporter of abuse (one who informs members of the legal system about the maltreatment of a family member)
- court-ordered witness (one who is subpoenaed to testify in court about a family seen in treatment)

Issues of Law in Family Therapy

Malpractice is a major legal issue and can occur through acts of omission as well as commission. In either case, negligence must be proved.

Advertising and record keeping are two other legal issues. The first involves protecting a title and representing one's skills adequately. The second focuses on keeping accurate and professional notes.

Liability insurance is a must if one is going to be legally protected as a family therapist.

Professional Identification as a Family Therapist

A family therapist's education, background, self-perception, and opportunities are associated with professional identity.

The five national professional associations related to family therapy are as follows:

- The AAMFT was established in 1942. It is the oldest and largest association devoted to family therapy. Its membership is interdisciplinary.
- The AFTA was established in 1977 by Murray Bowen. It is the most focused on teaching and research.
- Family Psychology (APA) was established in 1984 to allow psychology practitioners who work with families to keep their identity as psychologists.
- The IAMFC was established in 1986. It is the second largest family therapy association. It parallels many aspects of AAMFT but is more affiliated with counseling as a profession.
- NCFR was established in 1939, but only one group within the association is dedicated to working therapeutically with families.

Despite areas of overlap, there is still competition and some disagreement among these groups.

Research and Assessment in Family Therapy

---•---

As a child of five he played in leaves
his father raked on autumn days,
safe in the knowledge that the yard was home
and that dinner would be served at sunset.

Now middle-aged he examines fences,
where from within his own children frolic
in the deep shadowed light of dusk,
Aware that strong boundaries help create bonds
that extend time and memory beyond the present.

---•---

Gladding, 1992d

Research and assessment are vitally interlinked with family therapy and have a long association with it. From the time the term *family therapy* was first used in the 1950s until now, there has been a focus on assessment and healing among mental health professionals working with families (Baldwin & Huggins, 1998; Shields, Wynne, McDaniel, & Gawinski, 1994). Indeed, "the assessment of individuals and their family relationships has been and is an evolving part of the marriage and family counseling literature" (Sporakowski, 1995, p. 60).

Most of the pioneers in family therapy employed research-based procedures to evaluate and work with families. They were in effect "researcher-clinicians" (Sprenkle & Moon, 1996, p. 3). Although some of their research was soft by today's standards, initially, research came first and therapy was a secondary activity. Many early studies of therapeutic changes in families conducted by groups, such as those led by Bateson, Wynne, and Minuchin, excelled in family therapy research and assessment (Wynne, 1983). Historically, in the world of family therapy, there has been "a synergistic interplay among research, theory, and practice" (Sprenkle & Piercy, 1984, p. 226).

It is unfortunate but, after the genesis of family therapy, many practitioners drifted away from research and assessment. The reasons were multiple but included the tension between ethical, moral, and legal considerations connected with investigating family therapy as well as the complications involved in the process, such as conducting research in community agencies where most clinical services are delivered (Margolin et al., 2005; McCollum & Stith, 2002). This split is most dramatically seen today in some influential schools of family therapy whose advocates have gained considerable prominence but whose methods provide little empirical evidence to support their effectiveness (Gurman, Kniskern, & Pinsof, 1986). During the 1960s, therapists and researchers became two distinct groups, a fact lamented by Jay Haley (1978), among others.

In the 1990s, interest renewed in both the practice of family therapy and the conducting of research. Research became so prevalent that it was hard to keep up with it (Liddle, 1992). Research by family therapists started including methods such as "surveys, personal interviews, observational studies, and content analysis of historical documents" (Bird & Sporakowski, 1992, p. x). The 1990s "marked a dramatic increase in the incidence of empirical articles published using qualitative methodology" (Faulkner, Klock, & Gale, 2002, p. 73). Growth in the volume of family therapy research, and its more sophisticated procedures, added to the power and credibility of family therapy.

In the 21st century, family therapy is becoming even more refined in its research and focus on real-life context. The quantity and quality of research are improving dramatically (Spenkle, 2003). The researcher John Gottman has become well-known for his "love lab" that looks at real-time interactions between couples. Carrere, Buchlman, Gottman, Coan, & Ruckstruhl (2000) have found in studying the longitudinal course of marriages through social psychophysiological observations of marital interactions that they can predict with 81% accuracy what marriages will last at least 5 years. More emphasis is now placed on connecting process and outcome in family therapy research, too (Baldwin & Huggins, 1998), and making the translation of research findings into practical ways of working with dysfunctional families (Hawley & Gonzalez, 2005; Liddle, 1992). Whole issues of journals, such as the January 2002 issue of the *Journal of Marital and Family Therapy*, are being devoted to research as well.

The assessment of families is becoming stronger. **Assessment** focuses on dimensions of particular families and usually includes the administration of formal or informal tests or evaluation instrument(s) along with behavioral observations. Assessment is dependent on having a theoretical model of how families function and of the ways in which their functioning may go awry. Sometimes this type of information is easily obtained, but often it is not. The field of family assessment is less developed and more complex than that of individual evaluation (Drummond, 2004; Snyder, Cavell, Heffer, & Mangrum, 1995).

Ways of conducting assessment are covered in this chapter, and some of the most common assessment instruments are described. The most prominent features of family research are considered first.

Importance of Research in Family Therapy

Research is important in family therapy for many reasons, but three of the most important involve accountability, practicality, and uniqueness.

In regard to accountability, research studies provide family therapists with the means to prove they are not "witch doctors, snake oil peddlers, or overachieving do-gooders" (Hubble, 1993, p. 14). Research results are a necessary element in the increasing respectability of family therapy.

On the level of practicality, research also has a payoff. Although research studies sometimes do not yield immediate applicability, they do have "an influence on clinical practice" in the long run (Hubble, 1993, p. 15). Therefore, it is critical that practitioners in family therapy admit when they do not know something and challenge researchers to find answers (Young, 2005). It is also vital that practitioners, as well as statisticians, become familiar with family therapy research methods and outcomes.

In regard to uniqueness, it is through research that the field of family therapy establishes its common bond and point of departure with other mental health counseling approaches. By gaining knowledge about treatment methods and approaches, the profession of family therapy establishes itself as a type of entity that can make claims for its theories, practices, and clinicians (Schwartz & Breunlin, 1983). Thus, research is a vital link in the claim that family therapy should and does stand on its own as a type of specialized treatment (Piercy & Sprenkle, 1986).

Research Findings in Family Therapy

Most research studies are published in journals where scholars and practitioners can examine them for both process and outcomes (Hawley & Gonzalez, 2005). Research on the effectiveness of family therapy is no exception. Refereed periodicals such as the *Journal of Marital and Family Therapy, Family Process, Contemporary Family Therapy, The Family Journal: Counseling and Therapy with Couples and Families, Journal of Family Psychology,* and the *American Journal of Family Therapy* are some of the most common outlets for research studies.

Overall findings from research on family therapy indicate in general that most individuals and families improve when they receive couple and family therapy of any kind, especially when compared with a control group left on its own to resolve problems. Comprehensive reviews of family therapy research indicate specifically that:

- "Marriage and family interventions, both therapy and enrichment, are more effective than no treatment." Those effects tend to be maintained at follow-up (Shadish & Baldwin, 2003, p. 561).
- Improvement rates in marriage and family therapy are similar to improvement rates in individual therapy.

- Deterioration rates in marriage and family therapy are similar to deterioration rates in individual therapy.
- Deterioration can take place because the therapist:
  - has poor interpersonal skills
  - moves too quickly into sensitive topic areas and does not handle the situation well
  - allows family conflict to become exacerbated without moderating therapeutic intervention
  - does not provide adequate structure in the early stages of therapy
  - does not support family members (Fenell & Weinhold, 2003, p. 343)
- Family therapy is as effective as individual counseling for some personal problems such as depression (although severe psychological disorders may need additional interventions, e.g., schizophrenia is best treated through family psychoeducation and medication) (Goldstein & Miklowitz, 1995; Hernandez & Doherty, 2005).
- Family psychoeducation programs, which offer a treatment plan for the consumer and are usually diagnosis-specific, e.g., schizophrenia, bipolar disorder, decrease relapse and rehospitalization rates among patients whose families receive such services (McFarlane, Dixon, Lukens, & Lucksted, 2003).
- "Different kinds of marriage and family interventions tend to produce similar results" (Shadish & Baldwin, 2003, p. 561).
- Brief therapy of 20 sessions or less is as effective as open-ended or long-term therapy.
- Participation of fathers in family therapy is much more likely to bring about positive results than family therapy without them.
- Cotherapists and cotherapy have not been shown to be any more successful than sessions conducted by one therapist.
- Persons who receive "individual, marital, or family therapy" all reduce "their health care use after therapy," with the "largest reductions coming from those participants" who have "some form of conjoint therapy" (Law, Crane, & Berge, 2003, p. 353). This phenomenon of people reducing this health care after therapy is known as the **offset effect.**
- Just as in other types of therapy, therapists with good relationship skills are more successful than those with poor skills in fostering change and producing positive outcomes.
- "Marriage therapy tends to have better outcomes than family therapy, but this seems to occur because family therapists often deal with more difficult problems (e.g., schizophrenia)" (Shadish & Baldwin, 2003, p. 561).
- Psychosomatic, as well as substance abuse, problems can be treated successfully with a modified version of structural family therapy (Minuchin et al., 1978; Stanton & Todd, 1981, 1982).
- The type of family, its background, and its interactional style do not relate to the success or failure of family therapy (Gurman & Kniskern, 1981).
- Marriage and family therapy is moving more towards evidence-based treatments (similar to medicine and public health) (Shadish & Baldwin, 2003).

Some of the most promising research in the area of family therapy has been conducted by Jose Szapocznik and his associates at the Center for Family Studies at the University of Miami School of Medicine (Letich, 1993; Muir, Schwartz, & Szapocznik, 2004; Williams, 2005). This clinically based research has concentrated on Hispanic/Latino American and

African-American families since the early 1970s. While specific to these families, there are also some general implications. Among the contributions made by Szapocznik are:

- the development of Brief Strategic Family Therapy as a "family-based intervention that was responsive to the findings of a cross-cultural survey given to Cuban immigrants and White Americans in Miami" (Muir et al., 2004, p. 290)
- the formulation of Structural Ecosystems Therapy (SET) as "an ecological extension of BSFT, to address the need for extrafamilial as well as within-family intervention" with Hispanic and African-American adolescents (Muir et. al., 2004, p. 295)
- the development of the Strategic Family Systems Rating (SFSR), a research tool that objectively measures and evaluates family functioning on six dimensions: structure, resonance, developmental stage, identified patienthood, flexibility, and conflict resolution (Szapocznik et al., 1991)
- the creation of **one-person family therapy (OPFT),** in which strategic family therapy is offered to any person who comes to therapy in order to help that person make changes in the family system (Szapocznik, Kurtines, Perez-Vidal, Hervis, & Foote, 1990)
- a comparison of outcome in boys and their families of the efficacy of individual, psychodynamic, child therapy versus family therapy (a landmark study in supporting the family therapy concept of complementarity, that is, if one person gets better without changing the family structure, the rest of the family gets worse) (Szapocznik et al., 1989)
- the formulation of Structural Ecosystems Therapy for HIV-seropositive African-American women which identifies needs and concerns in these inner-city women's lives and seeks to provide them with the presence of "at least one supportive, involved, and concerned family member" (Muir et al., 2004, p. 297)

Szapocznik's research demonstrates a commitment to rigor and control with an orientation toward practical use. His work represents the best of clinical research. He and his colleagues have targeted interventions for ethnic minority families and in the process distinguished the culture of a given group from the culture of the inner city or the culture of poverty. This work is often idealized and serves as a model for the integration of research and theory within the field of family therapy.

Two Types of Family Therapy Research

The two types of family therapy research are qualitative and quantitative. **Qualitative research** is still in its infancy but is being used more and more (Hawley & Gonzalez, 2005). It is rooted in the traditions of anthropology and sociology (Moon, Dillon, & Sprenkle, 1990). "Qualitative researchers can capture and share their findings in a variety of ways" (Piercy & Benson, 2005, p. 109). For example, qualitative research can use aesthetic means such as drama, art, music or poetry as well as other means such as graphs and charts. There is even qualitative software, such as ATLASti (http://www.atlasti.de/), that allows "researchers to organize and analyze not only text documents, but also hyperlinks to audio, visual, and internet data, pictures, news clips, websites, and videotapes of interactions (Piercy & Benson, 2005, p. 109).

Present interest in qualitative methodology "appears to be part of a larger postmodern turn in the human sciences. Postmodernism represents a general loss of faith in ultimate truth, a 'knowable' reality, certainty, and determinacy" (Kleist & Gompertz, 1997, p. 137). According to Moon et al. (1990) most qualitative research is characterized by:

- open-ended, discovery-oriented questions that are holistic
- small samples carefully chosen to "fit research goals (criterion-based selection)" or to "help elaborate developing theory (theoretical selection)" (p. 369)
- participant-observer researchers who are subjectively explicit
- visual or verbal data reporting rather than numerical data reporting
- data analysis occurring simultaneously with data collection
- "analytic induction and constant comparison" (p. 369) by researchers who try to discern patterns in analyzing results of time- and labor-intensive investigations
- results that "take the form of theoretical assertions, discovered theory, or categorical systems (taxonomies)" (p. 369)
- reports that are well written, often as books, but with no standardized form
- reliability and validity based on journalistic reflections, thick descriptions of data, audits, comparison analysis, and "participant critiques of research reports" (p. 369)

Qualitative research, at its best, is found in extended interviews and autobiographies. A good example of a qualitative research study is the interview study of 10 couples with children in which both partners worked outside the home (Hochschild, 1989). In this research, written as a book, couples were asked who did what work around the house as well as information about their backgrounds. The researchers detected patterns and then made comments about them. The advantages of qualitative research over quantitative research include a more integrated and holistic view of client-families and greater interaction between researcher/clinicians and client-families (Sussman & Gilgun, 1997). Qualitative research also increases the flexibility of therapists to meet the needs of families (Hood & Johnson, 2002).

A particular type of qualitative research that is beginning to impact family therapy is participatory evaluation research (Piercy & Thomas, 1998). **Participatory evaluation research** has various forms but it differs from "other qualitative methods in the degree of participants' involvement" (p. 166). Instead of asking clients for information, a participatory researcher "might actually train clients as individual or focus group interviewers and involve them as co-researchers in data analysis interpretation and write-up" (p. 167). Overall, participatory research engages and empowers participants much more in the research process and is more democratic than other types of research.

Quantitative research grew out of the scientific traditions of physics, chemistry, and biology, and is the way most research is reported. Quantitative research is characterized by an emphasis on closed-ended questions, such as "Does a certain variable, such as working outside the home, have an impact on a family's happiness?" To answer this type of question, quantitative research utilizes large sample sizes to gather information. Objective researchers then focus on gathering data in a precise form, frequently using standardized instruments. Usually, the data from such studies is reported in a statistical format, such as averages of specific test scores. After the data are collected, they are analyzed and deductive conclusions are made based on the data analysis. The results tend to "prove" or "disprove" theories and assertions that formed the basis for the research in the first place.

A final report is then written in a standard and prosaic form. It describes what was done and how it was done. The report highlights characteristics of the population used; the reliability and validity of the instruments employed; and the process, conclusions, and recommendations for further research (Gay & Airasian, 2000; Goldman, 1990).

Quantitative research is one reason why family therapy is seen as a science as well as an art. By using quantitative methods, researchers are careful to define what they are doing and to record their results in a precise and scholarly manner. When they present their findings, quantitative researchers are likely to be able to focus on interventions that made a difference overall in their treatment. One example of an empirical study is the investigation of systemic and nonsystemic diagnostic processes by McGuirk, Friedlander, and Blocher (1987) in which they found that "systemic clinicians, in contrast with … nonsystemic ones, identified as relevant a greater number of different subsystems, more triads, and fewer monads" (p. 69).

Whether family therapy researchers choose qualitative or quantitative research methods, they must deal with complexities that are usually quite complicated. Most family therapy is premised on a systemic perspective that emphasizes circular causality (i.e., A and B affect each other) rather than linear thinking that stresses cause and effect (e.g., A caused B). Thus, the emphasis in treatment and research is on the interaction of family members with each other (West, 1988). Difficulties stemming from this model present themselves in many forms. Questions related to one's choices of research design, sampling, instrumentation, and procedure are critical. Theoretical and statistical choices are also important in regard to researching the process and outcome of family therapy.

Difficulties in Family Therapy Research

Many difficulties are associated with rigorously researching the effectiveness of family therapy. These include, but are not limited to, the complexity of relationships within families. In the study of family relationships, one question is "What within the family is the focus of attention?" For example, family therapy research can concentrate on the identified patient (IP), the marriage, the total family system, cross-generational relationships, and so forth (Gurman & Kniskern, 1981). The problems connected with studying families are further complicated by environmental factors. Are families studied within their environments or in a laboratory setting?

Furthermore, the time commitment needed to study the effects of family therapy is great—and the number of personnel who must be devoted to gathering and analyzing data is difficult and expensive to sustain over time. Many of John Gottman's longitudinal studies have lasted 10 or 15 years and have been both time-consuming and costly (Jencius & Duba, 2003). Finally, there is the matter of ethical and regulatory standards. "Family therapists are expected to engage in ethical and responsible research, while maintaining rigorous ethical standards and adhering to federal regulations that require protection for research participants" (Cain, Harkness, Smith, & Markowski, 2003, p. 47). That task is huge. It can be handled by adhering to professional ethical standards and federal and state regulations governing human research, e.g., the **National Research Act** (Public Law 94-348). In addition, the principles issued in the **Belmont Report** (National Commission for the Protection of Human Subjects of Biomedical and Behavioral Research, 1979) should be followed. These principles state that in basic human research there should be respect for persons (i.e., their autonomy and dignity), beneficence (i.e., minimize harm and risks, maximize benefits), and justice (i.e., select participants equitably).

Assuming that the questions of focus, environment, and ethical regulatory considerations can be handled properly, it becomes important to focus attention on another pertinent aspect of research—its design.

Design

The way in which research is designed ultimately affects the results (Gay & Airasian, 2000). Poorly designed studies yield worthless results; well-designed studies produce reports worth reading. In considering the design of a research study, investigators must make sure the design fits the families to be studied and that it is efficient (Miller, 1986).

The five categories of research design are exploratory, descriptive, developmental, experimental, and correlational. In **exploratory research** a qualitative approach is often taken because issues are still being defined. Therefore, many exploratory research designs consist of interviews between researchers and families. In **descriptive research,** the design is set up to describe specific variables, for example, subpopulations within the United States.

Developmental research designs focus on studying changes over time. The most characteristic of this type of design is a longitudinal study, although some cross-sectional studies are developmental in nature, too. A study focusing on the effects within families in which a member had AIDS is an example of a longitudinal study. **Experimental research** designs are those that adhere to classic "hard science" methodologies, such as an hypothesis and dependent/independent variables. In an experimental research design, at least one variable is manipulated.

In **correlational research designs,** the degree of association or relatedness between two variables is calculated. This type of research is usually ex post facto (after the fact) rather than a priori (before the fact). With correlational research, unlike experimental research, it is difficult to state in any precise way what factors were most influential and with whom. A correlational study might be one that examined the number of divorces in marriages of children of divorce.

Sampling

Because it is virtually impossible to study all families within a community, the sample that one chooses becomes extremely important. When conducted properly, a randomly chosen sample of families is representative of an entire group of families. "There is no substitute for randomly assigning families to treatment conditions. Without random assignment, group differences are uninterpretable; the study is not worth conducting" (Jacobson, 1985, p. 154).

In a **random assignment sampling** procedure, every family has an equal chance of being selected. Families are chosen by the luck of the draw. For instance, each family is assigned a number and then those numbers are blindly pulled out of a hat to set up a control and experimental group. The results of such studies are generalizable to the selected population of families as a whole.

When a sample is not chosen wisely, bias and/or misinformation result. Such has been the case with a large number of family studies (Gurman et al., 1986). Several creative ways have been devised to collect samples of families. Two of the most frequently used are those based on probability and those based on nonprobability. "Probability samples are drawn from a known population in such a way that it is possible to calculate the likelihood … of each case being included in the sample" (Miller, 1986, p. 70). In this method, it is also possible to estimate the margin of error between the sample data and the entire population. Ways of conducting probability sampling include conducting:

- a **simple random sample,** in which each family within a population has an equal chance of being selected
- a **systematic random sample,** in which the first family to be studied is selected at random, and then every nth family is automatically included

- a **stratified sampling,** in which random samples are drawn from different strata or groups of a population, such as families headed by women and families headed by men

Nonprobability samples are the opposite of probability samples. They may be used "when representativeness of a whole population is not as important as the information itself or when probability sampling is not feasible" (Nelson, 1996, p. 454). Despite a reluctance to use non-probability samples, they "have an important place in marriage and family research" (Miller, 1986, p. 70). This is especially true in studies that "are more exploratory and qualitative, hypothesis generating rather than hypothesis testing" (Miller, 1986, p. 71). Ways of collecting nonprobability samples are through:

- convenience (using local families or those known by the researcher)
- **snowballing** (asking participating families to refer other families)
- purposiveness (choosing families because they are thought by the researcher to be representative of the study population)

Instrumentation

Self-report instruments "provide family members an opportunity to systemically understand what the other members' concerns are" and "to self-disclose through paper and pencil rather than their usual method, which has failed" (Brock & Barnard, 1988, p. 41). The type of instrument used in a study has an influence on what is reported as outcome. A self-report instrument can yield a different result than a behaviorally based observation report. Self-reports also have an advantage in family therapy research in that they can be distributed to a large number of families at a relatively low cost. Their scoring is also objective, and this makes it relatively easy to establish external validity (i.e., generalization) (Copeland & White, 1991). On the other hand, self-reports are questionable in regard to **construct validity**—that is, measuring what they report to measure.

More open-ended or behaviorally based instruments have an advantage in that they focus on specific actions that can be observed in the present. They also allow researchers an opportunity to establish a baseline by which future interactions can be measured. This type of data is more complete than self-reports. However, it is more complicated to obtain:

> **Direct observational assessment** is characterized by the use of coders, raters, or judges, who usually are not participants in the interpersonal system being studied and whose task is to unitize and assign meaning to some aspects of the family therapy process. (Alexander, Newell, Robbins, & Turner, 1995, p. 355)

The weaknesses of open-ended and behaviorally based instruments include **interrater reliability** (i.e., the degree to which raters agree on what they observe) and other types of bias that may slip into the reports that are made (Copeland & White, 1991). Direct observation of families can also be very expensive and time-consuming (L'Abate & Bagarozzi, 1993). One attempt to resolve this problem has been to videotape families and have more than one observer evaluate their actions (Lewis, Beavers, Gossett, & Phillips, 1976).

Procedure

Procedure involves how families are studied. Methods are numerous and include the use of surveys, direct observation, phone calls, e-mails, and the examination of written records. Using more than one way of gathering data may be advantageous (Northey, 2005).

Regardless, research procedures and paradigms are not neutral. Instead they reflect the **epistemology** (i.e., worldview, knowledge) of the investigator (Colapinto, 1979). Researchers who are interested in proving the effectiveness of a theory or method generally concentrate on outcome research, that is, what is achieved as a result of a therapeutic intervention. In this type of research, families are exposed to a task or condition, and a measure is made of the impact (i.e., the behavioral reaction) (Beavers, 1985). On the other hand, researchers who wish to examine "the 'how' and the 'why' of effective or noneffective therapy" concentrate on doing process research (Diamond & Dickey, 1993, p. 23). Process research is time-consuming and labor intensive (Liddle, 1992). However, the results are often enlightening and clinically meaningful. They can inform practitioners of what treatments under what conditions and with what types of clients are most effective. Furthermore, process research "can assess the systemic and contextual processes that characterize family therapy" (Diamond & Dickey, 1993, p. 24).

Theory

Theory is an important element in research, and the interrelationship between theory, research, and practice is a crucial component in family therapy (Hawley & Geske, 2000). Well-designed research is based on questions that have usually arisen from a theory. Investigators conduct their inquiries to prove or disprove specific theoretical hypotheses, such as the importance of establishing permeable boundaries in family functioning. In using theory as a basis for conducting studies, researchers should pick a strong and relatively simple, clear theory that is logically connected (Shields, 1986).

Most family therapy is based on general systems theory. This theory has made specific inquiry into how families change (Reiss, 1988). Some theoretical research, such as that on addicts and their families by Stanton et al. (1982), has been successful because of the careful way it was set up. However, in numerous cases, the questions that have been asked and the answers that have been derived have been insignificant or even harmful.

An example of a group of detrimental inquiries not carefully based on general systems theory is found in some research studies on African-American families that employ "a deficit theoretical underpinning" (Turner, 1993, p. 9). In these studies, the focus is on African-American childhood aggression, within-race violence, household father absence, family disruption, and social/health problems. This type of approach assumes that African-American families can and should be compared with "ideal families" or families from other cultural groups. It "overlooks the political realities that individuals and families are affected by race, economic status, and cultural values" (Turner, 1993, p. 9). Research of this nature fails to view whatever family form or family group is being studied as embedded in larger social systems.

Statistics

Researchers can be excellent methodologists but weak statisticians. Likewise, statisticians may not be able to design research studies in a scientific manner. Regardless, when research results are reported in a statistical manner, they need to be clinically relevant and readable to practitioners as well as scientists (Gay & Airasian, 2000). One way to do this is to use descriptive statistics as a supplement to other statistical procedures. "By reporting the proportion of clients who improve to a clinically significant degree, the data from family therapy outcome research will be much more useful to family therapists than it will if researchers limit their reports to group means and statistical significance tests" (Jacobson, 1985, p. 151).

In general, statistics can show that a family is improved under the following circumstances:

- "if the posttherapy status places" the family "outside the distribution of dysfunctional clients (or families) and/or within the limits of a functional distribution of clients and
- if the amount of change during the course of therapy exceeds expectations" (Jacobson, 1988, p. 141)

Problems in reporting statistics are related to whether the sample they were based on was skewed or normally distributed.

Validity/Reliability

Validity "is the extent to which a measuring instrument measures what it was intended to measure" (Miller, 1986, p. 58). There are three main measures of validity:

1. **content validity,** which is aimed at actually tapping into representative beliefs or behaviors
2. **criterion validity,** which is the degree to which what is measured actually relates to life experience
3. **construct validity,** which is the degree to which a measured performance matches a theoretical expectation

Reliability refers to the consistency or dependency of a measure. Another way to conceptualize reliability is that it truly measures the differences between families. Perfect reliability is expressed as a correlational coefficient of 1.00, which is seldom achieved. "Measures can be reliable but not valid, but they cannot be valid unless they are reliable" (Miller, 1986, p. 59).

Family therapy research must have strong degrees of validity and reliability in order to be considered substantial. Consumers of research need to focus on the validity and reliability of outcomes in studies as they evaluate results.

The Importance of Assessing Families

An **assessment procedure** is any method "used to measure characteristics of people, programs, or objects" (American Educational Research Association, American Psychological Association, & National Council on Measurement in Education, 1985, p. 89). As opposed to testing, which is usually a task in which people are asked to do their maximum best, assessment evaluates typical performances, behaviors, or qualities. It is broader than any test measure. As such, assessment is a vital part of family therapy. Through assessment, therapists gain information that helps them diagnose and respond systemically and appropriately to the families with whom they are working (Gold, 1997). For example, therapists gain insight into a family's structure (i.e., roles, boundaries); control (i.e., power, flexibility); emotions/needs (i.e., affective expression, affective themes); culture (i.e., social position, cultural heritage); and development (stage of life) (Fisher, 1976).

In the past, the *Diagnostic and Statistical Manual* (*DSM*), which is published by the American Psychiatric Association and is the basis on which mental health disorders are assessed, has given little attention to marital and family diagnostic categories. Basically, the *DSM* is based on the medical model and is individually oriented. Thus, "the marriage and family field has been marginalized in the diagnosis process" (Hill & Crews, 2005, p. 179) because most of the key concerns of family therapists have been relationship-oriented (Simola,

Parker, & Froese, 1999). Rather than attach a disorder label to a relationship, the *DSM*'s approach has been to use **V codes** or the **Global Assessment of Relational Functioning Scale (GARF)** to describe these difficulties (Crews & Hill, 2005). The V code designation means that the condition described is "not attributable to a mental disorder" (American Psychiatric Association [APA], 1994, p. 9). The GARF is analogous to Axis V of the *DSM* GAF (Global Assessment of Functioning) scale that is used to assess individual functioning. It can be used to indicate an overall judgment of the functioning of a family on a hypothetical continuum ranging from competent, optimal relational functioning to a disrupted, dysfunctional relationship.

The fourth edition of the *DSM* (*DSM-IV*; APA, 1994) "brings slightly more focus on relational problems, such as parent–child, sibling, and partner relationships and physical and sexual abuse" (Sporakowski, 1995, p. 61). However, it is still not "user friendly" for clinicians working primarily with families because a V code diagnosis is not reimbursed by a third-party payer, such as an insurance company, regardless of its seriousness (Crews & Hill, 2005). Nevertheless, despite this obvious drawback, family therapists need to assess and diagnose when possible so that an appropriate treatment plan can be developed and followed (Gold, 1997).

Another advantage of assessment is that families and their members can be helped to understand the dynamics within their relationship better, enabling them to clarify goals, and to gain a sense of perspective (Hood & Johnson, 2002).

A final reason for the importance of assessment relates to accountability and professionalism. Therapy requires documentation of services and the reasons behind the services being offered. Family therapy is moving to become more scientific and precise. Family clinicians who wish to improve their skills and serve the public are increasingly likely to rely on assessment. Such reliance is a matter of being responsible.

Dimensions of Assessing Families

Most assessment with families is based on a systemic approach. This approach

> requires that one utilize the transactions between individuals, rather than the characteristics of each given individual, as primary data. Even when, for one reason or another, attention is focused on one person, his/her behavior is analyzed in terms of its power to affect and shape the behavior of other members of the system and in terms of the variables of the ecosystem that may have affected it. (Sluzko, 1978, p. 366)

When questions are asked in therapy sessions, they focus on transactions and relationships more than demographic data. They might include inquiries such as "When John gets angry, Mary, what do you do?" or "Carole, how do you react when the other children leave you out of their activities?"

Fishman (1988) states that therapists should consider four aspects of assessment: "contemporary developmental pressures on the family, history, structure, and process" (p. 14). He continues

> The four-dimensional model should give therapists, like cubist painters, a kaleidoscopic view of their subject. It allows therapists to look at a moving system from different perspectives. It also takes into consideration therapists' positions in the process as they move in and out of the system, sometimes as neutral observers, other times as involved protagonists who support a particular family member or suddenly realize the family's control. (p. 14)

This emphasis on processes and therapists' active place in them is what helps define family therapy as a therapy of experience.

Methods Used in Assessing Families

Assessment techniques available to family therapists "are many and varied" (Sporakowski, 1995, p. 61). Both informal and formal methods are used in the assessment of families. **Informal assessment** methods include observational data related to either natural or game-playing situations that may or may not be quantified. **Formal assessment** methods are usually field-tested instruments, some of which are based on a theoretical foundation and some of which are not (L'Abate & Bagarozzi, 1993).

Informal Methods of Assessing Families

There are a number of ways to informally assess couples and families. For instance, Sarnoff and Sarnoff (2005) have devised the *Couples Creativity Assessment Tasks (C-CAT)* to provide an "informal assessment of a couple's ability to create positive experiences in their relationship" (p. 83). The tasks in this assessment instrument include a focus on early memories, the future, perceptions of creative problem-solving ability, and divergent thinking. The assessment, which takes about 45 to 55 minutes to complete, is meant to be enjoyable and to bring "more positive, loving, and healthy interactions" into a couple's life together (p. 84).

One of the best informal methods of assessing a family is through using the *Family Assessment Form* (Piercy, McKeon, & Laird, 1983). Though concise, this form provides family therapists of all theoretical orientations with a means for fine-tuning their approach with a particular family. As can be seen from examining the family assessment form shown in Figure 17.1, therapists can gain a lot of knowledge in a relatively short amount of time. They can then tailor clarification questions and possible interventions accordingly.

Another way to informally assess families is through direct observation. In contrast to individual counseling, family therapy "offers the unique opportunity to observe directly the problematic interpersonal exchanges of clients and to contrast these with subjective appraisals of these events" (Snyder et al., 1995, pp. 163–164). Even though this process is complex because of the number of individuals in some sessions and possible expressions of hostility, it is an invaluable tool for picking up information that other instruments cannot provide.

Formal Methods of Assessing Families

More than 1,000 assessment instruments are available to family therapists (Fredman & Sherman, 1987; Grotevant & Carlson, 1989; Touliatos, Perlmutter, & Straus, 1990). They cover areas as diverse as intimacy, power, parenthood, and adjustment. "Instruments can enrich the practitioner's and the clients' assessment and treatment process when used in combination" (Thomas, 1995, p. 285). Figure 17.2 lists some of the most widely used assessment measures in marital and family therapy training programs, as reported by Gold (1997).

This text examines some of the best known and refined family and marital tests, many of which are on Gold's list. Nevertheless, clinicians need to consult reference works and abstracts for specific measures pertinent to their situations. It is important to note that with all assessment instruments, scales used in family therapy must be employed judiciously. These instruments should also be scrutinized in regard to the variables being measured, the scales and

Family Name _____ (Age)_____

Father _____(___) Mother _____(___)

Occupation _____ Occupation _____

Years Married _____

Children: _____(___) _____(___) _____(___)

_____(___) _____(___) _____(___)

Blended Family Relationships (Number of marriages, children by other marriages, etc.)

_____

_____

Referral Source _____

1. Presenting Problem/Change Desired (from each person's perspective)

2. Repetitive Nonproductive Behavioral Sequences (attempted solutions, attempts to maintain homeostatic balance)

3. Family Structure (family map; enmeshment, isolation or individuation, chaos, rigidity or flexibility; power structure; generational boundaries; spousal relationships, alliances, roles played, intrusions, etc.)

4. Communication and Interaction Styles (direct, clear, indirect, confused, vague, double binding, affective, cognitive, positive, supported, negative, aggressive, etc.)

5. Hypotheses Regarding Symptom Maintenance (how might the symptom serve a function)

6. Family Life Stages (courtship, early marriage, child bearing, child rearing, parents of teenagers, launching, middle years, retirement, etc.)

7. Pertinent Family-of-Origin Information (positive or negative influence from past generations)

8. External Sources of Stress and Support (relationships outside immediate family: community, work, friends, relatives)

9. Family Strengths

10. Significant Physical Conditions/Medication

11. Other Information (previous treatment, test results, etc.)

12. Therapeutic Goals:

13. Proposed Therapeutic Interventions (means for reaching goals)

_____   _____
Counselor's Signature   Date

Figure 17.1
Family assessment form.
From "A Family Assessment Process for Community Mental Health Clinics" by F. P. Piercy, D. McKeon, and R. A. Laird, 1983, *AMHCA Journal, 5*(3), pp. 94–104. Reprinted by permission of the publisher.

Marital assessment measures (*n* = 19)
>   Attitudes Toward Working Women Scale
>   Caring Days Inventory
>   Couples' Pre-Counseling Inventory
>   Dual-Career Family Scale
>   Dyadic Adjustment Scale
>   Evaluating and Nurturing Relationship Issues, Communication, and Happiness
>   Exchange-Orientation Instrument
>   Family of Origin Scale
>   Locke-Wallace Marital Adjustment Test
>   Marital Adjustment Balance Scale
>   Marital Communication Inventory
>   Marital Evaluation Checklist
>   Marital Satisfaction Inventory
>   Myers-Briggs Typology Inventory
>   Personal Assessment of Intimacy in Relationship
>   Sexual Attitudes and Beliefs Inventory
>   Sexual Interaction Inventory
>   Spouse Observation Checklist
>   Waring Intimacy Questionnaire

Parenting assessment measures (*n* = 2)
>   Parent-Adolescent Communication Inventory
>   Parenting Skills Inventory

Family assessment measures (*n* = 8)
>   Beavers-Timberlawn Family Evaluation Scales
>   Conflict Tactics Scale
>   Family Adaptability and Cohesion Scale
>   Family Inventory of Life Events and Change
>   Kveback Family Sculpture Test
>   McMaster Family Assessment Device
>   Quality of Life Scale
>   Taylor-Johnson Temperament Analysis

Figure 17.2
Widely used assessment measures in marital and family therapy training programs.
From "Assessing Education in Marriage and Family Counseling" by J. M. Gold, 1997, *The Family Journal: Counseling and Therapy for Couples and Families, 5*, 159–163. Copyright © 1997 by Sage Publications, Inc. Reprinted by permission of Sage Publications, Inc.

subscales being reported, the ease or difficulty of scoring directions and interpretation of test results, and the evidence available about validity and reliability (Sprenkle & Piercy, 1984).

Despite availability of an increasing number of family therapy measurement devices, clinicians are reticent to use them. One reason for this reticence is that using assessment instruments removes family therapists from the cutting edge of innovative practice (Shields et al., 1994). In addition, many practitioners lack adequate training in family assessment instruments (Thomas & Olson, 1993). Those family therapists who do employ measuring devices in their practices most often use individually focused assessment instruments, such as the MMPI-2 and the

Table 17.1
Model Conceptual Issues and Formal Assessment Techniques Across Family System Levels

Model Conceptual Issues	Formal Assessment
Individual	
How may cognitive style or abilities influence family members' response to therapy or each other?	Short-form Wechsler administrations (Silverstein, 1990) Peabody Picture Vocabulary Test–Revised (Dunn & Dunn, 1981) Attributional Style Questionnaire (Peterson & Villanova, 1988) Children's Attributional Style Questionnaire (Fielstein et al., 1985)
What dimensions of individual emotional or behavioral functioning influence family interaction? Which of these, if any, warrant separate treatment? Which reflect strengths?	Minnesota Multiphasic Personality Inventory–2 (Butcher, Dahlstrom, Graham, Tellegen, & Kaemmer, 1989) Millon Clinical Multiaxial Inventory–II (Millon, 1987) NEO Personality Inventory–Revised (Costa & McCrae, 1992) Schedule for Affective Disorders and Schizophrenia (Endicott & Spitzer, 1978)
How should current issues be viewed from a developmental perspective?	Child Behavior Checklist (Achenbach & Edelbrock, 1983) Personality Inventory for Children (Wirt, Lachar, Klinedinst, & Seat, 1984) Kiddie-Schedule for Affective Disorders and Schizophrenia (Puig-Antich & Chambers, 1978)
Dyad	
What are the sources and levels of distress or satisfaction in the marriage? In the parent–child relationships?	Marital Satisfaction Inventory (Snyder, 1981) Sexual Functioning Inventory (Derogatis, 1975) Parenting Stress Index (Abidin, 1986)
What patterns of communication typify these relationships?	Marital Interaction Coding System–Global (Weiss & Toiman, 1990) Rapid Couples Interaction Scoring System (Krokoff, Gottman, & Hass, 1989) Parent–Adolescent Interaction Coding System (Robin & Weiss, 1980)
How consistent and functional are relationship expectations? How do members view each other's behavior?	Relationship Brief Inventory (Edelson & Epstein, 1982) Relationship Attribution Measure (Fincham & Bradbury, 1992) Child's Report of Parental Behavior Inventory (Burger & Armentrout, 1971)
Nuclear family	
How close do family members feel to each other? How effective is the family in responding to daily challenges and crises?	Family Environment Scale (Moos & Moos, 1986) Children's Version–Family Environment Scale (Pino, Simons, & Slawinowski, 1984)

Myers-Briggs Type Indicator (Boughner, Bubenzer, Hayes, & West, 1993). Table 17.1 examines some conceptual issues and formal assessment techniques across family system levels.

Family Therapy Scales

To make an informed decision on what assessment instrument(s) would serve their clients best, therapists must conceptually clarify the areas in which they need to obtain information. A brief survey of some assessment devices in family therapy follows.

Model Conceptual Issues	Formal Assessment
	Family Assessment Measure–III (Skinner, Steinhauer, & Santa-Barbera, 1984)
	Family Adaptability and Cohesion Evaluation Scales III (Olson, Portner, & Lavee, 1985)
How is the family organized along dimensions of affect, authority, and control? What strategies do family members use to influence each other?	Child-Rearing Practices Report (Block, Block, & Morrison, 1981) Family Behavior Interview (Robin & Foster, 1989) Family Interaction Coding System (Reid, 1978)
Extended system	
To what extent do relationships with extended family, friends, or coworkers serve as sources of support or stress?	Genogram (McGoldrick & Gerson, 1985) Interpersonal Support Evaluation List (Cohen, Mermelstein, Kamarck, & Hoberman, 1985) Survey of Children's Social Support (Dubow & Ullman, 1989) My Family and Friends (Reid, Landesman, Treder, & Jaccard, 1989)
How do family members vary in their sources of external stress or support? How are these shared in the marriage or nuclear family?	
Community and culture	
What community resources are available to this family? Are these resources used? How does the community contribute to this family's distress or survival?	Mothers' Activities Checklist (Kelley & Carper, 1988) Community Interaction Checklist (Wahler, 1980) Eco-Map (Hartman, 1979)
To what extent do family members identify with a particular ethnic heritage?	Behavioral Acculturation Scale (Szapocznik, Kurtines, & Fernandez,1980)

From "Marital and Family Assessment: A Multifaceted, Multilevel Approach" by D. K. Snyder, T. A. Cavell, R. W. Heffer, and L. F. Mangrum in *Integrating Family Therapy* (pp. 163–182), edited by R. H. Mikesell, D. D. Lusterman, and S. H. McDaniel. Copyright © 1995 American Psychological Association. Reprinted with permission.

Family-of-Origin Scale

The family-of-origin scale (FOS) was developed to measure self-perceived healthiness in one's family of origin (Hovestadt, Anderson, Piercy, Cochran, & Fine, 1985). The scale is based on a five-point Likert format and contains 40 questions. Outcome scores can range from 40 to 200, with higher scores indicative of better overall family health. The test–retest reliability coefficient has been reported to be 0.97 for undergraduates on whom the scale was normed.

Two subscales of the FOS reflect 10 core constructs of family healthiness, principally derived from Lewis et al. (1976). "The Autonomy subscale emphasizes characteristics of healthiness such as clarity of expression, personal responsibility, respect for other family members, and openness to others within and outside the family system. The Intimacy subscale emphasizes characteristics such as expression of feelings, emotional warmth, conflict resolution without undue stress, sensitivity to other family members, and trust" (Wilcoxon, Walker, & Hovestadt, 1989, pp. 226–227).

The FOS can be used in the context of both family and couple therapy (Hovestadt, 2000). It has been found to distinguish between different cultural groups' (i.e., African Americans, European Americans, and Hispanic Americans) perceptions of their families of origin (Kane & Erdman, 1998). In this study African Americans rated their families of origin significantly higher than European Americans and Hispanic Americans on the major scales of Autonomy and Intimacy and on the Intimacy subscales Range of Feelings, Conflict Resolution, and Empathy. The researchers also found that there were no significant differences between males and females or between European Americans and Hispanic Americans.

The Personal Authority in the Family System Questionnaire

The Personal Authority in the Family System (PAFS) questionnaire is a self-report questionnaire based on the theoretical work of family systems theorists, such as Bowen, Boszormenyi-Nagy, and Williamson. It assesses relationships in three-generational families. It contains 132 items, all of which are scored on a five-point Likert scale. Five subscales measure intergenerational themes such as dependence/independence, intergenerational triangles, intergenerational intimidation, personal authority, and intergenerational fusion/individuation (Bray, Williamson, & Malone, 1984).

Reliability measures range from a test–retest low of 0.55 to an internal consistency of 0.95. Construct and concurrent validity are both solid. Overall, "the PAFS describes an individual's current interaction with his or her family of origin" (West, 1988, p. 176).

Family Adaptability and Cohesion Evaluation Scale III

The Family Adaptability and Cohesion Evaluation Scale III (FACES III) is similar to PRE-PARE/ENRICH in that it is based on the circumplex model of family functioning (i.e., adaptability and cohesion) (Olson et al., 1985). It is a self-report inventory "designed to measure an insider's perspective on family functioning" (Griffin & D'Andrea, 1998, p. 305). This instrument has undergone considerable refinement since it was introduced in 1978. Basically, it can be taken twice in order to derive ideal and perceived descriptions of a family. The discrepancy between these two outcome scores "provides a measure of family satisfaction with current levels of adaptability and cohesion" (West, 1988, p. 173). Reliability and validity are within acceptable limits.

FACES III has been used in a variety of ways including to investigate perceived family cohesion and adaptability in current relationships and family of origin, to assess cohesion and adaptability in violent couples, to predict future behavior, and to classify the relationship status of battered women (Griffin & D'Andrea, 1998).

Family Inventory of Life Events and Changes

The purpose of the Family Inventory of Life Events and Changes (FILE) instrument is to "investigate the impact of life stresses on family well-being" (L'Abate & Bagarozzi, 1993, p. 176).

As emphasized in this text, families undergo many transitions that affect them for better or worse. Sometimes stress events pile up on families and have negative consequences. FILE, as a 71-item self-report instrument, examines the normative and nonnormative events that have been experienced by families during a year, including financial, intrafamily, work, legal, loss, illness, marital, moving, and pregnancy/childbearing (Bretherson, Walsh, & Lependorf, 1996; McCubbin, Thompson, Pirner, & McCubbin, 1988). FILE scores can be summed according to family life event score, family-couple life events score, family-couple discrepancy score, family adjustment score, and family-couple readjustment score (Touliatos et al., 1990).

By gathering and scoring information on the family, therapists are more aware of where to address their interventions. The reliability and validity of FILE are high.

Family Environment Scale

The Family Environment Scale (FES) is "a 90-item, true-false, self-report questionnaire with 10 subscales designed to measure the social and environmental characteristics of a family" (Fredman & Sherman, 1987, p. 82). It is divided into 10 subscales that come under three major categories: (1) relationship (i.e., cohesion, expressiveness, and conflict subscales); (2) personal growth (i.e., independence, achievement orientation, intellectual-cultural orientation, active-recreational orientation, and moral-religious emphasis subscales); and (3) system maintenance (i.e., organization and control subscales).

The FES can be used to describe and compare family social environments, contrast parent and child perceptions, and examine actual and preferred family milieus (Moos & Moos, 1994). It is "probably the most widely accepted measure of the family climate" and "among the first" objectively scored methods of family assessment to be developed (Oliver, Handal, Enos, & May, 1988, p. 470). One of the reasons for the popularity of the FES is that it comprehensively addresses all aspects of family environment. It has a Real Form (which measures families' actual perceptions), an Ideal Form (which measures families' perceptions of how they would like their family to be), and an Expectations Form (which measures what people expect their families to be like).

In general, the FES has been shown to have sufficient measures of validity and reliability (Moos, 1990). It has been used in studies examining a wide variety of topics from academic performance to eating disorders.

Family Assessment Device

The Family Assessment Device (FAD) is a 60-item questionnaire geared toward assessing family functioning. It is based on the McMaster Model of Family Functioning (Epstein, Baldwin, & Bishop, 1983) and takes about 20 minutes to complete. The FAD has been translated into seven different languages and is one of the most researched family assessment tools available. This instrument examines seven dimensions of family functioning: (1) problem solving, (2) communication, (3) roles, (4) affective responsiveness (sharing of affection), (5) affective involvement (emotional sensitivity), (6) behavior control, and (7) general functioning (boundaries). The best way to read the results of the FAD is to use its general functioning subscale as a summary score since FAD subscales overlap substantially and do not assess unique dimensions of family functioning.

Family Strengths Scale

The Family Strengths Scale is a brief, 12-item inventory developed in 1983. It is appropriate for adults and adolescents (Olson, Larson, & McCubbin, 1985). It measures two areas of family functioning, family pride (e.g., loyalty, optimism, and trust) and family accord (e.g., ability to accomplish certain tasks, to deal with problems, to get along with one another).

The scale is scored on a five-point Likert index (Giblin, 1996). It is aimed at identifying how happy families resemble one another. Higher scores correlate with a higher level of family functioning. The inventory was initially based on the family strength work of Stinnet (1981), but the final version of the test is less comprehensive. Reliability for the total scale is reported at 0.83.

Family Coping Strategies Scale

The Family Coping Strategies Scale (F-COPES) is a measure of internal and external family coping strategies (McCubbin, Larsen, & Olsen, 1982). Internal strategies include reframing and passive appraisal; external strategies are those connected with acquiring social support, seeking spiritual support, and mobilizing the family to seek and accept help.

The scale assumes that family coping can potentially achieve the following:

- Decrease the family's vulnerability to stress
- Strengthen or maintain those family resources that serve to protect the family from the full impact of problems
- Reduce or eliminate the impact of stressor events
- Actively influence the environment by changing the social circumstances to make it easier for the family to adjust to the situation

The reliability of the instrument is in the 0.60 range.

Self-Report Family Inventory

The Self-Report Family Inventory (SFI) is a 36-item self-report family instrument that measures five family domains: health/competence, conflict resolution, cohesion, leadership, and emotional expressiveness (Beavers & Hampson, 1990). The inventory is based on a five-point Likert scale, except for the final two questions. The SFI has high reliability (between 0.84 and 0.93) and validity (0.62 and better). This instrument also "corresponds well with other self-report family scales measuring conceptually similar domains" (Hampson, Prince, & Beavers, 1999, p. 414). Included in the inventory is a husbands and wives demographic information form and an open-ended questionnaire on the family's evaluation of treatment.

Marital and Couple Therapy Scales

Marital and couple assessment is aimed at obtaining information in a fast and efficient manner so therapists can concentrate on particularly difficult relationship areas. Some of the earliest assessment instruments in the marital and family therapy areas were initially developed for this purpose. Those instruments described here are specifically geared for marital and couple use.

Locke-Wallace Marital Adjustment Test (MAT)

The Locke-Wallace Marital Adjustment Test (MAT) is one of the oldest and most widely used tests of global marital satisfaction. It consists of 15 items that are of a self-report nature.

It can be completed in about 10 minutes and is scored by the therapist. Higher scores (above 100 points) differentiate nondistressed from distressed couples (Sullivan, Parch, Eldridge, & Bradbury, 1998). This inventory has been successfully modified for use with premarital couples. It has been reported to have a split-half reliability of 0.90 (Locke & Wallace, 1959). Furthermore, the MAT is the standard by which other marriage adjustment inventories correlate their results (Fredman & Sherman, 1987). The main drawback to the MAT is that a few of its items are now considered out of date.

PREPARE/ENRICH

The PREPARE/ENRICH inventories are part of a package of material developed for couples striving to become more aware of or to nourish their relationships (Fredman & Sherman, 1987). PREPARE is designated for engaged couples; ENRICH is for already married couples. Both scales are composed of a 125-item inventory that is designed to identify relationship strengths and weaknesses in 10 specific areas of couple/family life. These areas are (1) personality issues, (2) communication, (3) conflict resolution, (4) financial management, (5) leisure activities, (6) sexual relationship, (7) children and marriage, (8) family and friends, (9) egalitarian roles, and (10) religious orientation (Olson, Fournier, & Druckman, 1987). Each scale also measures idealistic distortion, although PREPARE alone gets a reading on realistic expectations, and ENRICH alone obtains a score on marital satisfaction.

An individual score for each person on every scale is generated, and areas of agreement and disagreement are duly noted. Comparisons are coded as "relationship strength," "possible strength," "possible growth area," or "growth area." PREPARE and ENRICH both have strong reliability and validity scores in most areas. Both also have been found to have some predictive uses. In a 3-year follow-up of couples who took the PREPARE scale, scores were better than 80% accurate in predicting marital happiness versus separation/divorce (Flowers & Olson, 1986). The PREPARE scale has also been translated and adapted for use in some other cultures, such as Japanese (Asai & Olson, 2004).

Bienvenu Marital Communication Inventory (MCI)

The Bienvenu Marital Communication Inventory (MCI) is a 46-item, self-administered questionnaire that focuses on the perceived quality of marital communication. Each question is graded on a zero-to-four-point scale, with a range of scores from 0 to 138. Higher scores are indicative of better perceived couple communication patterns. The split-half reliability is 0.93 (Bienvenu, 1970).

This instrument is used in both marital and premarital counseling and can be interpreted as a measure of perceptions concerning the quality of communication (Schumm, 1983). Only a seventh-grade reading ability is required.

Dyadic Adjustment Scale

The Dyadic Adjustment Scale (DAS) is a 32-item, self-report, pencil-and-paper questionnaire of marital satisfaction (Spanier, 1976). Thirteen consensus items in areas such as household tasks, finances, recreation, friends, religion, and decision making are measured. The DAS possesses good reliability and discriminant validity. It yields an overall score up to 151 as well as scores for four subscales: dyadic consensus, satisfaction, cohesion, and affectional expression (Kramer & Conoley, 1992).

The usual cutoff point between distressed and nondistressed couples is 100, with higher scores indicating a better relationship (Floyd & Markman, 1983). The reliability of this instrument is high (0.96). Validity is also quite good (Fredman & Sherman, 1987). The DAS is reportedly the most commonly used self-report measure of marital adjustment (Glenn, 1990; Whisman, 2001). It has been used in more than 1,000 studies, translated into several languages (e.g., French and Chinese) and has been revised from a 32- to a 14-item instrument (Prouty, Markowski, & Barnes, 2000).

Marital Coping Questionnaire

The Marital Coping Questionnaire (MCQ) is an 18-item, self-report questionnaire in which respondents indicate how frequently they engage in each of a set of coping efforts (Fleishman, 1984; Menaghan, 1982; Pearlin & Schooler, 1978). The MCQ is situation-specific rather than global in its assessment.

The six most reliable coping factors are as follows:

1. seeking advice (e.g., ask the advice of relatives about getting along in marriage)
2. emotional discharge (e.g., yell or shout to let off steam)
3. positive comparison (e.g., how would you compare your marriage to that of most other people like yourself — better, the same, less good)
4. negotiation (e.g., try to find a fair compromise in marital problems)
5. resignation (e.g., just keep hurt feelings to yourself)
6. selective ignoring (e.g., try to ignore difficulties by looking only at good things) (Sabourin, Laporte, & Wright, 1990, pp. 91–92)

Primary Communication Inventory

The Primary Communication Inventory (PCI) is a 25-item, self-report questionnaire, with a five-point scale designed to measure a couple's verbal and nonverbal communication (Locke, Sabagh, & Thomas, 1956). It is one of the oldest and most frequently used marriage therapy indexes and has been the subject of several significant research studies (L'Abate & Bagarozzi, 1993). It distinguishes satisfied and dissatisfied couples from each other, but has some problems in regard to validity.

Marital Satisfaction Inventory-Revised

The Marital Satisfaction Inventory (MSI-R) is a 150-item, true/false, self-report questionnaire and measures "both the nature and intensity of distress in distinct areas of partners' interactions" (Means-Christensen, Snyder, & Negy, 2003, p. 72). The original MSI, with 280 questions, was initially compared with the MMPI because of both its length and number of scales (i.e., 11 scales). The revised scale includes two validity scales and 10 additional scales that assess specific dimensions of a relationship, e.g., time together, finances, sexual problems, role orientation, communication, and family history. The revised instrument just like the original also provides a global distress scale so clinicians can rate the overall level of distress within a marriage relationship (Means-Christensen et al., 2003; Snyder, 1981, 1997; Snyder & Regts, 1982).

The MSI is administered to each partner separately and requires about 25 minutes to complete. The MSI-R has a test–retest reliability on average of 0.89 for each subscale. It is one of the strongest marital satisfaction measures available in psychometric terms (Fowers, 1990). Overall, the MSI is a well-constructed inventory that is strong in regard to its research and clinical application. It has been used in cross-cultural situations and with gay and lesbian couples.

Marital Instability Inventory

The Marital Instability Inventory (MII) is a paper-and-pencil instrument designed to assess marital instability among intact couples (Booth & Edwards, 1983). It has a 20- and a 5-question form, both of which are scored from 0 (never) to 3 (now). Higher scores are more indicative of marital instability.

The MII is composed of two parts: cognitive (thoughts about the marriage) and behavior (actions based on thoughts about the marital relationship). Both reliability and validity factors are high, with the shorter form of the scale being less reliable.

Dyadic Trust Scale

The Dyadic Trust Scale (DTS) is an eight-item, pencil-and-paper questionnaire that takes less than 3 minutes to take. Its focus is on trust between marriage partners rather than trust in general (Larzelere & Huston, 1980). It has high internal consistency reliability (0.93), good face validity, and correlates well with scales of love and self-disclosure. The main drawback to this instrument is that its initial sample size was limited and, in norming the test, all participants were volunteers (Fredman & Sherman, 1987).

Marital Problem-Solving Scale

The Marital Problem-Solving Scale (MPSS) is a nine-item, seven-point Likert scale that measures problem-solving ability (Baugh, Avery, & Sheets-Haworth, 1982). It has strong internal consistency (0.95) and test–retest reliability (0.86). Validity is also good. An interesting aspect about the MPSS is that it "has demonstrated concurrent validity with behavioral coding assessments, enabling one to say that it is just as good as the time-consuming and expensive methods of behavior coding" (L'Abate & Bagarozzi, 1993, p. 145).

Couple Rating Scale

The Couple Rating Scale (CRS) is "a self-report assessment that encourages relationship insight for couples. Eight common areas of problems, consisting of 31 specific issues, are rated by each partner to assess both current level and desired level of functioning for the self and other" (Cron, 2000, p. 302). The eight areas addressed in the CRS are communication life, home life, work life, love life, sexual life, spiritual life, problem-solving life, and dream for the future life. Each area is rated from 1 to 10.

The CRS (Figure 17.3) is intended to operate on two levels—present reality and desired level of functioning for self and other. It is meant to be a measure that closes the gap in assessment on two specific couple misconceptions: external locus of control (e.g., "if my partner changed everything would be fine") and single-issue focus (e.g., money, sex).

Couple Rating Scale

Instructions: Rating scale is from 1 to 10, with 1 being the lowest and 10 being the highest. You will rate yourself in the first two columns. In Column 1, rate your current level of each trait. Column 2 is for the level you desire to reach. Columns 3 and 4 are for rating your partner. In Column 3, using your personal perception, rate his or her current level of each trait. In Column 4, rate the level desired by you for him or her to attempt.

Life Area	Self Current/Desired (1) (2)	Other Current/Desired (3) (4)	Life Area	Self Current/Desired (1) (2)	Other Current/Desired (3) (4)
Communication life			**Love life**		
Degree of listening skill	__/__	__/__	Degree of acceptance of other	__/__	__/__
Degree of sensitivity and respect	__/__	__/__	Degree of mutual understanding	__/__	__/__
Degree of honesty	__/__	__/__	Degree of trust in other	__/__	__/__
Degree of openness	__/__	__/__	Degree of expressed (spoken) love	__/__	__/__
Degree of flexibility/compromise	__/__	__/__	Degree of implied (unspoken) love	__/__	__/__
Home life			Degree of forgiveness in relationship	__/__	__/__
Degree of satisfaction with household responsibilities	__/__	__/__	**Spiritual life**		
Degree of completing household responsibilities	__/__	__/__	Degree of spiritual belief	__/__	__/__
Degree of role flexibility	__/__	__/__	Degree of religious practice	__/__	__/__
Degree of good parenting skills	__/__	__/__	Degree of comfort with spiritual expression	__/__	__/__
Work life			**Problem-solving life**		
Degree of fulfillment in own career	__/__	__/__	Ability to talk about problems (get them in the open)	__/__	__/__
Degree of comfort with partner's career	__/__	__/__	Ability to work through problems	__/__	__/__
Degree of balance between work and home life	__/__	__/__	Ability to fight fair	__/__	__/__
Sexual life			Ability to resolve family-of-origin problems	__/__	__/__
Degree of frequency	__/__	__/__	**Dream for the future life**		
Degree of satisfaction in lovemaking	__/__	__/__	Degree that your dream is also his or hers	__/__	__/__
Degree of excitement in lovemaking	__/__	__/__	Degree that your dream is mutually decided	__/__	__/__
Degree of variety in lovemaking	__/__	__/__			

Figure 17.3

Couple rating scale.

From "Couple Rating Scale: Clarifying Problem Areas" by E. A. Cron, 2000, *The Family Journal: Counseling and Therapy for Couples and Families, 8*(3), p. 303. Copyright © 2000 by Sage Publications, Inc. Reprinted by permission of Sage Publications, Inc.

Summary and Conclusion

Family research and assessment efforts have a long history. They began with the genesis of the field and have continued to the present. Research is the backbone of family therapy, because through it family therapists can prove that what they do is beneficial, unique, and practical. Fortunately, family therapy research indicates that treating families is at least equal in effectiveness to that of working with individuals. Particularly encouraging are findings that show the importance of therapists' relationship skills and the critical nature of having certain members of families, such as fathers, participate in treatment. From these data, clinicians/researchers, such as Jose Szapocznik, have advanced the field of family therapy even further through innovative research projects.

In examining family therapy research, keep in mind that many difficulties are associated with it because of the systemic nature of family therapy. Among problematic areas are those that involve whether to conduct qualitative or quantitative research. The design of the research, along with sampling procedures and choosing instruments, are also important. Equally crucial are considerations involving whether procedures should focus on process or outcome results, the statistical methods, if any, to employ, and the theoretical base on which to center the study. As the field of family therapy grows, efforts to incorporate research methods and findings into training/educational programs will increase, accompanied by renewed attention on the importance of research to practice (Liddle, 1992).

Like research, assessment is based on systemic theory and has been highlighted more in recent years. Assessment may take "many forms depending on the theory, practice, clients, and personal, professional development of the counselor" (Sporakowski, 1995, p. 63). There are a number of family assessment approaches, from those that consider limited data to those that encompass a broad perspective. Informal as well as formal methods of assessment are available. Formal methods, although well-researched, have still not been as utilized by family therapists as some popular, more individualized assessment tools, such as the Myers-Briggs Type Indicator and the MMPI-2. There is, nevertheless, an abundance of assessment instruments that will most likely grow in use and usefulness in the future.

Research and assessment are a vital part of the practice of family therapy. It is essential that clinicians keep current with advancements and related research. Otherwise, they will be handicapped in the treatment of their client families, and all will suffer as a result.

Summary Table

Research and Assessment in Family Therapy

Research and assessment has a long association with family therapy that dates back to the 1950s and pioneers in the field such as Bateson, Wynne, and Minuchin.

During the 1960s, therapists and researchers became two distinct groups.

In the 21st century, research in family therapy is growing again and is becoming increasingly sophisticated.

Assessment, which focuses on a family unit rather than a group of families, is also growing.

Good assessment instruments are based on theoretical models.

Importance of Research in Family Therapy

Empirical data are crucial to the future of treating families. The practitioner/research model needs to be highlighted.

Research is important in family therapy as a result of accountability, practicality, and uniqueness. Research results help family therapy gain respect.

Clinicians gain from research studies in the long run. Research also helps family therapists claim their area as a specialization.

Research Findings in Family Therapy

Family therapy is as effective as other psychotherapies, according to research. Some other salient findings include:

Deterioration in family therapy is related to poor skills and timing on the therapist's part.

Brief family therapy (20 sessions or less) is as effective as long-term family therapy.

Participation by the father in family therapy makes it more likely to have a positive outcome.

Less severe family problems are most successfully treated.

Some family therapies are more suited to certain types of problems than others.

The research of Jose Szapocznik is a good example of how research results can have practical application.

Two Types of Family Therapy Research

Qualitative and quantitative research methods are often used in measuring the impact of family therapy.

Qualitative research is characterized by its open-ended approach. It uses small samples, with the participant/observer/researcher gathering and analyzing data simultaneously in a narrative manner. A form of qualitative research, participatory evaluation research, involves participants even more in the research process and empowers them as well.

Quantitative research is characterized by its closed-ended questions, large sample sizes, objective data reporting, and numerical data analysis after the data are collected. Its conclusions are deductive, written in a prosaic form, with reference to standard measures of validity and reliability. It seeks to prove or disprove a theory or hypothesis.

Whether one chooses qualitative or quantitative research methods, studying families is complicated, especially if a systems model is followed.

Difficulties in Family Therapy Research

Difficulties in family therapy research are associated with

- where to focus (e.g., on the marriage, the identified patient, etc.)
- what environment to use (natural or laboratory)
- what research design to use (exploratory, descriptive, developmental, experimental, or correlational)
- sampling (random or nonprobable)
- instrumentation (self-report or behavioral open-ended)
- procedure (outcome or process based)
- theory (simple, clear, and systemic or not)
- statistics (descriptive and clinically relevant or not)
- validity (content, criterion, and construct)
- reliability (i.e., the consistency/dependability of a measure)

The Importance of Assessing Families

Assessment is the evaluation of families in particular cases with specific instruments. It is usually clinically relevant in regard to a family in treatment.

Assessment is related to diagnosis and, consequently, to treatment plans and outcomes.

Assessment is the basis for accountability with third-party providers.

For therapists, assessing families is necessary for survival as well as a matter of being responsible.

Dimensions of Assessing Families

Most assessment is conducted on a systematic level.

Dimensions of assessment are those related to:

- pressures on the family
- family history
- family structure
- family process

Assessment is a continuous process.

Methods Used in Assessing Families

Both informal and formal methods are used in assessment.

Informal methods include family assessment forms and observations.

Formal methods include the more than 1,000 assessment instruments available to family therapists.

Family therapy scales commonly used by clinicians include:

- Family-of-Origin Scale (FOS)
- Personal Authority in the Family System Questionnaire (PAFS)
- Family Adaptability and Cohesion Evaluation Scale III (FACES III)
- Family Inventory of Life Events and Changes (FILE)
- Family Environment Scale (FES)
- Family Assessment Device (FAD)
- Family Strengths Scale
- Family Coping Strategies Scale (F-COPES)
- Self-Report Family Inventory (SFI)

Marital therapy scales frequently used by clinicians include:

- Locke-Wallace Marital Adjustment Test (MAT)
- PREPARE/ENRICH
- Bienvenu Marital Communication Inventory (MCI)
- Dyadic Adjustment Scale (DAS)
- Marital Coping Questionnaire (MCQ)
- Primary Communication Inventory (PCI)
- Marital Satisfaction Inventory (MSI-R)
- Marital Instability Inventory (MII)
- Dyadic Trust Scale (DTS)
- Marital Problem-Solving Scale (MPSS)
- Couple Rating Scale (CRS)

Appendix A

— • —

Family Therapy Through the Decades

Before 1940	Cultural beliefs stress the individual, the use of community resources, and psychoanalytic theory.
	Ernest Groves, Alfred Adler, and county home extension agents teach family living/parenting skills.
	Abraham and Hannah Stone, Emily Mudd, and Paul Popenoe begin marriage counseling.
	National Council on Family Relations is founded (1938).
1940 to 1949	The American Association of Marriage Counselors (AAMC) is established (1942).
	Milton Erickson develops therapeutic methods that will later be adopted by family therapy.
	First account of concurrent marital therapy is published by Bela Mittleman (1948).
	Theodore Lidz and Lyman Wynne study schizophrenic families.
	World War II brings stress to families, and the divorce rate in the U.S. begins to rise rapidly.
	The National Mental Health Act of 1946 is passed by Congress.
1950 to 1959	A new cultural trend develops as the percentage of single-parent families created by divorce starts to exceed those created by death.
	Nathan Ackerman develops a psychoanalytical approach to working with families.
	Gregory Bateson's group begins studying patterns of communication in families.
	Don Jackson creates the Mental Research Institute (1958), which eventually lays the groundwork for strategic family therapy.
	Carl Whitaker sets up the first conference on family therapy at Sea Island, Georgia (1955).
	Murray Bowen begins the National Institute of Mental Health (NIMH) project of studying families with schizophrenics.
	Ivan Boszormenyi-Nagy begins work on contextual therapy.
1960 to 1969	Jay Haley refines and advocates therapeutic approaches of Milton Erickson. He moves from Palo Alto and leaves the Bateson group to join the Philadelphia Child Guidance Clinic (1967).
	Family Process, the first journal in family therapy, is cofounded by Nathan Ackerman and Don Jackson (1961).

(Continued)

Salvador Minuchin begins development of structural family therapy at Wiltwyck School in New York and continues at the Philadelphia Child Guidance Clinic. He coauthors *Families of the Slums* (1968).

John Bell publishes the first ideas about family group therapy (1961), an idea he originated earlier.

The marriage/family enrichment movement begins with Father Gabriel Calvo in Spain (1962).

The experiential branch of family therapy emerges out of the humanistic-existential psychology movement. It includes the work of Virginia Satir, Carl Whitaker, Fred and Bunny Duh, among others.

Virginia Satir publishes *Conjoint Family Therapy* (1964) and gains a national following.

Legislation authorizing community mental health centers is passed by Congress (1963).

First state licensure law regulating family counselors is passed in California (1963).

Nathan Ackerman publishes *Treating the Troubled Family* (1966).

Carl Whitaker moves from Georgia to the University of Wisconsin. He begins to write and lecture extensively.

Gerald Patterson begins the practice of applying behavioral theory to family problems.

General systems theory, formulated by Ludwig von Bertalanffy (1934/1968), becomes the basis for most family therapy.

Murray Bowen begins to formulate his own systemically oriented theory of family therapy as a result of his work with families having schizophrenic members and his own work on his family-of-origin.

Don Jackson dies (1968).

Training centers and institutes for family therapy are established in New York, Philadelphia, and Boston.

1970 to 1979	Membership in the American Association for Marriage and Family Therapy grows by 777% to 7,565 members. Nathan Ackerman dies (1971). David and Vera Mace establish the Association for Couple and Marriage Enrichment (ACME) on their 40th wedding anniversary (1973). The *Journal of Marital and Family Therapy* is founded (1974). *Families and Family Therapy* (1974) and *Psychosomatic Families* (1978) are published by Salvador Minuchin and associates. The *Family Therapy Networker* is created (1976).

Neil Jacobson begins his work as a theorist and researcher in behavioral family therapy.

The American Association of Marriage and Family Counselors becomes the American Association for Marriage and Family Therapy (1979). Its degree-granting programs are recognized by the Department of Health, Education, and Welfare.

The American Family Therapy Association is created (1977).

The Milan Group, originators of systemic family therapy, publishes *Paradox and Counterparadox* (1978). European family therapists gain influence in the U.S.

Feminist theorists, led by Rachel Hare-Mustin, begin questioning the premises of family therapy.

(Continued)

Jay Haley publishes *Uncommon Therapy* (1973) and *Problem Solving Therapy* (1976).

A focus on multiculturalism, a term used to refer to the cultural groups within a region or nation, begins to develop within American society.

1980 to 1989	Membership in the AAMFT grows to 14,000. Gregory Bateson dies (1980). Milton Erickson dies (1980). Division 43 (Family Psychology) of the American Psychological Association is established (1984). The International Association of Marriage and Family Counselors within the American Counseling Association is established (1986). New female leaders in family therapy emerge, such as Monica McGoldrick, Peggy Papp, Peggy Penn, Cloe Madanes, Fromma Walsh, and Betty Carter. Research procedures in family therapy are developed and refined. Publications in family therapy increase. *Family Therapy Networker* reaches a circulation of 50,000. Virginia Satir dies (1988).
1990 to 1999	Family therapy becomes more global as an approach to helping others. Murray Bowen dies (1990). Solution-focused family therapies of Steve deShazer and Bill O'Hanlon and narrative approach of Michael White and David Epston become popular. Other new theories are developed for working with couples and families, including constructionist theories. They challenge systems thinking. The integration and merger of family therapy theories occurs, with less emphasis on specialization. The new epistemology, which involves second-order cybernetics, emphasizes positive feedback in system transformation. The Basic Family Therapy Skills Project focuses on determining, defining, and testing the skills necessary for novice therapists to master, generically and specifically. Carl Whitaker dies (1995). John Weakland dies (1995). Jay Haley retires (1995). Salvador Minuchin retires (1996). Professional membership grows in AAMFT, IAMFC, AFTA, and Division 43 of APA. Accreditation of programs and licensure efforts at the state level increase with the term *family therapist* better defined in regard to course work, competencies, and clinical experience. The number of well-respected and researched theories practitioners can claim grows. Health care reform and mental health care provider status become increasingly important. Managed care becomes increasingly dominant. Tension between professional associations in family therapy develops. Neil Jacobson dies (1999).

(Continued)

2000 to present   Steve deShazer dies (2005).

Family based research becomes more prominent and culturally sensitive.

Family therapy becomes a more worldwide phenomenon.

Federal and state legislation becomes increasingly important in the practice and growth of family therapy.

Prepared by Trevor Buser, graduate student, Counseling Department, Wake Forest University, 2005. Used with permission.

Appendix B

•

AAMFT Code of Ethics

Effective July 1, 2001

Preamble

The Board of Directors of the American Association for Marriage and Family Therapy (AAMFT) hereby promulgates, pursuant to Article 2, Section 2.013 of the Association's Bylaws, the Revised AAMFT Code of Ethics, effective July 1, 2001.

The AAMFT strives to honor the public trust in marriage and family therapists by setting standards for ethical practice as described in this Code. The ethical standards define professional expectations and are enforced by the AAMFT Ethics Committee. The absence of an explicit reference to a specific behavior or situation in the Code does not mean that the behavior is ethical or unethical. The standards are not exhaustive. Marriage and family therapists who are uncertain about the ethics of a particular course of action are encouraged to seek counsel from consultants, attorneys, supervisors, colleagues, or other appropriate authorities.

Both law and ethics govern the practice of marriage and family therapy. When making decisions regarding professional behavior, marriage and family therapists must consider the AAMFT Code of Ethics and applicable laws and regulations. If the AAMFT Code of Ethics prescribes a standard higher than that required by law, marriage and family therapists must meet the higher standard of the AAMFT Code of Ethics. Marriage and family therapists comply with the mandates of law, but make known their commitment to the AAMFT Code of Ethics and take steps to resolve the conflict in a responsible manner. The AAMFT supports legal mandates for reporting of alleged unethical conduct.

The AAMFT Code of Ethics is binding on Members of AAMFT in all membership categories, AAMFT-Approved Supervisors, and applicants for membership and the Approved Supervisor designation (hereafter, AAMFT Member). AAMFT members have an obligation to be familiar with the AAMFT Code of Ethics and its application to their professional services. Lack of awareness or misunderstanding of an ethical standard is not a defense to a charge of unethical conduct.

The process for filing, investigating, and resolving complaints of unethical conduct is described in the current Procedures for Handling Ethical Matters of the AAMFT Ethics Committee. Persons accused are considered innocent by the Ethics Committee until proven guilty, except as otherwise provided, and are entitled to due process. If an AAMFT Member resigns in anticipation of, or during the course of, an ethics investigation, the Ethics Committee will complete its investigation. Any publication of action taken by the Association will include the fact that the Member attempted to resign during the investigation.

Contents

Principle I: Responsibility to Clients

Marriage and family therapists advance the welfare of families and individuals. They respect the rights of those persons seeking their assistance, and make reasonable efforts to ensure that their services are used appropriately.

1.1 Marriage and family therapists provide professional assistance to persons without discrimination on the basis of race, age, ethnicity, socioeconomic status, disability, gender, health status, religion, national origin, or sexual orientation.

1.2 Marriage and family therapists obtain appropriate informed consent to therapy or related procedures as early as feasible in the therapeutic relationship, and use language that is reasonably understandable to clients. The content of informed consent may vary depending upon the client and treatment plan; however, informed consent generally necessitates that the client: (a) has the capacity to consent; (b) has been adequately informed of significant information concerning treatment processes and procedures; (c) has been adequately informed of potential risks and benefits of treatments for which generally recognized standards do not yet exist; (d) has freely and without undue influence expressed consent; and (e) has provided consent that is appropriately documented. When persons, due to age or mental status, are legally incapable of giving informed consent, marriage and family therapists obtain informed permission from a legally authorized person, if such substitute consent is legally permissible.

1.3 Marriage and family therapists are aware of their influential positions with respect to clients, and they avoid exploiting the trust and dependency of such persons. Therapists, therefore, make every effort to avoid conditions and multiple relationships with clients that could impair professional judgment or increase the risk of exploitation. Such relationships include, but are not limited to, business or close personal relationships with a client or the client's immediate family. When the risk of impairment or exploitation exists due to conditions or multiple roles, therapists take appropriate precautions.

1.4 Sexual intimacy with clients is prohibited.

1.5 Sexual intimacy with former clients is likely to be harmful and is therefore prohibited for two years following the termination of therapy or last professional contact. In an effort to avoid exploiting the trust and dependency of clients, marriage and family therapists should not engage in sexual intimacy with former clients after the two years following termination or last professional contact. Should therapists engage in sexual intimacy with former clients following two years after termination or last professional contact, the burden shifts to the therapist to demonstrate that there has been no exploitation or injury to the former client or to the client's immediate family.

1.6 Marriage and family therapists comply with applicable laws regarding the reporting of alleged unethical conduct.

1.7 Marriage and family therapists do not use their professional relationships with clients to further their own interests.

1.8 Marriage and family therapists respect the rights of clients to make decisions and help them to understand the consequences of these decisions. Therapists clearly advise the clients that they have the responsibility to make decisions regarding relationships such as cohabitation, marriage, divorce, separation, reconciliation, custody, and visitation.

1.9 Marriage and family therapists continue therapeutic relationships only so long as it is reasonably clear that clients are benefiting from the relationship.

1.10 Marriage and family therapists assist persons in obtaining other therapeutic services if the therapist is unable or unwilling, for appropriate reasons, to provide professional help.

1.11 Marriage and family therapists do not abandon or neglect clients in treatment without making reasonable arrangements for the continuation of such treatment.

1.12 Marriage and family therapists obtain written informed consent from clients before videotaping, audio recording, or permitting third-party observation.

1.13 Marriage and family therapists, upon agreeing to provide services to a person or entity at the request of a third party, clarify, to the extent feasible and at the outset of the service, the nature of the relationship with each party and the limits of confidentiality.

Principle II: Confidentiality

Marriage and family therapists have unique confidentiality concerns because the client in a therapeutic relationship may be more than one person. Therapists respect and guard the confidences of each individual client.

2.1 Marriage and family therapists disclose to clients and other interested parties, as early as feasible in their professional contacts, the nature of confidentiality and possible limitations of the clients' right to confidentiality. Therapists review with clients the circumstances where confidential information may be requested and where disclosure of confidential information may be legally required. Circumstances may necessitate repeated disclosures.

2.2 Marriage and family therapists do not disclose client confidences except by written authorization or waiver, or where mandated or permitted by law. Verbal authorization will not be sufficient except in emergency situations, unless prohibited by law. When providing couple, family or group treatment, the therapist does not disclose information outside the treatment context without a written authorization from each individual competent to execute a waiver. In the context of couple,

family or group treatment, the therapist may not reveal any individual's confidences to others in the client unit without the prior written permission of that individual.

2.3 Marriage and family therapists use client and/or clinical materials in teaching, writing, consulting, research, and public presentations only if a written waiver has been obtained in accordance with Subprinciple 2.2, or when appropriate steps have been taken to protect client identity and confidentiality.

2.4 Marriage and family therapists store, safeguard, and dispose of client records in ways that maintain confidentiality and in accord with applicable laws and professional standards.

2.5 Subsequent to the therapist moving from the area, closing the practice, or upon the death of the therapist, a marriage and family therapist arranges for the storage, transfer, or disposal of client records in ways that maintain confidentiality and safeguard the welfare of clients.

2.6 Marriage and family therapists, when consulting with colleagues or referral sources, do not share confidential information that could reasonably lead to the identification of a client, research participant, supervisee, or other person with whom they have a confidential relationship unless they have obtained the prior written consent of the client, research participant, supervisee, or other person with whom they have a confidential relationship. Information may be shared only to the extent necessary to achieve the purposes of the consultation.

Principle III: Professional Competence and Integrity

Marriage and family therapists maintain high standards of professional competence and integrity.

3.1 Marriage and family therapists pursue knowledge of new developments and maintain competence in marriage and family therapy through education, training, or supervised experience.

3.2 Marriage and family therapists maintain adequate knowledge of and adhere to applicable laws, ethics, and professional standards.

3.3 Marriage and family therapists seek appropriate professional assistance for their personal problems or conflicts that may impair work performance or clinical judgment.

3.4 Marriage and family therapists do not provide services that create a conflict of interest that may impair work performance or clinical judgment.

3.5 Marriage and family therapists, as presenters, teachers, supervisors, consultants and researchers, are dedicated to high standards of scholarship, present accurate information, and disclose potential conflicts of interest.

3.6 Marriage and family therapists maintain accurate and adequate clinical and financial records.

3.7 While developing new skills in specialty areas, marriage and family therapists take steps to ensure the competence of their work and to protect clients from possible harm. Marriage and family therapists practice in specialty areas new to them only after appropriate education, training, or supervised experience.

3.8 Marriage and family therapists do not engage in sexual or other forms of harassment of clients, students, trainees, supervisees, employees, colleagues, or research subjects.

3.9 Marriage and family therapists do not engage in the exploitation of clients, students, trainees, supervisees, employees, colleagues, or research subjects.

3.10 Marriage and family therapists do not give to or receive from clients (a) gifts of substantial value or (b) gifts that impair the integrity or efficacy of the therapeutic relationship.

3.11 Marriage and family therapists do not diagnose, treat, or advise on problems outside the recognized boundaries of their competencies.

3.12 Marriage and family therapists make efforts to prevent the distortion or misuse of their clinical and research findings.

3.13 Marriage and family therapists, because of their ability to influence and alter the lives of others, exercise special care when making public their professional recommendations and opinions through testimony or other public statements.

3.14 To avoid a conflict of interest, marriage and family therapists who treat minors or adults involved in custody or visitation actions may not also perform forensic evaluations for custody, residence, or visitation of the minor. The marriage and family therapist who treats the minor may provide the court or mental health professional performing the evaluation with information about the minor from the marriage and family therapist's perspective as a treating marriage and family therapist, so long as the marriage and family therapist does not violate confidentiality.

3.15 Marriage and family therapists are in violation of this Code and subject to termination of membership or other appropriate action if they: (a) are convicted of any felony; (b) are convicted of a misdemeanor related to their qualifications or functions; (c) engage in conduct which could lead to conviction of a felony, or a misdemeanor related to their qualifications or functions; (d) are expelled from or disciplined by other professional organizations; (e) have their licenses or certificates suspended or revoked or are otherwise disciplined by regulatory bodies; (f) continue to practice marriage and family therapy while no longer competent to do so because they are impaired by physical or mental causes or the abuse of alcohol or other substances; or (g) fail to cooperate with the Association at any point from the inception of an ethical complaint through the completion of all proceedings regarding that complaint.

Principle IV: Responsibility to Students and Supervisees

Marriage and family therapists do not exploit the trust and dependency of students and supervisees.

4.1 Marriage and family therapists are aware of their influential positions with respect to students and supervisees, and they avoid exploiting the trust and dependency of such persons. Therapists, therefore, make every effort to avoid conditions and multiple relationships that could impair professional objectivity or increase the risk of exploitation. When the risk of impairment or exploitation exists due to conditions or multiple roles, therapists take appropriate precautions.

4.2 Marriage and family therapists do not provide therapy to current students or supervisees.

4.3 Marriage and family therapists do not engage in sexual intimacy with students or supervisees during the evaluative or training relationship between the therapist and student or supervisee. Should a supervisor engage in sexual activity with a former supervisee, the burden of proof shifts to the supervisor to demonstrate that there has been no exploitation or injury to the supervisee.

4.4 Marriage and family therapists do not permit students or supervisees to perform or to hold themselves out as competent to perform professional services beyond their training, level of experience, and competence.

4.5 Marriage and family therapists take reasonable measures to ensure that services provided by supervisees are professional.

4.6 Marriage and family therapists avoid accepting as supervisees or students those individuals with whom a prior or existing relationship could compromise the therapist's objectivity. When such situations cannot be avoided, therapists take appropriate precautions to maintain objectivity. Examples of such relationships include, but are not limited to, those individuals with whom the therapist has a current or prior sexual, close personal, immediate familial, or therapeutic relationship.

4.7 Marriage and family therapists do not disclose supervisee confidences except by written authorization or waiver, or when mandated or permitted by law. In educational or training settings where there are multiple supervisors, disclosures are permitted only to other professional colleagues, administrators, or employers who share responsibility for training of the supervisee. Verbal authorization will not be sufficient except in emergency situations, unless prohibited by law.

Principle V: Responsibility to Research Participants

Investigators respect the dignity and protect the welfare of research participants, and are aware of applicable laws and regulations and professional standards governing the conduct of research.

5.1 Investigators are responsible for making careful examinations of ethical acceptability in planning studies. To the extent that services to research participants may be compromised by participation in research, investigators seek the ethical advice of qualified professionals not directly involved in the investigation and observe safeguards to protect the rights of research participants.

5.2 Investigators requesting participant involvement in research inform participants of the aspects of the research that might reasonably be expected to influence willingness to participate. Investigators are especially sensitive to the possibility of diminished consent when participants are also receiving clinical services, or have impairments which limit understanding and/or communication, or when participants are children.

5.3 Investigators respect each participant's freedom to decline participation in or to withdraw from a research study at any time. This obligation requires special thought and consideration when investigators or other members of the research team are in positions of authority or influence over participants. Marriage and family therapists, therefore, make every effort to avoid multiple relationships with research participants that could impair professional judgment or increase the risk of exploitation.

5.4 Information obtained about a research participant during the course of an investigation is confidential unless there is a waiver previously obtained in writing. When the possibility exists that others, including family members, may obtain access to such information, this possibility, together with the plan for protecting confidentiality, is explained as part of the procedure for obtaining informed consent.

Principle VI: Responsibility to the Profession

Marriage and family therapists respect the rights and responsibilities of professional colleagues and participate in activities that advance the goals of the profession.

6.1 Marriage and family therapists remain accountable to the standards of the profession when acting as members or employees of organizations. If the mandates of an organization with which a marriage and family therapist is affiliated, through employment, contract or otherwise, conflict with the AAMFT Code of Ethics, marriage and family therapists make known to the organization their commitment to the AAMFT Code of Ethics and attempt to resolve the conflict in a way that allows the fullest adherence to the Code of Ethics.

6.2 Marriage and family therapists assign publication credit to those who have contributed to a publication in proportion to their contributions and in accordance with customary professional publication practices.

6.3 Marriage and family therapists do not accept or require authorship credit for a publication based on research from a student's program, unless the therapist made a substantial contribution beyond being a faculty advisor or research committee member. Coauthorship on a student thesis, dissertation, or project should be determined in accordance with principles of fairness and justice.

6.4 Marriage and family therapists who are the authors of books or other materials that are published or distributed do not plagiarize or fail to cite persons to whom credit for original ideas or work is due.

6.5 Marriage and family therapists who are the authors of books or other materials published or distributed by an organization take reasonable precautions to ensure that the organization promotes and advertises the materials accurately and factually.

6.6 Marriage and family therapists participate in activities that contribute to a better community and society, including devoting a portion of their professional activity to services for which there is little or no financial return.

6.7 Marriage and family therapists are concerned with developing laws and regulations pertaining to marriage and family therapy that serve the public interest, and with altering such laws and regulations that are not in the public interest.

6.8 Marriage and family therapists encourage public participation in the design and delivery of professional services and in the regulation of practitioners.

Principle VII: Financial Arrangements

Marriage and family therapists make financial arrangements with clients, third-party payors, and supervisees that are reasonably understandable and conform to accepted professional practices.

7.1 Marriage and family therapists do not offer or accept kickbacks, rebates, bonuses, or other remuneration for referrals; fee-for-service arrangements are not prohibited.

7.2 Prior to entering into the therapeutic or supervisory relationship, marriage and family therapists clearly disclose and explain to clients and supervisees: (a) all financial arrangements and fees related to professional services, including charges for canceled or missed appointments; (b) the use of collection agencies or legal measures for nonpayment; and (c) the procedure for obtaining payment from the client, to the extent allowed by law, if payment is denied by the third-party payor. Once services have begun, therapists provide reasonable notice of any changes in fees or other charges.

7.3 Marriage and family therapists give reasonable notice to clients with unpaid balances of their intent to seek collection by agency or legal recourse. When such action is taken, therapists will not disclose clinical information.

7.4 Marriage and family therapists represent facts truthfully to clients, third-party payors, and supervisees regarding services rendered.

7.5 Marriage and family therapists ordinarily refrain from accepting goods and services from clients in return for services rendered. Bartering for professional services may be conducted only if: (a) the supervisee or client requests it, (b) the relationship is not exploitative, (c) the professional relationship is not distorted, and (d) a clear written contract is established.

7.6 Marriage and family therapists may not withhold records under their immediate control that are requested and needed for a client's treatment solely because payment has not been received for past services, except as otherwise provided by law.

Principle VIII: Advertising

Marriage and family therapists engage in appropriate informational activities, including those that enable the public, referral sources, or others to choose professional services on an informed basis.

8.1 Marriage and family therapists accurately represent their competencies, education, training, and experience relevant to their practice of marriage and family therapy.

8.2 Marriage and family therapists ensure that advertisements and publications in any media (such as directories, announcements, business cards, newspapers, radio, television, Internet, and facsimiles) convey information that is necessary for the public to make an appropriate selection of professional services. Information could include: (a) office information, such as name, address, telephone number, credit card acceptability, fees, languages spoken, and office hours; (b) qualifying clinical degree (see subprinciple 8.5); (c) other earned degrees (see subprinciple 8.5) and state or provincial licensures and/or certifications; (d) AAMFT clinical member status; and (e) description of practice.

8.3 Marriage and family therapists do not use names that could mislead the public concerning the identity, responsibility, source, and status of those practicing under that name, and do not hold themselves out as being partners or associates of a firm if they are not.

8.4 Marriage and family therapists do not use any professional identification (such as a business card, office sign, letterhead, Internet, or telephone or association directory listing) if it includes a statement or claim that is false, fraudulent, misleading, or deceptive.

8.5 In representing their educational qualifications, marriage and family therapists list and claim as evidence only those earned degrees: (a) from institutions accredited by regional accreditation sources recognized by the United States Department of Education, (b) from institutions recognized by states or provinces that license or certify marriage and family therapists, or (c) from equivalent foreign institutions.

8.6 Marriage and family therapists correct, wherever possible, false, misleading, or inaccurate information and representations made by others concerning the therapist's qualifications, services, or products.

8.7 Marriage and family therapists make certain that the qualifications of their employees or supervisees are represented in a manner that is not false, misleading, or deceptive.

8.8 Marriage and family therapists do not represent themselves as providing specialized services unless they have the appropriate education, training, or supervised experience.

Appendix C

•

IAMFC Ethical Codes

Preamble

The IAMFC (International Association of Marriage and Family Counselors) is an organization dedicated to advancing the practice, training, and research of marriage and family counselors. Members may specialize in areas such as: premarital counseling, intergenerational counseling, separation and divorce counseling, relocation counseling, custody assessment and implementation, single parenting, stepfamilies, nontraditional family and marriage life-styles, healthy and dysfunctional family systems, multicultural marriage and family concerns, displaced and homeless families, interfaith and interracial families, and dual career couples. In conducting these professional activities, members commit themselves to protect and advocate for the healthy growth and development of the family as a whole, even as they conscientiously recognize the integrity and diversity of each family and family member's unique needs, situations, status, and condition. The IAMFC member recognizes that the relationship between provider and consumer services is characterized as an egalitarian process emphasizing co-participation, co-equality, co-authority, co-responsibility, and client empowerment.

This code of ethics promulgates a framework for ethical practice by IAMFC members and is divided into eight sections: client well-being, confidentiality, competence, assessment, private practice, research and publications, supervision, and media and public statements. The ideas presented within

Reprinted from *The Family Journal*, Vol. 1, January 1993, pp. 73–77. © ACA. Reprinted with permission.

these eight areas are meant to supplement the ethical standards of the American Counseling Association (ACA), formerly the American Association for Counseling and Development (AACD), and all members should know and keep the standards of our parent organization. Although an ethical code cannot anticipate every possible situation or dilemma, the IAMFC ethical guidelines can aid members in ensuring the welfare and dignity of the couples and families they have contact with, as well as assisting in the implementation of the Hippocratic mandate for healers: Do no harm.

Section I: Client Well-being

A. Members demonstrate a caring, empathic, respectful, fair and active concern for family well-being. They promote client safety, security, and a place-of-belonging in family, community, and society.

B. Members recognize that each family is unique. They strive to respect the diversity of personal attributes and do not stereotype or force families into prescribed attitudes, roles, or behaviors. Family counselors respect the client's definitions of families, and recognize diversity of families, including two-parent, single parent, extended, multigenerational, same gender, etc.

C. Members respect the autonomy and independent decision-making abilities of their clients. When working with families with children, counselors respect the parent's autonomy in child-rearing decisions.

D. Members seek to develop working, collaborative relationships with clients, which are egalitarian in nature. Counselors openly disclose information in sessions, including theoretical approach to understanding behavior, and processes for decision-making and problem-solving.

E. Members assist clients to develop a philosophy on the meaning, purpose, and direction of life. Counselors promote positive regard of self, family, and others.

F. Members do not impose personal values on families or family members. Members recognize the influence of worldview and cultural factors (race, ethnicity, gender, social class, spirituality, sexual orientation, educational status) on the presenting problem, family functioning, and problem-solving skills. Counselors are aware of indigenous healing practices and incorporate them into treatment when necessary or feasible. Members are encouraged to follow the guidelines provided in Multicultural Competencies (cf. Arredondo, P., Toporek, F., Brown, S., Jones, J., Locke, D.C., Sanchez, J., & Stadler, H. (1996). Operationalization of the multicultural counseling competencies. Alexandria, VA: American Counseling Association).

G. Members do not discriminate on the basis of race, gender, social class, disability, spirituality, religion, age, sexual orientation, nationality, language, educational level, marital status, or political affiliation.

H. Members do not engage in dual relationships with clients. In cases where dual relationships are unavoidable, family counselors are obligated to discuss and provide informed consent of the ramifications of the counseling relationship.

I. Members do not harass, exploit, or coerce current or former clients. Members do not engage in sexual harassment. Members do not develop sexual relationships with current or former clients.

J. Members must determine and inform all persons involved that the primary client is the family. Members must be sure that family members have an understanding of the nature of relationships, and the nature of reports to third parties (schools, teachers, managed care companies, etc.).

K. When a conflict of interest exists between the needs of the clients and the counselor's employers, family counselors must clarify commitments to all parties. Counselors recognize that the acceptance of employment implies agreement with policies, and therefore monitor their place of employment to make sure that the environment is conducive to the positive growth and development of clients. If after utilizing appropriate institutional channels for change, the counselor finds that the agency is not working toward the well-being of clients, the counselor has an obligation to terminate institutional affiliation.

L. Members should pursue the development of clients' cognitive, moral, social, emotional, spiritual, physical, educational, and career needs, as well as parenting, marriage, and family living skills, in order to prevent future problems.

M. Members terminate relationships if the continuation of services is not in the best interest of the client or would result in an ethical violation. If a client feels that the counseling relationship is no longer productive, the member has an obligation to assist in finding alternative services.

N. Members inform clients (in writing if feasible) about the goals and purpose of counseling, qualifications of the counselor(s), scope and limits of confidentiality, potential risks and benefits of the counseling process and specific techniques and interventions, reasonable expectations for outcomes, duration of services, costs of services, and alternative approaches.

O. Members refrain from techniques, procedures, or interventions that place families or members at risk of harm. Counselors should refrain from using intrusive interventions without a sound theoretical rationale and full consideration of the potential ramifications to families and members.

P. Members maintain accurate and up-to-date records. They make all file information available to clients unless the sharing of such information would be damaging to the status, goals, growth, and development of clients.

Q. Members are urged to consult with supervisors and consultants when facing an ethical dilemma. Counselors may contact the IAMFC executive director, president, executive board members, or chair of the ethics committee at any time for consultation or remedying ethical violations.

R. Members have the responsibility to confront unethical behavior conducted by other counselors. Counselors should attempt first informally to resolve the unethical behavior with the counselor. If the problem continues, the member should then use the procedures established by the employing institution. Counselors should also contact the appropriate licensing or certification board.

Section II: Confidentiality

A. Nature of confidentiality
  1. Members recognize that the proper functioning of the counseling relationship requires that clients must be free to discuss secrets with the counselor, and counselors must be free to obtain pertinent information beyond that which is volunteered by the client. Absent exceptions, this protection of confidentiality applies to all situations, including initial contacts by a potential client, the fact that a counseling relationship exists, and to all communications made as part of the relationship between a counselor and clients.
  2. Members protect the confidences and secrets of their clients. Counselors do not reveal information received from clients. Counselors do not use information received from a client to the disadvantage of the client. Counselors do not use information received from a client for the advantage of the counselor or of any other person.
  3. Unless alternate arrangements have been agreed upon by all participants, statements made by a family member to the counselor during an individual counseling or consulting contact are to be treated as confidential and not disclosed to other family members without the individual's permission.

B. Integration for legal and ethical limits on confidentiality
  1. Members make reasonable efforts to be knowledgeable about the legal status of confidentiality in their practice location.

  2. Members recognize that ethical standards are not intended to require counselors to violate clearly defined legal standards in their practice location.
  3. Members support professional activity to establish legal protection for confidentiality of communications between counselor and clients.

C. Exceptions to confidentiality
  1. Members may reveal a client's confidences with the consent of that client, but a counselor first makes reasonable efforts to make the client aware of the ramifications of the disclosure.
  2. Members may disclose confidences when required by a specific law such as a child abuse reporting statute.
  3. Members may disclose confidences when required to do so by a court of competent jurisdiction.
  4. Members may disclose an intention of a client to commit a crime, and may also disclose such other confidences as may be necessary to prevent the commission of the crime.
  5. Members may disclose confidences in order to prevent clearly identified bodily harm to the client or to some other clearly identified person.
  6. Members may reveal a client's confidences to the extent necessary to establish or collect a fee from that client.
  7. Members may reveal a client's confidences to the extent necessary to defend the counselor and/or associates against a charge of wrongful conduct brought by the client.

D. Informed consent about confidentiality
  1. Members inform clients about the nature and limitations of confidentiality, including the separate but related status of legal and ethical standards regarding confidentiality.
  2. Members use care not to explicitly or implicitly promise more protection of confidentiality than that which exists.
  3. Members use care to get informed consent from each family member concerning

limitations on confidentiality of communications made in the presence of a family or other group.

4. Members clearly define and communicate the boundaries of confidentiality agreed on by the counselor and family members prior to the beginning of a family counseling relationship. As changing conditions might necessitate a change in these boundaries, counselors get informed consent to the new conditions prior to proceeding with the counseling activities.

5. Members terminate the relationship and make an appropriate referral in cases where a client's refusal to give informed consent to the boundary of confidentiality interferes with the agreed upon goals of counseling.

E. Practice management concerning confidentiality

1. Members assert the client's right to confidentiality when the counselor is asked to reveal client confidences.

2. Members notify the client when the counselor receives a subpoena, which might lead to the counselor having to disclose the client's confidences.

3. When a member receives a subpoena to go to court, the counselor makes a reasonable effort to ask the court to recognize the value of the counseling relationship and the importance of confidentiality to that relationship, and consequently to excuse the counselor from disclosing confidential information.

4. When members are not excused from giving testimony, they exercise caution not to disclose information or relinquish records until directed to do so by the court.

5. Members exercise care in planning and monitoring their practices in order to assure that the counselors, their associates and staff, and the clients avoid any behavior that might be construed as a waiver of confidentiality.

6. Members make reasonable efforts to teach their clients to avoid behaviors, such as disclosing secrets under conditions which do not lead to an expectation of confidentiality, which might be construed as a waiver of confidentiality.

7. Members exercise professional judgment and discretion in deciding whether an exception to confidentiality applies in particular cases. In cases where the decision is not apparent, counselors utilize advice from consultants and the professional literature in making a decision.

8. When members make a good faith decision to disclose confidence based on one of the exceptions listed above, the amount and kind of information disclosed, the person(s) to whom the disclosure is made, and the method of communication all are limited to what is necessity to discharge the duty created by the exception.

9. Members get informed consent from all clients prior to making an electronic recording of a counseling session.

10. Members recognize that the normal operation of a counseling practice exposes confidential information to certain other counselors and to non-counseling staff, but counselors exercise care to limit access only to that which is necessary.

11. Members use care in screening, training, and supervising all paid and volunteer staff in order to assure that the staff members protect confidentiality in their role as an extension of the counselor.

12. Members use care in creating and maintaining office practices which protect confidentiality. For example, client reception areas are separate from counseling offices and work-stations where confidential files are handled, and clients are not allowed to have access to areas where they might hear or see other clients' secrets.

13. Members use care to assure clients' records are produced, stored, and disposed of in a way that protects confidentiality. Written records should be

kept in a locked and secure location, and computerized record systems should use appropriate safeguards to prevent unauthorized access.

14. Members create a system to protect the confidentiality of client records in the event of the death or incapacity of the counselor.

15. Members who disclose certain client information in order to get consultation from another counselor use care not to reveal the identity of the client or any other information beyond that which is necessary to get effective consultation. Members seek consultation only from other professional counselors who recognize their obligation to keep all shared information confidential.

16. Members who use client data for research, teaching, or publication purposes must use care to disguise the data in order to protect client's privacy rights and confidentiality rights.

Section III: Competence

A. Members have the responsibility to develop and maintain basic skills in marriage and family counseling through graduate work, supervision, and peer review. An outline of these skills is provided by the Council for Accreditation of Counseling and Related Educational Programs (CACREP) Environmental and Specialty Standards for Marriage and Family Counseling/Therapy. The minimal level of training shall be considered a master's degree in a helping profession.

B. Members recognize the need for keeping current with new developments in the field of marriage and family counseling. They pursue continuing education in forms such as books, journals, classes, workshops, conferences, and conventions.

C. Members accurately represent their education, areas of expertise, credentials, training and experience. They make concerted efforts to ensure that statements others make about them and/or their credentials are accurate.

D. Members do not attempt to diagnose or treat problems beyond the scope of their abilities and training. While developing new skills in specialty areas, marriage and family counselors take steps to ensure the quality of their work through training, supervision, and peer review.

E. Members do not undertake any professional activity in which their personal problems might impair their performance. They seek assistance for problems, and, if necessary, limit, suspend, or terminate their professional activities.

F. Members do not engage in actions that violate the "standards of practice" of their given professional counseling community.

G. Members are committed to gaining cultural competency, including awareness, knowledge, and skills to work with a diverse clientele. Members are aware of their own biases, values, and assumptions about human behavior. They employ techniques/assessment strategies that are appropriate for dealing with diverse cultural groups.

H. Members take care of their physical, mental, and emotional health in order to reduce the risk of burnout, and to prevent impairment and harm to clients.

Section IV: Assessment

A. Members have the responsibility of acquiring and maintaining skills related to assessment procedures and assessment instruments that promote the best interests and well-being of the client in clarifying concerns, establishing treatment goals, evaluating therapeutic progress, and promoting objective decision making.

B. Members provide clients with assessment results, interpretation, and conclusions drawn from assessment interviews and instruments. Members inform clients of how assessment information will be used.

C. Members use assessment methods that are current, reliable, valid, and germane to the goals of the client, including computer-assisted assessment. Members do not use inventories and tests that have outdated test items or lack normative data.

D. Members use assessment methods that are within the scope of their qualifications, training, or statutory limitations. Members using tests or inventories have a thorough understanding of measurement concepts.

E. Members are familiar with any assessment instrument prior to its use, including the testing manual, purpose of the instrument, and relevant psychometric and normative data.

F. Members only use instruments that have demonstrated validity in custody evaluations and do not make recommendations based solely on test and inventory scores. Members conducting custody evaluations recognize the potential impact that their reports can have on family members and use instruments that have demonstrated validity in custody evaluations.

G. Members strive to maintain the guidelines in the *Standards for Educational and Psychological Testing*, written in collaboration by the American Educational Research Association, American Psychological Association, and National Council on Measurement in Evaluation, as well as the *Code of Fair Testing Practices*, published by the Joint Committee on Testing Procedures.

Section V: Private Practice

A. Members in private practice have a special obligation to adhere to ethical and legal standards, because of the independent nature of their work.

1. Members keep informed of current ethical codes and ethical issues of the profession.
2. Members maintain a working knowledge of legal standards in the geographical area and areas of specialty in which they work, abiding by these standards in their practice.
3. Members continue professional growth and knowledge through consultation and supervision.

B. Members practice within the scope of their training

1. Members promote themselves only within the areas of their professional training, supervision, and experience.

2. Members refer to other practitioners clients who would benefit from services outside of their own areas of expertise.

C. Members in private practice are responsible and respectful of client needs in their setting and collection of fees for service.

1. Members provide a portion of their services at little or no cost as a service to the community.
2. Members appropriately refer clients who are unable to afford private services and cannot be seen pro bono by the private practitioner.
3. Members do not share or accept fees for offering or accepting referrals.
4. Bartering is discouraged because of the inherent potential for erosion of professional boundaries and introduction of dual relationships. If unavoidable and considered the standard of practice in the community, fair value for services/items exchanged should be included in a contract and reported as income.

D. Members do not terminate counseling with established clients that would benefit from further counseling without referring them to an appropriate practitioner or agency.

E. Members enter into professional partnerships only with others that adhere to ethical standards of the profession. Implicit in this standard is that members should not share or accept fees for accepting or offering referrals.

Section VI: Research and Publications

A. Members shall be fully responsible for their choice of research topics and the methods used for investigation, analysis, and reporting. They must be particularly careful that findings do not appear misleading, that the research is planned to allow for the inclusion of alternative hypotheses, and that provision is made for discussion of the limitations of the study.

B. Members safeguard the privacy of their research participants. Data about an individual participant are not released unless the individual is informed about the exact nature of the information to be released and gives written permission for doing so.

C. Members safeguard the safety of their research participants. Members receive approval from, and follow guidelines of, any institutional research committee. Prospective participants are informed, in writing, about any potential risk associated with a study and are notified that they can withdraw at any time.

D. Members make their original data available to other researchers.

E. Members only take credit for research in which they make a substantial contribution, and give credit to all such contributors. Authors are listed from greatest to least amount of contribution.

F. Members do not plagiarize. Ideas or data that did not originate with the author(s) and are not common knowledge are clearly credited to the original source.

G. Members are aware of their obligation to be a role model for graduate students and other future researchers and so act in accordance with the highest standards possible while engaged in research.

H. Family counselors should be cautious when assessing culturally diverse clients. Family counselors include cultural factors when assessing behaviors, functioning, and presenting symptoms of clients. Counselors are careful to use assessment techniques that have been appropriately formed and standardized on diverse populations. Counselors are also careful to interpret results from standardized assessment instruments in light of cultural factors.

Section VII: Supervision

A. Members who provide supervision demonstrate advanced skills in marriage and family counseling, and receive appropriate training and supervision-of-supervision prior to providing supervisory services. Members provide supervision only within the limits of their professional competence. Additionally, they accept supervisory responsibilities only for counselors they can appropriately and adequately oversee.

B. Members who provide supervision respect the inherent imbalance of power in supervisory relationships. Thus, they actively monitor and appropriately manage multiple relationships. They refrain from engaging in relationships or activities that increase risk of exploitation, or that may impair the professional judgement of supervisees. Sexual intimacy with students or supervisees is prohibited.

C. Members who provide supervision regard content of supervisory sessions as confidential. They provide the same level of security for documentation related to supervisees as they do for clients.

D. Members who are supervisors educate supervisees about professional ethics and standards of practice. Supervisors provide service to professional organizations and work to improve professional practices. They also encourage supervisees to participate in professional organizations.

E. Members who are supervisors provide accurate and complete information (e.g., areas of expertise, credentials, philosophy and approaches to supervision, procedures for evaluation, responses to client emergencies, ethical guidelines to which they adhere, etc.) to assure that potential supervisees engage in supervisory relationships with clear understanding for the supervisory arrangements. They articulate expectations surrounding skill building, knowledge acquisition, and the development of competencies. Members also provide ongoing and timely feedback to their supervisees.

F. Members who provide supervision are responsible for protecting the rights and well-being of their supervisees' clients. They monitor their supervisees' counseling on an ongoing basis, and create procedures to protect the confidentiality of clients whose sessions have been electronically recorded.

G. Members who provide supervision assure that supervisees' clients receive information about supervisees' level of training and credentials, parameters of supervision, the counseling processes and purposes, benefits and risks they may encounter, and limits of confidentiality prior to establishing contracts for counseling.

H. Members who provide supervision endorse for practice only those supervisees who demonstrate expectations for competency and professional judgement.

I. Supervisors assure that supervisees are knowledgeable about professional ethics and standards, and that they practice within those parameters.

J. Members who provide supervision strive to reach and maintain the guidelines provided in the Standards for Counseling Supervisors adopted by the ACA Governing Council and the Code of Ethics established by the Association for Counselor Education and Supervision.

K. Members understand the influence of cultural issues in the supervisory relationship, including issues of oppression and power structures within the relationship.

L. Members who provide supervision discuss cultural issues in the work of supervisees and clients, and promote cultural sensitivity and competence in the supervisees.

Section VIII: Advertising and Other Public Statements

A. Members accurately and objectively represent their education, training, professional qualifications, skills, and functions to the public. Members do not use membership in a professional organization to suggest endorsement of their competency.

B. Members ensure that all advertisements, announcements, or other public statements they make regarding their professional services are not false or misleading, either by commission or omission. Such public statements should focus on objective information that allows clients to make an informed decision about seeking services. Providing information such as highest relevant academic

degree earned, training and experience, professional credentials, types of services offered, office hours, fee structure, and languages spoken can help clients decide if the advertised services are appropriate for their needs.

C. Members advertise themselves as specialists within marriage and family counseling only in those areas in which they can demonstrate evidence of training, education, and supervised experiences in the area of specialization.

D. Members who engage others to advertise or promote their professional services remain responsible for all forms of public statements made. Members strive to make certain that statements about their professional services made by other persons are accurate. In addition, members do not ask for or accept testimonials from current or former clients regarding the uniqueness, effectiveness, or efficiency of counseling services.

E. Members promoting counseling-related products for commercial sale make every effort to ensure that advertisements and announcements are presented in a professional and factual manner. In addition, announcements and advertisements about workshops or training events should never contain false or misleading statements. Members make certain that advertisements and announcements regarding products or training events provide accurate and adequate information for consumers to make informed choices.

F. Members have the responsibility to provide information to the public that enhances marriage and family life. Such statements should be based on sound, professionally accepted theories, techniques, and approaches. When presenting information to the public, members only address issues for which they are adequately qualified and prepared. Due to the inability to complete a comprehensive assessment or provide follow-up, members do not give specific advice to an individual through the media or other public venues.

Glossary

•

ABC procedure   a procedure in Ellis's theory for disputing emotions where A stands for an event, B stands for the thought, and C stands for the emotion.

ABCX model of a crisis   In this model A represents the stressor event that happens to the family, B represents the resources at the family's disposal, and C represents the meaning or interpretation the family attaches to the experience. X is the combined effect of these factors (i.e., the crisis itself). This model highlights that the same type of event may be handled differently by different families.

absurdity   statements that are half-truths and even silly if followed to a conclusion. Whitaker and symbolic-experiential family therapists often work with families by using absurdities.

abuse   all forms of maltreatment within a family, such as physical, sexual, or emotional.

acceptance   (1) Neil Jacobson's term for loving your partner as a complete person and not focusing on differences. Such a strategy may promote change in couples. (2) the therapist's personal and professional comfortableness with a family.

accommodation   a process of joining in which the therapist makes personal adjustments in order to achieve a therapeutic alliance with a family.

acculturation   the modification of a culture as a result of coming into contact with another culture. In many instances, minority cultures incorporate many traditions and mores of majority cultures in attempts to "fit in."

acculturation gap   different rates of acculturation between immigrant parents and U.S.-raised children that complicates the normal generation gap. The results of this gap may result in greater misunderstandings, miscommunications, and eventual conflicts among family members than would otherwise happen.

act as if   a role-playing strategy where persons act as if they are the persons they want to be ideally.

action-oriented research   research that focuses on finding solutions to a problem, such as spouse abuse.

adding cognitive constructions   the verbal component of structural family therapy, which consists of advice, information, pragmatic fictions, and paradox.

administrative liability   where the therapist's license to practice is threatened by an investigation from the licensing board, which has the power to suspend a license. See also *civil liability; criminal liability; liability.*

administrative (regulatory) law   specialized regulations that pertain to certain specialty areas that are passed by authorized government agencies, for example, laws governing the use of federal land.

affect   feelings or emotions.

aging family   a family headed by those 65 years old and above.

alcohol use disorder   a term for alcohol problems that include two levels: **alcohol abuse**, a problem with drinking that interferes with work, school, and home life, and **alcohol dependency**, a disorder in which persons are unable to control their drinking of alcohol.

alignments   the ways family members join together or oppose one another in carrying out a family activity.

American Association for Marriage and Family Therapy (AAMFT)   the oldest and largest (23,000 members) professional family therapy organization in the world and dedicated to increasing understanding, research and education in the field of marriage and family therapy, and ensuring that the public's needs are met by trained practitioners (http://www.aamft.org/).

American Family Therapy Academy (AFTA)   a nonprofit organization of "leading family therapy teachers, clinicians, program developers, researchers and social scientists, dedicated to advancing systemic thinking and practices for families in their ecological context" (http://www.afta.org/).

amplifying feedback loops feedback loops that promote change. See *positive feedback loops*.

Anatomy of Intervention Model (AIM) a cognitive-behavioral strategy where the therapist learns to play many roles and be flexible. It involves five phases: (1) introduction, (2) assessment, (3) motivation, (4) behavior change, and (5) termination.

anxiety mental and physical nervousness associated with pressure to please and fear of failure.

asking question a primary tool of Bowen family therapists, often considered to be the "magic bullet" of this approach.

assertiveness (1) asking for what one wants in a timely and appropriate manner. (2) the act of asking for what one wants without being overly aggressive or passive.

assessment the administration of formal or informal tests or evaluation instrument(s) along with behavioral observations.

assessment procedure any method used to measure characteristics of people, programs, or objects.

assigned behaviors a strategic therapy technique where clients are asked to perform certain actions such as staying up when they begin to feel sleepy.

attachment theory John Bowlby's theory that is the underlying basis of emotionally focused therapy and much of experiential family therapy especially the communication/validation approach of Virginia Satir.

attenuating feedback loops feedback loops that promote a return to equilibrium. See *negative feedback loops*.

autonomy in Bowen theory, a designation for the level of differentiation in a person which signals the ability to think through a situation clearly. In ethics, the right of individuals to make decisions and choices.

Avanta Network an association that carries on the interdisciplinary work of training therapists in Satir's methods.

baseline a recording of the occurrence of targeted behaviors before an intervention is made.

Basic Family Therapy Skills Project a project that began in 1987 which focuses on determining, defining, and testing the skills essential for beginning family therapists to master for effective therapy practice.

battering violence that includes severe physical assault or risk of serious injury.

battle for initiative the struggle to get a family to become motivated to make needed changes.

battle for structure the struggle to establish the parameters under which family therapy is conducted.

behavioral analysis a procedure used in behavioral couples therapy to measure couple distress. It is based on interviewing, self reports on questionnaires, and making behavioral observations.

behavioral couple therapy a behavioral approach to working with couples based on an exchange/negotiation model and focused on negotiating pleasing behaviors as well as teaching problem solving and communication skills to partners.

behavioral family therapy an approach to treating families that focuses on dealing with behaviors directly in order to produce change. See also *cognitive-behavioral family therapy*.

behavioral therapy the therapeutic approach that proposes that all behavior is learned and that people act according to how they have been previously reinforced. Behavior is maintained by its consequences and will continue unless more rewarding consequences result from new behaviors.

behaviorism a form of treating individuals where therapists focus on changing observable behaviors through such methods as reinforcement, extinction, and shaping.

beneficience the ethical principle of first do no harm to individuals and work in their best interest.

binuclear family a term that describes two interrelated family households that comprise one family system, such as a remarried family.

blamer according to Satir, a person who attempts to place blame on others and not take responsibility for what is happening.

boomerang children adult children who, after being out on their own for awhile, return to live with their parents because of financial problems, unemployment, or an inability or reluctance to grow up.

boundaries the physical and psychological factors that separate people from one another and organize them.

brief therapy an approach to working with families that has to do more with the clarity about what needs to be changed rather than time. A central principle of brief therapy is that one evaluates which solutions have so far been attempted and then tries new and different solutions to the family's problem, often the opposite of what has already been attempted.

bug-in-the-ear supervision method a supervision model where the therapist working with a family receives messages from a supervisor through a telephone hookup device.

camera review where an impartial party, usually a judge, reviews a therapist's records and releases only those portions that are relevant to the situation at hand in a court case.

captitated contract a managed care method of cutting costs in which providers agree to provide treatment for a per-person, per-year fee.

cardboard kids children who appear fine on the surface, but who may lack depth, or the ability to be authentic with themselves or others.

care pathway guidelines instructions and directions in the managed care arena that delineate specific timelines in which diagnosis, interventions, decision-making processes, clinical services, and the potential interactions among multidisciplinary health care professionals should occur.

caring the idea that moral development and principles are centered in the social context of relationships and interdependency.

caring days part of a behavioral marital procedure in which one or both marital partners act as if they care about their spouse regardless of the other's action(s). This technique embodies the idea of a "positive risk"—a unilateral action not dependent on another for success.

case conceptualization a presession exercise where therapists ask themselves certain questions about couples or families they are going to see in order to form an initial impression of their future clients. This procedure helps them integrate theory with practice and come up with a treatment plan.

case law (court decisions) the type of law decided by decisions of courts at all levels from state to federal.

catalyst the role that a psychodynamic family therapist plays by moving into the "living space" of the family and stirs up interactions.

catharsis the release of pent up emotions.

centrifugal literally, directed away from a center. It describes how people move away from their family (i.e., family disengagement).

centripetal literally, directed toward a center. It describes a tendency to move toward family closeness.

certificates printed documents, often affixed with a logo, that are given at the end of narrative therapy to bring closure to the process and affirm that a problem has been defeated.

charting a procedure that involves asking clients to keep an accurate record of problematic behaviors. The idea is to get family members to establish a baseline from which interventions can be made and to show clients how the changes they are making work.

check mark diagram in the ABCX model of a crisis, the process that a family goes through in adjusting to situations, i.e., it initially tumbles down like the slope of a check mark and then after reaching bottom reestablishes itself like the upslope of a check mark from anywhere below, the same, or above where it was in the beginning. See also *ABCX model.*

child abuse maltreatment of a child through acts of commission.

child custody evaluator a family therapist who acts on behalf of a court to determine what is in the best interest of a child in a custody arrangement.

childhood sexual abuse such acts as unwanted touching, (i.e., fondling) intercourse, voyarism, making sexual remarks, oral sex, and pornography perpetrated by someone known or related to a child or by a stranger.

childless family a couple who consciously decides not to have a child or who remains childless as a result of chance, such as infertility.

child neglect maltreatment of a child through acts of omission.

child physical abuse the bodily abuse of a child which may range from mild to severe.

choreography a process in which family members are asked to symbolically enact a pattern or a sequence in their relationship to one another. Choreography is similar to mime or a silent movie.

circular causality the idea that actions are part of a causal chain, each influencing and being influenced by the other.

circular questioning a Milan technique of asking questions that focus attention on family connections and highlight differences among family members. Every question is framed so that it addresses differences in perception about events or relationships by various family members.

civil law that part of the law that pertains to acts offensive to individuals. Law involving family therapists pertains primarily to civil law—for example, divorce.

civil liability a lawsuit by a client against a therapist for professional malpractice (negligence) or gross negligence. See also *administrative liability; criminal liability; liability*.

classical conditioning the oldest form of behaviorism, in which a stimulus that is originally neutral is paired up with another event to elicit certain emotions through association.

clear boundaries rules and habits that allow and encourage dialogue and thus help family members to enhance their communication and relationships with one another.

clinical notes the written impressions of a couple or family soon after a session is over including progress toward a treatment plan.

clue an intervention in deShazer's brief therapy approach that mirrors the usual behavior of a family. It is intended to alert a family to the idea that some of their present behavior will continue.

coaching a technique by which a therapist helps individuals, couples, or families make appropriate responses by giving them verbal instructions.

coalition an alliance between specific family members against a third member. See also *detouring coalition; stable coalition*.

codependency a dynamic within a family where one member of the family underfunctions (such as a substance abuser) while another member of the family overfunctions (such as the codependent family member).

cognitions thoughts.

cognitive-behavioral family therapy an approach to working with families that takes into account the impact of cognitions (i.e., thoughts) and behaviors on modifying family interactions.

cognitive behavior couple therapy an approach to working with couples that takes into account the impact of cognitions (i.e., thoughts) and behaviors on modifying couple interactions.

cognitive behavior theory the idea that the cognitions individuals hold, shape how they think, feel, and behave.

cognitive distraction thinking of other than what one normally thinks of.

cohabitation the living together of a couple without being married.

commitment ambiguity a situation usually in gay and lesbian couple relationships where one partner is not sure about his or her place in the affiliation.

common law law derived from tradition and usage.

communication skills training a behavioral couple therapy approach where couples learn to use "I statements," stick to here-and-now problems rather than dwell on the past, describe their spouse's specific behavior rather than apply a label to it, and are taught how to provide positive feedback to their significant other.

communication stance an experiential family therapy procedure of Virginia Satir's in which family members are asked to exaggerate the physical positions of their perspective roles in order to help them "level." See also *leveling*.

communication/validation family therapy a term often used to describe Satir's model of working with families.

communications theory an approach to working with families that focuses on clarifying verbal and nonverbal transactions among family members. Much communication theory work is incorporated in experiential and strategic family therapy.

community reinforcement approach (CRA) use of systems and resources in the community in which these people live to help them recover from substance abuse.

complainant a solution-focused term to describe a client who complains about and describes a situation or problem.

complementarity the degree of harmony or reciprocity in the meshing of family roles.

complementary relationship relationships based on family member roles or characteristics that are specifically different from each other (e.g., dominant versus submissive, logical versus emotional). If a member fails to fulfill his or her role, such as being a decision maker or a nurturer, other members of the family are adversely affected.

compliment a written message used in brief family therapy designed to praise a family for its strengths and build a "yes set" within it. A compliment consists of a positive statement with which all members of a family can agree.

computer or rational analyzer according to Satir, a person who interacts only on a cognitive or intellectual level.

concerned significant others (CSOs) spouses, relatives, or children of a substance abuser who work to engage initially unmotivated problem abusers into treatment.

confidentiality the ethical duty to fulfill a contract or promise to clients that the information revealed during therapy will be protected from unauthorized disclosure.

confirmation of a family member a process that involves using a feeling word to reflect an expressed or unexpressed feeling of that family member or using a nonjudgmental description of the behavior of the individual.

conflictual triangles two individuals, such as a mother and father, arguing over and interacting with another, such as a rebellious son, instead of attending to their relationship.

confrontation a procedure through which the therapist points out to families how their behaviors contradict or conflict with their expressed wishes.

congruent communication see *leveling*.

conjoint couple therapy (dual therapy) a form of therapy devised by Whitaker.

conjoint family drawing a procedure in which families are initially given the instruction "Draw a picture as you see yourself as a family." Each member of the family makes such a drawing and then shares through discussion the perceptions that emerge.

conjoint therapy therapy with two or more members of a family together at the same time, often a married couple.

constructivism a philosophy that states reality is a reflection of observation and experience, not an objective entity. See *social constructionism*.

construct validity the degree to which an instrument measures what it reports to measure.

consultants the term given to the deShazer team in brief family therapy. Consultants observe a family session behind a one-way mirror and transmit messages to the therapist at a designated break time in the session.

consultation the use of a neutral third party expert in an area to enhance one's own knowledge and abilities in that area.

content the details and facts.

content validity the degree to which an instrument actually taps into representative beliefs or behaviors that it is trying to measure.

contextual therapy an approach developed by Ivan Boszormenyi-Nagy that stresses the healing of human relationships through trust and commitment which is done primarily by developing loyalty, fairness, and reciprocity.

contingency contracting a procedure in which a specific, usually written, schedule or contract describes the terms for the trading or exchange of behaviors and reinforcers between two or more individuals. One action is contingent, or dependent, on another.

contracting creating a formal agreement, often in writing, that describes what and when behavioral changes will be made. It is used when family interactions have reached a level of severe hostility. The contract contains built-in rewards for behaving in a certain manner.

correlational research a design that calculates the degree of association or relatedness between two variables. This type of research is usually ex post facto (after the fact) rather than a priori (before the fact). With correlational research it is difficult to state in any precise way what factors were most influential and with whom.

Couples Communication (CC) Program a marriage enrichment program which is divided into entry and advanced programs where couples learn about themselves and their partners better in addition to mastering 11 interpersonal skills for effective talking, listening, conflict resolution, and anger management.

couple therapy when a counselor works with two individuals to improve their relationship as a dyad. The couple may be married or unmarried, gay or straight, and have various levels of commitment to each other.

courage the ability to take calculated risks without knowing the exact consequences.

court-ordered witness the role a family therapist assumes when he or she must appear before a court to testify on behalf of or against a family or family member.

criminal law that part of the law that deals with acts offensive to society in general.

criminal liability the commission of a crime by a therapist, such as failing to report child abuse, engaging in sexual relations with a patient, or insurance fraud. See also *administrative liability; civil liability; liability.*

crisis resolution a treatment modality used in crisis situations where the therapist focuses most on supporting defenses and clarifying communication in order to help a family.

criterion validity the degree to which what an instrument measures actually relates to life experience.

cross-generational alliance (coalition) an inappropriate family alliance that contains members of two different generations within it, for example, a parent and child collusion.

cultural competency sensitivity to such factors as race, gender, ethnicity, socioeconomic status, and sexual orientation as well as the ability to respond appropriately in a therapeutic manner to persons whose cultural background differs from one's own.

culturally encapsulated counselors professional therapists who treat everyone the same and, in so doing, ignore important differences.

culture the customary beliefs, social forms, and material traits of a racial, religious, or social group.

culture-specific model of multicultural counseling a model of counseling that emphasizes the values, beliefs, and orientation of different ethnic cultural groups.

custodial parent a parent who has primary physical custody of a child.

customers a solution-focused term for clients who are not only able to describe a problem and how they are involved in it but who are willing to work to solve it.

cutoff when family members deal with fusion and a lack of differentiation by distancing themselves physically or emotionally from others.

cybernetics a type of systemic interrelatedness governed by rules, sequences, and feedback. The term was introduced as a concept to family therapy by Gregory Bateson. See also *new epistemology.*

cybernetics of cybernetics a type of systemic interrelatedness that stresses the impact on a family therapist's inclusion and participation in a family system. Also known as *second-order cybernetics.*

deconstruction a narrative family therapy procedure that uses questions as a therapeutic tool to help clients more closely examine taken-for-granted realities and practices.

descriptive research a design set up to describe specific variables, for example, subpopulations.

desensitization a behavioral approach to overcoming unnecessary and debilitating anxiety associated with a particular event.

detouring coalition a coalition in which a pair holds a third family member responsible for their difficulties or conflicts with one another.

detriangulation the process of being in contact with others and, yet, emotionally separate.

development predictable physical, mental, and social changes over life that occur in relationship to the environment.

developmental crises times of change in the life span, often accompanied by turmoil and new opportunity.

developmental research a design that focuses on studying changes over time such as a longitudinal study.

developmental stressors stressful events that are predictable and sequential, such as aging.

diagnosing a proactive structural family therapy technique where the systematic interrelationships of all family members is described early in the treatment process.

Diagnostic and Statistical Manual of Mental Disorders (DSM) a manual, now in its fourth edition, published by the American Psychiatric Association, that codifies psychiatric disorders.

differentiation (of self) a level of maturity reached by an individual who can separate his or her rational and emotional selves. Differentiation is the opposite of **fusion.**

diffuse boundaries arrangements that do not allow enough separation between family members, resulting in some members becoming fused and dependent on other members.

DINK an acronym meaning *dual income, no kids.*

direct and indirect suggestions a technique used in strategic family therapy that is a part of a usually purposefully ambiguous but important message to a client family such as "go slow" or "you may not want to change too quickly."

directive an instruction from a family therapist for a family to behave differently. A directive is to strategic therapy what the interpretation is to psychoanalysis—that is, the basic tool of the approach.

direct observational assessment a measurement characterized by the use of coders, raters, or judges, who usually are not participants in the interpersonal system being studied and whose task is to unitize and assign meaning to some aspects of the process.

disengaged   the state of being psychologically isolated from other family members.

disputing irrational thoughts   a cognitive-behavioral strategy in which irrational beliefs about an event are challenged.

distancing   the isolated separateness of family members from each other, either physically or psychologically.

distractor   according to Satir, a person who relates by saying and doing irrelevant things.

Division 43 of the American Psychological Association (APA): Family Psychology   a division of the APA established to enable psychologists who worked with families to keep their identity as psychologists. The division's mission is to expand both the study and the practice of Family Psychology, through education, research, and clinical practice (http://www.apa.org/divisions/div43/).

divorce mediation   an attempt to bring about a peaceful settlement or compromise between disputants through the objective intervention of a neutral third party.

divorce therapy   a part of marital therapy that seeks to help couples separate from each other physically, psychologically, and/or legally.

domestic violence   aggression that takes place in intimate relationships usually between adults.

Double ABCX model   a model for dealing with crises that builds on the ABCX model but focuses on family resolutions over time rather than in regard to a single happening. See also *ABCX model*.

double-bind   the theory that states that two seemingly contradictory messages may exist at the same time on different levels and lead to confusion, if not schizophrenic behavior, on the part of an individual who cannot comment on or escape from the relationship in which this is occurring.

dream and daydream analysis   a technique used in psychodynamic family therapy to uncover needs and wishes within family members.

dual-career families   those in which both marital partners are engaged in work that is developmental in sequence and to which they have a high commitment.

dual (multiple) relationship   a relationship that is not built on mutuality and where a therapist assumes a second role, for example, being a friend, business associate, lover, and so on.

dual therapy   the name for conjoint couple therapy devised by Carl Whitaker.

Duluth Model   a cognitive-behavioral model of domestic violence treatment premised on the idea that people learn violent behaviors because of being reinforced for them in cultural and social circles. They can therefore unlearn these behaviors and learn new ones through cognitive-behavioral means, such as education.

dysfunctional sets   are the family reactions, developed in response to stress, that are repeated without modification whenever there is family conflict. For example, one spouse might verbally attack the other, bringing charges and countercharges, until the fight escalates into physical violence or the couple withdraws from each other.

early recollections   an Adlerian concept that focuses on childhood memories before the age of 9. These memories often present patterns and recurring themes that relate to a person's present philosophy of life.

emotional deadness   a condition that exists when individuals in families either are not aware of or suppress their emotions.

emotionally cut off   a Bowen concept used to describe a family in which the members avoid each other, either physically or psychologically, because of an unresolved emotional attachment.

emotionally-focused couples therapy   a systemic therapeutic approach to working with couples originated by Susan Johnson that strives to foster the development of more secure attachment styles in couples by using emotions as a positive force for change in relationships.

emotionally overinvolved   see *fusion*.

empty nest   a term that describes couples who have launched their children and are without childrearing responsibilities.

enabler   a spouse or other family member on whom a substance abuser is most dependent and who allows the abuser to continue and become worse.

enactments   the actions of families that show problematic behavioral sequences to therapists, for example, having an argument instead of talking about one.

engagement   the process where experiential therapists become personally involved with their families through the sharing of feelings, fantasies, and personal stories.

enmeshment loss of autonomy due to overinvolvement of family members with each other, either physically or psychologically.

environmental influences the physical aspects of a family's life.

epistemology the study of knowledge.

equitability the proposition that everyone is entitled to have his or her welfare interests considered in a way that is fair from a multilateral perspective. Equitability is the basis for relationship ethics.

ESCAPE an acronym that stands for four major investments therapists must make: (1) Engagement with families and process, (2) Sensitivity to Culture, (3) Awareness of families' Potentials, and (4) knowledge of the Environment.

ethics the moral principles from which individuals and social groups, such as families, determine rules for right conduct. Families and society are governed by relationship ethics.

exceptions a term used in solution-focused family therapy for "negative" or "positive" space (or time when a family goal may be happening).

exceptions questions queries in narrative or solution-focused therapy directed toward finding instances when a situation reported to be a problem is not true. Most exceptions questions begin with "what" and challenge the family's view of the world as well as offer them hope that their lives can be different because some change has already taken place.

expected event a predictable event that occurs, such as getting married.

experiential symbolic family therapy the name of the approach (sometimes also known as symbolic experiential therapy) given to Carl Whitaker's theory of working with families.

experimental research a design that adheres to classic "hard science" methodologies, such as an hypothesis and dependent/independent variables. In an experimental research design, at least one variable is manipulated.

expert witness the role assumed by a family therapist who is asked to give testimony in regard to the probable causes of certain negative behaviors and to make recommendations in regard to a family member (e.g., an uncontrollable juvenile) displaying these behaviors.

exploratory research a qualitative approach often taken to define issues, the design usually consisting of interviews.

externalize problems a method of treatment in narrative therapy devised by White and Epston in which the problem becomes a separate entity outside of the family. Such a process helps families reduce their arguments about who owns the problem, form teams, and enter into dialogue about solving the problem.

extinction the process by which previous reinforcers of an action are withdrawn so that behavior returns to its original level. It involves the elimination of behavior.

family those persons who are biologically and/or psychologically related, who are connected by historical, emotional, or economic bonds, and who perceive themselves as a part of a household.

family adaptability the ability of a family to be flexible and change.

family clown a member of a substance abuse family whose function is to provide the family with humor and thus reduce tension.

family cohesion emotional bonding within a family.

family dance the verbal and nonverbal way a family displays its personality.

family development and environmental fit a concept that states that some environments are conducive to helping families develop and resolve crises, and others are not.

family/divorce mediation the process of helping couples and families settle disputes or dissolve their marriages in a nonadversarial way.

family group therapy a treatment approach that conceptualizes family members as strangers in a group. Members become known to each other in stages similar to those found in groups.

family hero an adult or child who functions to provide self-worth for the family of a substance abuser.

family homeostasis the tendency of the family to remain in its same pattern of functioning and resist change unless challenged or forced to do otherwise.

family life cycle the term used to describe the developmental trends within the family over time.

family life education the study of family life including developmental and situational factors that affect or change the life of families.

family life fact chronology a tool employed in family reconstruction in which the "star" creates a listing of all significant events in his or her life and that of the extended family having an impact on the people in the family.

family map   a visual representation of the structure of three generations of the "star's" family, with adjectives to describe each family member's personality.

family mediation   the process of helping couples and families settle disputes or dissolve a marriage in a nonadversarial way by having a family therapist, who is specially trained, act as an impartial, cognitive, neutral, third party to facilitate negotiation between disputing parties.

family of origin   the family a person was born or adopted into.

Family Process   the first journal in the field of family therapy.

family projection   the tendency of couples according to Bowen to produce offspring at the same level of differentiation as themselves.

family reconstruction   a therapeutic innovation developed by Satir to help family members discover dysfunctional patterns in their lives stemming from their families of origin.

family rules   the overt and covert rules families use to govern themselves, such as "you must only speak when spoken to."

family structure   "the invisible set of functional demands that organizes the ways in which family members interact" (Minuchin, 1974, p. 51).

family therapy supervision   a systemic type of supervision that includes a focus on interpersonal as well as intrapersonal issues.

fee-for-service health care system   a system where clients pay for services, such as family therapy, either directly or indirectly through insurance, without being accountable to a third party for specific ways of making interventions.

feedback   the reinsertion of results of past performances back into a system. Negative feedback maintains the system within limits; positive feedback signals a need to modify the system.

feminist family therapy   an attitude and body of ideas, but not clinical techniques, concerning gender hierarchy and its impact on conducting family therapy. Feminists recognize the overriding importance of the power structure in any human system.

fidelity   the ethical principle of being trustworthy and keeping one's promises.

filial therapy   a hybrid form of child-centered play therapy in which parents (or other primary caregivers) engage in play therapy with their own child in order to address the child's problem in the context of the parent/child relationship.

first-order change   the process whereby a family that is unable to adjust to new circumstances often repetitiously tries the same solutions or intensifies nonproductive behaviors, thus assuring that the basic organization of the family does not change.

focus on exceptions   a technique utilized by brief family therapists to help families realize that their symptoms are not always present and that they have some power in what they are presently doing to make changes.

focusing on strengths   a family therapy technique, originated by Nathan Ackerman, to change the focal point of a family in therapy from their weaknesses to their assets.

follow-up   an appointed time with the family several weeks or months after formal treatment has ended. The family is again reinforced by the therapist in regard to competencies and ability to maintain or continue change.

formal assessment   the use of field-tested instruments.

Four Horsemen of the Apocalypse   the term John Gottman and Nan Silver have given to four patterns of communication that tend to destroy a marriage when they become habits—criticism, contempt, defensiveness, and stonewalling (i.e., not responding to a spouse).

four phases of sexual responsiveness   excitement, plateau, orgasm, and resolution.

frame   a perception or opinion that organizes one's interactions.

functional family therapy   a type of behavioral family therapy that is basically systemic.

fused   when someone is emotionally overinvolved with someone else.

fusion   the merging of intellectual and emotional functions so that an individual does not have a clear sense of self and others. There is a discomfort with autonomy in relationships, wishes to psychologically merge with another, and difficulty tolerating differences of opinion. Fusion is the opposite of **differentiation.** See also *differentiation.*

games   a Milan concept that stresses how children and parents stabilize around disturbed behaviors in an attempt to benefit from them.

gay/lesbian family a same-sex couple with or without children from a previous marriage or artificial insemination.

gender roles traditionally prescribed roles for males and females in a society such as being sensitive or being brave. Individuals who ascribe to these roles often limit their behavior or try to behave in ways in which they are not comfortable or competent.

gender-sensitive issues in therapy an emphasis on the importance of gender rather than a focus on masculine or feminine concerns.

general systems theory see *systems theory*.

genogram a visual representation of a person's family tree depicted in geometric figures, lines, and words; originated by Bowen.

Global Assessment of Relational Functioning Scale (GARF) a scale that is analogous to Axis V of the DSM GAF (Global Assessment of Functioning) scale that is used to assess individual functioning. It can be used to indicate an overall judgment of the functioning of a family on a hypothetical continuum ranging from competent, optimal relational functioning to a disrupted, dysfunctional relationship.

going home again a Bowen technique in which the family therapist instructs the individual or family members with whom he or she is working to return home in order to better get to know the family in which they grew up. By using this type of information, individuals can differentiate themselves more clearly.

good enough mother a mother who lets an infant feel loved and cared for and thereby helps the infant develop trust and a true sense of self.

Great Start a program that utilizes PREPARE/ENRICH inventories and is designed for premarital and early marital relationships. It is a part of the Couples Communication Program.

Greek chorus the observers/consultants of a family treatment session (i.e., the team) as they debate the merits of what a therapist is doing to bring about change. They send messages about the process to the therapist and family. Through this process, the family is helped to acknowledge and feel their ambivalence.

grounding a disciplinary technique used primarily with adolescents where the individual is removed from stimuli, thus limiting his or her reinforcement from the environment. Grounding requires the adolescent to attend school, perform regular chores, follow house rules, and stay in his or her room unless eating meals, conducting chores, or attending school.

group family therapy seeing a number of unrelated families at one time in a joint family session.

guide a family therapist who helps the star or explorer, during family reconstruction, chart a chronological account of family events that include significant events in the paternal and maternal families, and the family of origin.

happenstance an unpredictable event, a chance circumstance.

health an interactive process associated with positive relationships and outcomes.

Hispanic or Latino a person born in any of the Spanish-speaking countries of the Americas (Latin America), Puerto Rico, or the United States who traces his or her ancestry to either Latin America or to Hispanic people from U.S. territories that were once Spanish or Mexican.

historical time the era in which people live. Historical times consist of forces that affect and shape humanity at a particular point in time, such as during an economic depression or a war.

home-based therapy a method of treatment that requires family therapists to spend time with families before attempting to help them.

homeostasis the tendency to resist change and keep things as they are, in a state of equilibrium.

homework tasks clients are given to do outside of therapy session. Marital and family therapies that are noted for giving homework assignments are behavioral, cognitive-behavioral, psychodynamic, systemic, structural, and postmodern approaches.

horizontal stressors stressful events related to the present, some of which are developmental, such as life cycle transitions, and others of which are unpredictable, such as accidents.

humor an initiative and therapeutic procedure family therapists may use with families by pointing out the absurdity of their rigid positions or relabeling a situation to make it seem less serious.

hypothesizing a technique central to the Milan approach that involves a meeting of the treatment team before the arrival of a family in order to formulate and discuss aspects of the family's situation that may be generating a symptom. Through hypothesizing, team members prepare themselves for treating the family.

"I" statements   statements that express feelings in a personal and responsible way that encourages others to express their opinions.

idealistic distortion   viewing one's marriage and spouse to be better than they actually are.

identified patient (IP)   a family member who carries the family's symptoms and who is seen as the cause of the family's problems.

incest   sexual relations between people who are closely related in a family, such as a parent/child or siblings, that is illegal or forbidden by custom.

indicated prevention   preventive efforts that focus on minimizing the harmful impact of serious problems in the early stages of their development, such as having a therapist work with a couple whose marriage is coming apart in order to prevent them from doing harm to one another or harm to their children.

individual time   the span of life between one's birth and death. Notable individual achievements are often highlighted in this perspective, for example, when recognized as "teacher of the year."

infidelity   a myriad of activities outside of a couple relationship including: having an affair, extramarital relationships, cheating, sexual intercourse, oral sex, kissing, fondling, emotional connections that are beyond friendships, friendships, internet relationships, pornography use, and others.

informal assessment   observational data related to either natural or game-playing situations that may or may not be quantified.

informed consent brochure   a brochure that includes all the information in a self-disclosure statement about therapy as well as a place for clients to sign off that they understand the policies and procedures involved.

Institute for Family Counseling   an early intervention program at the Philadelphia Child Guidance Center for community paraprofessionals that proved to be highly effective in providing mental health services to the poor.

institutional barrier   any hardship that minority populations must endure to receive mental health services, such as the inconvenient location of a clinic, the use of a language not spoken by one's family, and the lack of diversified practitioners.

integrative behavioral couple therapy (IBCT)   an approach that emphasizes the promotion of acceptance into the traditional focus of behavioral couple therapy.

intensity   the structural method of changing maladaptive transactions by having the therapist use strong affect, repeated intervention, or prolonged pressure with a family.

intercultural couple   individuals who elect to marry outside of their culture.

intergenerational coalitions   members from different generations, such as a mother and daughter, colluding as a team.

interlocking pathology   a term created by Ackerman to explain how families and certain of their members stay dysfunctional. In an interlocking pathology, an unconscious process takes place between family members that keeps them together.

International Association of Marriage and Family Counselors (IAMFC)   a division within the American Counseling Association that promotes excellence in the practice of couples and family counseling by creating and disseminating publications and media products, providing a forum for exploration of family-related issues, involving a diverse group of dedicated professionals, and emphasizing collaborative efforts with other marriage and family counseling and therapy groups (http://www.ifta-familytherapy.org/home.html).

International Family Therapy Association (IFTA)   an association formed in 1987, IFTA sponsors international conferences and reflects the growing interest in family therapy around the world (http://www.ifta-familytherapy.org).

interpersonal   pertaining to matters or relationships between two or more persons.

interpersonal couple conflict   aspects within a marriage such as distrust or discord that get in the way of couple functioning.

interpersonal processes   how people organize their interactions into patterns and cycles.

interpersonal stress   stress that is generated between two or more family members.

interrater reliability   the degree to which raters agree on what they observe.

intimate justice theory   a theory of ethics that is used in the treatment of abuse and violence in intimate relationships. The theory confronts disempowerment abuses of power in a partnership while challenging internalized beliefs on how one should treat one's partner.

intrapersonal thoughts, feelings, and processes within a person.

intrapersonal stress stress that is developed from within an individual.

intrapsychic conflict emotions such as guilt, trauma, or shame that keep a person from functioning well.

intrapsychic processes how people process their emotional experiences.

invariant/variant prescription a specific kind of ritual given to parents with children who are psychotic or anorexic in an attempt to break up the family's "dirty game" (i.e., power struggle between generations sustained by symptomatic behaviors). An **invariant prescription** requires parents to unite so that children cannot manipulate them as "winners" or "losers" and thereby side with them. A **variant prescription** is given for the same purpose as an invariant one. The difference is that a variant prescription is tailored to a particular family and considers unique aspects of that family.

invisible loyalties unconscious commitments that grown children make to help their families of origin, especially their parents.

involvement a stage in experiential family therapy where therapists concentrate on helping families try new ways of relating through the use of playfulness, humor, and confrontation.

job card grounding a behavior modification technique that is used with preadolescents and adolescents (ages 11–18) that is more age appropriate than the continuous use of time-out. In this procedure, parents make a list of small jobs, that take 15 to 20 minutes to complete, that are not a part of the adolescent's regular chores. When a problem behavior begins and the adolescent does not heed a warning behavior, he or she is given one of the jobs to complete and is grounded until the job is finished successfully. See *grounding*.

joining the process of "coupling" that occurs between the therapist and the family, leading to the development of the therapeutic system. A therapist meets, greets, and forms a bond with family members during the first session in a rapid but relaxed and authentic way and makes the family comfortable through social exchange with each member.

joint custody an arrangement where both divorced parents assume equal custody of their children.

joint family scribble an experiential family therapy technique in which family members individually make a brief scribble. Then, the whole family incorporates their scribbles collectively into a unified picture.

justice the ethical principle of treating people equally.

Latino a person of Hispanic, especially Latin American, descent.

law a body of rules recognized by a state or community as binding on its members.

legal the law or the state of being lawful.

letters a procedure in narrative family therapy where an epistle that is mailed to a client by a therapist serves as a medium for continuation of the dialogue between the therapist and family members and as a reminder of what has occurred in therapy sessions. In some cases, letters are case notes.

leveling "congruent communication" in which straight, genuine, and real expressions of one's feelings and wishes are made in an appropriate context.

liability a legal term dealing with obligation and responsibility. A liability may be civil, e.g., dealing with professional malpractice such as negligence; criminal, e.g., dealing with the committing of a crime; or administrative, e.g., investigation from a licensure board.

liability insurance insurance that protects therapists financially from legal claims that they have mishandled a clinical situation.

life cycle the events in life (individual or family) from birth to death.

life cycle transitions predictable movement from one stage of life to another, such as going from being married to being married with children.

life history a psychodynamic technique designed to affirm family members and assure them that they are valued and accepted regardless of their backgrounds. Taking a family life history promotes trust in the therapist and also provides family members with insight.

linear causality the concept of cause and effect—that is, forces being seen as moving in one direction, with each action causing another. Linear causality can be seen in, for example, the firing of a gun.

logico-scientific reasoning a way of thinking characterized by empiricism and logic.

long brief therapy another name for systemic family therapy. *Long brief therapy* refers to the length of time between sessions (usually a month) and the duration of treatment (up to a year).

lost child a child in a substance abuse family who suffers from rejection and loneliness.

making contact the first stage in Satir's human validation process model where attention is focused on each member of the family in an attempt to raise the level of the person's self-esteem and self-worth.

malpractice the failure to fulfill the requisite standard of care either because of omission (what should have been done, but was not done) or commission (doing something that should not have been done). In either case, negligence must be proved.

managed care the common name given to any type of managed health care.

managed health care a wide range of techniques and structures that are connected with obtaining and paying for medical care, including therapy. The most common are preferred provider organizations (PPOs) and health maintenance organizations (HMOs).

managed mental health care (MMHC) a branch of managed health care that focuses on mental health services.

mapping in brief therapy, the sketching out of a course of successful intervention; in structural family therapy, a mental process of envisioning how the family is organized.

marital distress situations in which marriage partners experience communication and problem-solving difficulties to the point that they find it hard to work together and have difficulty accepting each other's differences.

marital quality how a marriage relationship is functioning and how partners feel about and are influenced by such functioning.

marital schism overt marital conflict that is pathological.

marital skew a dysfunctional marriage in which one partner dominates the other.

marital stability whether a marriage ends by death, divorce, separation, desertion, or annulment.

marriage counseling see *marriage therapy*.

marriage education the use of didactic lectures, visual aids, books, handouts, and interactive discussions to help couples learn about the pitfalls and possibilities of marriage.

Marriage Encounter Program founded in 1962, the essence of this approach is to have a "team couple" lead a group of husbands and wives during a weekend in exercises that give them the opportunity to share their emotions and thoughts. In essence, couples are taught how to make effective communication a part of their everyday lives.

marriage enrichment the concept that couples stay healthy or get healthier by actively participating in certain activities, usually in connection with other couples.

marriage therapy when a therapist works with a couple that is legally married to help them improve their relationship.

mediation see *family mediation*.

metachange a changing of rules sometimes referred to as a change of change.

metacommunication the implied message within a message, typically conveyed nonverbally.

meta-ethical principles high level standards that guide clinicians as they make their ethical decisions. The five principles are: autonomy, nonmaleficence, beneficence, fidelity, and justice.

mimesis a way of joining in which the therapist becomes like the family in the manner or content of their communications—for example, when a therapist jokes with a jovial family.

miracle question a brief therapy technique in which a therapist poses a question such as "If a miracle happened tonight and you woke up tomorrow and the problem was solved, how would you know?"

modeling observational learning.

mourning stage the first stage in a family's adjustment following the death of a member where surviving family members release both positive and negative feelings about the deceased.

multicultural a term used to refer to the cultural groups within a region or nation.

multifamily therapy treating several families at the same time.

multigenerational families households that include a child, a parent, and a grandparent.

multigenerational transmission process the passing on from generation to generation in families of coping strategies and patterns of coping with stress. In poorly differentiated persons, problems may result, including schizophrenia.

multiple relationship see *dual relationship.*

multisystemic therapy a research-backed theory and treatment, originated by Scott Henggeler, that views individuals, especially "difficult-to-reach children," as nested within a complex of interconnected systems that encompass individual, family, and extrafamilial (peer, school, neighborhood) factors. Behavior is seen as the product of the reciprocal interplay between the individual and these systems and of the relations of the systems to each other. Developmental factors are included in assessment and cognitive-behavioral interventions are used.

mystification the actions taken by some families to mask what is going on between family members, usually in the form of giving conflicting and contradictory explanations of events.

narrative a lived experience (often conveyed through a story).

narrative reasoning a form of reasoning which is characterized by stories, substories, meaningfulness, and liveliness. Narrative reasoning is the basis on which narrative family therapy is built and is the opposite of empirical and logico-scientific reasoning.

National Council on Family Relations the oldest professional association dedicated to working with families. It was established in 1938, and many of its members helped to create and support the AAMFT. Throughout its history, the NCFR has concentrated on education. Its membership is interdisciplinary and includes family life educators, sociologists, family researchers, and family therapists (http://www.ncfr.org/).

National Institute of Relationship Enhancement the Guerneys' training program in filial therapy.

National Mental Health Act of 1946 legislation that authorized funds for research, demonstration, training, and assistance to states in order to find the most effective methods of prevention, diagnosis, and treatment of mental health disorders.

National Research Act (Public Law 94-348) the federal government's response to unethical research practices on human subjects prior to the mid-1970s. The National Research Act set up regulations governing human research including the establishment of institutional review boards (IRBs).

natural family group approach the name for John Bell's theory of working with families in groups.

negative feedback loops feedback loops that promote a return to equilibrium and help a family stabilize and maintain homeostasis. See also *positive feedback loops.*

neutrality literally value free; some family therapies pride themselves on operating around a neutrality framework. Critics of such a framework claim that all therapy has moral and political values. A neutrality stance has deep ethical implications.

new epistemology the idea that the general systems approach of Bateson, sometimes referred to as *cybernetics*, must be incorporated in its truest sense into family therapy with an emphasis on "second-order cybernetics" (i.e., the cybernetics of cybernetics). Basically, such a view stresses the impact of the family therapist's inclusion and participation in family systems.

noncustodial parent a parent who does not have primary physical custody of a child but who has the same rights as a custodial parent unless there is a court order expressively stating otherwise.

nonevent the nonmaterialization of an expected occurrence (e.g., the failure of a couple to have children).

nonmaleficence the avoidance of doing possible harm to a client from clinical action.

nonprobability samples a sample that is nonrepresentative of a population, i.e., one where not everyone has had an equal chance of being selected.

nonverbal messages messages that are given behaviorally, including eye glances, hands folded across one's body, facial expressions, and even the distancing of people through the arrangement or rearrangement of chairs.

nuclear family a core unit of husband, wife, and their children.

object a significant other (e.g., a mother) with whom children form an interactional, emotional bond.

object relations relations between persons involved in ardent emotional attachments.

object relations theory a psychoanalytic way of explaining relationships across generations. According to this theory, human beings have a fundamental motivation to seek objects (i.e., people) in relationships, starting at birth.

offset effect the phenomenon where people reduce their use of health care following some type of therapy, i.e., individual, marital, family, or another behavioral health intervention. The idea is that following therapy, people are better able to cope with life events more effectively thus reducing their need or tendency to express emotional concerns physically.

off-schedule events major life events, such as marriage, death, and the birth of children occurring at different times than is the norm.

old epistemology dated ideas that no longer fit a current situation.

old old that group of individuals aged 75 to 84.

oldest old that group of individuals aged 85 and over.

one-person family therapy (OPFT) when strategic family therapy is offered to any person who comes to therapy in order to help that person make changes in the family system.

ontology a view or perception of the world.

open assessment a type of assessment used in domestic violence cases where blame is not a primary emphasis and where the therapist emphasizes that the expression of violence in the family hurts the entire family rather than just one person.

open system a system with permeable or semipermeable boundaries.

operant conditioning a tenet of Skinner's behavioral theory that people learn, through rewards and punishments, how to respond to their environments.

operant interpersonal approach The term first used to describe Richard Stuart's initiatives in behavioral couple therapy.

ordeal a technique in which a therapist assigns a family or family member(s) the task of performing a specific activity (i.e., an ordeal) any time the family or individuals involved display a symptom they are trying to eliminate. The ordeal is a constructive or neutral behavior (e.g., doing exercise), but disagreeable to the person directed to engage in it.

organism a form of life composed of mutually dependent parts and processes standing in mutual interaction.

paradox a form of treatment in which therapists give families permission to do what they were going to do anyway, thereby lowering family resistance to therapy and increasing the likelihood of change.

parallel relationships relationships in which both complementary and symmetrical exchanges occur as appropriate.

parental subsystem the subsystem made up of those responsible for the care, protection, and socialization of children.

parentified child a child who is given privileges and responsibilities that exceed what would be considered developmentally consistent with his or her age. Such a child is often forced to give up childhood and act like a parent, even though lacking the knowledge and skills to do so.

parent-skills training a behavioral model in which the therapist serves as a social learning educator whose prime responsibility is to change parents' responses to a child or children.

Parents Without Partners a national organization that helps single parents and their children deal with the realities of single-parent family life in educational and experiential ways.

participatory evaluation research a type of research in which clients are trained as individuals or focus groups to be involved as coresearchers in data analysis interpretation and write-up.

patterns of communication the ways in which family members relate to one another, for example, double messages, withholding information, overgeneralization.

placater according to Satir, a person who avoids conflict at the cost of his or her integrity.

planful competence when adolescents have a reasonably realistic understanding of their intellectual abilities, social skills, and personal emotional responses in interrelationship with others.

play therapy a general term for a variety of therapeutic interventions that use play media such as toys as the basis for communicating and working with children.

pluralism a condition of society in which numerous distinct ethnic, religious, or cultural groups coexist in one nation.

positioning acceptance and exaggeration by the therapist of what family members are saying. If conducted properly, it helps the family see the absurdity in what they are doing.

positive connotation a type of reframing in which each family member's behavior is labeled as benevolent and motivated by good intentions.

positive feedback loops feedback loops that promote change. See also *negative feedback loops*.

positive reciprocity a mutual or cooperative exchange of rewarding and valued behaviors between partners.

positive reinforcer a material (e.g., food, money, or medals) or a social action (e.g., a smile or praise) that individuals are willing to work for.

positive risk a unilateral action that is not dependent on another for success.

possibility therapy another name for Bill O'Hanlon's solution-focused family therapy.

postgender relationship a symmetrical relationship where each partner is versatile and tries to become competent in doing necessary or needed tasks, e.g., either a man or a woman can work outside the home or take care of children.

power the ability to get something done. In families, power is related to both *authority* (the decision maker) and *responsibility* (the one who carries out the decision).

Practical Application of Intimate Relationship Skills (PAIRS) a marriage enrichment program developed by Lori Gordon that teaches attitudes, emotional understandings and behaviors that nurture and sustain healthy relationships.

pragmatic fictions pronouncements that help families and family members change, such as when a therapist tells children that they are acting younger than their years.

Premack principle a behavioral intervention in which family members must first do less pleasant tasks before they are allowed to engage in pleasurable activities.

premarital counseling working with a couple to enhance their relationship before they get married.

PREP (Prevention and Relationship Enhancement Program) a 12-hour structured enrichment program where couples, either married or unmarried, are taught to become effective communicators and problem solvers while enhancing their commitment to each other.

prescribing a strategic family therapy technique in which family members are instructed to enact a troublesome dysfunctional behavior in front of the therapist and to work it out past the point where they usually get stuck.

prescribing the symptom a type of paradox in which family members are asked to continue doing as they have done. This technique makes families either admit they have control over a symptom or give it up.

presuppositional question a question used in solution-focused therapy, such as "What good thing happened since our last session?", that supposes a certain type of response.

pretend technique a technique originated by Cloe Madanes in which the therapist asks family members to pretend to enact a troublesome behavior, such as having a fight. Through this procedure, individuals transform an involuntary action into one that is under their control.

primary rewards reinforcers that people will naturally work for, such as food.

private logic an Adlerian term for one's worldview.

privileged communication a client's legal right, guaranteed by statute, that confidences originating in a therapeutic relationship will be safeguarded.

probability sample a sample drawn from a known population in such a way that it is possible to calculate the likelihood of each case being included in the sample.

problem solving a behavioral couple therapy procedure where therapists help partners learn skills, such as specifying what they want, negotiating for it, and making a contract.

process how information is handled in a family or in therapy.

professional self-disclosure statement a statement given to the family by the therapist that outlines treatment conditions related to who will be involved, what will be discussed, the length and frequency of sessions, emergency numbers, information about confidentiality and exceptions to it, and fees.

programmed workbooks for parents instrumental behavioral books parents may employ to help their children, and ultimately their families, modify behaviors.

props materials such as ropes and blindfolds used to represent behaviors or to illustrate the impact of actions.

pseudo-individuation/pseudo-self a pretend self. This concept involves an attempt by young people who lack an identity and basic coping skills to act as if they had both.

pseudomutuality the facade of family harmony that many dysfunctional families display.

pseudo-self a pretend self where a person appears to be differentiated from his or her family of origin but is not.

psychoanalysis the method of treatment developed by Sigmund Freud in which methods such as free association, dream interpretation, transference, and analysis of resistance are used to uncover repressed memories and the unconscious and restore an individual to mental health or adjustment.

psychoeducation   a strategy that involves educational methods such as reading books, attending workshops, listening to audiovisual material and interactive discussions.

punctuation   the way a person describes a situation, that is, beginning and ending a sentence, due to a selective perception or emotional involvement in an event.

qualitative research   research that is characterized by an emphasis on open-ended questions and the use of extended interviews with small numbers of individuals/families. Results are written up in an autobiographical form. This research is often used in theory building.

quantitative research   research that is characterized by an emphasis on closed-ended questions and the use of large sample sizes to gather information. Data are gathered in a precise form, frequently using standardized instruments, and reported in a statistical format. Analyzed and deductive conclusions are made that tend to "prove" or "disprove" theories and assertions.

quasi kin   a formerly married person's ex-spouse, the ex-spouse's new husband or wife, and his or her blood kin.

quid pro quo   literally, something for something.

racism   discrimination or prejudice based on race.

random assignment sampling   a procedure where everyone has an equal chance of being selected.

rational emotive therapy (RET)   see *rational emotive behavior therapy (REBT)*.

rational emotive behavior therapy (REBT)   a cognitive behavioral theory originated by Albert Ellis that is sometimes used in couple therapy.

readjustment stage   the second stage in forming a single-parent family created by death where surviving members learn to do new tasks, drop old tasks, and/or reassign duties previously done by the ex-spouse to other members of the family.

reauthoring   a narrative family therapy approach for highlighting different stories in life than those that have been dominant. Such a process not only changes a family's focus but opens up new possibilities as well.

reciprocity   the likelihood that two people will reinforce each other at approximately equitable rates over time. Many marital behavior therapists view marriage as based on this principle.

records   remembrances in the form of written notes from sessions with couples and families. Records are important for treatment purposes and as a defense for the therapist if he or she is accused of wrongdoing.

redefining   a strategic family therapy technique of attributing positive connotations to symptomatic or troublesome actions. The idea is that symptoms have meaning for those who display them, whether such meaning is logical or not. Redefining is one way of lowering resistance.

redirection   where the therapist asks the couple or family to attend to the process of their relationship instead of the content of it.

redundancy principle   the fact that a family interacts within a limited range of repetitive behavioral sequences.

reframing   a process in which a perception is changed by explaining a situation from a different context. *Reframing* is the art of attributing different meaning to behavior.

reinforcer   a consequence of an action that increases its likelihood of occurring again.

relapse prevention   cognitive-behavioral strategies clients learn to gain self-control and prevent relapse.

relationship ethics   Boszormenyi-Nagy's term for ethics in a family that are based on the principles of equitability and caring.

reliability   the consistency or dependency of a measure.

remarried families   families that consist of two adults and step-, adoptive, or foster children. Sometimes, they are referred to as *stepfamilies, reconstituted families, recoupled families, merged families*, and *blended families*.

renewal and accomplishment stage   the last stage in a single-parent family created by death where family members, and the family as a whole, concentrate on finding and engaging in new growth opportunities resulting in new collective and individual identities and relationships.

reorient   an Adlerian process that focuses on helping families change what they are doing.

research design   the way a research study is set up. Five commonly used categories are (1) exploratory, (2) descriptive, (3) developmental, (4) experimental, and (5) correlational.

Resiliency Model of Family Stress, Adjustment, and Adaptation   a model of family adjustment that proposes that a family's capability to meet demands is dynamic and interactional.

resistance   anything a family does to oppose or impair progress in family therapy.

restraining   a type of paradox where therapists tell a client family that they are incapable of doing anything other than what they are doing. The intent is to get the family to show they can behave differently.

restructuring   changing the structure of the family. The rationale behind restructuring is to make the family more functional by altering the existing hierarchy and interaction patterns.

rigid boundaries   inflexible rules and habits that keep family members separated from each other.

rituals   specialized types of directives that are meant to dramatize significant and positive family relationships or aspects of problem situations.

role playing   procedures in which family members are asked to "act as if" they were the persons they ideally wanted to be. Members practice a number of behaviors to see which work best. Feedback is given and corrective actions are taken.

roles   prescribed and repetitive behaviors involving a set of reciprocal activities with other family members or significant others; behaviors family members expect from each other and themselves.

rules   implicit or explicit guidelines that determine behaviors of family members.

sample   a limited number of families representative of an entire group of families.

SAMHSA   Substance Abuse and Mental Health Administration. A component of the United States Department of Health and Human Services that provides information, statistics, and articles on improving the quality and availability of help for substance abuse and mental health problems (http://oas.samhsa.gov/).

SANCTUS   a theologically and psychologically based marriage enrichment program based on step-wise process that incorporates building a pattern of love and relationship with God, one's self, and others.

sandwich generation   couples who have adolescents and their aging parents to take care of and are squeezed psychologically and physically.

scaling   a solution-focused technique of asking questions using a scale of 1 (low) to 10 (high) to help clients assess situations.

scapegoat   a family member the family designates as the cause of its difficulties (i.e., the identified patient).

schema   core beliefs of an individual or couple.

schism   the division of the family into two antagonistic and competing groups.

sculpting   an experiential family therapy technique in which family members are molded during the session into positions symbolizing their actual relationships to each other as seen by one or more members of the family.

second-order change   a qualitatively different way of doing something; a basic change in function and/or structure.

second-order cybernetics   the *cybernetics of cybernetics*, which stresses the impact of the family therapist's inclusion and participation in family systems.

selective prevention   preventive efforts that focus on making interventions with at-risk groups in order to prevent problems such as conducting parenting classes for parents whose children are having difficulties in school.

self-control strategies   various ways individuals can help themselves cope, such as employing rational coping statements.

self-report instrument   an instrument where a person reports what he or she thinks or feels about a matter, e.g., like or dislike doing a certain activity.

self-worth   Satir's term that corresponds closely with self-esteem. Satir compared one's feelings of self-worth to a pot. The fuller the pot is the more persons feels alive and have faith in themselves.

senescence   a gradual physical decline of individuals related to age. This decline begins after overall growth stops and varies greatly from individual to individual.

shame attack   a process within role playing where someone does something he or she has previously dreaded, for example, asking for an allowance. Individuals who use this technique find that when they do not get what they asked for, they are not worse off for having asked.

shaping   the process of learning in small gradual steps; often referred to as *successive approximation*.

shaping competence   the procedure in which structural family therapists help families and family members become more functional by highlighting positive behaviors.

sibling rivalry   an Adlerian concept that focuses on the degree of competition between siblings.

sibling subsystem   that unit within the family whose members are of the same generation, for example, brothers and sisters. The concept of sibling position is important in both Adlerian and Bowen family therapy.

significance questions   queries in narrative and solution-focused therapy that are characterized as unique redescription questions. They search for and reveal the meanings, significance, and importance of the exceptions.

singlehood   being single.

single-parent family   families that include at least one parent who is biologically related to a child (or children) or who has assumed such a role through adoption. This parent is primarily alone in being responsible for taking care of self and a child (or children). Such families are created as a result of divorce, death, abandonment, unwed pregnancy, and adoption.

situational stressors   stressful events that are unpredictable, such as interpersonal relationships that are emotional.

skeleton keys   in deShazer's brief therapy approach, those interventions that have worked before and that have a universal application.

skew   see *marital skew.*

social constructionism   a philosophy that states experiences are a function of how one thinks about them and the language one uses within a specific culture. From this perspective all knowledge is time- and culture-bound. It challenges the idea that there is objective knowledge and absolute truth. Narrative and solution-focused therapy are based on social constructionism.

social exchange theory   an approach that stresses the rewards and costs of relationships in family life according to a behavioral economy.

social learning theory   a theory that stresses the importance of modeling and learning through observation as a primary way of acquiring new behaviors.

social time   time characterized by landmark social events such as marriage, parenthood, and retirement. Family milestones are a central focus in social time.

societal regression   the deterioration or decline of a society struggling against too many toxic forces (e.g., overpopulation and economic decline) countering the tendency to achieve differentiation.

soft emotions   those emotions like hurt, insecurity, loneliness, and fear that reveal personal vulnerability.

softening   an emotion-focused therapy process where a partner is transformed from a blaming or angry individual to one who is attached and bonded with the other partner through the use of soft emotions.

SOLAR   an acronym, each letter of which stands for the way professional skills may be shown. S stands for facing the couple or family squarely, either in a metaphorical or literal manner. The O is a reminder to adopt an open posture that is nondefensive. L indicates that the therapist should lean forward toward the client family to show interest. E represents appropriate eye contact. R stands for relaxation.

solid self   a Bowen term for developing a sense of one's own identity where beliefs and convictions are not simply adaptive to others.

solutions   desired behaviors in solution-focused therapy.

spillover   the extent to which participation in one domain, e.g., work, affects participation in another domain, e.g., the family.

splitting   viewing object representations as either all good or all bad. The result is a projection of good and bad qualities onto persons within one's environment. Through splitting, people are able to control their anxiety and even the objects (i.e., persons) within their environment by making them predictable.

spousal subsystem   the subsystem composed of marriage partners.

squeeze technique   an approach used in sexual therapy in which a woman learns to stimulate and stop the ejaculation urge in a man through physically stroking and firmly grasping his penis.

stable coalition   a fixed and inflexible union (such as that of a mother and son) that becomes a dominant part of a family's everyday functioning.

stages   an identifiable period in an individual's or family's life.

star or explorer   a central character in family reconstruction who maps his or her family of origin in visually representative ways.

statutory law   that group of laws passed by legislative bodies, such as state and national legislatures, and signed by an authorized source, such as a governor or the president.

stepfamily a family created when two people marry and at least one of them has been married previously and had a child.

stonewalling not responding to a spouse by withdrawing such as looking away, maintaining a stiff neck, and/or saying almost nothing.

strategic therapy a term coined by Jay Haley to describe the therapeutic work of Milton Erickson in which extreme attention was paid to details of client symptoms and the focus was to change behavior by manipulating it and not instilling insight.

stratified sampling a method in which random samples are drawn from different strata or groups of a population.

stress inoculation a process in which family members break down potentially stressful events into manageable units that they can think about and handle through problem-solving techniques. Units are then linked so that possible events can be envisioned and handled appropriately.

structural family therapy's major thesis a thesis stating that an individual's symptoms are best understood when examined in the context of family interactional patterns. A change in the family's organization or structure must take place before symptoms can be relieved.

structure an invisible set of functional demands by which family members relate to each other.

structuring behavior a general term in family therapy for describing the activity of a therapist in teaching and directing.

Substance Abuse and Mental Health Administration see *SAMHSA*.

subsystems smaller units of the system as a whole, usually composed of members in a family who because of age or function are logically grouped together, such as parents. They exist to carry out various family tasks.

successive approximation see *shaping*.

supportive behavior a general term in family therapy for describing the giving of warmth and care by a therapist.

symbolic drawing of family life space a projective technique in which the therapist draws a large circle and instructs family members to include within the circle everything that represents the family and to place outside of the circle those people and institutions not a part of the family. After this series of drawings, the family is asked to symbolically arrange themselves, through drawing, within a large circle, according to how they relate to one another.

symbolic experiential therapy the name of the approach (sometimes also known as experiential symbolic therapy) given to Carl Whitaker's theory of working with families.

symmetrical relationship a relationship in which each partner tries to gain competence in doing necessary or needed tasks. Members within these units are versatile. For example, either a man or a woman can work outside the home or care for children.

system a set of elements standing in interaction. Each element in the system is affected by whatever happens to any other element. Thus, the system is only as strong as its weakest part. Likewise, the system is greater than the sum of its parts.

systematic change agent the role a therapist takes when he or she tries to intervene on behalf of families in unhealthy and intolerant systems.

systematic desensitization a process in which a person's dysfunctional anxiety is reduced or eliminated through pairing it with incompatible behavior, such as muscular or mental relaxation. This procedure is gradual, with anxiety treated one step at a time.

systematic random sample a sampling design in which the first person to be studied is selected at random, and then every nth person is automatically included.

Systematic Training for Effective Parenting (STEP) an Adlerian based group that can help parents increase their understanding of family relations as well as improve their communications with their children.

systemic family therapy an approach, sometimes known as the Milan approach, that stresses the interconnectedness of family members as well as the importance of second-order change in families.

systems theory a theory, sometimes known as *general systems theory*, that focuses on the interconnectedness of elements within all living organisms, including the family. It is based on the work of Ludwig von Bertalanffy.

teasing technique a sexual therapy approach in which a woman learns how to start and stop sexually stimulating a man.

teleological literally meaning futuristic, this component is a major emphasis in Adlerian therapy.

temporary single-parent family a single-parent family formed out of uncontrollable circumstances, such as a war or a job change that involves one parent making an immediate move while the family stays behind.

theory systematically organized knowledge applicable in a rather wide area of circumstance to explain the behavior of a person, group, or phenomenon.

therapeutic neutrality accepting and nonjudgmental behavior by family therapists that keeps them from being drawn into family coalitions and disputes and gives them time to assess the dynamics within the family. Neutrality also encourages family members to generate solutions to their own concerns.

thought stopping a cognitive-behavioral technique in which family members are taught how to stop unproductive obsession about an event or person through overt mental procedures.

tickling of defenses Nathan Ackerman's term for provoking family members to open up and say what was on their mind.

TIME (Training in Marriage Enrichment) a 10-week enrichment program for married couples that is laid out developmentally and systemically. It includes a beginning session that focuses on accepting responsibility and final sessions that have a couple resolving an actual conflict based on skills they have learned.

time-in reinforcement in a positive environment.

time-out a process that involves the removal of persons (most often children) from an environment in which they have been reinforced for certain actions. Isolation, or withdrawal, from reinforcement for a limited amount of time (approximately 5 minutes) results in the cessation of the targeted behavior.

token economy a type of contract for earning points and reinforcing appropriate behavior, most often employed with children.

touch physical contact with a client by a family therapist which may be manifested in putting one's arms around another, patting a person on the shoulder, shaking hands, or even, in an extreme case, wrestling.

tracking a way of joining in which the therapist follows the content of the family (i.e., the facts).

transference the projection onto a therapist of feelings, attitudes, or desires.

transgenerational family therapy another term for Bowen family therapy.

triadic questioning asking a third family member how two other members of the family relate.

trial marriage a term among Whites for cohabitation.

triangle the basic building block of any emotional system and the smallest stable relationship system in a family.

triangulating projecting interpersonal dyadic difficulties onto a third person or object (i.e., a scapegoat).

typical day an Adlerian technique of having a family explore the processes and interactions they go through daily in order to understand themselves better.

unbalancing therapeutically allying with a subsystem. In this procedure, the therapist supports an individual or subsystem against the rest of the family.

undifferentiated an emotional dependency on one's family members, even if living away from them.

undifferentiated family ego mass according to Bowen, an emotional "stuck togetherness," or fusion, within a family.

unholy trinity sex, finances, and in-laws—3 of the main areas that couples disagree over or fight about.

unique outcomes clients' storied experiences that do not fit their problem-saturated story.

universal perspective model of multicultural counseling a model of counseling that assumes that counseling approaches already developed can be applied with minor changes to different cultural groups. Thus, cultural differences are recognized from a family systems perspective.

universal prevention prevention efforts that focus on preventing the development of problems in the general population, such as a media campaign promoting family togetherness.

unresolvable problems aspects of a couple's relationship that are unlikely to change.

utilization review the process in managed health care by which a therapist submits a written justification for treatment along with a comprehensive treatment plan to a utilization reviewer for approval.

validity   the extent to which an instrument measures what it was intended to.

values   beliefs and preferences, the ranking of an ordered set of choices from the most to the least preferable. Basically, there are four domains of values: personal, family, political/social, and ultimate. Each has an impact on the other. Ethics is based on values.

variant prescription   see *invariant/variant prescription.*

V code   a *Diagnostic and Statistical Manual (DSM)* designation meaning that the condition described is not attributable to a mental disorder. Interpersonal relationship problems are listed under V codes.

verbalizing presuppositions   an experiential technique in which a therapist helps a family take the first step toward change by talking of the hope that the family has.

vertical stressors   events dealing with family patterns, myths, secrets, and legacies. These are stressors that are historical and that families inherit from previous generations.

vicious cycle   a cycle of interactions that spiral downward.

virtuous cycle   a cycle of interactions that spiral upward.

visitors   a solution-focused term to describe clients who are not involved in a problem and are not part of a solution.

WASPs   white anglo-saxon protestants, often the group associated with the term "White."

wheel or circle of influence   that circle of individuals who have been important to the star or explorer through family reconstruction.

White   a term that is sometimes generalized and used to describe any person with white skin who has European ancestry.

worked through   when insights are translated into new and more productive ways of behaving and interacting.

working with spontaneous interaction   when a therapist spotlights attention on some particular disruptive or dysfunctional behavior. On such occasions, therapists can point out the dynamics and sequencing of behaviors and focus on the process. Such occasions are used to help families recognize patterns of interaction and what changes they might make to bring about modification.

worldview   the dominant perception or view of a specific group.

young old   that group of individuals aged 65 to 74.

References

Abudabeth, N., & Aseel, H. A. (1999). Transcultural counseling and Arab Americans. In J. McFadden (Ed.), *Transcultural counseling* (2nd ed., pp. 283–296). Alexandria, VA: American Counseling Association.

Accordino, M. P., & Guerney, B. G. Jr. (2002). The empirical validation of relationship enhancement couple and family therapy. In D. J. Cain (Ed.), *Humanistic psychotherapies: Handbook of research and practice.* (pp. 403–442). Washington, DC: American Psychological Association.

Accordino, M. P., & Guerney, B. G., Jr. (2003). Relationship enhancement couples and family outcome research of the last 20 years. *The Family Journal: Counseling and Therapy for Couples and Families, 11,* 162–166.

Accordino, M. P., Keat, D. B. II, & Guerney, B. G., Jr. (2003). Using relationship enhancement therapy with an adolescent with serious mental illness and substance dependence. *Journal of Mental Health Counseling, 25,* 152–164.

Ackerman, N. (1937). The family as a social and emotional unit. *Bulletin of the Kansas Mental Hygiene Society, 12.*

Ackerman, N. (1938). The unity of the family. *Archives of Pediatrics, 55,* 51–62.

Ackerman, N. (1956). Interlocking pathology in family relations. In S. Rado & G. Daniels (Eds.), *Changing concepts of psychoanalytic medicine* (pp. 135–150). New York: Grune & Stratton.

Ackerman, N. (1958). *The psychodynamics of family life.* New York: Basic Books.

Ackerman, N. (1962). Family psychotherapy and psychoanalysis: The implications of difference. *Family Process, 1,* 30–43.

Ackerman, N. (1966). *Treating the troubled family.* New York: Basic Books.

Ackerman, N. W., Beatman, F. L., & Sherman, S. N. (1961). *Exploring the base of family therapy.* New York: Family Service Association of America.

Adams, G. R., & Schvaneveldt, J. D. (1991). *Understanding research methods* (2nd ed.). London: Pearson Education.

Adams, J. (1987). A brave new world for private practice? *Family Therapy Networker, 11,* 18–25.

Ahrons, C. R. (1979). The binuclear family: Two households, one family. *Alternative Lifestyles, 2,* 499–515.

Ahrons, C. R. (1992, October). 21st-Century families: Meeting the challenges of change. *Family Therapy News, 23,* 3, 16.

Ahrons, C. R. (1996). *The good divorce: Keeping your family together when your marriage comes apart.* New York: HarperCollins.

Ahrons, C. R., & Rodgers, R. H. (1987). *Divorced families: A multi-disciplinary developmental view.* New York: Norton.

Albom, M. (1997). *Tuesdays with Morrie.* New York: Doubleday.

Alessandria, K. P. (2002). Acknowledging white ethnic groups in multicultural counseling. *The Family Journal: Counseling and Therapy for Couples and Families, 10,* 57–60.

Alexander, J. F. (1988). Phases of family therapy process: A framework for clinicians and researchers. In L. C. Wynne (Ed.), *The state of the art in family therapy research: Controversies and recommendations* (pp. 175–188). New York: Family Process Press.

Alexander, J., & Parsons, B. V. (1982). *Functional family therapy.* Pacific Grove, CA: Brooks/Cole.

Alexander, J. F., Newell, R. M., Robbins, M. S., & Turner, C. W. (1995). Observational coding in family therapy process research. *Journal of Family Psychology, 9,* 355–365.

Al-Krenawi, A., & Graham, J. R. (2005). Marital therapy for Arab Muslim Palestinian couples in the context of reacculturation. *The Family Journal: Counseling and Therapy for Couples and Families, 13,* 300–310.

Allen, B. P. (1990). *Personal adjustment.* Pacific Grove, CA: Brooks/Cole.

Allen, W. D., & Olson, D. H. (2001). Five types of African American marriages. *Journal of Marriage and Family Therapy, 27,* 301–314.

Almeida, R. (2000, March/April). Probing beyond the bruises. *Family Therapy Networker, 24,* 23–24.

Alonzo, D. J. (2005). Working with same-sex couples. In M. Harway (Ed.), *Handbook of couples therapy* (pp. 370–385). New York: Wiley.

Amato, P. R., Johnson, D. R., Booth, A., & Rogers, S. J. (2003). Stability and change in marital quality between 1980 and 2000. *Journal of Marriage and Family, 65,* 1–22.

American Association for Marriage and Family Therapy. (2001). *AAMFT Code of Ethics.* Washington, DC: Author.

American Association for Marriage and Family Therapy. (2001). *User's Guide to the AAMFT Code of Ethics.* Washington, DC: Author.

American Educational Research Association, American Psychological Association, & National Council on Measurement in Education (1985). *Standards for educational and psychological testing.* Washington, DC: Author.

American Psychiatric Association. (1994). *Diagnostic and Statistical Manual of Mental Disorders* (4th ed.). Washington, DC: Author.

Andersen, T. (1991). *The reflecting team: Dialogues and dialogues about dialogues.* New York: Norton.

Anderson, C. M. (1988). Psychoeducational model different than paradigm. *Family Therapy News, 19,* 10–12.

Anderson, C. M., & Stewart, S. (1983). *Mastering resistance: A practical guide to family therapy.* New York: Guilford.

Anderson, D. (1988, July/August). The quest for a meaningful old age. *Family Therapy Networker, 12,* 16–22, 72–75.

Anderson, H. (1994). Rethinking family therapy: A delicate balance. *Journal of Marital and Family Therapy, 20,* 145–149.

Anderson, R., Anderson, W., & Hovestadt, A. J. (1993, May/June). Family of origin work in family therapy: A practical approach. *Family Counseling and Therapy, 1,* 1–13.

Andolfi, M. (1996). Let it flow: Carl Whitaker's philosophy of becoming. *Journal of Marital and Family Therapy, 22,* 317–319.

Anonymous. (1972). Differentiation of self in one's family. In J. L. Framo (Ed.), *Family interaction.* New York: Springer.

Ansen, D., & Springen, K. (1992, April 13). A lot of not so happy endings. *Newsweek,* p. 58.

Anthony, M. (1993). The relationship between marital satisfaction and religious maturity. *Religious Education, 88,* 97–108.

Aponte, H. J. (1992). Training the person of the therapist in structural family therapy. *Journal of Marital and Family Therapy, 18,* 269–281.

Arditti, J. A., & Prouty, A. M. (1999). Change, disengagement, and renewal: Relationship dynamics between young adults and their fathers after divorce. *Journal of Marital and Family Therapy, 25,* 61–81.

Arnold, M. S., & Allen, N. P. (1996). Andrew Billingsley: The legacy of African American families. *The Family Journal: Counseling and Therapy for Couples and Families, 3,* 77–85.

Arthur, G. L., & Swanson, C. D. (1993). *Confidentiality and privileged communication.* Alexandria, VA: American Counseling Association.

Asai, S. G., & Olson, D. H. (2004). Culturally sensitive adaptation of PREPARE with Japanese premarital couples. *Journal of Marital and Family Therapy, 30,* 411–426.

Associated Press. (1993a, February 26). Single mothers growing in number. *Winston-Salem (NC) Journal,* p. 2.

Associated Press. (1993b, July 14). Study: More unwed women having babies. *Winston-Salem (NC) Journal,* p. 2.

Associated Press. (1999, September 15). Hispanic population in U.S. grew quickly in 1990s, report says. *Winston-Salem (NC) Journal,* pp. A1, A5.

Associated Press (2000, February 14). Half of black homes headed by single women. *Winston-Salem (NC) Journal,* p. A8.

Atkins, D. C., Eldridge, K. A., Baucom, D. H., & Christensen, A. (2005). Infidelity and behavioral couple therapy: Optimism in the face of betrayal. *Journal of Consulting and Clinical Psychology, 73,* 144–150.

Atwood, J. D. (1992). The field today. In J. D. Atwood (Ed.), *Family therapy: A systemic behavioral approach* (pp. 29–58). Chicago: Nelson-Hall.

Azar, S. T., Nix, R. L., & Makin-Byrd, K. N. (2005). Parenting schemas and the process of change. *Journal of Marital and Family Therapy, 31,* 45–58.

Bailey, G. (2002). Marital discord as pathway to healing and intimacy, utilizing emotionally focused couples' therapy. *Journal of Pastoral Counseling, 37,* 88–100.

Baldwin, C., & Huggins, D. (1998). Marital and family therapy research: Outcomes and implications for practice. *The Family Journal: Counseling and Therapy for Couples and Families, 6,* 212–218.

Baltimore, M. (1993). The training of marriage and family counselors/therapists: A "systemic" controversy among disciplines. *Alabama Counseling Association Journal, 19,* 34–44.

Bandura, A. (1969). *Principles of behavior modification.* New York: Holt, Rinehart, & Winston.

Bandura, A. (1977). *Social learning theory.* Upper Saddle River, NJ: Prentice Hall.

Bandura, A. (1982). The psychology of chance encounters and life paths. *American Psychologist, 37,* 747–755.

Bandura, A., & Walters, R. H. (1963). *Social learning and personality development.* New York: Rinehart & Winston.

Baptiste, D. A. (1987). Family therapy with Spanish-heritage immigrant families in cultural transition. *Contemporary Family Therapy, 9,* 229–251.

Barker, P. (2001). *Basic family therapy* (4th ed.). New York: Blackwell Publishing.

Barnes, G. G. (1999). Divorce transitions: Identifying risk and promoting resilience for children and their parental relationships. *Journal of Marital and Family Therapy, 25,* 425–441.

Barnhill, L. R. (1979). Healthy family systems. *Family Coordinator, 28,* 94–100.

Barton, C., & Alexander, J. F. (1981). Functional family therapy. In A. S. Gurman & D. P. Kniskern (Eds.), *Handbook of family therapy* (pp. 403–443). New York: Brunner/Mazel.

Baruth, L. G., & Burgraff, M. Z. (1991). Counseling single-parent families. In J. Carlson & J. Lewis (Eds.), *Family counseling: Strategies and issues* (pp. 157–173). Denver, CO: Love Publishing.

Bateson, G. (1955). A theory of play and fantasy. *Psychiatric Reports, 2,* 177–193.

Bateson, G. (1971). The cybernetics of "self": A theory of alcoholism. *Psychiatry, 34,* 1–18.

Bateson, G. (1972). *Steps to an ecology of mind.* New York: Ballantine.

Bateson, G. (1979). *Mind and nature: A necessary unity.* New York: E. P. Dutton.

Bateson, G., Jackson, D. D., Haley, J., & Weakland, J. (1956). Toward a theory of schizophrenia. *Behavioral Science, 1,* 251–264.

Baucom, D. H., & Epstein, N. (1990). *Cognitive-behavioral marital therapy.* New York: Brunner/Mazel.

Baugh, C. W., Avery, A. W., & Sheets-Haworth, K. L. (1982). Marital Problem Solving Scale: A measure to assess relationship conflict negotiation ability. *Family Therapy, 9,* 43–51.

Bean, R. A., Perry, B. J., & Bedell, T. M. (2002). Developing culturally competent marriage and family therapists: Treatment guidelines for non-African-American therapists working with African-American families. *Journal of Marital and Family Therapy, 28,* 153–161.

Beavers, W. R. (1985). *Successful marriage.* New York: Norton.

Beavers, W. R., & Hampson, R. B. (1990). *Successful families: Assessment and intervention.* New York: Norton.

Beck, A. T. (1976). *Cognitive therapy and the emotional disorders.* New York: International Universities Press.

Beck, M., Springen, K., & Foote, D. (1992, April 13). Sex and psychotherapy. *Newsweek,* pp. 52–57.

Beckerman, N. L. (2004). The impact of post-traumatic stress disorder on couples: A theoretical framework for assessment and intervention. *Family Therapy, 31,* 129–144.

Beckerman, N., & Sarracco, M. (2002). Intervening with couples in relationship conflict: Integrating emotionally focused couple therapy and attachment theory. *Family Therapy, 29,* 23–31.

Beels, C., & Ferber, A. (1969). Family therapy: A view. *Family Process, 8,* 280–332.

Bell, J. E. (1961). Family group therapy. *Public Health Monograph #64.* Washington, DC: U.S. Government Printing Office.

Benedek, R., & Benedek, E. (1979). Children of divorce. Can we meet their needs? *Journal of Social Issues, 35,* 155.

Benedetto, R. (1992, December 16). Hispanics feeling at home. *USA Today,* p. 5A.

Berenson, D. (1992). The therapist's relationship with couples with an alcoholic member. In E. Kaufman & P. Kaufman (Eds.), *Family therapy of drug and alcohol abuse* (pp. 224–235). Boston: Allyn & Bacon.

Bernstein, B. E., & Collins, S. K. (1985). Remarriage counseling: Lawyers and therapists help with the second time around. *Family Relations, 34,* 387–391.

Bertalanffy, L. von (1934). *Modern theories of development: An introduction to theoretical biology.* London: Oxford University Press.

Bertalanffy, L. von (1968). *General systems theory: Foundation, development, and application.* New York: Braziller.

Beitin, B. K., & Allen, K. R. (2005). Resilience in Arab American couples after September 11, 2001: A systems perspective. *Journal of Marital and Family Therapy, 31,* 251–267.

Bienvenu, M. J. (1970). Measurement of marital communication. *The Family Coordinator, 19,* 26–31.

Billingsley, A. (1968). *Black families in White America.* Upper Saddle River, NJ: Prentice Hall.

Billingsley, A. (1992). *Climbing Jacob's ladder: The enduring legacy of African American families.* New York: Simon & Schuster.

Bing, E. (1970). The conjoint family drawing. *Family Process, 9,* 173–194.

Bird, G., & Sporakowski, M. J. (1992). Introduction. In G. Bird & M. J. Sporakowski (Eds.), *Taking sides: Clashing views on controversial issues in family and personal relationships* (pp. x–xv). Guilford, CT: Dushkin Publishing.

Bird, G. W., & Sporakowski, M. J. (1992). The study of marriage and the family. In G. Bird & M. J. Sporakowski (Eds.), *Taking sides* (pp. x–xv). Guilford, CT: Dushkin.

Bitter, J. R. (2000). Dissolving a problem: Structuring externalization interviews with couples. In R. E. Watts (Ed.), *Techniques in marriage and family counseling* (pp. 91–94). Alexandria, VA: American Counseling Association.

Bitter, J. R. (2004). Two approaches to counseling a parent alone: Toward a Gestalt-Adlerian integration. *The Family Journal: Counseling and Therapy for Couples and Families, 12,* 358–367.

Bittner, S., Blalek, E., Nathiel, S., Ringwald, J., & Tupper, M. (1999). An alternative to managed care: A "guild" model for the independent practice of psychotherapy. *Journal of Marital and Family Therapy, 25,* 99–111.

Black, C. (1990). *Double duty.* New York: Ballantine.

Blacker, L. (1999). The launching phase of the life cycle. In B. Carter & M. McGoldrick (Eds.), *The expanded family life cycle* (3rd ed., pp. 287–306). Boston: Allyn & Bacon.

Blaisure, K. R., & Geasler, M. J. (2000, March). Divorce interventions. *AAMFT Clinical Update, 2*(2), 1–8.

Bloch, D., & Simon, R. (1982). *The strength of family therapy: Selected papers of Nathan W. Ackerman.* New York: Brunner/Mazel.

Blow, A. J., & Hartnett, K. (2005a). Infidelity in committed relationships I: A methodological review. *Journal of Marital and Family Therapy, 31,* 183–216.

Blow, A. J., & Hartnett, K. (2005b). Infidelity in committed relationships I: A substantive review. *Journal of Marital and Family Therapy, 31,* 217–233.

Bodin, A. (1981). The interactional view: Family therapy approaches to the Mental Research Institute. In A. S. Gurman & D. P. Kniskern (Eds.), *Handbook of family therapy* (Vol. I, pp. 267–309). New York: Brunner/Mazel.

Bograd, M. (1992). Values in conflict: Challenges to family therapists' thinking. *Journal of Marital and Family Therapy, 18,* 245–256.

Bograd, M. (1999). Strengthening domestic violence theories: Intersections of race, class, sexual orientation, and gender. *Journal of Marital and Family Therapy, 25,* 275–289.

Bograd, M., & Mederos, F. (1999). Battering and couples therapy: Universal screening and selection of treatment modality. *Journal of Marital and Family Therapy, 25,* 291–312.

Booth, A., & Edwards, J. (1983). Measuring marital instability. *Journal of Marriage and Family, 45,* 387–393.

Bornstein, P. H., & Bornstein, M. T. (1986). *Marital therapy: A behavioral-communications approach.* New York: Pergamon.

Boscolo, L., Cecchin, G., Hoffman, L., & Penn, P. (1987). *Milan systemic family therapy.* New York: Basic Books.

Boszormenyi-Nagy, I. (1987). *Foundations of contextual therapy: Collected papers of Ivan Boszormenyi-Nagy.* New York: Brunner/Mazel.

Boszormenyi-Nagy, I., & Spark, G. M. (1973). *Invisible loyalties: Reciprocity in intergenerational family therapy.* New York: Brunner/Mazel.

Boszormenyi-Nagy, I., & Ulrich, D. N. (1981). Contextual family therapy. In A. S. Gurman & D. P. Kniskern (Eds.), *Handbook of family therapy* (pp. 159–186). New York: Brunner/Mazel.

Boughner, S., Bubenzer, D. L., Hayes, S., & West, J. (1993). *Use of standardized assessment instruments by marital and family practitioners.* Atlanta, GA: American Counseling Association annual convention.

Bowling, T. K., Hill, C. M., & Jencius, M. (2005). An overview of marriage enrichment. *The Family Journal: Counseling and Therapy for Couples and Families, 13,* 87–94.

Bowen, G., & Orthner, D. (1990). *The Organization Family: Work and Family Linkages in the U.S. Military.* New York: Praeger.

Bowen, M. (1960). A family concept of schizophrenia. In D. Jackson (Ed.), *The etiology of schizophrenia.* New York: Basic Books.

Bowen, M. (1961). Family psychotherapy. *American Journal of Orthopsychiatry, 31,* 40–60.

Bowen, M. (1965). Family psychotherapy with schizophrenia in the hospital and in private practice. In I. Boszormenyi-Nagy & J. T. Framo (Eds.), *Intensive family therapy* (pp. 213–243). Hagerstown, MD: Harper & Row.

Bowen, M. (1972). Toward the differentiation of self in one's family of origin. In F. D. Andres & J. P. Lorio (Eds.), *Georgetown Family Symposia* (pp. 70–86). Washington, DC: Georgetown University.

Bowen, M. (1974). Alcoholism as viewed through family systems theory and family psychotherapy. *Annals of the New York Academy of Sciences, 233,* 125–132.

Bowen, M. (1975). Family therapy after twenty years. In S. Arieti, D. X. Freedman, & J. E. Dyrud (Eds.), *American handbook of psychiatry V: Treatment* (2nd ed.). New York: Basic Books.

Bowen, M. (1976). Theory in the practice of psychotherapy. In P. J. Guerin (Ed.), *Family therapy: Theory and practice* (pp. 42–90). New York: Gardner Press.

Bowen, M. (1978). *Family therapy in clinical practice.* New York: Jason Aronson.

Bowen, M. (1981). The use of family theory in clinical practice. In J. Haley (Ed.), *Changing families.* Philadelphia: Grune & Stratton.

Bowlby, J. (1988). *A secure base: Parent/child attachment and healthy human development.* New York: Basic Books.

Boyd-Franklin, N. (1987). The contribution of family therapy models to the treatment of black families. *Psychotherapy, 24,* 621–629.

Boyd-Franklin, N. (1993, July/August). Pulling out the arrows. *Family Therapy Networker, 17,* 54–56.

Boylin, W. M., Doucette, J., & Jean, M. F. (1997). Multifamily therapy in substance abuse treatment with women. *American Journal of Family Therapy, 25,* 39–47.

Boynton, G. (1987). Cross-cultural family therapy: The ESCAPE model. *American Journal of Family Therapy, 15,* 123–130.

Bradley, B., & Johnson, S. M. (2005). EFT: An integrative contemporary approach. In M. Harway (Ed.), *Handbook of couples therapy* (pp. 179–193). New York: Wiley.

Brammer, L. M., & MacDonald, G. (2003). *The helping relationship: Process and skills* (8th ed.). Boston: Allyn & Bacon.

Braver, S. L., Wolchik, S. A., Sandler, I. N., Sheets, V. L., Fogas, B., & Bay, R. C. (1993). A longitudinal study of noncustodial parents: Parents without children. *Journal of Family Psychology, 7,* 9–23.

Bray, J. H. (1988). Children's development during early remarriage. In E. M. Hetherington & J. Arastek (Eds.), *The impact of divorce, single-parenting, & stepparenting on children* (pp. 279–298). Hillsdale, NJ: Lawrence Erlbaum.

Bray, J. H. (1993). Becoming a stepfamily: Developmental issues for new stepfamilies. *The Family Journal: Counseling and Therapy for Couples and Families, 1,* 272–275.

Bray, J. H. (1993). Families in demographic perspective: Implications for family counseling. *The Family Journal: Counseling and Therapy for Couples and Families, 1,* 94–96.

Bray, J. H. (1994). What does a typical stepfamily look like? *The Family Journal: Counseling and Therapy for Couples and Families, 2,* 66–69.

Bray, J. H., & Berger, S. H. (1992). Stepfamilies. In M. E. Procidano & C. B. Fisher (Eds.), *Contemporary families: A handbook for school professionals* (pp. 57–79). New York: Teachers College Press.

Bray, J. H., & Hetherington, E. M. (1993). Families in transition: Introduction and overview. *Journal of Family Psychology, 7,* 3–8.

Bray, J. H., Williamson, D. S., & Malone, P. E. (1984). Personal Authority in the Family System: Development of a questionnaire to measure personal authority in intergenerational family processes. *Journal of Marital and Family Therapy, 10,* 167–178.

Brendel, J. M., & Nelson, K. W. (1999). The stream of family secrets: Navigating the islands of confidentiality and triangulation involving family therapists. *The Family Journal: Counseling and Therapy for Couples and Families, 7,* 112–117.

Bretherson, I., Walsh, R., & Lependorf, M. (1996). Social support in postdivorce families. In G. R. Pierce, B. R. Sarason, & I. G. Sarason (Eds.), *Handbook of social support and the family* (pp. 345–373). New York: Plenum Press.

Bridges, S. K., Lease, S. H., & Ellison, C. R. (2004). Predicting sexual satisfaction in women: Implications for counselor education and training. *Journal of Counseling and Development, 82,* 158–166.

Brock, G. W., & Barnard, C. P. (1988). *Procedures in family therapy.* Boston: Allyn & Bacon.

Brock, G. W., & Barnard, C. P. (1999). *Procedures in marriage and family therapy* (3rd ed.). Boston: Allyn & Bacon.

Broderick, C. B., & Schrader, S. S. (1981). The history of professional marriage and family therapy. In A. S. Gurman & O. P. Kniskern (Eds.), *Handbook of family therapy* (pp. 5–38). New York: Brunner/Mazel.

Broderick, C. B., & Schrader, S. S. (1991). The history of professional marriage and family therapy. In A. S. Gurman & O. P. Kniskern (Eds.), *Handbook of family therapy, II* (pp. 3–40). New York: Brunner/Mazel.

Brown, F. H. (1988). The impact of death and serious illness on the family life cycle. In B. Carter & M. McGoldrick (Eds.), *The changing family life cycle* (2nd ed., pp. 457–482). New York: Brunner/Mazel.

Brown, S. L. (2002). We are, therefore I am: A multisystems approach with families in poverty. *The Family Journal: Counseling and Therapy with Couples and Families, 10*, 405–409.

Bruhn, D. M., & Hill, R. (2004). Designing a premarital counseling program. *The Family Journal: Counseling and Therapy for Couples and Families, 12*, 389–391.

Bry, B. H. (1994). Preventing substance abuse by supporting families' efforts with community resources. *Child and Family Behavior Therapy, 16*, 21–26.

Bubenzer, D. L., & West, J. D. (1993). William Hudson O'Hanlon: On seeking possibilities and solutions in therapy. *The Family Journal: Counseling and Therapy for Couples and Families, 1*, 365–379.

Bubenzer, D. L., West, J. D., & Boughner, S. R. (1994). Michael White and the narrative perspective in therapy. *The Family Journal: Counseling and Therapy for Couples and Families, 2*, 71–83.

Bullis, R. K. (1993). *Law and the management of a counseling agency or private practice.* Alexandria, VA: American Counseling Association.

Bumpass, L. L. (1990). What's happening to the family? Interactions between demographic and institutional change. *Demography, 27*, 483–498.

Bumpass, L., & Sweet, J. A. (1989). Children's experience in single-parent families: Implications of cohabitation and marital transitions. *Family Planning Perspectives, 6*, 256–260.

Burgess, T. A., & Hinkle, J. S. (1993). Strategic family therapy of avoidance behavior. *Journal of Mental Health Counseling, 15*, 132–140.

Burkemper, E. M. (2002). Family therapists' ethical decision-making processes in two duty-to-warn situations. *Journal of Marital and Family Therapy, 28*, 203–211.

Burr, W. R., Hill, R., Nye, F. I., & Reiss, I. L. (1979). *Contemporary theories about the family.* New York: Free Press.

Burton, L. M., Winn, D-M, Stevenson, H., & Clark, S. L. (2004). Working with African American clients: Considering the "homeplace" in marriage and family therapy practices. *Journal of Marital and Family Therapy, 30*, 397–410.

Calvo, G. (1975). *Marriage encounter: Official national manual.* St. Paul, MN: Marriage Encounter, Inc.

Campbell, J., & Moyers, B. (1988). *The power of myth.* New York: Doubleday.

Campbell, D., Draper, R., & Crutchley, E. (1991). The Milan systemic approach to family therapy. In A. S. Gurman & D. P. Kniskern (Eds.), *Handbook of family therapy* (Vol. II, pp. 325–362). New York: Brunner/Mazel.

Canino, I., & Canino, G. (1982). Cultural syntonic family for migrant Puerto Ricans. *Hospital and Community Psychiatry, 33*, 299–303.

Cano, A., Christian-Herman, J., O'Leary, K. D., & Avery-Leaf, S. (2002). Antecedents and consequences of negative marital stressors. *Journal of Marital and Family Therapy, 28*, 145–151.

Carey, A. R., & Bryant, W. (1996a, June 25). Living alone. *USA Today,* p. A1.

Carey, A. R., & Rechin, K. (1996b, July 5). Nation of "empty nests." *USA Today,* p. A1.

Carlson, J., & Dinkmeyer, D. (2003). *TIME for a better marriage.* Alascadero, CA: Impact.

Carlson, J., & Ellis, C. M. (2004). Treatment agreement and relapse prevention strategies in couple and family therapy. *The Family Journal: Counseling and Therapy for Couples and Families, 12*, 352–357.

Carlson, J., & Fullmer, D. (1992). Family counseling: Principles for growth. In R. L. Smith & P. Stevens-Smith (Eds.), *Family counseling and therapy* (pp. 27–52). Ann Arbor, MI: ERIC/CAPS.

Carlson, J., & Sperry, L. (1993, January/February). The future of families: New challenges for couple and family therapy. *Family Counseling and Therapy, 1*, 1–14.

Carlson, J., Hinkle, J. S., & Sperry, L. (1993). Using diagnosis and DSM-III-R and IV in marriage and family counseling and therapy: Increasing treatment outcomes without losing heart and soul. *The Family Journal: Counseling for Couples and Families, 1*, 308–312.

Carlson, J., Kurato, Y., Ruiz, E., Ng, K-M, & Yang, J. (2004). A multicultural discussion about personality development. *The Family Journal: Counseling and Therapy for Couples and Families, 12*, 111–121.

Carrere, S., Buchlman, K. T., Gottman, J. M., Coan, J. A., & Ruckstruhl, L. (2000). Predicting marital stability and divorce in newlywed couples. *Journal of Family Psychology, 14*, 42–58.

Carter, B. (1986). Success in family therapy. *Family Therapy Networker, 10*, 16–22.

Carter, B. (1992, January/February). Stonewalling feminism. *Family Therapy Networker, 16*, 64–69.

Carter, B. (1999). Becoming parents: The family with young children. In B. Carter & M. McGoldrick (Eds.), *The expanded family life cycle* (3rd ed., pp. 249–273). Boston: Allyn & Bacon.

Carter, B., & McGoldrick, M. (1988). Overview: The changing family life cycle—A framework for family therapy. In B. Carter & M. McGoldrick (Eds.), *The changing family life cycle* (2nd ed., pp. 3–28). New York: Gardner.

Carter, B., & McGoldrick, M. (1999). *The expanded family life cycle* (3rd ed.). Boston: Allyn & Bacon.

Carter, E. A., & McGoldrick-Orfanidis, M. (1976). Family therapy with one person and the family therapist's own family. In P. J. Guerin, Jr. (Ed.), *Family therapy* (pp. 119–219). New York: Gardner.

Castro-Martin, T., & Bumpass, L. (1989). Recent trends and differentials in marital disruption. *Demography, 26*, 37–51.

Caudill, O. B., Jr. (2000, February/March). Long distance liability. *Family Therapy News, 31*(1), 10–12.

Cavan, R. S. (1969). *The American family* (4th ed.). New York: Thomas Y. Crowell Co.

Chan, J. G. (2003). An examination of family-involved approaches to alcoholism treatment. *The Family Journal: Counseling and Therapy for Couples and Families, 11,* 129–138.

Chen-Hayes, S. F. (1997). Counseling lesbian, bisexual, and gay persons in couple and family relationships: Overcoming the stereotypes. *The Family Journal: Counseling and Therapy for Couples and Families, 5,* 236–240.

Cheng, W. D. (1996, Spring). Pacific perspective. *Together, 24,* 8.

Cherlin, A. J. (1992). *Marriage, divorce, remarriage* (rev. ed.). Cambridge, MA: Harvard University Press.

Christensen, A., & Jacobson, N. S. (2000). *Reconcilable differences.* New York: Guilford Press.

Christensen, A., Atkins, D. C., Berns, S., Wheeler, J., Baucom, D. H., & Simpson, L. E. (2004). Traditional versus integrative behavioral couple therapy for significantly and chronically distressed married couples. *Journal of Consulting and Clinical Psychology, 72,* 176–191.

Chronister, K. M., & McWhirter, E. H. (2003). Applying social cognitive career theory in the empowerment of battered women. *Journal of Counseling and Development, 81,* 418–425.

Clausen, J. A. (1993). *American lives.* New York: Free Press.

Clawson, T. W., Henderson, D. A., & Schweiger, W. K. (2004). *Counselor preparation* (11th ed.). New York: Brunner-Routledge.

Clemens, A., & Axelson, L. (1985). The not-so-empty-nest: The return of the fledgling adult. *Family Relations, 34,* 259–264.

Cleveland, P. H., & Lindsey, E. W. (1995). Solution-focused family interventions. In A. C. Kilpatrick & T. P. Holland (Eds.), *Working with families* (pp. 145–160). Boston: Allyn & Bacon.

Cloutier, P. F., Manion, I. G., Walker, J. G., & Johnson, S. M. (2002). Emotionally focused interventions for couples with chronically ill children: A 2-year follow-up. *Journal of Marital and Family Therapy, 28,* 391–398.

Coale, H. W. (1994). Therapeutic use of rituals with stepfamilies. *The Family Journal: Counseling and Therapy for Couples and Families, 2,* 2–10.

Coates, J. F. (1996, September/October). What's ahead for families: Five major forces of change. *The Futurist,* pp. 27–35.

Cobia, D. C., & Boes, S. R. (2000). Professional disclosure statements and formal plans for supervision: Two strategies for minimizing the risk of ethical conflicts in post-master's supervision. *Journal of Counseling and Development, 78,* 293–296.

Cobia, D. C., Sobansky, R. R., & Ingram, M. (2004). Female survivors of childhood sexual abuse: Implications for couples' therapists. *The Family Journal: Counseling and Therapy for Couples and Families, 12,* 312–318.

Cohen, E. (1993, August). Who are Latinos? *Family Therapy News, 24,* 13.

Colapinto, J. (1979). The relative value of empirical evidence. *Family Process, 18,* 427–441.

Colapinto, J. (2000). Structural family therapy. In A. M. Horne (Ed.), *Family counseling and therapy* (3rd ed., pp. 140–169). Itasca, IL: F. E. Peacock.

Coleman, M., & Ganong, L. H. (1989). Financial management in stepfamilies. *Lifestyles, 10,* 217–232.

Coleman, S. (1985). *Failures in family therapy.* New York: Guilford.

Collins, W. E., Newman, B. M., & McKenry, P. C. (1995). Intrapsychic and interpersonal factors related to adolescent psychological well-being in stepmother and stepfather families. *Journal of Family Psychology, 9,* 433–445.

Combrinck-Graham, L. (1985). A developmental model for family systems. *Family Process, 24,* 139–150.

Constantine, J. A., Stone Fish, L. S., & Piercy, F. P. (1984). A systematic procedure for teaching positive connotation. *Journal of Marital and Family Therapy, 10,* 313–316.

Coontz, S. (1997). *The way we really are: Coming to terms with America's changing families.* New York: Basic Books.

Coontz, S. (2000). *The way we never were: American families and the nostalgia trap.* New York: Basic Books.

Coontz, S. (2005). *Marriage, a history: From obedience to intimacy, or how love conquered marriage.* New York: Viking.

Cooper, C., & Costas, L. (1994, Spring). Ethical challenges when working with Hispanic/Latino families: Personalismo. *The Family Psychologist, 10,* 32–34.

Copeland, A. P., & White, K. M. (1991). *Studying families.* Newbury Park, CA: Sage.

Cordova, J. V., Jacobson, N. S., & Christensen, A. (1998). Acceptance versus change interventions in behavioral couple therapy: Impact on couples' in-session communication. *Journal of Marital and Family Therapy, 24,* 437–455.

Corey, G., Corey, M. S., & Callanan, P. (2002). *Issues and ethics in the helping professions* (6th ed.). Pacific Grove, CA: Brooks/Cole.

Cormier, L. S., & Hackney, H. (2004). *Counseling strategies and interventions* (6th ed.). Boston: Allyn & Bacon.

Costa, L. (1991). Family sculpting in the training of marriage and family counselors. *Counselor Education and Supervision, 31,* 121–131.

Costa, L., & Sorenson, J. (1993). Feminist family therapy: Ethical considerations for the clinician. *The Family Journal: Counseling and Therapy for Couples and Families, 1,* 17–24.

Cottone, R. R., & Claus, R. E. (2000). Ethical decision-making models: A review of the literature. *Journal of Counseling and Development, 78,* 275–283.

Coyne, J. C. (1985). Toward a theory of frames and reframing: The social nature of frames. *Journal of Marital and Family Therapy, 11,* 337–344.

Crespi, T. D., & Howe, E. A. (2000, March). Families in crisis: Considerations and implications for school counselors. *Counseling Today, 42*(9), 6.

Crethar, H. C., Snow, K., & Carlson, J. (2005). Theories of family therapy (Part II). In R. H. Combs (Ed.), *Family Therapy Review* (pp. 143–168). Mahwah, NJ: Lawrence Erlbaum.

Crews, J. A., & Hill, N. R. (2005). Diagnosis in marriage and family counseling: An ethical double bind. *The Family Journal: Counseling and Therapy for Couples and Families, 13*, 63–66.

Crohn, H., Sager, C. J., Brown, H., Rodstein, E., & Walker, L. (1982). A basis for understanding and treating the remarried family. In J. C. Hansen & L. Messinger (Eds.), *Therapy with remarriage families*. Rockville, MD: Aspen.

Cron, E. A. (2000). Couple Rating Scale: Clarifying problem areas. *The Family Journal: Counseling and Therapy for Couples and Families, 8*, 302–304.

Croyle, K. L., & Walz, J. (2002). Emotional awareness and couples' relationship satisfaction. *Journal of Marital and Family Therapy, 28*, 435–444.

Cuber, J., & Harroff, P. (1966). *Sex and the significant Americans*. Baltimore: Penguin.

Curich, M. S., & Stone, M. H. (1998). The targeted dysfunctional behavior cycle applied to family therapy. *The Family Journal: Counseling and Therapy for Couples and Families, 6*, 328–333.

Curran, D. (1985). *Stress and the healthy family*. San Francisco: Harper & Row.

Cutler, H. A., & Radford, A. (1999). Adult children of alcoholics: Adjustment to a college environment. *The Family Journal: Counseling and Therapy for Couples and Families, 7*, 148–153.

Dahl, A. S., Cowgill, K. M., & Asmundsson, R. (1987). Life in remarriage families. *Social Work, 32*, 40–44.

Darden, E. C., & Zimmerman, T. S. (1992). Blended families: A decade review, 1979–1990. *Family Therapy, 19*, 25–31.

Dattilio, F. M. (Ed.). (1998). *Case studies in couples and family therapy: Systemic and cognitive perspectives*. New York: Guilford.

Dattilio, F. M. (2001). Cognitive-behavior family therapy: Contemporary myths and misconceptions. *Contemporary Family Therapy, 23*, 3–18.

Dattilio, F. M. (2005). The restructuring of family schemas: A cognitive-behavior perspective. *Journal of Marital and Family Therapy, 31*, 15–30.

Dattilio, F. M., & Bevilacqua, L. J. (2000). A cognitive-behavioral approach. In F. M. Dattilio & L. J. Bevilacqua (Eds.), *Comparative treatments for relationship dysfunction* (pp. 137–159). New York: Springer.

Dattilio, F. M., & Epstein, N. B. (2005). Introduction to the special section: The role of cognitive-behavioral interventions in couple and family therapy. *Journal of Marital and Family Therapy, 31*, 7–13.

Davey, M. (2004, May 31). For soldiers back from Iraq, basic training in resuming life. *New York Times*, A1, A15.

David, J. R. (1979). The theology of Murray Bowen or the marital triangle. *Journal of Psychology and Theology, 7*, 259–262.

Davis, R. F., & Borns, N. F. (1999). *Solo dad survival guide: Raising your kids on your own*. New York: NTC/Contemporary Publishing.

Davis, S. D., & Butler, M. H. (2004). Enacting relationships in marriage and family therapy: A conceptual and operational definition of enactment. *Journal of Marital and Family Therapy, 30*, 319–333.

Daw, J. L. (1995, December). Alcohol problems across the generations. *Family Therapy News, 26*, 19.

DeMaria, R., & Hannah, M. T. (Eds.). (2003). *Building intimate relationships*. New York: Brunner-Routledge.

DeMaria, R. (2005). Distressed couples and marriage education. *Family Relations, 54*, 242–253.

Depner, C. E., & Bray, J. H. (Eds.). (1993). *Nonresidential parents. New vistas in family living*. Newbury Park, CA: Sage.

deShazer, S. (1982). *Patterns of brief family therapy*. New York: Guilford.

deShazer, S. (1984). The death of resistance. *Family Process, 23*, 11–21.

deShazer, S. (1985). *Keys to solution in brief therapy*. New York: Norton.

deShazer, S. (1988). *Clues: Investigating solutions in brief therapy*. New York: Norton.

deShazer, S. (1989). Resistance revisited. *Contemporary Family Therapy, 11*, 227–233.

deShazer, S. (1991). *Putting differences to work*. New York: Norton.

deShazer, S., & Molnar, A. (1984). Four useful interventions in brief family therapy. *Journal of Marital and Family Therapy, 10*, 297–304.

Diamond, G., & Dickey, M. (1993, Spring). Process research: Its history, intent and findings. *The Family Psychologist, 9*, 23–25.

Diamond, J. (2000, July/August). Making friends with your addiction. *Family Therapy Networker*, pp. 40–47.

DiBlasio, F. (2000). Decision-based forgiveness treatment in cases of marital infidelity. *Psychotherapy, 37*, 149–158.

Dickerson, V. C., & Zimmerman, J. (1992). Families with adolescents: Escaping problem lifestyles. *Family Process, 31*, 341–353.

Dicks, H. V. (1963). Object relations theory and marital studies. *British Journal of Medical Psychology, 36*, 125–129.

DiGuiseppe, R. (1988). A cognitive-behavioral approach to the treatment of conduct disorder in children and adolescents. In N. Epstein, S. E. Schlesinger, & W. Dryden (Eds.), *Cognitive-behavioral therapy with families* (pp. 183–214). New York: Brunner/Mazel.

Dinkmeyer, D. C., & McKay, G. D. (1989). STEP: *The parents handbook*. Circle Pines, MN: American Guidance Service.

Dinkmeyer, D. C., Dinkmeyer, D. C., Jr., & Sperry, L. (2000). *Adlerian counseling and psychotherapy* (3rd ed.). Upper Saddle River, NJ: Merrill/Prentice Hall.

Disque, J. G., & Morrow, B. (2002). Gus Napier: Reflections on the field of family therapy. *The Family Journal: Counseling and Therapy for Couples and Families, 10*, 112–118.

Doherty, W. J. (1995). *Soul searching: Why psychotherapy must promote moral responsibility*. New York: Basic Books.

Doherty, W. J., & Boss, P. G. (1991). Values and ethics in family therapy. In A. S. Gurman & D. P. Kniskern (Eds.), *Handbook of family therapy* (Vol. II, pp. 606–637). New York: Brunner/Mazel.

Doherty, W. J., & Simmons, D. S. (1996). Clinical practice patterns of marriage and family therapists: A national survey of therapists and their clients. *Journal of Marital and Family Therapy, 22*, 9–25.

Doss, B. D., Atkins, D. C., & Christensen, A. (2003). Who's dragging their feet? Husbands and wives seeking marital therapy. *Journal of Marital and Family Therapy, 29*, 165–177.

Doss, B., Simpson, L., & Christensen, A. (2004). Why do couples seek marital therapy? *Professional Psychology: Research and Practice, 35*, 608–614.

Drummet, A. R., Coleman, M., & Cable, S. (2003). Military families under stress: Implications for family life education. *Family Relations, 52*, 279–287.

Drummond, R. J. (2004). *Appraisal procedures for counselors and helping professionals* (5th ed.). Upper Saddle River, NJ: Merrill/Prentice Hall.

Duckett, E., & Richards, M. H. (1995). Maternal employment and the quality of daily experience for young adolescents of single mothers. *Journal of Family Psychology, 9*, 418–432.

Duhl, B. S. (1983). *From the inside out and other metaphors.* New York: Brunner/Mazel.

Duhl, B. S., & Duhl, F. J. (1981). Integrative family therapy. In A. S. Gurman & D. P. Kniskern (Eds.), *Handbook of family therapy* (pp. 483–513). New York: Brunner/Mazel.

Duhl, F. J., Kantor, D., & Duhl, B. S. (1973). Learning, space, and action in family therapy: A primer of sculpture. In D. A. Bloch (Ed.), *Techniques of family psychotherapy* (pp. 69–76). New York: Grune & Stratton.

Duncan, S. F., & Brown, G. (1992). RENEW: A program for building remarried family strengths. *Families in Society, 73*, 149–158.

Duncan, S. F., & Duerden, D. S. (1990). Stressors and enhancers in the marital/family life of the family professional. *Family Relations, 39*, 211–215.

Duncan, S. F., & Wood, M. M. (2003). Perceptions of marriage preparation among college-educated young adults with greater family-related risks for marital disruption. *The Family Journal: Counseling and Therapy with Couples and Families, 11*, 342–352.

Dunn, A. B., & Levitt, M. M. (2000). The genogram: From diagnostics to mutual collaboration. *The Family Journal: Counseling and Therapy for Couples and Families, 8*, 236–244.

Duvall, E. (1977). *Marriage and family development* (5th ed.). Philadelphia: Lippincott.

Eaves, S. H., Sheperis, C. J., Blanchard, T., Baylot, L., & Doggett, R. A. (2005). Teaching time-out and job card grounding procedures to parents: A primer for family counselors. *The Family Journal: Counseling and Therapy for Couples and Families, 13*, 252–258.

Eccles, J. S., Midgley, C., Wigfield, A., Buchanan, C. M., Reuman, D., Flanagan, C., & MacIver, D. (1993). Development during adolescence: The impact of stage-environment fit on young adolescents' experiences in schools and families. *American Psychologist, 48*, 90–101.

Eckstein, D. (2004). The "A's and H's" of healthy and unhealthy relationships: Three relationship renewal activities. *The Family Journal: Counseling and Therapy for Couples and Families, 12*, 414–418.

Eckstein, D., & Jones, J. E. (1998). Thirty-three suggestions for relationship renewal. *The Family Journal: Counseling and Therapy for Couples and Families, 6*, 334–336.

Edwards, M. E., & Steinglass, P. (1995). Family therapy treatment outcomes for alcoholism. *Journal of Marital and Family Therapy, 4*, 475–509.

Egan, G. (2002). *The skilled helper* (7th ed.). Pacific Grove, CA: Brooks/Cole.

Elam, G. A., & Kleist, D. M. (1999). Research on the long-term effects of child abuse. *The Family Journal: Counseling and Therapy for Couples and Families, 7*, 154–160.

Elder, G. H., Jr. (1975). Age differentiation and the life course. *Annual Review of Sociology, 1*, 165–190.

Elias, M. (1992, June 19–21). Parenting turns men's lives on end. *USA Today*, pp. 1A, 2A.

Elias, M. (1996, August 22). Teens do better when dads are more involved. *USA Today*, p. D1.

Elkin, M. (1984). *Families under the influence.* New York: W.W. Norton.

Ellis, A. (1977). The nature of disturbed marital interactions. In A. Ellis & R. Greiger (Eds.), *Handbook of rational-emotive therapy* (pp. 77–92). New York: Springer.

Ellis, A. (1978). Family therapy: A phenomenological and active-directive approach. *Journal of Marriage and Family Counseling, 4*, 43–50.

Ellis, A. (1985). *Overcoming resistance: Rational-emotive therapy with difficult clients.* New York: Springer.

Ellis, A. (1993). The rational-emotive therapy (RET) approach to marriage and family therapy. *The Family Journal: Counseling and Therapy for Couples and Families, 1*, 292–307.

Ellis, A. (2000). Rational-emotive behavioral marriage and family therapy. In A. M. Horne (Ed.), *Family counseling and therapy* (3rd ed., pp. 489–514). Itasca, IL: F. E. Peacock.

Ellis, A., & Harper, R. A. (1961). *A guide to rational living.* Upper Saddle River, NJ: Prentice Hall.

Ellis, A., Sichel, J. L., Yeager, R. J., DiMattia, D. J., & DiGuiseppe, R. (1989). *Rational-emotive couple therapy.* Itasca, IL: F. E. Peacock.

Ellis, G. F. (1986). Societal and parental predictors of parent–adolescent conflict. In G. K. Leigh & G. W. Peterson (Eds.), *Adolescents in families* (pp. 155–178). Cincinnati: South-Western.

El Nasser, H., & Grant, L. (2005, June 9a). Diversity tints new kind of generation gap. *USA Today*, p. 4A.

El Nasser, H., & Grant, L. (2005, June 9b). Immigration causes age, race split. *USA Today*, p. 1A.

Enns, C. Z. (1992). Dilemmas of power and equality in marital and family counseling: Proposals for a feminist perspective. In R. L. Smith & P. Stevens-Smith (Eds.), *Family counseling and therapy* (pp. 338–357). Ann Arbor, MI: ERIC/CAPS.

Epstein, N. B., & Bishop, D. S. (1981). Problem centered systems therapy of the family. *Journal of Marital and Family Therapy, 7*, 23–31.

Epstein, N. B., Baldwin, L. M., & Bishop, D. S. (1983). The McMaster Family Assessment Device. *Journal of Marital and Family Therapy, 9*, 171–180.

Epstein, N., Schlesinger, S. E., & Dryden, W. (1988). Cognitive-behavioral family therapy: Summary and future directions. In N. Epstein, S. E. Schlesinger, & W. Dryden (Eds.), *Cognitive-behavioral therapy with families* (pp. 361–366). New York: Brunner/Mazel.

Epston, D. (1994). Extending the conversation. *Family Therapy Networker, 18*, 30–37, 62–63.

Erbe, B. (1993, July 19). Stop surge of unwed mothers. *USA Today*, p. 11A.

Erdman, P. (2000). Bringing a symbol: An experiential exercise for systematic change. In R. E. Watts (Ed.), *Techniques in marriage and family counseling* (pp. 99–102). Alexandria, VA: American Counseling Association.

Ericksen, J. A., Yancey, W. L., & Ericksen, E. P. (1979). The division of family roles. *Journal of Marriage and Family, 41*, 301–313.

Erikson, E. H. (1950). *Childhood and society*. New York: Norton.

Erikson, E. H. (1959). *Identity and the life cycle: Psychological issues*. New York: International Universities Press.

Erikson, E. H. (1968). *Identity: Youth and crisis*. New York: Norton.

Evans, D. L., Foa, E. B., Gur, R. E., Hendin, H., O'Brien, C. P., Seligman, M. E. P., & Walsh, B. T. (2005). *Treating and preventing adolescent mental health disorders*. New York: Oxford.

Evans, M. (1988). *This is me and my two families*. New York: Brunner/Mazel.

Evans, M. (1989). *This is me and my single parent*. New York: Brunner/Mazel.

Everett, C. A., & Volgy, S. S. (1991). Treating divorce in family-therapy practice. In A. S. Gurman & D. P. Kniskern (Eds.), *Handbook of family therapy* (Vol. II, pp. 508–524). New York: Brunner/Mazel.

Everett, C. A., Livingston, S. E., & Bowen, L. D. (2005). Separation, divorce, and remarriage. In R. H. Combs (Ed.), *Family therapy review* (pp. 257–275). Hillsdale, NJ: Lawrence Erlbaum.

Facundo, A. (1990). Social class issues in family therapy: A case study of a Puerto Rican migrant family. *Journal of Strategic and Systemic Therapies, 9*, 14–34.

Fairbairn, W. R. (1954). *An object-relations theory of personality*. New York: Basic Books.

Falloon, I. R. (1988). *Handbook of behavioral family therapy*. New York: Guilford.

Falloon, I. R. H. (1991). Behavioral family therapy. In A. S. Gurman & D. P. Kniskern (Eds.), *Handbook of family therapy* (Vol. II, pp. 65–95). New York: Brunner/Mazel.

Fals-Stewart, W. (2003). The occurrence of partner physical aggression on days of alcohol consumption: A longitudinal diary study. *Journal of Consulting and Clinical Psychology, 71*, 41–52.

Faulkner, R. A., Klock, K., & Gale, J. E. (2002). Qualitative research in family therapy: Publication trends from 1980 to 1999. *Journal of Marital and Family Therapy, 28*, 69–74.

Fay, A. (1999). *Making it as a couple*. Essex, CT: FMC Books.

Fenell, D. L., & Weinhold, B. K. (1992). Research in marriage and family therapy. In R. L. Smith & P. Stevens-Smith (Eds.), *Family counseling and therapy* (pp. 331–337). Ann Arbor, MI: ERIC/CAPS.

Fenell, D. L., & Weinhold, B. K. (1996, March). Treating families with special needs. *Counseling and Human Development, 28*, 1–12.

Fenell, D. L., & Weinhold, B. K. (2003). *Counseling families* (3rd ed.). Denver: Love.

Ferstenberg, R. L. (1992). Mediation versus litigation in divorce and why a litigator becomes a mediator. *American Journal of Family Therapy, 20*, 266–273.

Figley, C. R. (1989). *Helping traumatized families*. San Francisco: Jossey-Bass.

Figley, C. R., & McCubbin, H. (1983). *Stress and the family: Vol. 2: Coping with catastrophe*. New York: Brunner/Mazel.

Figley, C. R., & Nelson, T. S. (1990). Basic family therapy skills, II: Structural family therapy. *Journal of Marital and Family Therapy, 16*, 225–239.

Filaccio, M. L. (2005). Discovery, confidentiality, and in camera review: Is it possible to serve two masters? *The Family Journal: Counseling and Therapy for Couples and Families, 13*, 68–70.

Fish, J. M. (1988, July/August). Reconciling the irreconcilable. *Family Therapy Networker, 12*, 15.

Fisher, L. (1976). Dimensions of family assessment: A critical review. *Journal of Marriage and Family Counseling, 2*, 367–382.

Fisher, L., Ransom, D., Terry, H. E., & Burge, S. (1992). The California family health project: IV. Family structure/organization and adult health. *Family Process, 31*, 399–419.

Fishman, C. H. (1988). *Treating troubled adolescents*. New York: Basic Books.

Fleishman, J. A. (1984). Personality characteristics and coping patterns. *Journal of Health and Social Behavior, 25*, 229–244.

Fleming, J. S., & Rickord, B. (1997). Solution-focused brief therapy: One answer to managed mental health care. *The Family Journal: Counseling and Therapy for Couples and Families, 5*, 286–294.

Flowers, B., & Olson, D. (1986). Predicting marital success with PREPARE: A predictive validity study. *Journal of Marital and Family Therapy, 12*, 403–413.

Floyd, F. J., & Markman, H. J. (1983). Observational biases in spouse interaction: Toward a cognitive/behavioral model of marriage. *Journal of Consulting and Clinical Psychology, 51*, 450–457.

Foos, J. A., Ottens, A. J., & Hill, L. K. (1991). Managed mental health: A primer for counselors. *Journal of Counseling and Development, 69*, 332–336.

Footlick, J. K. (1990, Winter/Spring). What happened to the family? *Newsweek*, pp. 15–20.

Foucault, M. (1965). *Madness and civilization: A history of insanity in the use of reason*. New York: Random House.

Foucault, M. (1980). *Power/knowledge: Selected interviews and other writings*. New York: Pantheon Books.

Foucault, M. (1982). The subject and power. In H. Dreyfus & P. Rabinow (Eds.), *Michel Foucault: Beyond structuralism and hermeneutics*. Chicago: University of Chicago Press.

Foucault, M. (1984). Space, knowledge and power. In P. Rabinow (Ed.), *The Foucault reader*. New York: Pantheon.

Fowers, B. J. (1990). An interactional approach to standardized marital assessment: A literature review. *Family Relations, 39,* 368–385.

Fowers, B. J., Lyons, E. M., & Montel, K. H. (1996). Positive marital illusions: Self-enhancement or relationship enhancement? *Journal of Family Psychology, 10,* 192–208.

Frame, M. W. (1998). The ethics of counseling via the Internet. *The Family Journal: Counseling and Therapy for Couples and Families, 5,* 328–330.

Frame, M. W. (2000). Constructing religious/spiritual genograms. In R. E. Watts (Ed.), *Techniques in marriage and family counseling* (pp. 69–74). Alexandria, VA: American Counseling Association.

Framo, J. L. (1981). The integration of marital therapy with sessions with family of origin. In A. S. Gurman & D. P. Kniskern (Eds.), *Handbook of family therapy*. New York: Brunner/Mazel.

Framo, J. L. (1996). A personal retrospective of the family therapy field: Then and now. *Journal of Marital and Family Therapy, 22,* 289–316.

Fraenkel, P., Markman, H., & Stanley, S. (1997). The prevention approach to relationship problems. *Sexual and Marital Therapy, 12,* 249–258.

Franklin, A. J. (1993, July/August). The invisibility syndrome. *Family Therapy Networker, 17,* 32–39.

Fraser, J. S. (1982). Structural and strategic family therapy: A basis for marriage or grounds for divorce? *Journal of Marital and Family Therapy, 8,* 13–22.

Fredman, N., & Sherman, R. (1987). *Handbook of measurements for marriage and family therapy*. New York: Brunner/Mazel.

Freedman, J., & Combs, G. (1996). *Narrative therapy: The social construction of preferred reality*. New York: Norton.

Freeman, A., & Zaken-Greenberg, F. (1989). A cognitive-behavioral approach. In C. R. Figley (Ed.), *Treating stress in families* (pp. 97–121). New York: Brunner/Mazel.

Freeman, M. G. (1985). *The concepts of love and marriage* (film). Atlanta, GA: Emory University.

Friedlander, M. L., Wildman, J., & Heatherington, L. (1991). Interpersonal control in structural and Milan systemic family therapy. *Journal of Marital and Family Therapy, 17,* 395–408.

Friedlander, M. L., Wildman, J., Heatherington, L., & Skowron, E. A. (1994). What we do and don't know about the process of family therapy. *Journal of Family Psychology, 8,* 390–416.

Friedman, E. H. (1985). *Generation to generation: Family process in church and synagogue*. New York: Guilford.

Friedman, E. H. (1991). Bowen theory and therapy. In A. S. Gurman & D. P. Kniskern (Eds.), *Handbook of family therapy* (Vol. II, pp. 134–170). New York: Brunner/Mazel.

Freud, S. (1940). *An outline of psychoanalysis. In The standard edition of the complete psychological works of Sigmund Freud* (Vol. 23, pp. 139–171). London: Hogarth Press.

Friesen, J. D. (1985). *Structural-strategic marriage and family therapy*. New York: Gardner.

Fulmer, R. H. (1988). Lower-income and professional families: A comparison of structure and life cycle process. In B. Carter & M. McGoldrick (Eds.), *The changing family life cycle* (2nd ed., pp. 545–578). New York: Gardner.

Furstenberg, F. F. (1990). Divorce and the American family. *Annual Review of Sociology, 16,* 379–403.

Gale, J. E. (1991). *Conversion analysis of therapeutic discourse: The pursuit of a therapeutic agenda*. Norwood, NJ: Ablex.

Galvin, K. M., & Brommel, B. J. (1986). *Family communication: Cohesion and change* (2nd ed.). Glenview, IL: Scott Foresman.

Garcia-Preto, N. (1986, November/December). Puerto Rican families. *Family Therapy Networker, 10,* 33–34.

Gardner, R. A. (1971). *The boys and girls book about stepfamilies*. New York: Bantam.

Gardner, R. (1984). Counseling children in stepfamilies. *Elementary School Guidance and Counseling, 19,* 40–49.

Garfield, R. (1982). Mourning and its resolution for spouses in marital separation. In J. C. Hansen & L. Messinger (Eds.), *Therapy with remarriage families* pp. 1–16). Rockville, MD: Aspen.

Garrett, M. T. (2006). When Eagle speaks: Counseling Native Americans. In C. C. Lee (Ed.), *Multicultural issues in counseling: New approaches to diversity* (3rd ed., pp. 25–53). Alexandria, VA: American Counseling Association.

Gaston, J. (1996, July 8). Roots of disunion. *Winston-Salem (NC) Journal,* pp. D1–D2.

Gay, L. R., & Airasian, P. (2000). *Educational research: Competencies for analysis and applications* (6th ed.). Upper Saddle River, NJ: Merrill/Prentice Hall.

Geddes, M., & Medway, J. (1977). The symbolic drawing of family life space. *Family Process, 16,* 219–228.

Gelles, R. J. (1989). Child abuse and violence in single-parent families: Parent absence and economic deprivation. *American Journal of Orthopsychiatry, 59,* 492–501.

Gelles, R. J. (1997). *Intimate violence in the family* (3rd ed.). Thousand Oaks, CA: Sage Publications.

Gerson, R. (1995). The family life cycle: Phases, stages, and crises. In R. H. Mikesell, D. Lusterman, & S. H. McDaniel (Eds.), *Integrating family therapy* (pp. 91–112). Washington, DC: American Psychological Association.

Giblin, P. (1993). Values: Family and other. *The Family Journal: Counseling and Therapy for Couples and Families, 1,* 240–242.

Giblin, P. (1994). Marital satisfaction. *The Family Journal: Counseling and Therapy for Couples and Families, 2,* 48–50.

Giblin, P. (1995). Identity, change, and family rituals. *The Family Journal: Counseling and Therapy for Couples and Families, 3,* 37–41.

Giblin, P. (1996). Family strengths. *The Family Journal: Counseling and Therapy for Couples and Families, 4,* 339–348.

Gibson, J. M., & Donigian, J. (1993). Use of Bowen theory. *Journal of Addictions and Offender Counseling, 14,* 25–35.

Gibson, P. A. (2002). Caregiving role affects family relationships of African American grandmothers as new mothers again: A phenomenological perspective. *Journal of Marital and Family Therapy, 28,* 341–353.

Gilbert, L. A. (1994). Current perspectives on dual-career families. *Current Directions in Psychological Science, 3,* 101–105.

Gilbert, M., & Shmukler, D. (1997). *Brief therapy with couples: An integrative approach.* New York: Wiley.

Gilbert, S. (2005, April 19). Married with problems? Therapy may not help. *New York Times,* F1.

Gilligan, C. (1982). *In a different voice: Psychological theory and women's development.* Cambridge, MA: Harvard University Press.

Giordano, J., & Carini-Giordano, M. A. (1995). Ethnic dimensions in family treatment. In R. H. Mikesell, S. H. McDaniel, & D-D. Lusterman (Eds.), *Integrating family therapy* (pp. 347–356). Washington, DC: American Psychological Association.

Gladding, S. T. (1988). *Milestones.* Unpublished manuscript.

Gladding, S. T. (1991d). *Eli.* Unpublished manuscript.

Gladding, S. T. (1991c). *Monday nights.* Unpublished manuscript.

Gladding, S. T. (1991a). *Present vows and memories.* Unpublished manuscript.

Gladding, S. T. (1991b). *The fight.* Unpublished manuscript.

Gladding, S. T. (1992b). *A life in a day of aging.* Unpublished manuscript.

Gladding, S. T. (1992c). *Blendings.* Unpublished manuscript.

Gladding, S. T. (1992d). *Differences in awareness.* Unpublished manuscript.

Gladding, S. T. (1992a). *On the death of Paul.* Unpublished manuscript.

Gladding, S. T. (1992e). *Past presence.* Unpublished manuscript.

Gladding, S. T. (1993a). *Beecher Road.* Unpublished manuscript.

Gladding, S. T. (1993b). *First request.* Unpublished manuscript.

Gladding, S. T. (1993c). *Birth and Resolve.* Unpublished manuscript.

Gladding, S. T. (1993d). *Nervous beginnings.* Unpublished manuscript.

Gladding, S. T. (1996). *Small change.* Unpublished manuscript.

Gladding, S. T. (2002). *Becoming a counselor: The light, the bright, and the serious.* Alexandria, VA: American Counseling Association.

Gladding, S. T. (2004a). *Counseling: A comprehensive profession* (5th ed.). Upper Saddle River, NJ: Merrill/Prentice Hall.

Gladding, S. T. (2004b). *From whom I am descended.* Unpublished manuscript.

Gladding, S. T. (2005a). *Counseling as an art: The creative arts in counseling* (3rd ed.). Alexandria, VA: American Counseling Association.

Gladding, S. T. (2005b). *Going beyond pretend.* Unpublished manuscript.

Gladding, S. T., Remley, T. P., Jr., & Huber, C. H. (2001). *Ethical, legal and professional issues in the practice of marriage and family therapy* (3rd ed.). Upper Saddle River, NJ: Merrill/Prentice Hall.

Gladding, S. T., Wilcoxon, S. A., Semon, M. G., & Myers, P. (1992). Individual and marriage/family counseling supervision: Similarities, differences, and implications for training. *Journal of the Florida Association for Counseling and Development, 1,* 58–71.

Gladow, N. W., & Ray, M. P. (1986). The impact of informal support systems on the well-being of low income single-parents. *Family Relations, 35,* 113–123.

Glang, C., & Betis, A. (1993). Helping children through the divorce process. *PsychSpeak, 13,* 1–2.

Glenn, N. D. (1990). Quantitative research on marital quality in the 1980s: A critical review. *Journal of Marriage and Family, 52,* 818–831.

Glenn, N., & McLanahan, S. (1982). Children and marital happiness: A further specification of the relationship. *Journal of Marriage and Family, 43,* 63–72.

Glenwick, D. S., & Mowrey, J. D. (1986). When parent becomes peer: Loss of intergenerational boundaries in single-parent families. *Family Relations, 35,* 57–62.

Glick, P. C. (1988). The role of divorce in the changing family structure: Trends and variations. In S. A. Wolchik & P. Karoly (Eds.), *Children of divorce: Empirical perspectives on adjustment* (pp. 3–34). New York: Gardner.

Glick, P. C. (1989). Remarried families, stepfamilies, and stepchildren: A brief demographic profile. *Family Relations, 38,* 24–27.

Gold, J. M. (1997). Assessing education in marriage and family counseling. *The Family Journal: Counseling and Therapy for Couples and Families, 5,* 159–163.

Gold, J. M., & Morris, G. M. (2003). Family resistance to counseling: The initial agenda for intergenerational and narrative approaches. *The Family Journal: Counseling and Therapy for Couples and Families, 11,* 374–379.

Gold, J. M., & Wilson, J. S. (2002). Legitimizing the child-free family: The role of the family counselor. *The Family Journal: Counseling and Therapy for Couples and Families, 10,* 70–74.

Gold, J. M., Bubenzer, D. L., & West, J. D. (1993). Differentiation from ex-spouses and stepfamily marital intimacy. *Journal of Divorce and Remarriage, 19,* 83–95.

Goldberg, J. R. (1993, August). Is multicultural family therapy in sight? *Family Therapy News, 24,* 1, 7, 8, 16, 21.

Golden, L. B. (Ed.). (2004). *Case studies in marriage and family therapy* (2nd ed.). Upper Saddle River, NJ: Prentice Hall.

Goldenberg, H., & Goldenberg, I. (1993). Multiculturalism and family systems: Progress. *Family Systems Research and Therapy, 2,* 7–12.

Goldenberg, H., & Goldenberg, I. (2002). *Counseling today's families* (4th ed.). Pacific Grove, CA: Brooks/Cole.

Goldiamond, I. (1965). Self-control procedures in personal behavior problems. *Psychological Reports, 17,* 851–868.

Goldin, E., & Mohr, R. (2000). Issues and techniques for counseling long-term, later-life couples. *The Family Journal: Counseling and Therapy for Couples and Families, 8,* 229–235.

Goldman, L. (1990). Qualitative assessment. *The Counseling Psychologist, 18,* 205–213.

Goldsmith, J. (1982). The postdivorce family system. In F. Walsh (Ed.), *Normal family processes* (pp. 297–330). New York: Guilford.

Gorden, R. (1992). *Basic interviewing skills*. Itasca, IL: F. E. Peacock.

Gordon, K. C., Baucom, D. H., & Synder, D. K. (2004). An integrative intervention for promoting recovery from extramarital affairs. *Journal of Marital and Family Therapy, 30*, 213–231.

Gordon, L. H., Temple, R. R., & Adams, D. W. (2005). Premarital counseling from the PAIRS perspective. In M. Harway (Ed.), *Handbook of couples therapy* (pp. 7–27). New York: Wiley.

Gordon, S. B., & Davidson, N. (1981). Behavioral parent training. In A. S. Gurman & D. P. Kniskern (Eds.), *Handbook of family therapy*. New York: Brunner/Mazel.

Gorman-Smith, D., Tolan, P. H., Zelli, A., & Huesmann, L. R. (1996). The relation of family functioning to violence among inner-city minority youth. *Journal of Family Psychology, 10*, 115–129.

Gose, B. (1996, July 12). Study finds children of divorced parents less likely to enroll at selective colleges. *Chronicle of Higher Education, XLII*, A35–A36.

Gottman, J. M. (1994). *What predicts divorce? The relationship between marital processes and marital outcomes*. Hillsdale, NJ: Lawrence Erlbaum.

Gottman, J. M., Gonso, J., Notarius, C., & Markman, H. (1978). *A couple's guide to communication*. Champaign, IL: Research Press.

Gottman, J. M., Jacobson, N. S., Rushe, R. H., Wu Shortt, J., Babcock, J., La Tallade, J. J., & Waltz, J. (1995). The relationship between heart rate reactivity, emotionally aggressive behavior, and general violence in batterers. *Journal of Family Psychology, 9*, 227–248.

Gottman, J. M., Coan, J., Carrere, S., & Swanson, C. (1998). Predicting marital happiness and stability from newlywed interactions. *Journal of Marriage and Family, 60*, 5–22.

Gottman, J. M., & Silver, N. (1999). *The seven principles of making marriage work*. New York: Three Rivers Press.

Gould, R. L. (1972). The phases of adult life: A study in developmental psychology. *American Journal of Psychiatry, 129*, 521–531.

Gould, R. L. (1978). *Transformations*. New York: Simon and Schuster.

Gray, R. E. (1987). Adolescent response to the death of a parent. *Journal of Youth and Adolescence, 16*, 511–525.

Gray, R. E. (1988). The role of school counselors with bereaved teenagers: With and without peer support. *The School Counselor, 35*, 185–193.

Gray, R. E. (1989). Adolescent's perceptions of social support after the death of a parent. *Journal of Psychosocial Oncology, 7*, 127–144.

Greene, G. J., Hamilton, N., & Rolling, M. (1986). Differentiation of self and psychiatric diagnosis: An empirical study. *Family Therapy, 8*, 187–194.

Green, S. L., & Hansen, J. C. (1986). Ethical dilemmas in family therapy. *Journal of Marital and Family Therapy, 12*, 225–230.

Green, S. L., & Hansen, J. C. (1989). Ethical dilemmas faced by family therapists. *Journal of Marital and Family Therapy, 15*, 149–158.

Greenberg, L. S., & Johnson, S. M. (1986). Emotionally focused couple therapy. In N. Jacobson & A. Gurman (Eds.), *Clinical handbook of marital therapy* (pp. 253–276). New York: Guilford.

Greenwalt, B. C., Sklare, G., & Portes, P. (1998). The therapeutic treatment provided in cases involving physical child abuse: A description of current practices. *Child Abuse and Neglect, 22*, 71–78.

Gregory, M. A., & Leslie, L. A. (1996). Different lenses: Variations in clients' perception of family therapy by race and gender. *Journal of Marital and Family Therapy, 22*, 239–251.

Griffin, J. E., & D'Andrea, L. M. (1998). Using FACES II to classify the relationship status of battered women. *The Family Journal: Counseling and Therapy for Couples and Families, 5*, 303–308.

Griffith, B. A., & Rotter, J. C. (1999). Families and spirituality: Therapists as facilitators. *The Family Journal: Counseling and Therapy for Couples and Families, 7*, 161–164.

Grosser, G. H., & Paul, N. L. (1964). Ethical issues in family group therapy. *American Journal of Orthopsychiatry, 34*, 875–884.

Grotevant, H. D., & Carlson, C. I. (1989). *Family assessment: A guide to methods and measures*. New York: Guilford.

Grove, D. R., & Haley, J. (1993). *Conversations on therapy: Popular problems and uncommon solutions*. New York: Norton.

Groze, V. (1991). Adoption and single-parents: A review. *Child Welfare, 70*, 321–332.

Guerin, P. J. (1976). Family therapy: The first twenty-five years. In P. J. Guerin (Ed.), *Family therapy: Theory and practice* (pp. 2–22). New York: Gardner.

Guerney, B. G., Jr. (1977). *Relationship enhancement*. San Francisco: Jossey-Bass.

Guerney, L. (1991). Parents as partners in treating behavior problems in early childhood settings. *Topics in Early Childhood Special Education, 11*, 74–90.

Guerney, L. F., & Guerney, B. G. (1994). Child relationship enhancement: Family therapy and parent education. In C. E. Schaefer & L. J. Carey (Eds.), *Family play therapy* (pp. 127–138). Northvale, NJ: Aronson.

Gurel, L. (1999, June). John Elderkin Bell (1913–1995). *American Psychologist, 54*, 434.

Gurman, A. S., & Fraenkel, P. (2002). The history of couple therapy: A millennial review. *Family Process, 41*, 199–260.

Gurman, A. S., & Kniskern, D. P. (1981). Family therapy outcome research: Knowns and unknowns. In A. S. Gurman & D. P. Kniskern (Eds.), *Handbook of family therapy*. New York: Brunner/Mazel.

Gurman, A. S., & Kniskern, D. P. (1981). Preface. In A. S. Gurman & D. P. Kniskern (Eds.), *Handbook of family therapy* (pp. xiii–xviii). New York: Brunner/Mazel.

Gurman, A. S., Kniskern, D. P., & Pinsof, W. M. (1986). Research on the process and outcome of marital and family therapy. In S. L. Garfield & A. E. Bergin (Eds.), *Handbook of psychotherapy and behavioral change* (3rd ed., pp. 565–624). New York: Wiley.

Gushue, G. V. (1993). Cultural-identity development and family assessment: An interactive model. *The Counseling Psychologist, 21*, 487–513.

Gutterman, J. T., Mecias, A., & Ainbinder, D. L. (2005). Solution-focused treatment of migraine headache. *The Family Journal: Counseling and Therapy for Couples and Families, 13,* 195–198.

Guy, J. D. (1987). *The personal life of the psychotherapist.* New York: Wiley.

Hackney, H., & Cormier, L. S. (2005). *The professional counselor: A process guide to helping* (5th ed.). Boston: Allyn & Bacon.

Hafner, R. J. (1986). *Marriage & mental illness.* New York: Guilford.

Hahlweg, K., Baucom, D. H., & Markman, H. (1988). Recent advances in therapy and prevention. In I. R. H. Falloon (Ed.), *Handbook of behavioral family therapy.* New York: Guilford.

Haley, J. (1963). *Strategies of psychotherapy.* New York: Grune & Stratton.

Haley, J. (1969). *The power tactics of Jesus Christ and other essays.* New York: Grossman.

Haley, J. (1973). *Uncommon therapy: The psychiatric techniques of Milton Erickson, M.D.* New York: Norton.

Haley, J. (1976a). Development of a theory: A history of a research project. In C. E. Sluzki & D. C. Ransom (Eds.), *Double-bind: The foundation of the communication approach to the family.* New York: Grune & Stratton.

Haley, J. (1976b). *Problem-solving therapy.* San Francisco: Jossey-Bass.

Haley, J. (1978). Ideas which handicap therapists. In M. M. Berger (Ed.), *Beyond the double bind.* New York: Brunner/Mazel.

Haley, J. (1980). *Leaving home: The therapy of disturbed young people.* New York: McGraw-Hill.

Haley, J. (1984). *Ordeal therapy.* San Francisco: Jossey-Bass.

Haley, J. (1987). *Problem solving therapy* (2nd ed.). San Francisco: Jossey-Bass.

Haley, J. (1990). Interminable therapy. In J. Zeig & S. Gilligan (Eds.), *Brief therapy: Myths, methods, and metaphors.* New York: Brunner/Mazel.

Halford, W. K., Markman, H. J., Kline, G. H., & Stanley, S. M. (2003). Best practice in couple relationship education. *Journal of Marital and Family Therapy, 29,* 385–406.

Hampson, R. B., Beavers, W. R., & Hulgus, Y. (1990). Cross-ethnic family differences: Interactional assessment of white, black, and Mexican-American families. *Journal of Marital and Family Therapy, 16,* 307–319.

Hampson, R. B., Prince, C. C., & Beavers, W. R. (1999). Marital therapy: Qualities of couples who fare better or worse in treatment. *Journal of Marital and Family Therapy, 25,* 411–424.

Hannon, K. (1996, May 13). Upset? Try cybertherapy. *U.S. News and World Report,* pp. 81–83.

Hanson, S. M. (1986). Healthy single-parent families. *Family Relations, 35,* 125–132.

Hare-Mustin, R. T. (1978). A feminist approach to family therapy. *Family Process, 17,* 181–194.

Hare-Mustin, R. T. (1987). The problem of gender in family therapy theory. *Family Process, 26,* 15–27.

Harrigan, M. P. (1992). Advantages and disadvantages of multigenerational family households: Views of three generations. *Journal of Applied Gerontology, 11,* 457–474.

Hartigan, J., Jr. (1997). When White Americans are a minority. In L. L. Naylor (Ed.), *Cultural diversity in the United States* (pp. 103–115). Westport, CT: Bergin & Garvey.

Haslam, D., & Harris, S. (2004). Informed consent documents of marriage and family therapists in private practice: A qualitative analysis. *American Journal of Family Therapy, 32,* 359–374.

Hawley, D. R., & Geske, S. (2000). The use of theory in family therapy research: A content analysis of family therapy journals. *Journal of Marital and Family Therapy, 26,* 17–22.

Hawley, D. R., & Gonzalez, C. (2005). Publication patterns of faculty in Commission on Accreditation for Marriage and Family Therapy Education programs. *Journal of Marital and Family Therapy, 31,* 89–98.

Hayes, R. L., & Hayes, B. A. (1986). Remarriage families: Counseling parents, stepparents, and their children. *Counseling and Human Development, 18*(7), 1–8.

Hayes, R. L., & Hayes, B. A. (1991). Counseling remarried families. In G. Carlson & J. Lewis (Eds.), *Family counseling: Strategies and issues* (pp. 175–188). Denver: Love.

Heiman, J. R., LoPiccolo, L., & LoPiccolo, J. (1981). The treatment of sexual dysfunction. In A. S. Gurman & D. P. Kniskern (Eds.), *Handbook of family therapy.* New York: Brunner/Mazel.

Henderson, M. C. (1987). Paradoxical process and ethical consciousness. *Family Therapy, 14,* 187–193.

Henry, R., & Miller, R. (2004). Marital problems occurring in midlife: Implications for couples therapists. *American Journal of Family Therapy, 32,* 405–417.

Hernandez, B. C., & Doherty, W. J. (2005). Marriage and family therapists and psychotropic medications: Practice patterns from a national study. *Journal of Marital and Family Therapy, 31,* 177–189.

Herring, R. D. (1989). The Native American family: Dissolution by coercion. *Journal of Multicultural Counseling and Development, 17,* 4–13.

Herring, R. D. (1991). Counseling Native American youth. In C. C. Lee & B. L. Richardson (Eds.), *Multicultural issues in counseling: New approaches to diversity* (pp. 37–47). Alexandria, VA: American Counseling Association.

Hershenson, D. B., & Power, P. W. (1987). *Mental health counseling: Theory and practice.* New York: Pergamon.

Hetherington, E. M. (1990). Coping with family transitions: Winners, losers, and survivors. *Child Development, 60,* 1–14.

Hetherington, E. M. (1991). Families, lies and videotapes. *Journal of Research on Adolescence, 1,* 323–348.

Hetherington, E. M. (2004). Marriage and divorce American style. In K. R. Glibert (Ed.), *Annual editions: The family 2004/2005* (pp. 166–168). Guilford, CT: McGraw-Hill/Dushkin.

Hetherington, E. M., & Kelly, J. (2003). *For better or for worse: Divorce reconsidered.* New York: Norton.

Hetherington, E. M., Cox, M., & Cox, R. (1981). The aftermath of divorce. In E. M. Hetherington & R. D. Parke

(Eds.), *Contemporary readings in child psychology* (2nd ed., pp. 99–109). New York: McGraw-Hill.

Hickey, D., Carr, A., Dooley, B., Guerin, S., Butler, E., & Fitzpatrick, L. (2005). Family and marital profiles of couples in which one partner has depression or anxiety. *Journal of Marital and Family Therapy, 31*, 171–182.

Hill, A. (1989). Treatment and prevention of alcoholism in the Native American family. In G. W. Lawson & A. W. Lawson (Eds.), *Alcoholism and substance abuse in special populations* (pp. 247–272). Rockville, MD: Aspen.

Hill, N., & Crews, J. (2005). The application of an ethical lens to the issue of diagnosis in marriage and family counseling. *The Family Journal: Counseling and Therapy for Couples and Families, 13*, 176–180.

Hill, R. (1949). *Families under stress: Adjustment to the crisis of war, separation, and reunion.* Westport, CT: Greenwood.

Hill, R. (1972). *The strengths of black families.* New York: Emerson-Hall.

Hill, R. (1986). Life cycle stages for types of single-parent families: Of family developmental theory. *Family Relations, 35*, 19–29.

Hines, M. (1988). Similarities and differences in group and family therapy. *Journal for Specialists in Group Work, 13*, 173–179.

Hines, M. (1998). Acceptance versus change in behavior therapy: An interview with Neil Jacobson. *The Family Journal: Counseling and Therapy for Couples and Families, 6*, 244–251.

Hines, P., & Boyd-Franklin, N. (1996). African American families. In M. McGoldrick, J. Giordano, & J. K. Pearce (Eds.), *Ethnicity and family therapy* (2nd ed.). New York: Guilford.

Hines, P. M., Garcia-Preto, N., McGoldrick, M., Almeida, R., & Weltman, S. (1992). Intergenerational relationships across cultures. *Families in Society: The Journal of Contemporary Human Services, 73*, 323–338.

Hines, P. M., Preto, N. G., McGoldrick, M., Almeida, R., & Weltman, S. (1999). Culture and the family life cycle. In B. Carter & M. McGoldrick (Eds.), *The expanded family life cycle* (3rd ed., pp. 69–87). Boston: Allyn & Bacon.

Ho, M. K. (1987). *Family therapy with ethnic minorities.* Newbury Park, CA: Sage.

Hochschild, A. (1989). *The second shift: Working parents and the revolution at home.* New York: Viking.

Hodas, G. R. (1994). Reversing narratives of failure through music and verse in therapy. *The Family Journal: Counseling and Therapy for Couples and Families, 2*, 199–207.

Hodges, M. (1989). Culture and family therapy. *Journal of Family Therapy, 11*, 117–128.

Hohenshil, T. H. (2000). High tech counseling. *Journal of Counseling and Development, 78*, 365–368.

Holland, J. L. (1973). *Making vocational choices: A theory of vocational personalities and work environments* (3rd ed.). Sarasota, FL: Psychological Assessment Resource.

Hollist, C., & Miller, R. (2005). Perceptions of attachment style and marital quality in midlife marriages. *Family Relations, 54*, 46–57.

Holmes, T. H., & Rahe, R. H. (1967). The social readjustment rating scale. *Journal of Psychosomatic Research, 2*, 213–228.

Hong, G. K. (1989). Application of cultural and environmental issues in family therapy with immigrant Chinese Americans. *Journal of Strategic and Systemic Therapies, 8*, 14–21.

Hood, A. B., & Johnson, R. W. (2002). *Assessment in counseling* (3rd ed.). Alexandria, VA: American Counseling Association.

Hopkins, B. R., & Anderson, B. S. (1990). *The counselor and the law* (3rd ed.). Alexandria, VA: American Counseling Association.

Horne, A., & Sayger, T. V. (2000). Behavioral approaches to couple and family therapy. In A. M. Horne (Ed.), *Family counseling and therapy* (3rd ed., pp. 454–488). Itasca, IL: F. E. Peacock.

Horne, K. B., & Hicks, M. W. (2002). All in the family: A belated response to Knudson-Martin's feminist revision of Bowen theory. *Journal of Marital and Family Therapy, 28*, 103–113.

Hovestadt, A. J. (2000). Unresolved couple conflict: Clinical use of the family of origin scale. In R. E. Watts (Ed.), *Techniques in marriage and family counseling* (pp. 75–80). Alexandria, VA: American Counseling Association.

Hovestadt, A. J., Anderson, W. T., Piercy, F. P., Cochran, S. W., & Fine, M. (1985). A family of origin scale. *Journal of Marital and Family Therapy, 11*, 287–297.

Howell, L. C., Weers, R., & Kleist, D. M. (1998). Counseling blended families. *The Family Journal: Counseling and Therapy for Couples and Families, 6*, 42–45.

Hubble, M. A. (1993, Spring). Therapy research: The bonfire of the uncertainties. *The Family Psychologist, 9*, 14–16.

Huber, C. H. (1993). Balancing family health and illness. *The Family Journal: Counseling and Therapy for Couples and Families, 1*, 69–71.

Huber, C. H. (1995). Counselor responsibility within managed mental health care. *The Family Journal: Counseling and Therapy for Couples and Families, 3*, 42–44.

Huber, C. H., Mascari, J. B., & Sanders-Mascari, A. (1991). Family mediation. In J. Carlson & J. Lewis (Eds.), *Family counseling: Strategies and issues.* Denver: Love.

Hudson, P. O., & O'Hanlon, W. H. (1991). *Rewriting love stories: Brief marital therapy.* New York: Norton.

Hughes, F. P., & Noppe, L. D. (1991). *Human development across the life span.* Upper Saddle River, NJ: Merrill/Prentice Hall.

Hundert, E. M. (1987). A model for ethical problem solving in medicine, with practical applications. *American Journal of Psychiatry, 144*, 839–846.

Hurvitz, N. (1967). Marital problems following psychotherapy with one spouse. *Journal of Consulting and Clinical Psychology, 31*, 38–47.

Hutchins, J. (1995, December). Barrett calls for MFT mediation for false memory families. *Family Therapy News, 26*, 21.

Hutchins, J. (1995, December). Industry downsizing, increased provider risk, and niche marketing are trends, say experts. *Family Therapy News, 26*, 15.

Hutchins, J. (1996, April). Beyond office sharing: Starting a group practice. *Family Therapy News, 27, 7,* 22.

Hyde, C., Bentovim, A., & Monck, E. (1995). Some clinical and methodological implications of a treatment outcome study of sexually abused children. *Child Abuse and Neglect, 19,* 1387–1399.

Ihinger-Tallman, M., & Pasley, K. (1987). *Remarriage.* Newbury Park, CA: Sage.

Imber-Black, E. (1988a). *Families and larger systems: A family therapist's guide through the labyrinth.* New York: Guilford.

Imber-Black, E. (1988b). Normative and therapeutic rituals in couple therapy. In E. Imber-Black, J. Roberts, & R. Whiting (Eds.), *Rituals in families and family therapy.* New York: Norton.

Imber-Black, E. (1989, July/August). Creating rituals in therapy. *Family Therapy Networker, 13,* 39–47.

Imber-Black, E. (1999). Creating meaningful rituals for new life cycle transitions. In B. Carter & M. McGoldrick (Eds.), *The expanded family life cycle* (3rd ed., pp. 202–214). Boston: Allyn & Bacon.

Imber-Black, E., Roberts, J., & Whiting, R. (1989). *Rituals in families and in family therapy.* New York: Norton.

Inclan, J. (1990). Understanding Hispanic families: A curriculum outline. *Journal of Strategic and Systemic Therapies, 9,* 64–82.

Ingrassia, M. (1993, August 30). Endangered family. *Newsweek,* pp. 17–27.

International Association of Marriage and Family Counselors. (2002). Ethical standards. Retrieved July 4, 2005, from http://iamfc.com/ethical_codes.html.

Irwin, E., & Malloy, E. (1975). Family puppet interview. *Family Process, 14,* 179–191.

Jacobson, N. S. (1985). Family therapy outcome research: Potential pitfalls and prospects. *Journal of Marital and Family Therapy, 11,* 149–158.

Jacobson, N. S. (1988). Guidelines for the design of family therapy outcome research. In L. C. Wynne (Ed.), *The state of the art in family therapy research* (pp. 139–155). New York: Family Process.

Jacobson, N. S. (1994). Rewards and dangers in researching domestic violence. *Family Process, 33,* 81–85.

Jacobson, N. S., Gottman, J. M., & Wu Shortt, J. (1995). The distinction between Type I and Type II batterers—Further considerations. *Journal of Family Psychology, 9,* 272–279.

Jaffe, D. T. (1991). *Working with the ones you love.* Berkeley, CA: Conari.

Janson, G. R., & Steigerwald, F. J. (2002). Family counseling and ethical challenges with Gay, Lesbian, Bisexual, and Transgendered (GLBT) clients: More questions than answers. *The Family Journal: Counseling and Therapy for Couples and Families, 10,* 415–418.

Jayson, S. (2005a, June 22). Hearts divide over marital therapy. *USA Today,* pp. 1D, 2D.

Jayson, S. (2005b, July 18). Divorce declining, but so is marriage. *USA Today,* p. 3A.

Jefferson, C. (1978). Some notes on the use of family sculpture in therapy. *Family Process, 17,* 69–76.

Jencius, M. (2003). The thing called love: An interview with Susan Johnson. *The Family Journal: Counseling and Therapy for Couples and Families, 11,* 427–434.

Jencius, M., & Duba, J. D. (2003). The marriage of research and practice: An interview with John M. Gottman. *The Family Journal: Counseling and Therapy for Couples and Families, 11,* 216–223.

Jester, S. (1995, December). Legal and risk management plan and Practice Strategies newsletter join growing list of AAMFT member benefits. *Family Therapy News, 26,* 7.

Johnson, A. C. (1995). Resiliency mechanisms in culturally diverse families. *The Family Journal: Counseling and Therapy for Couples and Families, 3,* 316–324.

Johnson, L., & Thomas, V. (1999). Influences on the inclusion of children in family therapy. *Journal of Marital and Family Therapy, 25,* 117–123.

Johnson, L., Bruhn, R., Winek, J., Krepps, J., & Wiley, K. (1999). The use of child-centered play therapy and filial therapy with Head Start families: A brief report. *Journal of Marital and Family Therapy, 25,* 169–176.

Johnson, M. E., Fortman, J. B., & Brems, C. (1993). *Between two people: Exercises toward intimacy.* Alexandria, VA: American Counseling Association.

Johnson, S. M. (1998). Emotionally focused couple therapy. In F. M. Dattilio (Ed.), *Case studies in couple and family therapy* (pp. 450–472). New York: Guilford.

Johnson, S. M. (2003). The revolution in couple therapy: A practitioner-scientist perspective. *Journal of Marital and Family Therapy, 29,* 365–384.

Johnson, S. M. (2004). *The practice of emotionally focused marital therapy: Creating connections* (2nd ed.). New York: Brunner/Routledge.

Johnson, S. M., & Lebow, J. (2000). The "coming of age" of couple therapy: A decade review. *Journal of Marital and Family Therapy, 26,* 23–38.

Johnson, T. W., & Colucci, P. (1999). Lesbians, gay men, and the family life cycle. In B. Carter & M. McGoldrick (Eds.), *The expanded family life cycle* (3rd ed., pp. 346–361). Boston: Allyn & Bacon.

Jones, C. (1993, April 12). Alone: Marriage rate for blacks is declining. *Winston-Salem (NL) Journal,* pp. 43–44.

Jordan, K., & Stevens, P. (1999). Revising the ethical code of the IAMFC–A training exercise for counseling psychology and counselor education students. *The Family Journal: Counseling and Therapy for Couples and Families, 7,* 170–175.

Jory, B., & Anderson, D. (1999). Intimate justice II: Mutuality, reciprocity, and accommodation in therapy for psychological abuse. *Journal of Marital and Family Therapy, 25,* 349–364.

Jory, B., & Anderson, D. (2000). Intimate justice III: Healing the anguish of abuse and embracing the anguish of accountability. *Journal of Marital and Family Therapy, 26,* 329–340.

Jory, B., Anderson, D., & Greer, C. (1997). Intimate justice: Confronting issues of accountability, respect, and freedom in treatment for abuse and violence. *Journal of Marital and Family Therapy, 23,* 399–419.

Jourard, S. M., & Landsman, T. (1980). *Healthy personality* (4th ed.). New York: Macmillan.

Juarez, R. (1985). Core issues in psychotherapy with Hispanic children. *Psychotherapy, 22*, 441–448.

Jung, M. (1984). Structural family therapy: Its application to Chinese families. *Family Process, 23*, 365–374.

Juhnke, G. A. (1993). *Effective family counseling: Applications for school counselors.* Paper presented at the 66th annual convention of the North Carolina Counseling Association, Raleigh, NC.

Kalima, I. (2005). The technique of "redirection" in couple therapy. *The Family Journal: Counseling and Therapy for Couples and Families, 13*, 199–200.

Kane, C. M. (1994). Family making: A Satir approach to treating the H. family. *The Family Journal: Counseling and Therapy for Couples and Families, 2*, 256–258.

Kane, C. M., & Erdman, P. (1998). Differences in family-of-origin perceptions among African American, Anglo-American, and Hispanic college students. *The Family Journal: Counseling and Therapy for Couples and Families, 6*, 13–18.

Kaplan, D. M. (2000a). Using an informed consent brochure to help establish a solid therapeutic relationship. In R. E. Watts (Ed.), *Techniques in marriage and family counseling* (pp. 3–10). Alexandria, VA: American Counseling Association.

Kaplan, D. M. (2000b). Who are our giants? *The Family Digest, 12*(4), 1, 6.

Kaplan, D. M., & Allison, M. (1993a). Family ethics. *The Family Journal: Counseling and Therapy for Couples and Families, 1*, 72–77.

Kaplan, D. M., & Allison, M. (1993b). Family ethics. *The Family Journal: Counseling and Therapy for Couples and Families, 1*, 246–248.

Kaplan, D. M., & Culkin, M. (1995). Family ethics: Lessons learned. *The Family Journal: Counseling and Therapy for Couples and Families, 3*, 335–338.

Kaplan, H. S. (1974). *The new sex therapy.* New York: Quadrangle.

Kaslow, F. W. (1980). History of family therapy in the United States: A kaleidoscopic overview. *Marriage and Family Review, 3*, 77–111.

Kaslow, F. (1990). *Voices in family psychology.* Newbury Park, CA: Sage.

Kaslow, F. W. (1991). The art and science of family psychology. *American Psychologist, 46*, 621–626.

Katkin, E. S. (1978). Charting as a multipurpose treatment intervention in family therapy. *Family Process, 17*, 465–468.

Kaufman, S. R. (1986). *The ageless self: Sources of meaning in later life.* Madison, WI: University of Wisconsin Press.

Kay, E. (2003). *Heroes at home.* Minneapolis, MN: Bethany House.

Kazdin, A. E., Stolar, M. J., & Marciano, P. L. (1995). Risk factors for dropping out of treatment among white and black families. *Journal of Family Psychology, 9*, 402–417.

Keeney, B. (1983). *The aesthetics of change.* New York: Guilford.

Keeney, B. P. (1986). Cybernetics of the absurd: A tribute to Carl Whitaker. *Journal of Strategic and Systemic Therapies, 5*, 20–28.

Keeney, B. (1990). *Improvisational therapy.* St. Paul, MN: Systemic Therapy.

Keim, J. (2000). Strategic family therapy. In A. Horne (Ed.), *Family counseling and therapy* (3rd ed., pp. 170–207). Itasca, IL: F. E. Peacock.

Keim, J. (2000). Strategic family therapy: The Washington School. In A. M. Horne (Ed.), *Family counseling and therapy* (3rd ed., pp. 170–207). Itasca, IL: F. E. Peacock.

Keith, D. V. (1987). Intuition in family therapy: A short manual on post-modern witchcraft. *Contemporary Family Therapy, 9*, 11–22.

Keith, D. V., & Whitaker, C. A. (1982). Experiential/symbolic family therapy. In A. M. Horne & M. M. Ohlsen (Eds.), *Family counseling and therapy* (pp. 43–74). Itasca, IL: F. E. Peacock.

Kemp, A. (1998). *Abuse in the family: An introduction.* Pacific Grove, CA: Brooks/Cole.

Kempler, W. (1968). Experiential psychotherapy with families. *Family Process, 7*, 88–89.

Kernberg, O. F. (1976). *Object-relations theory and clinical psychoanalysis.* New York: Jason Aronson.

Kerr, M. E. (1981). Family systems theory and therapy. In A. S. Gurman & D. P. Kniskern (Eds.), *Handbook of family therapy.* New York: Brunner/Mazel.

Kerr, M. E. (1988). Chronic anxiety and defining a self. *The Atlantic Monthly, 262*, 35–37, 40–44, 46–58.

Kerr, M. E. (2003, August). *Process of differentiation.* Paper presented at the 111th Annual Convention of the American Psychological Association, Toronto, Canada.

Kerr, M. E., & Bowen, M. (1988). *Family evaluation: An approach based on Bowen theory.* New York: Norton.

Keyes, C. (1977). *The golden peninsula.* New York: Macmillan.

Kier, F. J., & Lawson, D. M. (1999). A comparison of family-of-origin perceptions of doctoral student psychotherapists with doctoral students in other fields: Implications for training. *The Family Journal: Counseling and Therapy for Couples and Families, 7*, 118–124.

Kilpatrick, A. C. (1980). The Bowen family intervention theory: An analysis for social workers. *Family Therapy, 7*, 167–178.

Kilpatrick, A. C., & Holland, T. P. (1995). *Working with families* (pp. 175–197). Boston: Allyn & Bacon.

Kim, E. Y-K., Bean, R. A., & Harper, J. M. (2004). Do general treatment guidelines for Asian American families have applications to specific ethnic groups? The case of culturally-competent therapy with Korean Americans. *Journal of Marital and Family Therapy, 30*, 359–372.

Kim, J. M. (2003). Structural family therapy and its implications for the Asian American family. *The Family Journal: Counseling and Therapy for Couples and Families, 11*, 388–392.

Kinnier, R. T., Brigman, S. L., & Noble, F. C. (1990). Career indecision and family enmeshment. *Journal of Counseling and Development, 68*, 309–312.

Kiser, D. J., Piercy, F. P., & Lipchik, E. (1993). The integration of emotion in solution-focused therapy. *Journal of Marital and Family Therapy, 19*, 233–242.

Kitson, G. C., & Holmes, W. M. (1992). *Portrait of divorce: Adjustment to marital breakdown*. New York: Guilford.

Klagsbrun, F. (1985). *Married people*. New York: Bantam.

Klein, M. (1948). *Contributions to psychoanalysis, 1921–1945*. London: Hogarth.

Klein, W. (Ed.). (1992). *Austria*. Singapore: Hofer.

Kleinke, C. L. (2002). *Coping with life challenges*. Long Grove, IL: Waveland.

Kleist, D. M. (1999). Single-parent families: A difference that makes a difference? *The Family Journal: Counseling and Therapy for Couples and Families, 7*, 373–378.

Kleist, D. M., & Gompertz, K. (1997). Current use of qualitative research methodology in couples and family counseling. *The Family Journal: Counseling and Therapy for Couples and Families, 5*, 137–143.

Knudson-Martin, C., & Mahoney, A. R. (2005). Moving beyond gender: Processes that create relationship equality. *Journal of Marital and Family Therapy, 31*, 235–246.

Kohut, H. (1971). *The analysis of self*. New York: International Universities Press.

Kohut, H. (1977). *The restoration of the self*. New York: International Universities Press.

Kok, C. J., & Leskela, J. (1996). Solution-focused therapy in a psychiatric hospital. *Journal of Marital and Family Therapy, 22*, 397–406.

Kottler, J. A. (1991). *The compleat therapist*. San Francisco: Jossey-Bass.

Kowal, J., Johnson, S. M., & Lee, A. (2003). Chronic illness in couples: A case for emotionally focused therapy. *Journal of Marital and Family Therapy, 29*, 299–310.

Kral, R., & Hines, M. (1999). A survey study on developmental stages in achieving a competent sense of self as a family therapist. *The Family Journal: Counseling and Therapy for Couples and Families, 7*, 102–111.

Kramer, J. J., & Conoley, J. C. (Eds.). (1992). *The eleventh mental measurements yearbook*. Lincoln, NE: Buros Institute of Mental Measurement.

Krasner, L., & Houts, A. C. (1984). A study of the "value" systems of behavioral scientists. *American Psychologist, 39*, 840–850.

Krauth, L. D. (1995, December). Single-parent families: The risk to children. *Family Therapy News, 26*(6), 14.

Krauth, L. D. (1995, December). Strength-based therapies. *Family Therapy News, 26*, 24.

Krein, S. F. (1986). Growing up in a single-parent family: The effects on education and earnings of young men. *Family Relations, 35*, 161–168.

Krestan, J., & Bepko, C. (1988). Alcohol problems and the family life cycle. In B. Carter & M. McGoldrick (Eds.), *The changing family life cycle* (2nd ed., pp. 483–511). New York: Gardner.

Krysan, M., Moore, K. A., & Zill, N. (1990). *Identifying successful families: An overview of constructs and selected measures*. Washington, DC: Child Trends.

Kurilla, V. (1998). Multicultural counseling perspectives: Culture specificity and implications in family therapy. *The Family Journal: Counseling and Therapy for Couples and Families, 6*, 207–211.

Kurpius, D. J., & Fuqua, D. R. (1993). Fundamental issues in defining consultation. *Journal of Counseling & Development, 71*, 598–600.

Kurtz, P. D., & Tandy, C. C. (1995). Narrative family interventions. In A. C. Kilpatrick & T. P. Holland (Eds.), *Working with families* (pp. 177–197). Boston: Allyn & Bacon.

Kwiatkowska, H. Y. (1967). Family art therapy. *Family Process, 6*, 37–55.

L'Abate, L. (1992). Family psychology and family therapy: Comparisons and contrasts. *American Journal of Family Therapy, 20*, 3–12.

L'Abate, L., & Bagarozzi, D. A. (1993). *Sourcebook of marriage and family evaluation*. New York: Brunner/Mazel.

LaFountain, R. M., & Mustaine, B. L. (1998). Infusing Adlerian theory into an introductory marriage and family course. *The Family Journal: Counseling and Therapy for Couples and Families, 6*, 189–199.

Laing, R. D. (1965). Mystification, confusion, and conflict. In I. Boszormenyi-Nagy & J. L. Framo (Eds.), *Intensive family therapy: Theoretical and practical aspects*. New York: Harper & Row.

Laing, R. D. (1970). *Knots*. New York: Pantheon.

Laird, J. (1993). Lesbian and gay families. In F. Walsh (Ed.), *Normal family processes* (2nd ed., pp. 282–328). New York: Guilford.

Lambert, S. (2005). Gay and lesbian families: What we know and where to go from here. *The Family Journal: Counseling and Therapy for Couples and Families, 13*, 43–51.

Lambie, R., & Daniels-Mohring, D. (1993). *Family systems within educational contexts*. Denver, CO: Love.

Laqueur, H. P. (1976). Multiple family therapy. In P. Guerin (Ed.), *Family therapy*. New York: Gardner.

Larson, J., & Lamont, C. (2005). The relationship of childhood sexual abuse to the marital attitudes and readiness for marriage of single young adult women. *Journal of Family Issues, 26*, 415–430.

Larson, J. H., Anderson, J. O., & Morgan, A. (1984*). Effective stepparenting*. New York: Family Service Association of America.

Larson, J. H., Newell, K., Topham, G., & Nichols, S. (2002). A review of three comprehensive premarital assessment questionnaires. *Journal of Marital and Family Therapy, 28*, 233–239.

LaSala, M. C. (2002). Walls and bridges: How coupled gay men and lesbians manage their intergenerational relationships. *Journal of Marital and Family Therapy, 28*, 327–339.

Larzelere, R., & Huston, T. (1980). The Dyadic Trust Scale: Toward understanding interpersonal trust in close relationships. *Journal of Marriage and Family, 43*, 595–604.

Lavee, Y., McCubbin, H. I., & Olson, D. H. (1987). The effects of stressful life events and transitions on family functioning and well-being. *Journal of Marriage and Family, 49*, 857–873.

Law, D. D., Crane, D. R., & Berge, J. M. (2003). The influence of individual, marital, and family therapy on high utilizers of health care. *Journal of Marital and Family Therapy, 29*, 353–363.

Lawson, A. W. (1994). Family therapy and addictions. In J. A. Lewis (Ed.), *Addiction: Concepts and strategies for treatment* (pp. 211–232). Gaithersburg, MD: Aspen.

Lawson, D. M. (2003). Incidence, explanations, and treatment of partner violence. *Journal of Counseling and Development, 81,* 19–32.

Lazarus, A. A. (1968). Behavior therapy and group marriage counseling. *Journal of the American Society of Medicine and Dentistry, 15,* 49–56.

Lazarus, A. A. (2000). Working effectively and efficiently with couples. *The Family Journal: Counseling and Therapy for Couples and Families, 8,* 222–228.

Learner, S. (1983). *Constructing the multigenerational family genogram: Exploring a problem in context* (videotape). Topeka, KS: Menninger Video Productions.

Lebow, J. (1995). Open-ended therapy: Termination in marital and family therapy. In R. H. Mikesell, D.-D. Lusterman, & S. H. McDaniel (Eds.), *Integrating family therapy.* (pp. 73–86) Washington, DC: American Psychological Association.

Lebow, J. (2005, May/June). Marital distress. *Family Therapy Magazine,* pp. 38–45.

Lee, C. C. (1991). Cultural dynamics: Their importance in multicultural counseling. In C. C. Lee & B. L. Richardson (Eds.), *Multicultural issues in counseling: New approaches to diversity* (pp. 11–17). Alexandria, VA: American Counseling Association.

Lee, C. C. (1995). Empowering the African American family: New perspectives on single parenthood. *The Family Digest, 8,* 1, 3, 11.

Lee, C. C., & Ramsey, C. J. (2006). Multicultural counseling: A new paradigm for a new century. In C. C. Lee (Ed.), *Multicultural issues in counseling: New approaches to diversity* (pp. 3–11). Alexandria, VA: American Counseling Association.

Lee, C. C., Armstrong, K. L., & Brydges, J. L. (1996). The challenges of a diverse society: Counseling for mutual respect and understanding. *Counseling and Human Development, 28*(5), 1–8.

Lee, M. Y., & Mjelde-Mossey, L. (2004). Cultural dissonance among generations: A solution-focused approach with East Asian elders and their families. *Journal of Marital and Family Therapy, 30,* 497–513.

Lee, R. M. Choe, J., Kim, G., & Ngo, V. (2000). Construction of the Asian American family conflicts scale. *Journal of Counseling Psychology, 47,* 211–222.

Lerner, S. (1999). Interactions between the therapist's and client's life cycle stages. In B. Carter & M. McGoldrick (Eds.), *The expanded life cycle* (3rd ed., pp. 512–519). Boston: Allyn & Bacon.

Leslie, R. S. (2004a, May/June). Termination of treatment: Ethical and legal considerations. *Family Therapy Magazine,* pp. 46–48.

Leslie, R. S. (2004b, July/August). Minimizing liability. *Family Therapy Magazine,* pp. 46–48.

Letich, L. (1993, September/October). A clinician's researcher. *Family Therapy Networker, 17,* 77–82.

Levant, R. F. (2003, August). Couples and couples therapy in a time of social change. Paper presented at the 111th Annual Convention of the American Psychological Association, Toronto, Canada.

Lever, K., & Wilson, J. J. (2005). Encore parenting: When grandparents fill the role of primary caregiver. *The Family Journal: Counseling and Therapy for Couples and Families, 13,* 167–171.

Levine, A. (1990, January 29). The second time around: Realities of remarriage. *U.S. News and World Report,* pp. 50–51.

LeVine, E., & Padilla, A. (1980). *Cross cultures in therapy: Pluralistic counseling for the Hispanic.* Pacific Grove, CA: Brooks/Cole.

Levinson, D. J. (1978). *The seasons of a man's life.* New York: Knopf.

Levinson, D. J. (1986). A conception of adult development. *American Psychologist, 41,* 3–13.

Levitan, S. A., & Conway, E. A. (1990). *Families in flux.* Washington, DC: Bureau of National Affairs.

Levy, P. A., & Hadley, B. J. (1998). Family-of-origin relationships and self-differentiation among university students with bulimic-type behavior. *The Family Journal: Counseling and Therapy for Couples and Families, 6,* 19–23.

Lewis, J. A. (Ed.). (1994). *Addictions: Concepts and strategies for treatment.* Gaithersburg, MD: Aspen.

Lewis, J. M., Beavers, W. R., Gossett, J. T., & Phillips, V. A. (1976). *No single thread: Psychological health in family systems.* New York: Brunner/Mazel.

Lewis, R., Freneau, P., & Roberts, C. (1979). Fathers and the postparental transition. *Family Coordinator, 28,* 514–520.

Liberman, R. P. (1970). Behavioral approaches to family and couple therapy. *American Journal of Orthopsychiatry, 40,* 106–118.

Liberman, R. P., Wheeler, E., deVisser, L. A. J. M., Kuehnel, J., & Kuehnel, T. (1980). *Handbook of marital therapy: A positive approach to helping troubled relationships.* New York: Plenum.

Libow, J. A., Raskin, P. A., & Caust, B. L. (1982). Feminist and family systems therapy: Are they irreconcilable? *American Journal of Family Therapy, 10,* 3–12.

Liddle, H. A. (1992, October). Assessing research productivity and impact. *Family Therapy News, 23,* 17, 29.

Lidz, R. W., & Lidz, T. (1949). The family environment of schizophrenic patients. *American Journal of Psychiatry, 106,* 332–345.

Lidz, T., Cornelison, A., Fleck, S., & Terry, D. (1957). The intrafamilial environment of schizophrenic patients. II: Marital schism and marital skew. *American Journal of Psychiatry, 114,* 241–248.

Locke, H., & Wallace, K. (1959). Short marital adjustment and prediction tests: The reliability and validity. *Marriage and Family Living, 21,* 251–255.

Locke, H. J., Sabagh, G., & Thomas, M. (1956). Correlates of primary communication and empathy. *Research Studies of the State College of Washington, 24,* 116–124.

London, H., & Devore, W. (1992). Layers of understanding: Counseling ethnic minority families. In R. L. Smith & P. Stevens-Smith (Eds.), *Family counseling and therapy* (pp. 358–371). Ann Arbor, MI: ERIC/CAPS.

Long, L. L., & Burnett, J. A. (2005). Teaching couples counseling: An integrative model. *The Family Journal:*

Counseling and Therapy for Couples and Families, 13, 321–327.

Lopez, F. G. (1986). Family structure and depression: Implications for the counseling of depressed college students. *Journal of Counseling and Development, 64,* 508–511.

Lopez, F. G. (1995). Attachment theory as an integrative framework for family counseling. *The Family Journal: Counseling and Therapy for Couples and Families, 3,* 11–17.

Lopez, F. G., Melendez, M. C., & Rice, K. G. (2000). Parental divorce, parent–child bonds, and adult attachment orientation among college students: A comparison of three racial/ethnic groups. *Journal of Counseling Psychology, 47,* 177–186.

LoPiccolo, J. (1978). Direct treatment of sexual dysfunction. In J. LoPiccolo & L. LoPiccolo (Eds.), *Handbook of sex therapy.* New York: Plenum.

LoPiccolo, J. (2002). Postmodern sex therapy. In F. W. Kaslow (Ed.), *Comprehensive handbook of psychotherapy: Integrative/eclectic,* Vol. 4. (pp. 411–435). New York: Wiley.

LoPiccolo, J. (2004). Sexual disorders affecting men. In L. Hass (Ed.), *Handbook of primary care psychology* (pp. 485–494). New York, NY, US: Oxford University Press.

Loy, E., Machen, L., Beaulieu, M., & Greif, G. (2005). Common themes in clinical work with women who are domestically violent. *American Journal of Family Therapy, 33,* 33–44.

Luepnitz, D. A. (1988). *The family interpreted: Feminist theory in clinical practice.* New York: Basic Books.

Lumpkin, P. (1999). *The Stepkin stories: Helping children cope with divorce and adjust to stepfamilies.* Portland, OR: BookPartners.

Lynch, J. J. (1977). *The broken heart: The medical consequences of loneliness.* New York: Basic Books.

Ma, J. L. C. (2005). Family treatment for a Chinese family with an adolescent suffering from anorexia nervosa: A case study. *The Family Journal: Counseling and Therapy for Couples and Families, 13,* 19–26.

Mace, D. (1983). *Prevention in family services.* Beverly Hills, CA: Sage.

Mace, D. (1987). Three ways of helping married couples. *Journal of Marital and Family Therapy, 13,* 179–186.

Mace, D., & Mace, V. (1977). *How to have a happy marriage: A step-by-step guide to an enriched relationship.* Nashville: Abington.

Madanes, C. (1981). *Strategic family therapy.* San Francisco: Jossey-Bass.

Madanes, C. (1984). *Behind the one-way mirror: Advances in the practice of strategic therapy.* San Francisco: Jossey-Bass.

Madanes, C. (1990). *Sex, love, and violence.* New York: Norton.

Madanes, C. (1991). Strategic family therapy. In A. S. Gurman & D. P. Kniskern (Eds.), *Handbook of family therapy* (Vol. II, pp. 396–416). New York: Brunner/Mazel.

Madden-Derdich, D. A., Estrada, A. U., Updegraff, K. A., & Leonard, S. A. (2002). The boundary violations scale: An empirical measure of intergenerational boundary violations in families. *Journal of Marital and Family Therapy, 28,* 241–254.

Maddock, J. W. (1989). Healthy family sexuality: Positive principles for educators and clinicians. *Family Relations, 38,* 130–136.

Magnuson, S., & Shaw, H. E. (2003). Adaptations of the multifaceted genogram in counseling, training, and supervision. *The Family Journal: Counseling and Therapy for Couples and Families, 11,* 45–54.

Main, F., & Oliver, R. (1988). Complementary, symmetrical and parallel personality priorities as indicators of marital adjustment. *Journal of Individual Psychology, 44,* 324–332.

Mamalakis, P. M. (2001). Painting a bigger picture: Forgiveness therapy with premarital infidelity: A case study. *Journal of Family Psychotherapy, 12,* 39–54.

Manson, S. M., Tatum, E., & Dinges, N. G. (1982). Prevention research among American Indian and Alaska Native communities: Charting further courses for theory and practice in mental health. In S. M. Manson (Ed.), *New directions in prevention among American Indian and Alaska Native Communities* (pp. 1–61). Portland, OR: Oregon Health Sciences University.

Marano, H. E. (2004). Divorced? Don't even think of remarrying until you read this. In K. R. Gilbert (Ed.), *Annual Editions: The family 2004/2005* (pp. 178–182). Guilford, CT: McGraw-Hill/Dushkin.

Margolin, G., Chien, D., Duman, S., Fauchier, A., Gordis, E., Oliver, P., Ramos, M., & Vickerman, K. (2005). Ethical issues in couple and family research. *Journal of Family Psychology, 19,* 157–167.

Marine, E. (1995, December). Preserving your records. *Family Therapy News, 26*(6), 11.

Marino, T. W. (1996, August). Families often merge onto a highway of frustration. *Counseling Today,* p. 8.

Markham, H. J., Stanley, S. M., & Blumberg, S. L. (2002). *Fighting for your marriage: Positive steps for preventing divorce and preserving a lasting love.* San Francisco: Jossey-Bass.

Markman, H. J., Renick, M. J., Floyd, F. J., Stanley, S. M., & Clements, M. (1993). Preventing marital distress through communication and conflict management training: A 4- and 5-year follow-up. *Journal of Consulting and Clinical Psychology, 61,* 70–77.

Martin, D., & Martin, M. (1992). *Stepfamilies in therapy.* San Francisco: Jossey-Bass.

Martin, T. C., & Bumpass, L. (1989). Recent trends and differentials in marital disruption. *Demography, 26,* 37–51.

Mason, M. G. (2005). Theoretical considerations of "resistant families." *The Family Journal: Counseling and Therapy for Couples and Families, 13,* 59–62.

Mason, M. J. (1991). Family therapy as the emerging context for sex therapy. In A. S. Gurman & D. P. Kniskern (Eds.), *Handbook of family therapy* (Vol. II, pp. 479–507). New York: Brunner/Mazel.

Masters, W. H., & Johnson, V. E. (1966). *Human sexual response.* Boston: Little, Brown.

Masters, W. H., & Johnson, V. E. (1970). *Human sexual inadequacy.* Boston: Little, Brown.

Mattessich, P., & Hill, R. (1987). Life cycle and family development. In M. B. Sussman & S. K. Steinmetz (Eds.),

Handbook of marriage and the family (p. 447). New York: Plenum.

Maturana, H., & Varela, F. (1987). *The tree of knowledge*. Boston: New Science Library.

May, J. C. (2005). Family attachment narrative therapy: Healing the experience of early childhood maltreatment. *Journal of Marital and Family Therapy, 31*, 221–237.

May, K. M. (1994, Winter). Gay and lesbian families. *The Family Digest, 7*, 1, 3.

May, K. M. (1998). A feminist and multicultural perspective in family therapy. *The Family Journal: Counseling and Therapy for Couples and Families 6*, 123–124.

Maynard, P. E., & Olson, D. H. (1987). Circumplex model of family systems: A treatment tool in family counseling. *Journal of Counseling and Development, 65*, 502–504.

McAdoo, H. P. (1982). Stress absorbing systems in black families. *Family Relations, 31*, 479–488.

McCollum, E. E., & Stith, S. M. (2002). Leaving the ivory tower: An introduction to the special section on doing marriage and family therapy research in community agencies. *Journal of Marital and Family Therapy, 28*, 5–7.

McCourt, F. (1996). *Angela's Ashes*. New York: Simon & Schuster.

McCoy, C. W. (1996). Reexamining models of healthy families. *Contemporary Family Therapy, 18*, 243–256.

McCubbin, H. I., & Figley, C. R. (1983). Bridging normative and catastrophic family stress. In H. I. McCubbin & C. R. Figley (Eds.), *Stress and the family*. New York: Brunner/Mazel.

McCubbin, H. I., & Patterson, J. M. (1981). *Systematic assessment of family stress, resources, and coping: Tools for research, education, and clinical intervention*. St. Paul, MN: Department of Family Social Science.

McCubbin, H. I., & McCubbin, M. A. (1991). Family stress theory and assessment. In H. I. McCubbin & A. I. Thompson (Eds.), *Family assessment inventories for research and practice* (pp. 3–32). Madison, WI: University of Wisconsin-Madison.

McCubbin, H. I., Larsen, A., & Olson, D. H. (1982). F-COPES: Family coping strategies. In D. H. Olson, H. I. McCubbin, H. I. Barnes, A. Larsen, M. Maxen, & M. Wilson (Eds.), *Family inventories: Inventories used in a national survey of families across the family life cycle* (pp. 101–120). St. Paul, MN: University of Minnesota.

McCubbin, H. I., Thompson, A. I., Pirner, P. A., & McCubbin, M. A. (1988). *Family types and strengths: A life cycle and ecological perspective*. Edina, MN: Burgess.

McCullough, P. G., & Rutenberg, S. K. (1988). Launching children and moving on. In B. Carter & M. McGoldrick (Eds.), *The changing family life cycle* (2nd ed., pp. 285–309). New York: Gardner.

McCurdy, K. G., & Murray, K. C. (2003). Confidentiality issues when minor children disclose family secrets in family counseling. *The Family Journal: Counseling and Therapy for Couples and Families, 11*, 393–398.

McDowell, T., Fang, S-R, Young, C. G., Khanna, A., Sherman, B., & Brownlee, K. (2003). Making space for racial dialogue: Our experience in a marriage and family therapy training program. *Journal of Marital and Family Therapy, 29*, 179–194.

McFarlane, W. R., Dixon, L., Lukens, E., & Lucksted, A. (2003). Family psychoeducation and schizophrenia: A review of the literature. *Journal of Marital and Family Therapy, 29*, 223–245.

McGoldrick, M. (1986, November/December). Irish families. *Family Therapy Networker, 10*, 31.

McGoldrick, M. (1986, November/December). Mourning rituals. *Family Therapy Networker, 10*, 29–30.

McGoldrick, M. (1999). Women and the family life cycle. In B. Carter & M. McGoldrick (Eds.), *The expanded family life cycle* (3rd ed., pp. 106–123). Boston: Allyn & Bacon.

McGoldrick, M., & Carter, E. A. (1982). The family life cycle. In F. Walsh (Ed.), *Normal family processes* (pp. 167–195). New York: Guilford.

McGoldrick, M., & Carter, B. (1988). Forming a remarried family. In B. Carter & M. McGoldrick (Eds.), *The changing family life cycle* (2nd ed., pp. 399–429). New York: Gardner.

McGoldrick, M., & Carter, B. (1999a). Remarried families. In B. Carter & M. McGoldrick (Eds.), *The expanded family life cycle* (3rd ed., pp. 417–435). Boston: Allyn & Bacon.

McGoldrick, M., & Carter, B. (1999b). Self in context: The individual life cycle in systemic perspective. In B. Carter & M. McGoldrick (Eds.), *The expanded family life cycle* (3rd ed., pp. 27–46). Boston: Allyn & Bacon.

McGoldrick, M., & Giordano, J. (1996). Overview: Empathy and family therapy. In M. McGoldrick, J. Giordano, & J. K. Pearce (Eds.), *Ethnicity and family therapy* (2nd ed., pp. 1–27). New York: Guilford.

McGoldrick, M., & Rohrbaugh, M. (1987). Researching ethnic family stereotypes. *Family Process, 1*, 89–100.

McGoldrick, M., & Walsh, F. (1999). Death and the family life cycle. In B. Carter & M. McGoldrick (Eds.), *The expanded family life cycle* (3rd ed., pp. 185–201). Boston: Allyn & Bacon.

McGoldrick, M., Gerson, R., & Shellenberger, S. (1999). *Genograms: Assessment & intervention*. New York: Norton.

McGoldrick, M., Preto, N. G., Hines, P. M., & Lee, E. (1991). Ethnicity and family therapy. In A. S. Gurman & D. P. Kniskern (Eds.), *Handbook of family therapy* (Vol. II, pp. 546–582). New York: Brunner/Mazel.

McGuirk, J. G., Friedlander, M. L., & Blocher, D. H. (1987). Systemic and nonsystemic diagnostic processes: An empirical comparison. *Journal of Marital and Family Therapy, 13*, 69–76.

McLaughlin, I. G., Leonard, K. E., & Senchak, M. (1992). Prevalence and distribution of premarital aggression among couples applying for a marriage license. *Journal of Family Violence, 7*, 309–319.

McWey, L. M. (2004). Predictors of attachment styles of children in foster care: An attachment theory model for working with families. *Journal of Marital and Family Therapy, 30*, 439–452.

McWhirter, J. J., & McWhirter, E. H. (1989). Poor soil yields damaged fruit: Environmental influences. In D. Capuzzi & D. R. Gross (Eds.), *Youth at risk* (pp. 19–40). Alexandria, VA: American Counseling Association.

Mead, D. E. (2002). Marital distress, co-occurring depression, and marital therapy: A review. *Journal of Marital and Family Therapy, 28*, 299–314.

Mead, M. (1972). *Blackberry winter*. New York: Morrow.

Means-Christensen, A. J., Snyder, D. K., & Negy, C. (2003). Assessing nontraditional couples: Validity of the Marital Satisfaction Inventory-Revised with Gay, Lesbian, and cohabitating heterosexual couples. *Journal of Marital and Family Therapy, 29*, 69–83.

Meichenbaum, D. H. (1977). *Cognitive-behavior modification: An integrative approach*. New York: Plenum.

Meichenbaum, D. H. (1985). *Stress inoculation training*. New York: Pergamon.

Meidonis, G. G., & Bry, B. H. (1995). Effects of therapist exceptions questions on blaming and positive statements in families with adolescent behavior problems. *Journal of Family Psychology, 9*, 451–457.

Melito, R. (2003). Values in the role of the family therapist: Self determination and justice. *Journal of Marital and Family Therapy, 29*, 3–11.

Melli, M. S. (1986). The changing legal status of the single-parent. *Family Relations, 35*, 31–35.

Menaghan, E. (1982). Measuring coping effectiveness: A panel analysis of marital problems and coping efforts. *Journal of Health and Social Behavior, 23*, 220–234.

Mercado, M. M. (2000). The invisible family: Counseling Asian American substance abusers and their families. *The Family Journal: Counseling and Therapy for Couples and Families, 8*, 267–272.

Merscham, C. (2000). Restorying trauma with narrative therapy: Using the phantom family. *The Family Journal: Counseling and Therapy for Couples and Families, 8*, 282–286.

Meyers, R. J., Apodaca, T. R., Flicker, S. M., & Slesnick, N. (2002). Evidence-based approaches for the treatment of substance abusers by involving family members. *The Family Journal: Counseling and Therapy for Couples and Families, 10*, 281–288.

Miller, B. C. (1986). *Family research methods*. Beverly Hills, CA: Sage.

Miller, V. S., & Ullery, E. K. (2002). A holistic treatment approach to male erectile disorder. *The Family Journal: Counseling and Therapy for Couples and Families, 10*, 443–447.

Miller, R. B., Anderson, S., & Keala, D. K. (2004). Is Bowen theory valid? A review of basic research. *Journal of Marital and Family Therapy, 30*, 453–466.

Miller, S., Nunnally, E., & Wackman, D. B. (1977). *Couple communication instructor's manual*. Littleton, CO: Interpersonal Communication Programs.

Miller, S., Nunnally, E. W., & Wackman, D. B. (1979). *Couple communication: Talking together*. Littleton, CO: Interpersonal Communication Programs.

Miller, S., & Sherrard, P. (1999). Couple Communication: A system for equipping partners to talk, listen, and resolve conflicts effectively. In R. Berger & M. T. Hannah (Eds.), *Preventative approaches to couples therapy* (pp. 125–148). Philadelphia: Routledge.

Miller, T. W., Veltkamp, L. J., Lane, T., Bilyeu, J., & Elzie, N. (2002). Care pathway guidelines for assessment and counseling for domestic violence. *The Family Journal: Counseling and Therapy for Couples and Families, 10*, 41–48.

Miller, W. R., Meyers, R. J., & Tonigan, J. S. (1999). Engaging the unmotivated in treatment for alcohol problems: A comparison of three strategies for intervention through family members. *Journal of Consulting & Clinical Psychology, 67*, 688–697.

Milstein, K., & Baldwin, C. (1997). Coalitions in primary triads: Reexamining the theoretical constructs from a feminist perspective. *The Family Journal: Counseling and Therapy for Couples and Families, 5*, 125–131.

Minuchin, P. (1995). Children and family therapy: Mainstream approaches and the special care of the multicrisis poor. In R. H. Mikesell, D. Lusterman, & S. H. McDaniel (Eds.), *Integrating family therapy* (pp. 113–140). Washington, DC: American Psychological Association.

Minuchin, S. (1974). *Families and family therapy*. Cambridge, MA: Harvard University Press.

Minuchin, S. (1993). *Family healing: Tales of hope and renewal from family therapy*. New York: Free Press.

Minuchin, S., & Fishman, C. H. (1981). *Family therapy techniques*. Cambridge, MA: Harvard University Press.

Minuchin, S., & Nichols, M. P. (1998). *Family healing: Strategies for hope and understanding*. New York: Free Press.

Minuchin, P., Colapinto, J., & Minuchin, S. (1999). *Working with families of the poor*. New York: Guilford.

Minuchin, S., Lee, W.-Y., & Simon, G. M. (1997). *Mastering family therapy: Journeys of growth and transformation*. New York: Wiley.

Minuchin, S., Rosman, B., & Baker, L. (1978). *Psychosomatic families: Anorexia nervosa in context*. Cambridge, MA: Harvard University Press.

Minuchin, S., Montalvo, B., Guerney, B. G., Rosman, B. L., & Schumer, F. (1967). *Families of the slums*. New York: Basic Books.

Mitchell, R. W. (1991). *Documentation in counseling records*. Alexandria, VA: American Counseling Association.

Mitten, T. J., & Connell, G. M. (2004). The core variables of symbolic-experiential therapy: A qualitative study. *Journal of Marital and Family Therapy, 30*, 467–478.

Mittleman, B. (1948). The concurrent analysis of married couples. *Psychoanalytic Quarterly, 17*, 182–197.

Molina, B., Estrada, D., & Burnett, J. A. (2004). Cultural communities: Challenges and opportunities in the creation of "Happily Ever After" stories of intercultural couplehood. *The Family Journal: Counseling and Therapy for Couples and Families, 12*, 139–147.

Monarch, N. D., Hartman, S. G., Whitton, S. W., & Markman, H. J. (2002). The role of clinicians in the prevention of marital distress and divorce. In J. H. Harvey & A. Wenzel (Eds.), *A clinicians guide to maintaining and enhancing close relationships* (pp. 233–258). Hillsdale, NJ: Lawrence Erlbaum.

Monk, G. (1998). Narrative therapy: An exemplar of the postmodern breed of therapies. *Counseling and Human Development, 30*(5), 1–14.

Moody, F. (1992). Divorce: Sometimes a bad notion. In O. Pocs (Ed.), *Marriage and family 92–93* (pp. 171–176). Guilford, CT: Dushkin.

Moody, R. A., & Moody, C. P. (1991). A family perspective: Helping children acknowledge and express grief following the death of a parent. *Death Studies, 15,* 587–602.

Moon, S. M., Dillon, D. R., & Sprenkle, D. H. (1990). Family therapy and qualitative research. *Journal of Marital and Family Therapy, 16,* 357–374.

Moos, R. H. (1990). Conceptual and empirical approaches to developing family-based assessment procedures: Resolving the case of the family environment. *Family Process, 29,* 199–208.

Moos, R. H., & Moos, B. S. (1994). *The family environment scale manual.* Palo Alto, CA: Consulting Psychologists Press.

Moreno, J. L., & Elefthery, D. G. (1975). An introduction to group psychodrama. In G. M. Gazda (Ed.), *Basic approaches to group psychotherapy and group counseling* (pp. 69–100). Springfield, IL: Thomas.

Morgan, O. J. (1998). Addiction, family treatment, and healing resources: An interview with David Berenson. *Journal of Addiction and Offender Counseling, 18,* 54–61.

Morrison, J., Layton, B., & Newman, J. (1982). Ethical conflict in clinical decision making: A challenge for family therapists. In J. Hansen (Ed.), *Values, ethics, legalities and the family therapists.* Rockville, MD: Aspen.

Morrison, N. C. (1995). Successful single-parent families. *Journal of Divorce and Remarriage, 22,* 205–219.

Muir, J. A., Schwartz, S. J., & Szapocznik, J. (2004). A program of research with Hispanic and African American families: Three decades of intervention development and testing influenced by the changing cultural context of Miami. *Journal of Marital and Family Therapy, 30,* 285–303.

Mullen, P. E., Martin, J. L., Anderson, J. C., Romans, S. E., & Herbison, G. P. (1995). The long-term impact of physical, emotional, and sexual abuse of children: A community study. *Child Abuse and Neglect, 20,* 7–21.

Mullins, M. E. (1993, July 14). Divorcing couples growing older. *USA Today,* p. D1.

Murdock, C. V. (1980). *Single parents are people too.* New York: Butterick.

Murphy, J. P. (1984). Substance abuse and the family. *Journal for Specialists in Group Work, 9,* 106–112.

Murray, C. E. (2005). Prevention work: A professional responsibility for marriage and family counselors. *The Family Journal: Counseling and Therapy for Couples and Families, 13,* 27–34.

Murray, C. E., & Murray, T. L., Jr. (2004). Solution-focused premarital counseling: Helping couples build a vision for their marriage. *Journal of Marital and Family Therapy, 30,* 349–358.

Murray, K. A. (2002). Religion and divorce: Implications and strategies for counseling. *The Family Journal: Counseling and Therapy for Couples and Families, 10,* 190–194.

Murray, P. E., & Rotter, J. C. (2002). Creative counseling techniques for family therapists. *The Family Journal: Counseling and Therapy for Couples and Families, 10,* 203–206.

Naaman, S., Pappas, J. D., Makinen, J., Zuccarini, D., & Johnson-Douglas, S. (2005). Treating attachment injured couples with emotionally focused therapy: A case study approach. *Psychiatry, 68,* 55–77.

Nance-Nash, S. (2005). Managing a blended family. In K. R. Gilbert (Ed.), *Annual editions: The family 05/06* (pp. 179–181). Dubuque, IA: McGraw-Hill/Dushkin.

Napier, A. Y., & Whitaker, C. A. (1978*). The family crucible.* New York: Harper & Row.

Napoliello, A. L., & Sweet, E. S. (1992). Salvador Minuchin's structural family therapy and its application to Native Americans. *Family Therapy, 19,* 155–165.

National Center for Health Statistics. (1991). *Advanced report of final natality statistics, 1989* (Monthly vital statistics report). Hyattsville, MD: Public Health Service.

National Center for Health Statistics. (2005). Unmarried childbearing. Retrieved August 28, 2005, from http://www.cdc.gov/nchs/fastats/unmarry.htm.

National Commission for the Protection of Human Subjects of Biomedical and Behavioral Research. (1979). *The Belmont report: Ethical principles and guidelines for the protection of human subjects of research* (Department of Health, Education, and Welfare Publication No. OS 78–0012). Washington, DC: U.S. Government Printing Office.

Nelson, P. T. (1986). Newsletters: An effective delivery mode for providing educational information and emotional support to single-parent families? *Family Relations, 35,* 183–188.

Nelson, T. S. (1996). Survey research in marriage and family therapy. In D. H. Sprenkle & S. M. Moon (Eds.), *Research methods in family therapy* (pp. 447–468). New York: Guilford.

Nelson, T. S., Heilbrun, G., & Figley, C. R. (1993). Basic family therapy skills, IV: Transgenerational theories of family therapy. *Journal of Marital and Family Therapy, 19,* 253–266.

Nerin, W. F. (1986). *Family reconstruction: Long day's journey into light.* New York: Norton.

Neugarten, B. L. (1976). Adaptation and the life cycle. *Counseling Psychologist, 6,* 16–20.

Neugarten, B. L. (1979). Time, age, and the life cycle. *American Journal of Psychiatry, 136,* 887–894.

Newlon, B. J., & Arciniega, M. (1991). Counseling minority families: An Adlerian perspective. In J. Carlson & J. Lewis (Eds.), *Family counseling: Strategies and issues* (pp. 189–223). Denver, CO: Love.

Ng, K. S. (2005). The development of family therapy around the world. *The Family Journal: Counseling and Therapy for Couples and Families, 13,* 35–42.

Nichols, M. P., & Schwartz, R. C. (2004). *Family therapy: Concepts and methods* (6th ed.). Boston: Allyn & Bacon.

Nichols, M. P., & Schwartz, R. C. (2005). *The essentials of family therapy* (2nd ed.). Boston: Allyn & Bacon.

Nichols, W. C. (1993). *The AAMFT: 50 years of marital and family therapy.* Washington, DC: American Association for Marriage and Family Therapy.

Nichols, W. C., & Everett, C. A. (1986). *Systemic family therapy: An integrated approach.* New York: Guilford.

Nicholson, B., Anderson, M., Fox, R., & Brenner, V. (2002). One family at a time: A prevention program for at-risk parents. *Journal of Counseling and Development, 80,* 362–371.

Nixon, J. A. (1993). Gender considerations in the case of "The Jealous Husband": Strategic therapy in review. *The Family Journal: Counseling and Therapy for Couples and Families, 1,* 161–163.

Norsworthy, K. L. (2000). Feminist family therapy. In A. M. Horne (Ed.), *Family counseling and therapy* (3rd ed., pp. 515–538). Itasca, IL: F. E. Peacock.

Northey, W. F., Jr. (2002). Characteristics and clinical practices of marriage and family therapists: A national survey. *Journal of Marital and Family Therapy, 28,* 487–494.

Northey, W. F., Jr., Wells, K. C., Silverman, W. K., & Bailey, C. E. (2003). Childhood behavioral and emotional disorders. *Journal of Marital and Family Therapy, 29,* 523–545.

Northey, W. F., Jr. (2004a, November/December). Clients of marriage and family therapists. *Family Therapy Magazine,* pp. 14–17.

Northey, W. F., Jr. (2004b, November/December). Who are marriage and family therapists? *Family Therapy Magazine,* pp. 10–13.

Northey, W. F., Jr. (2005). Studying marriage and family therapists in the 21st century: Methodological and technological issues. *Journal of Marital and Family Therapy, 31,* 99–105.

Norton, A. J., & Glick, P. C. (1986). One parent families: A social and economic profile. *Family Relations, 35,* 9–17.

Notarius, C., & Markman, H. (1993). *We can work it out: How to solve conflicts, save your marriage, and strengthen your love for each other.* New York: Putnam.

Nurse, A. R. (1994, Spring). A 60–year study of normals through time: Implications for practice. *The Family Psychologist, 10,* 35–36, 38.

Nurse, A. R. (1996, Spring). The cardboard kids. *The Family Psychologist, 13,* 22–23.

Oates, R. K., & Bross, D. C. (1995). What have we learned about treating child physical abuse? A literature review of the last decade. *Child Abuse and Neglect, 19,* 463–473.

Odell, M., & Quinn, W. H. (1998). Therapist and client behaviors in the first interview: Effects on session impact and treatment duration. *Journal of Marital and Family Therapy, 24,* 369–388.

Odom, M., Snow, J. N., & Kern, R. M. (1999). Use of the identified patient as the helper in family therapy. *The Family Journal: Counseling and Therapy for Couples and Families, 7,* 181–184.

O'Farrell, T. J. (1996). Marital and family therapy in the treatment of alcoholism. In *The Hatherleigh Guide to Treating Substance Abuse, Part I* (pp. 101–127). New York: Hatherleigh.

O'Farrell, T. J., & Fals-Stewart, W. (2003). Alcohol abuse. *Journal of Marital and Family Therapy, 29,* 121–146.

O'Halloran, M. S., & Weimer, A. K. (2005). Changing roles: Individual and family therapy in the treatment of anorexia nervosa. *The Family Journal: Counseling and Therapy for Couples and Families, 13,* 181–187.

O'Hanlon, W. H. (1987). *Taproots: Underlying principles of Milton Erickson's therapy and hypnosis.* New York: Norton.

O'Hanlon, W. H., & Weiner-Davis, M. (1989). *In search of solutions: A new direction in psychotherapy.* New York: Norton.

O'Hanlon, W. H., & Wilk, J. (1987). *Shifting contexts: The generation of effective psychotherapy.* New York: Guilford.

Okun, B. F. (1984). *Working with adults: Individual, family, and career development.* Pacific Grove, CA: Brooks/Cole.

Okun, B. F., & Rappaport, L. J. (1980). *Working with families: An introduction to family therapy.* North Scituate, MA: Duxbury.

O'Leary, K. D., & Murphy, C. (1999). Clinical issues in the assessment of partner violence. In R. Ammerman & M. Hersen (Eds.), *Assessment of family violence: A clinical and legal sourcebook* (pp. 46–94). New York: Wiley.

O'Leary, K. D., & Smith, D. A. (1991). Marital interactions. *Annual Review of Psychology, 42,* 191–212.

Oliver, C. J. (1992). Legal issues facing families in transition: An overview for counselors. *New York State Journal for Counseling and Development, 7,* 41–52.

Oliver, J. M., Handal, P. J., Enos, D. M., & May, M. J. (1988). Factor structure of the family environment scale: Factors based on items and subscales. *Educational and Psychological Measurement, 48,* 469–477.

Olkin, R. (1993, Winter). Teaching family therapy to graduate students: What do we teach and when do we teach it? *Family Psychologist, 9,* 31–34.

Olowu, A. A. (1990). Helping children cope with death. *Early Child Development and Care, 61,* 119–123.

Olson, D. H. (1986). Circumplex model VII: Validation studies and FACES III. *Family Process, 25,* 337–351.

Olson, D. H. (2000). *Marriage and the family: Diversity and strengths* (3rd ed.). Mountain View, CA: Mayfield.

Olson, D. H., & Olson, A. (2000). *Empowering couples: Building on your strengths.* Minneapolis: Life Innovations Inc.

Olson, D. H., Fournier, D. G., & Druckman, J. M. (1987). *Counselor's manual for PREPARE/ENRICH* (rev. ed.). Minneapolis, MN: PREPARE/ENRICH Inc.

Olson, D. H., Larsen, A. S., & McCubbin, H. I. (1985). Family strengths. In D. Olson, H. I. McCubbin, H. Barnes, A. Larsen, M. Muxen, & M. Wilson (Eds.), *Family inventories* (rev. ed., pp. 78–92). St Paul, MN: Family Social Science, University of Minnesota.

Olson, D. H., McCubbin, H. I., Barnes, H., Larsen, A., Muxen, M., & Wilson, M. (1985). *Family inventories: Inventories used in a national survey of families across the family life cycle.* St Paul, MN: Family Social Science, University of Minnesota.

Olson, M. M., Russell, C. S., Higgins-Kessler, M., & Miller, R. B. (2002). Emotional processes following disclosure of an extramarital affair. *Journal of Marital and Family Therapy, 28,* 423–434.

O'Malley, P. (1995, December). Confidentiality in the electronic age. *Family Therapy News, 26,* 9.

Ooms, T., & Wilson, P. (2004). The challenges of offering relationship and marriage education to low-income populations. *Family Relations, 53,* 440–447.

Orthner, D. K., Bowen, G. L., & Beare, V. G. (1990). The organization family: A question of work and family boundaries. *Marriage and family review, 15,* 15–36.

Page, S. (1998). *How One of You Can Bring the Two of You Together.* Louisville, KY: Broadway.

Pals, S., Piercy, F., & Miller, J. (1998). Factors related to family therapists' breaking confidence when clients disclose high-risks-to-HIV/AIDS sexual behaviors. *Journal of Marital and Family Therapy, 24,* 457–472.

Papernow, P. L. (1993). *Becoming a stepfamily.* San Francisco: Jossey-Bass.

Papero, D. V. (1990). *Bowen family systems theory.* Boston: Allyn & Bacon.

Papero, D. V. (1991). The Bowen theory. In A. M. Horne & J. L. Passmore (Eds.), *Family counseling and theory* (2nd ed., pp. 47–76). Itasca, IL: F. E. Peacock.

Papp, P. (1976). Family choreography. In P. J. Guerin, Jr. (Ed.), *Family therapy* (pp. 465–479). New York: Gardner.

Papp, P. (Ed.). (1977). *Family therapy: Full-length case studies.* New York: Gardner.

Papp, P. (1980). The Greek chorus and other techniques of paradoxical therapy. *Family Process, 19,* 45–57.

Papp, P. (1984, September/October). The creative leap. *Family Therapy Networker, 8,* 20–29.

Pardeck, J. T., & Pardeck, J. A. (1987). Using bibliotherapy to help children cope with the changing family. *Social Work in Education, 9,* 107–116.

Pardeck, J. T., & Pardeck, J. A. (1997). Recommended books for helping young children deal with social and developmental problems. *Early Child Development and Care, 136,* 57–63.

Parke, M. (2004). Are married parents really better for children? In K. R. Gilbert (Ed.), *Annual editions: The family 2004/2005* (pp. 110–112). Guilford, CT: McGraw-Hill/Dushkin.

Parrott, L. III, & Parrott, L. (2003). The SYMBIS approach to marriage education. *Journal of Psychology and Theology, 31,* 208–212.

Pasley, K., Rhoden, L., Visher, E. B., & Visher, J. S. (1996). Successful stepfamily therapy: Clients' perspectives. *Journal of Marital and Family Therapy, 22,* 343–357.

Patten, J. (1992, October). Gay and lesbian families. *Family Therapy News, 23,* 10, 34.

Patterson, C. H. (1996). Multicultural counseling: From diversity to universality. *Journal of Counseling and Development, 74,* 227–231.

Patterson, G. R. (1975). *Families: Applications of social learning to family life.* Champaign, IL: Research Press.

Patterson, G. R., & Brodsky, A. (1966). A behavior modification programme for a child with multiple behavior problems. *Journal of Child Psychology and Psychiatry, 7,* 277–295.

Patterson, G. R., & Gullion, M. E. (1971). *Living with children: New methods for parents and teachers* (rev. ed.). Champaign, IL: Research Press.

Patterson, G. R., Jones, R., Whittier, J., & Wright, M. (1965). A behavior modification technique for a hyperactive child. *Behavior Research and Therapy, 2,* 217–226.

Patterson, G. R., McNeal, S., Hawkins, N., & Phelps, R. (1967). Reprogramming the social environment. *Journal of Child Psychology and Psychiatry, 8,* 181–195.

Patterson, T. (2005). Cognitive behavioral couple therapy. In M. Harway (Ed.), *Handbook of couples therapy* (pp. 119–140). New York: Wiley.

Pavao, J. M. (1998). *The family of adoption.* Boston: Beacon.

Pavlicin, K. M. (2003). *Surviving deployment: A guide for military families.* St. Paul, MN: Elva Resa.

Pedersen, P. (1996). The importance of similarities and differences in multicultural counseling: Reaction to C. H. Patterson. *Journal of Counseling and Development, 74,* 236–237.

Pearlin, L. T., & Schooler, C. (1978). The structure of coping. *Journal of Health and Social Behavior, 19,* 2–21.

Pearson, J. C. (1993). *Communication in the family* (2nd ed.). New York: HarperCollins.

Peluso, P. R. (2003). The ethical genogram: A tool for helping therapists understand their ethical decision-making style. *The Family Journal: Counseling and Therapy for Couples and Families, 11,* 286–291.

Pence, E., & Paymar, M. (1993). *Education groups for men who batter: The Duluth Model.* New York: Springer.

Penn, C. D., Hernandez, S. L., & Bermudez, J. M. (1997). Using a cross-cultural perspective to understand infidelity in couples therapy. *American Journal of Family Therapy, 25,* 169–185.

Perosa, L. (1996). Relations between Minuchin's structural family model and Kohut's self-psychology constructs. *Journal of Counseling and Development, 74,* 385–392.

Perry, V. (1992). *An examination of attention deficit disorders without hyperactivity: A case study from a strategic family systems perspective.* Unpublished master's research report, Wake Forest University, Winston-Salem, North Carolina.

Peterman, L. M., & Dixon, C. G. (2003). Domestic violence between same-sex partners: Implications for counseling. *Journal of Counseling and Development, 81,* 40–47.

Peterson, A., & Jenni, C. B. (2003). Men's experience of making the decision to have their first child: A phenomenological analysis. *The Family Journal: Counseling and Therapy for Couples and Families, 11,* 353–363.

Peterson, K. S. (1992, November 25). Traditions that put life in context. *USA Today,* pp. D1–2.

Peterson, K. S. (2000c, March 8). Black couples stay the course. *USA Today,* p. 8D.

Peterson, K. S. (2000a, March 30). Sweet nothings help marriages stick. *USA Today,* p. A1.

Peterson, K. S. (2000b, April 18). Changing the shape of the American family. *USA Today,* pp. D1, D2.

Phillips, J., & Sweeney, M. (2005). Premarital cohabitation and marital disruption among White, Black, and Mexican American Women. *Journal of Marriage and Family, 67,* 296–314.

Pickens, M. E. (1997, January). Evolving family structures: Implications for counseling. *Counseling and Family Development, 29,* 1–8.

Piercy, F. P. (2000, March/April). To tell or not to tell? *Family Therapy Networker, 24,* 21.

Piercy, F. P., & Benson, K. (2005). Aesthetic forms of data representation in qualitative family therapy research. *Journal of Marital and Family Therapy, 31,* 107–119.

Piercy, F. P., & Lobenz, N. M. (1994). *Stop marital fights before they start.* New York: Berkeley Press.

Piercy, F. P., & Sprenkle, D. H. (1986). *Family therapy sourcebook.* New York: Guilford.

Piercy, F. P., & Sprenkle, D. H. (1990). Marriage and family therapy: A decade review. *Journal of Marriage and Family, 52,* 1116–1126.

Piercy, F. P., & Thomas, V. (1998). Participatory evaluation research: An introduction for family therapists. *Journal of Marital and Family Therapy, 24,* 165–176.

Piercy, F. P., McKeon, D., & Laird, R. A. (1983). A family assessment process for community mental health clinics. *AMHCA Journal, 5,* 94–104.

Piercy, F. P., Sprenkle, D. H., & Wetchler, J. L. (1997). *Family therapy sourcebook* (2nd ed.). New York: Guilford.

Pietrzak, D., & L'Amoreaux, N. (1998). Robert Smith. *The Family Journal: Counseling and Therapy for Couples and Families, 6,* 159–162.

Pill, C. J. (1990). Stepfamilies: Redefining the family. *Family Relations, 39,* 186–193.

Pinsof, W., & Wynne, L. (Eds.). (1995). Special issue: The effectiveness of marital and family therapy. *Journal of Marital and Family Therapy, 21*(4), 339–613.

Pinsof, W. M., & Wynne, L. C. (2000). Toward progress research: Closing the gap between family therapy practice and research. *Journal of Marital and Family Therapy, 26,* 1–8.

Pinson-Milburn, N. M., Fabian, E. S., Schlossberg, N. K., & Pyle, M. (1996). Grandparents raising grandchildren. *Journal of Counseling and Development, 74,* 548–554.

Piore, A. (2004). Home alone. In K. R. Gilbert (Ed.), *Annual editions: The family 2004/2005* (pp. 164–165). Guilford, CT: McGraw-Hill/Dushkin.

Pistole, M. C., & Marson, G. (2005). Commentary on the family's vitality: Diverse structures with TV illustrations. *The Family Journal: Counseling and Therapy for Couples and Families, 13,* 10–18.

Pistorello, J., & Follette, V. M. (1998). Childhood sexual abuse and couples' relationships: Female survivors' reports in therapy group. *Journal of Marital and Family Therapy, 24,* 473–485.

Pittman, F. (1991). *Private lies: Infidelity and betrayal of intimacy.* New York: Norton.

Pittman, F. (1995, November/December). Turning tragedy into comedy. *Family Therapy Networker, 19,* 36–40.

Pittman, F., & Wagers, T. P. (1995). Crises of infidelity. In N. S. Jacobson & A. S. Gurman (Eds.), *Clinical handbook of couple therapy* (pp. 295–316). New York: Guilford.

Ponce, A. (1995, Winter). The Hispanic family. *The Family Digest, 7,* 7, 11.

Ponterotto, J. G. (1987). Counseling Mexican-Americans: A multimodal approach. *Journal of Counseling and Development, 65,* 308–312.

Ponzetti, J. J., Jr. (2005). Family beginnings: A comparison of spouses' recollections of courtship. *The Family Journal: Counseling and Therapy for Couples and Families, 13,* 132–138.

Pope, K. S., & Vasquez, M. J. T. (1998). *Ethics in psychotherapy and counseling: A practical guide.* San Francisco: Jossey-Bass.

Popenoe, D. (1993, April 14). Scholars should worry about the disintegration of the American family. *Chronicle of Higher Education, 39,* A48.

Premack, D. (1965). Reinforcement theory. In D. Levine (Ed.), *Nebraska symposium on motivation.* Lincoln, NE: University of Nebraska Press.

Prest, L. A., & Keller, J. F. (1993). Spirituality and family therapy: Spiritual beliefs, myths, and metaphors. *Journal of Marital and Family Therapy, 19,* 137–148.

Priebe, S., & Pommerien, W. (1992). The therapeutic system as viewed by depressive inpatients and outcome: An expanded study. *Family Process, 31,* 433–439.

Prouty, A. M., Markowksi, E. M., & Barnes, H. L. (2000). Using the Dyadic Adjustment Scale in marital therapy: An exploratory study. *The Family Journal: Counseling and Therapy for Couples and Families, 8,* 250–257.

Puente, M. (1993, July 16). Hispanics debating their "destiny" in USA. *USA Today,* p. 10A.

Pulleyblank, E. (1996, January/February). Hard lessons. *Family Therapy Networker, 20,* 42–44, 46, 49.

Rait, D. (1988). Survey results. *Family Therapy Networker, 12,* 52–56.

Ray, W. A. (2000). Don D. Jackson—A re-introduction. *Journal of Systemic Therapies, 19*(2), 1–6.

Reiss, D. (1988). Theoretical versus tactical inferences. In L. C. Wynne (Ed.), *The state of the art in family therapy research* (pp. 33–46). New York: Family Process.

Remley, T. P. (1991). *Preparing for court appearances.* Alexandria, VA: American Counseling Association.

Remley, T. P., Jr., & Miranti, J. (1992). Child custody evaluator: A new role for mental health counselors. *Journal of Mental Health Counseling, 13,* 334–342.

Renk, K., Liljequist, L., Simpson, J. E., & Phares, V. (2005). Gender and age differences in the topics of parent-adolescent conflict. *The Family Journal: Counseling and Therapy for Couples and Families, 13,* 139–149.

Renshaw, D. C. (2005). Fathering today. *The Family Journal: Counseling and Therapy for Couples and Families, 13,* 7–9.

Resnikoff, R. O. (1981). Teaching family therapy: Ten key questions for understanding the family as patient. *Journal of Marital and Family Therapy, 7,* 135–142.

Rhodes, A. R. (2002). Long-distance relationships in dual-career commuter couples: A review of counseling issues. *The Family Journal: Counseling and Therapy for Couples and Families, 10,* 398–404.

Rice, J. K. (2005). Divorcing couples. In M. Harway (Ed.), *Handbook of couples therapy* (pp. 405–430). New York: Wiley.

Richardson, B. L., & June, L. N. (2006). Developing effective partnerships in order to utilize and maximize the resources of the African American church: Strategies and tools for counseling professionals. In C. C. Lee

(Ed.), *Multicultural issues in counseling* (pp. 113–124). Alexandria, VA: American Counseling Association.

Rickert, V. (1989). *The initial family interview.* Presentation at the annual convention of the American Association for Marriage and Family Therapy, San Francisco, CA.

Riley, L. D., & Bowen, C. P. (2005). The sandwich generation: Challenges and coping strategies of multigenerational families. *The Family Journal: Counseling and Therapy for Couples and Families, 13,* 52–58.

Ripley, J. S., & Worthington, E. L., Jr. (2002). Hope-focused and forgiveness-based group interventions to promote marital enrichment. *Journal of Counseling and Development, 80,* 452–463.

Riseman, B. J. (1986). Can men "mother"? Life as a single father. *Family Relations, 35,* 95–102.

Roberto, L. A. (1991). Symbolic-experiential family therapy. In A. S. Gurman & D. P. Kniskern (Eds.), *Handbook of family therapy* (Vol. II, pp. 444–476). New York: Brunner/Mazel.

Roberts, J., & Imber-Black, E. (1992). *Rituals for our times: Celebrating, healing, and changing our lives and our relationships.* New York: HarperCollins.

Roberts, T. W., & Price, S. J. (1986). A systems analysis of the remarriage process: Implications for the clinician. *Journal of Divorce, 9,* 1–25.

Robertson, P. K. (2004). The historical effects of depathologizing homosexuality on the practice of counseling. *The Family Journal: Counseling and Therapy for Couples and Families, 12,* 163–169.

Robinson, J. (1998). *Communication Miracles for Couples: Easy and Effective Tools to Create More Love and Less Conflict.* Conari.

Rolland, J. S. (1999). Chronic illness and the family life cycle. In B. Carter & M. McGoldrick (Eds.), *The expanded family life cycle* (3rd ed., pp. 492–510). Boston: Allyn & Bacon.

Rotter, J. C. (2000). Family grief and mourning. *The Family Journal: Counseling and Therapy for Couples and Families, 8,* 275–277.

Rotter, J. C., & Houston, I. S. (1999). Treating family violence: Risks and limitations. *The Family Journal: Counseling and Therapy for Couples and Families, 7,* 58–63.

Rowe, C. L., & Liddle, H. A. (2003). Substance abuse. *Journal of Marital and Family Therapy, 29,* 97–120.

Rowe, W., Bennett, S. K., & Atkinson, D. R. (1994). White racial identity models: A critique and alternative proposal. *The Counseling Psychologist, 22,* 129–146.

Ryder, R., & Hepworth, J. (1990). AAMFT ethical code: "Dual relationships." *Journal of Marital and Family Therapy, 16,* 127–132.

Ruiz, A. (1981). Cultural and historical perspectives in counseling Hispanics. In D. W. Sue (Ed.), *Counseling the culturally different: Theory & practice* (pp. 186–215). New York: Wiley.

Saba, G. W., Karrer, B. M., & Hardy, K. V. (Eds.). (1996). *Minorities and family therapy.* New York: Haworth.

Sabourin, S., Laporte, L., & Wright, J. (1990). Problem solving self-appraisal and coping efforts in distressed and nondistressed couples. *Journal of Marital and Family Therapy, 16,* 89–97.

Sager, C. J., Brown, H. S., Crohn, H., Engel, T., Rodstein, E., & Walker, L. (1983). *Treating the remarried family.* New York: Brunner/Mazel.

Sager, D. E., & Sager, W. G. (2005). SANTUS marriage enrichment. *The Family Journal: Counseling and Therapy for Couples and Families, 13,* 212–218.

Saginak, K. A., & Saginak, M. A. (2005). Balancing work and family: Equity, gender, and marital satisfaction. *The Family Journal: Counseling and Therapy for Couples and Families, 13,* 162–166.

Sanik, M. M., & Mauldin, T. (1986). Single versus two parent families: A comparison of mothers' time. *Family Relations, 35,* 53–56.

Santisteban, D. A., & Szapocznik, J. (1994). Bridging theory, research and practice to more successfully engage substance abusing youth and their families into therapy. *Journal of Child & Adolescent Substance Abuse, 3,* 9–24.

Santrock, J. W. (2004). *Life-span development* (9th ed). New York: McGraw-Hill.

Sarnoff, D. P., & Sarnoff, P. (2005). Assessing interactive creativity in couples. *The Family Journal: Counseling and Therapy for Couples and Families, 13,* 83–86.

Satir, V. M. (1964). *Conjoint family therapy.* Palo Alto, CA: Science and Behavior.

Satir, V. M. (1972). *Peoplemaking.* Palo Alto, CA: Science and Behavior.

Satir, V. M. (1982). The therapist and family therapy: Process model. In A. M. Horne & M. M. Ohlsen (Eds.), *Family counseling and therapy.* Itasca, IL: F. E. Peacock.

Satir, V. M. (1986). A partial portrait of a family therapist in process. In H. C. Fishman & B. L. Rosman (Eds.), *Evolving models for family change: A volume in honor of Salvador Minuchin* (pp. 278–293). New York: Guilford.

Satir, V. M. (1987). The therapist story. *Journal of Psychotherapy and the Family, 3,* 17–25.

Satir, V. M. (1988). *The new peoplemaking.* Mountain View, CA: Science and Behavior.

Satir, V. M., & Baldwin, M. (1983). *Satir step by step.* Palo Alto, CA: Science and Behavior.

Satir, V. M., & Bitter, J. R. (2000). The therapist and family therapy: Satir's human validation process model. In A. M. Horne (Ed.), *Family counseling and therapy* (3rd ed., pp. 62–101). Itasca, IL: F. E. Peacock.

Satir, V. M., Bitter, J. R., & Krestensen, K. K. (1988). Family reconstruction: The family within a group experience. *Journal for Specialists in Group Work, 13,* 200–208.

Satir, V. M., Stachowiak, J., & Taschman, H. A. (1975). *Helping families to change.* New York: Aronson.

Satir, V. M., Banmen, J., Gerber, J., & Gomori, M. (1991). *The Satir model: Family therapy and beyond.* New York: Science and Behavior.

Sauber, S. R., L'Abate, L., & Weeks, G. R. (1985). *Family therapy: Basic concepts and terms.* Rockville, MD: Aspen.

Sayger, T. V., Homrich, A. M., & Horne, A. M. (2000). Working from a family focus. In A. M. Horne (Ed.), *Family counseling and therapy* (pp. 12–40). Itasca, IL: F. E. Peacock.

Scanzoni, L. D., & Scanzoni, J. (1988). *Men, women, and change* (3rd ed.). New York: McGraw-Hill.

Scarf, M. (1992, July/August). The middle of the journey. *Family Therapy Networker, 16*, 51–55.

Scarf, M. (1995). *Intimate worlds: Life inside the family.* New York: Random House.

Schacht, A. J., Tafoya, N., & Mirabla, K. (1989). Home-based therapy with American Indian families. *American Indian and Alaska Native Mental Health Research, 3*, 27–42.

Scharff, J. (Ed.). (1989). *The foundations of object relations family therapy.* New York: Jason Aronson.

Schecter, S., & Ganley, A. (1995). *Domestic violence: A national curriculum for family preservation practitioners.* San Francisco: Family Violence Prevention Fund.

Scheinkman, M. (2005). Beyond the trauma of betrayal: Reconsidering affairs in couples therapy. *Family Process, 44*, 227–244.

Schlesinger, S. E. (1988). Cognitive-behavioral approaches to family treatment of addiction. In N. Epstein, S. E. Schlesinger, & W. Dryden (Eds.), *Cognitive-behavioral therapy with families* (pp. 254–291). New York: Brunner/Mazel.

Schlossberg, N. K., Waters, E. B., & Goodman, J. (1996). *Counseling adults in transition: Linking practice with theory* (2nd ed.). New York: Springer.

Schroeder, E. (1989). Therapy for the chemically dependent family. *Journal of Chemical Dependency Treatment, 2*, 95–129.

Schulman, G. L. (1972). Myths that intrude on the adaptation of the stepfamily. *Social Casework, 53*, 131–139.

Schumm, W. R. (1983). Theory and measurement in marital communication training programs. *Family Relations, 32*, 3–11.

Schumm, W. R., Stilliman, B., & Bell, D. B. (2000). Perceived premarital counseling outcomes among recently married army personnel. *Journal of Sex and Marital Therapy, 26*, 177–186.

Schwartz, L. L. (1992). Children's perceptions of divorce. *American Journal of Family Therapy, 20*, 324–332.

Schwartz, R. (1994). *Internal family systems therapy.* New York: Guilford.

Schwartz, R. C. (1999). Narrative therapy expands and contracts family therapy's horizons. *Journal of Marital and Family Therapy, 25*, 263–267.

Schwartz, R. C., & Breunlin, D. (1983). Research: Why clinicians should bother with it. *Family Therapy Networker, 7*, 22–27, 57–59.

Schwartz, R. C., Liddle, H. A., & Breunlin, D. C. (1988). Muddles in live supervision. In H. A. Liddle, D. C. Breunlin, & R. C. Schwartz (Eds.), *Handbook of family therapy training* (pp. 172–182). New York: Guilford.

Schwartzberg, A. Z. (1987). The adolescent in the remarriage family. *Adolescent Psychiatry, 14*, 259–270.

Schwebel, A. I., & Fine, M. A. (1992). Cognitive-behavioral family therapy. *Journal of Family Psychotherapy, 3*, 73–92.

Schwebel, A. I., & Fine, M. A. (1994). *Understanding and helping families: A cognitive behavioral approach.* Hillsdale, NJ: LEA Press.

Sciarra, D. T., & Ponterotto, J. G. (1991). Counseling the Hispanic bilingual family: Challenges to the therapeutic process. *Psychotherapy, 28*, 473–479.

Seligman, D. (1981, November 16). Luck and careers. *Fortune*, pp. 60–75.

Seligman, M., & Darling, R. B. (1997). *Ordinary families, special children* (2nd ed.). New York: Guilford.

Seltzer, J. A. (1991). Relationships between fathers and children who live apart: The father's role after separation. *Journal of Marriage and Family, 53*, 79–101.

Selvini Palazzoli, M. (1974). *Self-starvation.* London: Human Context.

Selvini Palazzoli, M. (1981). *Self-starvation: From the intrapsychic to the transpersonal approach to anorexia nervosa.* New York: Jason Aronson.

Selvini Palazzoli, M. (1986). Towards a general model of psychotic family games. *Journal of Marital and Family Therapy, 12*, 339–349.

Selvini Palazzoli, M. (1988). *The work of Mara Selvini Palazzoli.* Northvale, NJ: Jason Aronson.

Selvini Palazzoli, M., Boscolo, L., Cecchin, G., & Prata, G. (1980). Hypothesizing-circularity-neutrality. *Family Process, 19*, 73–85.

Selvini Palazzoli, M., Cecchin, G., Prata, G., & Boscolo, L. (1978). *Paradox and counterparadox.* New York: Jason Aronson.

Selye, H. (1976). *The stress of life* (2nd ed.). New York: McGraw-Hill.

Seppa, N. (1996, August). Supreme Court protects patient-therapist privilege. *APA Monitor, 27*, 39.

Seward, R. (1978). *The American family: A demographic history.* Newbury Park, CA: Sage.

Sexton, T. L., & Montgomery, D. (1994). Ethical and therapeutic acceptability: A study of paradoxical techniques. *The Family Journal: Counseling and Therapy for Couples and Families, 2*, 215–228.

Shadish, W. R., & Baldwin, S. A. (2003). Meta-analysis of MFT interventions. *Journal of Marital and Family Therapy, 29*, 547–570.

Shadish, W. R., & Baldwin, S. A. (2005). Effects of behavioral marital therapy: A meta-analysis of randomized control trials. *Journal of Consulting & Clinical Psychology, 73*, 6–14.

Sharpe, T. S. (2003). Adult sexuality. *The Family Journal: Counseling and Therapy for Couples and Families, 11*, 420–426.

Shapiro, L. (1993, April 19). Rush to judgment. *Newsweek*, pp. 54–60.

Sheehy, G. (1977). *Passages.* New York: Bantam.

Sheehy, G. (1981). *Pathfinders.* New York: Bantam.

Sherman, R. (1993). The intimacy genogram. *The Family Journal: Counseling and Therapy for Couples and Families, 1*, 91–93.

Sherman, R. (1999). Family therapy: The art of integration. In R. E. Watts & J. Carlson (Eds.), *Interventions and strategies in counseling and psychotherapy* (pp. 101–134). Philadelphia: Francis & Taylor.

Sherman, R., & Dinkmeyer, D. (1987). *Systems of family therapy: An Adlerian integration.* New York: Brunner/Mazel.

Sherman, R., & Fredman, N. (1986). *Handbook of structural techniques in marriage and family therapy.* New York: Brunner/Mazel.

Shertzer, B., & Stone, S. (1980). *Fundamentals of counseling* (3rd ed.). Boston: Houghton Mifflin.

Shields, C. G. (1986). Critiquing the new epistemologies: Toward minimum requirements for a scientific theory of family therapy. *Journal of Marital and Family Therapy, 12*, 359–372.

Shields, C. G., King, D. A., & Wynne, L. C. (1995). Interventions with later life families. In R. H. Mikesell, D. Lusterman, & S. H. McDaniel (Eds.), *Integrating family therapy* (pp. 141–160). Washington, DC: American Psychological Association.

Shields, C. G., Wynne, L. C., McDaniel, S. H., & Gawinski, A. (1994). The marginalization of family therapy: An historical and continuing problem. *Journal of Marital and Family Therapy, 20*, 117–138.

Sholevar, G. P., & Schwoeri, L. D. (2003). *Textbook of family and marital therapy: Clinical applications.* Arlington, VA: American Psychiatric Publishing.

Shumway, S. T., & Wampler, R. S. (2002). A behaviorally focused measure for relationships: The couple behavior report (CBR). *American Journal of Family Therapy, 30*, 311–321.

Silverstein, L. B., & Levant, R. F. (1996, Spring). Children need fathers not patriarchs. *The Family Psychologist, 13*, 18–19.

Simms, L. J. (2002). The application of attachment theory individual behavior and functioning in close relationships: Theory, research, and practical applications. In J. H. Harvey & A. Wenzel (Eds.), *A clinicians guide to maintaining and enhancing close relationships* (pp. 63–80). Hillsdale, NJ: Lawrence Erlbaum.

Simola, S. K., Parker, K. C. H., & Froese, A. P. (1999). Relational V-code conditions in a child or adolescent population do warrant treatment. *Journal of Marital and Family Therapy, 25*, 225–236.

Simon, F., Stierlin, H., & Wynne, L. (1985). *The language of family therapy.* New York: Family Process.

Simon, G. M. (2004). An examination of the integrative nature of emotionally focused therapy. *The Family Journal: Counseling and Therapy for Couples and Families, 12*, 254–262.

Simon, R. (1982, September/October). Behind the one-way mirror: An interview with Jay Haley. *Family Therapy Networker, 6*, 18–25, 28–29, 58–59.

Simon, R. (1984, November/December). Stranger in a strange land: An interview with Salvador Minuchin. *Family Therapy Networker, 8*, 20–31.

Simon, R. (1985, September/October). Take it or leave it: An interview with Carl Whitaker. *Family Therapy Networker, 9*, 27–34.

Simon, R. (1986, September/October). Behind the one-way kaleidoscope: An interview with Cloe Madanes. *Family Therapy Networker, 10*, 19–29, 64–67.

Simon, R. (1987, September/October). Good-bye paradox, hello invariant prescription: An interview with Mara Selvini Palazzoli. *Family Therapy Networker, 11*, 16–33.

Simon, R. M. (1988). Family life cycle issues in the therapy system. In B. Carter & M. McGoldrick (Eds.), *The changing family life cycle* (2nd ed., pp. 107–117). New York: Gardner.

Simon, R. (1989, January/February). Reaching out to life: An interview with Virginia Satir. *Family Therapy Networker, 13*, 36–43.

Sinclair, S. L., & Monk, G. (2004). Moving beyond the blame game: Toward a discursive approach to negotiating conflict within couple relationships. *Journal of Marital and Family Therapy, 30*, 335–347.

Skinner, B. F. (1948). *Walden two.* New York: Macmillan.

Skinner, B. F. (1953). *Science and human behavior.* New York: Macmillan.

Skowron, E. A. (2000). The role of differentiation of self in marital adjustment. *Journal of Counseling Psychology, 47*, 229–237.

Skowron, E. A., & Platt, L. F. (2005). Differentiation of self and child abuse potential in young adulthood. *The Family Journal: Counseling and Therapy for Couples and Families, 13*, 281–290.

Skynner, A. C. R. (1981). An open-systems, group-analytic-approach to family therapy. In A. S. Gurman & D. P. Kniskern (Eds.), *Handbook of family therapy* (pp. 39–84). New York: Brunner/Mazel.

Slesnick, N., & Prestopik, J. L. (2004). Perceptions of the family environment and youth behaviors: Alcohol-abusing runaway adolescents and their primary caregivers. *The Family Journal: Counseling and Therapy for Couples and Families, 12*, 243–253.

Slipp, S. (1988). *The technique and practice of object relations family therapy.* New York: Aronson.

Sluzko, C. E. (1978). Marital therapy from a systems theory perspective. In T. J. Paolino & B. C. McCrady (Eds.), *Marriage and marital therapy.* New York: Brunner/Mazel.

Smith, R. L. (1991). Marriage and family therapy: Direction, theory, and practice. In J. Carlson & J. Lewis (Eds.), *Family counseling* (pp. 13–34). Denver: Love.

Smith, R. L., & Stevens-Smith, P. (1992a). A critique of healthy family functioning. In R. L. Smith & P. Stevens-Smith (Eds.), *Family counseling and therapy* (pp. 3–13). Ann Arbor, MI: ERIC/CAPS.

Smith, R. L., & Stevens-Smith, P. (1992b). Future projections for marriage and family counseling and therapy. In R. L. Smith & P. Stevens-Smith (Eds.), *Family counseling and therapy* (pp. 433–440). Ann Arbor, MI: ERIC/CAPS.

Smith, S., Mullis, F., Kern, R. M., & Brack, G. (1999). An Adlerian model for the etiology of aggression in adjudicated adolescents. *The Family Journal: Counseling and Therapy for Couples and Families, 7*, 135–147.

Snead, E. (1993, July 13). Lesbians in the limelight. *USA Today,* pp. D1, D2.

Snider, M. (1992). *Process family therapy.* Boston: Allyn & Bacon.

Snyder, D. K. (1981). *Marital Satisfaction Inventory manual.* Los Angeles: Western Psychological Services.

Snyder, D. K. (1997). *Manual for the Marital Satisfaction Inventory—revised.* Los Angeles: Western Psychological Services.

Snyder, D. K., & Regts, J. M. (1982). Factor scales for assessing marital disharmony and disaffection. *Journal of Consulting and Clinical Psychology, 50*, 736–743.

Snyder, D. K., & Whisman, M. A. (2004). Treating distressed couples with coexisting mental and physical disorders: Directions for clinical training and practice. *Journal of Marital and Family Therapy, 30*, 1–12.

Snyder, D. K., Cavell, T. A., Heffer, R. W., & Mangrum, L. F. (1995). Marital and family assessment: A multifaceted, multilevel approach. In R. H. Mikesell, D.-D. Lusterman, & S. H. McDaniel (Eds.), *Integrating family therapy* (pp. 163–182). Washington, DC: American Psychological Association.

Soehner, G., Zastowny, T., Hammond, A., & Taylor, L. (1988). The single-parent family project: A community-based, preventive program for single-parent families. *Journal of Child and Adolescent Psychiatry, 5*, 35–43.

Softas-Nall, B. C., Baldo, T. D., & Tiedemann, T. R. (1999). A gender-based, solution-focused genogram case: He and she across the generations. *The Family Journal: Counseling and Therapy for Couples and Families, 7*, 177–180.

Solovey, A. D., & Duncan, B. L. (1992). Ethics and strategic therapy: A proposed ethical direction. *Journal of Marital and Family Therapy, 18*, 53–61.

Spanier, G. B. (1976). Measuring dyadic adjustment: New scales for assessing the quality of marriage and similar dyads. *Journal of Marriage and Family, 38*, 15–28.

Sperry, L. (2005). Case conceptualizations: The missing link between theory and practice. *The Family Journal: Counseling and Therapy for Couples and Families, 13*, 71–76.

Spiegel, H., & Linn, L. (1969). The "ripple effect" following adjunct hypnosis in analytic psychotherapy. *American Journal of Psychiatry, 126*, 53–58.

Spiegel, J. (1971). *Transactions: The interplay between individual, family, and society*. New York: Science House.

Spillman, J. A., Deschamps, H. S., & Crews, J. A. (2004). Perspectives on nonresidential paternal involvement and grief: A literature review. *The Family Journal: Counseling and Therapy for Couples and Families, 12*, 263–270.

Sporakowski, M. J. (1995). Assessment and diagnosis in marriage and family counseling. *Journal of Counseling & Development, 74*, 60–64.

Sprenkle, D. H. (1990). The clinical practice of divorce therapy. In M.R. Textor (Ed.), *The divorce and divorce therapy book*. Northvale, NJ: Aronson.

Sprenkle, D. H. (2003). Effectiveness research in marriage and family therapy: Introduction. *Journal of Marital and Family Therapy, 29*, 85–96.

Sprenkle, D. H., & Moon, S. M. (1996). Toward pluralism in family therapy research. In D. H. Sprenkle & S. M. Moon (Eds.), *Research methods in family therapy* (pp. 3–19). New York: Guilford.

Sprenkle, D. H., & Piercy, F. P. (1984). Research in family therapy: A graduate level course. *Journal of Marital and Family Therapy, 10*, 225–240.

Sprenkle, D. H., & Piercy, F. P. (2006). *Research Methods in Family Therapy* (2nd ed.). New York: Guilford.

Stabb, S. D. (2005). What the research tells us. In M. Harway (Ed.), *Handbook of couples therapy* (pp. 431–456). New York: Wiley.

Stanton, M. D. (1981). An integrated structural/strategic approach to family therapy. *Journal of Marital and Family Therapy, 7*, 427–439.

Stanton, M. D. (1999, May). Alcohol use disorders. *AAMFT Clinical Update, 1*(3), 1–8.

Stanton, M. D., & Todd, T. (1981). Family treatment approaches to drug abuse problems. *Family Process, 18*, 251–280.

Stanton, M. D., Todd, T., & Associates. (1982). *The family therapy of drug abuse and addiction*. New York: Guilford.

Stanton, M. D., Todd, T. C., Heard, D. B., Kirschner, S., Kleiman, J. I., Mowatt, D. T., Riley, P., Scott, S. M., & Van Deusen, J. M. (1982). A conceptual model. In M. D. Stanton, T. C. Todd, & Associates (Eds.), *The family therapy of drug abuse and addiction* (pp. 7–30). New York: Guilford.

Steinberg, E. B., Sayger, T. V., & Szykula, S. A. (1997). The effects of strategic and behavioral family therapies on child behavior and depression. *Contemporary Family Therapy, 19*, 537–551.

Steinhauser, P. D., Santa-Barbara, J., & Skinner, H. (1984). The process model of family functioning. *Canadian Journal of Psychiatry, 29*, 77–88.

Stern, P. N. (1978). Stepfather families: Integration around child discipline. *Issues in Mental Health Nursing, 1*, 50–56.

Stevens-Smith, P., & Hughes, M. M. (1993). *Legal issues in marriage and family counseling*. Alexandria, VA: American Counseling Association.

Stevenson, H. C. (1994, Spring). Research on African-American family life: Learning to interpret the dance. *The Family Psychologist, 10*, 38–40, 46.

Stinnet, N. (1981). In search of strong families. In N. Stinnet, B. Chesser, & J. DeFrain (Eds.), *Building family strengths: Blueprints for action*. Lincoln, NE: University of Nebraska Press.

Stinnett, N., & DeFrain, J. (1985). *Secrets of strong families*. Boston: Little, Brown.

Stith, S. M., Rosen, K. H., & McCollum, E. E. (2003). Effectiveness of couples treatment for spouse abuse. *Journal of Marital and Family Therapy, 29*, 407–426.

Stith, S. M., Rosen, K. H., McCollum, E. E., & Thomsen, B. J. (2004). Treating intimate partner violence within intact couple relationships: Outcomes of multi-couple versus individual couple therapy. *Journal of Marital and Family Therapy, 30*, 305–318.

Stoltz-Loike, M. (1992). Couple and family counseling. In R. L. Smith & P. Stevens-Smith (Eds.), *Family counseling and therapy* (pp. 80–108). Ann Arbor, MI: ERIC/CAPS.

Stone, C. (2005, March/April). Rights for noncustodial parents. *ASCA School Counselor, 6–7*.

Storm, C. L. (1991). Placing gender at the heart of MFT masters programs: Teaching a gender sensitive systemic view. *Journal of Marital and Family Therapy, 17*, 45–52.

Stovall, T. (2000). *A love supreme: Real-life stories of black love*. New York: Warner.

Strong, B., & DeVault, C. (1986). *The marriage and family experience* (3rd ed.). St. Paul, MN: West.

Strong, B., & DeVault, C. (1998). *The marriage and family experience* (7th ed.). Belmont, CA: Wadsworth.

Strong, B., DeVault, C., & Sayad, B. W. (2001). *The marriage and family experience* (8th ed.). Belmont, CA: Wadsworth.

Strong, B., DeVault, C., & Sayad, B. W. (2005). *The marriage and family experience: Intimate relationships in a changing society* (9th ed.). Belmont, CA: Wadsworth.

Stuart, R. B. (1969). Operant-interpersonal treatment of marital discord. *Journal of Consulting and Clinical Psychology, 33,* 675–682.

Stuart, R. B. (1980). *Helping couples change: A social learning approach to marital therapy.* New York: Guilford.

Stuart, R. B. (1998). Updating behavior therapy with couples. *The Family Journal: Counseling and Therapy for Couples and Families, 6,* 6–12.

Substance Abuse and Mental Health Services (1999). *National survey on drug use and health.* Retrieved July 20, 2005 from http://oas.samhsa.gov/.

Sue, D. (1994, Spring). Incorporating cultural diversity in family therapy. *The Family Psychologist, 10,* 19–21.

Sue, D. W., & Sue, D. (2002). *Counseling the culturally diverse: Theory and practice* (4th ed.). New York: Wiley.

Sue, S., & Morishima, J. K. (1982). *The mental health of Asian Americans.* San Francisco: Jossey-Bass.

Sugarman, S. (1987). Teaching symbolic-experiential family therapy: The personhood of the teacher. *Contemporary Family Therapy, 9,* 138–145.

Sullivan, B. F., & Schwebel, A. I. (1995). Relationship beliefs and expectations of satisfaction in marital relationships: Implications for family practitioners. *The Family Journal: Counseling and Therapy for Couples and Families, 3,* 298–305.

Sullivan, K. T., & Anderson, C. (2002). Recruitment of engaged couples for premarital counseling: An empirical examination of the importance of program characteristics and topics to potential participants. *The Family Journal: Counseling and Therapy for Couples and Families, 10,* 388–397.

Sullivan, K. T., Parch, L. A., Eldridge, K. A., & Bradbury, T. N. (1998). Social support in marriage: Translating research into practical applications for clinicians. *The Family Journal: Counseling and Therapy for Couples and Families, 6,* 263–271.

Sussman, M., & Gilgun, J. F. (Eds.). (1997). *The methods and methodologies of qualitative family research.* New York: Haworth.

Sweeney, D. S., & Rocha, S. L. (2000). Using play therapy in assessing family dynamics. In R. E. Watts (Ed.), *Techniques in marriage and family counseling* (pp. 33–47). Alexandria, VA: American Counseling Association.

Sweet, J. A., Bumpass, L. L., & Call, V. (1988). *The design and content of the National Survey of Families and Households* (Working paper NSFH-1). Madison, WI: University of Wisconsin, Center for Demography and Ecology.

Szapocznik, J., & Kurtines, W. M. (1993). Family psychology and cultural diversity: Opportunities for theory, research, and application. *American Psychologist, 48,* 400–407.

Szapocznik, J., Kurtines, W., Perez-Vidal, A., Hervis, O., & Foote, F. (1990). One person family therapy. In R. A. Wells & V. A. Gianetti (Eds.), *Handbook of brief psychotherapies* (pp. 493–510). New York: Plenum.

Szapocznik, J., Rio, A., Hervis, O., Kurtines, W., Faraci, A. M., & Mitrani, V. (1991). Assessing change in family functioning as a result of treatment: The structural family systems rating scale (SFSR). *Journal of Marital and Family Therapy, 17,* 295–310.

Szapocznik, J., Rio, A., Murray, E., Cohen, R., Scopetta, M., Rivas-Vasquez, A., Hervis, O., Posada, V., & Kurtines, W. (1989). Structural family therapy versus psychodynamic child therapy for problematic Hispanic boys. *Journal of Consulting and Clinical Psychology, 57,* 571–578.

Tafoya, T. (1989). Circles and cedar: Native Americans and family therapy. *Journal of Psychotherapy and the Family, 6,* 71–98.

Tafoya, T. (1994, Spring). Epistemology of native healing and family psychology. *The Family Psychologist, 10,* 28–31.

Tennant, G. P., & Sperry, L. (2003). Work-family balance: Counseling strategies to optimize health. *The Family Journal: Counseling and Therapy for Couples and Families, 11,* 404–408.

Thibaut, J., & Kelley, H. H. (1959). *The social psychology of groups.* New York: Wiley.

Thomas, A. J. (1998). Understanding culture and worldview in family systems: Use of the multicultural genogram. *The Family Journal: Counseling and Therapy for Couples and Families, 6,* 24–32.

Thomas, M. B. (1992). *An introduction to marital and family therapy: Counseling toward healthier family systems across the life span.* Upper Saddle River, NJ: Merrill/Prentice Hall.

Thomas, V. (1995). The clinical report: Integrating family assessment instruments into family counseling practice. *The Family Journal: Counseling and Therapy for Couples and Families, 3,* 284–297.

Thomas, V., & Olson, D. H. (1993). Problem families and the circumplex model: Observational assessment using the Clinical Rating Scale (CRS). *Journal of Marital and Family Therapy, 19,* 159–175.

Titelman, P. (1987). *The therapist's own family: Toward the differentiation of self.* Northvale, NJ: Jason Aronson.

Todd, T. (1992). Brief family therapy. In R. L. Smith & P. Stevens-Smith (Eds.), *Family counseling and therapy* (pp. 162–175). Ann Arbor, MI: ERIC/CAPS.

Todd, T. C., & Selekman, M. D. (1991). *Family therapy approaches with adolescent substance abusers.* Boston: Allyn & Bacon.

Toman, W. (1961). *Family constellation: Its effects on personality and social behavior.* New York: Springer.

Tomes, H. (1996, August). Are we in denial about child abuse? *APA Monitor, 27,* 55.

Tomm, K. M. (1984a). One perspective on the Milan approach: Part I. Overview of development, theory, and practice. *Journal of Marital and Family Therapy, 10,* 113–125.

Tomm, K. M. (1984b). One perspective on the Milan approach: Part II. Description of session format, interviewing style, and interventions. *Journal of Marital and Family Therapy, 10,* 253–271.

Tomm, K. (1987). Interventive interviewing: Part 1. Strategizing as a fourth guideline for the therapist. *Family Process, 26,* 3–13.

Tootle, A. E. (2003). Neuroscience applications in marital and family therapy. *The Family Journal: Counseling and Therapy with Couples and Families, 11,* 185–190.

Touliatos, J., Perlmutter, B. F., & Straus, M. A. (Eds.) (1990). *Handbook of family measurement techniques.* Newbury Park, CA: Sage.

Treadway, D. (1987, July/August). The ties that bind. *Family Therapy Networker, 11,* 16–23.

Trepper, T. S. (2005, January/February). Family therapy around the world—An introduction. *Family Therapy Magazine,* pp. 10–12.

Trotzer, J. P. (1988). Family theory as a group resource. *Journal for Specialists in Group Work, 13,* 180–185.

Trotzer, J. P., & Trotzer, M. A. (1986). *Marriage and family: Better ready than not.* Muncie, IN: Accelerated Development.

Tseng, W.-S., & Hsu, J. (1991). *Culture and family.* Binghamton, NY: Haworth.

Tuason, M. T., & Friedlander, M. L. (2000). Do parents' differentiation levels predict those of their adult children? and other tests of Bowen theory in a Philippine sample. *Journal of Counseling Psychology, 47,* 27–35.

Turner, W. L. (1993, April). Identifying African-American family strengths. *Family Therapy News, 24,* 9, 14.

Turner, W. L., Wieling, E., & Allen, W. D. (2004). Developing culturally effective family-based research programs: Implications for family therapists. *Journal of Marital and Family Therapy, 30,* 257–270.

Urschel, J. (1993, April 8). Stopping high-risk marriages. *USA Today,* p. 12A.

U.S. Census Bureau. (2000a). *Fertility and family statistics.* Washington, DC: Author.

U.S. Census Bureau. (2000b). *Statistical abstract of the United States, 2000* (120th ed.). Washington, DC: U.S. Government Printing Office.

U.S. Census Bureau. (2003). *Alternative income estimates in the United States: 2003.* Retrieved August 29, 2005, from http://www.census.gov/prod/2005pubs/p60-228.pdf.

U.S. Department of Health and Human Services. (2004). *Child maltreatment.* Washington, DC: U.S. Government Printing Office.

Usdansky, M. L. (1993, August 23). Census shows diversity of Hispanics in USA. *USA Today,* p. A1.

Van Alstine, G. T. (2002). A review of research about an essential aspect of emotionally focused couple therapy: Attachment theory. *Journal of Pastoral Counseling, 37,* 101–118.

Van Deusen, J. M., Stanton, M. D., Scott, S. M., Todd, T. C., & Mowatt, D. T. (1982). Getting the addict to agree to involve his family or origin: The initial contact. In M. D. Stanton, T. C. Todd, & Associates (Eds.), *The family therapy of drug abuse and addiction* (pp. 39–59). New York: Guilford.

VanFleet, R. (1994*). Filial therapy: Strengthening parent–child relationships through play.* Sarasota, FL: Professional Resource Press.

Van Hoose, W. H., & Kottler, J. (1985). *Ethical and legal issues in counseling and psychotherapy* (2nd ed.). San Francisco: Jossey-Bass.

Viere, G. M. (2005). Examining family rituals. In K. R. Gilbert (Ed.), *Annual editions: The family 05/06* (pp. 197–199). Dubuque, IA: McGraw-Hill/Dushkin.

Visher, E. B., & Visher, J. S. (1978). Common problems with stepparents and their spouses. *American Journal of Orthopsychiatry, 48,* 252–262.

Visher, E. B., & Visher, J. S. (1979). *Stepfamilies: A guide to working with stepfamilies and stepchildren.* New York: Brunner/Mazel.

Visher, E. B., & Visher, J. S. (1985). Stepfamilies are different. *Journal of Family Therapy, 7,* 9–18.

Visher, E. B., & Visher, J. S. (1986). *Stepfamily workbook manual.* Baltimore, MD: Stepfamily Association of America.

Visher, E. B., & Visher, J. S. (1988). *Old loyalties; new ties: Therapeutic strategies with stepfamilies.* New York: Brunner/Mazel.

Visher, E. B., & Visher, J. S. (1993). Remarriage families and stepparenting. In F. Walsh (Ed.), *Normal family processes* (2nd ed., pp. 235–253). New York: Guilford.

Visher, E. B., & Visher, J. S. (1994). The core ingredients in the treatment of stepfamilies. *The Family Journal: Counseling and Therapy for Couples and Families, 2,* 208–214.

Visher, E. B., & Visher, J. S. (1996). *Therapy with stepfamilies.* New York: Brunner/Mazel.

Vontress, C. E., Johnson, J. A., & Epp, L. R. (1999). *Cross-cultural counseling: A casebook.* Alexandria, VA: American Counseling Association.

Waite, L. J., & Gallagher, M. (2000). *The case for marriage: Why married people are happier, healthier, and better off financially.* New York: Doubleday.

Wald, E. (1981). *The remarried family: Challenges and promise.* New York: Family Service Association of America.

Walen, S., & Perlmutter, R. (1988). Cognitive-behavioral treatment of adult sexual dysfunctions from a family perspective. In N. Epstein, S. E. Schlesinger, & W. Dryden (Eds.), *Cognitive-behavioral therapy with families* (pp. 325–360). New York: Brunner/Mazel.

Walker, L. D. (1990). Problem parents and child custody. *American Journal of Family Law, 4,* 155–168.

Waller, M., & McLanahan, S. (2005). "His" and "her" marriage expectations: Determinants and consequences. *Journal of Marriage and Family, 67,* 53–67.

Wallerstein, J. S. (1986). Women after divorce: Preliminary report from a 10-year follow up. *American Journal of Orthopsychiatry, 56,* 65–77.

Wallerstein, J. S. (1990). *Second chances.* New York: Ticknor & Fields.

Wallerstein, J. S. (1992). Children after divorce. In O. Pocs (Ed.), *Marriage and family 92–93* (pp. 163–168). Guilford, CT: Dushkin.

Wallerstein, J. S., & Kelly, J. B. (1980). *Surviving the break up: How children and parents cope with divorce.* New York: Basic Books.

Walsh, F. (1982). Conceptualization of normal family functioning. In F. Walsh (Ed.), *Normal family processes* (pp. 3–44). New York: Guilford.

Walsh, F. (1991). Promoting healthy functioning in divorced and remarried families. In A. S. Gurman & D. P. Kniskern (Eds.), *Handbook of family therapy* (Vol. II, pp. 525–545). New York: Brunner/Mazel.

Walsh, F. (1995). From family damage to family challenge. In R. H. Mikesell, D.D. Lusterman, & S. H. McDaniel (Eds.), *Integrating family therapy* (pp. 587–606). Washington, DC: American Psychological Association.

Walsh, F. (1999). Families in later life: Challenges and opportunities. In B. Carter & M. McGoldrick (Eds.), *The expanded family life cycle* (3rd ed., pp. 307–326). Boston: Allyn & Bacon.

Walsh, F., & Pryce, J. (2003). The spiritual dimension of family life. In F. Walsh (Ed.), *Normal family processes: Growing diversity and complexity* (3rd ed., pp. 337–372). New York: Guilford.

Walsh, W. M. (1993). Gender and strategic marital therapy. *The Family Journal: Counseling and Therapy for Couples and Families, 1*, 160–161.

Walsh, W. M., & McGraw, J. A. (2002). *Essentials of family therapy* (2nd ed.). Denver, CO: Love.

Walter, J., & Peller, J. (1993). Solution-focused brief therapy. *The Family Journal: Counseling and Therapy for Couples and Families, 1*, 80–81.

Walters, M., Carter, B., Papp, P., & Silverstein, O. (1992). *The invisible web: Gender patterns in family relationships.* New York: Guilford.

Watts, R. E. (2000). Using the how I remember my family questionnaire in couples counseling. In R. E. Watts (Ed.), *Techniques in marriage and family counseling* (pp. 53–56). Alexandria, VA: American Counseling Association.

Watts, R. E. (2001). Integrating cognitive and systemic perspectives: An interview with Frank M. Dattilio. *The Family Journal: Counseling and Therapy for Couples and Families, 9*, 472–476.

Watts, R. E. (2003a). Reflecting "as if": An integrative process in couple counseling. *The Family Journal: Counseling and Therapy for Couples and Families, 11*, 73–75.

Watts, R. E. (2003b). Adlerian therapy as a relational constructivist approach. *The Family Journal: Counseling and Therapy for Couples and Families, 11*, 139–147.

Watts, R. E., & Broaddus, J. L. (2002). Improving parent-child relationships through filial therapy: An interview with Garry Landreth. *Journal of Counseling and Development, 80*, 372–379.

Watzlawick, P. (1976). *How real is real?* New York: Random House.

Watzlawick, P. (1978). *The language of change.* New York: Basic Books.

Watzlawick, P. (1983). *The situation is hopeless but not serious.* New York: Norton.

Watzlawick, P., Beavin, J. H., & Jackson, D. D. (1967). *Pragmatics of human communication.* New York: Norton.

Watzlawick, P., Weakland, J. H., & Fisch, R. (1974). *Change: Principles of problem formation and problem resolution.* New York: Norton.

Waxman, G. L., & Press, S. (1991). Mediation: Part II. Mediation in Florida. *Nova Law Review, 15*, 1212–1225.

Weber, T., & Levine, F. (1995). Engaging the family: An integrative approach. In R. H. Mikesell, D.-D. Lusterman, & S. H. McDaniel (Eds.), *Integrating family therapy* (pp. 45–71). Washington, DC: American Psychological Association.

Weber, T., McKeever, J. E., & McDaniel, S. H. (1992). A beginner's guide to the problem-oriented first family interview. In R. L. Smith & P. Stevens-Smith (Eds.), *Family counseling and therapy* (pp. 202–212). Ann Arbor, MI: ERIC/CAPS.

Weeks, G. R., Gambescia, N., Jenkins, R. E. (2003). *Treating infidelity: Therapeutic dilemmas and effective strategies.* New York: Norton.

Weiner, J. P., & Boss, P. (1985). Exploring gender bias against women: Ethics for marriage and family therapy. *Counseling and Values, 30*, 9–21.

Weiner-Davis, M. (1993). *Divorce Busting: A step-by-step Approach to Making Your Marriage Loving Again.* New York: Simon & Schuster.

Weiner-Davis, M. (2003). *The Divorce Remedy: The Proven 7–Step Program for Saving Your Marriage.* New York: Simon & Schuster.

Weiss, R. (1979). *Going it alone: The family life and social situation of the single parent.* New York: Basic Books.

Weitzman, S. (2000). *"Not to people like us": Hidden abuse in upscale marriages.* New York: Basic Books.

Welfel, E. R., Danzinger, P. R., & Santoro, S. (2000). Mandated reporting of abuse/maltreatment of older adults: A primer for counselors. *Journal of Counseling and Development, 78*, 284–292.

Weltner, J. S. (1982). A structural approach to the single-parent family. *Family Process, 21*, 203–210.

Wendorf, D. J., & Wendorf, R. J. (1992). A systemic view of family therapy ethics. In R. L. Smith & P. Stevens-Smith (Eds.), *Family counseling and therapy* (pp. 304–320). Ann Arbor, MI: ERIC/CAPS.

West, G. D., Hosie, T. W., & Zarski, J. J. (1987). Family dynamics and substance abuse: A preliminary study. *Journal of Counseling and Development, 65*, 487–490.

West, J. D. (1988). Marriage and family therapy assessment. *Counselor Education and Supervision, 28*, 169–180.

West, J. D., Bubenzer, D. L., Smith, J. M., & Hamm, T. L. (1997). Insoo Kim Berg and solution-focused therapy. *The Family Journal: Counseling and Therapy for Couples and Families, 5*, 346–354.

West, P. L., & MohdZain, A. Z. (2000). Marriage counseling and the TFA model: An application. *The Family Journal: Counseling and Therapy for Couples and Families, 8*, 293–299.

Westcot, M. E., & Dries, R. (1990). Has family therapy adapted to the single-parent family? *American Journal of Family Therapy, 18*, 363–372.

Wetchler, J. L., & Piercy, F. P. (1986). The marital/family life of the family therapist: Stressors and enhancers. *American Journal of Family Therapy, 14*, 99–108.

Whisman, M. A. (2001). The association between depression and marital dissatisfaction. In S. R. H. Beach (Ed.),

Marital and family processes in depression: A scientific foundation for clinical practice. Washington, DC: American Psychological Association.

Whitaker, C. A. (1958). Psychotherapy with couples. *American Journal of Psychotherapy, 12,* 18–23.

Whitaker, C. A. (1975). Psychotherapy of the absurd: With a special emphasis on the psychotherapy of aggression. *Family Process, 14,* 1–16.

Whitaker, C. A. (1976). The hindrance of theory in clinical work. In P. J. Guerin, Jr. (Ed.), *Family therapy: Theory and practice.* New York: Gardner.

Whitaker, C. A. (1989). *Midnight musings of a family therapist.* New York: Norton.

Whitaker, C. A. (1990). 'I had to learn because I wasn't being taught.' *Contemporary Family Therapy, 12,* 181–183.

Whitaker, C. A., & Bumberry, W. M. (1988). *Dancing with the family: A symbolic-experiential approach.* New York: Brunner/Mazel.

Whitaker, C. A., & Keith, D. V. (1981). Symbolic-experiential family therapy. In A. Gurman & D. Kniskern (Eds.), *The handbook of family therapy* (pp. 187–225). New York: Brunner/Mazel.

White, H. (1978). *Your family is good for you.* New York: Random House.

White, L. K., & Booth, A. (1985). The quality and stability of remarriages: The role of children. *American Sociological Review, 50,* 689–698.

White, M. (1986). Negative explanation, restraint, and double description: A template for family therapy. *Family Process, 25,* 169–184.

White, M. (1989). *Selected papers.* Adelaide, South Australia: Dulwich Centre.

White, M. (1991). Deconstruction and therapy. *Dulwich Centre Newsletter, 3,* 21–40.

White, M. (1992). Deconstruction and therapy. In M. White & D. Epston (Eds.), *Experience, contradiction, narrative, and imagination* (pp. 109–151). Adelaide, South Australia: Dulwich Centre.

White, M. (1993). The histories of the present. In S. Gilligan (Ed.), *Therapeutic conversations.* New York: Norton.

White, M. (1995). *Re-authoring lives.* Adelaide, South Australia: Dulwich Centre.

White, M., & Epston, D. (1990). *Narrative means to therapeutic ends.* New York: Norton.

Whitehead, B. D. (1993). Dan Quayle was right. *The Atlantic Monthly, 271,* 47–84.

Whiteside, M. F. (1989). Family rituals as a key to kinship connections in remarried families. *Family Relations, 38,* 34–39.

Whiteside, M. F. (1998). The parental alliance following divorce: An overview. *Journal of Marital and Family Therapy, 24,* 3–24.

Whittinghill, D. (2002). Ethical considerations for the use of family therapy in substance abuse treatment. *The Family Journal: Counseling and Therapy for Couples and Families, 10,* 75–78.

Wilcoxon, S. A. (1985). Healthy family functioning: The other side of family pathology. *Journal of Counseling and Development, 63,* 495–499.

Wilcoxon, S. A. (1993, March/April). Ethical issues in marital and family counseling: A framework for examining unique ethical concerns. *Family Counseling and Therapy, 1,* 1–15.

Wilcoxon, S. A., Walker, M. R., & Hovestadt, A. J. (1989). Counselor effectiveness and family-of-origin experiences: A significant relationship? *Counseling and Values, 33,* 225–229.

Willbach, D. (1989). Ethics and family therapy: The case management of family violence. *Journal of Marital and Family Therapy, 15,* 43–52.

Williams, R. A. (2005). A short course in family therapy: Translating research into practice. *The Family Journal: Counseling for Couples and Families, 13,* 188–194.

Willis, J. T. (1988). An effective counseling model for treating the Black family. *Family Therapy, 15,* 185–194.

Willis, J. T. (1990). Some destructive elements in African-American male–female relationships. *Family Therapy, 17,* 139–147.

Wills, T. A., Weiss, R. L., & Patterson, G. R. (1974). A behavioral analysis of the determinants of marital satisfaction. *Journal of Consulting and Clinical Psychology, 42,* 802–811.

Wilson, L. L., & Stith, S. M. (1991). Cultural sensitive therapy with black clients. *Journal of Multicultural Counseling and Development, 19,* 32–43.

Winnicott, D. W. (1965). *The maturational processes and the facilitation of environment.* London: Hogarth.

Winter, J. (1989). *Family research project: Treatment outcomes and results.* Unpublished manuscript, The Family Institute of Virginia, Richmond.

Woestendiek, J. (1992, August 15). You are not my mother. *Winston-Salem (NC) Journal,* pp. 22–23.

Wolff, Z. (2005, June 16). Going to the therapist in route to the alter. *New York Times,* pp. E1–E2.

Wolin, S. J., & Wolin, S. (1993). *The resilient self: How survivors of troubled families rise above adversity.* New York: Villard.

Wolpe, J. (1969). *The practice of behavior therapy.* New York: Pergamon.

Wood, L. F., & Jacobson, N. S. (1990). Behavioral marital therapy: The training experience in retrospect. In F. W. Kaslow (Ed.), *Voices in family psychology* (Vol. 2, pp. 159–174). Newbury Park, CA: Sage.

Woods, M. D., & Martin, D. (1984). The work of Virginia Satir: Understanding her theory and technique. *American Journal of Family Therapy, 12,* 3–11.

Woody, R. H. (1988). *Fifty ways to avoid malpractice.* Sarasota, FL: Professional Resource Exchange.

Worden, M. (1992). *Adolescents and their families.* New York: Haworth.

Wrenn, C. G. (1962). The culturally-encapsulated counselor. *Harvard Educational Review, 32,* 444–449.

Wrenn, C. G. (1985). Afterward: The culturally-encapsulated counselor revisited. In P. B. Pedersen (Ed.), *Handbook of cross-cultural counseling and therapy.* Westport, CT: Greenwood.

Wycoff, S., & Cameron, S. C. (2000). The Garcia family: Using a structural systems approach with an alcohol-dependent family. *The Family Journal: Counseling and Therapy for Couples and Families, 8,* 47–57.

Wylie, M. S. (1990, March/April). Brief therapy on the couch. *Family Therapy Networker, 14,* 26–35, 66.

Wylie, M. S. (1991, March/April). Family therapy's neglected prop. at. *Family Therapy Networker, 15,* 24–37, 77.

Wylie, M. S. (1992, January/February). The evolution of a revolution. *Family Therapy Networker, 16,* 17–29, 98–99.

Wylie, M. S. (1999, September/October). Neil S. Jacobson, 1949–1999. *Family Therapy Networker, 23*(5), 14, 16–18.

Wylie, M. S., & Cooper, G. (2000, March/April). Remembering Mara Selvini Palazzoli. *Family Therapy Networker, 24,* 11.

Wynne, L. C. (1983). Family research and family therapy: A reunion? *Journal of Marital and Family Therapy, 9,* 113–117.

Wynne, L., Ryckoff, I., Day, J., & Hirsh, S. (1958). Pseudomutuality in the family relations of schizophrenics. *Psychiatry, 21,* 205–220.

Wynne, L. C., Shields, C. G., & Sirkin, M. I. (1992). Illness, family theory, and family therapy: I. Conceptual issues. *Family Process, 31,* 3–18.

Young, M. A. (2004). Healthy relationships: Where's the research? *The Family Journal: Counseling and Therapy for Couples and Families, 12,* 159–162.

Young, M. A. (2005). Creating a confluence: An interview with Susan Johnson and John Gottman. *The Family Journal: Counseling and Therapy for Couples and Families, 13,* 219–225.

Young, M. E., & Long, L. L. (1998). *Counseling and therapy for couples.* Pacific Grove, CA: Brooks/Cole.

Zal, H. M. (2002). *The Sandwich Generation: Caught Between Growing Children and Aging Parents.* New York: Perseus Publishing.

Name Index

Subject Index

•